THE CITIES BOOK

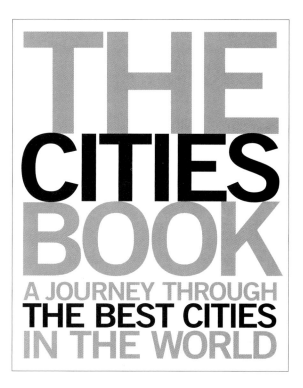

THE CITIES BOOK

A JOURNEY THROUGH THE BEST CITIES IN THE WORLD

MELBOURNE · OAKLAND · LONDON

Foreword

Much like the cities explored within its pages, this book has become like a living, breathing organism, developing its own vibrant, vivacious and decidedly urbane personality. This character is vividly expressed through a combination of amazing imagery (much of it taken especially for this book by Lonely Planet photographers on the road), judicious and insightful text (thanks to our hardworking authors for that – what a job they have!) and our in-house team who have nurtured, shaped and moulded the content and design to create this lovely book.

The heart of this book was set beating by our travellers, however, who provided us with the list of 200 cities for inclusion in the book, via a survey we ran on www.lonelyplanet.com asking travellers (and our staff) to nominate their favourite cities.

The top five held no major surprises – Paris, New York, Sydney, Barcelona and London – although a quick glance at the top 25 cities certainly speaks to the adventurous spirit of our travellers. In the top 10 we have Cape Town and Bangkok, and the top 25 features Kathmandu, Buenos Aires and Jerusalem. In the 200 cities selected, we were able to display the great diversity of city life as it is experienced all over the globe: in the classic Western European cities such as Paris; ancient South American cities such as La Paz and Quito; island cities such as Apia in Samoa; trading centres such as Nairobi, hi-tech/futuristic cities such as Hong Kong and Tokyo; and those iconic cities like London, Florence or Rome, where time appears to stand still and accelerate in the same moment. The incredible diversity of day-to-day life explored through these pages challenges our very notion of a consistent 'city lifestyle', and yet something about the energy, pace and commonality of experiences connects these cities.

We don't set too much store by the 'rating' of these cities, but it was interesting to see just how the city standard is set by Paris. There are several other cities in this book that claim the reputation by association: Budapest, as the Paris of Eastern Europe; Beirut, as the Paris of the Middle East; Buenos Aires, as the Paris of the South; and Melbourne, as the Paris of the southern hemisphere!

Partly in recognition of that much-used cliché about discovering the heart and soul of the city (and partly because it just seemed like a fun idea), we decided to approach each city as if it were a person. Thus, factual information such as when the city was founded (date of birth), which country it is located in (address), or what is good and bad about it (strengths and weaknesses), are treated as if a person. This approach allowed us to absorb and reflect the natural energy and life force of each city.

A little tongue-in-cheek, we also asked authors to provide a 'gold star' for each city. Far from the stock standard responses of 'food', 'history' or 'architecture', these gold stars really encapsulate what's unique and defining about the city. The gold star for hanging out? San Francisco, of course. The best hospitality? Cape Town. Murals? Mexico City. The best silk boutiques in the world? Head to Ho Chi Minh City. The most beautiful city square in the world? It must be Marrakesh. Need to regain your mojo? Book a flight to Salvador da Bahia. And the gold star for hope goes to Hiroshima, and for survival to Sarajevo.

The 'import' and 'export' sections provided an interesting way of thinking about how cities inhale and exhale traditions, personalities and icons. The 'urban myths' were interpreted somewhat differently by different authors; some are strictly myths and others more legendary (and true!) stories about the city. Although not 'urban myths' in the strict sense of the term, these colourful stories provide a unique insight into each city.

We gave Lonely Planet founder and 'most travelled man' Tony Wheeler the last word. We asked him to suggest his favourite cities that hadn't made the vote – the cities, in his view, that simply couldn't be left out. It was a close thing Detroit, Jakarta, Karachi, Mandalay, Oslo, Papeete, Stanley, Tehran, Tunis and Warsaw, but you made it!

I hope you get pleasure from this book. It has been a real privilege to work with such great material – the images and text – but most of all to discover the rich textures of humanity that are woven throughout these remarkable cities all over our planet. Cities are often chaotic, frequently overpopulated, polluted, bursting at the seams with energy, buckling at the knees with the weight of history, and propelled ever forward by the driving force of technology And we wouldn't have it any other way.

Roz Hopkins
Trade & Reference Publisher
Lonely Planet Publications

Introducing Cities
Past, Present & Future

When you look at a city, it's like reading the hopes, aspirations and pride of everyone who built it. – Hugh Newell Jacobsen

The Cities Book is a celebration. Of the physical form, in stone, glass, metal and wood, that is taken by these remarkable spiritual, cultural, political and technological bastions. Of the people whose energy spills out into the city, transforming itself into music, art and culture. Of the myriad sights, smells, sounds and other temptations awaiting travellers at the end of a plane, train or boat journey. By celebrating the majesty of cities on every continent we are pausing to marvel at the contribution they have made to the collective richness of humankind over more than six millennia.

Hence it made sense to us to begin this book with a look at the evolution of the city – the roots of cities in the first civilisations, the characteristics that we associate with the great cities of today, and the possible directions that they will take in the future.

Like so many other things, cities come to us as a gift from the ancients. Although capable of great foresight, our urban ancestors could not possibly have predicted the way in which cities were to change the world we live in. According to the UN, the urban populace is increasing by 60 million people per year, about three times the increase in the rural population. To get a sense of the impact that cities have made, try picturing the world without them. Imagine fashion without Milan, theatre without London's West End, hip-hop without New York, classical music without Vienna, or technology without Tokyo.

UN Secretary-General Kofi Annan summed it up best when he said: 'We have entered the urban millennium. At their best, cities are engines of growth and incubators of civilization. They are crossroads of ideas, places of great intellectual ferment and innovation…cities can also be places of exploitation, disease, violent crime, unemployment, and extreme poverty…we must do more to make our cities safe and livable places for all.'

THE PAST GREETS THE FUTURE: A GEISHA PLACIDLY AWAITS THE INCOMING TOKYO BULLET TRAIN.
Photographer: Paul Chesley

Past

The story of how cities evolved is the story of civilisation. The link is encoded in the words themselves: 'civilisation' comes from the Latin *civitas*, meaning 'city'. We can catch a glimpse of the past in the preserved walls of castles, palaces and places of worship that have survived, albeit haphazardly, for centuries, and which influence the colour and flavour of our present-day cities. Cuzco in Peru is the perfect example. The city's strongest walls remain those constructed by the Inca who, unfathomably, erected enormous stone monoliths carved by hand and laid the blocks so precisely, without mortar, that it is impossible to slide paper between them. Following the Spanish conquest, the ancient Inca stones were used to build palaces and cathedrals, but the stones were so mighty that many could not be brought down and so continue to make up the streets and foundations of newer buildings to this day.

Paradoxically, with the advent of the first sedentary settlements, where people flocked together to settle in large groups instead of roaming the countryside as small bands of hunter-gatherers, came the advent of inter-city travel. Initially people travelled (as they still do) for trade and business, war, or religious pilgrimages, but eventually cities gave birth to the leisured classes who could travel for curiosity and pleasure. Even in ancient times there were hoteliers who ran a roaring trade for prototypal backpackers and travel writers and historians who made their livings from the fantastical tales of their wanderings.

Sumerian Cities

Divine Nature gave the fields, human art built the cities.
– Marcus Terentius Varro

Current archaeological records indicate that the oldest cities are those found scattered along the banks of the Tigris and Euphrates Rivers in Mesopotamia, modern Iraq.

Five thousand years ago merchants travelling upriver from Egypt would have entered the great Sumerian capital of Uruk by boat, sailing swiftly past the fertile shores lined with irrigation ditches that had been dug centuries before. These ditches, filled with water from the Euphrates River, had allowed the Sumerians to begin farming the land, producing surpluses of food that were used to feed an army of construction workers, possibly slaves, to raise the first cities the world had ever seen. The most ancient of these was Uruk and with its construction the door was firmly closed on the prehistoric epoch.

The city of Uruk was famous for its giant defensive walls, luscious gardens and the sophistication of its ruling elite, chief among them the god-king Gilgamesh, who became the subject for the world's oldest epic, the *Song of Gilgamesh*, which is still in print today. Excavation of the vast site where the city once stood, an area covering 450 hectares, has yielded astonishing finds. In the 1900s a cuneiform tablet found at Uruk happened to contain what is regarded as the best and most accurate description of the legendary Tower of Babel, an architectural feat referred to in the Bible.

But the real fascination is with the form of the city itself. In 2003 Jorg Fassbinder, part of a German-led archaeological team conducting excavations at the site, said that in its heyday Uruk must have been 'like Venice in the desert'. The dig covered more than 100 hectares, uncovering extensive gardens as well as an extremely sophisticated network of canals by which the Sumerians swanned around their idyllic city in absolute luxury.

It is incredible to think that after more than 5000 years the legacy of Sumerian culture could still remain potent. Not only did they invent the wheel and come up with the world's first written language (Sumerian cuneiform script, which emerged around 3500 BC), but they also dreamt up the sexagesimal number system, which we still use to measure time. Every time you count down the minutes to an event, you have the Sumerians to thank.

What we know of ancient Sumer has been deduced through careful analysis and interpretation of the discoveries made by archaeologists. These include stone tablets inscribed with ancient stories (the first ever recorded); gold necklaces inlaid with lapis lazuli that were once worn by Sumer's elite; weathered fragments of beautiful vases depicting the conquest and subjugation of rival cities; and the broken outlines of once-feared cities that stretched for kilometres. Interpreting these finds with a little imagination only whets our appetite and makes us want to learn more about these strange worlds that have been lost in time.

Rome – Antiquity's Great Melting Pot

A great city, whose image dwells in the memory of man, is the type of some great idea. Rome represents conquest; Faith hovers over the towers of Jerusalem; and Athens embodies the pre-eminent quality of the antique world, Art. – Benjamin Disraeli

Sicilian writer Vincenzo Salerno said that despite everything that came after it, the blueprint for Western civilisation was the society of ancient Rome. The Romans gave us our alphabet (minus *u* and *w*), and many of the words we still use are derived from ancient Latin. They gave us the 12-month lunar calendar; the rudiments of classical architecture; the pope; straight roads; a system of government; literature; public-ablution facilities; and endless subject matter for Shakespearian plays and even movies, such as *Gladiator* and *I, Claudius*. The Romans came, saw and conquered, and left enough behind that they would never be forgotten. And at the heart of the mighty empire was the imperial capital, a monolith of power carved in brilliant marble, home of the Senate and generations of megalomaniac emperors. Ancient Rome's former pagan glory is still visible if you take a stroll around the modern city, notably the remains of the Roman Forum, the Pantheon and the Colosseum.

Quite clearly, the Romans were a pretty remarkable bunch. But they were not the first people to become civilised, and nor did they develop in a vacuum. They were great assimilators, subsuming the skills, knowledge, literary conventions and even deities from neighbouring or past civilisations – a process hastened through conquest. From afar Rome admired in particular the Greek and Egyptian civilisations, centred on the capitals of Athens and Alexandria, which were already melting pots of ideas, racial groups and culture.

Alexandria the Great

It was in Alexandria, during the six hundred years beginning around 300 BC, that human beings, in an important sense, began the intellectual adventure.
– Carl Sagan

In 332 BC Alexander the Great thrashed the Persians and then conquered Egypt for the Greeks. The following year, after being crowned pharaoh, he ordered the construction of a fortified port which he named, in a moment of egotism, Alexandria. The city was to replace Memphis as the capital of ancient Egypt and, had Alexander not died of fever during the conquest of Babylon, would have become the capital of his enormous empire. As it happened, the empire was carved up by Alexander's generals following his death and Ptolemy Soter took over as pharaoh and king of Alexandria.

During antiquity the Egyptian capital was famous for its wonderful papyrus and had a reputation for producing great medicines, perfume, jewellery and gold work. But most of all, the city was, and still is, legendary for the Pharos Lighthouse, one of the Seven Wonders of the Ancient World, and for its library, established under Ptolemy III. It is alleged that he composed a letter 'to all sovereigns on earth, requesting them to send him works by every kind of author, including poets and prose-writers, rhetoricians and sophists, doctors and soothsayers, historians and all the others too'. Such was his zealousness in collecting knowledge that he gave orders for any books on board ships calling at Alexandria to be copied, and only the copies were returned to the owners. As a secure port city, an industrial and manufacturing base, and a hub of knowledge, Alexandria had a celebrated liberal system of governance that championed diversity.

Less than 500 years after Ptolemy Soter had ascended the throne, Alexandria was reduced to smouldering rubble, destroyed through a combination of Caesar's aggression, petty-minded Christian rebels, earthquake and flood. The coastal Egyptian city we know today as Alexandria bears almost no trace of its amazing history. But through the advanced system of trade and communications that existed throughout antiquity, at least some of the knowledge contained in the library (such as details of the Archimedes screw, a pump that Archimedes invented while staying at the Mouseion, the city university), was not completely lost. Then as now, the great powers adopted and adapted the successful tricks and strategies of their contemporaries and in so doing ensured that the legacies of civilisations dating back countless millennia would be recorded.

Lost Cities – Atlantis to Great Zimbabwe

Towered cities please us then,
And the busy hum of men.
– John Milton

For thousands of years fabled lost cities have had a vicelike grip on our imagination. Even such a wise philosopher as Plato would get excited thinking about how these advanced civilisations could just be mysteriously wiped out. His fascination with lost cities has trickled down hundreds of generations and given us the most tantalising and well-known mysterious lost city of all, Atlantis.

The legend of the lost city of Atlantis has captivated scholarly and public imagination since it was first recorded over two millennia ago. The source of the great legend stems from an account written by Plato (427–347 BC) in *Critias* and *Timaeus*. Plato's account was originally derived from Solon (640–560 BC), the great lawmaker of Athens. It is alleged that Solon was told of the disappearance of a vast and worldly island civilisation by Egyptian priests while he was visiting the Nile delta. This story was told to Plato by Critias (a poet, philosopher and controversial political figure), via his great-grandfather, who had learned the story with Solon. In *Timaeus*, Plato quotes Critias' account of the legend:

> *Now in this island of Atlantis there was a great and wonderful empire*
> *which had ruled over the whole island and several others, and over parts*
> *of the continent… But, there occurred violent earthquakes and floods,*
> *and in a single day and night of misfortune…the island of Atlantis…*
> *disappeared in the depths of the sea.*

Right now there are still people out there trying to find the site of this ancient Utopia. Based on the scant detail in Plato's account, it is highly unlikely we could identify Atlantis even it were to be discovered. But there has been no shortage of possible candidates. Over the past few years a spate of potential Atlantises have been found in waters off India, Cuba and Japan.

In May 2001 underwater archaeologists at India's National Institute of Ocean Technology detected signs of an ancient submerged settlement in the Gulf of Cambay, off Gujarat. Acoustic-imaging analysis identified a 9km-long stretch of what had once been a river now lying 40m beneath the waves. Evidence retrieved from the site, including pottery, beads, broken sculpture, wood and human teeth, has been carbon dated, and a conservative estimate of the age of the site puts it at around 7500 BC. It is not clear whether the Cambay site represents a city or a smaller type of settlement. If it is a city, then the belief that the Sumerians built the first city would be proved wrong, and the whole theory of the origin and spread of ancient civilisations would need to be revised.

But wait, it gets better. In December 2001 another lost city was discovered, this time off the west coast of Cuba in the Yucatán Channel by scientists innocently engaged in sonar imaging for a Canadian company that was hoping to discover sunken ships laden with Spanish treasure. The fact that some of the buildings alleged to be part of the city appear to be shaped like pyramids got dozens of Internet Atlantean hopefuls extremely fired up.

Although the jury is still out on whether this Cuban discovery is a lost city or just an anomaly that showed up on the radar, there is no doubt that a strange megalithic structure discovered in Japanese waters off the island of Yonaguni is genuinely man-made. The huge stone structure, which is over 100m long, was discovered by a diver in 1985. By itself the megalith isn't enough to signify the existence of a whole civilisation or even a city, but the estimated age of the structure, put minimally at 6000 years, represents another spanner in the works for those attempting to piece together the chronology of ancient human civilisation.

Each new archaeological find is a puzzle, and as much likely to inspire fear and prejudice as it is joy. Nowhere is this tenet illustrated more plainly than at the site of one of Africa's great lost cities, Great Zimbabwe. The first rumours of a magnificent lost city began circulating around the Portuguese colony of Mozambique during the 16th century. However, the spectacular ruins, with their massive curved walls raised without mortar, were not discovered by Europeans until nearly the end of the 19th century, when a young German explorer named Carl Mauch was directed to the site by a German trader who told him of some large ruins 'that could never have been built by blacks'.

It was almost another 20 years before a full exploration of the site was conducted by J Theodore Bent, an amateur archaeologist at best, bankrolled by British imperialist Cecil Rhodes, a notorious racist and diamond entrepreneur. Despite unearthing masses of evidence that pointed to the indigenous origins of Great Zimbabwe, Bent concluded that the impressive curved-walled enclosures, which stretched over 40.5 hectares and were over 9.1m high, were the work either of Phoenicians or Egyptians who had travelled down from North Africa.

The inability of conquering civilisations to appreciate the achievements of those whom they have conquered has added significantly to the numbers of lost cities and ruined sites on all continents save Antarctica. The ruins of the World Heritage–listed site at Machu Picchu, picturesquly perched among the clouds high in the mountains of Peru, were once the spiritual capital of the Incan population that was decimated by the Spanish conquistadors, and are now an enigma. With the Inca gone and their knowledge lost, the ruins they left behind can never be interpreted with any certainty. But perhaps that only adds to the allure of the lost city. And the dim, irrational thought that perhaps, upon spending time wandering the ruins with the ghosts of our spiritual ancestors, it is possible to catch a glimmer of understanding in these sacred places.

THE LABYRINTHINE WALLS OF URUK'S BIT RESH TEMPLE, WHICH DATES BACK TO THE FOURTH MILLENNIUM BC.
Photographer: Nik Wheeler

6

Present

In the days of the European Grand Tour of the 19th century, it was fashionable for young aristocrats to complete their education by travelling to the great cities of the Continent to study their history and art. These 'tourists' are the origin of our modern word. But travel was still time-consuming, difficult and expensive and therefore only really available to the privileged classes. Today, modern transport means that we can travel between cities in hours, not days. The world is becoming smaller while correspondingly people's interests are becoming broader, thanks to our greater access to the world through the media. Recent travel trends show that short-break city trips are one of the most popular kinds of travel, and that the main motivators are education and exploring other cultures, escaping the stresses of everyday life for a while, and a sense of adventure. Travellers claim that travel has had a considerable impact on their lives, helping define a social conscience and positively impacting personal goals and values. Today, the most difficult part of city travel is deciding which city to visit next.

Stormy Weather

Not houses finely roofed or the stones of walls well builded, nay nor canals and dockyards make the city, but men able to use their opportunity. – Alcaeus

In 2004 the reality of a disaster such as that which may have destroyed Alexandria and Atlantis was brought home, literally, when it was beamed into TV sets around the world. The devastating tsunami that struck in December that year, causing widespread coastal damage, affecting 12 countries and causing the loss of hundreds of thousands of lives, was followed by two further brutal natural disasters in the form of Hurricanes Katrina and Rita in 2005.

When Katrina lashed into New Orleans at the end of August, it was confirmation, if such was needed, that in the future even cities with significant defences could not take their safety for granted.

New Orleans lies below sea level in a wide, shallow bowl on delicate marshlands, with the Mississippi River running through the centre. It is situated under the lip of a vast lake more than twice its size, while to the south and east lies the Gulf of Mexico, one of the world's most fertile hurricane zones. Following the devastation that occurred when the Mississippi burst its banks in 1927, engineers designed and built a complex system of flood defences, enough to protect it from a Category 5 storm. Even though New Orleans did not take the full brunt of the storm, the historic city lost a large number of its priceless old buildings, became engulfed by toxic waters, and many inhabitants suffered significant physical and psychological damage. Many people feel that to avoid a rebuilding process that will benefit property developers rather than those made homeless by the disaster, the authorities should entrust the power and responsibility of reconstructing the old jazz capital to its former citizens.

One thing is certain: however much equity goes into the reconstruction, the next system of levees will have to be a vast improvement on the ones that broke under the weight of Katrina. If New Orleans needs help choosing its future direction, the city's mayor could do a lot worse than turn to the example set by the world's most livable city, Vancouver.

Plan for Living

The chief function of the city is to convert power into form, energy into culture, dead matter into the living symbols of art, biological reproduction into social creativity. – Lewis Mumford

If anyone is surprised that Vancouver has emerged as the world's most livable city in 2005, as nominated by William M Mercer quality-of-life survey and the *Economist*, then it certainly is not the city's planners or its residents. Over more than three decades the idyllic Canadian city has earned this accolade through the introduction of a simple yet revolutionary approach to city planning and design.

In 1972 the city's planning office took a bold step often feared by public servants scared of opening a Pandora's box. They decided to look beyond the computer models, livability indicators and programme plans they had created and ask the public what they thought would make the city most livable. The more they tried to answer the question 'what is livability?', the more they realised they didn't have the answer. So they decided to phone a friend – millions of friends.

Another instance where Vancouver looked to the needs of its citizens was the Art Underfoot initiative, a competition in which members of the public came up with the best designs for the city's manhole covers. The idea was to help make city infrastructure more visible to the public. How much more a part of the city would you feel if you had a chance to design illustrations that would appear on manhole covers everywhere?

The city's public discourse about livability eventually led to a plan that recognised the city as an organic entity in itself. A discussion paper on Vancouver prepared by the Vancouver-based International Centre for Sustainable Cities stated:

The brain and nervous system of a livable city refers to participatory processes by which a city develops visions and plans, monitors the implementation of its plans and adjusts to changing circumstances. The heart is the common values and public space of a city that define its essential identity. The neighborhoods, industrial clusters, downtown, parks and other hubs form the organs of a city. Similar to the circulatory system and neural networks that weave connections within a living organism, transportation routes, infrastructure, waste disposal, communication lines, water flows, and green space connect these nodes.

The essence of livability was found to be about quality of life, which is tied to the ability of citizens to access food; clean air; affordable housing; infrastructure (transportation, communication, water and sanitation); meaningful employment; and green parks and spaces, and is also determined by the access that its residents have to participate in decision-making to meet their needs.

The *Economist* survey, published in October 2005, assesses living conditions in 127 cities around the world by looking at these factors. Vancouver is the highest ranked city, but a further two Canadian cities (Montréal and Toronto) feature in the top five. Alongside Canada, Australia has some of the most livable places in the world, with Melbourne ranked joint second overall. Perth, Adelaide and Sydney join Zürich, Toronto and Calgary in joint fifth place. Not far behind is Brisbane in joint 11th place.

A SURVIVOR OF HURRICANE KATRINA PULLS HIS BOAT DOWN SUBMERGED PARIS ST, CHALMETTE, JUST OUTSIDE NEW ORLEANS.
Photographer: Jason Reed

Elsewhere in the Asian region, cities in Japan, New Zealand, Hong Kong, South Korea, Singapore and Taiwan all offer a good standard of living, and it is only a humid climate that brings scores down slightly. The influx of investment in China alongside the increased availability of goods has helped all six Chinese cities surveyed perform relatively well, along with other emerging business centres such as Bangkok and Kuala Lumpur.

Although higher crime rates and a greater threat of terror put US cities below those of Canada, US cities are still among the world's most livable. Cleveland and Pittsburgh are the joint best scoring cities in the US, in joint 26th place in the global ranking. Although no Latin American city surveyed manages to present ideal living conditions, neither do any fall into the category where extreme difficulties are faced. Montevideo (Uruguay), Santiago (Chile) and Buenos Aires (Argentina), which share joint 64th place, offer the best living conditions in Latin America.

Africa and the Middle East fare the worst of any region. Instability, the threat of terror and many cultural restrictions bring the ratings down, although strong anti-crime measures in many Arab states are a stabilising factor, and in Israel the negatives are offset by a generally high level of development that makes Tel Aviv the best destination surveyed there.

Rapt in Wander

We all become great explorers during our first few days in a new city, or a new love affair. – Mignon McLaughlin

Cities are places to wander, without a map, relishing the freedom that comes of being lost in a strange new world. Whether you're taking a leisurely stroll along the wide, cobblestone pathways of Antigua or letting a doe-eyed dog lead you aimlessly round the busy streets of Bangkok, exploring on foot can easily be the highlight of any trip around a city.

The best thing about walking is that you have control. Whenever you come across something interesting you can stop and check it out, take your time and really savour the experience. Often the most ancient cities are the most rewarding ones to walk through. Perhaps it's because they were built for walking, in a time before cars were invented and carriages and horses were reserved for a small elite. Small cities also lend themselves to walking, as it is easy to learn your way around and to get a feel for their human scale. The slow pace of walking allows us to meditate and absorb the ambiance of a place, particularly in holy cities.

Passing along the decorated walls of the streets of Varanasi in India, winding through the hustle and bustle, can be a dreamlike experience. The myriad temples and sumptious buildings of the place nicknamed 'the eternal city' may help you to understand the Hindu belief that anyone who dies and is cremated in the city automatically ends the cycle of death and reincarnation and ascends immediately to nirvana. Lost in thought, wandering slowly, meandering like the Ganges as it flows through the centre of the city, you might feel as if your sins have been washed away and your mind made clear.

In Mecca, a city where you are required to walk, the sense of renewal and rejuvenation comes from the river of humanity you will find yourself caught up in in the haj pilgrimage. Every year well over two million Muslims perform the sacred pilgrimage, forming a human mass that has to be seen to be comprehended. The focal point of Mecca is the Kaaba, the 'House of God', believed by Muslims to have been built by Abraham (peace be upon him) and his son Ishmael (peace be upon him), and which is covered in a large black-and gold-embroidered cloth. The pilgrims who have made the journey to Islam's holiest city wait patiently to circle the Kaaba seven times before they try to touch or kiss its cornerstone, the Black Stone, which is believed to be a meteorite. The process can take several hours simply due to the unbelievable numbers of pilgrims. This is one walk you won't forget in a hurry.

Tasty Travel

To be tempted and indulged by the city's most brilliant chefs. It's the dream of every one of us in love with food. – Gael Greene

Food is the foundation of city and human life and a trip to any city would be much the worse for not savouring the flavours favoured by the locals. The quality of a city's restaurants can reveal much about its inhabitants – the importance of their traditions and their openness to new ideas.

Cities around the world, and many in this book, would all claim to be top or near the top of the epicure food chain. New York, Paris, London, Toronto, Melbourne, Montréal would certainly stake a fierce claim, as would San Francisco. Some cities have nice weather, others have nice beaches, but San Francisco has both (most of the time) and great food to boot. Whether you're sampling the city's best seafood with the leather-clad crowd in the Castro, chewing on dim sum (yum cha) in one of the world's biggest Chinatowns, going Mexican in the Mission District or dining sophisto in California's oldest restaurant, Tadich Grill, this is one city that demands you eat, and eat well.

But of course sampling a city's cuisine isn't always about eating the very best. The locals in any city have their own peculiar favourites, often in marked contrast to all the grand fare served up by gastronomic wizards in the finest restaurants at the fashionable end of town. As a general rule Londoners like nothing better than a serving of fish and chips or a juicy kebab of an evening, while the *porteños* of Buenos Aires prefer snacking on *empanadas* (turnovers) and *lomitos* (steak sandwiches). Sometimes it's all about discovering the local secrets, trying something a little different that you wouldn't find at home.

When you're in Minsk and need something to help keep your strength up against the Belarusian wind, make sure you gobble down a couple of fish in jelly. They're a lot tastier than you might think.

In Lahore it pays to explore the full range of Pakistani delicacies and there is no better place to achieve this goal than at the conveniently dubbed 'Gawalmandi food street'. The whole street is cordoned off to traffic, and from where you sit you can order whatever appeals from any of the stalls. Balti and tandoori dishes are most popular, but the more adventurous can tuck into *karai kaleji* (chicken livers), *gurda* (kidneys), *kapureh* (testicles) and *magaz* or *bheja* (brains).

Cro-Magnon men everywhere should make their way immediately to Nairobi to sample the ultimate meat-lover's fantasy at the Carnivore restaurant, on the outskirts of town. As the name of the place suggests, this is one hard-core serving of animal flesh. Dinner or lunch provides the opportunity to get stuck into zebra, giraffe, impala, wildebeest, crocodile and other game meats. Waiters will bring the skewers straight from the fire to the table, and no-one will object if you wolf it down.

In Celebration of Diversity

This is the most happening place in the city, and it happens to be gay. I don't think it's a coincidence. – Paul Colombo

There's something about the Berlin Love Parade, Sydney's Mardi Gras and Rio's Carnaval that makes it hard to picture them taking place in a tiny, sleepy country village with a population of 50 where everyone knows your name and if you go back far enough the inhabitants are all blood related.

One of the great opportunities cities offer new residents is the chance for people to be themselves. Sharing a living space with millions of others is often regarded as a profoundly liberating experience. Anonymity allows for freedom and the chance to become the person you want to be.

Cities have a long history of attracting people who are seeking a fresh start or need to outrun the demons of prejudice and intolerance more common in villages and rural areas. During medieval times throughout Europe, peasants, not to mention thieves and vagabonds, would escape the attentions of despotic landlords by fleeing to the cities, hence the old expression 'city air is free air'. In 19th-century England, following the abolition of slavery in the British Empire, slave ships bound for the Caribbean continued to dock in port cities such as Liverpool. Occasionally slaves would be helped to escape and would hide among the throng of the busy city before eventually being integrated into society. Cities are also centres of migration, from rural areas and from abroad. The relative peace and stability that is enjoyed by people of different races, sexual orientation, cultural backgrounds and political views, who live together side by side in thousands of cities worldwide, is a wonderful advertisement for urbanisation.

The residents of Tbilisi in Georgia take pride in their city's reputation for multiculturalism. It is home to more than 100 ethnic groups, including Georgians, Russians, Armenians, Azeris, Ossetians, Abkhazians, Ukranians, Greeks, Jews, Estonians, Germans and Kurds. On the other side of the world in Puerto Vallarta (Mexico), locals celebrate the city's rich cultural diversity by eating out at the famous mix of restaurants.

Meanwhile, in the 'gayborhoods' of San Francisco, Sydney, Paris, New York and London, predominantly gay, lesbian, bisexual and transgender trendsetters continue to make a vital contribution to their city's economy by attracting curious tourists keen to hang out in a cool part of town. The Chueca barrio in Madrid is one of the city's best-known gay areas, with a totally chilled atmosphere where gay and straight people intermingle, and same-sex kissing and hand-holding is commonplace.

Tolerance and acceptance subsequently gives rise to amazing public spectacles that succeed in uniting everyone in a celebration of diversity. Take the Berlin Love Parade, first held in 1989 on a whim by a German DJ, Dr Motte, who thought it would be cool to hold a free, mobile acid-house street party. The first Love Parade attracted 150 revellers, who followed two cars with cassette recorders along the Kurfürstendamm. Ten years later 1.4 million people were jiving after 51 floats past Germany's most important landmarks in a beautifully outrageous celebration of 'Love, Freedom and Techno'. Although the Love Parade was cancelled in 2004 and 2005, allegedly due to lack of funding, Berlin's largest outdoor party is set to make a stunning comeback in 2006 when Germany hosts the football world cup. The mayor has already publicly stated his support for the event, saying that it puts the city at the centre of the world stage in a very positive way and draws young people to Berlin.

Endless Nights

Cities, like cats, will reveal themselves at night. – Rupert Brooke

No matter how many natural, cultural or culinary charms a city may have, it is often judged by the quality of its nightlife. And having explored the delights of your chosen city by day, it's only natural that you should want to check out what happens between dusk and dawn, just to make sure you haven't missed anything.

Often the best nights out are those that are unplanned. Similarly, some of the best nightlife can be found in the cities where you'd least expect to find it.

Take Belgrade for example. Just five years after protestors stormed the city, set fire to its Parliament building and forced President Slobodan Milošević to step down, the Serbian capital is already back in full swing as soon as the sun sets over the Danube. Along the river you will find dozens of *splavovi* (floating raft clubs) blaring out funky, folksy Balkan beats as they slide out of view. But the real action is around the historic Kalemegdan Park. Founded by the Romans and recognised as one of the most glorious parks in the world, the buildings around Kalemegdan should probably be heritage listed. Instead, the most popular promenade in Belgrade boasts some of the wickedest clubs in Europe playing the weirdest range of music, from Gypsy, rock, electro, folk and Serbia's own uniquely bizarre brand of fusion known as turbofolk. Belgrade nightlife is like a postman on a Sunday – it delivers when you least expect it.

In contrast, you expect New York to deliver – and it does. Whenever, wherever, whatever, however you want it, the world's most extravagant city has it all, 24/7. The clearest indication that NY, NY, is indeed the world's flashiest beacon for those in search of nocturnal entertainment is the number of results listed if you search for 'New York nightlife' on Google. The search engine listed a whopping 11,600,000 results compared to just 6,220,000 if you do a similar search for nightlife in London.

To maintain its pole position, the city has even spawned the New York Nightlife Association (NYNA), an orderly gang of owners, managers and staff from many of the city's top establishments, who in their own words believe New York City is the nightlife capital of the world and want to keep it that way. In the pursuit of their own best interests, they also play a key role in making sure New York is still a fun place to hang out. Currently the NYNA's greatest challenge is staying ahead of the beast of gentrification that sees snazzy apartments springing up in areas usually reserved for noisy venues where decadence beats high-cost living. The Meatpacking District, between 14th and 19th Sts, and the West Chelsea manufacturing district on 27th and 28th Sts, are prime residential development opportunities in the eyes of property tycoons. The same areas are also home to awesome nightclubs and cabaret venues so cool they have no phones and don't advertise. In an interview with the *New York Times,* NYNA lawyer Robert Bookman said what was happening now is '…the same story that has been repeated over the years in Soho, Noho, Tribeca and the Flatiron district'. Does this mean that one day New York will lose its lustre? Not likely, but following the closure of legendary punk-rock club CBGB it's clear that even in the world's nocturnal cultural capital, fun cannot be taken for granted.

Future

Having lured us out of the wild and into homes that for many are packed with creature comforts, fridges, running hot water, electricity, heating, ADSL connections, telephones and the rest, what more does the city have up its sleeve? One thing is certain and that is that there will be change.

The challenges for the future faced by cities mainly revolve around sustainability and managing growing populations. Among the UN's Millennium Development Goals is a target to 'significantly improve' the lives of at least 100 million people living in urban slums by the year 2020. At the same time, cities must also plan to be less enviromentally damaging. Economic factors and the desire for unparallelled luxury are also motivators for city planners of the future. Technology moves ahead in leaps and bounds, and ultimately the only thing that can limit a city is the imaginations of the people who are building it. And today, perhaps more than at any time in history, ordinary people are nearer to turning their own city daydreams into something real.

New Real Estate

In a real estate man's eye, the most expensive part of the city is where he has a house to sell. – Will Rogers

In an essay entitled 'The Rise of the Ephemeral City' published in *Metropolis Magazine*, Joel Kotkin has suggested that we are witnessing the emergence of a new urban environment populated by 'non-families' and the nomadic rich whose needs are attended to by a subservient service class. He calls it the ephemeral city and suggests that it prospers merely through its ability to provide an 'alternative' – and one suspects extravagantly decadent – lifestyle for the wealthy few who can afford it. Even though Kotkin wasn't referring to the city of Dubai, he might well have been describing the glittering, paradisal playground for the rich, famous and, especially, the nouveau riche.

Often the difference between the possible and the impossible is someone brave enough to have a vision. In the coastal city of Dubai, part of the United Arab Emirates, Sheikh Mohammed bin Rashid Al Maktoum is such a man.

In 2001 he ordered construction work to begin on two palm tree–shaped artificial islands. According to the European Space Agency, whose satellite has been monitoring the construction, the islands comprise approximately 100 million cubic metres of rock and sand and are set to increase Dubai's shoreline by 120km.

When complete, the Palm Islands will support over 60 luxury hotels, 5000 residential villas, 5000 apartments, marinas, water theme parks, restaurants, shopping malls, sports facilities, health spas, cinemas and numerous dive sites. It is hoped the development, dubbed by proud locals as the Eighth Wonder of the World, will further secure the city's reputation as a top tourist destination and fantasy playground for the fabulously wealthy. Football ace David Beckham is rumoured to have purchased an apartment.

To prove that less is not more, the sheikh announced in 2004 that a third and even grander Palm island, the Deira Palm, was to begin construction. This palm tree–shaped island will become the largest artificial island in the world, with an area of 80 sq km, and will consist of a trunk, a crown with 41 fronds and a surrounding crescent island that acts as a breaker. The residential area, located on the fronds, will consist of 8000 two-storey town houses.

And just in case there was any shadow cast over Dubai's ambition to remain completely over the top, the sheikh has also commissioned the erection of the enormous Burj Dubai, which will be the world's tallest tower when completed. In keeping with the plant theme, the tower's triple-lobed design is based, according to the press release, 'on an abstracted version of a desert flower, while the silhouette of the lobes resonate the onion-dome constructions of an Islamic culture'.

Another epic urban-development project, considered to be the largest private commercial real-estate development in the world, is underway in South Korea. At an initial cost of US$15 billion, New Songdo City is under construction on a 556-hectare landfill connected to mainland Seoul by bridge. When complete it is planned to be home to almost half a million people and an economic hub to rival Hong Kong. The picturesque, high-density city aims to attract multinational corporations wishing to set up new headquarters for their Northeast Asian operations. Developers have declared New Songdo will be a free economic zone, with tax incentives and low-interest loans. It will feature international schools, hospitals and pharmacies, canals, a water shuttle, a golf course and a 'green lung' modelled on New York's Central Park. The city will also become a test-bed for new technology.

Seoul residents have already shown tremendous interest in the project and New Songdo apartments are rumoured to be selling fast. The first building stage will be complete in 2008, when the inaugural residents will move in. Whereas in the past real estate developers would build houses, office and apartment blocks, it seems that the 21st century has ushered in a new era of real estate where developers construct entire cities.

Raising the Dream

The city is a fact in nature, like a cave, a run of mackerel or an ant-heap. But it is also a conscious work of art, and it holds within its communal framework many simpler and more personal forms of art. Mind takes form in the city; and in turn, urban forms condition mind. – Lewis Mumford

Some city planners have a vastly different vision from the property developers, some would say less mercenary and certainly more environmentally sustainable. In the Arizona desert, north of Phoenix, a revolutionary city has been under construction since 1970. Its founder, Italian architect Paolo Soleri, hopes Arcosanti will inspire a change in the prevailing culture. Arcosanti is said to resemble the modernist urban Utopian designs of Le Corbusier and Sant'Elia. However, the principles of design are based on Soleri's concept of 'arcology' (a fusion of architecture and ecology). His vision is for an organic sustainable city that fits into the ecological system rather than imposing itself upon it. For example, greenhouses beneath residential buildings generate solar energy for heating, as well as producing food. Soleri insists that when people come to Arcosanti they will be inspired and that when they leave they will begin to insist that genuinely sustainable principles start being applied to the development of their own cities.

With an average of only 50 permanent residents who also work to construct the city, Arcosanti is on too small a scale to provide the technical solutions for the challenges that face the world's major urban centres. However, in terms of the principles he has applied to his design, Soleri fulfils the role of a visionary, in that he believes that cities must become confluent with the example set by nature if they are not to be destroyed by the same forces that give them life. He writes:

In nature, as an organism evolves it increases in complexity and it also becomes a more compact or miniaturized system. Similarly a city should function as a living system… The city is the necessary instrument for the evolution of humankind.

Citizen City

I have an affection for a great city. I feel safe in the neighbourhood of man, and enjoy the sweet security of the streets. – Henry Wadsworth Longfellow

While old-school realists take a deep breath and get on with it, dreamers continue to dream. Anyone who has played Sim City knows the allure of being able to construct your own metropolis. Deciding whether the citizens have a greater need for a new university or a high-security prison can be fun, but for an increasing number of ordinary folk the fun is turning into reality.

THE HELIPAD OF THE EXTRAVAGANT BURJ AL ARAB HOTEL, DUBAI.
Photographer: David Cannon

Constructing cities started off as the sole preserve of warrior god-kings, then it passed into the hands of elected politicians, and now it seems anyone with enough passion, perseverance and financial backing can give it a go.

In the USA the Laurent Company, in rural South Dakota, is trying to recruit a vice president of construction to help it build 'the world's first fully integrated signing community'. The plan is to build a city that centres on the needs of hearing-impaired people who use sign as their first language; Phase 1 is due for completion in late 2006. The built environment will be constructed to take into account the special needs of its proposed citizenry, expected to number between 1250 and 4000.

The company says homes and businesses will encourage easy visibility for signing across wide distances through the use of glass and open spaces. Fire and police services will be designed with more lights and fewer sirens. High-speed Internet connections will be made available throughout, as the Internet and video relay service have become vital modes of communication for deaf people. Some critics have warned that the proposed city is segregation, albeit voluntary, and argue that there would be widespread moral outrage had the criteria for entry been factors such as ethnicity or gender (such as at a monastery). Still, the city seems likely to be raised and with the full support of signers, who are already signing up to buy property.

For Florida-based Freedom Ship International (FSI), getting its city off the ground and into the ocean has been far from smooth sailing. FSI has plans to construct a 1371m-long, 228m-wide, 106m-tall, ocean-going vessel known as the *Freedom Ship*. The structure is billed as 'an international, cosmopolitan, full-spectrum, residential, commercial, and resort city that circles the globe once every three years'. If the project ever finds serious investors, the mobile modern city with its 518,160-sq-metre floor-space will have 18,000 living units costing from US$180,000 to US$44 million; 3000 commercial units; 2400 time-share units; 10,000 hotel units; a casino; world-class medical facilities; schools; an international trade centre; and more than 40 hectares of outdoor park, recreation and community space for residents to enjoy when they are not flying to the mainland in the ship's aircraft.

So far Norman Nixon, FSI's CEO, has reported the project has been inundated with offers of finance from bogus investors. But he hasn't given up hope of finding someone real who can turn the dream into reality. If only he could team up with Dubai's Sheikh Mohammed bin Rashid Al Maktoum, perhaps it would be full steam ahead for the world's first mobile floating city.

Clearly if you're looking to set up your own city it would be helpful to have loads of money. Then you could just buy a ready-made city like the one in Wiltshire being sold off by Britain's Ministry of Defence. With an asking price of only UK£5 million, 'Burlington', with its 97 hectares, 100 miles of roads, private railway station and even its own pub, the Rose and Crown, sounds like a snip. The catch is that the Cold War relic, built during the 1950s to house the government, British Royal family and 4000 civil servants in the event of a Soviet nuclear attack, is located underground on the site of a disused and rather dangerous stone mine. However, as an added incentive to prospective buyers, the city will come fully furnished with government-issue ashtrays, lavatory brushes, tea sets and office chairs unpacked from 1959.

Paying Your Part

Man's course begins in a garden, but it ends in a city. – Alexander MacLaren

As the evidence about the impact of climate change mounts there is a growing awareness among city-dwellers that something needs to be done.

The British Council estimates that over 75% of energy consumption is directly related to cities and that in many cases cities are highly vulnerable to the effects of climate change. At the same time, it says that cities have a great potential to 'instigate innovative solutions to the impacts of climate change'. Feeling guilty? Try this then.

The UK's Climate Care Trust offers organisations and individuals a way to live guilt-free in the city by simultaneously selling carbon offsets while funding and managing projects that help to reduce further emissions elsewhere. How does it work? Simple. Using the trust's Car & Home Calculator, you can work out the amount of carbon dioxide emissions (which cause the negative effects referred to as climate change) for which you are responsible by entering how much electricity, petrol, gas and oil you use per annum. The calculator then works out how much carbon dioxide was ejected into the atmosphere as a result of the energy consumption you've admitted to, revealing a total in pounds that the environmentally conscious are then morally obliged to pay in the form of carbon offsets.

According to the nifty Car & Home Calculator, an average one-car household uses about 9.5 tonnes of carbon dioxide, which would cost around £60 to offset. That £60 would in turn go towards funding worthy conservation projects such as disseminating efficient cooking stoves in Honduras or providing finance for renewable-energy cooking stoves in schools in India.

But the Climate Care Trust doesn't just work out your household and car emissions. To ensure guilt-free travel between cities, they have developed the Air Travel calculator that tells you how much carbon dioxide you are responsible for if you take a flight from, say, Boston to Delhi. Such a journey would emit 3.21 tonnes of carbon dioxide and would cost you £20.87 to offset. It may sound like a bit of a scam and critics often ask why the organisation isn't run as a charity. The trust responds with this message: 'The answer is simple: we do not believe that it should be left to the charitable sector to clear up pollution.' Whether or not you advocate the approach taken by the trust, the message that we have a responsibility to behave in a sustainable fashion to preserve the built heritage for future generations is one that is worth taking seriously.

In 2005 London mayor Ken Livingstone hosted a meeting of leaders from 20 cities in order to exchange ideas on ways to combat the effects of climate change. Representatives from cities including Beijing, São Paulo, Delhi, Stockholm and Kingston attended the World Cities Leadership Climate Change Summit and cited some examples where cities had been successful in finding ways to reduce emissions. In Berlin nearly all new buildings must include solar panels in their design; in Toronto, cold water pumped from the depths of Lake Ontario is circulated around the city as part of the Deep Lake Water Cooling Project to keep buildings cool, rather than using conventional air conditioners; in Mexico City, which suffers from the worst air pollution of any city, they have vowed to replace 80,000 taxis with low-emissions vehicles by 2006; and in Chicago, the government is trying to find new ways to encourage the use of rooftop gardens in order to keep buildings cool.

Overall, delegates who attended the meeting said the event was a success and that they would take back valuable lessons to their home cities. Let's hope they all paid Climate Care Trust to offset the emissions generated by what must have amounted to thousands of air miles.

Fly Me to the Moon

In Rome you long for the country; in the country – oh inconstant! – you praise the distant city to the stars. – Horace

Sometimes the only way is up. And when it comes to building the cities of the future, Professor Ouyang Ziyuan, author and member of the Chinese Academy of Sciences, couldn't agree more. He reckons that within our lifetime work will already be seriously underway to construct a lunar city, and it won't be made out of cheese.

Ouyang outlined his vision for a moon city in *Academicians Envisioning the 21st Century*, a book published in 2000 to encourage children to get interested in science. He predicted that by 2005 astronauts would have begun turning the moon into a 'natural space station' that would have pressurised modules, electricity-generating facilities and groovy roving vehicles. By 2010 the completed and fully equipped station would allow human explorers to stay up there for weeks and in 2015, a small-scale but permanent moon base would appear. Humans living in the base would then start to build experimental factories and farms, gradually developing a fully fledged moon city before realising the dream of a self-sufficient 'earth village' by 2020.

Ouyang's predictions may have been a bit premature, as, in spite of claims by conspiracy theorists that NASA has already established colonies on the moon and Mars, there doesn't appear to have been much work in establishing a lunar base as yet. But those who can predict the future often seem to have a problem with dates – Nostradamus springs to mind – so perhaps we should wait a bit longer before giving the Chinese scholar's ideas the brush-off. After all, with China now spending well over US$1.2 billion on its space programme, maybe it won't be too long before Ouyang is proved correct. And we should hope so, because he also predicts that the moon city will feature a network of mining operations using solar power that will be able to generate enough surplus energy for it to be transmitted back to earth as a long-term, stable energy supply. Now that's got to be better than burning all that coal.

No two cities are the same. Some have great food, others great nightlife, some stunning architecture, some are rich with history and others have an eye on the future. Cities are individuals. Like a human being, a city is a mass of genes, chosen at random by forces beyond our control, fused together in a secret furnace, acted on by nature, reared through infinite probabilities of nurture before finally growing up and trying to make its own way in the world. Only by taking an interest in someone, spending time with them, observing their mannerisms, conversing with them, engaging with their likes and dislikes, strengths and weaknesses, learning their idiosyncrasies and funny habits, listening to them sing in the shower and snore at night, only by walking the path with them and imagining what it would be like if you were wearing their shoes, can you begin to realise how special someone is. And the city is the same, except maybe a little bit bigger.

ENVIRONMENTALLY SUSTAINABLE GEOTHERMAL ENERGY IS PRODUCED IN A FUTURISTIC-LOOKING DOME IN HELLISHEIDI, ICELAND.
Photographer: Stephen Toner

16

Map 1: THE WORLD

ARCTIC OCEAN

Chukchi Sea

Arctic Circle

Bering Strait

Bering Sea

Alaska (US)

•Anchorage

Gulf of Alaska

Beaufort Sea

Banks Island (Canada)

Victoria Island (Canada)

Ellesmere Island (Canada)

CANADA

Hudson Bay

Baffin Bay

Baffin Island (Canada)

Greenland (Denmark)

Davis Strait

•Nuuk

Denmark Strait

•Reykjavik

ICELAND

Faroe Islands (Denmark)

Norwegian Sea

NOR

UNITED KINGDOM

IRELAND

Nor Se NE

BELGIUM

FRANCE L

•Vancouver
•Seattle

•Québec City
•Montréal

Detroit•
Chicago• •Toronto

San Francisco•

UNITED STATES OF AMERICA

•New York City
•Washington DC

Newfoundland (Canada)

St Pierre & Miquelon (France)

NORTH ATLANTIC OCEAN

Azores Islands (Portugal)

PORTUGAL SPAIN

MONACO ANDO

Med

•Las Vegas

Los Angeles•

•Memphis

•Savannah

Bermuda (UK)

Gibraltar (UK)

MOROCCO

ALGERI

Canary Islands (Spain)

Hawaii (US)

Tropic of Cancer

•Austin

•New Orleans

•Miami

THE BAHAMAS

Gulf of Mexico

MEXICO

Turks & Caicos Islands (UK)

Cayman Islands (UK)

CUBA

Virgin Islands (UK & US)

Anguilla (UK)
ST KITTS & NEVIS
ANTIGUA & BARBUDA
Montserrat (UK)
Guadeloupe (France)
DOMINICA
Martinique (France)
ST LUCIA
BARBADOS
ST VINCENT & THE GRENADINES
GRENADA
TRINIDAD & TOBAGO

MAURITANIA MALI

CAPE VERDE

•Dakar
SENEGAL

THE GAMBIA
GUINEA-BISSAU
GUINEA

•Bamako

NI

BURKINA FASO

BENIN

NORTH PACIFIC OCEAN

JAMAICA

BELIZE

GUATEMALA
HONDURAS
EL SALVADOR
NICARAGUA

COSTA RICA PANAMA

Caribbean Sea

HAITI
DOMINICAN REPUBLIC

Puerto Rico (US)

Aruba (Neth)

Netherlands Antilles

SURINAME

VENEZUELA

GUYANA

French Guiana (France)

CÔTE D'IVOIRE
SIERRA LEONE
LIBERIA

TOGO
GHANA

Gulf of Guinea

EQUATORIAL GUINEA

SÃO TOMÉ & PRÍNCIPE

EQUATOR

Galápagos Islands (Ecuador)

See Map 4: Central America

COLOMBIA

ECUADOR

BRAZIL

PERU

Ascension (UK)

SAMOA

American Samoa (US)
Niue (NZ)

Cook Islands (NZ)

Tahiti (France)

French Polynesia (France)

•Cuzco

•Arequipa

•Salvador da Bahia

St Helena (UK)

SOUTH ATLANTIC OCEAN

•La Paz

BOLIVIA

TONGA

•Pape'ete

Tropic of Capricorn

Pitcairn Islands (UK)

Easter Island (Chile)

PARAGUAY

•Rio de Janeiro

CHILE

•Valparaíso

•Mendoza

URUGUAY

Tristan da Cunha (UK)

•Santiago

•Buenos Aires

•Montevideo

ARGENTINA

SOUTH PACIFIC OCEAN

Falkland Islands (UK)

•Stanley

•Ushuaia

South Georgia (UK)

Antarctic Circle

ANTARCTICA

ANTARCTIC

Map 2: AFRICA

Map 3: EUROPE

21

Map 4: CENTRAL AMERICA

Map 5: SOUTH ASIA

The Cities

Paris

VITAL STATISTICS

NAME: PARIS

NICKNAME: CITY OF LIGHT

DATE OF BIRTH: 52 BC; WHEN JULIUS CAESAR ESTABLISHED LUTETIA ON THE BANKS OF THE SEINE

ADDRESS: FRANCE (MAP 3, G9)

HEIGHT: 75M

SIZE: 105 SQ KM

POPULATION: 2.15 MILLION

Paris has it all: celebrity monuments, manicured parks, taste-bud–tingling cuisine, endless museums, frenetic flea markets and *haute couture* – and like its well-groomed citizens, it always looks good, with no hair out of place.

ANATOMY

Ringed by the terrifying blvd Périphérique, France's capital city is made up of 20 *arrondissements* (districts). The Seine River flows through the city and around two islands, Île de la Cité (site of Notre Dame) and Île St-Louis. The arty, intellectual Left Bank (south of the Seine) houses the Sorbonne University, the vibrant, touristy Latin Quarter and upmarket St-Germain. The Right Bank is home to the Champs-Élysées and the Louvre, as well as trendy shopping in the Marais, nightlife in the Bastille district and Paris's two opera houses. Overlooking the city to the north is the 126m-high Butte de Montmartre (Montmartre hill), the Moulin Rouge and Pigalle (the red-light district). The Eiffel Tower is directly south of the Arc de Triomphe on the southern side of the Seine. Walk or take the wonderfully efficient Métro.

PEOPLE

Officially, 17% of Paris' population are immigrants, with the largest numbers arriving from Algeria, Portugal, Morocco, Tunisia, China and Mali (in descending numerical order). The rest are French.

TYPICAL PARISIAN

Parisians are typically crazy drivers and park with their handbrakes off to allow their neighbouring parker the inevitable bumping. They are stylish, chic and will wear lipstick for putting the rubbish out. They can come across as snooty and see the rest of France as rather provincial. Etiquette is very important and one false move will meet a barely detectable raising of the eyebrows and semiaudible sigh. They are well educated and ambitious, but never brash. They are also expert conversationalists and very respectful and proud of French cuisine and culture. Finally, despite burgeoning nonsmoking laws, Parisians still smoke – a lot.

DEFINING EXPERIENCE

Coffee and croissants on Place de la Contrescarpe, then strolling through the Latin Quarter and over the river to the quietly charming Île St-Louis, on to the Marais for some retail indulgence then lunch and a *vin rouge* (red wine) on Place des Vosges.

STRENGTHS

◢ Successful modern masterpieces eg the Eiffel Tower, the Louvre Pyramid and the Centre Pompidou
◢ Musée du Louvre
◢ Musée d'Orsay
◢ Sacré Cœur
◢ Dazzling department stores – La Samaritaine, Galeries Lafayette
◢ Shakespeare & Co bookshop
◢ *Haute couture*
◢ Cathédrale de Notre Dame de Paris
◢ Cimetière du Père Lachaise
◢ Château de Versailles
◢ *Café terrasses* (café terraces)
◢ Quirky museums eg the Musée des Égouts de Paris (sewers) and Catacombes de Paris (catacombs)
◢ Philosophers and intellectuals
◢ Paris Plage
◢ French Open
◢ Compulsory cleaning of building façades every 10 years
◢ Art in the Métro
◢ Heavenly food and wine

WEAKNESSES

◢ Mad drivers
◢ Underwhelming Eurostar terminal
◢ Tiny, expensive hotel rooms
◢ Rude waiters
◢ Dog poo
◢ Strikes
◢ August – much of Paris closes as Parisians flee the city

GOLD STAR

Landmarks – so much of Paris is iconic.

CITYSPEAK

◢ The Iraq war and anti-American sentiment
◢ Food and the best new restaurants
◢ Muslim headscarves and other religious clothing banned in schools – is this fair?

STARRING ROLE IN...

◢ *Before Sunset* (2004)
◢ *Le Fabuleux Destin d'Amélie Poulin* (Amélie, 2001)
◢ *Subway* (1985)
◢ *Last Tango in Paris* (1972)
◢ *À Bout de Souffle* (1959)
◢ *Les Misérables* by Victor Hugo

IMPORT

◢ Valentine's Day visitors
◢ James Joyce
◢ Samuel Beckett
◢ Henry Miller
◢ Ernest Hemingway
◢ Pablo Picasso
◢ Man Ray
◢ Salvador Dalí
◢ Jim Morrison

EXPORT

◢ Existentialism
◢ Jean-Paul Sartre
◢ Marcel Proust
◢ Brigitte Bardot
◢ Serge Gainsbourg
◢ Simone de Beauvoir
◢ Johnny Halliday
◢ Charles Baudelaire
◢ François Voltaire
◢ Molière
◢ Édith Piaf
◢ Jacques Chirac
◢ Claude Monet
◢ The French Revolution
◢ Auguste Rodin
◢ The Statue of Liberty

SEE Leonardo da Vinci's *Mona Lisa* at possibly the world's best art gallery, the Louvre.

EAT delectable patisseries and creamy confections at historic Ladurée on rue Royale, founded in 1862.

DRINK martinis or mojitos (a cocktail made of rum, lime, sugar, mint and soda water) at the classy China Club and imagine you're in a gentleman's club.

DO sunbathe by the Seine at Paris Plage – imported sand and pebble beaches complete with plastic palm trees.

WATCH the Eiffel Tower light up from the balcony of Georges restaurant in the Centre Pompidou.

BUY Hermès and Yves Saint Laurent on rue du Faubourg St-Honoré.

AFTER DARK take to the water with a techno night at Le Batofar, a tugboat-turned-club on the Seine.

URBAN MYTH

Who actually uttered the infamous phrase 'let them eat cake' is a source of much debate. It is usually attributed to Marie Antoinette, who apparently suggested cake as a response to riots about bread shortages in 1789. The mob, seething with hunger and rage, stormed the Château de Versailles, forcing Marie Antoinette to flee down a secret passage. The story, as we know, ends badly for the lady. Whether or not she said 'let them eat cake', she and her husband Louis XVI had become sufficiently unpopular as to lose their role as monarchs and were summarily guillotined a few years later.

LIFE IMITATES ART IN THE CAFÉ OF THE MUSÉE GREVIN WHERE THE KISSING IS AS FRENCH AS THE CUISINE.
Photographer: Carole Martin (1)

IN THE HEART OF THE CAPITAL, CAFÉS ON COBBLED RUE COQUILLIÈRE EXUDE A PROVINCIAL ELEGANCE.
Photographer: Greg Johnston (2)

DWARFED BY THE EIFFEL TOWER CROWDS OF TOURISTS QUEUE FOR A VIEW FROM THE GREAT ICON OF PARIS.
Photographer: Kevin Levesque (3)

THE CRÈME DE LA CRÈME ON DISPLAY AT A PARISIAN PÂTISSERIE.
Photographer: Russell Mountford (4)

New York City

VITAL STATISTICS

NAME: NEW YORK CITY

NICKNAME: THE BIG APPLE; THE CAPITAL OF THE WORLD; GOTHAM

DATE OF BIRTH: 1609; WHEN DUTCH WEST INDIA COMPANY EMPLOYEE HENRY HUDSON ARRIVED

ADDRESS: USA (MAP 1, M9)

HEIGHT: 96M

SIZE: 1572 SQ KM

POPULATION: 9.3 MILLION

RIDING IN STYLE ON THE SUBWAY, NEW YORK'S UNDERGROUND HUB OF TRANSPORT AND SOCIAL INTERACTION.
Photographer: Corey Wise (1)

TAXIS TAKE OFF LIKE RALLY CARS ON THE MANIC STREETS OF THE WORLD'S MOST IMPATIENT CITY.
Photographer: Corey Wise (2)

HARLEM'S FAMOUS APOLLO THEATER, HOME OF MUSIC LEGENDS FROM ELLA FITZGERALD TO LAURYN HILL.
Photographer: Corey Wise (3)

GALLERY GOERS PAUSE FOR A BREATH OF INSPIRATION AT MOMA.
Photographer: Angus Oborn (4)

Not much about New York City is subtle – it boasts vibrant architecture, world-class art, fashion and entertainment, snarling traffic, spirited politics, and a rich and radical history infused with the tradition of immigration that endures today.

ANATOMY

New York Harbor has 105 sq km of inland waterways and 1240km of direct shoreline. Grid systems are at work on the city streets in the five boroughs of this fairly flat city. Transport is a mixture of subway, buses, honking cabs, ferries all crammed into roads, tunnels and bridges.

PEOPLE

New York is a city for the young; the median age of residents is 34. Sixty-two percent of the population is white, while 16% is black, 15% Latino and 5.5% Asian. A whopping 32% of the population is foreign-born (46% in Queens), and hundreds of languages are spoken. Religiously, New York is much more Semitic than the rest of the country: about 2% of the national population is Jewish, but in the city it's about 12%. Around 70% are Christian.

TYPICAL NEW YORKER

New Yorkers have attitude, and they're not afraid to use it. They're tough, brave, jaded, overworked and intensely focused. Ask one of those blank-faced strap-hanging subway travellers for directions, however, and they'll respond with explicit instructions and a smile, and perhaps even escort you themselves if it's on the way to where they're headed. A lot of it is drama: barking into mobile (cell) phones, marching down the street – these are citizens for whom being swamped with work becomes a point of pride, frequently trying to one-up each other with tales of endless responsibilities and deadlines.

DEFINING EXPERIENCE

Hopping on a subway and heading to Little Italy in the Bronx, going for a sunset run around the sparkling Central Park reservoir, and kicking off the evening with a martini somewhere fabulous.

STRENGTHS

- Restaurant week
- US Open tennis tournament
- New York City Marathon
- Macy's Thanksgiving Day Parade
- Rockefeller Center Christmas tree lighting
- Dean & DeLuca
- Lower Broadway
- Central Park
- The Dakota Building
- Brownstone streets in Brooklyn that look like Sesame St
- Greenwich Village
- Alphabet City
- Gourmet delivery
- Sylvia's on Lenox in Harlem
- Narrow skyscraper canyons

WEAKNESSES

- The Donald and his glitzy building escapades
- The coffee
- The way most New Yorkers dress – with all that's available, so many still look so dull
- The relentless keeping up
- The mobile (cell) phones
- The blinkered New York focus
- The super size–me effect in supermarkets

GOLD STAR

Manhattan, the isle of joy, is a thing of wonder. Nothing quite beats the pleasure of walking out onto the streets to be surrounded by the incredible variety of life, the brusqueness and the energy.

CITYSPEAK

- The homelessness situation – forever with us?
- Gentrification – just what are we doing to housing prices?
- I'll be trapped in my rent-stabilised apartment forever

STARRING ROLE IN...

- *Breakfast at Tiffany's* by Truman Capote
- *The Catcher in the Rye* by JD Salinger
- *The Great Gatsby* by F Scott Fitzgerald
- *Underworld* by Don DeLillo
- *New York, New York* (1977)
- *Basketball Diaries* (1995)
- *Desperately Seeking Susan* (1985)
- *Kids* (1995)
- *Manhattan* (1979)
- *Midnight Cowboy* (1969)
- *Saturday Night Fever* (1977)
- *Taxi Driver* (1976)

IMPORT

- The Statue of Liberty
- Ivana Trump
- The Cloisters
- Fine sensibilities
- Millions of émigrés from all over
- Foreign Cuisines
- Truman Capote
- Alistair Cooke
- John Lennon and Yoko Ono
- Dorothy Parker
- Andy Warhol
- Tom Wolfe

EXPORT

- Irving Berlin
- Miles Davis
- Hip-hop music and culture
- Thelonious Monk
- The New York Dolls and the Ramones
- Rap band Run-DMC
- Broadway musicals
- Sonic Youth
- *Friends*
- Martin Scorsese
- *Seinfeld*
- Sarah Vaughan
- The Velvet Underground
- *Sex & the City*
- Woody Allen
- J Lo

SEE the 360-degree view from the Empire State Building.

EAT good on-the-go grub from street vendors hawking everything from hot dogs and tacos to home-made soups and falafel sandwiches.

DRINK New York State wine from the excellent new wine bar Il Posto Accanto.

DO visit the Metropolitan Museum of Art, with extensive collections of American, European, Asian, African, Egyptian and Graeco-Roman art.

WATCH conspicuous consumption all over Manhattan.

BUY quirk at the gallery stores at the Museum of Modern Art (MoMA) or cutting-edge fashion in the streets around Lower Broadway.

AFTER DARK the city is still jumping, so find somewhere locally or jump in a cab for downtown.

URBAN MYTH

New York is just about the most dangerous place on earth! Not any more. Many, many out-of-towners still expect to visit here and find the New York of the '70s. They are shocked – pleasantly so – by the absence of graffiti-covered subway cars and muggers. The murder rate is also down a startling 69% since the early '90s. These days, it's nearly impossible to even *find* a Manhattan neighbourhood that's off-limits after dark.

Sparkling in the sunlight and revelling in the limelight, Sydney is all glitz and glam – and catching sight of Sydney Harbour for the first time is one of life's memorable experiences.

ANATOMY

Sydney sits on Australia's populous east coast and is centred on Port Jackson, spreading south to Botany Bay, north to Palm Beach and west to the foothills of the Blue Mountains. It's a hilly city, with numerous bays and headlands and sits atop a vast sandstone shelf. Its architecture is predominantly modern, although some sandstone gems from the 19th century remain. It is crisscrossed by a bus and train network, with light rail and a monorail in the city centre.

PEOPLE

Sydney is avowedly multicultural, although before WWII most Sydneysiders were predominantly of British or Irish stock. English is the official language, although about 15% of people speak a different language (such as Greek or Vietnamese) at home. Sydney's Aboriginal population is about 1% of the total population.

TYPICAL SYDNEYSIDER

'Work hard, play hard' is something of a mantra for Sydneysiders. So is the phrase 'smart casual'. People are expected to combine such things at the workplace and still find time to cultivate a buffed, bronzed body, a binge-drinking habit, an ability to cook fusion cuisine and a have wide circle of friends. All this and finding a place to park your car means that they are always talking (on their mobile phones) about how busy they are.

DEFINING EXPERIENCE

Starting your day with a dip in an ocean beach such as Bronte then scoffing breakfast with colleagues who've become mates, cruising around one of the markets such as Balmain before late-afternoon beers on a pub's veranda, then seeing a performance at the Opera House.

Sydney 003

VITAL STATISTICS

NAME: SYDNEY

NICKNAME: SIN CITY

DATE OF BIRTH: 1788; WHEN CAPTAIN ARTHUR PHILLIP LANDED THE FIRST FLEET AT SYDNEY COVE

ADDRESS: AUSTRALIA (MAP 1, MM21)

HEIGHT: 42M

SIZE: 1800 SQ KM

POPULATION: 4 MILLION

THE AUSTRALIAN CRAWL IS ALIVE AND KICKING AT BONDI BEACH ROCK POOL.
Photographer: Paul Beinssen (1)

STRENGTHS

- Glorious sunshine when you need it most
- The world's best harbour at your tippy toes
- Beachside swimming pools
- Mardi Gras
- 2500 shows a year at the Sydney Opera House
- Sydney Film Festival
- Sydney Harbour Bridge climb
- Proliferation of coffee and juice vendors
- Multiculturalism
- BYO restaurants
- Museum of Contemporary Art
- Friendly locals
- Hills and vantage points

WEAKNESSES

- Ridiculous housing prices
- Crowded (and late) public transport
- GDP-style bills at trendy eateries
- Incessant mobile phone usage
- Narcissism
- Pollution
- Trying to get a cab at 3am change-over time
- The Cahill Expressway
- Speed bumps and roundabouts
- Brashness

GOLD STAR

Accessibility – Sydney understood long ago that the great outdoors should be enjoyed by as many people as possible, hence the ease of access to beaches, national parks and walking paths.

CITYSPEAK

- How much did you pay for your terrace house?
- Nicole Kidman sightings
- How crap is the train system?
- Gossip about disgraced business identities

STARRING ROLE IN...

- *Mission: Impossible 2* (2000)
- *Lantana* (2001)
- *Finding Nemo* (2003)
- *Puberty Blues* (1981)
- 'Love This City', song by The Whitlams

IMPORT

- New Zealanders
- Starbucks and chain restaurants
- Backpacking, construction and hospitality workers
- Fuel
- Cars
- Designer footwear
- Chinese, Japanese and Thai cuisine
- Reality TV
- Blockbuster movies

EXPORT

- Nicole Kidman
- Sass & Bide
- Collette Dinnigan
- Opals
- Chefs
- Marc Newson's Lockheed Lounge
- Patrick White
- Cricketers
- Soap stars
- Vegemite
- Rising inflections
- Shark nets
- Blockbuster movie crews

SEE the view from on high in Sydney Tower.

EAT fabulous Thai food at Longrain.

DRINK schooners at the Hollywood Hotel.

DO the Bondi to Coogee walk.

WATCH the stars of the theatre scene at a Company B performance.

BUY the best swimsuit from a local designer at a funky Paddington boutique.

AFTER DARK watch movies under the stars at the annual OpenAir cinema in the Domain.

URBAN MYTH

From 1930 to 1967, the word 'eternity' – beautifully executed in perfect copperplate by yellow chalk – appeared almost half a million times on the pavements of Sydney. It was written by Arthur Stace, an almost illiterate metho drinker who, after attending a fire-and-brimstone sermon at a Baptist church in 1930, dropped the bottle and picked up the chalk. He was inspired after hearing the words of Isaiah 57:15: 'For thus saith the high and lofty One that inhabiteth eternity, whose name is Holy'. Arthur rose at 4am almost every day to record the word 'eternity' on the streets of Sydney. Every now and again it reappears on Sydney's streets.

THE SETTING SUN THROWS THE IRON GIRDERS OF THE SYDNEY HARBOUR BRIDGE INTO SHARP RELIEF.
Photographer: Dallas Stribley (2)

IMPROVISED GUITAR RIFFS ESCAPE FROM A MUSIC SHOP IN THE BACKSTREETS OF KING'S CROSS.
Photographer: Gillianne Tedder (3)

ATMOSPHERE IS EVERYTHING AT WILL AND TOBY'S BAR WHERE GLOWING FURNITURE SETS A MODERN MOOD.
Photographer: Greg Elms (4)

Barcelona

004

VITAL STATISTICS

NAME: BARCELONA

DATE OF BIRTH: 3RD CENTURY BC; WHEN ROMANS ESTABLISHED BARCINO

ADDRESS: SPAIN (MAP 3, G14)

HEIGHT: 93M

SIZE: 487 SQ KM

POPULATION: 1.6 MILLION

EITHER AN ALIEN SPACESHIP OR THE TORRE AGBAR FROM ACROSS THE MOTORWAY.
Photographer: Dennis Gilbert (1)

The city of Gaudí and Miró captivates with its proud Catalan identity, roaring nightlife, fabulous cuisine, sunny weather, sandy beaches and sheer style – Barcelona is addictive.

ANATOMY

The wide tree-lined boulevard La Rambla is Barcelona's main thoroughfare, leading from the port up to Plaça de Catalunya where you'll find buses and taxis. East of La Rambla is the Barri Gòtic with its medieval winding streets and Catedral (cathedral). Over the road, El Raval, the more run-down part of the old quarter, is slowly being gentrified. North of here, L'Eixample is home to most of Barcelona's Modernista architecture. To the southwest stands the 173m hill of Montjuïc. Along the coast are Port Vell, the working-class district of La Barceloneta and Port Olímpic beyond.

PEOPLE

Bilingual Barcelona (Catalan and Castilian Spanish) has become a multicultural city, with around 13% of the population coming from as far afield as Ecuador, Argentina, Morocco and Pakistan. The city is not as predominantly Catalan as the rest of the region and many residents come from other parts of Spain.

TYPICAL BARCELONIN

Barcelonins who live in the city generally inhabit apartments – a lack of space means a lack of houses. All dream of an apartment with a *terrassa* (terrace). Many residents escape the city to a second property at weekends. Barcelonins are known for being serious and hard-working but party just as hard as other Spaniards. *Tapear* (tapas-bar-hopping) is popular but with rising prices, dinner parties are gaining ground. People take pride in their appearance and follow fashion. Football is almost a religion and most people support FC Barcelona. Remember that Barcelonins live in Catalonia, not Spain.

DEFINING EXPERIENCE

Breathing in the morning air on La Barceloneta beach before strolling into El Born for a coffee, then heading up to L'Eixample for Gaudí architecture at La Pedrera and a spot of shopping.

STRENGTHS

- *Bolets* (wild mushrooms)
- *Arròs negre* (rice in black cuttlefish ink)
- Late-night partying
- Festes de la Mercè, the city's main festival
- Proximity to the Pyrenees for skiing and hiking
- The Costa Brava
- Romanesque and Gothic churches
- Modernista architecture
- FC Barcelona football and basketball teams
- Reduced levels of air pollution
- Natural-gas buses
- Hosing down the street every night
- Museu Picasso
- La Sagrada Familia
- Parc Güell
- Affordable Spanish fashion
- La Pedrera
- Museu Marítim
- *Sardana* folk dance

WEAKNESSES

- Expensive real estate
- Suppression of Catalan interests within Spain
- Litter
- Dog poo
- Illegal bill posting
- Heroin abuse
- Els Boixos Nois (The Mad Boys), local football hooligans
- Noise pollution

GOLD STAR

Modernista architecture

CITYSPEAK

- Is it really a good idea to have only two hours of school taught in Spanish per week?
- Property prices – how can anyone afford to buy an apartment?
- FC Barcelona's latest results

STARRING ROLE IN...

- *El Gran Gato* (2003)
- *L'Auberge Espagnol* (The Spanish Apartment, 2002)
- *Todo Sobre Mi Madre* (All About My Mother, 1999)
- *Gaudí Afternoon* (2001)

IMPORT

- Purificación García
- Cruise ships
- The Olympics in 1992
- Pablo Picasso
- Jean Genet
- Stag and hen parties

EXPORT

- Antoni Gaudí
- Salvador Dalí
- Joan Miró
- Cava
- Chef Ferran Adrià
- Chupa Chups
- Joaquim Verdú
- Antonio Miró
- Custo Dalmau (aka Custo Barcelona)
- Mango clothes shop
- Seat
- Carmen Amaya

SEE Gaudí's huge architectural confection, La Sagrada Familia, unfinished and yet awe-inspiring.

EAT *melindros* (soft sugar-coated biscuits) dipped into *cacaolat* (thick hot chocolate) at Salvador Dalí's favourite dairy bar, Granja Dulcinea.

DRINK cocktails at the 1933 Art Deco Boadas whose founder served Hemingway in Havana.

DO learn about Picasso's early works at the fascinating Museu Picasso.

WATCH men offering women roses and women giving men books on Día de Sant Jordi, the feast of Catalonia's patron saint.

BUY affordable Spanish fashion at Mango or Zara in L'Eixample.

AFTER DARK bump and grind down to Port Olímpic for your pick of the clubs.

URBAN MYTH

Gaudí didn't start or finish the building for which he is probably most famous – La Sagrada Familia. Having replaced another architect in 1884, he became obsessed by the project, planning three superbly ornate façades devoted to the Nativity, Passion and Glory, each to be crowned by four towers. The design was so complicated that he only saw the creation of the Nativity. When asked why he was fussing about the top of the towers Gaudí replied, 'the angels will see them'. When funds ran out, he sold all his possessions and started sleeping on the site. In 1926 he was tragically hit by a tram and died. In 1952 work restarted and the still unfinished architectural masterpiece is visited by millions every year.

KEEPING ONE'S HEAD IS A CHALLENGE AMIDST ALL THE BEACHGOERS AT LA PLAYA.
Photographer: IML Image Group Ltd (2)

D IS FOR DOZING: OUTSIDE THE MUSEUM OF MODERN ART.
Photographer: Luke Peters (3)

THE FANTASTIC ENTRANCE TO GAUDÍ'S SURREAL PARC GÜELL.
Photographer: Martin Child (4)

THE BRIGHT LIGHTS OF THE FUTURE BECKON IN THE ULTRAMODERN DESIGNS OF THE LLOYDS BUILDING (FOREGROUND) AND THE SWISS RE TOWER.
Photographer: Ashley Cooper (1)

London

005

VITAL STATISTICS

NAME: LONDON

NICKNAME: THE BIG SMOKE

DATE OF BIRTH: AD 43; EMPEROR CLAUDIUS LED
AN ARMY TO ESTABLISH A PORT CALLED LONDINIUM

ADDRESS: ENGLAND (MAP 3, F8)

HEIGHT: 5M

SIZE: 1572 SQ KM

POPULATION: 7.2 MILLION

Britain's economic motor, London is one of the most vibrant, multiculturally diverse spots on earth, where you can listen to any style of music, view any kind of art and sample world cuisines.

ANATOMY

Above ground the River Thames meanders through the capital, while underground is a warren of tube lines. Within the yellow one (Circle Line) you'll find the main tourist sights, nightlife and shops except a few that dot the regenerated South Bank. Thirty percent of the city is parkland, making it the greenest city of its size in the world. The skyline is punctured by a few skyscrapers, most notably the 'Erotic Gherkin' (the Swiss Re Tower), and Canary Wharf's flashing pyramid roof.

PEOPLE

London's nonwhite population is the largest of any European city. With an estimated 33 ethnic communities and 300 languages spoken, it's no empty boast when the mayor calls it 'a world in one city'.

TYPICAL LONDONER

Londoners work the longest hours in the EU and live in its most expensive city. They are polite (yes they queue), tolerant and unfazed by outrageous dress or behaviour. They are always in a rush but won't refuse a request for help. They go to the pub after work and will coolly ignore any famous faces. They frequently take weekend breaks in Europe courtesy of discount airlines. They complain about London a lot but wouldn't live anywhere else.

DEFINING EXPERIENCE

Sun-bathing in Hyde Park with champagne and strawberries, Coldplay on the iPod, then walking into Notting Hill for a pint outside the Cow to dissect last night's missed penalty before catching an art-house film at the Electric.

STRENGTHS

◢ History around every corner
◢ Hyde Park, Battersea Park etc
◢ Pubs and pints
◢ Victorian swimming baths
◢ London Fashion Week
◢ Multiculturalism
◢ Underground music scene (eg bangra and dancehall)
◢ Comedy nights at the Comedy Store
◢ Cheap flights to Europe
◢ West End theatre
◢ The congestion charge
◢ Deified football clubs eg Arsenal and Chelsea
◢ Free museums and galleries
◢ Notting Hill Carnival (second largest in the world after Rio de Janeiro)
◢ Magic and Heart FM
◢ Ethnic and designer cuisine
◢ The Tate Modern
◢ Tower Bridge
◢ Royal Palaces eg Buckingham Palace, Kensington Palace
◢ Mediterranean summers

WEAKNESSES

◢ Vertiginous house prices
◢ High cost of living
◢ Armpit ambience on crowded rush-hour tubes
◢ 11pm pub closing time
◢ Litter
◢ Friday night traffic leaving London
◢ Confusing bus maps and timetables
◢ 1950s to 1970s architecture
◢ Its size
◢ Speed bumps

GOLD STAR

Theatre – London is still the world leader, with Hollywood stars seeking credibility treading West End boards.

CITYSPEAK

◢ Anti-terrorism laws – good or bad idea?
◢ Antisocial behaviour orders eg no hooded tops in shopping centres
◢ The death of Routemaster buses
◢ House prices…Rising? Falling?

STARRING ROLE IN…

◢ *Vera Drake* (2005)
◢ *Harry Potter and the Half-Blood Prince* (2005)
◢ *Closer* (2004)
◢ *Bridget Jones's Diary* and *Bridget Jones: The Edge of Reason* (2001, 2004)
◢ *28 Days Later* (2002)
◢ *Lock, Stock and Two Smoking Barrels* (1998)

IMPORT

◢ Other EU citizens
◢ Starbucks and chain restaurants
◢ New Zealand lamb
◢ Doctors and nurses
◢ Hollywood stars – for West End shows
◢ French footballers
◢ Fashion – clothes, shoes, trainers
◢ Kylie Minogue
◢ Gwyneth Paltrow
◢ Madonna
◢ Roman Abramovich
◢ Karl Marx
◢ Charles Dickens

EXPORT

◢ The *London Underground Map*
◢ Queen Elizabeth II and the Royal Family
◢ Michael Caine
◢ Twinings Tea
◢ Jamie Oliver and Gordon Ramsey
◢ Convicts
◢ The circus – invented in London in 1768
◢ Zebra crossings
◢ Fuel-cell technology
◢ Harrods
◢ Cockney rhyming slang
◢ Beefeater Gin
◢ Ian Fleming's James Bond
◢ Charlie Chaplin
◢ David Beckham
◢ Alfred Hitchcock

SEE the 40km view from the London Eye.

EAT Michelin-star Chinese food in sophisticated Hakkasan.

DRINK organic bitter at the 18th-century Jerusalem Tavern.

DO a London walk and discover the haunted corners of the city of London.

WATCH Shakespeare performed as it was meant to be at the Globe Theatre.

BUY cutting-edge fashion at Spitalfields Market.

AFTER DARK check out the world-famous dance floor and amazing weekend DJ line-ups at Fabric.

URBAN MYTH

Jack the Ripper was the first serial killer of the multimedia age. Newspaper reports of his vicious killing and mutilation of prostitutes in the backstreets of the East End sent shivers through Victorian middle-class England. Letters, apparently from the killer himself, appeared in print. He became legend, with rumours riding rampant about his identity and the extent of his depravity. Some blamed him for four murders and some put the toll at eight. Who was he? Alas, the Ripper evaded police and his name remains a mystery.

A BOY SKIPS THROUGH THE TRADEMARK LONDON FOG UNDER THE WATCHFUL GAZE OF BIG BEN.
Photographer: Jez Coulson (2)

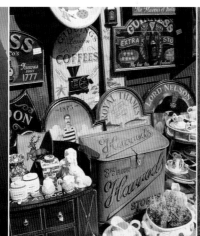

ESSENTIAL TEA-, COFFEE- AND BEER-DRINKING ACCESSORIES ON OFFER AT THE PORTOBELLO RD MARKET.
Photographer: Andrea Pistolesi (3)

A DECKCHAIR DEVOTEE CATCHES UP ON RAYS AND READING IN HYDE PARK.
Photographer: Doug McKinlay (4)

THE TIMELESS FACE OF THE DIOSCURI STATUE LOOKS TO ROME'S GLORIOUS PAST.
Photographer: Martin Moos (1)

Whether they're romantics, art-lovers, gourmands or historians, when you tell people you're going to Rome, they'll sigh – even if they haven't been there.

ANATOMY

Rome's best-known geographical features are its seven hills: the Palatine, Capitoline, Aventine, Caelian, Esquiline, Viminal and Quirinal. Two other hills, the Gianicolo, which rises above Trastevere, and the Pincio, above Piazza del Popolo, were never part of the ancient city. From the Gianicolo you can see how the River Tiber winds through town. Rome has myriad bus routes that cover the city and a semi-useless two-line metro system (Linea A and Linea B) which traverses the city in an X-shape.

PEOPLE

The majority of Romans (over 80%) still consider themselves Catholic, although church attendance isn't what it used to be. Of the non-Catholics in the city, it's the Muslims who are making the furthest inroads – 36.5% of immigrants to Italy are Muslim. The Muslim community in Rome is based around the city mosque, inaugurated in 1995.

TYPICAL ROMAN

The typical Roman works for the government, drives rather than catches public transport, lives at home with the family despite being over 30 years old and is fairly conformist when it comes to matters of style, preferring to look like most other Romans – stylish, groomed and labelled. They share their city with millions of tourists and 150,000 stray cats.

DEFINING EXPERIENCE

Taking your morning espresso at Caffè Sant'Eustachio, walking the streets and getting lost only to stumble upon the perfect trattoria and losing all sense of time over *saltimbocca alla romana* (jump-in-the-mouth veal) and a good wine, crossing Piazza del Popolo and having your breath taken away by Caravaggio's the *Calling of St Matthew*.

STRENGTHS

- History everywhere you look
- Stylish dressing as a widespread art form
- Gelato
- Passeggiata di Gianicolo walk for beautiful views of the city
- AS Roma
- The Pantheon
- The Forum
- Domus Aurea
- Via del Governo Vecchio
- Villa Borghese
- Baroque architecture
- Morning coffee on a piazza
- Crossing the Tiber on foot
- Al dente pasta
- Trastevere

Rome 006

VITAL STATISTICS

NAME: ROME

NICKNAME: THE ETERNAL CITY

DATE OF BIRTH: 21 APRIL 753 BC; ANCIENT ROMANS DATED THE CITY FOUNDATION FROM THIS DATE

ADDRESS: ITALY (MAP 3, K13)

HEIGHT: 17M

SIZE: 150 SQ KM

POPULATION: 3.8 MILLION

THE COBBLED DISTRICT OF TRASTEVERE IS ALWAYS A BLUR OF ACTION.
Photographer: Glenn Beanland (2)

BERNINI'S COLONNADE, THE GRAND GATEWAY TO THE VATICAN, PIAZZA DI SAN PIETRO.
Photographer: Martin Moos (3)

TWO OLD FRIENDS BASK IN THE SUNSET GLOW OF PIAZZA GARIBALDI, WITH CENTRAL ROME IN THE BACKGROUND.
Photographer: Martin Moos (4)

WEAKNESSES

- Overcrowded buses and an all but useless metro
- Too many menus in English/French/German
- Bureaucracy
- Tame nightlife
- Trying to walk in stylish shoes on cobblestones (unless you're a local)
- Tripe
- Dreary modern high-rise buildings in the outer suburbs
- Lack of public toilets

GOLD STAR

History – Rome knows that no-one's coming here for the modern architecture, and so a lot of money gets spent on keeping the past alive for tourists.

CITYSPEAK

- Do you think they'll ever spend money on Rome for Romans?
- Whatever ruins have been found this week
- Whether or not the new Pope is settling in
- I reckon this government won't last six months

STARRING ROLE IN...

- *Roma, città aperta* (Rome, Open City, 1945)
- *Ladri di biciclette* (The Bicycle Thief, 1948)
- *Roman Holiday* (1953)
- *La Dolce Vita* (1961)

IMPORT

- Other countries' citizens
- Irish theme pubs
- Caravaggio
- Helmet laws for Vespa and motorcycle riders
- Smart cars
- Knock-off handbags
- John Keats
- The current Pope
- Drugs
- Telecommunications technology

EXPORT

- Rules and regulations
- Pasta
- Roads
- Bread-and-circuses politics
- Conservation techniques
- Roman numerals
- Toga parties

SEE the Vatican.

EAT Rome's favourite pizza at Da Baffetto.

DRINK a glass of Torre Ercolana, an opulent local red from Anagni, in a little *enoteca* (wine bar).

DO as the Romans do.

WATCH some of the tightest reverse parking you'll ever see.

BUY something beautiful from a household name on Via dei Condotti.

AFTER DARK go sightseeing when everyone's in bed and the traffic's negligible – you won't get inside the big sights, but you will get to see the outside with no hassles.

URBAN MYTH

According to the legend of Romulus and Remus, the twin sons of Rhea Silvia (a Latin princess) and the war god Mars were raised by a she-wolf after being abandoned on the banks of the River Tiber. The myth says Romulus killed his brother during a battle over who should govern, and then established the city of Rome on the Palatine, making himself the first king. Later he disappeared, poetically taken up by the gods or, more prosaically, secretly murdered by senators.

San Francisco

007

VITAL STATISTICS

NAME: SAN FRANCISCO

NICKNAME: FRISCO (ALTHOUGH NOBODY FROM SAN FRANCISCO WOULD EVER SAY THIS); CITY BY THE BAY

DATE OF BIRTH: 1776; WHEN A MILITARY POST WAS ESTABLISHED BY SPANISH MISSIONARIES FROM MEXICO

ADDRESS: USA (MAP 1, G10)

HEIGHT: 16M

SIZE: 121 SQ KM

POPULATION: 750,000

Post dot-gone, the City by the Bay sparkles on with literary luminaries, artsy stars and a blinding array of cultures.

ANATOMY

The city is on the tightly packed tip of a peninsula bordered by the Pacific Ocean and San Francisco Bay. The central part resembles a generous slice of pie, with Van Ness Ave and Market St marking the two sides and the Embarcadero bend serving as the outer crust. Squeezed into this compact area are Union Sq, the Financial District, Civic Center, Chinatown, North Beach, Nob Hill, Russian Hill and Fisherman's Wharf. San Francisco's principal public transport system is Muni (San Francisco Municipal Railway), which operates nearly 100 bus lines (many of them electric trolleybuses), streetcars and the famous cable cars.

PEOPLE

Long ago an Anglo-Celtic town, the face of San Francisco has changed significantly since the early days. Though still predominantly a white population, the Asian community follows at a close second, as evidenced by the world's largest Chinatown outside Asia. The balance of the city's residents are Latino, the majority being Mexican, and black, with a significant 10% who classify themselves as 'other'. Best estimates say at least 11% of city residents – some 80,000 people – are gays or lesbians. San Francisco also ranks as fairly young, with a median age of 36.5 years old.

TYPICAL SAN FRANCISCAN

Native San Franciscans are few and far between. San Francisco is a city of transplants, and the diversity of the city attracts eccentrics, individualists, free spirits and nature lovers. Everyone you meet will be writing a novel, producing a short film or performing their interpretive dance, but somehow still have a better tan than you could imagine. They usually do it in between wine tasting in Marin County, being dazzled by the bay and bracing themselves for the next big one.

DEFINING EXPERIENCE

Hanging out in Haight Ashbury and getting a piercing or tat, browsing the latest wordy *wunderkind* works at the 826 Valencia bookstore, grabbing a boa constrictor of a burrito on Mission St, making new friends with leather chaps and handle-bar moustaches at Harvey's, chowing down on dim sum in Chinatown and then spotting the Golden Gate through a curtain of fog.

STRENGTHS

- Golden Gate Bridge
- The Presidio
- Mexican food
- Diverse sexuality
- World-class restaurants
- Eccentricity
- The Giants
- Alcatraz
- Beat poetry
- Carlos Santana
- The Ferry Plaza Farmers Market
- San Francisco 49ers
- City Lights bookstore
- Haight Ashbury
- Grateful Dead

WEAKNESSES

- Haight Ashbury
- Grateful Dead
- Panhandlers
- Fog
- The Tenderloin
- San Andreas Fault
- Real-estate prices

GOLD STAR

Hanging out – Kerouac came here to learn how to do nothing and the city is still a great place to people-watch or just tune into the universe, man.

CITYSPEAK

- Parental leave for sperm/egg donors – should the state pay?
- Where to buy the best not dogs and soy milk
- Are there any decent apartments for under two grand a month?

STARRING ROLE IN...

- *The Golden Gate* by Vikram Seth
- *On the Road* by Jack Kerouac
- *Tales of the City* by Armistead Maupin
- *Memento* (2000)
- *Basic Instinct* (1992)
- *Dirty Harry* (1971)
- *American Graffiti* (1973)
- *Birdman of Alcatraz* (1962)
- *Guess Who's Coming to Dinner* (1967)
- *The Joy Luck Club* (1993)

IMPORT

- Alice Walker
- Tom Waits
- Miles Davis
- Isabel Allende
- Amy Tan
- Jack Kerouac
- Mark Twain
- Hippies
- Allen Ginsberg
- Lawrence Ferlinghetti
- Robin Williams
- Dave Eggers

EXPORT

- Birkenstocks
- George Lucas
- Carlos Santana
- Web developers
- Grateful Dead
- Dead Kennedys
- William Randolph Hearst
- Martinis
- Performance poetry
- Jack London
- Levi's jeans
- Harvey Milk
- Gertrude Stein
- Gordon Getty
- OJ Simpson
- Joe DiMaggio
- Sam Spade
- Granola
- Thomas Pynchon

SEE

SEE the almost inescapable Alcatraz, which hosted Al Capone and a bird fancier or two.

EAT a juicy burrito at La Taquería on Mission St.

DRINK an English beer pumped straight from the cellar at Magnolia Pub Brewery.

DO the cycle around the Presidio as a warm-up for mountain biking in Marin County.

WATCH and heckle a spoken word performance (that's poetry reading to you and me) at Café Du Nord.

BUY an old vinyl copy of the Grateful Dead at Amoeba Records on Haight St.

AFTER DARK catch a brew and beating at Bondage A Go Go at the Cat Club.

URBAN MYTH

Emperor Norton I came to San Francisco as a young man and made a fortune from the city's boomtown economy, but lost everything in a business gamble in 1852 and never recovered. After eight years of increasing poverty, he snapped, at least in one key respect: he declared himself the Emperor of the United States, and within a month he added the title Protector of Mexico. Norton never appeared without his uniform, including a plumed hat and sword. He issued his own money, which was good-naturedly accepted by many shopkeepers. Norton also made an injunction against the word 'Frisco' with a princely penalty of $25. In 1880, thousands of people attended Norton's royal funeral. He now rests in Colma Cemetery under a headstone proclaiming him 'Emperor of the United States & Protector of Mexico'.

SALUTING THE SAN, ARTIST PETER RABBIT PAYS HOMAGE TO HIS HOME TOWN.
Photographer: Anthony Pidgeon (1)

DANCERS SWITCH ON THE COLOURFAST SPIN CYCLE AT THE CARNIVAL ON MEMORIAL DAY WEEKEND.
Photographer: Rick Gerharter (2)

THE NEON WONDERLAND OF CHINATOWN BY NIGHT.
Photographer: John Elk III (3)

I'M PLASTIC AND I'M BEAUTIFUL! – A DOLL-FACED ACTIVIST AT THE GAY DAY PARADE.
Photographer: Rick Gerharter (4)

Bangkok
008

VITAL STATISTICS

NAME: BANGKOK OR *KRUNG THEP MAHANAKHON AMON RATTANAKOSIN MAHINTHARA AYUTHAYA MAHADILOK PHOP NOPPHARAT RATCHATHANI BURIROM UDOMRATCHANIWET MAHASATHAN AMON PIMAN AWATAN SATHIT SAKKATHATTIYA WITSANUKAM PRASIT* (TRANSLATION: THE CITY OF ANGELS, THE GREAT CITY, THE ETERNAL JEWEL CITY, THE IMPREGNABLE CITY OF GOD INDRA, THE GRAND CAPITAL OF THE WORLD ENDOWED WITH NINE PRECIOUS GEMS, THE HAPPY CITY, ABOUNDING IN AN ENORMOUS ROYAL PALACE THAT RESEMBLES THE HEAVENLY ABODE WHERE REIGNS THE REINCARNATED GOD, A CITY GIVEN BY INDRA AND BUILT BY VISHNUKARN)

NICKNAME: VENICE OF THE EAST

DATE OF BIRTH: MID-16TH CENTURY; FOUNDED AS A TRADING POST

ADDRESS: THAILAND (MAP 5, K8)

HEIGHT: 2M

SIZE: 1569 SQ KM

POPULATION: 8 MILLION

It's a city of contrasts: glass and steel buildings shaped like cartoon robots standing next to glittering temple spires; wreaths of jasmine flowers dangling from the rear-view mirrors of buses and taxis; shaven-headed, orange-robed monks walking barefoot along the street beneath a bank of giant Sony screens blasting MTV Asia.

ANATOMY

Bangkok is located in the basin of the Chao Phraya River. The land is crisscrossed with canals and rivers. The sky is littered with high-rises in the form of shopping malls and major hotel chains but the side streets (*sois*) harbour canals and traditional Thai buildings and, perhaps, even a few teak houses. The Skyrail is an efficient and air-conditioned mode of transportation that circumnavigates the city. A túk-túk (motorised rickshaw) will take you wherever you want to go.

PEOPLE

The population is mostly Thai, although there are many Chinese immigrants and an increasing number of Indians.

TYPICAL BANGKOKIAN

About one in every ten Thais is said to be from Bangkok. Patriotic taxi drivers will welcome you and wax lyrical about their city, with a polite smile on their face. They are down-to-earth and remarkably calm, despite the bureaucracy and traffic congestion.

DEFINING EXPERIENCE

Heralding in the day with a bit of t'ai chi in Lumphini Park and, if your muscles can manage to move after a gruelling massage at the Wat Pho school of massage, taking a spot of high tea in the Author's Lounge at the Oriental, alongside the ghosts of Joseph Conrad and Graham Greene.

STRENGTHS

- You can buy anything for a (very cheap) price, anything
- Markets around every corner
- Vegetarian cafés
- Crazy Patpong entertainment
- One-hour Thai massage for less than the price of a Happy Meal
- Five-star hotels for a song
- DVDs of films that are still making their way onto the big screen
- Open 24 hours
- Beautiful fabrics
- Gilt stupas in the centre of the madness

WEAKNESSES

- Pollution – you may as well smoke a packet a day
- *Faràng* (Caucasians) with beer guts, wearing silk shirts and with sweaty arms around young Thai boys
- Traffic congestion despite an organised skyrail network
- Black-as-tar river (don't ask why the river taxis have covered windows)
- Count-down traffic lights

GOLD STAR

Ayuthaya Historical Park – a Unesco World Heritage site, Ayuthaya's historic temples are scattered throughout this once magnificent city and along the encircling rivers.

CITYSPEAK

- Gun-toting teachers
- Bangkok Fashion City: is Bangkok set to become the Milan of the East?
- The Thailand Elite card continues to disappoint despite the discounts, VIP treatment and potential access to easy acquisition of land by foreigners

STARRING ROLE IN...

- *Bangkok Hilton* (1989)
- *Nang Nak* (1998)
- *The Shutter* (2004)
- *A Siamese Fairy Tale* by Somerset Maugham

IMPORT

- Japanese investment
- The flora at Rama IX Park
- Fake IDs on Khao San Rd
- Football
- Thai democracy – modelled on the UK system of government where parliamentarians have the go-ahead to lampoon one another
- Jim Thompson
- Virgin Radio
- Scrabble – used as a learning aid
- Zebra crossings (largely ignored by drivers)

EXPORT

- Coconut curries
- Go-go bars and ping-pong shows
- Thai massage
- Sarongs
- Exquisite silk
- Gems (read: scams)
- Red Bull (you can still get the original formula in Thailand)
- Siamese cats
- Reproduction couture

SEE the dizzying mobile-phone floor at MBK shopping centre.

EAT a bag of green mango wedges coated in sugar, lime juice and chilli – not for a weak stomach.

DRINK Singha Beer while people-watching on Khao San Rd.

DO have a heavy-duty one-hour massage on the sprawling king-size beds at the Wat Pho school of massage.

WATCH river life and longboats cruise languidly by from a riverside café.

BUY a protective amulet from the amulet market near the Grand Palace or the funkiest clothing for your pooch at the Chatuchak weekend market.

AFTER DARK wander around Patpong and take in a show.

URBAN MYTH

According to legend, the Emerald Buddha, which was created in 43 BC in Pataliputra, India, was rediscovered when lightning struck a pagoda in a temple in Chiang Rai. It was covered in stucco but a small chip on its nose revealed a hint of green. The emerald was later revealed to be jade but the name stuck. The Emerald Buddha now resides at Wat Phra Kaew.

FROM SILVER SCREEN TO CITY SCENE, AN ARTIST APPLIES FINISHING TOUCHES TO A MOVIE POSTER.
Photographer: John Borthwick (1)

A YOUNG MONK AT THE BUDDHA BENCHAMABOPHIT IN DUSIT.
Photographer: Richard I'Anson (2)

ALL FIRE AND SPICE, A NIGHT MARKET HOTS UP ON THE CITY STREETS.
Photographer: Jerry Alexander (3)

JUVENILE WATER PISTOL COMMANDOS WREAK HAVOC AT THE SONGKHRAN 'WATER-SPLASHING FESTIVAL' TO CELEBRATE NEW YEAR.
Photographer: Richard I'Anson (4)

Cape Town 009

VITAL STATISTICS

NAME: CAPE TOWN

NICKNAME: THE MOTHER CITY

DATE OF BIRTH: 1652; WHEN THE DUTCH PULLED UP AT THE BASE OF TABLE MOUNTAIN AND ESTABLISHED SOUTH AFRICA'S FIRST EUROPEAN SETTLEMENT

ADDRESS: SOUTH AFRICA (MAP 2, F27)

HEIGHT: 17M

SIZE: 300 SQ KM

POPULATION: 2.98 MILLION

AFTER-DARK AMBIENCE IN THE STYLISHLY RENOVATED 19TH-CENTURY METROPOLE HOTEL ON LONG ST.
Photographer: Brent Stirton (1)

SUNSET SETTLES OVER THE AZURE WATERS AND LONG WHITE SANDY STRETCH OF CAMPS BAY BEACH.
Photographer: Brent Stirton (2)

A FISHERMAN SELLS HIS CATCH STRAIGHT OFF THE BOAT.
Photographer: Brent Stirton (3)

THE OLD MALAY QUARTER OF BO-KAAP, WITH ITS STRING OF HIP BARS AND EATERIES, IS A RICH CULTURAL AND SOCIAL CENTRE.
Photographer: Brent Stirton (4)

Even transient visitors can't help but devote a few million brain cells to storing images of Cape Town's grandeur, from its striking Table Mountain backdrop to its glorious beaches and strange and wonderful wildlife.

ANATOMY

A major part of Cape Town's allure is the 1073m-high mountain slap-bang in the centre of the 'City Bowl': Table Mountain and its attendant peaks – Devil's Peak and Lion's Head – are Cape Town's most enduring image. If you drive (or ride a bus) 70km south, you'll find the fabled Cape of Good Hope. While Cape Town has a good rail and bus network, taxis, although a little on the pricey side, are well worth considering late at night.

PEOPLE

Of Cape Town's population, more than half are coloured: blacks account for about a third of the total and whites and other groups comprise the balance. In the Cape Town area three of South Africa's 11 official languages are prominent: Afrikaans (spoken by many whites and coloureds), English (spoken by nearly everyone) and Xhosa (spoken mainly by blacks).

TYPICAL CAPETONIAN

There is no such thing as a 'typical' Capetonian – the city's range of cultures and ethnicities put paid to that. However, more than a decade after the fall of apartheid, all citizens, regardless of background, generally share a political optimism. While Cape Town is reasonably safe, citizens living in the townships on the Cape Flats endure a neighbourhood rife with crime and poverty.

DEFINING EXPERIENCE

Hiking Table Mountain then making the exhilarating abseil down (lazy bones could ride the cable car) before taking in a glorious Cape Town sunset and South African wine or few on a harbour cruise of Table Bay.

STRENGTHS

- Robben Island
- The Bo-kaap
- Lively music and cultural scene
- Company's Gardens
- Table Mountain
- Cape of Good Hope Nature Reserve
- District Six Museum
- Drum Café
- Houses of Parliament
- Rust-en-Vreugd
- Kirstenbosch Botanical Gardens
- South African National Gallery

WEAKNESSES

- Rampant crime and poverty on the Cape Flats
- The wealthy indifference
- The black/white/coloured divide
- Suspicion and mistrust among different cultural groups

GOLD STAR

Hospitality – Cape Town's mix of trendy hostelries match up favourably to those in any other cosmopolitan city, and, for all of the city's contradictions, you'll find Capetonians likeable, (generally) open-minded and relaxed.

CITYSPEAK

- AIDS babies – who will care for South Africa's generation of orphans?
- Patricia de Lille – the next South African president?

STARRING ROLE IN…

- *Long Walk to Freedom* by Nelson Mandela
- *Sachs Street* by Rayda Jacobs
- *In My Country* (2004)
- *Lord of War* (2005)
- *The Last Face* (2005)

IMPORT

- The Dutch
- Computer software and services
- Agricultural products
- Pharmaceutical products
- Tourism

EXPORT

- Nelson Mandela
- Archbishop Desmond Tutu
- Gold
- Diamonds
- Wine
- Arts and crafts
- Textiles
- JM Coetzee

SEE Unesco World Heritage site Robben Island, used as a prison from the early days of the VOC (Dutch East India Company) right up until the first years of majority rule.

EAT decadent chocolate chilli fillets at Madame Zingara's, a popular mid-priced haunt decked out like a gypsy caravan on Loop St.

DRINK potent straw rum as you rock the casbah Cape Town–style at Fez on Hout St – roundly toasted as the city's hippest bar.

DO forgo the cable car and hike up Table Mountain for an unforgettable view, taking the time to sniff over 1400 species of flowering plants.

WATCH any one of Cape Town's three teams in the national Premier Soccer League.

BUY a colourful, highly patterned 'Madiba' shirt from Greenmarket Sq – as popularised by Nelson Mandela.

AFTER DARK pick up your own *djembe* drum and fold into the mesmerising rhythm of the drum circle at the Drum Café, an African institution spreading around the world.

URBAN MYTH

For centuries, sailors (most famously King George V) have spotted the ghost of the schooner the *Flying Dutchman* sailing the waters of Cape Point. Before the ship went down en route to Holland in 1641, her foolhardy captain, Hendrik Van der Decken, vowed to the devil that he would sail to the ends of the earth. More than 360 years on, let's hope that Van der Decken has some able seamen on board to take the wheel occasionally.

IN THE WARM GLOW OF A GAS LAMP, TWO WOMEN PURCHASE A LATE-NIGHT CORN SNACK NEAR SULTANAHMET MOSQUE.
Photographer: Scott Barbour (1)

The masterpiece of the Byzantine and Ottoman Empires in its former incarnations as Byzantium and Constantinople, and the jewel of the modern Turkish state, Istanbul is a bustling, rambunctious, energetic and bewitching city.

ANATOMY

The only city to straddle two continents, Istanbul is separated into European and Asian districts by the Bosphorus. The heart of Old Istanbul is at Sultanahmet and the nearby Bazaar district on the European side. Across the Golden Horn is the former diplomatic quarter of Beyoğlu, now a swish shopping district. Buses connect all corners of the city and yellow taxis are ubiquitous, but the best way to cross the city is on the ferries that ply the turgid waters of the Bosphorus.

PEOPLE

Istanbul is largely Turkish, but the fabric of the city and its citizens is interwoven with diverse influences. There are small Greek, Armenian and Jewish communities, as well as Russian and Georgian traders. Many Istanbul families can trace their origins to the years of the Ottoman Empire, but many villagers from Anatolia have also arrived in recent years, seeking the opportunities that the thriving metropolis provides.

TYPICAL ISTANBULLU

Istanbullus are gregarious and talkative and admirably relaxed for citizens of such an enormous city. They love a cup of çay (tea) and an opportunity to discuss the matters of the day. Istanbul residents are increasingly proud of the history and legacy of their great city. They are uniformly football mad and love green spaces in which to conduct elaborate and lengthy picnics. Family plays an integral role in everyday life, and many Istanbullus holiday in ancestral villages in Anatolia.

Istanbul
010

VITAL STATISTICS

NAME: ISTANBUL

NICKNAME: THE CITY OF THE WORLD'S DESIRE

DATE OF BIRTH: 657 BC; WHEN BYZAS, SON OF THE GOD POSEIDON AND A NYMPH, ESTABLISHED THE CITY

ADDRESS: TURKEY (MAP 3, R14)

HEIGHT: 114M

SIZE: 1991 SQ KM

POPULATION: 9.6 MILLION

BEER AND BANTER ARE THE ORDER OF THE DAY AT A CAFÉ IN NEVIZADE SOKAK.
Photographer: Scott Barbour (2)

FLAG SELLERS WAVE THEIR WARES IN FRONT OF NEW MOSQUE, EMINÖNÜ.
Photographer: Scott Barbour (3)

FOOD FOR BODY AND SOUL – A MOTHER BREAKS TO FEED HER CHILD OUTSIDE NEW MOSQUE, EMINÖNÜ.
Photographer: Scott Barbour (4)

DEFINING EXPERIENCE

Contemplating the mighty soaring domes of Aya Sofya and the Blue Mosque, getting lost in the arcades of the Grand Bazaar, going underground at the Basilica Cistern beneath the heart of Sultanahmet, window-shopping on cosmopolitan İstiklal Caddesi, chilling out with a *nargileh* (water pipe), catching a ferry to Ortaköy and having a drink on the waterfront.

STRENGTHS

- Vibrant arts, music and fashion scenes
- History around every corner
- Bosphorus cruises
- Gregarious Turks
- Eating baklava and *lokum* (Turkish delight)
- Commuting on ferries
- *Meyhanes* (taverns) on Nevizade Sokak
- Topkapı Palace
- Carpets, textiles and Turkish handicrafts
- Architecture – from Byzantine to ultramodern
- Old books and maps at Sahaflar Çarşısı
- The Fish Market at Beyoğlu
- Wrought-iron balconies and cobbled streets
- Sea views

WEAKNESSES

- Carpet-shop touts
- Traffic
- Smokers everywhere
- Old neighbourhoods being swallowed up
- Wooden houses, dripping with character, falling into disrepair

GOLD STAR

The interaction of air, water, land and architecture – to truly appreciate this, climb the Galata Tower at twilight to watch the sun retreat across two continents and silhouette the voluptuous skyline of Old Istanbul.

CITYSPEAK

- The bid to join the EU
- Should we have removed all those zeros from the currency?
- Are we due for the next big quake?
- The Eurovision song contest

STARRING ROLE IN...

- *From Russia with Love* (1974)
- *Topkapi* (1964)
- *Hamam* (1996)
- *Distant* (2003)
- *The Black Book* and *Istanbul: A Memoir* by Orhan Pamuk
- *The Birds Are Also Gone* by Yashar Kemal
- *Portrait of a Turkish Family* by Irfan Orga
- *The Turkish Embassy Letters* by Lady Mary Wortley Montagu
- *Istanbul the Imperial City* by John Freely
- The Inspector Ikmen crime novels of Barbara Nadel

IMPORT

- Anatolian workers and their families

EXPORT

- Guest workers to Germany
- Rifat Özbek
- Hussein Chalayan
- Cars, appliances, consumer goods
- Carpets, leather, ceramics

SEE the treasures of the Ottoman sultans at the Topkapı Palace.

EAT a fish sandwich from the vendors on the boats at Eminönü.

DRINK *rakı* (aniseed spirit) accompanied by savoury *meze* (selection of hot and cold starters traditionally served at the beginning of Middle Eastern meals).

DO a Bosphorus cruise, bumping between rickety piers on the European and Asian shores.

WATCH commuters at Eminönü in the late afternoon – the whole world is on the move.

BUY carpets or traditional craftwork in the Grand Bazaar – come prepared to haggle.

AFTER DARK head across to Beyoğlu to the bars and clubs around İstiklal Caddesi.

URBAN MYTH

English prime minister Benjamin Disraeli spent time in Istanbul in 1830, claiming 'the life of this people greatly accords with my taste, being somewhat indolent and melancholy... To repose on voluptuous ottomans, to smoke superb pipes, daily to indulge in the luxuries of the bath...is I think a far more sensible life...'

Melbourne

011

VITAL STATISTICS

NAME: MELBOURNE

NICKNAME: PARIS OF THE SOUTHERN HEMISPHERE

DATE OF BIRTH: 1835; BY TASMANIAN ENTREPRENEURS KEEN ON A MAINLAND BASE

ADDRESS: AUSTRALIA (MAP 1, LL21)

HEIGHT: 35M

SIZE: 2025 SQ KM

POPULATION: 3.2 MILLION

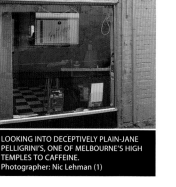

LOOKING INTO DECEPTIVELY PLAIN-JANE PELLIGRINI'S, ONE OF MELBOURNE'S HIGH TEMPLES TO CAFFEINE.
Photographer: Nic Lehman (1)

Suave, sophisticated, and stark-raving sports mad, Melbourne is an arty powerhouse with an eye on the Melbourne Cup and a mouthful of world-class cuisine.

ANATOMY

Melbourne lines Port Phillip Bay and stretches into the plains to the west and east and out to the foothills of the Dandenong Ranges. The city is divided by the muddy Yarra River, with the CBD on the north bank, set in a neat grid that suits its kitschy tram transport perfectly. To the CBD's north is the dining precinct of Carlton and grungy Fitzroy, which vies for coolest-suburb honours with St Kilda to the south of the Yarra with its ace of beaches and backpackers. Trams and trains are the best way to get around the city.

PEOPLE

Melbourne's population is drawn from around the world, with postwar migrations of Italian, Greek and Jewish people giving it a unique cultural make-up. Melbourne, famously, has the highest population of Greeks of any city outside of Greece itself. More recently Vietnamese, Indonesian and Malaysian people have arrived, with Melbourne having a particularly high population of international students (the fourth-largest in the world). Melbourne's original people, the Wurundjeri, have survived all of these waves of immigration.

TYPICAL MELBURNIAN

Dressed in black and swilling a coffee, Melburnians have been known to argue about their city's best restaurant for hours and spend most of Monday talking about how their footy team went. You could say lifestyle is more important than career, but Melburnians are passionate about their politics, with the city holding the largest protests against federal government change to industrial relations reforms. While many talk about the 'great divide' between the north and south side of the Yarra, many more live in suburbs far from the river.

DEFINING EXPERIENCE

Running a lap of the Botanic Gardens, then catching a tram to the Melbourne Cricket Ground (MCG) for Saturday's big AFL (Australian Football League) game, hunkering down in a Fitzroy pub to watch local band the Lucksmiths, then spotting possums in Carlton Gardens on the way home.

STRENGTHS

- Flinders St Station
- Trams
- Secret city laneways and back alleys
- St Kilda beaches
- Live music
- Federation Sq
- Melbourne Zoo
- Sports-obsessed culture
- National Gallery of Victoria
- Melbourne Cricket Ground (MCG, or more simply, the G)
- Esplanade Hotel (The Espy)
- Royal Exhibition Buildings and Carlton Gardens
- Snazzy new Docklands
- 'Paris end' of Collins St
- St Kilda bars and restaurants
- Melbourne Museum
- Diverse cuisine
- Funky Fitzroy
- Lygon St cafés
- Artsy Southgate

WEAKNESSES

- Tricky traffic hook turns
- St Kilda beaches
- Tea-coloured Yarra River
- Controversial Crown Casino

GOLD STAR

Multiculturalism – from postwar Italian and Greek immigrants to more recent Vietnamese and Eritrean families, Melbourne has a diverse ethnicity.

CITYSPEAK

- Premier Steve Bracks' chance at another term
- How 'your' footy club went on the weekend – having a team is compulsory
- What is Spencer St Station designed to look like: a dragon or a dog's breakfast?
- What are you seeing at this year's film/comedy/arts/writers'/fringe/ midsumma festival?
- Have you got your tickets for the 2006 Commonwealth Games yet?

STARRING ROLE IN...

- *Ghost Rider* (2006)
- *Three Dollars* (2005)
- *The Wog Boy* (2000)
- *The Bank* (2001)
- *Malcolm* (1986)
- *Proof* (1991)
- *Crackerjack* (2002)
- *Mallboy* (2001)
- *The Castle* (1997)
- *Love and Other Catastrophes* (1996)
- *Death in Brunswick* (1991)
- *Dogs in Space* (1987)
- *Harvie Krumpet* (2003)
- *Street Hero* (1984)

IMPORT

- Paul Kelly
- Steve Bracks
- Great coffee
- Cathy Freeman
- Formula One Grand Prix

EXPORT

- Eddie McGuire
- AFL
- *Neighbours*
- Kylie Minogue
- Peter Carey
- AC/DC
- Nick Cave
- Melbourne Cup
- The Australian Ballet
- Jet
- Heidelberg School
- Dame Edna Everage and her alter-ego, Barry Humphries
- Adam Elliot
- Lonely Planet
- The Cat Empire
- John Farnham

SEE the patchwork design of Federation Sq.

EAT the sumptuous Peking duck at the Flower Drum, Melbourne's foodie apogee.

DRINK an espresso (anything else isn't *autentico*) at Pellegrini's, Mario's or a fabulous new place that absolutely no-one has ever heard of.

DO the adrenaline rush of kite-surfing at St Kilda Beach.

WATCH local band Architecture in Helsinki at the iconic live-music venue, the Corner Hotel.

BUY an edgy outfit on Chapel St, only to spot a bargain knock-off on Bridge Rd.

AFTER DARK check out the back alleys that hide bars like Honky Tonks and Movida.

URBAN MYTH

On 17 December 1967, Australia's prime minister Harold Holt popped out for a swim on Cheviot Beach not far from Melbourne and disappeared without a trace. Speculation was rife about what happened to the head of state, with theories ranging from suicide to defection to China. The latter conspiracy theory speculated that Holt had arranged to be picked up by a Chinese submarine as a pay-off for creating closer trade relationships with Asia. When told of this idea, his wife, Zara, reputedly scoffed that Holt 'didn't even like Chinese food'. Regardless of his diet, Holt's disappearance remains a part of Melbourne culture through the rhyming-slang expression 'to do a Harold Holt' (or bolt) and Glen Iris' ironic Harold Holt Swimming Centre.

WORSHIPPERS CONGREGATE A THE MCG, THE GREAT CATHEDRAL OF AUSTRALIAN RULES FOOTBALL, MELBOURNE'S ORTHODOX RELIGION.
Photographer: Dallas Stribley (2)

A MAN JOGS ALONG SOUTH MELBOURNE BEACH BENEATH BROODING STORM CLOUDS.
Photographer: Regis Martin (3)

NOT JUST FOR SQUARES – AWESTRUCK DEVOTEES OF MELBOURNE'S OTHER RELIGION AT THE AUSTRALIAN CENTRE FOR CONTEMPORARY ART. Photographer: Phil Weymouth (4)

WORDSMITHS IN WANCHAI DWARFED BY THEIR NEON CREATION IN THE CITY OF LIGHTS.
Photographer: Lawrence Worcester (1)

Hong Kong

012

VITAL STATISTICS

NAME: HONG KONG

NICKNAME: THE CITY OF LIGHTS

DATE OF BIRTH: 206 BC; WHEN THE EASTERN HAN DYNASTY RULED

ADDRESS: CHINA (MAP 5, P5)

HEIGHT: 33M

SIZE: 1100 SQ KM

POPULATION: 6.8 MILLION

Hong Kong is a noisy, vibrant fusion of West and East, packed with businesspeople, markets, temples, futuristic buildings, double-decker trams and boats crisscrossing the harbour – it is unlike anywhere else on earth.

ANATOMY

Four main areas make up Hong Kong. To the south lies Hong Kong Island containing most major businesses and government offices and many top-end hotels and restaurants, all overlooked by Victoria Peak. Over the harbour to the north bustles the Kowloon Peninsula, where you'll find even more people and tempting shopping opportunities. The New Territories, which spread from Kowloon towards mainland China, and the 234 outlying islands, complete the puzzle. Public transport is cheap, fast, widely used and generally efficient. Take your pick of buses and trains.

PEOPLE

Approximately 94% of Hong Kong's population is ethnic Chinese, but only about 57% of Hong Kong Chinese were born in the territory. Of the foreign community, the three largest groups are Filipinos, Indonesians and Canadians, with Americans not far behind. Australians and Britons make up the smallest portion. The largest religious groups in Hong Kong are Buddhists and Christians.

TYPICAL HONG KONG CITIZEN

Beneath the Western consumerist energy of Hong Kong, Chinese beliefs and traditions remain. Top concerns are the appeasement of spirits and predicting the future. Memories of economic oppression, war and hunger mean the pursuit of wealth also scores highly. People used to have a reputation for rudeness, but this has noticeably reduced. Etiquette is important without being overwhelming (here's a tip: always carry business cards and hand them over with two hands not one). Hong Kong society is highly educated, with a literacy rate of about 93%. Hong Kong consumes more oranges than anywhere else on earth and has the world's highest per-capita consumption of cognac. Popular pastimes include dining together, betting on horses and watching or participating in sport. The city is also very fashion conscious. Finally, Hong Kong citizens are proud of China's successes.

DEFINING EXPERIENCE

Riding the *Star Ferry* to Tsim Sha Tsui for a stroll before heading to Kowloon Park for some t'ai chi, soaking up the buzz of Nathan Rd, then refuelling with afternoon tea at the Peninsula Hong Kong hotel.

STRENGTHS

- Victoria Peak
- Glittering modern architecture
- Star Ferry
- Hong Kong trams
- Temple St night market
- Tian Tan Buddha statue
- Shopping in Central and Causeway Bay
- Easy business dealings
- Beaches and hiking on Lamma
- 600 temples
- Low taxes
- Central Escalator
- Fashion eg Walter Ma, Barney Cheng
- Noodle restaurants
- Karaoke bars and Canto-pop
- Low crime rate
- Happy hours
- Fortune-tellers
- Hong Kong Museum of History
- Rugby Sevens

WEAKNESSES

- Noise, water and air pollution
- Crowds
- Overexcited air-conditioning
- Expensive beer

GOLD STAR

Business

CITYSPEAK

- Business, business, business
- Top tips for the next Happy Valley race

STARRING ROLE IN...

- *Tomb Raider 2* (2003)
- *Rush Hour* (1998)
- *Double Impact* (1991)
- *Year of the Dragon* (1985)
- *The Man with the Golden Gun* (1974)

IMPORT

- Water supplies and food (most of this is imported from the mainland)
- Expats
- Money
- Sports stars for international tournaments

EXPORT

- John Woo
- Jackie Chan
- John Rocha
- Chow Yun Fat
- Clothing
- Costume jewellery
- Handbags
- Umbrellas
- Artificial flowers
- Toys
- Clocks
- Telecommunications
- Banking and money

SEE the jaw-dropping view from the summit of Victoria Peak and enjoy the gravity-challenging ride there on the Peak tram.

EAT dim sum delights at the noisy, authentic Maxim's Palace.

DRINK bubbly at the Grand Hyatt Champagne Bar and enjoy live blues in the Art Deco surroundings.

DO take a nocturnal lantern-festooned *Star Ferry* from Tsim Sha Tsui to Central and enjoy the cityscape by night.

WATCH thousands make the pilgrimage to the *Tian Tan Buddha* statue on Buddha's Birthday in May.

BUY a custom-made suit from Sam's Tailor or try your luck on Nathan Rd.

AFTER DARK hit fur-lined C Club, where you can groove to house music then relax on the double bed.

URBAN MYTH

On 15 January 1857, 400 Europeans living in Hong Kong collapsed, writhing in agony as a result of eating arsenic-laced bread from the E-Sing Bakery in Wan Chai. At the time anti-foreigner sentiment was rampant and people were calling for the Chinese to overthrow the colonial power. The owner of the bakery, Cheong, was assumed to be an activist and taken to trial. However it transpired that he too had been poisoned and the jury found him not guilty. (Popular opinion forced him into voluntary exile for five years anyway.) The culprit was never found, E-Sing Bakery closed and the gourmet goods emporium Lane, Crawford and Company set up its own bakery, managed, of course, by Europeans. The 'poisoned bread case' remains unsolved.

A WINDOW CATCHES THE REFLECTION OF A TAXI IN A SWIRL OF MOVEMENT AND ELECTRIC LIGHT.
Photographer: Andrea Pistolesi (2)

A YOUNG DINER HELPS HERSELF AT FOOK YING HOT POT RESTAURANT.
Photographer: Oliver Strewe (3)

THE FUTURISTIC SKYLINE OF HONG KONG BY NIGHT.
Photographer: Ray Laskowitz (4)

Kathmandu

013

VITAL STATISTICS

NAME: KATHMANDU

NICKNAME: THE DOORWAY TO THE HIMALAYA

DATE OF BIRTH: AD 723; FOUNDED BY KING GUN KAMDEV

ADDRESS: NEPAL (MAP 5, F3)

HEIGHT: 1338M

SIZE: 395 SQ KM

POPULATION: 729,000

This amazing city seems, in places, unchanged since the Middle Ages; at other times it is just another developing-world capital rushing into a modern era of concrete and traffic pollution.

ANATOMY

In the high, fertile Kathmandu Valley, surrounded by terraced hills, the valley is the cultural and political heart of Nepal. Most of the interesting things to see in Kathmandu are clustered in the old part of town from Kantipath (the main north–south road) west towards the Vishnumati River. There are taxis (cheap) and buses (crowded).

PEOPLE

Kathmandu's population is fairly homogeneous, but Tibetans and other Nepali ethnic groups contribute to its populace. The valley was a meeting place of Mongoloid peoples from the Tibetan plateau (Buddhist) and a large influx of Indo-Aryan people (Hindu) from the south.

TYPICAL KATHMANDU CITIZEN

Although these days there is more money around, most of it has remained in the pockets of the upper class. Kathmandu has one of the highest inflation rates in Asia, so the cost of living can really take it out of the average pay packet. And while the city's literacy and health have improved over the last 20 years, they're still under par. Despite all this, people retain a good-humoured self-respect and integrity.

DEFINING EXPERIENCE

Strolling around the medieval-like old town and exploring Hanuman Dhoka (Old Royal Palace) before lunching at Babar Mahal Revisited, chilling out in the late afternoon in a rooftop garden and then choosing from the many Thamel restaurants for dinner.

STRENGTHS

- Thamel
- Pashupatinath
- Svayambunath
- Hanuman Dhoka
- Bodhnath
- Durbar Sq
- The flight in and out with awe-inspiring views of the Himalaya

WEAKNESSES

- Pollution
- The political situation
- The poverty
- The failings of democracy
- The failings of autocracy

GOLD STAR

Within the city itself are four Unesco World Heritage sites: Durbar Sq, Svayambunath, Bodhnath and Pashupatinath.

CITYSPEAK

- Democracy – are we going to get it back? Do we want it back?
- How bad is the pollution going to get?

STARRING ROLE IN...

- *The Tutor of History* by Manjushree Thapa
- *Forget Kathmandu: An Elegy for Democracy* by Manjushree Thapa
- *Escape from Kathmandu* by Kim Stanley Robinson
- *The Window of the House Opposite* by Govinda Bahadur Malla
- *The Guru of Love* by Samrat Upadhyay
- *Arresting God in Kathmandu* by Samrat Upadhyay

IMPORT

- Tibetan refugees
- Ethnic Nepalis from Bhutan
- Trekkers
- Pilgrims
- Hippies
- Polluting vehicles
- NGOs
- Democracy
- Guerrilla movements

EXPORT

- Dazed hippies
- Ambitious guidebook writers
- Gurkhas
- Giardia
- Students

SEE Mt Everest and the Himalaya on a one-hour mountain flight.

EAT very good Thai food or Himalayan perch at Yin Yang Restaurant in Thamel.

DRINK at New Orleans Café – a very mellow vibe.

DO wander from Pashupatinath temple, the Hindu funeral site on the banks of the Bagmati River, across the fields to Bodhnath, the Buddhist stupa.

WATCH the devotees climb the steps and circle the stupa in prayer at Svayambunath.

BUY clothes, cushions and bags from Maheela, part of the Women's Foundation (50% of monies go back to the producers).

AFTER DARK have a drink and listen to some music at Jatra in Thamel.

URBAN MYTH

Not only does Nepal have countless gods, goddesses and deities, but it also has a real living goddess. The Kumari Devi is a young girl who lives in the building known as the Kumari Bahal, right beside Kathmandu's Durbar Sq. The Kumari is selected from a particular caste of Newari gold- and silversmiths. Customarily, she is somewhere between four years old and puberty and must meet 32 strict physical requirements, ranging from the colour of her eyes and shape of her teeth to the sound of her voice. Her horoscope must also be appropriate, of course. Once suitable candidates have been found they are gathered together in a darkened room where terrifying noises are made, while men dance by in horrific masks and gruesome buffalo heads are on display. Naturally these goings-on are unlikely to frighten a real goddess, particularly one who is an incarnation of Durga, so the young girl who remains calm and collected throughout this ordeal is clearly the new Kumari. In a process similar to the selection of the Dalai Lama, the Kumari then chooses items of clothing and decoration worn by her predecessor as a final test.

COLOUR FOR SALE – TRADITIONAL TIKKA BRIGHTENS UP AN OPEN-AIR MARKET.
Photographer: Mark Andrew Kirby (1)

TWO SOLEMN TAMANG BOYS SETTLE IN FOR A TEA BREAK.

Photographer: Bill Wassman (2)

BUSINESS IS BLOOMING AT A FLOWER STALL ON THE BUSY JUNCTION OF ASAN TOLE.
Photographer: Greg Elms (3)

GOING STRAIGHT TO THE SOURCE – MEN CONGREGATE AROUND NEWSPAPER VENDORS TO CATCH THE LATEST NEWS.
Photographer: Andrew Peacock (4)

Prague

014

VITAL STATISTICS

NAME: PRAGUE

NICKNAME: MATIČKA PRAHA (LITTLE MOTHER PRAGUE)

DATE OF BIRTH: 4000 BC; WHEN FARMING COMMUNITIES WERE ESTABLISHED BY GERMANIC AND CELTIC TRIBES; THE SLAVS ARRIVED AROUND AD 600

ADDRESS: CZECH REPUBLIC (MAP 3, L9)

HEIGHT: 262M

SIZE: 496 SQ KM

POPULATION: 1.21 MILLION

With its fairy-tale cityscape, solid cultural heritage and perfect pilsner, Prague continues to captivate.

ANATOMY

Prague straddles the Vltava River, its two halves joined by the Charles Bridge, one of the world's loveliest. The centre consists of five historical towns: Hradčany, the castle district, on a hill above the west bank; Malá Strana (Little Quarter), between the river and castle; Staré Město, the Gothic 'Old Town' on the east bank; adjacent Josefov, the former Jewish ghetto; and Nové Město (New Town – new in the 14th century, that is), to the south and east. This compact maze is best appreciated on foot, aided by Prague's fine Soviet-era metro, tram and bus system.

PEOPLE

For a modern European city, the Czech capital is fairly homogeneous – Praguers are almost all Czechs. Most notable exceptions are the Slovak and Roma minorities (the latter, formerly known as Gypsies, are often the target of vicious racism), as well as significant numbers of German and American expatriates who now call Prague home.

TYPICAL PRAGUER

Praguers pay dearly for the privilege of living in one of Europe's best-preserved and most-visited cities – at least half their wages can go on rent, and many restaurants, bars and consumer goods are out of their reach. They still manage to drink enormous amounts of beer, and indulge decidedly highbrow cultural tastes (and dress up for the symphony). First impressions may suggest mild manners and old-fashioned values, but Praguers often harbour a surreal sense of humour, and a steely sense of their rights and their place in history.

DEFINING EXPERIENCE

Taking the dog for a run through Vrtbov Gardens and up Petřín Hill, refuelling on strudel and browsing for antique books in Staré Město, then drinking beer and scoffing sausage at riverside Letenske sady, laughing about David Černý's latest stunt and deciding whether it's to be an all-nighter at Akropolis or a jazz jam at Little Glen's.

STRENGTHS

- A thousand years of well-preserved European architecture
- Pilsner, pilsner and more pilsner
- Poignant, picturesque Josefov
- Old Town Sq, despite the tack
- Fab futurist Metro stations
- The Velvet Revolution
- The Havel/Pistek-designed uniforms of the castle guards
- Jan Švankmajer
- The morally instructive Astronomical Clock

WEAKNESSES

- Shuffling crowds of camcorder-wielding tourists
- Jazz-fusion fanatics
- Grumpy service
- Pickpockets
- Tacky souvenir shops
- Meter-meddling taxi drivers

GOLD STAR

Romance – despite the tourists, Prague's riverside setting and architectural heritage cannot fail to pull the heart strings.

CITYSPEAK

- Public toilets – what's the government doing about them?
- Will the ring road ever get built?
- What's the EU ever done for us?
- Staropramen beer – has it gone downhill since the brewery went multinational?

STARRING ROLE IN...

- *Comfortably Numb* (2005)
- *Van Helsing* (2004)
- *A Knight's Tale* (2001)
- *Mission: Impossible* (1996)
- *The Unbearable Lightness of Being* (1988)
- *Metamorphoses* by Franz Kafka

IMPORT

- Coca-Cola
- American trustafarians (a marijuana-smoking, rich, white university student)
- Soviet-era watches and fur hats
- Mexican restaurants
- British and Irish stag parties

EXPORT

- Animation
- Pilsner
- Franz Kafka
- Anton Dvořák
- Absinthe
- Textiles
- Milan Kundera
- Ivan Klima

SEE the splendid gilt-set slabs of semiprecious stones in the Chapel of St Wenceslas in St Vitus Cathedral, then take in the splendid view from the ramparts outside.

EAT posh pork and dumplings at the Kolkovna in Staré Město, a modern take on the trad beer hall.

DRINK light, dark or waywardly flavoured Czech lager, made on the premises at Nové Město's Pivovarský Dům.

DO a Sunday afternoon football match at AC Sparta Praha's stadium.

WATCH Smetana performed at the glorious, golden-roofed Národní Divadlo, a living monument to the Czech National Revival.

BUY a 16th-century aquatint of an angel at Antikvariát U Karlova Mostu, right near the Charles Bridge.

AFTER DARK dance with the Bohemians, or discover the lethal combination of *pivo* (beer) and poetry, at the venerable Radost FX, near Wenceslas Sq.

URBAN MYTH

Those who were involved in the Velvet Revolution – '89ers – often tell a story about 'the Japanese guy'. Student activists where having a hard time keeping under the police radars and were using ancient 300-baud modems to communicate via Fidonet, an early Internet bulletin-board system, but it wasn't an easy task. Out of the blue, a quiet Japanese man turned up at the university and presented the students with a suitcase full of brand-new 2400-baud Taiwanese modems. No-one got his name or saw him again, although everyone agrees he existed. The modems were vital to the cause and were used to coordinate demonstrations, circulate manifestos and keep one step ahead of the secret police. Soon the older-generation dissident intelligentsia joined in and the rest, as they say, is history.

LOVERS SHARE AN INTIMATE EMBRACE ON THE CITY'S NUMBER ONE MUST-SEE MONUMENT, THE STONE GOTHIC CHARLES BRIDGE .
Photographer: Sean Gallup (1)

THE PLAYFUL ARCHITECTURE OF THE DANCING HOUSE.
Photographer: Sean Gallup (2)

A DAILY STREAM OF PRAGUERS CROSS CHARLES BRIDGE INTO PICTURESQUE MALÁ STRANA AT THE FOOT OF PRAGUE CASTLE. Photographer: Sean Gallup (3)

REVAMPED SOVIET-ERA METRO STATIONS GIVE THE CITY'S TRANSPORT SYSTEM A LIFT.
Photographer: Sean Gallup (4)

A BRUNCH WITH A VIEW – LAID-BACK DINING AT ONE OF THE RESTAURANTS ON GRANVILLE ISLAND.
Photographer: Chris Cheadle (1)

Casual but cosmopolitan, freewheeling offbeat Vancouver is framed by a mountain backdrop with the sea kissing its edges.

ANATOMY

Straddling the lowlands of the Fraser River and the Coast Mountains of southwest British Columbia, Vancouver sits atop the most active earthquake zone in Canada. There are many bays, inlets and river branches shaping the city and coastline. Skyscrapers, big business and high finance sit just blocks from Stanley Park's thick rainforest. The city spreads east and north, and is well served by an elevated skytrain, buses, trains and the sea-bus crossing to North Vancouver.

PEOPLE

Vancouver's population comes from all over the world. By the end of the 20th century it had the largest Asian population in North America with an influx of Hong Kong Chinese. Forty percent of Vancouver residents are foreign-born.

TYPICAL VANCOUVERITE

With the knowledge that they live in an all-round 'top foreign city' known for its 'best quality of life', Vancouverites have a laid-back mind-set, happy to be part of a pioneering Pacific Rim city where marijuana is tolerated and the foodie scene has exploded. Vancouverites are aggressively outdoors oriented (they don't wear all that Gore-Tex for nothing), skiing in the winter but also cycling, blading, paddling on False Creek and sailing on English Bay.

DEFINING EXPERIENCE

Strolling through Stanley Park, lunching on the terrace at the Vancouver Art Gallery (having wandered through the permanent collection of local artists and caught the latest temporary exhibition), taking the sea bus across to North Van and watching for seals in the harbour before heading out to the university campus and the huge collection of First Nation artefacts at the Museum of Anthropology then finishing the day by dining on Pacific Northwest cuisine on Granville Island.

Vancouver

015

VITAL STATISTICS

NAME: VANCOUVER

NICKNAME: HOLLYWOOD NORTH; HONGKOUVER; CITY OF GLASS

DATE OF BIRTH: 1867; FIRST NAMED GASTOWN, A SALOON WAS OPENED NEXT TO A SAWMILL AND A TOWN SPRANG UP AROUND IT

ADDRESS: CANADA (MAP 1, G8)

HEIGHT: 14M

SIZE: 107 SQ KM

POPULATION: 2 MILLION

CANADA'S LONGEST POOL, KITSILANO SALT POOL (137M), IS OFFSET BY THE NATURAL BEAUTY OF THE NORTH SHORE MOUNTAINS. Photographer: Chris Cheadle (3)

DAWN'S SOFT LIGHT MUTES THE GLITTERING GLASS FAÇADE OF THE EVENTS VENUE 'PLAZA OF NATIONS' AND ITS ATTENDANT PLEASURE BOATS. Photographer: Chris Cheadle (2)

A MERCHANT DISPLAYS HIS WARES AT THE 'CLOTHING OPTIONAL' WRECK BEACH. Photographer: Chris Cheadle (4)

STRENGTHS

- Vancouver Art Gallery
- Wreck Beach
- Stanley Park
- Museum of Anthropology
- The startling Coast Mountains north of the city
- Coal Harbour Seawalk
- Marijuana cafés
- Eating outside all year round
- Star-spotting on film sets
- Dr Sun-Yat Sen Garden
- Illuminares Lantern Festival
- Bare Buns Fun Run
- 200-plus ice-cream flavours at La Casa Gelato – wasabi or balsamic anyone?
- The tiny ferries across to Granville Island

WEAKNESSES

- The rain – 170 days a year
- House prices
- Rapidly gentrifying neighbourhoods fuelling those house prices
- Eating out year-round – 'Can we please go inside, now?'
- Fleece/Gore-Tex – does everyone have to wear it?
- Blocked-off streets for film sets
- Always substituting for somewhere else

GOLD STAR

Granville Island – not really an island but an enclave of artists, artisans, theatre companies and restaurants with great views over the city any time of the day.

URBAN MYTH

There is a haunted house on the southeast corner of King Edward and Cambie Sts. A doctor killed his wife there in the 1930s…or maybe someone else was murdered and now Chinese monks that summon the dead live there and things fly around in the house. Or the house was bought by a group of nuns from Taiwan, who later sold the house. Or the house that stands there now is a newer dwelling but the ground that the house sits on is still cursed and the spirits of the dead have not left. Exorcisms have failed – in one case, a priest, or some other holy person, went to sleep inside the house and woke up in the middle of the night somewhere outside the house. Or maybe, just maybe, locals are getting themselves worked up over nothing.

CITYSPEAK

- Safe injecting sites – controlling drug use or promoting drug abuse?
- The Winter Olympics in 2010 – financial boon or burden?
- House prices…Rising? Falling?

STARRING ROLE IN...

- *The X Files* (1993–98)
- *Double Jeopardy* (1999)
- Douglas Coupland novels

IMPORT

- Hong Kong Chinese citizens
- Hong Kong Chinese money
- Hollywood productions
- South Asian communities
- William Gibson

EXPORT

- Greenpeace
- Generation X
- kd lang
- Michael J Fox
- Pamela Anderson
- Jason Priestley
- Carrie-Ann Moss
- Hayden Christensen
- Diana Krall
- Bryan Adams
- Michael Bublé
- Smoked salmon
- Maple syrup
- Salmon jerky

SEE the steam-powered clock in Gastown.

EAT Pacific Northwest food – salmon with a hazelnut and maple crust?

DRINK Maple Cream Ale at Granville Island Brewery.

DO explore Dr Sun Yat-Sen Park, a tranquil oasis where every pebble and brook has its place.

WATCH First Nations carvers working at the Museum of Anthropology.

BUY up-and-coming local fashion on the decidedly inappropriately named Main St.

AFTER DARK catch some jazz or blues at Café Deux Soleil or Bukowski's on Commercial Drive.

One of the world's most seductive, sophisticated and cool cities, Buenos Aires is the pounding trade and cultural heart of Argentina, and is probably the only major capital you can experience *without* busting your budget.

ANATOMY

The city sits beside the Atlantic on the edge of an agriculturally rich pampas on the River Plate. It is by far Argentina's richest city and the eighth-largest in the world, with one of the highest skyscraper counts anywhere (over 1500). Buenos Aires is divided into 47 *barrios* (neighbourhoods), each with its own fascinating idiosyncrasies. Acres of parkland, wide boulevards and graceful historic architecture give the city a distinctly European edge. Buenos Aires' rail network services the suburbs surrounding the city area, while the Subte (Underground) is South America's oldest subway and still a quick, efficient and easy way to get around. Buses also ply the streets of Buenos Aires.

PEOPLE

Greater Buenos Aires holds around 40% of Argentina's population. The majority are descended from Spanish and Italian immigrants but there are also significant German, British, Jewish, central and eastern European, and Middle Eastern communities, known collectively as *turcos*. Mestizos (people of mixed Native Indian and European heritage) are a growing minority, making up over a quarter of the inner-city population. The Spanish spoken here is rhythmically closer to Italian and the locals also use colourful slang expressions known as *lunfardo*.

TYPICAL PORTEÑO

Locals refer to themselves as *porteños* (port people) and have a reputation outside Buenos Aires for being arrogant know-it-alls. They are refreshingly proud of their city and willing to sing its praises at great length. Whatever the occasion they are always meticulously turned out, earning them a further reputation as some of the sexiest people on the planet. They work hard and play harder, and exude a seductive charisma through their uniquely lyrical language.

Buenos Aires

016

VITAL STATISTICS

NAME: BUENOS AIRES

NICKNAME: PARIS OF THE SOUTH

DATE OF BIRTH: 1536; FOUNDED AS SANTA MARÍA DEL BUEN AIRE (ST MARY OF THE GOOD AIR) BY SPANISH SAILOR PEDRO DE MENDOZA

ADDRESS: ARGENTINA (MAP 1, N20)

HEIGHT: 27M

SIZE: 200 SQ KM

POPULATION: 3 MILLION

DANCERS GIVE AN IMPROMPTU PERFORMANCE ALONGSIDE BUSKERS, LA BOCA.
Photographer: Donald C & Priscilla Alexander Eastman (1)

DEFINING EXPERIENCE

Feeling the world change as you go through the different neighbourhoods, rubbing shoulders with the city's elite around the Cementerio de la Recoleta, taking a cheeky siesta in one of Palermo's gorgeous parks, catching your breath on the riverside patio at club Mint, wandering 'home' via Plaza Serrano as the sun comes up, amazed at how good the *porteños* still manage to look.

STRENGTHS

- Plaza de Mayo
- Gay-friendly
- Buenos Aires International Tango Festival
- Safe neighbourhoods
- Neighbourhood diversity
- Unpredictable
- Cheap prices
- Beautiful people
- Underground jungle scene
- Hot and humid weather
- Cementerio de la Recoleta
- Succulent beef steaks
- Friendly locals
- Parks
- Botanical Gardens
- Theatre

WEAKNESSES

- Air pollution
- Crowded streets
- A few dodgy neighbourhoods
- Flooding
- Unemployment
- Can be a pedestrians' nightmare

GOLD STAR

Nightlife – the *boliches* (discos) are the throbbing heart of the city's world-famous nightlife. Dress hot, dance cool, and arrive well after 2am.

CITYSPEAK

- Traffic-police corruption
- The latest sex scandal affecting the Catholic Church
- Smoking restrictions in public places – good or bad?

STARRING ROLE IN...

- *Evita* (1996)
- *Motorcycle Diaries* (2004)
- *A Social Genocide* (2004)
- *Pin Boy* (2004)
- *Ronda Nocturna* (2005)
- *Labyrinths; Selected Stories and other writings* by Jorge Luis Borges
- *The Flight* by Horacio Verbitsky

IMPORT

- Aristotle Onassis
- Catwalk fashion
- Latin spirit
- Drainage technology

EXPORT

- Tango
- Eva Perón
- Che Guevera
- Diego Maradona
- Latin playboy image
- Jorge Luis Borges
- Grain
- Julio Cortázar
- Biro pens – first made here in 1944
- Beef
- Champion polo players
- Shellfish

SEE Buenos Aires' hip-shakin' young things at Cocoliche, an electronic-music paradise based in a glamorous old mansion.

EAT *flan casera* (home-made flan) at Munich Recoleta, where legendary poet Jorge Luis Borges was once a regular.

DRINK maté at the trendy Nucha café.

DO hire a bicycle one weekend and check out the city's parks, including the Reserva Ecológica Costanera Sur.

WATCH majestic mayhem unfold at a Boca Juniors versus River Plate *fútbol* (football) match.

BUY outrageous sexy and crazy fashion from the weird and wonderful collection at Objeto.

AFTER DARK funk it up to some wicked hip-hop beats at Club 69.

URBAN MYTH

Nowadays the tango epitomises high-society glamour, but its origins were in the brothels of 19th-century Buenos Aires. Successive waves of immigrants, drawn to the city's 'houses of ill repute', invented the tango as a means to vent their sorrow at finding themselves 'strangers in a strange land'. The rhythm is attributed to the beats pumped out by African slaves on their drums, known as tan-go, fused with the milonga music of the pampas, and Latin sounds already familiar to the early Spanish colonists. The dance developed as an 'acting out' of the pimp-prostitute relationship, and the early tangos not only represented a kind of sexual choreography, but often a duel between men competing for the sexual favours of a woman, which resulted in the symbolic death of an opponent.

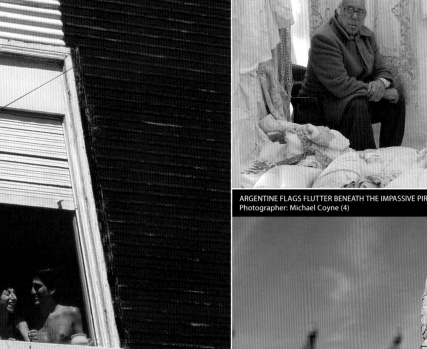

COLOURFUL AND HOT – AND THAT'S JUST OUTSIDE THE WALLS!
Photographer: Jane Sweeney (2)

SURROUNDED BY THEIR WARES, SHOPKEEPERS AWAIT CUSTOMERS AT THE PLAZA DORREGO SUNDAY MARKET.
Photographer: Michael Coyne (3)

ARGENTINE FLAGS FLUTTER BENEATH THE IMPASSIVE PIRAMIDE DE MAYO MONUMENT.
Photographer: Michael Coyne (4)

Rio de Janeiro

017

VITAL STATISTICS

NAME: RIO DE JANEIRO

NICKNAME: CIDADE MARAVILHOSA (MARVELLOUS CITY)

DATE OF BIRTH: 1567; THE PORTUGUESE SET UP THE FIRST SETTLEMENT; RIO BECAME THE CAPITAL IN 1763

ADDRESS: BRAZIL (MAP 1, P19)

HEIGHT: 61M

SIZE: 1200 SQ KM

POPULATION: 6.2 MILLION

With 37 beaches, green mountainous surrounds and streets that seethe with sensuality, Rio has more than its fair share of natural and cultural riches.

ANATOMY

Rio is a tale-of two cities: the upper and middle classes reside in the Zona Sul, the lower class in the Zona Norte. *Favelas* (shantytowns) cover steep hillsides on both sides of town. Most industry is in the Zona Norte, as is most of the pollution. The ocean beaches are in the Zona Sul. Buses are easily caught, but they're often crowded, slowed by traffic and driven by maniacs. The excellent subway system is limited to points north of the middle-class neighbourhood of Botafogo.

PEOPLE

The racial composition of Rio's population reflects its past: a mix of Africans, Europeans and Indians who have intermarried freely since colonial times. The Portuguese gave the country its religion and language, while Indian culture helped shape the legends, dance, music and other aspects of modern Brazilian culture. The influence of African culture is also prominent as the early slaves brought with them their religion, music and cuisine, all of which profoundly shaped Brazilian identity. Rio's rich melting pot is also a product of many immigrants who began arriving in the late 19th century – Italians, Spaniards, Germans, Japanese, Russians and Lebanese among others.

TYPICAL CARIOCA

The Cariocas – as Rio's inhabitants are called – thrive on dance, drink, the beach, sport and sun. They are spontaneous, friendly and prone to kicking footballs. However, it is class more than anything that separates Rio's citizens. At least one in five Cariocas live in a *favela*.

DEFINING EXPERIENCE

Celebrating with Fluminense fans over a hard-won football match at a sidewalk café in Flamengo, then heading to Lapa and wandering among the bars and old music halls in search of the soul of samba, and, finally, dancing in the streets with fellow Friday night revellers.

STRENGTHS

- Ipanema Beach
- The enormous cone-shaped Catedral Metropolitana
- *Bolo* (cake) and thick *cafezinho* (little coffee)
- Samba clubs in Lapa
- Antique stores of Rua do Lavradio
- A game of *futebol* at Maracanã stadium
- The statue *Cristo Redentor* (Christ the Redeemer) on Corcovado (Hunchback) mountain
- Centro Cultural Banco do Brasil, which often hosts some of the city's best (and avant-garde–leaning) exhibits
- Riding the *bonde* (tram) to the lovely hilltop neighbourhood of Santa Teresa
- Rio's weekend Feira Nordestina

WEAKNESSES

- Pollution
- Poverty
- Street kids
- Materialism
- *Favelas*
- Inadequate education and medical care for the poor
- Drug abuse
- Violence
- Police corruption

GOLD STAR

The birthplace of bossa nova today hosts samba, jazz, half a dozen regional styles, hip-hop (called 'black music'), reggae, funk, electronic music, Música Popular Brasileiro (MPB), and many fusions among them, such as samba-jazz, samba-funk, electro-samba and bossa-jazz.

CITYSPEAK

- Football. What's wrong with the national team?
- Will Rio be ready for the Pan Am games in 2007?

STARRING ROLE IN...

- *Pixote* (1981)
- *Central do Brasil* (Central Station, 1998)
- *Cidade de Deus* (City of God, 2002)
- *Motorcycle Diaries* (2004)
- *The Alchemist* by Paulo Coelho

IMPORT

- Soap operas
- Tourists
- Guns
- Football
- Multiculturalism
- The Portuguese
- Shopping malls
- Beach volleyball

EXPORT

- Supermodels
- Football stars
- Samba
- Carnaval
- *Fio dental* (dental-floss bikinis)
- *Havaianas* (rubber sandals)
- Formula One world champions
- 'The Girl from Ipanema'
- Bossa nova
- *Capoeira* (combination of martial arts, dance, acrobatics and music)

SEE the city unfold beneath the outstretched arms of the *Cristo Redentor*.

EAT the best *churrasco* (traditional barbecued meat) in Rio at Porcão, with stunning views and all the juicy steak you can eat.

DRINK cocktails and take in the ambient sounds (mixed by a changing crew of house and drum and bass hands) at the sleek Sitio Lounge.

DO take a *voleibol* (volleyball) class on Ipanema Beach and learn why it's the Cariocas' second-most popular sport (after football, of course).

WATCH Rio's new breed of hip-hop (pronounced hippie-hoppie) aficionados at a hip-hop jam in Humaitá or Botafogo.

BUY some vintage vinyl or pick up a CD at the open-air Feira de Música market in Centro.

AFTER DARK check out a *baile* (literally a 'dance' or 'ball') and try on your best dance moves alongside 10,000 locals.

URBAN MYTH

Carioca was the name the Tupi Indians gave to the Portuguese settlers. It comes from *'kara 'i oca,'* which means white house, in reference to the white masonry the newcomers used in their buildings.

THE BEACH AT COPACABANA IS INHABITED BY AN ODD SPECIES OF DANGLING PRIMATE.
Photographer: John Maier Jnr (1)

A SAMBA DANCER SHOWS HOW IT'S DONE DURING A CARNAVAL PARADE.
Photographer: Stephanie Maze (2)

A VOLLEYBALL APPEARS TO SOAR ABOVE DISTANT PEAKS AT A SUNSET GAME ON IPANEMA BEACH.
Photographer: Ricardo Gomes (3)

THE GIGANTIC FIGURE OF *CRISTO REDENTOR* ON CORCOVADO DWARFS A HELICOPTER PASSING IN THE
BACKGROUND. Photographer: Judy Bellah (4)

IN A BLUR OF ACTIVITY A BARTENDER AT BERLIN'S REINGOLD BAR OFFERS BRISK SERVICE.
Photographer: Richard Nebesky (1)

Berlin is constantly evolving, adapting, throwing up surprises and questioning its identity; while filled with history, she is determined to move ever forward.

ANATOMY

Apart from rivers and lakes, the city lacks distinctive geographical features – you're more likely to use buildings as a way of orienting yourself. Some of the city's rare hills were actually made from WWII rubble. Berlin's spread-out nature means you'll be relying on its U-bahns, S-bahns, buses and trams.

PEOPLE

Berliners enjoy a reputation for being liberal and well educated and the city itself is a patchwork of people from 185 countries. The most obvious immigrant group is the Turkish community. English is widely spoken, although less so among people of the former East, who will have learnt Russian as a second language.

TYPICAL BERLINER

Polite, friendly and fond of dry, sharp humour, Berliners are hard to shock. They live in high-ceilinged, airy apartments full of art and Ikea, make weekend brunches an essential experience and always seem to know where the 'scene' is and what's happening culturally.

DEFINING EXPERIENCE

Losing oneself in any of the city's blockbuster galleries and museums, keeping up with the locals by attending one of the 1500 cultural events that are crammed into Berlin's calendar, and reminding yourself that Potsdamer Platz was once 'No Man's Land'.

STRENGTHS

- History around every corner
- Willingness to make modern architectural statements
- Entrepreneurial spirit of young Berliners
- Imaginative protests
- Coffee and cake as a ritual
- Talking trash cans
- Efficient public transport
- Citywide love of new ideas
- Multiculturalism
- Vital contemporary arts scene
- Late-night kebabs
- Tiergarten (zoo)
- Schloss Charlottenburg
- Parades

Berlin 018

VITAL STATISTICS

NAME: BERLIN

NICKNAME: EUROPE'S BIGGEST BUILDING SITE

DATE OF BIRTH: 1307; TRADING POSTS BERLIN AND CÖLLN JOINED TO FORM A CITY

ADDRESS: GERMANY (MAP 3, L7)

HEIGHT: 55M

SIZE: 892 SQ KM

POPULATION: 3.38 MILLION

AN ABSTRACT STAR OF DAVID CRISS-CROSSES THE ZINC FAÇADE OF THE JEWISH MUSEUM.
Photographer: Andrea Schulte-Peevers (2)

URBANITES RELAX ON A SUNNY AFTERNOON IN HALENSEE PARK.
Photographer: Guy Moberly (3)

PEACE, LOVE AND BODY PAINT – REVELLERS AT THE LOVE PARADE.
Photographer: Guy Moberly (4)

WEAKNESSES
- ◢ 'The wall in the mind'
- ◢ Mullet hangovers
- ◢ Dog poo on the streets of Friedrichshain
- ◢ Confusing transport maps
- ◢ Needing to take public transport between attractions
- ◢ Racial tensions
- ◢ Techno doof doof when you're trying to sleep
- ◢ Weather

GOLD STAR
Nightlife – Berlin is determined to remain one of the coolest clubbing spots and her citizens throw themselves into the fray with abandon.

CITYSPEAK
- ◢ The 2006 World Cup
- ◢ The GDR: those were the days…
- ◢ Hot spots – where's in, what's out, what's new, what's still being built and where
- ◢ Has anyone seen the economy?

STARRING ROLE IN...
- ◢ *Die Fetten Jahre sind vorbei* (The Edukators, 2004)
- ◢ *Good Bye Lenin!* (2003)
- ◢ *Der Himmel über Berlin* (Wings of Desire, 1987)
- ◢ *Lola rennt* (Run Lola Run, 1997)
- ◢ *Herr Lehmann* (Berlin Blues, 2003)
- ◢ *Berlin: Sinfonie einer Großstadt* (Berlin: Symphony of a City, 1927)

IMPORT
- ◢ Doner kebabs
- ◢ Ikea
- ◢ Christopher Isherwood
- ◢ David Bowie
- ◢ Lou Reed
- ◢ Iggy Pop
- ◢ Nick Cave
- ◢ U2
- ◢ Bertolt Brecht
- ◢ Stem cells for research
- ◢ Spelling changes
- ◢ Fruit and veg

EXPORT
- ◢ Marlene Dietrich
- ◢ George Grosz
- ◢ Einstürzende Neubauten
- ◢ Tangerine Dream
- ◢ Currywurst
- ◢ Nina Hagen
- ◢ Dadaism
- ◢ Leni Riefenstahl
- ◢ Techno
- ◢ Günter Grass
- ◢ Siemens
- ◢ Helmut Newton
- ◢ Squatting as a way of life

SEE what all the fuss is about at the domed Reichstag.

EAT wonderful Vietnamese food cheek by jowl with locals at Monsieur Vuong.

DRINK while checking out the other patrons at Cookies.

DO a tour of the cutting-edge galleries in the former East Berlin.

WATCH the most exciting developments in the cinematic world at the Berlin Film Festival.

BUY a GDR-era souvenir at Flohmarkt am Arkonaplatz.

AFTER DARK graffiti-bedecked Tacheles can still throw up night-time surprises for arty partiers.

URBAN MYTH
Europe's first (hand-operated) traffic light was installed in Potsdamer Platz in 1924. A replica can be found in the same spot today.

UNCOVERING HISTORY'S CRACKED FOUNDATIONS – A WORKER MAKES REPAIRS IN FRONT OF THE DOME OF THE ROCK.
Photographer: Spencer Platt (1)

Jerusalem
019

VITAL STATISTICS

NAME: JERUSALEM

NICKNAME: J-TOWN

DATE OF BIRTH: AROUND 2000 BC; ORIGINALLY A SMALL JEBUSITE SETTLEMENT, JERUSALEM OCCUPIED THE SLOPES OF MT MORIAH, WHERE, ACCORDING TO THE OLD TESTAMENT, ABRAHAM OFFERED HIS SON ISAAC AS A SACRIFICE; IN 997 BC, KING DAVID CAPTURED THE CITY AND MADE IT HIS CAPITAL

ADDRESS: ISRAEL AND THE PALESTINIAN TERRITORIES (MAP 2, L2)

HEIGHT: 557M

SIZE: 122 SQ KM

POPULATION: 693,200

Jerusalem's place in the hearts and minds of so many people gives it a charged atmosphere unlike any other city.

ANATOMY

Built on a series of hills, Jerusalem is on the watershed, the edge of the narrow fertile strip that clings to the Eastern Mediterranean. To the west there are green hills, spotted with villages. To the east, the brown desert hills are only rarely blessed with rain, which covers them in a ghostly sprinkling of bright green. There are two city centres, one Palestinian and one Israeli, both fairly compact and about 1.2km from each other. Jerusalem is laced with a very good network of city bus routes.

PEOPLE

Officially, Jews make up 68% of the population and Arabs 32%, but these figures are skewed by the inclusion of outlying Jewish settlements. The Jewish population comes from almost every corner of the earth, and ranges from long-bearded ultra-orthodox men in their traditional 17th-century Polish gabardine, to secular Moroccans partying in the latest American fashions. Hebrew and Arabic are the dominant languages, but many people speak English, especially in West Jerusalem.

TYPICAL JERUSALEMITE

Jerusalemites are both rude and hospitable. They'll keep you waiting 10 minutes before serving you at a counter, then invite you home to dinner. They will gladly get involved in an argument with you about anything, but usually about politics, religion, or why a good-looking girl/guy like you isn't married yet. Living on a holy mountain, they look down, literally and figuratively, on the sweaty plains-dwellers.

DEFINING EXPERIENCE

Sharing coffee and stories with an old man at the Damascus Gate, watching the sunset ignite the Dome of the Rock from the Mount of Olives, making a do-it-yourself falafel on Ben Yehuda St, before beer and live Russian music at the Pargod Theatre.

STRENGTHS

- An architectural patchwork of cultures and historical periods
- Hilltop views
- The old city
- Hezekiyah's Tunnel
- Local hospitality
- Empty highways on Yom Kippur
- Sabbath quiet
- Mild and dry weather
- A centre of traditional Jewish learning
- The Russian church
- The Mount of Olives
- Home to many idealists

WEAKNESSES

- Bombings (sometimes)
- Violent demonstrations (sometimes)
- High police presence in Arab suburbs (sometimes)
- Tension (always)
- Crazy drivers
- Too much machismo
- High prices on anything imported
- Home to many idealists

GOLD STAR

There's no substitute for standing where *those feet* actually trod.

CITYSPEAK

- When will the ultra-orthodox take over West Jerusalem and shut down all the nightspots on the one and only day of rest in the week?
- The latest mismatch on 'Sof Haderech', an amazing race-style TV show that teams up people from the opposite ends of Israeli society – religious guy with secular homosexual, farmer with professor, and so on

STARRING ROLE IN...

- The Bible
- *A Beggar in Jerusalem* by Elie Wiesel
- *Jerusalem* by Larry Collins and Dominique Lapierre
- *Kadosh* (1999)
- *Rana's Wedding* (2004)

IMPORT

- Jews from half the countries in the world
- Journalists
- American fashions
- Pilgrims
- Tourists
- Human-rights activists
- Water
- Students
- Rough diamonds

EXPORT

- Religions
- News footage
- Holy relics
- Edward Said
- Nobel Prize winners
- Antiquities
- Sirhan Sirhan (shot Bobby Kennedy)
- Natalie Portman (Queen Amidala in *The Phantom Menace*)
- Yasser Arafat (birthplace disputed)
- Cut diamonds
- Pharmaceuticals
- Amos Oz
- Jewellery
- Yitzhak Rabin
- Pottery

SEE the hills of Judea from the road to Jericho.

EAT Yemenite *haute cuisine* at the Yemenite Step.

DRINK sweet cardamom coffee.

DO the ramparts walk on the walls of the old city.

WATCH the best of Israeli cinema at Cinematheque.

BUY traditional Palestinian embroidery at Maher Natsheh's on Christian Quarter Rd.

AFTER DARK sample Hebrew blues or trilingual rap at Mike's Place.

URBAN MYTH

People say that Jerusalem means 'city of peace' (*shalom*), then shake their heads at how little peace there is. In fact, the city is named after the old patron god, Shalem, who was worshipped by the city's Canaanite inhabitants in his hilltop temple, but evicted when the Israelites built their own temple. Today, the Muslim Dome of the Rock stands on the same hill, over a rock said to bear the Prophet Mohammed's last footprint on earth. Jerusalem is like a religious onion – layered and tearful.

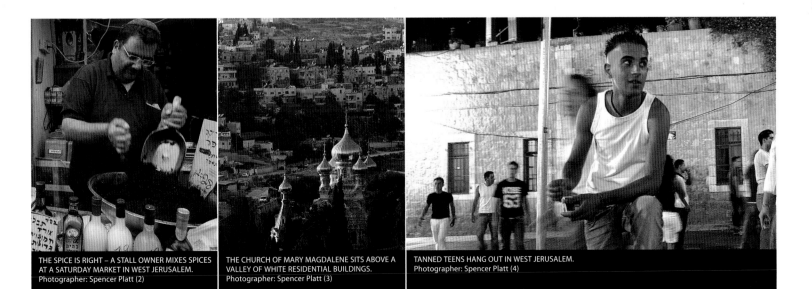

THE SPICE IS RIGHT – A STALL OWNER MIXES SPICES AT A SATURDAY MARKET IN WEST JERUSALEM.
Photographer: Spencer Platt (2)

THE CHURCH OF MARY MAGDALENE SITS ABOVE A VALLEY OF WHITE RESIDENTIAL BUILDINGS.
Photographer: Spencer Platt (3)

TANNED TEENS HANG OUT IN WEST JERUSALEM.
Photographer: Spencer Platt (4)

Montréal

020

VITAL STATISTICS

NAME: MONTRÉAL

DATE OF BIRTH: 1642; WHEN THE LURE OF FUR AND SAVAGE SOULS IN NEED OF SAVING – IN THIS CASE IROQUOIS – SAW PAUL DE CHOMEDEY DE MAISONNEUVE FOUND VILLE-MARIE

ADDRESS: CANADA (MAP 1, M9)

HEIGHT: 57M

SIZE: 449 SQ KM

POPULATION: 3.6 MILLION

FORTY YEARS AFTER IT WAS BUILT, THE BIOSPHERE REMAINS THE CITY'S CENTRE OF ENVIRONMENTAL AWARENESS.
Photographer: Chris Cheadle (1)

As the locals say, it's Europe and America rolled into one: achingly hip, proudly diverse, bilingual, and all set in a rousing frontier landscape.

ANATOMY

Montréal occupies an island on the north shore of the St Lawrence River. Modern skyscrapers mix with 18th- and 19th-century greystones in the distinct neighbourhoods that cluster around Mont Royal, known locally as 'the mountain'. 'The Main', the busy and cosmopolitan rue Saint Denis and the blvd Saint Laurent, delineates traditional French–English boundaries. Its grid pattern streets don't often see gridlock, with commuters happy to use the excellent metro and bus system or, for those not deterred by the city's steep inclines, pedal power.

PEOPLE

Although almost 70% of Montréalers claim French as their first language, today almost half speak both French and English. Traditional cultural and linguistic boundaries are fast eroding, due to a younger, globally focused generation and the city's large number of migrants. Montréal boasts a diverse ethnic profile: 10% of the population has Italian heritage and there are also significant Haitian, Chinese, Portuguese, Jewish, Greek and various Middle Eastern communities.

TYPICAL MONTRÉALER

They still might not earn as much as their New York or Toronto counterparts, but Montréalers are increasingly happy to stay put, citing charming but affordable housing, a fantastic festival calendar, a sense of cultural renaissance and new business confidence as just some of the reasons to stay. Many may have grown up with traditional religious values – statistically over 70% are Roman Catholic – but more often than not are laid-back, liberal and a little eccentric. Montréalers are famously stylish, fanatical about food and fond of a party. They also love the outdoors and pounding the puck, hockey being the city's favourite spectator sport.

DEFINING EXPERIENCE

White-water rafting at the Lachine rapids, then home for some DIY on the apartment (it's on the market), then agonising over the outfit (Kamkyl or Marc Jacobs?), then a quiet meal at the little Plateau *bistrot*, finishing with some Québécois *lait cru* (raw milk) cheese, nabbing a sofa at Jello, bouncing ideas around about a sound-installation project and deciding, tonight at least, not to go to clubbing.

STRENGTHS

- The Mountain
- Nightlife
- Underground City (all 29km of it)
- Father Emmett 'Pops' Johns
- Habitat 67, architect Moshe Safdie's iconic vision of urban life
- Tam Tams on summer Sundays
- Basilique Notre Dame
- Franco-frontier cuisine
- Gay Village
- Chic sartorial style (think Rufus Wainwright)
- Mile End and Plateau
- Musée d'Art Contemporain de Montréal
- Thriving indie band scene spawning the likes of Arcade Fire
- Quartier Latin
- Festival International de Jazz de Montréal – North America's largest
- Thousands of restaurants (many of them BYO)
- Grande Bibliothèque
- Hôtel Godin

WEAKNESSES

- Second-fiddle chip on shoulder
- Spiralling rents
- Subarctic cold snaps of 40°C below
- Anglophone–Francophone tension on St Jean-Baptiste Day
- Céline Dion
- Gas-guzzling habits

GOLD STAR

Cuisine – affordable, eclectic, sophisticated and symbolic of Montréal's contented multiculturalism

CITYSPEAK

- Just how much did the government pay to keep the Grand Prix?
- I can't believe I didn't buy that Plateau apartment when I could
- Do you think Cité Multimédia is really a metaphor for the Internet?
- So when is your sister moving back from Toronto?
- I'm not rooting for anybody (in reference to baseball)
- The Megacity

STARRING ROLE IN...

- *The Decline of the American Empire* (1986)
- *Jesus of Montreal* (1989)
- *The Score* (2001)
- *Les Invasions barbares* (The Barbarian Invasions, 2003)
- *Le Survenant* (2005)
- *The Apprenticeship of Duddy Kravitz* by Mordecai Richler
- *Bonheur d'Occasion* by Gabrielle Roy

IMPORT

- Hollywood film shoots
- Catholicism
- Siphay Southidara, creator of fashion label YSO, originally from Laos
- Students
- Corneille, Rwandan-born R&B star
- Pizza, bagels and Portuguese chicken
- Football

EXPORT

- Cirque du Soleil
- Oscar Peterson
- Hockey studs
- Softimage-generated 3D animation (think *Jurassic Park* and *Titanic*)
- Fur
- Leonard Cohen
- Montréal melons
- William Shatner
- The Stills
- Pierre Elliott Trudeau
- Fashion
- The Expos – all the way to DC

SEE the Old Port from the observation tower of the Chapelle Notre Dame de Bonsecours, the pretty Sailors' Church.

EAT *poutine foie gras* (French fries with pork gravy, cheese curds and foie gras) at the Plateau's Au Pied de Cochon.

DRINK a *Païenne* (blond ale) at the Mile End brewpub, Brasserie Dieu du Ciel.

DO an icy lap at the blissfully bucolic Lac Aux Castors rink.

WATCH Cinémathèque québécoise's Ciné-Jazz program (maybe rare footage of Duke in Paris in the '40s), part of the behemoth annual Jazz Fest.

BUY fur without the guilt: recycled pelt products from stylish Harricana, in Downtown.

AFTER DARK and, in true Montréal style, after day has dawned, shake your thing at Stereobar or Jet.

URBAN MYTH

It's true – Montréalers will eat anything. Every summer, thousands of adventurous diners fill up on crickets, mealworms, caterpillars and locusts at the Insectarium in the Jardin Botanique. Apparently, wax-moth larvae taste like bacon and the fried African locusts are just like potato chips with wings.

A RIGHT ROYAL JAM – EVERY SUNDAY IN SUMMER HUNDREDS TURN OUT TO BEAT THE DRUM AT MOUNT ROYAL PARK.
Photographer: Chris Cheadle (2)

LUSH STREET GARDENS, LIKE THESE IN THE QUARTIER LATIN, LINE THE CITY'S RESIDENTIAL AREAS.
Photographer: Chris Cheadle (3)

THE FLAGS OF MONTRÉAL, QUÉBEC AND CANADA APPEAR THROUGH THE COLOURED FAÇADE OF THE MONTRÉAL CONVENTION CENTER. Photographer: Chris Cheadle (4)

Since the reinstatement of the Scottish Parliament in 1999, Edinburgh has been booming with rising property prices, new building projects, and wealthy inhabitants – in financial and cultural terms.

ANATOMY

Edinburgh is very hilly and green, with Castle Rock being the most prominent inhabited hill and Hollyrood Park (home to the 251m-high Arthur's Seat) the largest green space. The only river, the water of Leith, runs along the northwestern border of New Town. New Town is characterised by regular Georgian terraces and squares. It is separated from the Old Town, which lies to the south, by the valley of Princes St Gardens. Old Town is a delightful maze of medieval alleys trickling off the Royal Mile, which climbs from the Palace of Holyroodhouse up to Edinburgh Castle. The only public transport is buses, which have the city carefully covered. Otherwise the best way to get around is on a bicycle.

PEOPLE

Edinburgh is Scotland's most cosmopolitan and middle-class city. Many Irish and English people have settled here and there are smaller ethnic communities, including Indians, Pakistanis, Bangladeshis, Italians, Poles, Chinese and Spanish. During the Edinburgh Festival the city's population swells to twice its size.

TYPICAL EDINBURGHER

Years of living almost on top of each other in densely packed tenements is often the reason given for Edinburghers' interest in each other's business. That said, people can appear shy and are unlikely to start chatting to strangers. Although Leith (Edinburgh's port) became part of the city in 1920, its inhabitants are Leithers and not Edinburghers. A typical young professional in Edinburgh probably spends his/her salary earned in financial services paying off a large mortgage on a tenement flat in the Southside. They enjoy eating out, and eschew beer and tea for wine and cappuccino. They aspire to owning property abroad and ski once a year if they can.

Edinburgh
021

VITAL STATISTICS

NAME: EDINBURGH

NICKNAME: ATHENS OF THE NORTH; AULD REEKIE (OLD SMOKY)

DATE OF BIRTH: 900 BC; THERE ARE SIGNS OF HUMAN HABITATION AT CASTLE ROCK AND ARTHUR'S SEAT FROM THIS TIME

ADDRESS: SCOTLAND (MAP 3, D5)

HEIGHT: 134M

SIZE: 260 SQ KM

POPULATION: 430,000

THE ROYAL MILE, AS SEEN THROUGH THE LEGS OF A DEFIANT KILT-WEARER.
Photographer: Chris Furlong (1)

DEFINING EXPERIENCE

Sipping a latte in Grassmarket before wandering down the Royal Mile to Hollyrood Park and climbing up Arthur's Seat, followed by some restorative shopping in Harvey Nichols and a dish of oysters on ice at the Café Royal Oyster Bar.

STRENGTHS

- Museum of Scotland
- Adventure Centre
- Cycling on Union Canal towpath
- Elegant Georgian terraces of New Town
- Arthur's Seat
- Scottish Enlightenment
- Scottish Parliament Building
- Princes St Gardens
- Low unemployment
- Victorian tenements south of the centre
- More restaurants per capita than any other UK city
- Modern Scottish cuisine
- The cleaning of soot-blackened buildings
- The Edinburgh Festival Fringe
- The Military Tattoo
- Hogmanay
- Royal Mile
- Clubbing in Cowgate

WEAKNESSES

- Soaring house prices
- Dearth of parking spaces
- Traffic jams

GOLD STAR

The Edinburgh Festival Fringe

CITYSPEAK

- Scottish Parliament Building – an architectural accomplishment or a big waste of money?
- How can first-time buyers get on the property ladder?

STARRING ROLE IN...

- *Trainspotting* (1996)
- *The Prime of Miss Jean Brodie* (1969)
- *Complicity* by Ian Banks
- *The Falls* by Ian Rankin

IMPORT

- Theatrical students for the Edinburgh fringe
- MTV awards in October 2003
- JK Rowling
- Ian Rankin
- Alexander McCall Smith
- Hugh MacDiarmid

EXPORT

- Sir Sean Connery
- Robert Louis Stevenson
- Howie Nicholsby of 21st Century Kilts
- The *Encyclopaedia Britannica* and *Chambers Encyclopaedia* (first published in Edinburgh)
- Sir Walter Scott
- Royal Bank of Scotland and HBOS
- Irvine Welsh
- Sir Arthur Conan Doyle (creator of Sherlock Holmes)
- Dame Muriel Spark
- The Proclaimers
- Finlay Quaye
- The Scottish Colourists
- National Gallery of Scotland
- Malt whisky
- Irn-Bru softdrink
- Salmon
- Trout
- Oats

SEE Edinburgh Castle on its perfectly defensible perch, Castle Rock.

EAT chargrilled Aberdeen Angus fillet steak at the Tower, and peer over at the castle.

DRINK one or two of the 100 malts on offer at Victorian Bennet's Bar.

DO walk up Arthur's Seat for an unbeatable view of the city.

WATCH obscure plays with an audience of one at the Edinburgh Festival Fringe.

BUY exquisite, contemporary jewellery from Scottish jeweller Annie Smith.

AFTER DARK enjoy a night of theatre cabaret at the unusual Bongo Club.

URBAN MYTH

One of Edinburgh's most gruesome myths comes from the time of the plague in 1645. Legend has it that the stricken inhabitants of Mary King's Close (now the site of the City Chambers) were bricked into their houses to die and rot. Apparently when workmen eventually came to remove the bodies, rigor mortis meant limbs had to be severed in order to extricate the dead from their claustrophobic dwellings. Although this story is not true, people who lived there afterwards and who have since visited have reported sightings of grotesque ghouls and floating body parts. Spooky!

A COUPLE KISS TO A VIOLIN'S TUNE DURING FESTIVAL MONTH.
Photographer: Chris Furlong (2)

A TEA HUGGER COLLECTS HER THOUGHTS AT THE FOREST CHARITY CAFÉ.
Photographer: Chris Furlong (3)

THE FAMOUS CONTEMPLATION WINDOWS OF THE CONTROVERSIAL SCOTTISH PARLIAMENT BUILDING AT HOLYROOD. Photographer: Chris Furlong (4)

Venice 022

VITAL STATISTICS

NAME: VENICE

NICKNAME: LA SERENISSIMA; THE QUEEN OF THE ADRIATIC

DATE OF BIRTH: 5TH AND 6TH CENTURIES AD; WHEN THE ISLANDS OF THE VENETIAN LAGOON WERE FIRST SETTLED DURING THE BARBARIAN INVASIONS

ADDRESS: ITALY (MAP 3, K11)

HEIGHT: 1M

SIZE: 458 SQ KM

POPULATION: 63,000

There's no city on earth whose visual impact has the same power as Venice – the Adriatic island republic is reluctantly part of Italy, but in reality belongs to the entire world as one of the great cultural treasures anywhere on the planet.

ANATOMY

Spread over an incredible 117 islands, connected by over 400 bridges and divided by some 150 canals, Venice is in many places a cramped and dark city whose astonishing colours and vibrancy suddenly become apparent in the plentiful open spaces and along the magnificent Grand Canal, the main artery of the city, which hums with traffic day and night. Few cities reward walkers so generously as Venice. A vaporetto is the other essential method of getting around, and it can be equally rewarding: you won't find too many public transport routes as unforgettable as vaporetto No 1's trip along the Grand Canal. Taking a ride in a gondola is corny, expensive, embarrassing and…well, if you really want to, why not? Water taxis are almost as expensive as gondolas, but their pilots don't wear stripy shirts or sing 'O Sole Mio'.

PEOPLE

Venetians are sadly a declining breed, if not necessarily a dying one. The lack of jobs outside the tourist industry has led to many young people leaving the city for the mainland at the earliest opportunity, and as such the native population is in sharp decline. House prices – high enough already – are forced higher by large numbers of non-Venetians purchasing second homes here.

TYPICAL VENETIAN

Defined by their own dialect of Italian, a separate history and an island mentality, Venetians are somewhat reluctant Italians and define themselves far more in terms of their city than in terms of their country. There's a love-hate relationship going on here though – Venetians will tell you the disadvantages of living in their unique overpriced and sinking city, but will expect nothing but praise from you as a visitor!

DEFINING EXPERIENCE

Taking a trip across the lagoon at dawn to see San Marco before the crowds, stopping off at a café to sip coffee, getting lost in the back alleys, discovering a magnificent church, vaporetto-hopping up and down the Grand Canal and munching some top-notch seafood for dinner.

STRENGTHS

- Discovering that despite the crowds, the smells and the high prices there's absolutely nowhere like this remarkable city
- The Giardini – Venice's green lung beyond San Marco
- The Lido – roads! And a beach!
- The annual film festival, which sees Hollywood royalty rubbing shoulders with the locals
- The Venice Biennale, one of the greatest art shows on earth.

WEAKNESSES

- The crowds
- The smelly canals (particularly foul when they are being dredged)
- The high prices

GOLD STAR

The Venice Carnival is a once-in-a-lifetime experience that will thrill and exhaust in equal measure. Held in February or March, the city parties nonstop, although you'll feel out of place if you haven't spent a lot of time and money on your costume.

CITYSPEAK

- The controversial new bridge over the Grand Canal (only the fourth ever)
- Should there be a daily tourist tax imposed on every non-Venetian in town?
- Will the new sea barriers ever be finished and will they work?

STARRING IN…

- *Death in Venice* (1971)
- *Don't Look Now* (1973)
- *The Merchant of Venice* by Shakespeare
- *Everyone Says I Love You* (1996)
- *The Talented Mr Ripley* (1999)
- *The Aspern Papers* by Henry James

IMPORT

- Tourists, tourists and more tourists
- Hollywood royalty (annually)
- Artistic royalty (biennially)

EXPORT

- Murano glass
- Marco Polo
- Titian
- Giacomo Casanova
- Dramatist Carlo Goldoni
- Vivaldi

SEE the extraordinary interior of the Basilica di San Marco early in the morning before the crowds arrive.

EAT superb seafood, but avoid anywhere with a *menu turistico*.

DRINK the world's most expensive espresso on Piazza San Marco.

DO try to get there for the Carnival, or one of Venice's other big municipal celebrations.

WATCH opera at the stunningly rebuilt La Fenice opera house.

BUY Murano glass (admittedly an acquired taste) at bargain prices.

AFTER DARK enjoy a world-famous Bellini (Venice's native cocktail, made with champagne and peaches) at Harry's Bar.

URBAN MYTH

Many are now arguing that Venice is no longer sinking, although the jury's out until conclusive proof is produced. The major sinking of the city occurred in the first half of the 20th century, when artesian wells were dug into the periphery of the lagoon to draw water for local industry. This caused subsidence, which has been enormously reduced by the banning of the wells in the 1960s. However, the city is not out of danger – as a result of the subsidence it is at constant risk from the *acqua alta* – the high tides that come in regularly from the Adriatic.

PEAK HOUR ON THE GRAND CANAL WHERE GONDOLAS LINE UP BEFORE LAUNCHING OFF.
Photographer: Jon Davison (1)

WASHING DAY NEAR CATHEDRAL SAN PIETRO DI CASTELLO.
Photographer: Juliet Coombe (2)

SIBLINGS TAKE TIME OUT TO SKETCH AND RELAX AT SIESTA TIME.
Photographer: Roberto Soncin Gerometta (3)

EERILY EMPTY, THE FAMOUS PIAZZA SAN MARCO GLISTENS AFTER A STORM.
Photographer: Juliet Coombe (4)

Hanoi 023

VITAL STATISTICS

NAME: HANOI

DATE OF BIRTH: 1010; WHEN IT WAS TRANSFERRED FROM THE MOUNTAINS TO ITS PRESENT LOCATION

ADDRESS: VIETNAM (MAP 5, M5)

HEIGHT: 16M

SIZE: 2146 SQ KM

POPULATION: 4.1 MILLION

Hanoi's beguiling boulevards, *belle époque* architecture and peaceful parks and pagodas are enough to recommend it, but there's also the bonus of a vibrant, optimistic population and fantastic food.

ANATOMY

Hanoi sprawls along the Red River (Song Hong), which is spanned by three bridges. The city is divided into seven central districts *(quan)*, surrounded by outlying neighbourhoods called *hyyen*. Peaceful Hoan Kiem Lake lies between the imploding maze of the Old Quarter in the north, and the architecturally elegant Ba Dinh district (French Quarter) to the south. Go west for the monument-strewn former Imperial City, or north to the lovely West Lake. Here two wheels *are* better than four: motorbike, bicycle and *cyclo* (pedicab) beat the buses every time.

PEOPLE

Ethnic Vietnamese *(kihn)* dominate Hanoi, though there are a small number of ethnic minorities from around Vietnam. Second languages reflect a historical chronology: those under 30 (almost three-quarters of the population) speak English, the middle-aged may have a smattering of Russian and German and the elderly are often fluent in French.

TYPICAL HANOI CITIZEN

Hanoi residents are known for their reserve and strength of character, coupled with energy and resourcefulness. After a history of colonisation, war and Communist rule, they tend to be suspicious both of authority and of outsiders but are also hospitable and incredibly adaptive to change. Family values abound – beneath the nonchalant cool-kid-on-motorbike pop-culture persona there's usually a strong sense of Confucian responsibility and discipline. The younger generation are well educated and optimistic about the future.

DEFINING EXPERIENCE

Having your shoes shined at 5am, watching merchants setting up their stalls, then off to the flower market to buy blooms, padded bras and some plastic baskets, followed by *pho* (beef-noodle soup) for breakfast with ground pork and mushrooms at the little place next to the Binh Minh Hotel.

STRENGTHS

- Youthful energy
- Long Bien Bridge
- Temple of Literature
- Communist monuments – drab and spectacular in turns
- City lights reflecting on Hoan Kiem Lake
- Mung dumplings with sweet ginger sauce in winter
- Hotel Metropole and other French colonial architecture
- Tree-lined boulevards
- *Ga Tan* (stewed chicken with medicinal herbs, dates and grilled baguettes)
- Wacky water puppets
- One Pillar Pagoda
- Coffee – strong and sweet
- Tight-knit sense of community

WEAKNESSES

- Traffic
- Bureaucracy
- Censorship
- Over-the-top architectural styles of the newly wealthy
- Overcrowding
- Government surveillance

GOLD STAR

Bustling authentic retail landscape – the 36 streets of the Old Quarter combine hundreds of years of history with intriguing shopping and an insight into Hanoi's heart.

CITYSPEAK

- The future
- The latest government proclamation on 'social evils'

STARRING ROLE IN...

- *Les Filles du botaniste chinois* (2005)
- *The Quiet American* (2002)
- *Daughter from Danang* (2002)
- *Vertical Ray of the Sun* (2000)
- *Marché à Hanoi* (1903)

IMPORT

- Architecture: French and Soviet
- Canto-pop
- Buddhism
- Picasso-era modernism
- Existentialism
- Russian salads
- Catholicism
- Padma cars
- Minsk motorbikes
- Stalinist labour camps
- French food legacies: pastry, baguettes, crème caramel and yoghurt
- Confucianism
- Japanese food
- Cable TV

EXPORT

- Diaspora
- Stone carving
- Silk
- Water puppets
- *Pho*-culture

SEE the t'ai chi practice at Hoan Kiem Lake at dawn.

EAT fried squid with dill, tofu with tomatoes and grilled chicken at a *bia hoi* (beer tavern) in the old town – maybe Bia Hoi Viet on Pho Tong Dan.

DRINK *xeo* (rice wine) and hang with the Minsk motorcycle club.

DO play a game of badminton in Lenin Park.

WATCH the circus at Cong Vien Le Nin: bears, tigers, elephants and girls on roller skates.

BUY bolts of silk or order bespoke shirts along Pho Hang Gai.

AFTER DARK catch a Vietnamese pop star performing at the Hanoi Opera House then go for a motorbike ride around West Lake.

URBAN MYTH

Hoan Kiem, the name of Hanoi's enchanting lake, means 'the returned sword'. Legend has it that the 15th-century king, Le Loi, had a magical sword that proved invaluable in driving back the Chinese. One day as he was boating on the lake, a giant turtle rose from the depths and seized the sword, vowing to return it to the gods. A turtle that was found and preserved in the 1970s is thought to be more than 500 years old, making it old enough to be the turtle of the legend. There are still sightings of giant turtles in the lake, the last in 1998, and scientists believe they could be a unique species.

A SHOULDER TO LEAN ON: SCHOOLCHILDREN STICK TIGHTLY TOGETHER.
Photographer: Keren Su (1)

SHORT BACK AND SIDES FOR A YOUNG CUSTOMER AT A STREET SALON.
Photographer: Owen Franken (2)

HOMEWARD BOUND, A FARMER CARRIES BASKETS OF PRODUCE THROUGH DONG ANH DISTRICT AT SUNSET.
Photographer: Kevin R Morris (3)

WOMEN IN WHITE CYCLE THROUGH THE CITY STREETS AT SUNRISE.
Photographer: Jean Reay (4)

Amsterdam 024

VITAL STATISTICS

NAME: AMSTERDAM

NICKNAME: MOKUM, VENICE OF THE NORTH

DATE OF BIRTH: 1275; WHEN THE COUNT OF HOLLAND LIFTED TOLLS FOR RESIDENTS ON THE AMSTEL DAM

ADDRESS: THE NETHERLANDS (MAP 3, H7)

HEIGHT: 1M

SIZE: 220 SQ KM

POPULATION: 735,328

FRIENDS ABANDON THEIR BIKES FOR A LEISURELY JUGGLE IN VONDELPARK.
Photographer: Barry Lewis (1)

SAY CHEESE – HOLLAND'S FAMOUS YELLOW RIND VARIETY LINES THE SHELVES OF A CITY SHOP.
Photographer: Esbin Anderson (2)

LIKE A SCENE FROM A DREAM, BUILDINGS IN KEIZERSGRACHT TILT AT BIZARRE ANGLES.
Photographer: Frans Lemmens (3)

A SIGN OF THINGS TO COME AT THE ENTRANCE TO THE MODERN WING OF THE VAN GOGH MUSEUM AMSTERDAM.
Photographer: Richard Nebesky (4)

Forget images of red lights, drug addicts and coffee shops – Amsterdam's truly liberal, laid-back atmosphere, beautiful watery setting, picturesque houses, excellent museums and infamous nightlife give it a unique appeal.

ANATOMY

The central area of Amsterdam is Centrum, home to impressive Dam Sq, great shops, and those notorious red lights. Heading east from here, you pass through the market of Waterlooplein, the museums of the Plantage, the Eastern Islands and the new residential district, IJburg. The main tourist spots are in the Southern Canal Belt, while the fashionable shops of Jordaan are west of Centrum. Not far from the Van Gogh Museum is the leafy haven of Vondelpark. Bicycles are the most popular way to get around the city.

PEOPLE

The Netherlands is the world's third-most densely populated country, after Bangladesh and South Korea. Around 47% of the city's residents come from somewhere else, mainly Suriname, Morocco, Turkey and Indonesia.

TYPICAL AMSTERDAMMER

Only 10% of Dutch people own their own homes, but nearly all residents of Amsterdam have a bicycle (the city had 600,000 bikes at last count). The unemployment rate is just under 10%. As you would expect, Amsterdammers are a pretty relaxed bunch with liberal approaches to drugs, abortion, prostitution, euthanasia and homosexuality. That said, they say what they think and can come across as rude. They like a good time and don't take themselves too seriously. Like the English, queuing is a religion – woe betide anyone who tries to jump.

DEFINING EXPERIENCE

Taking a bike ride along the canals, then visiting the Van Gogh Museum and pottering in the antiques shops of Nieuwe Spiegelstraat, before enjoying a well-earned beer on one of the many café terraces.

STRENGTHS

- 160 canals and 90 islands, all reclaimed from the sea
- 7000 registered historical buildings
- Bicycles everywhere
- Dutch-Renaissance architecture eg Bartolotti House
- Those coffee shops
- Dutch beer served frothy and cold
- Clubbing at Bloemendaal beach
- Biggest gay scene in Europe
- Golden Age painters
- Liberal attitudes (the world's first homosexual marriage and legal euthanasia)
- Van Gogh Museum
- Rijksmuseum
- Anne Frankhuis
- Blijburg Beach
- Vondelpark
- Artis Zoo
- Nederlands Scheepvaartmuseum (Maritime Museum)
- Shopping in Negen Straatjes
- Beurs van Berlage and the Amsterdam School

WEAKNESSES

- Pushy dealers
- The Heineken Experience
- Bicycle theft – 200,000 get nicked every year
- Smelly backstreets
- Turbine noise from Schiphol, Europe's fastest-growing airport
- If the dams burst, 25% of the Netherlands would flood

GOLD STAR

Liberal attitudes

CITYSPEAK

- Who's swiped my bicycle?
- Where are we going clubbing tonight?
- Are house prices still going down?

STARRING ROLE IN...

- *Deuce Bigalow: European Gigolo* (2005)
- *Ocean's 12* (2004)
- *Traffic* (1971)
- *The Acid House* by Irvine Welsh

IMPORT

- Anne Frank
- Rembrandt
- Travel writer Lieve Joris
- Artist Marlene Dumas
- Stag nights

EXPORT

- Vincent Van Gogh
- Baruch Spinoza
- Piet Mondrian
- Jacob van Ruysdael
- Albert Cuyp
- Jan Steen
- Cornelis Troost
- Jacob de Wit
- Golden Earring
- Shocking Blue
- Jan Akkerman
- Arts and crafts
- Heineken
- Dennis Bergkamp
- Tulips
- Modern dance
- Clogs
- Cheese

SEE Dutch masterpieces by Rembrandt and others in the fantastic Rijksmuseum.

EAT spicy Indonesian cuisine to the sounds of the sax at Coffee & Jazz.

DRINK in the sun at arty Finch on one of Jordaan's most attractive squares.

DO visit Anne Frankhuis and see the attic where Anne Frank wrote her incredible diary in hiding.

WATCH the city go mad on Koninginnedag (Queen's Day), with street parties, live music and endless beer.

BUY upmarket fashion and vintage clothing along the Western Canal Belt.

AFTER DARK hit the dance floor at trendy Eleven and drink in the cityscape views.

URBAN MYTH

Prostitution was legalised in the Netherlands in 1810, and brothels were made legal in 2000. Seventy-eight percent of Dutch people have no problem with prostitution. There are 380 red-light windows in the city where 1000 to 1200 prostitutes work each day. Prostitutes rent their windows for between €40 and €100 per day and pay tax on their earnings. Services rendered by prostitutes start at €30. There is a union and if a client gets violent prostitutes can press a button to alert the police. Finally, why the red light? Apparently it is so flattering it makes teeth sparkle. In the 1300s, ladies of the night carried red lanterns to welcome the sailors to shore.

An island city that's a country unto itself all tricked-out with Southeast Asia's latest tech toys, Singapore is at a cultural crossroads that includes Indian, Malay and Chinese communities best served up at a hawker stall.

ANATOMY

The Singapore River weaves through the city centre, with the hippest dining and club spots lining the riverbanks at Boat, Clarke and Robertson Quays. Change into a suit to head south of the river to the central business district, or switch to a sari further north for Little India and Kampung Glam, the Muslim quarter. The southern island is the plastic theme park of Sentosa, while the eastern stretch of coast hosts the airport. The far north offers Bukit Timur, the last chunk of surviving wilderness. The west keeps it wild with Jurong's bird sanctuary but is largely industrial. Singapore's public transport is plentiful and varied.

PEOPLE

Predominantly Chinese (76.7% of the population), Singapore's population follows many traditional customs of mainland China, including speaking Cantonese or dialect languages. Neighbouring Malaysia has contributed 14% of the population, bringing an Islamic influence, while India has bought 8% of the population, many from the south, particularly Madras. The loud minority (1.7%) are expats who have made English the most spoken language.

TYPICAL SINGAPOREAN

Singaporeans love gadgetry and their traditional cultures so a Mass Rapid Transit (MRT) ride will usually feature images of kids listening to Goan hip-hop on the latest MP3 players while texting on their mobile for the latest Chinese horoscopes. The stomach of the Lion City roars for the best food and everyone has an opinion on the best hawker stalls. Privately Singaporeans might hold opinions on the government and its tough policies, but publicly they're too busy filling their mouths with excellent cuisine to speak out. Shopping rivals eating as a national passion, with many Singaporeans jetting over to China or Indonesia on low-cost flights for bargains. The Hokkien word *kiasu* (afraid to lose) is a guiding philosophy along Orchard Rd around sale times, when bargain frenzies dismiss any notion of reserve.

Singapore

025

VITAL STATISTICS

NAME: SINGAPORE

NICKNAME: THE LION CITY

DATE OF BIRTH: MID-13TH CENTURY; WHEN THE REGION WAS ESTABLISHED AS A MINOR TRADING POST FOR THE POWERFUL SUMATRAN SRIVIJAYA EMPIRE

ADDRESS: SINGAPORE (MAP 5, L13)

HEIGHT: 10M

SIZE: 682.3 SQ KM

POPULATION: 4.24 MILLION

A TYPICALLY CONSERVATIVE SINGAPOREAN REVS UP THE CHINESE NEW YEAR PARADE.
Photographer: Alain Evrard (1)

DEFINING EXPERIENCE

Breakfasting on *roti paratha* (grilled stuffed flat bread) in Little India and grabbing a discounted sari before heading over for some serious shopping in Orchard Rd, chilling out in the Botanic Gardens, then working up an appetite by strolling along the river to Boat Quay, where you'll find tasty Malay satays.

STRENGTHS

- ◢ Newly redeveloped Clarke Quay
- ◢ Hyper-efficient MRT
- ◢ Asian Civilisations Museum
- ◢ Orchard Rd shopping
- ◢ Hawker food at budget prices
- ◢ Cable-car ride from Mt Faber to Sentosa
- ◢ Club St
- ◢ World-class Changi Airport
- ◢ Cheap, abundant hawker cuisine
- ◢ Hi-tech gadgetry at Sim Lim Sq and the Tekka Centre
- ◢ Bargain flights to China, India and Southeast Asia
- ◢ Limited traffic
- ◢ Little India

WEAKNESSES

- ◢ Censorship
- ◢ Fines for jaywalking, eating on the MRT and chewing gum
- ◢ Freezing air-con
- ◢ High-priced booze
- ◢ Sentosa's overpriced, overhyped rides
- ◢ Touts hounding you along Temple St

GOLD STAR

Changi Airport – it has churches of every denomination, cinemas, restaurants and free Internet, plus it's got zippy public transport straight to the city centre.

CITYSPEAK

- ◢ New casino – moral decay or government payday?
- ◢ Who's hot in *Singapore Idol*?
- ◢ Best hawker stalls, especially if they've moved recently
- ◢ High cost of car licences

STARRING ROLE IN...

- ◢ *Army Daze* (1996)
- ◢ *Rogue Trader* (1999)
- ◢ *King Rat* by James Clavell
- ◢ *Saint Jack* by Paul Theroux

IMPORT

- ◢ Chicken rice
- ◢ Sir Thomas Stamford Raffles
- ◢ *Dosa* (an Indian pancake stuffed with potato)
- ◢ *Roti paratha*
- ◢ Coffee Bean & Tea Leaf outlets
- ◢ Satay
- ◢ Water from Malaysia

EXPORT

- ◢ Tiger balm
- ◢ Singapore Sling
- ◢ Lee Kuan Yew
- ◢ Chilli crab
- ◢ Self-proclaimed Makan food guru KF Seetoh
- ◢ Garbage to the nearby island of Pulau Semakau

SEE Clarke Quay on a romantic evening cruise lit with red lanterns.

EAT garlic stingray from a hectic Newtown Circus hawker stall.

DRINK a Singapore Sling at the Long Bar at the Raffles Hotel – a compulsory cliché.

DO a wet and weird Duck Tour on the river and through the colonial district.

WATCH a dazzling lion dance in front of Ngee Ann City on the lunar New Year.

BUY a Slurping Ape T-shirt from the hippest outlets along Orchard Rd.

AFTER DARK dance the night away at the multilevel institutional club, Zouk.

URBAN MYTH

The laws are the quirkiest part of Singapore and while you can find yourself wearing a fine for drinking water on the MRT there are good reasons behind some of the laws. Chewing gum was reputedly banned after an accident involving the doors of the MRT being wedged open using a humble piece of gum. You can now carry gum (for personal use) and buy it through a prescription-like system. Spitting and littering have always been cracked down on, but as a response to SARS the city took public hygiene to a new level, with fines, public education and a group of concerned volunteers who regularly patrol public toilets, awarding prizes for the cleanest.

GLITTERING WITH LIGHT, BUILDINGS ABOVE SINGAPORE RIVER BRIGHTEN UP THE NIGHT SKYLINE.
Photographer: Alain Evrard (2)

STUDENTS FOR PEACE! PUPILS AT AN ELEMENTERY SCHOOL THROW THEIR HANDS IN THE AIR LIKE THEY JUST DON'T CARE. Photographer: Alain Evrard (3)

SURREAL UNDERWATER SCENES AT THE CHINESE NEW YEAR PARADE.
Photographer: Alain Evrard (4)

Tokyo

026

VITAL STATISTICS

NAME: TOKYO (FORMERLY EDO)

NICKNAME: EASTERN CAPITAL

DATE OF BIRTH: 10,000–300 BC; DURING THE JŌMON PERIOD, WHEN PEOPLE ENJOYED GOOD HUNTING IN THE MARSHY REGION

ADDRESS: JAPAN (MAP 1, KK10)

HEIGHT: 6M

SIZE: 616 SQ KM

POPULATION: 12 MILLION

TRENDY VENDORS IN HARAJUKU DEMONSTRATE THE ART OF AIR ORIGAMI.
Photographer: Simon Charles Rowe (1)

Japan's mighty metropolis rises manga-style from economic ashes and earthquake fears to take on the world by transforming from business-as-usual salaryman to gadget-wielding monster and protector of Edo's tradition.

ANATOMY

Tokyo's massive size is only understandable in terms of the spaghetti-tangle rail map that includes three different train systems. Tourists stick to the Japan Railway's (JR) Yamanote line, which takes in the Imperial Palace with Ginza and Marunouchi (business district) in the east. To the west lies club-paradise Roppongi and then more nightlife in Shibuya and Shinjuku. Addresses are determined not by street name (few have actual names) but by indicating the *ku* (ward), then the *chō* or *machi* (like suburbs) and then *chōme* (roughly a couple of blocks). It's no wonder even taxi drivers ask for directions.

PEOPLE

Japan's famous homogeneity is disturbed by cosmopolitan Tokyo, but only slightly. Non-Japanese number less than 400,000 and form a *gaijin* (foreigner) population of business visitors, English-language teachers and Korean communities. Broadly, the population is Japanese, some of whom have a grasp of English, but many know only their native tongue.

TYPICAL TOKYOITE

In a city where there's half a vending machine for every citizen, you can expect a consumer culture to be important, with an obsession for owning the latest. Foreigners often snap up bargains of last-season electronics or clothing. And the bursting of the economic bubble means real estate is finally becoming more affordable. Expressing *honne* (personal views) is frowned upon socially with a need for *tatamae* (or safer views)…unless the sake is flowing, when even karaoke seems like a good idea.

DEFINING EXPERIENCE

Breakfasting on sushi in gumboots with the fisherfolk at Tsukiji Central Fish Market, striking a pose with the *Cos-play-zoku* (dress-up gangs) near Meiji Shrine, getting spiritual at the shrines of Sensō-ji, then polishing off the night with beer and snacks at an *izakaya* (pub/eatery).

STRENGTHS

- *Cos-play-zoku*
- Ginza
- Ueno Park
- 'Bullet' trains
- Tokyo National Museum
- Bonsai Park
- Shinjuku
- Mt Fuji
- *Kaijū* (monster movie)
- Imperial Palace
- Meiji Shrine and surrounding Harajuku and Aoyama areas
- Kabuki-za Theatre
- *Hanami* (cherry-blossom viewing) in spring
- Kite Museum

WEAKNESSES

- High cost of living
- Eating *unagi* (eel)
- Impossible traffic
- Distant Nairita airport
- Yakuza (Japanese mafia)
- Earthquakes

GOLD STAR

Low crime – three people will stoop to help if you drop your wallet, and the streets are safe at all hours.

CITYSPEAK

- Only-child syndrome – punish the parents for these spoiled children!
- *Bosozoku* (motorcycle gangs) – is there no way to stop their obnoxious engine revving?
- How to solve the problem of *mukekkon sedai* (nonmarriage generation)

STARRING ROLE IN…

- *Lost in Translation* (2003)
- *Kill Bill: Vol 1* (2003)
- *Shinjuku Boys* (1995)
- *Tora! Tora! Tora!* (1970)

IMPORT

- Tokyo Disneyland
- Coffee
- *Gaijin* (foreigners)
- Whisky
- Korean labourers
- The Beatles

EXPORT

- Sony
- 17th-century haiku poet Bashō
- 'Bullet' trains
- Yohji Yamamoto
- Hayao Miyazaki
- Issey Miyake
- Asahi beer
- *Yu-Gi-Oh!* trading cards and TV series
- Manga
- *Sailor Moon* animated TV series
- Dragon Ball
- Nikon
- J-pop
- *Denki* (electronic music)
- Banana Yoshimoto
- *Iron Chef* TV series
- Haruki Murakami

SEE the Meiji Shrine, a tranquil Shinto sanctuary.

EAT the after-work favourite, *yakitori* (grilled skewers of chicken or vegetables), at the ever-busy Akiyoshi

DRINK *shōchū* – distilled liquor used as a disinfectant during the Edo period – at any trendy Shinjuku bar.

DO soak and scrub your cares away at Jakotsu-yu, an Edo-era *onsen* (traditional bathhouse).

WATCH sumo at the Ryōgoku Kokugikan Stadium, though you'd have to join the *yakuza* to get a seat.

BUY cold Big Boss coffee from a vending machine, undrinkable but *very* Tokyo.

AFTER DARK pack your fangs for a night out at the vampy campy movie-tribute bar Dusk Till Dawn.

URBAN MYTH

Tokyo's apparent political conformity is often disturbed by mysterious black vans that prowl the streets blasting out right-wing patriotic songs, which bear an uncanny resemblance to children's *manga* theme songs. This is the propaganda arm of the *uyoku* – a collection of seriously far-right political parties. Most Tokyoites studiously ignore them, but the *uyoku* have been known to police criticism of the emperor either through threats and, occasionally, violence.

TRAINEE WRESTLERS POSE FOR A 'BEFORE' PHOTO AT A SUMO ACADEMY.
Photographer: Martin Moos (2)

BASEBALL FANS WAVE THEIR SCARVES IN TRIBUTE TO THE YOMIURI GIANTS AT TOKYO DOME.
Photographer: Greg Elms (3)

FUSSY BUYERS INSPECT ROWS OF TUNA AT TSUKIJI FISH MARKET.
Photographer: Paul Dymond (4)

PIAZZA SANTA CROCE HOSTS THE ANNUAL FLORENTINE FOOTBALL MATCH, A TRADITIONAL 16TH-CENTURY GAME COMBINING ELEMENTS OF RUGBY, FOOTBALL AND WRESTLING.
Photographer: Tony Gentile (1)

Florence
027

VITAL STATISTICS

NAME: FLORENCE

DATE OF BIRTH: 30 BC; JULIUS CAESAR NAMED HIS GARRISON TOWN ON THE ARNO FLORENTIA

ADDRESS: ITALY (MAP 3, K12)

HEIGHT: 38M

SIZE: 3514 SQ KM

POPULATION: 374,500

Star of the Renaissance, Florence is an aesthetic feast of world-famous paintings and sculpture, stunning churches and palaces, and beautiful people.

ANATOMY

Florence's city centre is relatively compact. The River Arno flows through the town, with the striking dome of Florence's Duomo (cathedral) and the *centro storico* (historic centre) on the northern side. The famous Ponte Vecchio crosses the river directly south of the cathedral and not far from the main square, Piazza della Signoria, and the Uffizi. On the other side of the Arno is the Oltrarno area, which is quieter and far less touristy. Walking or catching a bus is the best way to get around.

PEOPLE

The population comprises Italians originating from Florence and other parts of Italy and illegal migrants from Africa (Tunisia and Senegal) or the Balkans. Makeshift settlements on the edge of the city house immigrants from Albania and Kosovo. Around 85% of Florentines are Catholic, while Muslims, Protestants and Buddhists make up the rest.

TYPICAL FLORENTINE

Most Florentines are unfairly good-looking and known for taking care of their appearance. They are polite and friendly, although they can sometimes appear standoffish – with the constant invasion of tourists, this is perhaps forgivable. They tend to be conservative, and modern architectural proposals cause massive controversy. They like it if visitors attempt to speak Italian, and may even award lower prices in return. Smoking is forbidden in many bars and restaurants, but a Florentine who wants to smoke will light up anyway.

DEFINING EXPERIENCE

Craning your neck admiring the ceiling of the Duomo, before ambling through the historic centre, strolling over the Ponte Vecchio and enjoying a gelato in Piazza Pitti.

STRENGTHS

◢ Art everywhere you turn
◢ Building restoration
◢ Medieval historic centre
◢ *Bistecca alla fiorentina* (Florentine steak)
◢ Enviable fashion sense
◢ Delicious wine eg Chianti and Brunello
◢ Cosimo de' Medici
◢ Duomo
◢ Uffizi
◢ Michelangelo's *David*
◢ Campanile
◢ Ponte Vecchio
◢ Palazzo Vecchio
◢ Haggling at San Lorenzo market
◢ Profusion of shoes and handbags to buy
◢ Boboli Gardens
◢ Electric buses
◢ Fine-arts faculty at the Università degli Studi di Firenze
◢ Skiing the Abetone pistes north of Pistoia

WEAKNESSES

◢ Air pollution
◢ Constant restoration means things are often closed
◢ Crowds
◢ Snooty sales assistants
◢ Smelly streets
◢ Traffic
◢ Street prostitution
◢ Pigeons and rats

GOLD STAR

The Renaissance – it was born in Florence

CITYSPEAK

◢ Isozaki's modern exit for the Nuovi Uffizi – is it beautiful or a travesty?
◢ AC Fiorentina football club has its old name back, so who cares about a little scandal?
◢ Cough, cough – with all the mopeds we need more electric buses!

STARRING ROLE IN...

◢ *Hannibal* (2001)
◢ *La Vita è Bella* (Life is Beautiful, 2001)
◢ *Tea with Mussolini* (1999)
◢ *A Room with a View* (1986)

IMPORT

◢ Raphael
◢ Leonardo da Vinci
◢ Tourists
◢ Other Italians
◢ Michelangelo
◢ Galileo Galilei

EXPORT

◢ Leather goods
◢ Tuscan wines
◢ Pecorino cheese
◢ Olive oil
◢ Franco Zeffirelli
◢ Pinocchio
◢ Machiavelli
◢ Dante Alighieri
◢ Filippo Brunelleschi
◢ Gucci
◢ Salvatore Ferragamo
◢ Pucci
◢ Furniture
◢ Cheque books

SEE Botticelli's *Birth of Venus*, Leonardo da Vinci's *Annunciation* and other artistic marvels at the Uffizi (book in advance to beat the crowds).

EAT devilishly good chocolate confections on the terrace of Caffè Rivoire and savour the view of the Palazzo Vecchio.

DRINK a glass of Chianti Classico with the locals on Piazza Santo Spirito.

DO cross the Ponte Vecchio and mosey through the quieter streets of the Oltrarno.

WATCH 27-a-side football matches at the Gioco del Calcio Storico.

BUY a Pucci bikini and guarantee future beach cred.

AFTER DARK head to the outdoor dance area of Central Park and enjoy a moonlight mosh.

URBAN MYTH

Whether or not the statue of David by Michelangelo is a self-portrait, many visitors sneer at the size of his manhood. In fact, viewers are lucky to see it at all. Prudish church authorities used to insist that nudes in art had their privates hidden, either by a judiciously painted fig leaf or by removing the area altogether – Michelangelo's *Bacchus* had his bits chopped off. It's no surprise then that some artists, such as Brunelleschi with his *Crucifix*, gave up representing the naughty bits altogether.

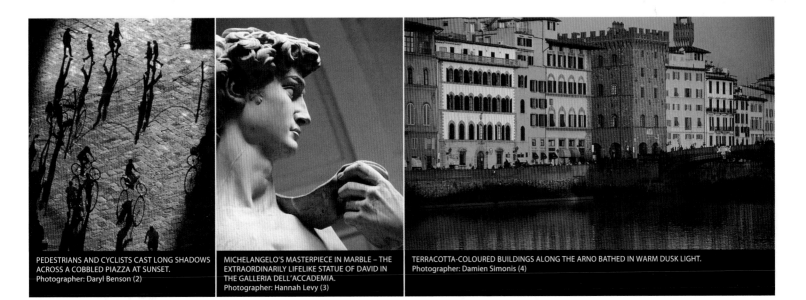

PEDESTRIANS AND CYCLISTS CAST LONG SHADOWS ACROSS A COBBLED PIAZZA AT SUNSET.
Photographer: Daryl Benson (2)

MICHELANGELO'S MASTERPIECE IN MARBLE – THE EXTRAORDINARILY LIFELIKE STATUE OF DAVID IN THE GALLERIA DELL'ACCADEMIA.
Photographer: Hannah Levy (3)

TERRACOTTA-COLOURED BUILDINGS ALONG THE ARNO BATHED IN WARM DUSK LIGHT.
Photographer: Damien Simonis (4)

Dublin may not be a particularly pretty city, but for poetry, pubs, sporting life and garrulous sociability, you can't do better.

ANATOMY

Dublin sprawls around Dublin Bay with the River Liffey dividing the city. North of the river, busy O'Connell St leads to Parnell Sq and, to the west, revitalised Smithfield. On the south side lie the increasingly tedious Temple Bar and the stately houses and elegant parks of Georgian Dublin. The DART train line links the seaside suburbs, and the new LUAS light-rail system connects the south to the centre.

PEOPLE

Traditionally, a Dubliner hails from between the canals, but it's now hard to put your finger on the city's physical or social boundaries. Expats returning home and migrants from the rest of Ireland are joined by significant numbers of Nigerians, Chinese, Romanians and Bosnians. A long way from the *Gaeltacht* (Irish-speaking region), Dubliners may speak a smattering of Irish, but are more famous for their own particularly colourful take on the English language.

TYPICAL DUBLINER

Dublin is one of Europe's most expensive cities, but with over half the population under 30, there's a youthful exuberance and open, optimistic spirit evident. Dubliners pride themselves on their irreverent humour, razor wit and keenness to debate. Although still overwhelmingly Roman Catholic, they tend to be relatively liberal; they're also fabulously self-deprecating and have a strong aversion to pretence of any kind. The rest of Ireland – pejoratively known as bogmen or *culchies* in the local vernacular – may not see this easy-going side, and tend to think that Dubliners are overly smug.

DEFINING EXPERIENCE

Skipping the fry-up because you can't be arsed with the weekend crowds at your local café, instead scoffing a bun and a cup of tea in Bewley's, then heading off to an international rugby test at Lansdowne Rd, seeing Ireland getting the lard beaten out of them, and then going to Ba Mizu for pints and a plate of stew, though not getting too bladdered because you've got tickets to see a gig at Whelan's.

Dublin 028

VITAL STATISTICS

NAME: DUBLIN

NICKNAME: DUB

DATE OF BIRTH: 6TH CENTURY AD; ESTABLISHED AS A MONASTIC SETTLEMENT

ADDRESS: IRELAND (MAP 3, C7)

HEIGHT: 47M

SIZE: 921 SQ KM

POPULATION: 1.16 MILLION

ALL HAIRSTYLES ARE WELCOME AT THE MARKET BAR.
Photographer: Jonathan Smith (1)

STRENGTHS

- Cracking nightlife, every night of the week
- Well-preserved Georgian streetscapes
- Burgeoning restaurant scene, including great Modern Irish
- St Stephen's Green
- Proud literary heritage
- Kilmainham Gaol
- The banter
- Trinity College
- The Liffey's bridges
- Sports-obsessed culture
- Fitzwilliam Sq
- Irish Museum of Modern Art, both the collections and the site

WEAKNESSES

- City-centre traffic, especially on the quays
- Crass, soulless 'theme' bars
- Overpriced pints
- The stench of vomit in Temple Bar
- Urban planning, or lack of it
- The rain

GOLD STAR

Pub culture – despite the onslaught of gastropubs and chains, Dublin is still the best place for a pint in the world.

CITYSPEAK

- The M50
- Shock jocks
- Have you seen yer man's new phone?
- The cost of the LUAS – you could've put a man on the moon for less
- Have you been to Ikea yet?

STARRING ROLE IN...

- *Veronica Guerin* (2003)
- *Intermission* (2003)
- *The General* (1997)
- *Circle of Friends* (1995)
- *Into the West* (1992)
- *The Commitments* (1991)
- *My Left Foot* (1989)
- *The Dead* (1988)
- *Ulysses* by James Joyce
- *Paddy Clarke Ha Ha Ha* by Roddy Doyle
- *Cowboys and Indians* by Joseph O'Connor

IMPORT

- Football
- Nurses and doctors
- Espresso
- Summer vegetables
- John Rocha
- Australian bar staff
- British stags and hens
- Damon Hill and Eddie Irvine
- Musician Phil Lynott (born in Birmingham, raised in Dublin)

EXPORT

- Guinness
- James Joyce
- U2
- Georgian door knockers
- Boyzone/Westlife/Ronan Keating
- Organic meat
- Bob Geldof
- Sinead O'Connor
- Francis Bacon
- Gabriel Byrne
- Colin Farrel
- Jameson whiskey
- Sean Scully

SEE panoramic views of the city through the bottom of a pint glass at the Gravity Bar – part of the Guinness Storehouse.

EAT a potato and mackerel terrine at Jacob's Ladder, gazing over the playing fields of Trinity.

DRINK the porter at Grogan's on South William St.

DO everything in your power to get a ticket to the All-Ireland Hurling Finals at Croke Park in September.

WATCH a play at the Abbey Theatre during the Dublin Theatre Festival.

BUY a luxe Lainey Keogh sweater from Brown Thomas on Grafton St.

AFTER DARK take advantage of the late licence and the mood lighting upstairs at Hogan's in SoDa.

URBAN MYTH

Everyone, it seems, *has* got a Bono story. Although arguably Ireland's most famous musical export, the members of U2 have continued to live in or around Dublin throughout their stellar international career. Most Dubliners will have a tale involving the seemingly ubiquitous Bono. These range from the banal to the mildly disturbing: being a waitress and serving him gravy; seeing him scribbling (a song perhaps?) on Killiney Beach; hearing him sing at the Dandelion Market in 1979; having him offer you a hand with the shopping; minding your business, sitting by the Grand Canal Docks and himself turning up in a *currach* (small boat), waving and shouting 'Thank you, Ireland!'. The phenomenon is so widespread that a novel entitled *Everyone's Got a Bono Story*, by Anne-Marie O'Connor, was based on the idea.

HURTLING THROUGH HURLING PRACTICE.
Photographer: Martin Moos (2)

TAIL-LIGHTS BLAZE A BUSY TRAIL THROUGH DAME ST.
Photographer: Olivier Cirendini (3)

THE HA'PENNY BRIDGE GRACEFULLY ARCHES OVER THE LIFFEY.
Photographer: Richard Cummins (4)

Mexico City

VITAL STATISTICS

NAME: MEXICO CITY

NICKNAME: EL DF; CHILANGOTLÁN; CHILANGOLANDIA; LA CIUDAD DE LOS PALACIOS (CITY OF PALACES); LA CIUDAD DE LA ESPERANZA (CITY OF HOPE)

DATE OF BIRTH: 1325; WHEN THE AZTECS RULED IT AS TENOCHTITLÁN, BUT IT WAS REBUILT AS NUEVA ESPAÑA BY THE CONQUISTADORS AROUND 1550

ADDRESS: MEXICO (MAP 4, C4)

HEIGHT: 2309M

SIZE: 5000 SQ KM

POPULATION: 22 MILLION

For sheer scale, Mexico City impresses; it's also North America's oldest metropolis, and its layering of European nostalgia, rich indigenous culture and modern urban energy are as exhilarating as its size.

ANATOMY

Set in a high, flat valley, Mexico City's 350 crowded *colonias* neighbourhoods) sprawl. The heart of the city, El Zócalo, and its surrounding museum-packed neighbourhoods and green expanses of the Alameda, form the Centro Histórico. Architectural styles range across the spectrum, from the baroque to early 20th-century delights, from millennial-gated communities to the outer rings of slum dwellings. There is horrendous traffic congestion, despite a metro, a large network of buses and trolley cars, and countless (and infamous) taxis.

PEOPLE

The majority of *capitalinos* or *chilangos,* as residents are known, are Spanish-speaking mestizos, a typically Mexican melange of Spanish and indigenous ancestry, often with some European or African-slave heritage in the mix as well. The city's enormous population continues to be swelled by immigrants from other parts of the country, usually from the rural south.

TYPICAL CAPITALINO

Young *capitalinos* from the fashionable inner neighbourhoods tend to be politically engaged (though cynical), culturally switched on, and a little hedonistic. Although deep-held values – family, machismo, Catholicism – still endure, for the middle class at least, there are profound shifts in social attitudes, particularly around gender equality. *Capitalinos* may know they are living in a city that is safer than ever, increasingly stylish and certainly cosmopolitan, but not all of them get to share in the glamour; over 20% of citizens live in poverty, mainly in the dire outer sprawl.

DEFINING EXPERIENCE

Brunching late at El Pendulo, listening to the guitarist and discussing the presidential election, taking a stroll around the Mercado de la Merced with your *abuela* (grandmother), then having a prickly-pear ice cream at Nevería Roxy, stopping by Chic By Accident and bargaining for that antique mirror you've been coveting for the conversion in El Centro, followed by drinks on the rooftop at Condesa DF.

STRENGTHS

- Improving air quality
- Museo Nacional de Antropología
- The new 'Mexican chic' epitomised by Hotel Habita and Condesa DF
- Palacio de las Bellas Artes
- Self-deprecation
- Thousands of taco stands
- Photography collection at Galería Casa Lamm
- Camino Real's Mex-modernist décor
- Colour
- Art Deco in Condesa
- Art Nouveau in Colonia Roma
- Casa Azul and Museo Casa Estudio Diego Rivera y Frida Kahlo (key cult-of-Kahlo sites)
- Church of Santa Veracruz and the baroque Church of San Juan de Dios
- Castillo de Chapultepec
- The pyramids at Teotihuacán Tenochtitlán
- Never-say-die nightlife

WEAKNESSES

- Sprawl
- Pollution
- Decrepit infrastructure
- Extreme social inequalities
- It's sinking
- Happy-handed rush hour commuters on the metro
- The 5am trumpet wake-up call in the Zócalo
- Altitude

GOLD STAR

Murals: Mexico City's spirited, incendiary murals, especially those by Rivera, Siqueiros and Orozco, which capture the history and psyche of the city and the nation.

CITYSPEAK

- Taxis – to call or not to call
- The José Vasconcelos Library
- US neo-imperialism
- The elevated highway's 'second floor'

STARRING ROLE IN...

- *Los Olvidados* (1950)
- *The Falcon and the Snowman* (1985)
- *Love in the Time of Hysteria* (1991)
- *The Beginning and the End* (1993)
- *Amores Perros* (2000)
- *Y Tu Mama Tambien* (2001)
- *Frida* (2002)
- *The Death of Artemio Cruz* by Carlos Fuentes

IMPORT

- Leon Trotsky
- André Breton
- Baseball
- Luis Buñuel
- Bullfighting
- Tina Modotti
- US fast-food chains
- Gabriel García Márquez
- Sushi
- Football

EXPORT

- Mural art
- Octavio Paz
- Cement
- Textiles
- Silver
- *Antojitos* (small tortillas with various fillings)
- Musicians Rodrigo y Gabriela
- Plastics
- Hammocks
- Hugo Sánchez

SEE the Gothic, baroque *and* neoclassical Catedral Metropolitana and the Aztec Templo Mayor from the balcony bar of the Holiday Inn.

EAT Patricia Quintana's *nueva cocina mexicana* (new Mexican cuisine) at Izote: Mexican standards and indigenous ingredients (think yucca flower) get a considered reworking.

DRINK *pulque* (maguey liquor) at Las Duelistas, a traditional working-class *cantina* (bar).

DO escape to the shaded waterways of pre-Hispanic Xochimilco and take in the music from aboard a *trajinera* (a gondola-like vessel).

WATCH Astrid Hadad skewer the powerful in her bawdy take-no-prisoners cabaret, upstairs at Condesa's La Bodega.

BUY vintage embroidered dresses and antique silver at the Bazar Sábado in San Angel.

AFTER DARK grab a *pinindia* (cocktail that includes tequila and pineapple juice) at Prima, then get to the Dos Naciones for contemporary sounds and *cantina* atmosphere, finishing up at a 24-hour café on 5 de Mayo.

URBAN MYTH

Frida Kahlo is one of Mexico's most well known artists. Kahlo's exquisitely sensuous work uses the pain and heartbreak of her life as a central motif. Her physical pain was all too real, the result of appalling injuries sustained in a bus accident. The teenage Kahlo's leg and spine were shattered and she was impaled by a handrail's steel shaft ('I lost my virginity', she wryly observed). Kahlo lay naked, the force of the crash having torn off her clothes, bleeding profusely and covered in the gold powder paint that a fellow passenger had been carrying. Surreally, she came to resemble a figure from a gruesome *santa sangre* (a form of Mexican folk painting), an image that would later haunt her work.

A COOL CUSTOMER CUTS A GLAMOROUS FIGURE IN A CONDESA DISTRICT SHOP.
Photographer: Lynsey Addario (1)

COLUMNS OF PINK AND FLUFFY CANDY FLOSS FOR SALE ON A STREET CORNER IN COLONIAL COYOACAN.
Photographer: Mireille Vautier (2)

¡QUÉ PADRE! DANCERS OF THE BALLET FOLCLÓRICO KEEP TO A TRADITIONAL TEMPO.
Photographer: David Ryan (3)

A YELLOW VOLKSWAGEN BEETLE TAXI PROCLAIMS ITS INDIVIDUALITY AMONG THE MASSES.
Photographer: Chris Cheadle (4)

Kraków 030

VITAL STATISTICS

NAME: KRAKÓW

NICKNAME: POLAND'S ROYAL CITY

DATE OF BIRTH: 7TH CENTURY AD; WHEN SETTLEMENT WAS FIRST RECORDED HERE

ADDRESS: POLAND (MAP 3, N9)

HEIGHT: 209M

SIZE: 327 SQ KM

POPULATION: 870,000

Kraków is a whimsical, beautiful city: tatters of the iron curtain can still be found in the city's grey, identikit suburbs, but these only throw into relief the pale, lazy loops of the Vistula River curling around the old town, or the flower stalls, which make the centre of the old town and its marketplace so vivid.

ANATOMY

Relatively flat, save for some scattered rocky formations, Kraków is bisected by the Vistula River, Poland's longest river (wending its way 1047km to the Baltic). Most districts, including the historic quarter, are on the northern, left bank and very walkable. The Old Town is only 800m wide and 1200m long, with the Main Market Sq in the middle. Both buses and trams are used to travel further out.

PEOPLE

Ethnically homogeneous, Poles make up 98% of Kraków's population. Only about 150 Jews remain in the city, compared with the 70,000 in the late 1930s. About 95% of the population is Roman Catholic.

TYPICAL KRAKÓW CITIZEN

Residents of Kraków are more conservative than their fellow countrymen in Warsaw. They are friendly and hospitable but polite and formal – they are passionate hand-shakers. They are firmly religious.

DEFINING EXPERIENCE

Reflecting on Poland's long Catholic tradition at St Mary's Church in Rynek Glowny, then leisurely strolling around the Main Market Sq, passing through the Cloth Hall, finding an appetising lunch on ul Grodzka, then heading to the Czartoryski Museum before ambling to Wawel Royal Castle and watching the stunning views over the Vistula River.

STRENGTHS

- Wawel Palace
- Wawel Cathedral
- Czartoryski Museum
- Rynek Glowny
- Cloth Hall
- The jazz scene
- Wieliczka salt mine
- A vast collection of artworks
- Wierzynek, Poland's oldest restaurant, dating from 1364

WEAKNESSES

- Weather
- Nowa Huta
- Sauerkraut with everything

GOLD STAR

Main Market Sq – the largest medieval town square in Poland (and reputedly in all of Europe) – and the Cloth Hall. The 1257 layout has been retained to this day – the façades might look neoclassical, but most of the buildings are much older.

CITYSPEAK

- We're in the EU now – is it helping us?
- Warsaw – who needs it?

STARRING ROLE IN...

- *La Double vie de Véronique* (The Double Life of Véronique, 1991)
- *Schindler's List* (1993)

IMPORT

- Capitalism
- Nigel Kennedy
- Karol Wojtyla (Pope John Paul II)
- Nowa Huta
- *Lady with the Ermine* by Leonardo da Vinci
- Lenin

EXPORT

- Pope John Paul II
- Copernicus
- Film-maker Roman Polanski
- Musician Zbigniew Preisner

SEE the Chapel of the Blessed Kinga, a church deep in the salt mine at Wieliczka.

EAT excellent Polish fare at Restuaracja pod Aniolami in vaulted cellars, beautifully decorated with traditional household implements and old crafts.

DRINK beer (Zywiec, Okocim or EB) or vodka (clear, or flavoured with juniper berries, cherries or rowan berries).

DO make the trip out to Auschwitz, possibly the most moving experience in the whole of Poland.

WATCH experimental theatre (knowledge of the language is not necessary).

BUY amber in striking colours – from ivory and pale yellow to reddish and brownish hints.

AFTER DARK vaulted cellar pubs and bars are the place to head for; there are 100 pubs and/or bars in the Old Town alone.

URBAN MYTH

According to legend, once upon a time there lived a powerful prince, Krak or Krakus, who built a castle on a hill named Wawel on the banks of the Vistula and founded a town named after himself. It would have been para-dise if not for a dragon living in a cave underneath the castle. This fearsome and ever-hungry huge lizard deci-mated cattle and sheep, and was not averse to human beings, especially pretty maidens. The wise prince or-dered a sheep's hide to be filled with sulphur, which was set alight, and the whole thing was hurled into the cave. The voracious beast devoured the bait in one gulp, only then feeling the sulphur burning in its stomach. The dragon rushed to the river, and drank and drank and finally exploded, giv-ing the citizens a spectacular fire-works display. The town was saved. The dragon has become the symbol of the city, immortalised in countless images, and the dragon's monument has been placed where the beast once lived.

A LOCAL WOMAN AND A HOTEL ADVERTISEMENT COME FACE TO FACE ON A STREET CORNER.
Photographer: Bruce Yuanyue Bi (1)

LOVERS LOUNGE BENEATH THE OPULENT FRIEZES OF ST MARY'S CHURCH.
Photographer: Bruce Yuanyue Bi (2)

PIGEONS AND FAMILIES ALIKE FLOCK TO MAIN MARKET SQ, THE HEART AND SOUL OF THE CITY.
Photographer: Bruce Yuanyue Bi (3)

COLD BEER AND WARM ATMOSPHERE DEFINES KRAKÓW'S PERSONABLE PUB SCENE.
Photographer: Bruce Yuanyue Bi (4)

Toronto 031

VITAL STATISTICS

NAME: TORONTO

NICKNAME: THE MEGACITY; HOGTOWN; TO

DATE OF BIRTH: 1793; WHEN LOYALISTS FROM THE AMERICAN REVOLUTIONARY WAR FLED NORTH

ADDRESS: CANADA (MAP 1, L9)

HEIGHT: 116M

SIZE: 641 SQ KM

POPULATION: 650,000

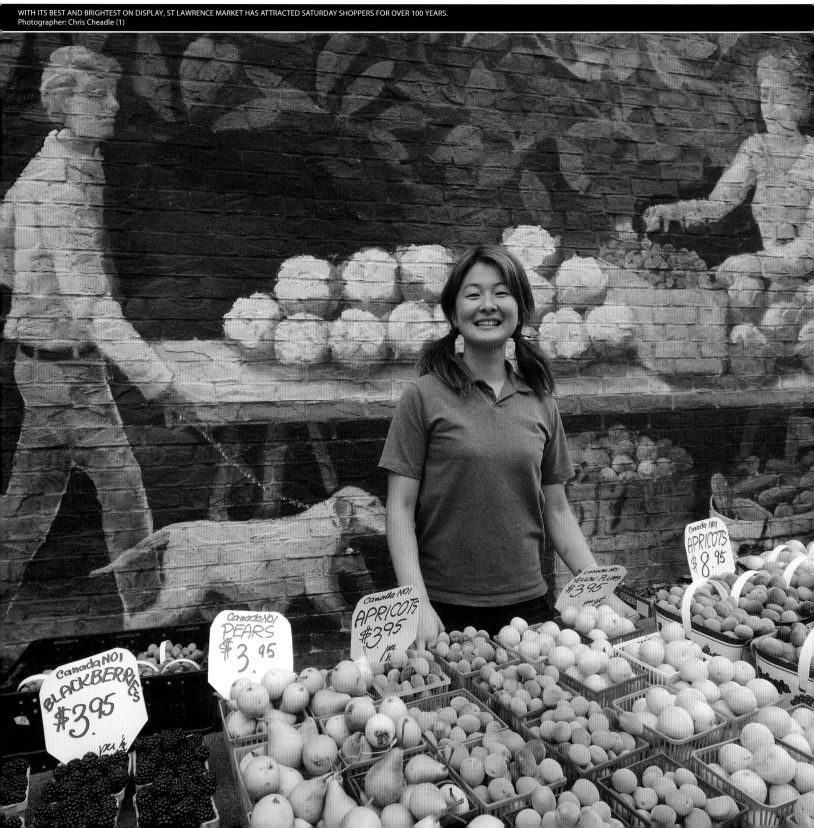

WITH ITS BEST AND BRIGHTEST ON DISPLAY, ST LAWRENCE MARKET HAS ATTRACTED SATURDAY SHOPPERS FOR OVER 100 YEARS.
Photographer: Chris Cheadle (1)

FROM ACROSS LAKE ONTARIO, THE ROGER'S CENTER 'SKYDOME' RADIATES IN ANTICIPATION OF AN ACTION-PACKED NIGHT MATCH.
Photographer: Chris Cheadle (2)

IN FRONT OF UNION STATION FRANCESCO PERILLI'S 'MONUMENT TO MULTICULTURALISM' CELEBRATES THE CITY'S CULTURAL DIVERSITY.
Photographer: Chris Cheadle (3)

PUNK-STYLE CAFÉ CULTURE ADORNS THE STREETS NEAR KENSINGTON MARKET.
Photographer: Chris Cheadle (4)

Toronto is Canada's boldest metropolis, where the world is available at the cost of a subway token and tolerance is a reigning virtue.

ANATOMY

Toronto itself was once under the waters of Lake Iroquois. Today the modern city sits beside Lake Ontario, part of the chain of Great Lakes shared between Canada and the USA. The Toronto Islands, originally a 9km-long sandbar peninsula, were created by a violent 19th-century storm. Quiet residential blocks scattered throughout the city centre boast shady trees, one-way streets (called 'traffic-calming zones') and Victorian row houses. Overall, the land around Toronto is flat, making it easy for walking. TO has a model public-transport system of integrated subway, bus and streetcar services.

PEOPLE

Toronto is one of the most multicultural cities in the world, with about 36% of its population comprising visible minorities. The remainder of the population is of European origin, chiefly of British, Irish, French, Italian and Portuguese descent. Chinese and South Asian communities each make up about 10% of the population. Half of all black Canadians live in Toronto, and they constitute around 8.3% of the population. Over 100 languages and dialects are spoken here, and over one third of Toronto residents speak a language other than English at home.

TYPICAL TORONTONIAN

Diversity is what Toronto rightly uses to define its character. Tolerance is a way of life. In general, Torontonians are still very mannerly, if a bit standoffish. They think seriously about how to live their daily lives, meaning everything from recycling to how to treat one's neighbour and the future of indie music. Although Torontonians are less hesitant to speak their mind than other Canadians, especially when it comes to criticising Americans, tolerance remains a virtue. Eating and drinking are major pursuits, with life lived outdoors as much as possible, especially during summer.

DEFINING EXPERIENCE

Having a quick breakfast at the St Lawrence Market, strolling down to the Harbourfront and catching the ferry over to Centre Island, then cycling along the boardwalk and stopping to admire the flower gardens on Ward's Island before heading back to the mainland, riding the subway north from Union Station and strolling to leafy Baldwin Village for lunch at an outdoor café.

STRENGTHS

- Art Gallery of Ontario
- Royal Ontario Museum
- International Dragon Boat Festival
- Caribana
- Du Maurier Downtown Jazz Festival
- Caravan multicultural festival
- Scream in High Park
- Molson Indy
- Toronto Star Bluesfest
- Toronto International Film Festival
- Toronto Islands
- St Lawrence Market
- Harbourfront
- Queen West
- Legalised gay marriage

WEAKNESSES

- Winter weather
- Summer humidity
- Increased numbers of homeless people on the streets
- Snarled traffic on major expressways

GOLD STAR

Location, location, location. This lakeside city has its very own islands in the waters of the lake, facing off against the downtown skyline, and a string of gorgeous beaches. Just beyond the city limits are the fertile vineyards of the Niagara Peninsula, and of course, the mighty falls themselves.

CITYSPEAK

- What disaster next – after West Nile virus and SARS?
- Who cares about the Toronto International Film Festival?
- Can the Libs really be trusted after almost a decade of Tory rule?
- What happened to the Maple Leaf Gardens?

STARRING ROLE IN...

- *Queer as Folk* (2003–)
- *X-Men* (2000)
- *Good Will Hunting* (1997)
- *Bulletproof Monk* (2003)
- *Chicago* (2002)

IMPORT

- Immigrants from everywhere
- Draft dodgers
- Cuisine from all over the world

EXPORT

- Ice hockey
- Maple syrup
- Conrad Black
- Marshall McLuhan
- Keanu Reeves
- Jim Carrey
- David Cronenberg
- Atom Egoyan
- Frank Gehry
- Glenn Gould
- Norman Jewison
- Gilda Radner
- Dan Aykroyd
- Mike Myers

SEE the view from the CN Tower.

EAT Canadian *nouvelle cuisine* at Canoe and Auberge du Pommier – unusual, fresh (often organic) local ingredients with classic French stylings and daring fusion from Asia.

DRINK Niagara Peninsula wines, particularly ice-wine vintages.

DO make the trip to Niagara Falls for a good drenching.

WATCH a baseball game at SkyDome or ice hockey in winter.

BUY from the eclectic shops on Queen St W – west of Spadina the street gets funkier the further you go.

AFTER DARK sample the variety at Cameron House; get down with soul, R&B, acid jazz and other alternative music at this veteran Queen West venue.

URBAN MYTH

Toronto was known as York until 1834, when William Lyon Mackenzie, the first mayor, renamed it Toronto, an aboriginal name meaning 'meeting place'. The Victorian city, controlled by conservative politicians, became known as 'Toronto the Good', a tag that only began to fade in the 1970s. Religious restraints (for instance, it was illegal to hire a horse on Sunday) and strong anti-vice laws were largely responsible. Not all that long ago, curtains were drawn in department-store windows on Sunday, because window-shopping was considered sinful, and movies couldn't be screened on the holy day.

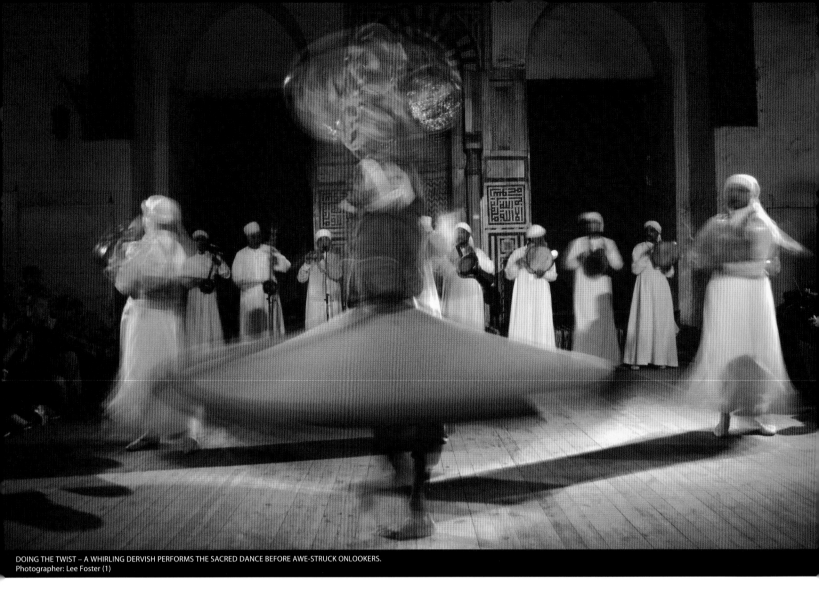

DOING THE TWIST – A WHIRLING DERVISH PERFORMS THE SACRED DANCE BEFORE AWE-STRUCK ONLOOKERS.
Photographer: Lee Foster (1)

Cairo dominates Egypt with one of the world's highest population densities, its minarets dominate the skyline and ancient obelisks and extraordinary works of art greet you in the most unlikely places.

ANATOMY

Cairo is relatively easy to navigate. Islamic Cairo is the medieval centre of the city. Heading east, Downtown ends at Midan Ataba and the old but still kicking medieval heart of the city known as Islamic Cairo takes over. Bordering Downtown to the west is the Nile River, which is obstructed by two sizable islands. The more central of these, connected directly to Downtown by three bridges, is Gezira, home to the Cairo Tower and the Opera House complex. The west bank of the Nile is less historical and much more residential. Giza stretches some 20km west on either side of the long, straight road that ends at the foot of the pyramids. The Metro is startlingly efficient, but the masses still use minibuses.

PEOPLE

More than a quarter of Egyptians live in Cairo, Africa's largest city. The majority of its population is Egyptian, with a small number of Bedouins, Nubians from Sudan and an almost negligible number of Greeks, Armenians, Italians and French. While Muslim is the official religion, around 10% of Cairenes are Coptic Christian.

TYPICAL CAIRENE

The people of Cairo are both curious and generous. They'll gladly help you across the maddening roads with cars that never stop for anything and at the same time ask you a million questions about where you're from and even offer to show you some ancient treasures that are hidden to tourists.

DEFINING EXPERIENCE

Smoking a *sheesha* (a tobacco water pipe, often flavoured with honey or apple) surrounded by dusty gilt mirrors, tourists, travellers and locals alike at the renowned El Fishawi café in the Khan el-Khalili souq (market).

STRENGTHS

⊿ Khan el-Khalili
⊿ Pyramids and Sphinx at your doorstep
⊿ The Egyptian Museum
⊿ King Tutankhamun's relics
⊿ The land of a million guides

Cairo 032

VITAL STATISTICS

NAME: CAIRO

NICKNAME: THE CITY OF A THOUSAND MINARETS

DATE OF BIRTH: AD 150; THE ROMAN BABYLON FORT WAS THE FIRST SETTLEMENT ON THE LOCATION OF MODERN CAIRO

ADDRESS: EGYPT (MAP 2, K3)

HEIGHT: 116M

SIZE: 214 SQ KM

POPULATION: 16.5 MILLION

A LONE FIGURE POLISHES THE TILES IN THE BEAUTIFUL INTERIOR OF THE MAUSOLEUM OF BARQUQ.
Photographer: Patrick Horton (3)

SMOKE OBSCURES THE FACE OF A MAN IN THE BACKSTREETS OF CENTRAL CAIRO.
Photographer: Phil Weymouth (2)

RUSH HOUR ON CAIRO'S SUBWAY: A MODERN SYSTEM SERVING AN ANCIENT CITY.
Photographer: Phil Weymouth (4)

WEAKNESSES

- Guides – they'll take you anywhere, as long as you visit a papyrus 'museum', jewellery shop, camel rental etc
- Cars that sink into the melting bitumen
- The heat in June
- Tourist police who, for a little baksheesh, know where everything is
- Tourists falling out of tour buses at the Egyptian Museum wearing short shorts

GOLD STAR

The pyramids and the Sphinx – both larger and smaller than you could ever imagine, respectively.

CITYSPEAK

- Foreign belly dancers – should the government enact a permanent ban?
- The preservation of cultural heritage – will the Café Riche, Cairo's first cultural and intellectual hub of the 20th century, survive the Abdeen district council's suggestion to knock down its landmark building?

STARRING ROLE IN...

- *Death on the Nile* (1978)
- *Gallipoli* (1981)
- *Malcolm X* (1992)
- *The Spy Who Loved Me* (1977)
- *The Ten Commandments* (1956)
- *The Purple Rose of Cairo* (1985)
- *The Cairo Trilogy: Palace Walk, Palace of Desire, Sugar Street* by Naguib Mahfouz
- *The Map of Love* by Ahdaf Soueif (1999)
- *Under the Same Sky – Rooftops in Cairo*, 2002–2003 by photographer Randa Shaath

IMPORT

- Metro German supermarket chain
- Pizza Hut
- Barbie
- Classical music at the Cairo Opera House
- Eating disorders among teenage girls

EXPORT

- Omar Sharif
- Mummies
- Backgammon
- Hand-blown glass perfume bottles
- Naguib Mahfouz – winner of the 1988 Nobel Prize for Literature
- Belly dancer Fifi Abdou
- The sounds of singer Om-Kalthoum
- Boutros Boutros-Ghali

SEE the pyramids during the heat of the day – you'll be guaranteed that there will be few tourists around and you can sit within the depths of Cheops listening only to the sound of your own beating heart.

EAT a great spread of falafel, salads, *fuul* (seasoned chickpeas), bread, tahini and omelettes at Akher Sa'a.

DRINK *karkadeh* (hibiscus tea) – found everywhere.

DO get a Coptic cross tattooed on your wrist in the Coptic Christian quarter.

WATCH feluccas sail down the Nile.

BUY pure jasmine oil in a hand-blown glass bottle from one of the many stalls in the Khan.

AFTER DARK check out the light-and-sound show at the pyramids after a spectacular sunset.

URBAN MYTH

Old Cairo is also home to the city's remaining Jewish population. The area's Ben Ezra Synagogue, Egypt's oldest, is said to be where the prophet Jeremiah gathered the Jews after they fled from Nebuchadnezzar, the destroyer of their Jerusalem temple. There is also a spring that is supposed to mark the place where the pharaoh's daughter found Moses in the reeds, and where Mary drew water to wash the baby Jesus.

Budapest

033

VITAL STATISTICS

NAME: BUDAPEST

NICKNAME: PARIS OF EASTERN EUROPE

DATE OF BIRTH: 1873; WHEN HILLY, RESIDENTIAL BUDA AND HISTORIC ÓBUDA ON THE WESTERN BANK OF THE DANUBE RIVER MERGED WITH FLAT, INDUSTRIAL PEST ON THE EAST TO FORM WHAT WAS AT FIRST CALLED PEST-BUDA

ADDRESS: HUNGARY (MAP 3, N10)

HEIGHT: 139M

SIZE: 525 SQ KM

POPULATION: 1.8 MILLION

IN THE SHADOW OF VAJDAHUNYAD CASTLE, CROUCHING SPEED SKATERS WHIZ AROUND THE ARTIFICIAL LAKE AT SZÉCHENYI PARK.
Photographer: David Greedy (1)

Budapest has a multifarious and often embittered history, incredible architecture and a rich cultural heritage.

ANATOMY

Budapest is a large, sprawling city. Two ring roads – Nagykörút (the big one) and the semicircular Kiskörút (the little ring road) – link three of the bridges across the Danube and essentially define central Pest. Budapest is divided into 23 kerület (districts), which usually have traditional names such as Lipótváros (Leopold Town) in district XIII or Víziváros (Watertown) in district I. The Roman numeral appearing before each street address signifies the district. Budapest has an ageing but safe, inexpensive and efficient public-transport system that won't have you waiting more than five to 10 minutes.

PEOPLE

With just under two million inhabitants, Budapest is home to almost one-fifth of the national population. Most are Magyars, an Asiatic people of obscure origins who do not speak an Indo-European language and make up the vast majority of Hungary's 10.2 million people. Life expectancy is very low by European standards: about 67 years for men and just over 76 for women.

TYPICAL BUDAPESTER

Well-educated, reserved and somewhat formal, Budapesters are extremely polite in social interaction, shake hands profusely on greeting, love a drink and are comfortable with public displays of affection. In summer, going topless is almost the norm for women in Budapest's parks. Citizens of all ages love to overindulge their dogs.

DEFINING EXPERIENCE

Taking in the grand views at Castle Hill, wandering Old Town on foot or in a horse-drawn carriage, bathing at the cathedral-like Gellért Baths, visiting the Royal Palace and, finally, dining at Menza, whose parody of Communist colours and styles (a menza was a state-run canteen) give insight as to what much of '70s Budapest looked like – well into the '90s.

STRENGTHS

- Castle Hill
- Hungarian State Opera
- Thermal baths
- The Basilica of St Stephen
- Crown of St Stephen
- Aquincum Museum
- Buda Castle Labyrinth
- The bridges of Budapest
- Wonderfully restored Great Market Hall
- Hungarian National Museum
- Traditional markets
- Budapest History Museum (Castle Museum)
- House of Hungarian Photographers
- Applied Arts Museum

WEAKNESSES

- Margaret Island after dark
- 'Accidentally' inflated restaurant bills
- Scammers
- Hailing cabs
- Polluting waste created by the Soviet military
- Scapegoating of Hungarian Roma (formerly known as Gypsies)

GOLD STAR

The view from Fisherman's Bastion on Castle Hill.

CITYSPEAK

- Has privatisation gone too far?
- Will Fidesz make a come-back?

STARRING ROLE IN...

- *A Life in Suitcases* (2005)
- *Underworld* (2003)
- *Napoleon* (2002)
- *I Spy* (2002)
- *Spy Game* (2001)
- *I Love Budapest* (2001)
- *Werckmeister Harmonies* (2000)
- *Sunshine* (2000)
- *Evita* (1996)
- *The Vampire of Budapest* (1995)

IMPORT

- Coca-Cola
- McDonald's

EXPORT

- Franz Liszt
- Rubik Cubes
- Biros
- Vitamin C
- Photographer Brassaï
- Estée Lauder
- GM automobiles
- Béla Lugosi
- Royal Philips Electronics appliances
- Béla Bartók
- Zoltán Kodály
- Eva and Zsa Zsa Gabor
- A plethora of literary figures

SEE the two icons of Hungarian nationhood: the crown of St Stephen in the Parliament building and the saint-king's mortal remains in the Basilica of St Stephen.

EAT excellent goose-liver dishes at the traditional but elegant Kisbuda Gyöngye.

DRINK coffee at Gerbeaud, the most famous of Budapest's famous cafés, bar none.

DO have a soak at any of the city's celebrated thermal baths, especially the Gellért, Rudas or Széchenyi.

WATCH and listen to opera in incredibly rich surrounds at the beautiful neo-Renaissance Hungarian State Opera House.

BUY hot salami, paprika, a bottle of boutique Hungarian wine and some colourful folk embroidery.

AFTER DARK head to a *táncház* (literally, a dance house) to hear authentic Hungarian music and learn a dance to go along with it.

URBAN MYTH

One of Hungary's best-loved writers, the novelist Gyula Krúdy (1878–1933), moonlighted at Kéhli (arguably home to the best traditional Hungarian food in town) as a restaurant critic and enjoyed bone marrow on toast (better than it sounds) so much he included it in one of his novels.

THE OPULENT INTERIOR OF THE NEO-RENAISSANCE OPERA HOUSE, DESIGNED IN 1884.
Photographer: Martin Moos (2)

A BUSKER DOES HIS THING UNDER THE WATCHFUL EYE OF AN ENORMOUS AD.
Photographer: Martin Moos (3)

THE CLASSICAL OPULENCE OF THE GELLÉRT THERMAL BATHS, AN OTHER-WORLDLY OASIS IN THE HEART OF THE METROPOLIS. Photographer: Christer Fredriksson (4)

BASEBALL FANS KEEP A CLOSE EYE ON THE GAME DURING THE PLAYOFFS AT WRIGLEY FIELD.
Photographer: Ray Laskowitz (1)

Chicago
034

VITAL STATISTICS

NAME: CHICAGO

NICKNAME: THE WINDY CITY; HOG BUTCHER FOR THE WORLD; SECOND CITY

DATE OF BIRTH: 1779; WHEN CHICAGO'S FIRST SETTLER, JEAN BAPTISTE POINTE DU SABLE, ESTABLISHED A TRADING POST ON THE NORTH BANK OF THE CHICAGO RIVER

ADDRESS: USA (MAP 1, K9)

HEIGHT: 251M

SIZE: 588 SQ KM

POPULATION: 3 MILLION

Though it ranks third behind Los Angeles and New York size-wise, the Windy City is a vast and vibrant metropolis – a place where running shoes and a good train map are a must if you even *hope* to make a dent in the city's copious and unique attractions.

ANATOMY

The Windy City sprawls along the western side of Lake Michigan, with towering buildings constructed on swampy land forming an artificial landmark. The Loop is the city's historic heart, sitting on a small peninsula where the Chicago River meets the lake. The city and suburbs fan out across the prairie in all directions. Public transport includes trains and buses.

PEOPLE

Chicago's 'diversity index' – a percentage likelihood that two randomly chosen people in an area will be of different races – is 74%, a full 25% higher than the USA as a whole. Blacks outnumber whites in Chicago, with Latinos running a close third. Catholicism is running strong in the Windy City. Chicago has the largest Catholic archdiocese in the country, and a sizable Jewish population as well.

TYPICAL CHICAGOAN

The quintessential Midwesternness of the natives – cheerful, hard-working, and a little conservative – acts as a steadying anchor for the city's more adventurous impulses. Despite the high diversity, integrated neighbourhoods are rare in Chicago, with blacks tending to live in the city's south and west sides, Latinos showing a strong presence in Pilsen and many areas on the North Side, and Asians in Chinatown and along Argyle St in Uptown. Segregation is a fact of life in Chicago.

DEFINING EXPERIENCE

Starting a high-speed day with a laid-back breakfast at the Original Pancake House in Bellevue Plaza, followed by a quick cab ride down to the Art Institute, then to the Berghoff for lunch, followed by some top-tier window-shopping on Michigan Ave, dining on deep-dish pizza at Giordano's nearby, followed by sunset drinks way, way up on the 96th floor of the John Hancock Center's Signature Lounge.

STRENGTHS

- The lake
- Chicago Blues Festival
- Art Institute
- Navy Pier Ferris Wheel
- Chicago Mercantile Exchange
- Store-front churches
- Frank Lloyd Wright's Prairie School–style houses

WEAKNESSES

- The cold in winter
- Weather
- Rats
- Blizzards
- So much salt on the roads
- Corruption in city politics
- The cost of motel and hotel rooms
- Ice on pavements

GOLD STAR

The Art Institute of Chicago is as impressive a museum as can be found anywhere. Turn any corner and you find yet another breathtaking piece of art, from medieval armour to Mondrian abstracts. So this is where it ended up! On the shores of Lake Michigan, the institute has a wondrous collection of impressionist paintings as well as 20th-century modernist and realist works.

CITYSPEAK

- The new Soldier Field is exactly the creative jolt Chicago architecture needed
- Yuppies moving to the South Side will be the saviours of the neighbourhood
- The Cabrini-Green housing projects should be renovated, not destroyed
- The sooner Chicago bans smoking in bars, the safer everyone will be

STARRING ROLE IN...

- *The Adventures of Augie March* by Saul Bellow
- *Nowhere Man* by Aleksandar Hemon
- *North by Northwest* (1959)
- *Blues Brothers* (1980)
- *Ferris Bueller's Day Off* (1986)
- *Chicago* (2003)

IMPORT

- Conrad Black
- Louis Armstrong
- Frank Lloyd Wright
- Al Capone
- Sara Paretsky
- Saul Bellow

EXPORT

- Oprah and *Oprah*
- John Belushi
- Hillary Rodham Clinton
- Raymond Chandler
- Sam Cooke
- Walt Disney
- Studs Terkel
- Mahalia Jackson
- Harrison Ford
- Hugh Hefner
- Herbie Hancock
- Ernest Hemingway
- *The Jerry Springer Show*

SEE Steppenwolf Theater, the legendary ensemble group that helped put Chicago theatre on the map.

EAT on Division St in Ukrainian Village, the hipster's dining paradise that includes several of the best brunch places in town – Smoke Daddy Rhythm & Bar-B-Que, Leo's Lunchroom or Mirai.

DRINK from the hundreds of beers on offer at Quencher's.

DO check out Second City, a must-see club (John Belushi, Bill Murray, Dan Aykroyd and Elaine May got their start here) where performers give sharp and biting commentaries on life, politics and love.

WATCH the beaches in smelt season, when the tiny fish swarming into Chicago harbours to spawn are met by amateur anglers, nets and deep-fat fryers.

BUY clothes, accessories, anything on Milwaukee Ave (Wicker Park), where the funkier cousin to Damen Ave features blocks and blocks of hip stores.

AFTER DARK check out the multigenerational dance scene – Chicago was one of the hotbeds of house in the early '80s, and the audiences have aged with the music.

URBAN MYTH

It's certainly true that Chicago is windy, but meteorology is not the reason for the moniker 'Windy City'. The most popular of various legends as to the origin of the name claims it is to do with the city's politicians and journalists, who are 'full of wind'. Apparently, the name was popularised by a writer in the New York Sun, who claimed that despite its boasts, 'that windy city' would not beat New York in the competition to hold the World's Fair of 1893. Not only did Chicago win, but the fair was a huge success.

A SMURF'S-EYE VIEW OF THE SMURFIT-STONE TOWER ON MICHIGAN AVE.
Photographer: Richard Cummins (2)

A COMMUTER TRAIN NEAR GRANT PARK HEADS TO THE OTHER SIDE OF THE TRACKS.
Photographer: Ray Laskowitz (3)

HOW MUCH DO YOU LOVE CHICAGO? A BOY MAKES A SPLASH AT LAKE MICHIGAN.
Photographer: Lou Jacobs Jr (4)

The jewel of the Caribbean, Havana's faded colonial grandeur, magnificent Malecón (waterfront promenade) and charming old town make it an instant hit with anyone lucky enough to visit.

ANATOMY

The city faces the Straits of Florida (a big temptation for many sick of Castro) with its vast seafront, the legendary Malecón, which is one of the most impressive in the world, despite the crumbling colonial buildings, peeling paint and general sense of neglect. The centre of the city is divided up into La Habana Vieja (Old Havana), a Unesco World Heritage site and the best-preserved Spanish colonial town in the Americas, and Centro Habana, the modern city and seat of most major government ministries to the west. Train is the best way to get around.

PEOPLE

Havana is almost entirely populated by Cubans, with a small business and diplomatic community. Sixty percent of citizens are of Spanish descent, 22% are of mixed race, 11% of African descent and 1% Chinese. There's almost no ethnic tension – Havana is a great example of total racial harmony. Forty-seven percent are Catholic, 4% Protestant and 2% Santería (many Catholics also practice Santería). Spanish is the official language.

TYPICAL HABANERO

Definitely a highlight of the trip, the Habaneros are great fun. Forget any preconceptions you might have of life under a totalitarian government – Habaneros carry on regardless, with an almost bloody-minded determination to be as happy and unfazed by the problems of everyday life as possible.

DEFINING EXPERIENCE

Knocking back an ice-cold mojito (a cocktail made of rum, lime, sugar, mint and soda water) at almost any bar in the old town, as locals stare down at you from their dilapidated balconies (a hobby among Habaneros, particularly the elderly).

Havana

035

VITAL STATISTICS

NAME: HAVANA

DATE OF BIRTH: 1514; WHEN THE PORT OF SAN CRISTÓBAL DE LA HAVANA WAS FOUNDED BY DIEGO VELÁZQUEZ

ADDRESS: CUBA (MAP 4, I2)

HEIGHT: 24M

SIZE: 740 SQ KM

POPULATION: 2.2 MILLION

RIDING IN STYLE, TWO GIRLS KEEP AN EYE ON CENTRO HABANA FROM THE WINDOWS OF THEIR CLASSIC CAR.
Photographer: Richard I'Anson (1)

STRENGTHS

- Extraordinarily friendly and fun-loving locals
- Mind-blowing buildings and bright colours everywhere
- Few better places to drink superb cocktails and listen to great live music
- Yet to be conquered by massive American tour groups

WEAKNESSES

- The food can be extremely unexciting after a few days
- The appalling human-rights record
- Beach resorts that keep Cubans apart from foreigners in a form of apartheid

GOLD STAR

La Habana Vieja – the best-preserved colonial Spanish complex in the Americas – is a joy to walk round. True, much of it has been sanitised far more than is proper, but stray into the backstreets from the revamped roads and you'll be mesmerised by the sultry Caribbean charm of Havana once more.

CITYSPEAK

- What will happen after Fidel? Few can imagine life in Havana post-Castro
- The latest restoration works in La Habana Vieja or on the Malecón
- The US blockade of Cuba – its consequences, victims and chances of change

STARRING ROLE IN...

- *Fresa y Chocolate* (1994)
- *The Buena Vista Social Club* (1999)
- *Before Night Falls* (2000)
- *Dirty Dancing: Havana Nights* (2004)

IMPORT

- Tour groups
- Music lovers
- Cigar aficionados
- Convinced Communists
- Fidelologists

EXPORT

- Rum
- Sugar
- Political dissidents
- Families in dinghies crossing the Straits of Florida

SEE the Capitolio Nacional, former seat of the Cuban government and one of the highlights of Havana's rich architectural heritage.

EAT ice cream at the famous Coppelia Ice Cream parlour for the true Habanero experience.

DRINK plenty of delicious mojitos and Cuba Libre cocktails at the fabulous neoclassical Inglaterra Hotel in Parque Central.

DO not forget that there's more to Havana than the old town – explore the further-flung parts and don't miss the Playas del Este.

WATCH the monthly display of hundreds of singers and musicians performing in Plaza de la Catedral.

BUY from an endless array of books and posters from the unofficial stands on Plaza Vieja.

AFTER DARK head to one of Cuba's famous nightspots or cabaret clubs in La Habana Vieja.

URBAN MYTH

Fidel Castro, despite having outlived entire generations of CIA staff, has remained the subject of relentlessly innovative and bizarre schemes to see him assassinated or otherwise wrested from power. Most famously there was the assassination attempt using the exploding cigar (which failed), but the CIA tried many other methods of discrediting Castro – from poisoning him so his famous beard would fall out, to impregnating a diving costume with lethal bacteria and then presenting it to Castro as a present. Amazingly, Castro has survived all these attempts on his life and has gone on to be one of the longest-serving leaders of modern times.

SHADES OF CHE – A COOL COMMIE SHOWS OFF HIS TRUE COLOURS.
Photographer: Rick Gerharter (2)

A QUEUE FORMS BENEATH THE ARCHWAYS OF A GRACEFULLY DECAYING COLONIAL BUILDING IN THE CITY CENTRE.
Photographer: Martin Fojtek (3)

ON THE STREETS OF THE OLD TOWN, A GLAMOROUS HABANERA PAUSES FOR A PUFF.
Photographer: Dominic Arizona Bonuccelli (4)

Madrid

036

VITAL STATISTICS

NAME: MADRID

DATE OF BIRTH: 85 AD; WHEN MOHAMMED I, EMIR OF CÓRDOBA, ESTABLISHED A FORTRESS HERE

ADDRESS: SPAIN (MAP 3, D14)

HEIGHT: 660M

SIZE: 607 SQ KM

POPULATION: 3.09 MILLION

Madrid's city centre is the most vibrant, versatile and exciting in Europe – La Movida may technically be over, but you'll be hard-pressed to believe it on a weekend night at 4am.

ANATOMY

Madrid is Europe's highest capital. Most major sights are within walking distance of a very short metro ride. The historic centre features a mix of old and new low-rise buildings and hundreds of plazas, with skyscrapers predominantly in the northern part of the city. Madrid's metro is the quickest and easiest way to get around the city, with *cercanías* (regional trains) and buses close runners-up.

PEOPLE

Many locals aren't from Madrid proper, and often come from all over Spain. Some 600,000 foreign migrants live in the Comunidad de Madrid (the region around Madrid) – more than two-thirds of them in the city. The biggest groups are Ecuadorians, Colombians and Moroccans. In the working-class neighbourhoods of Lavapiés and around, you will encounter North Africans rubbing shoulders with Pakistanis, black Africans and Latin Americans.

TYPICAL MADRILEÑO

Doesn't seem to need any sleep! They might be *gatos* (born-and-bred locals, from the Spanish word for 'cat') or they might be from somewhere else in Spain or North Africa, but they'll work long hours, spend a fortune on keeping a roof over their heads and appreciate that none of it's worth it without regular tapas-fuelled catch-ups with friends and family.

DEFINING EXPERIENCE

Waking up late, having coffee and *churros* (doughnuts), then browsing for trash (maybe treasure) at El Rastro flea market before enjoying a long Sunday lunch in a nearby restaurant, having a rest in El Retiro afterwards, and then waiting to hear if your plans for the evening come to fruition.

STRENGTHS

- Tolerance
- Chatty locals
- Efficient public transport
- Cheap taxis
- Thousands of tapas bars
- Regional Spanish and ethnic cuisine
- Siesta
- Nightlife
- Major art museums
- Los Austrias, La Latina and Lavapiés *barrios* (neighbourhoods)
- Plazas brimming with friends and neighbours catching up
- Green parks in the early morning
- Real Madrid
- Acoustics at Teatro Real

WEAKNESSES

- Endless roadworks
- Noise pollution
- Dog poo on the streets
- Traffic jams at 4am
- Late-night/early-morning rubbish collection
- Packed peak-hour metro trains in summer
- Freezing winters and hellish summers
- Drunken teens on the streets at weekends
- The exodus to Valencia on Friday
- Trying to score Real Madrid tickets

GOLD STAR

Art – Madrid has three blockbuster museums in the Museo del Prado, the Museo Thyssen Bornemisza and the Centro d'Arte Reina Sofía.

CITYSPEAK

- The Windsor skyscraper fire – arson or accident?
- Are they really going to move El Rastro?
- Which big name will Real Madrid sign next – and will they be any good?
- Is this real-estate bubble ever going to burst?
- Are gay wedding presents any different from straight wedding presents?

STARRING ROLE IN...

- *Abre los Ojos* (Open Your Eyes, 1997)
- *Amantes* (The Lovers, 1991)
- *Live Flesh* (1997)
- *Bad Education* (2003)

IMPORT

- Expensive footballers
- Flamenco
- Asian cuisine
- Picasso's *Guernica*
- Queen Sofía
- Asturian cider
- Galician octopus
- Basque *pintxos* (tapas)
- Navarran wine
- Air-conditioning units

EXPORT

- Gal lip balm
- Colourful fans
- Real Madrid strips
- Lladró porcelain
- Pedro Almodóvar
- Capes
- Tapas
- Bullfighting posters
- Sexy actresses

SEE Picasso's *Guernica* and weep.

EAT tapas every chance you get.

DRINK eye-crossingly potent cocktails in any of the party *barrios*.

DO as the locals do and take it easy for the siesta with a long lunch.

WATCH a soul-stirring flamenco performance at a backstreet *tablao* (flamenco bar).

BUY a beautiful embroidered and fringed silk *mantón* (shawl) from El Corte Ingles.

AFTER DARK try staying awake for as long as the Madrileños – say 6am on weekends.

URBAN MYTH

Full-blooded Madrileños are often known as *gatos* (cats) a nice image to reflect their city savvy. The term quite appeals to the locals, as it has come to reflect their tendency to crawl around the city like cats until all hours. They say the term was coined as one of Alfonso VI's soldiers artfully scaled the formidable walls of Muslim Magerit (now Madrid) in 1085. 'Look', cried his comrades, 'he moves like a cat!'

TRADITIONAL CÓRDOBAN HATS COME IN MANY COLOURS AT A CARNIVAL COSTUMERY NEAR PUERTA DEL SOL.
Photographer: Christopher Wood (1)

THE STUNNING SYMMETRIES OF THE PATIO DE LOS EVANGELISTAS IN THE PALACE OF SAN LORENZO EL ESCORIAL.
Photographer: Michael George (2)

NEWSPAPER IN HAND, A LOCAL MAN STROLLS PAST THE ELABORATE TILE WORK ON THE FAÇADE OF A CITY SHOP.
Photographer: Patrick Ward (3)

GIGGLING FOR FORGIVENESS – CHEEKY WOMEN PENITENTS AT THE EASTER HOLY WEEK PROCESSIONS.
Photographer: Juan Carlos Rojas (4)

Munich 037

VITAL STATISTICS

NAME: MUNICH

DATE OF BIRTH: 1158; WHEN HEINRICH DER LÖWE (HENRY THE LION) BECAME RULER

ADDRESS: GERMANY (MAP 3, K10)

HEIGHT: 524M

SIZE: 310 SQ KM

POPULATION: 1.2 MILLION

Regularly voted by Germans as the most desirable place to live, the capital of Bavaria's beguiling résumé includes grand architecture, world-class museums, plentiful beer halls, well-dressed people and the world-famous Oktoberfest.

ANATOMY

The *Altstadt* (old town) is home to most of the city's major attractions, which unfurl from the central Marienplatz. North of here is the museum and theatre district, the Residenz. East of the Residenz buzzes bohemian Schwabing (home to the university), and the enormous Englischer Garten (one of the largest city parks in Europe). Across the Isar River, which runs through the eastern part of the city from south to north, are trendy Haidhausen and moneyed Bogenhausen. The Olympiapark, captivating Schloss Nymphenburg and multicultural Neuhausen, lie to the northwest of the *Altstadt*. Besides walking, Munich's excellent public-transport network (MVV) is the best way to get around.

PEOPLE

Munich is Germany's third-largest city. Around one in five of the population is not of German origin, with the largest ethnic groups coming from Turkey and Eastern Europe. The majority of inhabitants are Catholic, but there are also many Lutherans in the city.

TYPICAL MÜNCHENER

Müncheners are a mix of cultural sophistication and traditional values. They are hugely proud of their Bavarian heritage. They often assert their traditions by wearing *Tracht* (lederhosen for the men and dirndls for the ladies), particularly at Oktoberfest. They are characterised by an independent streak, with Bavaria holding a special legal status as a 'free state'. Bavaria was the first German state to appoint an environment minister and virtually everyone recycles. The people of Munich are known for being cultured, affluent and groomed. They are polite and greet each other by shaking hands or kissing. Nude bathing and sunbathing are common and allowed in the Englischer Garten.

DEFINING EXPERIENCE

Admiring the Renaissance art at the Alte Pinakothek then soaking up the sun in the Englischer Garten and cooling off with a stein at the Chinesischer Turm, before hitting the shops on Maximilianstrasse and bar hopping down Schwabing's Leopoldstrasse.

STRENGTHS

- Sausages, particularly the *Weisswurst* (veal sausage)
- Breweries (half of Germany's breweries are in Bavaria), beer halls (eg Hofbräuhaus), beer gardens and steins
- Englischer Garten
- Marienplatz
- Oktoberfest
- Schloss Nymphenburg
- Lenbachhaus
- Pinakothek museums
- *Blaue Reiter* art
- Residenzmuseum
- *Tracht* (traditional costume)
- Frauenkirche
- Low unemployment rate
- Low air-pollution levels
- The Wittlesbachs, who ruled Bavaria for over 700 years
- FC Bayern
- Opera and Bayerische Staatsoper
- Münchener Philharmoniker
- *Jugendstil* (German Art Nouveau)
- Skiing in the Bavarian Alps

WEAKNESSES

- Meat-heavy cuisine
- Increased levels of crime during Oktoberfest
- The Föhn – static-charged wind from the south gives people headaches and makes them irritable
- Hitler's Beer Hall Putsch on 8 November 1923

GOLD STAR

Bavarian culture

CITYSPEAK

- The integration of immigrants – should we make them integrate or not?

STARRING ROLE IN...

- *Munich* (2005)
- *Marlene* (1999)
- *Das Boot* (1981)
- *Herr und Hund* by Thomas Mann

IMPORT

- International sporting teams
- Thomas Mann
- Wim Wenders
- Rainer Werner Fassbinder
- Adolf Hitler
- Paul Klee
- Lola Montez

EXPORT

- Audi
- BMW
- Siemens
- Bertelsmann
- Pharmaceutical research and medical technology
- Aviation and aeronautics
- Hitler's *Mein Kampf*
- Werner Herzog
- FC Bayern
- Eva Braun
- Alfred Einstein
- Heinrich Himmler
- Richard Strauss
- Winter-sports champions Rosi Mittermaier, Martina Ertle, Hilde Gerg, Alois Vogl
- Beer

SEE the stunning Schloss Nymphenburg with its majestic interiors and sculpted gardens.

EAT traditional Bavarian fare in the tiny but authentic Hundskugel (Munich's oldest restaurant), founded in 1440.

DRINK as much beer as you can bear at the mammoth Oktoberfest.

DO take a stroll around the endlessly enticing Englischer Garten and feel free to strip off and sunbathe.

WATCH the characters of the delightful glockenspiel (carillon) dance and celebrate on Marienplatz.

BUY funky street fashion in the boutiques of Schwabing and Haidhausen.

AFTER DARK pick your best party clothes and mix with celebs at P1.

URBAN MYTH

The Fischbrunnen (Fish Fountain) in the *Altstadt* is said to bring you wealth if you dip your purse into it on Ash Wednesday. In medieval times it was used to keep river fish alive at the markets; later it received many butcher's apprentices for wetting the head (and body) ceremonies. Every year Munich's mayor and council officials routinely dip a purse in the fountain in the hope of fuller council coffers the following year.

QUENCHING A BIG THIRST, THIS WOMAN SAMPLES THE MERCHANDISE IN THE BEER GARDEN OF THE AUGUSTINER BREWERY.
Photographer: Johannes Simon (1)

A SHRINE TO PAULANER (BREWED IN MUNICH SINCE 1634) IN FRONT OF ST PAUL'S CHURCH.
Photographer: Johannes Simon (2)

BEER SWILLING IS TAKEN TO A WHOLE NEW LEVEL ON THE OKTOBERFEST MERRY-GO-ROUND.
Photographer: Johannes Simon (3)

SETTING THE MOOD FOR THE EXHIBITS – THE STYLISH ENTRANCE HALL OF THE SPACIOUS PINAKOTHEK DER MODERNE.
Photographer: Johannes Simon (4)

Athens 038

VITAL STATISTICS

NAME: ATHENS

DATE OF BIRTH: 1400 BC; FOUNDED BY THE MYCENAEANS

ADDRESS: GREECE (MAP 3, P15)

HEIGHT: 107M

SIZE: 428 SQ KM

POPULATION: 3.27 MILLION

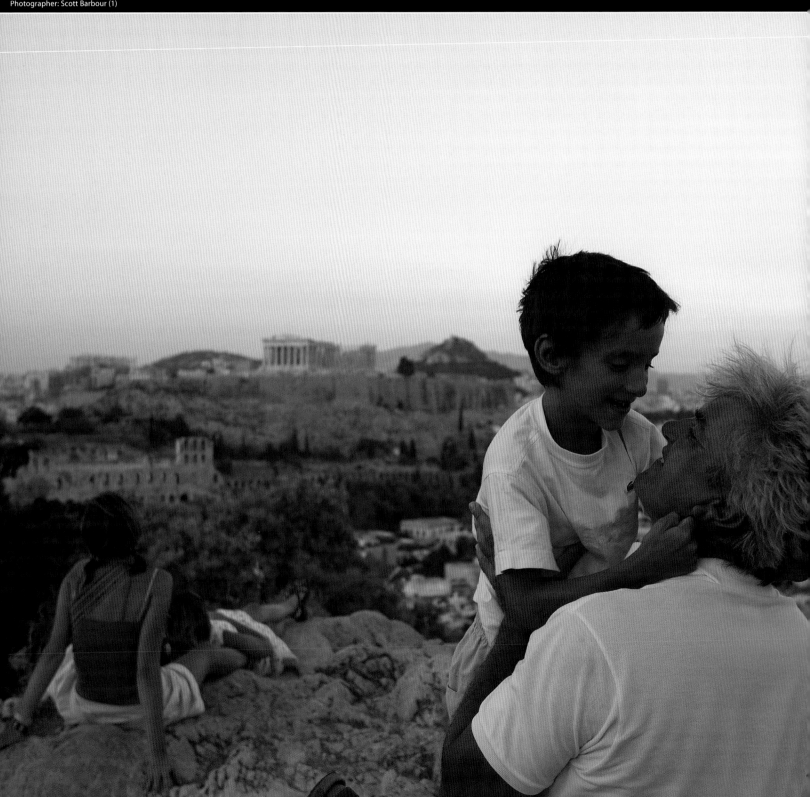

FATHER AND SON FROLIC ON FILOPAPPOU HILL OVERLOOKING THE ACROPOLIS.
Photographer: Scott Barbour (1)

GILT-EDGED MIRRORS CATCH THE REFLECTIONS OF PASSING SHOPPERS AT THE SUNDAY PLATEIA MONASTIRAKIOU FLEA MARKET.
Photographer: Scott Barbour (2)

SEEN FROM THE ACROPOLIS, THE CRADLE OF CIVILISATION NURTURES AN URBAN JUNGLE.
Photographer: Scott Barbour (3)

A REMBETIKA PLAYER ENLIVENS A RESTAURANT IN PLAKA.
Photographer: Scott Barbour (4)

Redolent with mythology, smeared with grime, Athens is an affable city enlivened by outdoor cafés, pedestrian streets, parks, gardens and urban eccentrics.

ANATOMY

The city is bounded on three sides by Mt Parnitha, Mt Pendeli and Mt Hymettos. Within Athens there are eight hills, of which the Acropolis and Lykavittos are the most prominent. The city's boundary on the southern side is the Saronic Gulf. The new metro system has made getting around the centre of Athens relatively painless. There's also an extensive bus and trolleybus network.

PEOPLE

A large proportion of Athens's residents today are relative newcomers to the city, who migrated here from other parts of Greece or from Greek communities around the world. Greece, which lost much of its population to mass migration, is now attracting large numbers of migrants, both legal and illegal, including many Albanians and refugees from the Balkans, the former Soviet Union, Bangladesh, Pakistan, Iran and Iraq.

TYPICAL ATHENIAN

Athenians are affable, warm and welcoming. The pace of life in Athens can be fast (the public service aside) but people still take time out for endless coffees. The younger generations of Athenians are highly literate, with a large number studying abroad. A high proportion speak English and are in tune with world trends, fashion and music. About 98% of the Greek population belong to the Greek Orthodox Church.

DEFINING EXPERIENCE

Emerging from the hectic U-Matic dance club at 5am then heading to the darkened central meat market, where the tavernas turn out huge pots and trays of tasty, traditional home-style dishes, 24 hours a day.

STRENGTHS

- The Acropolis standing sentinel over Athens
- The many city streets and squares fringed with orange trees
- National Archaeological Museum
- Refreshing your eyes and lungs in the delightfully shady National Gardens
- The Plateia Monastirakiou flea market
- Shopping for antiques in Antiqua
- The Bohemian Exarhia district – home to many cheap tavernas, good cafés, alternative book, music and clothing stores, *rembetika* clubs and small live-music venues
- *Loukoumades* (Greek-style doughnuts) served with honey and walnuts
- Dining on the terrace at Pil Poul, with views of the illuminated Acropolis
- Seeing Euripides performed in the Odeon of Herodes Atticus
- Lively *rembetika* clubs
- Benaki Museum
- Balconies bulging with geraniums

WEAKNESSES

- *Nefos* (smog)
- Concrete
- Lack of public toilets
- Traffic
- Smoking
- Greek bureaucracy
- Summer heat

GOLD STAR

The Acropolis – time, war, pilfering, earthquakes and pollution have taken their toll on the sacred hill, yet it stands defiant and dignified over Athens.

CITYSPEAK

- And the winner of the Eurovision Song Contest 2005 is…Helena Paparizou for Greece!
- Is the Nescafé *frappé* on the way out?
- And who is Paris Latsis dating now?

STARRING ROLE IN...

- *Anthismeni Amigdhalia* (Almond Trees in Bloom, 1959)
  Landscape in the Mist (1988)
- *The Last Temptation* by Nikos Kazantzakis

IMPORT

- Bad driving
- Paris Hilton
- Mini Chinatown
- Haute couture
- Nescafé
- Concrete
- Tourists
- Jackie Onassis

EXPORT

- Souvlaki
- Greeks, who have migrated all over the world
- The Olympics
- Philosophy
- Democracy
- Olive oil
- Ouzo
- Shipping magnates
- Maria Callas

SEE dusk settle on the symbol of the glory of ancient Greece, the Parthenon (Virgin's Chamber), which stands on the highest point of the Acropolis.

EAT the best, fresh traditional-style *tiropites* (cheese pastries) in Athens (and many other tasty variations) at Ariston.

DRINK a home-made brew from one of the many on offer at Brettos, a quaint little bar with a stunning array of coloured bottles, old wine barrels and a refreshingly old-fashioned feel.

DO get lost among the little whitewashed cube houses in Anafiotika before ascending to explore the Acropolis.

WATCH a film at the outdoor cinema in the Zappeio Gardens, where you can get a wine and gourmet snack-pack to add to your viewing pleasure.

BUY a pair of traditional Jesus sandals from septuagenarian sandal-maker Stavros Melissinos's store in the market district of Monastiraki.

AFTER DARK check out Baroc'e, right next to the old Olympic Stadium, where a regular procession of well-heeled Athenians spill out onto the footpath in summer.

URBAN MYTH

Despite a popular perception, there is not much plate-smashing to be had in Greece these days. It's not the done thing in restaurants. At some bars in Athens, party animals throw stacks of paper napkins everywhere when the night heats up. But be warned – these acts of merrymaking can be very pricey (you pay for the napkins!).

IN THE CITY'S FRENCH QUARTER, A LOCAL PO BOYS SHOP SETS A NEON SCENE.
Photographer: Jerry Alexander (1)

Despite the devastation of Hurricane Katrina in August 2005, New Orleans will always seduce with soulful jazz wafting out of saloon doors, people leaning over wrought-iron balconies on sultry summer nights and masked party-goers turning up the heat at Carnival.

ANATOMY

New Orleans lies in reclaimed swampland sandwiched between the Mississippi to the south and Lake Pontchartrain to the north. The heart of the original city is the historic French Quarter (the Vieux Carré). Southwest of here is the Central Business District (CBD). The arty Warehouse District and bohemian Lower Garden District are upriver (paradoxically this is south) of the French Quarter. Adjacent to the Lower Garden District are the historic homes of the Garden District. Faubourg Marigny to the east attracts a mostly gay crowd, while the mainly black neighbourhood of Faubourg Tremé to the north is known for its music. Catch a local bus or streetcar to get around town.

PEOPLE

Well over half (around 62%) of New Orleans' population is black. Whites make up 35% while Hispanics number around 3%. A group of Asian immigrants live mainly in the Versailles area and on the West Bank. Thanks to its French and Spanish heritage, the population is predominantly Roman Catholic.

TYPICAL NEW ORLEANIAN

New Orleans is a fairly poor city with a small tax base to support its social services and education. Wages in Louisiana, as measured in income per capita, are the lowest in the USA after Mississippi and Arkansas, and one in four people live on or near the poverty line (most of the poor people are black). New Orleanians are a friendly bunch and welcoming towards visitors (although you're not really part of the club unless you have generations of New Orleans blood coursing through your veins). Life in the Big Easy is for enjoying and service can occasionally be slow. But New Orleanians don't worry about that – they know that having a good time is more important than having a quick time!

New Orleans

039

CARNIVAL BEADS AND JAZZY TRINKETS OVERLAY AN EMBLEMATIC IMAGE OF MARDI GRAS.
Photographer: Richard Cummins (2)

CAJUN COOKING IN THE BUSY KITCHENS OF NOLA'S RESTAURANT IN THE FRENCH QUARTER.
Photographer: Jerry Alexander (3)

THE FURIOUS SOUNDS OF NEW ORLEANS JAZZ RAISING THE ROOF AT PRESERVATION HALL.
Photographer: John Elk III (4)

DEFINING EXPERIENCE

Starting the day with a coffee at Café du Monde before wandering around the French Quarter, relaxing in Jackson Sq and gearing up for an evening of live music at Funky Butt on Congo Sq.

STRENGTHS

- New Orleans Jazz & Heritage Festival
- Mardi Gras
- Gay and lesbian scene
- The beautiful Garden District
- Audubon Zoo
- Riverboat calliope music
- Buskers in Jackson Sq
- St Charles Ave streetcar
- The balconies and courtyards of Royal St
- St Louis Cemetery No 1
- Creole restaurants of Royal St and Bourbon St
- The French Market
- The French Quarter
- Ursuline Convent
- Aquarium of the Americas
- Tranquil Bayou St John
- New Orleans Museum of Art

WEAKNESSES

- Racial inequality during the Civil War and Reconstruction
- Risks of flooding and sudden storms, Hurricane Katrina being the worst and most recent example
- Faint petroleum smell in parts of the city

GOLD STAR

Jazz

CITYSPEAK

- Strong feelings over whether authorities have done enough to help those displaced by the hurricane
- 'Katrina fatigue' – will the generosity of the American people run dry before the city can be rebuilt?
- The latest news on which restaurants and businesses are open again

STARRING ROLE IN...

- *JFK* (2001)
- *Dead Man Walking* (1996)
- *Easy Rider* (1969)
- *A Streetcar Named Desire* (1951)
- *The Big Easy* (1987)

IMPORT

- Professor Longhair
- Trent Reznor
- Benjamin Henry Latrobe
- Tennessee Williams
- William Faulkner
- King Oliver

EXPORT

- Louis Armstrong
- Buddy Bolden
- Truman Capote
- Harry Connick Jr
- Fats Domino
- Randy Newman
- Lee Harvey Oswald
- Aaron Neville
- Jelly Roll Morton
- Anne Rice
- Grain
- Steel
- The cocktail (allegedly invented in New Orleans)

SEE the city from aboard a riverboat.

EAT gumbo at local favourite K-Paul's Louisiana Kitchen.

DRINK in the candlelit Lafitte's Blacksmith Shop, apparently an old pirate haunt.

DO wander through the French Quarter, discovering New Orleans' history at the Louisiana State Museum and soaking up the atmosphere.

WATCH the parades, floats, seminaked revellers and dazzling debauchery of Mardi Gras.

BUY local tunes from the Louisiana Music Factory, which also has live music on Saturday.

AFTER DARK Donna's Bar & Grill is hopping with the best local jazz musicians – if they're not on the bill they'll pop in to jam.

URBAN MYTH

Shotgun houses can be found all over the city and are popular for their high ceilings and Victorian styling. They are called 'shotgun' not because of the speed of their construction as you might think but because of their shape. With each room back to back and the whole house one room wide, they were specifically designed in the 19th century so as to allow a bullet to pass through the house without stopping. There are also double-shotguns (duplexes with a separately owned mirror-image) and even camel-back shotguns, with a 2nd floor above the back of the house.

Vienna

040

VITAL STATISTICS

NAME: VIENNA

DATE OF BIRTH: AD 8; WHEN VINDOBONA WAS FOUNDED BY THE ROMANS

ADDRESS: AUSTRIA (MAP 3, M10)

HEIGHT: 203M

SIZE: 415 SQ KM

POPULATION: 1.55 MILLION

THE FAÇADE OF THE SCHLOSS BELVEDERE ROYAL PUTS IN A BID FOR BEST POSTCARD VIEW IN VIENNA.
Photographer: Martin Brent (1)

Once the most sparkling gem in the Hapsburg crown, Vienna remains a city of culture, class and beauty, famous for its opera and classical music; but peer beneath this tradition and you'll see experimental arts, world food and green living.

ANATOMY

The blue Danube runs through Vienna, nudging the old city and most tourist attractions to the west. Heading south from the river, the Danube Canal creates one rim of the historic centre (Innere Stadt). In the middle of the Danube River, the long Donauinsel promises fun with many beaches and playgrounds. The beloved Wienerwald (Vienna Woods) undulates appealingly to the west and north of the city. The greenery doesn't stop there – almost half the city comprises green spaces, more than any other European capital. Trams trundle through the city, while the U-Bahn whizzes around below ground.

PEOPLE

Almost a quarter of today's population hails from outside Austria, with the largest ethnic communities being Yugoslavian and Turkish, followed by Bosnian and Croatian. Seventy-four percent of the population is Roman Catholic; Protestants and Muslims come next.

TYPICAL VIENNESE

Despite their reputation for being grumpy, the Viennese are consistently inconsistent, being cheery one day and dour the next. Their dark sense of humour is often self-deprecating and utterly beguiling, and they have a strange fascination with death – fancy visiting a museum devoted to funerals and undertakers (Bestattungs-museum)? Politeness is important – look your co-drinker in the eye when clinking glasses, to avoid appearing insincere. Employees receive extra salary payments for the summer and Christmas holidays, and rents are low. Around 8.3% of households own a dog, which approximates to 65,000 dogs. The Viennese are politically engaged and Austria's strongest advocates of socialism. Not surprisingly, they are also cultural, enjoying their theatre, music, opera, art, food and wine.

DEFINING EXPERIENCE

Gazing at Schiele's work in the Leopold Museum, before lapping up some sun and coffee in the MuseumsQuartier's courtyard, then heading to the Old Danube for a leisurely swim and refuelling at a *Heuriger* (wine tavern) in Stammersdorf.

URBAN MYTH

Disputes over the origin of the rich chocolate *Sacher Torte* cake raged between Hotel Sacher and Demel café in 1938 and 1953, with the crucial debate centring on whether the apricot jam should go under the icing or in the middle of the cake. The Hotel Sacher bakes 500 to 600 *Sacher Torte* a day and up to 3000 during Christmas – no wonder the recipe is fiercely protected. The Hotel Sacher claims that Japanese spies have infiltrated their kitchen in an attempt to discover the mysteries of the cake (and stage a cake coup?). But the hotel are determined that the ingredients should remain secret.

STRENGTHS

- ◢ Magnificent imperial palaces eg Schönbrunn
- ◢ Gothic Stephansdom (St Stephen's Cathedral)
- ◢ Secessionism and Secession Hall
- ◢ Otto Wagner's metro stations
- ◢ *Beisln* (pubs/bistros)
- ◢ *Heuriger*
- ◢ *Würstelstände* (sausage stands)
- ◢ The Danube
- ◢ The Wienerwald
- ◢ Vineyard day trips
- ◢ Christmas markets
- ◢ Vienna Boys' Choir
- ◢ The Spanish Riding School and its Lipizzaner stallions
- ◢ Staatsoper (the opera house)
- ◢ *Sacher Torte* (a rich chocolate cake)
- ◢ Hapsburg history
- ◢ The *Wiener Zeitung* (the oldest newspaper in the world, first published in 1703)
- ◢ Compulsory recycling
- ◢ Abundant cycle lanes
- ◢ The Vienna Philharmonic
- ◢ Avant-garde art eg Viennese Actionism
- ◢ Low crime
- ◢ Efficient trams
- ◢ The Naschmarkt (a market dating back to the 16th century)

WEAKNESSES

- ◢ Home-grown fashion (except Helmut Lang)
- ◢ Occasional xenophobia
- ◢ Bureaucratic hoops for budding entrepreneurs
- ◢ Labyrinthine one-way system
- ◢ Confusing or nonexistent WC labels
- ◢ Ubiquitous dog turds
- ◢ Grumpy waiters

GOLD STAR

Opera and classical music

CITYSPEAK

- ◢ The latest bargains at Ikea and Hofer
- ◢ Horse nappies for the *Fiaker* (horse and carriage) – good idea or a bit weird?
- ◢ The latest bicycles and cycling equipment
- ◢ Anything to do with politics

STARRING ROLE IN...

- ◢ *The Piano Teacher* (2001)
- ◢ *Before Sunrise* (1995)
- ◢ *The man with Two Brains* (1983)
- ◢ *The Third Man* (1949)

IMPORT

- ◢ High street fashion shops
- ◢ Wolfgang Amadeus Mozart
- ◢ Wiener schnitzel (this originated in Milan)
- ◢ World food
- ◢ Music fans

EXPORT

- ◢ Helmut Lang
- ◢ Josef Haydn
- ◢ Franz Schubert
- ◢ The waltz
- ◢ Egon Schiele
- ◢ Gustav Klimt
- ◢ Ludwig Wittgenstein
- ◢ Novelist and playwright Peter Handke
- ◢ Sigmund Freud
- ◢ Container transloading
- ◢ Riesling and Veltliner wines

SEE as many museums as you can on the evening of 20 September, Lange Nacht der Museen.

EAT *Kaffee und Kuchen* (coffee and cake) in Konditorei Oberlaa Stadthaus.

DRINK in the Palmenhaus, a beautifully renovated Palm house, complete with high, arched ceilings, glass walls and steel beams.

DO a gentle but illuminating bicycle tour of Vienna's parks and waterways.

WATCH the Vienna Boys' Choir doing their sensational stuff in the Hofburg's Royal Chapel.

BUY a very traditional but exquisite porcelain ornament from the Wiener Porzellanmanufaktur Augarten.

AFTER DARK throw some shapes on the dance floor at Flex to the soundtrack of Viennese and international DJs.

WHAT'RE YOU LOOKIN' AT?' A PUNK COMPETES WITH A MOZART IMPOSTOR FOR MOST INTERESTING HAIRSTYLE.
Photographer: Martin Brent (2)

THE VIEW OF SOME CLASSIC VIENNESE TILING FROM STEPHANSDOM SOUTH TOWER.
Photographer: Martin Brent (3)

A WAITER PEERS THROUGH SMOKE TO MAKE SURE ALL'S WELL WITH THE BILL IN CAFÉ HAWELKA.
Photographer: Martin Brent (4)

Ho Chi Minh City

VITAL STATISTICS

NAME: HO CHI MINH CITY

NICKNAME: HCMC; ALSO KNOWN AS SAIGON, BUT CAREFUL HOW YOU USE THIS – IT'S BEST TO STICK TO HO CHI MINH CITY WHEN DEALING WITH GOVERNMENT OFFICIALS

DATE OF BIRTH: 6TH CENTURY AD; WHEN THE FUNANESE CONSTRUCTED A CANAL SYSTEM THAT MOST LIKELY EXTENDED TO THE SITE OF PRESENT-DAY HO CHI MINH CITY

ADDRESS: VIETNAM (MAP 5, M9)

HEIGHT: 9M

SIZE: 2356 SQ KM

POPULATION: 6.12 MILLION

Crazy-making and seductive, HCMC (formerly known as Saigon) beats with a palpable energy, day and night.

ANATOMY

HCMC is not so much a city as a small province, with rural regions making up the majority of the land area of HCMC (but only holding a fraction of the city's population). HCMC is divided into 16 urban districts (quan, derived from the French quartier) and five rural districts (huyen). District 1 (once Saigon) is the downtown area and the location of most of the city's sights, while District 5 encompasses the huge Chinese neighbourhood called Cholon (Big Market). The city's neoclassical and international-style buildings and pavement kiosks selling French rolls and croissants give neighbourhoods such as District 3 an attractive, vaguely French atmosphere. Travelling the chaotic streets of HCMC is not for the faint-hearted. Metered taxis, cyclos (pedicabs) and motorbike 'taxis' are the most common forms of transport.

PEOPLE

HCMC has the largest ethnic Chinese community in Vietnam, mostly found in Cholon. While most fled in 1975, a small community of Indians remains; Vietnam's other minorities (Khmers, Chams and Hill Tribes) tend to live in other regions of the country.

TYPICAL HO CHI MINH CITY CITIZEN

At first sight, HCMC may seem to be populated with a million bandana-bedecked women bandits on the verge of a giant traffic accident. And, in fact, the pattern in the streets reflects a generalised, organised chaos in a city that attracts people from all over the country hoping to better their fortunes. A young office worker manoeuvres her Honda Future through rush-hour traffic, long hair flowing, high heels working the brake pedal. The sweating Chinese businessman chats on his mobile phone, cursing his necktie in the tropical heat. A desperate beggar suddenly grabs your arm – a rude reminder that this is still a developing city, despite the trimmings. It is here that the economic changes sweeping Vietnam – and their negative social implications – are most evident.

DEFINING EXPERIENCE

Strolling through the crisscross streets of historic District 1, wrangling a cyclo into Cholon, sniffing around local markets and browsing the sumptuous shops around Dong Khoi, before journeying further afield to the Cao Dai Temple and Cu Chi Tunnels.

STRENGTHS

- The bustling, dynamic and spirited atmosphere
- Cyclo drivers who give you an insight into their city
- Proximity to the Mekong Delta
- Smiling, friendly residents
- Colourful shops
- Bustling, intriguing Cholon

WEAKNESSES

- Pickpockets
- Taxi drivers who only take you to the hotels for which they receive a commission
- Cyclo drivers who overcharge
- Confusingly named streets
- Traffic
- Pollution

GOLD STAR

Silk boutiques – more diverse, less traditional and cheaper than those in Hanoi

CITYSPEAK

- Government corruption and the responsibility of the press: the trial of Ho Chi Minh City's crime lord Nam Can, which exposed many police and officials on his payroll, is fresh in everyone's memory, and the prime minister has recently vowed to crack down on under-the-table dealings with local crime lords
- Whether the city's burgeoning building and development industry is serving the needs of the rising middle class or causing environmental havoc

STARRING ROLE IN...

- The Quiet American (2002)
- Indochine (1992)

IMPORT

- French and Americans expats
- Rural peasants
- Pubs
- Croissants
- Joint-venture capitalists

EXPORT

- Ao dai (Vietnamese national dress)
- Pirated DVDs and CDs

SEE the War Remnants Museum for a graphic depiction of the impact of US military action from the point of view of 'the other side'.

EAT traditional banh xeo (rice-flour crepe stuffed with bean sprouts, prawns and pork), especially at the swoon-worthy restaurant Banh Xeo 46A.

DRINK cocktails while taking in the city view and cool breezes at the Rex Hotel's rooftop bar.

DO take a cyclo trip through the city before the municipal government phases them out.

WATCH hordes of young people checking each other out in the Dong Khoi area every weekend.

BUY a carved seal featuring your name in Vietnamese.

AFTER DARK join HCMC's fashion-conscious, alternative crowd at Q Bar near the Municipal Theatre.

URBAN MYTH

The legend goes that Quan Am Thi Kinh was a woman unjustly turned out of her home by her husband. She disguised herself as a monk and went to live in a pagoda, where a young woman accused her of fathering her child. She accepted the blame – and the responsibility that went along with it – and again found herself out on the streets, this time with her 'son'. Much later, about to die, she returned to the monastery to confess her secret. When the emperor of China heard of her story, he declared her the Guardian Spirit of Mother and Child. It is believed that she has the power to bestow male offspring on those who fervently believe in her and, as such, is extremely popular with childless couples.

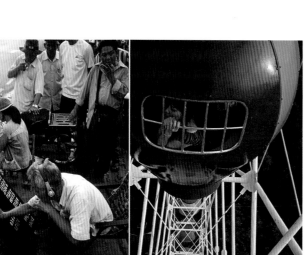

HOPING FOR A LUCKY BREAK, A STREET VENDOR JOTS DOWN WEEKEND LOTTERY NUMBERS ANNOUNCED OVER THE RADIO.
Photographer: Kris LeBoutillier (1)

A PASSENGER ON THE COLOSSAL FERRIS WHEEL AT DAM SEN PEERS DOWN OVER THE CITY.
Photographer: Kris LeBoutillier (2)

MAN OF STEEL – STREET PERFORMERS BEND METAL AROUND A STRONGMAN'S NECK.
Photographer: Kris LeBoutillier (3)

COLOURFULLY CLAD SCHOOL CHILDREN FORM A DISORDERLY LINE BEFORE CLASS.
Photographer: Kris LeBoutillier (4)

Marrakesh 042

VITAL STATISTICS

NAME: MARRAKESH

NICKNAME: THE RED

DATE OF BIRTH: 1062; WHEN THE CONQUERING ALMORAVID GENERAL YOUSSEF BEN TACHFINE ESTABLISHED A FORTIFIED CAMP

ADDRESS: MOROCCO (MAP 3, B19)

HEIGHT: 460M

SIZE: 70 SQ KM

POPULATION: 998,000

SHADOWS LENGTHEN AGAINST THE STARK LIGHT OF DUSK AS LOCALS HURRY ABOUT THEIR BUSINESS.
Photographer: Jaume Pages Pinyol (1)

IN FINE RED ROBES A PERFORMER ENTERTAINS THE PUBLIC IN DJEMAA EL FNA.
Photographer: John Elk III (2)

FRAMED BY THE INTRICATE WINDOW OF A STUDENT CELL IN THE ALI BEN YOUSSEF MEDERSA, A BURNOOSE WEARER CONTEMPLATES THE SCENE BELOW. Photographer: Martin Harvey (3)

FINGERS OF SUNLIGHT THREAD THEIR WAY INTO A BUSY SHOE SOUQ.
Photographer: Andrea Pistolesi (4)

One of Morocco's most important cultural centres, Marrakesh is a lively former capital famed for its markets and festivals set in breathtaking surroundings.

ANATOMY

Built around an oasis at the foot of the High Atlas Mountains, Marrakesh is a Moroccan rail and road hub. The old city is a maze of red mud-brick buildings. The French-built Ville Nouvelle (New Town) is next door, with its wide boulevards and Art Deco/Moorish architecture, while breeze-block modern suburbs sprawl out to the north and east. Extensive gardens and palm groves preserved within the New Town provide an escape from the bustling centre. Walking is usually the best way to get around, but for longer distances, *petits taxis* (local taxis) are fairly cheap.

PEOPLE

Marrakesh is a Berber town. The Romans called them Barbari, or barbarians, and the Arab conquerors continued the practice. The Berbers themselves prefer the term Amazigh (free men), but they rarely get their own way. The language spoken by the tribes in the area is called Tashilhayt. Arabic is more common among the city's established residents, but Marrakesh is a market town for the Amazigh, and so you will hear Tashilhayt spoken as well. There is also a substantial expat community of French, Germans and English, drawn by the climate and the culture.

TYPICAL MARRAKSHI

Marrakshis are more laid-back than most urban Moroccans. The Berber culture is more relaxed in matters of religion and formality. Marrakshi woman have freedoms that would be frowned upon further north, and the city is relatively gay-friendly. Marrakshis are known for their warmth, directness and sense of humour. But beware, commerce is a passion for Marrakshis, and they have developed the hard-sell haggle to a fine art.

DEFINING EXPERIENCE

Strolling through the souq (market) without buying anything, retreating from the clamour to the shade of the Menara gardens, then sitting on the terrace of Café Glacier, overlooking the Djemaa el Fna, drinking mint tea and watching the sunset turn the mud bricks from red to pink to orange, discussing which of the Gueliz nightclubs is the least touristy, but enjoying the conversation and the fire jugglers too much to leave.

STRENGTHS

- ◢ Beautiful architecture
- ◢ Colourful markets
- ◢ The Koutoubia
- ◢ The Saadian Tombs
- ◢ The gardens
- ◢ The relaxed atmosphere
- ◢ The Festival of Popular Arts
- ◢ Berber music
- ◢ Street theatre
- ◢ Sunny winters
- ◢ Relatively gay-friendly

WEAKNESSES

- ◢ Overcrowding
- ◢ Poverty
- ◢ Sex tourists
- ◢ High prices (for Morocco)
- ◢ Pickpockets
- ◢ Scammers
- ◢ Bureaucratic sluggishness

GOLD STAR

Marrakesh has one of the most beautiful and exotic city squares in the world, Djemaa el Fna.

CITYSPEAK

- ◢ The brain drain – the loss of Morocco's finest to Europe and America
- ◢ The elaborate schemes and grisly deaths of the 'burners' – Moroccans trying to get to Europe illegally
- ◢ The expat influence on house prices and morals
- ◢ The war on terror and its effects on tourism
- ◢ Discrimination against Berbers

STARRING ROLE IN...

- ◢ *Hideous Kinky* (1999)
- ◢ *Marrakesh* by George Orwell
- ◢ *The Sand Child* by Tahar Ben Jelloun
- ◢ *Voices of Marrakesh* by Elias Canetti
- ◢ *Lords of the Atlas* by Gavin Maxwell
- ◢ 'Marrakesh Express' by Crosby Stills and Nash
- ◢ *Our Man in Marrakesh* (1966)

IMPORT

- ◢ Tourists
- ◢ Expats
- ◢ Berber street performers
- ◢ Cotton
- ◢ Raw animal hides
- ◢ Henna
- ◢ Fruit and vegetables
- ◢ Camel bones
- ◢ Olives
- ◢ Saints – for burial
- ◢ Rural immigrants

EXPORT

- ◢ Painters
- ◢ Oil lamps
- ◢ Singers
- ◢ Leatherwork
- ◢ Carpets
- ◢ Just Fontaine
- ◢ Intricate pottery
- ◢ Islamic scholars
- ◢ Jewellery

SEE the old city from a rooftop terrace at sunset.

EAT the best couscous at El Fassia restaurant.

DRINK green tea with mint and sugar.

DO a walk through the Ben Youssef Medersa.

WATCH the Fantasia horse dance at the festival of Popular Arts in June.

BUY hand-woven Berber carpets.

AFTER DARK dance to the latest hits at Le Diamant Noir.

URBAN MYTH

Marrakesh was once the capital, and Europeans came to call the whole country after the city, corrupting the name to Morocco. However, the origin of the name itself is still a subject of dispute. Some say it means 'mountain pass', and some that it means 'the land of the sons of Kutch', the biblical grandson of Noah. Others will tell you that Marrakesh means 'do not linger', reflecting the danger once faced by travellers in the area, and joke that the pickpockets and charlatans of today are working to keep the name current.

The crossroads of east and west since antiquity, Sarajevo nestles by the Miljacka River, surrounded by hills and mountains, and encompasses the essence of Bosnia's cultural diversity – a powerful merge of dance, music, food and hope for the future after centuries of war.

ANATOMY

Sarajevo lies in a wide valley created by the Miljacka River. The distant mountains of Jahorina and Bjelašnica (host to the 1984 Winter Olympics) flank the city to the south. From the airport, 6.5km to the southwest, the main road runs up to the suburb of Ilidža, then swings east through Novo Sarajevo. The bus and train stations are to the north. Near the town centre the road runs alongside the Miljacka River, before leaving it at Baščaršija (the bustling old Turkish Quarter), which occupies the eastern end of town.

PEOPLE

Serbs, Croats and Bosnian Muslims are all Southern Slavs of the same ethnic stock. Physically they are indistinguishable. The pre-war population was incredibly mixed and intermarriage was common. Ethnic cleansing has concentrated Muslims in Sarajevo, but there are also high numbers of people who are Orthodox and Roman Catholic. Inhabitants are known as Bosnian Serbs, Bosnian Croats or Bosniaks (Muslims). Across Bosnia and Hercegovina, churches and mosques are being built (or rebuilt) at lightning speed. This is more symptomatic of strong nationalism than religion, as most people are fairly secular.

TYPICAL SARAJEVAN

For any city it's a stretch to summarise the general character of its denizens, and that goes for Sarajevo 10-fold. Their differences are both their greatest challenge and greatest strength. What is certain is that they are proud, patriotic and traditionally minded but also very cosmopolitan and friendly. Given the speed and diligence with which they are rebuilding their city, to say that they were hard-working and determined would be an understatement.

Sarajevo
043

VITAL STATISTICS

NAME: SARAJEVO

DATE OF BIRTH: AD 1461; TURKISH SARAJEVO WAS FOUNDED BY ISA-BEY ISAKOVIC AND LATER BECAME A MILITARY, ADMINISTRATIVE, AND COMMERCIAL CENTRE

ADDRESS: BOSNIA & HERCEGOVINA (MAP 3, N12)

HEIGHT: 630M

SIZE: 142 SQ KM

POPULATION: 602,500

THE CROWDED SKYLINE TELLS OF THE CITY'S RICH CULTURAL PAST AND ITS ASPIRATIONS FOR THE FUTURE.
Photographer: Doug McKinlay (1)

DEFINING EXPERIENCE

Exploring the polished-cobble laneways of Baščaršija, shopping for a handmade watch, then spending the afternoon cycling the old road that leads alongside the Miljacka River towards the Turkish bridge (Goat Bridge).

STRENGTHS

◢ Fresh *burek* (small round filo-pastry balls stuffed with minced beef or spinach and feta)
◢ Gazi-Husrevbey Mosque
◢ Baščaršija
◢ Multiculturalism
◢ National Museum
◢ The indoor and outdoor markets
◢ 20km ski run at Mt Jahorina
◢ The Sebilj fountain
◢ Latin Bridge
◢ Morića Han

WEAKNESSES

◢ Land mines
◢ Nationalism
◢ Confusing street-numbering system
◢ Limited vegetarian options
◢ War damage

GOLD STAR

Survival – for enduring a war that took it to the cusp of destruction and remaining a strong and enigmatic mix of cultures.

CITYSPEAK

◢ The whereabouts of the war's most elusive war criminals, most notably Bosnian Serb leader Radovan Karadžić and his military henchman Ratko Mladić
◢ The rebuilding of the city

STARRING ROLE IN...

◢ *No Mans Land* (2002)
◢ *The Perfect Circle* (1997)
◢ *Welcome to Sarajevo* (1997)

IMPORT

◢ Turkish food and culture
◢ Foreign aid for reconstruction
◢ Islam
◢ International investment
◢ Western political influence

EXPORT

◢ Textiles
◢ Director Emir Kusturica
◢ Cigarettes
◢ Metalwork
◢ Handmade watches

SEE the Sarajevo roses (skeletal handlike indentations where a shell has exploded) on the pavements – some are symbolically filled in with red cement, often accompanied by a series of brass plaques giving the names of those killed by that shell.

EAT Turkish *ćevapčići* (grilled minced lamb or beef), usually accompanied by a half-loaf of spongy *somun* bread, in one of the many of the restaurants in Baščaršija.

DRINK shots of *šlivovica* (plum brandy) or *loza* (grape brandy) savoured with a meal at the Bosanska Kuća.

DO take in some of the rich local art and culture at the art gallery and National Museum.

WATCH the dance, music and street theatre of Baščaršija Noći (Nights of Baščaršija) – an annual festival in July.

BUY colourful woven items from Bosnian Handicrafts in Baščaršija – a nonprofit organisation working with refugees to produce these wonderful pieces.

AFTER DARK indulge in a local beer at the cavernous bar of the Sarajevo Brewery.

URBAN MYTH

During the recent conflict, Sarajevo's heritage of six centuries was pounded into rubble and its only access to the outside world was via a tunnel, which saved it. Most of the tunnel's 800m stretch under the airport has collapsed, but the Tunnel Museum, on the far (southwestern) side of the airport, gives visitors a glimpse of what it must have been like. The house that provided the tunnel's cover holds a small museum of digging equipment and photos from the days when the tunnel was in use.

A YOUNG MUSLIM WOMAN PLANS HER DAY FROM THE STEPS OF GAZI-HUSREVBEY MOSQUE.
Photographer: Doug McKinlay (2)

MAKING HIS OWN FUN, A YOUNG BOY PLAYS AMONG THE PESKY PIGEONS IN THE MAIN SQUARE OF BAŠČARŠIJA.
Photographer: Doug McKinlay (3)

A BURLY BROLLY SALESMAN WAITS FOR THE CLOUDS TO GATHER IN THE TURKISH QUARTER.
Photographer: Doug McKinlay (4)

Seville 044

VITAL STATISTICS

NAME: SEVILLE

DATE OF BIRTH: MID-2ND CENTURY BC; WHEN IT BECAME A SIGNIFICANT TRADING PORT FOR THE ROMANS

ADDRESS: SPAIN (MAP 3, C16)

HEIGHT: 9M

SIZE: 5.2 SQ KM

POPULATION: 710,000

The historic heart of the city retains the picturesque decay that attracted 19th-century Romantics.

ANATOMY

Seville straddles the Río Guadalquivir, with most places of interest on the east bank. The central area is mostly a tangle of narrow, twisting old streets and small squares. Spain's fourth-largest city is easily walkable, and with the concentration of motor vehicles, foot traffic is preferable. Seville has an extensive and affordable bus network that covers the whole of the greater city area.

PEOPLE

Seville's citizens are quite homogeneously Andalucian, with a Spanish and Moorish heritage. Seville has the largest concentration of *gitanos* (Roma people, formerly known as Gypsies) in Spain. Spanish (Castilian) is the official language. Around 80% of the population is Roman Catholic.

TYPICAL SEVILLANO

Sevillanos when comparing themselves to other Spaniards, and more particularly to their Andalucian neighbours in Granada, declare themselves to be more *simpáticos* (genial) and more polite in everything. They love socialising and partying – thought of as gregarious, emotional and in love with colour and action, they have helped set a universal Spanish stereotype. Their southern outlook – lethargic, with a fondness for their afternoon siesta – is balanced by their tendency to spontaneity, exaggerated sense of tragedy and robust sense of humour. They have a strong sense of tradition and are very family-oriented, with gender roles being fairly strict.

DEFINING EXPERIENCE

Visiting the cathedral then wandering through the Barrio de Santa Cruz and enjoying lunch at the Corral del Agua, then in the afternoon heading over to the Río Guadalquivir and visiting Plaza de Toros and the Museo de Bellas Artes before devoting the evening to a relaxed tour of a few tapas bars.

STRENGTHS

- The mix of Muslim and Hispanic building styles
- Chocolate and *churros* (Spanish doughnuts) for breakfast
- Plaza de España
- Traditional Moorish-influenced sweets
- Street life on balmy evenings
- Flamenco
- Alcázar – the palace-fortress
- La Giralda – the remaining minaret of the 12th-century mosque
- Archivo General de Indias – Spanish late-Renaissance architecture
- Spectacular new bridges over the Guadalquivir
- Bullfighting

WEAKNESSES

- Traffic
- Parking
- Drunk teenagers at weekend Botellon
- Bullfighting

GOLD STAR

The sultry nightlife is wondrous. To be out and about till the small hours with this sense of gaiety and brilliance, appreciated for its theatricality and intensity of life, is an unforgettable experience.

CITYSPEAK

- Where will we go tonight?

STARRING ROLE IN...

- *Novelas Ejemplares* (Exemplary Novels) by Cervantes
- *Star Wars Episode II: Attack of the Clones* (2002)
- *Lawrence of Arabia* (1962)
- *Mission: Impossible II* (2000)
- *Nadie conoce a nadie* (Nobody Knows Anybody, 1999)

IMPORT

- Expo '92
- Tourists
- 19th-century romantics

EXPORT

- Oranges
- Sherry
- *Carmen*
- *The Barber of Seville*
- *Don Juan*
- Flamenco
- Velázquez
- Murillo
- Zurbarán

SEE the paintings from the Siglo de Oro (Golden Century), in the Museo de Bellas Artes.

EAT tapas at Bar Giralda, a converted Moorish bathhouse.

DRINK local wines Aljafe and Los Palacios, when you tire of sherry.

DO climb La Giralda, the minaret of the former mosque, to see the view over the largest Gothic cathedral in the world.

WATCH spectacular and slightly creepy Santa Semana (Holy Week) processions, with candlelit parades of hooded penitents going by with grotesque solemnity.

BUY, or at least browse through, all manner of goodies at the Sunday-morning *mercadillo* (flea market) in Alamede de Hercules.

AFTER DARK nightlife is jumping – wander the streets and find what's happening – flamenco, jazz, dance…

URBAN MYTH

The Sevillana flamenco dance, the one most people think of when they think 'flamenco', did not originate in Seville. But the folksongs called *sevillanas* are authentically Sevillean, as is the four-part dance that goes with them.

THE ELEGANT FAÇADE OF THE PLAZA DE ESPAÑA.
Photographer: Christopher Groenhout (1)

TWO OLD FRIENDS SHARE A COFFEE IN A LOCAL CAFÉ WHERE MAGNIFICENT MOORISH TILEWORK ADORNS THE WALLS.
Photographer: Dan Herrick (2)

FROM PIG TAILS TO PIROUETTES – AN INSTRUCTOR CALLS THE ROLL FOR SEVILLE'S UP-AND-COMING BALLERINAS.
Photographer: Oliver Strewe (3)

THE DEFIANT INSCRIPTION ON AN OLD EARTHENWARE WINE CROCK AT THE CASA MORALES BAR: '1850–UNTIL GOD WILLS…'
Photographer: Oliver Strewe (4)

Kyoto 045

VITAL STATISTICS

NAME: KYOTO

DATE OF BIRTH: 7TH CENTURY AD; LITTLE MORE THAN A VAST, FERTILE PLAIN, KYOTO – THEN KNOWN AS YAMASHIRO-NO-KUNI – BECAME HOME TO THE HATA CLAN FROM KOREA

ADDRESS: JAPAN (MAP 1, KK10)

HEIGHT: 41M

SIZE: 610 SQ KM

POPULATION: 1.5 MILLION

Cultural heart of Japan, Kyoto's raked pebble gardens, sensuously contoured temple roofs and latter-day geishas fulfil the Japanese fantasy of every Western cliché hunter.

ANATOMY

The city is divided into five sections designating the central (*raku-chu*), eastern (*raku-to*), northern (*raku-hoku*), western (*raku-sai*) and southern (*raku-nan*) areas, plus *raku-gai*, the city's outskirts. With a rectangular grid system, it's easy to navigate. The main business district is in the south and centre; the less populated northern parts have a greener feel, with rice fields sandwiched between apartment buildings. Although many major sights are in the centre, the best sightseeing is on the fringes in the north, east and west. It's easy to get around by walking, cycling, taking the bus or subway.

PEOPLE

Kyoto is home to one of the largest concentrations of colleges and universities in Japan, however, the majority of students leave after graduation for the bigger economic centres of Tokyo and Osaka. There are also an estimated 33,000 Japanese-Koreans living here, particularly in the neighbourhood south of Kyoto station.

TYPICAL KYOTOITE

Kyotoites are sometimes described as cold, unnecessarily formal and snobbish towards outsiders, though short-term tourists are made to feel welcome. The Kyoto dialect can be extremely vague, masking true feelings behind veiled smiles and nebulous wording. Known for their sense of style, Kyotoites prefer small and refined over large and flashy.

DEFINING EXPERIENCE

Visiting Nanzen-ji temple and its expansive grounds, including the classic Zen garden, then viewing the cherry blossoms in bloom (April only) in Kyoto Imperial Palace Park, before relaxing in a *sentō* (public bath) as a prelude to an evening stroll around Ponto-chō's restaurants, bars and teahouses.

STRENGTHS

◢ Japan's cultural treasure-house – 17 ancient structures and gardens are World Heritage sites
◢ 1600 Buddhist temples
◢ 400 Shintō shrines
◢ Three palaces
◢ Dozens of gardens and museums
◢ Cherry-blossom festival (April)
◢ Nightlife in Ponto-chō and Gion's 'floating world'
◢ 500 *matsuri* (festivals) every year
◢ Growing environmental awareness among young Kyotoites
◢ Kyoto station

WEAKNESSES

◢ Ugly urban development
◢ Widespread environmental apathy
◢ Kyoto Tower – great views, not so great to look at

GOLD STAR

Nanzen-ji Temple, for the combination of temple, grounds, Zen garden and hidden shrine in a forest hollow behind the main precinct

CITYSPEAK

◢ Destruction of historic *kyō-machiya* (wooden townhouses)
◢ 'Stop idling' campaign targeting people sleeping in cars with the engine running for heat/air-con

STARRING ROLE IN...

◢ *Katakuri-ke no kôfuku* (The Happiness of the Katakuris, 2001)
◢ *The Pillow Book* (1996)
◢ *Ai no corrida* (In the Realm of the Senses, 1976)
◢ *Rashômon* (1950)

IMPORT

◢ Beer
◢ Western junk food
◢ Soccer
◢ Baseball
◢ Doughnuts
◢ Foreign artists, musicians, teachers, scholars, writers and people 'just passing through'
◢ Whisky
◢ Coffee

EXPORT

◢ The *sensu* (folding fan)
◢ Kyoto Protocol to reduce greenhouse-gas emissions
◢ *Kiyomizu-yaki* pottery and ceramics
◢ Nintendo
◢ Film director Jūzō Itami
◢ Kyocera cameras
◢ *Kyō-ryōri* (cuisine emphasising subtlety, utilising fresh seasonal vegetables)
◢ *Shōjin-ryōri* (vegetarian cuisine with origins in Buddhist asceticism)
◢ Film director Oshima Nagisa
◢ *Kyō-yūzen* (silk-dyeing method)
◢ *Kyō-komon* (stencil dyeing)
◢ Tie-dyeing (*kyō-kanoko shibori*), in the 6th century (slightly before Grateful Dead fans rediscovered it)
◢ *Kyō-ningyo* (handcrafted dolls)

SEE a panoramic 360-degree view of the city from Kyoto Tower.

EAT sukiyaki in a traditional tatami room at Morita-ya.

DRINK sake at Ing, a favourite spot for a drink in Kyoto.

DO belt out a number or three at Jumbo Karaoke Hiroba.

WATCH a traditional kabuki performance at Minami-za, the oldest kabuki theatre in Japan.

BUY distinctive ceramics at To-ji market, held on the 21st of every month.

AFTER DARK wander the 'floating world' of traditional entertainment areas Gion and Ponto-chō.

URBAN MYTH

Kyoto's fortune in escaping US bombing during WWII is commonly believed to be due to American scholar Langdon Warner, said to have urged US military authorities to spare the city, thereby preserving its artistic and historical treasures. Despite this popular account, other theories have surfaced, along with documentation pointing to an elaborate conspiracy to quell anti-American sentiment. Some historians now suggest that, in fact, Kyoto was on a list of 180 cities earmarked for air raids, and was also a prime target for atomic annihilation.

'AND DON'T FORGET TO PUBLISH YOUR MEMOIRS' – AN APPRENTICE GEISHA RECEIVES ADVICE FROM AN OLDER WOMAN.
Photographer: Oliver Strewe (1)

THE EXTRATERRESTRIAL KYOTO TOWER LOOMS OVER THE CITY AT NIGHT.
Photographer: Martin Moos (2)

LIKE A BRUSH PAINTING COME TO LIFE, THE BLOSSOMING BANKS OF THE KAMO GAWA RIVER PRESENT AN IDYLLIC SCENE.
Photographer: Frank Carter (3)

HELLO KITTY – PUNK PUPPIES IN GANG COLOURS.
Photographer: Frank Carter (4)

Las Vegas 046

VITAL STATISTICS

NAME: LAS VEGAS

NICKNAME: SIN CITY

DATE OF BIRTH: 1821; WHEN ANTONIO ARMIJO TOOK A DETOUR EN ROUTE TO LOS ANGELES, BUT NATIVE AMERICAN SETTLEMENTS HAVE BEEN HERE SINCE ANCIENT TIMES

ADDRESS: USA (MAP 1, H10)

HEIGHT: 612M

SIZE: 293 SQ KM

POPULATION: 517,000

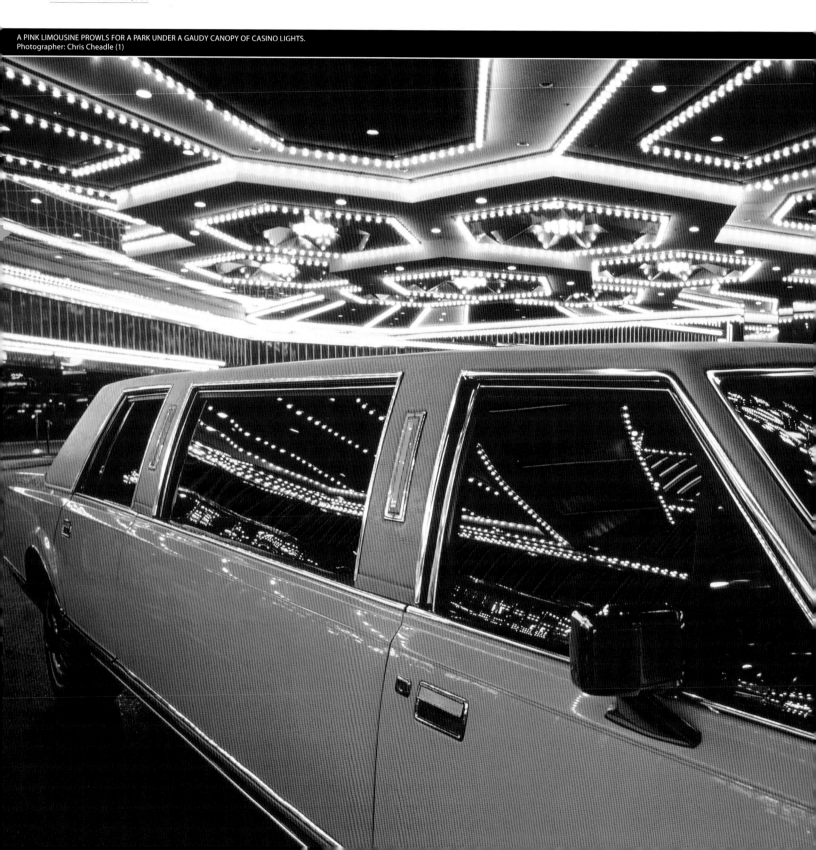

A PINK LIMOUSINE PROWLS FOR A PARK UNDER A GAUDY CANOPY OF CASINO LIGHTS.
Photographer: Chris Cheadle (1)

THE BRIGHT LIGHTS OF FREMONT ST LURE FORTUNE-SEEKERS LIKE MOTHS TO THE FLAME.
Photographer: Curtis Martin (2)

PAST ITS PRIME, A GIGANTIC W RESTS IN PEACE IN THE NEVADA DESERT.
Photographer: Neil Emmerson (3)

SEQUIN-POPPING SHOWGIRLS GLAM IT UP AT THE CIRCUS HOTEL AND CASINO.
Photographer: Ray Laskowitz (4)

There's nowhere like Vegas, baby – come here to marry a stranger you met on the plane, gamble your life savings away or just lap up the glorious oddness and kitsch of the whole place.

ANATOMY

Centred on the world-famous strip (or Las Vegas Blvd to purists), the city can seem to be little else for those just in town for a few days. Las Vegas proper is centred on Fremont St and the downtown area to the north of the big hotel-casino complexes of the strip.

PEOPLE

The vast majority of Las Vegans were born outside Nevada. It's impossible to define this mixed bunch. There's a Bible-toting Elvis bumming smokes from the guy hawking his first hip-hop album in what appears to be Tuscany. At the strip joint off the strip the drunken guy on his last fling is throwing dollars at the perky-breasted gal dancing on the pole. She's telling him the money's so good she commutes from the West Coast.

TYPICAL LAS VEGAN

Your typical Las Vegan loves this city, as they've chosen to live here, coming from other towns in the US and beyond. The population loves its sport (particularly golf and tennis) and is oblivious to the tourist crowds on the strip, avoiding them by living and hanging out downtown, and so experiencing a very different lifestyle (despite many working in the casinos and hotels of the strip) from that enjoyed by most visitors to the city.

DEFINING EXPERIENCE

Strolling down the strip through the animated crowds in the summer evening heat, wandering from Venice (the Venetian Hotel) to Polynesia (the Mirage Hotel, complete with on-site erupting volcano) to Paris (the Paris-Las Vegas Hotel) to New York (New York-New York) to Egypt (the Luxor Hotel) in the space of half an hour, constantly being amazed at what an insane place Las Vegas is.

STRENGTHS

⊿ 24-hour gambling and drinking
⊿ Huge choice of hotels, all with their own ridiculous theme
⊿ Delicious food and extraordinarily attentive service
⊿ No need to worry about being rained out

WEAKNESSES

⊿ Sometimes you just want some normality and a little less neon
⊿ The need to take a taxi almost everywhere
⊿ The heat makes staying in an air-conditioned casino such an attractive idea
⊿ There's nothing to make you feel you should be having anything but fun…

GOLD STAR

There's only one reason for Vegas being here – it's the undisputed gambling capital of the world, with more choice and more casinos than anywhere else on earth.

CITYSPEAK

⊿ The latest multi-multi-million dollar development to muscle in on the city's skyline
⊿ The latest populist act of mafia-lawyer-turned-hugely-successful mayor, Oscar Goodman
⊿ Is anyone in town actually from Nevada?

STARRING ROLE IN...

⊿ *Viva Las Vegas* (1964)
⊿ *Rain Man* (1988)
⊿ *Leaving Las Vegas* (1995)
⊿ *Casino* (1995)
⊿ *Oceans Eleven* (1960 and 2001)

IMPORT

⊿ Gamblers from all over the world
⊿ Nicholas Cage (he's made more films here than anywhere else)
⊿ Water
⊿ Divas on their last legs (Liza, Céline, Elton)

EXPORT

⊿ Andre Agassi
⊿ Broke gamblers
⊿ Newlyweds

SEE the incredible dancing fountains outside the Bellagio Hotel.

EAT in vast hotel buffets – the only way Vegas can realistically feed its teeming thousands of hungry gamblers.

DRINK for free as you play – just grab a cocktail waitress and don't forget to tip.

DO get married to someone you barely know at short notice in one of the hilarious chapels on the strip.

WATCH the neon-clad city from the sky by ascending the Stratosphere at night.

BUY more chips, regularly…and remember, the house always wins.

AFTER DARK bring your sunglasses out with you to deal with all the fabulous neon.

URBAN MYTH

It's actually a myth that you can pitch up at any chapel in Las Vegas and get married there and then. You need to go first to the Clark County Court House and obtain a marriage licence. The courthouse is open daily, but only until midnight, so it's not always plain sailing and you can't just drunkenly arrive at the chapel and demand an instant union.

SUN WORSHIPPERS PERFORM THEIR ABLUTIONS OUTSIDE INDIA TEAHOUSE, COTTESLOE BEACH.
Photographer: Peter Ptschelinzew (1)

This city on sand epitomises the wild frontier character of Australia's emptiest and largest state, but despite its isolation, easy-going Perth rivals its east-coast brethren for quality of life, with top-class food and wine, vibrant nightlife, and more days of sunshine than any other capital city in the country.

ANATOMY

Perth's compact city centre sits on a sweeping bend of the Swan River. Shoppers buzz through the Hay St and Murray St Malls, while the city's suits wheel and deal along St George's Tce, the centre of Perth's business district. Jump on a free Transperth bus or train and head west to the sprawling Kings Park or cross the railway line to the north, and you'll find Northbridge, heart of the city's nightlife. West and northwest of the city are the popular Indian Ocean beaches, Cottesloe and Scarborough.

PEOPLE

The city is home to people born in more than 200 different countries, speaking 170 different languages and practising more than 100 religious faiths.

TYPICAL PERTH CITIZEN

Sandgropers (as residents of Western Australia are known) just have to 'get out', but once away they pine for their unspoilt west coast and sleepy small-town values. Everyone plays something, be it tennis, football, golf or a Fender. There are enough baby-boomer Poms to fill the Burswood Lyric Theatre for Jerry and the Pacemakers three nights running. And the America's Cup *will* come back to the Royal Perth Yacht Club.

DEFINING EXPERIENCE

Heading down to Scarborough Beach for a surf, breakfasting at Cottesloe, then walking through the wildflowers at Kings Park, making sure you have time to catch the sardine fishermen unloading at Fremantle before barbecuing the catch on a rise overlooking the Swan as the sun sets golden in the west.

Perth 047

VITAL STATISTICS

NAME: PERTH

NICKNAME: CITY OF LIGHTS

DATE OF BIRTH: 1829; WHEN THE SWAN RIVER SETTLEMENT WAS FOUNDED ON LAND THAT WAS OCCUPIED BY THE ABORIGINAL NYOONGAR TRIBE

ADDRESS: AUSTRALIA (MAP 1, II20)

HEIGHT: 60M

SIZE: 1075 SQ KM

POPULATION: 1.8 MILLION

HISTORIC SWAN BELLS, ORIGINALLY DATING TO THE 14TH CENTURY AND BROUGHT OVER FROM ENGLAND IN 1988.
Photographer: Wayne Walton (2)

THE CITY SKYLINE AT DAY'S END.
Photographer: Peter Ptschelinzew (3)

YEAR-ROUND BEACH WEATHER MEANS RIGOROUS SURF CLUB TRAINING AT THE POPULAR COTTESLOE BEACH.
Photographer: Peter Bennetts (4)

STRENGTHS

- Stunning city beaches
- Sunshine
- Federation Walkway through the tree tops in Kings Park
- Fremantle
- Maritime Museum
- The Eagles (local football team)
- Subiaco on a Saturday
- The Fremantle Doctor
- Indonesian food
- A drive into Margaret River
- The boutique brews
- Proximity to Asia
- Free inner-city transport

WEAKNESSES

- The empty seats at the Opera
- The ballot for a place on Rottnest
- Lack of iconic buildings
- Cost of flights

GOLD STAR

Perth locals swear they have the best city beaches in Australia, and with that clean white sand and warm aquamarine water, who can argue?

CITYSPEAK

- When will bottle shops be able to trade on Sunday?
- What time's sunrise so I can hit the beach for a surf?

STARRING ROLE IN...

- *The Shark Net* by Robert Drewe
- *Let's Get Skase* (2001)
- *Japanese Story* (2003)

IMPORT

- Alan Bond
- Asian food
- The Swan Bells (eighteen church bells)
- The Outram Hotel – a little bit of Paris in West Perth
- Kite-surfing

EXPORT

- Models, and a lot of them
- Aluminium
- Wheat
- Iron ore
- Gold
- Pavlova
- Nashi pears
- Wine
- Heath Ledger
- Judy Davis
- Bob Hawke

URBAN MYTH

Rose Porteous, a housekeeper-turned-socialite-turned-suspect in the death of her third very wealthy mining magnate husband, is one of Perth's larger-than-life characters. Like watching *The Bold and the Beautiful*, it's hard to keep up with flamboyant Rose and her oh-so-public intrigues. Locals drive slowly past her Mosman Park home hoping to catch Rose in her scarlet lipstick and fluffy slippers. But not for much longer. After recently declaring Perth 'too boring for me and my poodles', her $17.5 million *Gone with the Wind*-style manor, Prix d'Amour, complete with 16 rooms and one of the biggest Waterford crystal chandeliers in the southern hemisphere, is set to be bulldozed. Rose reckons Melbourne will be more fun.

SEE locals sucking back the eucalyptus-flavoured oxygen at the popular O2U bar.

EAT Malay king-prawn curry, or hand-pick your fish from the market adjoining Kailis Bros Fish Café in groovy Leederville.

DRINK a pale ale on the outside deck at Little Creatures in Fremantle.

DO catch the ferry to Rottnest for a day of cycling around the virtually car-free island.

WATCH humpback whales pass by Perth on their annual journey to Antarctic waters.

BUY a case of Margaret River wine.

AFTER DARK grab a mate and trawl for prawns and crabs in the shallows of the Swan.

Shanghai

048

VITAL STATISTICS

NAME: SHANGHAI

NICKNAME: PEARL OF THE ORIENT; PARIS OF THE EAST

DATE OF BIRTH: 3900 BC; WHEN THE FIRST SETTLEMENTS APPEARED

ADDRESS: CHINA (MAP 5, R1)

HEIGHT: 7M

SIZE: 6341 SQ KM

POPULATION: 13.4 MILLION

THE SCIENCE FICTION CITYSCAPE OF NANJING LU SHOPPING PRECINCT. Photographer: Walter Bibikow (1)

China's most chichi city wows with its sharp fashion and dazzling architecture but still manages to keep it traditional.

ANATOMY

Central Shanghai is divided into Pudong (east of the Huangpu River) and Puxi (west of the Huangpu River), though there is no single focus to the city. Most attractions are in Puxi, including the Bund – the tourist centrepiece. West of the Bund is the former international settlement and one of Shanghai's main shopping streets, Nanjing Lu. South of the Bund is the Chinese city, a maze of narrow lanes. West of the old town and hidden in the backstreets north and south of Huaihai Lu (Shanghai's premiere shopping street) is the former French Town, with a major collection of Western-style restaurants and bars. Western Shanghai is dominated by Hongqiao, a hotel/conference centre/ office zone with the expat area of Gubei further out. East of the Huanpu, Pudong is a 'special economic' zone of banks, skyscrapers and new residential complexes. Walking and catching buses can be a nightmare, but the metro and light railway system work like a dream.

PEOPLE

Most Shanghainese residents are the descendants of poor migrants who came to the city from the two adjacent provinces of Northern Jiangsu and Zhejiang, where Wu Chinese is the favoured dialect. Recent immigration from other parts of China has meant that Mandarin is more commonly spoken, but other languages are rare. To make Shanghai an 'international city' the government has a target of 5% foreign residents, so Shanghainese are welcoming of foreigners even if they can't speak their language.

TYPICAL SHANGHAINESE

The rest of China may view Shanghai as being in the thrall of the West with their interest in plastic surgery, fashion and progress, but the Shanghainese know they're just jealous. Shanghai's women are said to be the most beautiful in China and even the men are known for being fashionable, even if it just means having the latest mobile or knowing the hippest bar. There's a strong pride in the city, with other Chinese seen as *waidìrén* (outlanders) and the Taiwanese sniggered at as *táibazi* (Taiwanese hicks).

DEFINING EXPERIENCE

Snapping up fashion firsts along Huaihai Lu, queuing for *xiǎlóngbaō* (dragon balls) outside Nanxiang Steamed Bun Restaurant, people-watching on Nanjing Lu, and browsing the pirated CDs at Wushan Night Market.

STRENGTHS

- French Town
- The Bund
- Volkswagen taxis
- Jinmao Tower
- Nanjing Lu
- *Nòngtángs* (back-alley communities)
- Yuyuan Gardens and Bazaar
- Huzhou Pagoda

WEAKNESSES

- Bad public transport
- Pollution haze
- Little personal space
- Spitting

GOLD STAR

Architecture – from whopping Jinmao Tower to the disco-ball of the Oriental Pearl Tower, there's plenty to dazzle.

CITYSPEAK

- The death of the live-music scene
- Shanghai is so much better than Beijing – just look at the new 100-storey development to prove it
- The growing traffic problem

STARRING ROLE IN...

- *Shanghai Express* (1932)
- *Empire of the Sun* (1986)
- *Purple Butterfly* (2003)
- *The Red Violin* (1998)
- *The Blue Lotus* by Hergé
- *When We Were Orphans* by Kazuo Ishiguro

IMPORT

- Emily Hahn
- *Baiwēi* (Budweiser)
- Western influence
- Formula One Grand Prix
- *Màidāngláo* (McDonald's)
- Kooky architecture
- Mobile phones
- JG Ballard

EXPORT

- Clothing and textiles
- Zhou Xuan
- Movies
- Snakehead gangsters
- Ruan Lingyu, 'China's Garbo' of the 1930s
- Liao Changyong

SEE the daunting Jinmao Tower after a stroll along the ritzy Bund.

EAT the authentically Uygur *dapánjī* (fried chicken and potatoes) for a taste of China's colonies at Afanti Restaurant.

DRINK martinis in the Glamour Bar at M while enjoying evening views of the Bund.

DO a Chinese martial-arts course at the kick-arse Longwu International Kung Fu Centre.

WATCH the gymnastic genius of the Shanghai Acrobatics Troupe, bending most nights at Shanghai Centre Theatre.

BUY a *qipao* (cheongsam) tailored to any figure at Dongjiadu Cloth Market.

AFTER DARK head for Loft, a converted cinema with the chance to dance, drink and dine.

URBAN MYTH

The godfather of Shanghai's under-world, which covertly ran the city during the 1930s, was Du Yuesheng, or 'Big-Eared' Du, as he was called out of earshot. By 1927 he led the Green Gang, controlling the city's prostitution, drug-running and protection rackets. His favourite scheme was to kidnap the wealthy and then negotiate their release, pocketing half the ransom as commission. Du prowled town in a bulletproof sedan with armed bodyguards crouched on the running boards, styling himself as the Chinese Al Capone. In 1931 – after playing a part in Chiang Kaishek's anti-Communist massacre – he was elected to the municipal council and reigned as unofficial mayor until the Japanese invasion, when he fled to Chongqing, and then Hong Kong, where he died a billionaire in 1951.

FANS OF T'AI CHI EXPRESS GRACE AND POISE DURING MORNING EXERCISES ON THE BUND.
Photographer: Ray Laskowitz (2)

SOME PEOPLE CALL IT AN EXTREME SPORT, BUT TO THESE SHANGHAIESE WINDOW WASHERS, IT'S JUST PART OF THE JOB. Photographer: Bradley Mayhew (3)

EXPRESS TO THE FUTURE – A GLITTERY RIDE THROUGH THE ELECTRO-PSYCHODELIC BUND TUNNEL.
Photographer: John Borthwick (4)

FIELD OF DREAMS – A YOUNG AFICIONADO TAKES A FRONT PEW AT DODGER STADIUM.
Photographer: Ray Laskowitz (1)

Los Angeles
049

VITAL STATISTICS

NAME: LOS ANGELES

NICKNAME: LA; CITY OF ANGELS

DATE OF BIRTH: 1781; SPANISH MISSIONARIES FOUNDED THE SETTLEMENT

ADDRESS: USA (MAP 1, H11)

HEIGHT: 95M

SIZE: 1215 SQ KM

POPULATION: 10.1 MILLION

Los Angeles may be the world capital of myth-making but it thrives beyond its own highly constructed clichés with a mosaic of cultures and a beautiful setting between desert and sea.

ANATOMY

Los Angeles, in fact an enormous concatenation of independent cities, stretches down the Pacific coast, and sandwiched inland by the Santa Monica and San Gabriel Mountains. Inland, the skyscrapers of Downtown are the only recognisable centre. East LA, a Latino-dominated area, edges against Downtown, as do the historically African-American neighbourhoods of South Central and Compton. Westward are iconic Hollywood, West Hollywood, Bel Air and Beverly Hills. The car is king, but there is a large bus and limited light-rail network.

PEOPLE

Angelinos are a diverse lot. Almost half the population are Hispanic by birth or heritage, and Spanish is spoken almost as widely as English. There is a fast-growing Asian and Pacific Islander population, who join significant African-American and Native American communities.

TYPICAL ANGELINO

Angelinos don't care what the world thinks of them (narcissistic, vapid, flaky and superficial), or their city (dystopian, ugly, soulless) because they are too busy keeping fit, self-actualising, working the room, or just out there enjoying the place. They will admit to their notoriety for aggression behind the wheel, and are all too aware of the appalling economic disparities on display (and the simmering tensions it can generate), but that's because they are generally a tolerant, open-minded and cosmopolitan lot.

DEFINING EXPERIENCE

Running along the beach, then off to morning service at a happening little nondenominational (spirituality is on the list of things to improve this year), grabbing some cheddar enchiladas at the Venice Cantina before going to a Lucha Libre match (those wrestler's masks are *so* hot…), stopping by Wordtheatre's reading to check out your actor friend doing Raymond Carver, and then heading home to blog all the latest gossip.

STRENGTHS

- 300-plus days of sunshine per year
- Excellent contemporary-art museums and galleries
- Nuevo-Latino cuisine
- Downtown renewal
- Walt Disney Concert Hall
- LA Metro
- Getting into trouble at the Marmont
- Hollywood Forever Cemetery
- Griffith Park
- David Lynch's online weather report
- Farmers Market
- Mid-century modern furniture on tap
- Las Posadas and other Mexican festivals
- Thriving alternative art scene
- Jacarandas in bloom
- Kilometres of beaches
- Kelly Wearstler's OTT interiors
- Vibrant Latino culture

WEAKNESSES

- June gloom
- Sprawl
- Cooler-than-thou bouncers and shop assistants
- Stop-and-go freeways
- Persisting racial inequality
- Bad pizza
- Aggressive surfers
- Gang violence
- New York 'transplants' who do nothing but criticise
- San Andreas fault line

GOLD STAR

Built environment – for fans of modernist architecture, LA is the most innovative and diverse city in the USA.

CITYSPEAK

- Of course she's had work…
- LAPD
- Is that the Hiltons skanking up the dance floor?
- The LA River – just a crazy dream?

STARRING ROLE IN…

- *Double Indemnity* (1944)
- *The Big Sleep* (1946)
- *Sunset Boulevard* (1950)
- *Rebel without a Cause* (1955)
- *Touch of Evil* (1958)
- *Point Blank* (1967)
- *Chinatown* (1974)
- *Barfly* (1987)
- *La Bamba* (1987)
- *Boyz n the Hood* (1991)
- *The Player* (1992)
- *Short Cuts* (1993)
- *LA Story* (1991)
- *Pulp Fiction* (1994)
- *LA Confidential* (1997)
- *Mulholland Drive* (2001)
- *Crash* (2004)

IMPORT

- Eucalypts
- Actors
- Film and TV industry workers
- Charles and Ray Eames
- Igor Stravinsky
- Water
- Mexican domestic labourers
- William Faulkner
- F Scott Fitzgerald
- Bertolt Brecht
- Richard Neutra
- Chet Baker
- Mike Davis

EXPORT

- Film
- TV
- Porn
- Surf and skate culture
- McDonald's
- The word 'smog'
- Charles Bukowski
- San Pedro punk (Minutemen et al)
- Bikram yoga teachers
- Art Pepper
- Cobb salad
- NWA
- California rolls (*kashu-maki*)
- MFK Fisher
- Beach Boys

SEE nature *and* culture: the mountain and sea views plus David Hockney's Californian scenes at Richard Meier's glorious Getty Center.

EAT meat and drink vodka, Atkins-style, in the rococo-camp surrounds of the Lincoln Steakhouse Americana, Santa Monica.

DRINK an apple martini holed up in a poolside pleasure pod on the rooftop at the Standard Downtown.

DO a Friday-night yoga session with live DJs at Bala Yoga on La Brea, the ultimate in LA chill.

WATCH a Hollywood blockbuster in Hollywood, at the hipster-favoured ArcLight on Sunset Boulevard.

BUY preloved rock-and-roll lifestyle clothing – perhaps an ultra-rare Ziggy Stardust T-shirt – from Lo-Fi in West Hollywood.

AFTER DARK entertain or be entertained by Marty and Elayne at the Dresden Room in Los Feliz.

URBAN MYTH

Kenneth Anger's 'delicious box of poisoned bonbons', *Hollywood Babylon* dishes the dirt on the world's most self-mythologising city, purporting to uncover the seedier side of LA's entertainment industry. From the Fatty Arbuckle rape trial in the '20s and Errol Flynn's predilection for underage girls to Marilyn Monroe's death and the Manson murders, the book is full of half-truths, unsubstantiated rumour and outright fiction, but has gone on to inspire a whole genre of ironically tabloid-style 'LA uncovered' books.

THE SURF-INSPIRED ARCHITECTURE OF THE GETTY CENTER.
Photographer: Richard Cummins (2)

SURFER DUDES CARVE UP THE WEEKEND WAVES WITH PANACHE.
Photographer: David Peevers (3)

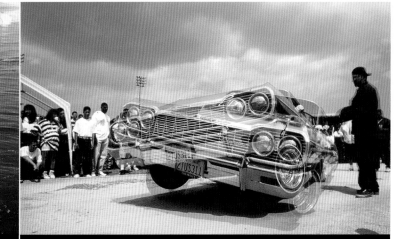

A CHEVY SHAKES ITS BOOTY AT A CAR DANCE-OFF WHERE VEHICLES WITH HYDRAULIC AXLES SHIMMY FOR SHOW.
Photographer: Robert Yager (4)

Lisbon is as romantic as Paris, as fun as Madrid, as laid-back as Rome, but small enough to fit into their handbags.

ANATOMY

Lisbon sits atop seven hills on the northern side of Portugal's finest natural harbour, the wide mouth of the Rio Tejo (Tagus River). On each hill is a castle, church or stunning *miradouro* (viewpoint). Many of the medieval buildings were destroyed in a huge earthquake in 1755 and the city was rebuilt in a baroque style along a formal grid. The ancient maze-like Alfama district, relatively unscathed, still exists near the narrow streets of the Bairro Alto *fin-de-siècle* decadence with snaking cobbled streets. Trams, both very old and very new, and funiculars exist alongside an extensive metro system.

PEOPLE

Greater Lisbon's citizens represent one-third of the country's population. Portugal's population breakdown has seen dramatic changes in the last few decades. The country's emigration rate has long been among Europe's highest, but its immigration rate shot up during the mid-1970s when around one million African *retornados* (refugees) immigrated from former Portuguese colonies. They have especially big communities in Lisbon. Another influx resulting from Portugal's empire building is of Brazilians. There's a small resident Roma (formerly known as Gypsies) population and there are also increasing numbers of immigrant workers from central and Eastern Europe.

TYPICAL LISBONITE

Lisbonites, like most Portuguese, return to home villages in August, drawn by family ties and a longing for home. They are known to suffer bouts of *saudade*, a particularly Portuguese melancholia, or longing, for something past. The city and its inhabitants have benefited greatly from EU membership, with floods of foreign investment and an overhaul of the city centre. Despite this, recent studies have declared the Portuguese the laziest people and heaviest drinkers in Europe. Lisbonites will have none of it.

Lisbon 050

VITAL STATISTICS

NAME: LISBON

DATE OF BIRTH: 1000 BC; WHEN THE PHOENICIANS FIRST SETTLED HERE

ADDRESS: PORTUGAL (MAP 3, B15)

HEIGHT: 77M

SIZE: 87 SQ KM

POPULATION: 564,660

ONE OF LISBON'S TRADEMARK TRAMS PREPARES TO POUNCE FROM A NARROW STREET CORNER.
Photographer: Bruno Morandi (1)

DEFINING EXPERIENCE

Wandering Baixa (Lower Town), Lisbon's heartbeat, taking a tram to Belém for a custard tart, then spending the afternoon with art and antiquities at the Museu Calouste Gulbenkian before choosing from an eclectic range of restaurants in Bairro Alto (some as big as a dining room).

STRENGTHS

- ◢ The Lisbon metro – an art gallery in itself
- ◢ *Azulejos* – the decorative glazed tiles found everywhere
- ◢ Mosteiro dos Jerónimos
- ◢ Torre de Belém
- ◢ Royal Palaces
- ◢ Mammoth baroque Palacio Nacional de Mafra
- ◢ Gare do Oriente
- ◢ 17km-long Ponte de Vasco da Gama
- ◢ African jazz scene
- ◢ Laid-back clubs
- ◢ Dining late
- ◢ Custard tarts
- ◢ Rickety trams
- ◢ Cobblestone streets

WEAKNESSES

- ◢ The rivalry between Cape Verdean and Angolan gangs
- ◢ *Bacalhau* (salt cod) – there is such a thing as too much
- ◢ Mateus Rosé

GOLD STAR

A city in thrall to its past, Lisbon has baroque cafés, 1960s diners, velvet-lined bars and Art Deco bakeries. This city has not been renovated into oblivion.

CITYSPEAK

- ◢ How will they fare in the next European Football championships (having lost in the final to Greece in 2004)?
- ◢ Economic slowdown – has the shine gone off economic expansion?
- ◢ Will Portugal lose out now that the EU has expanded eastwards?

STARRING ROLE IN...

- ◢ *The Lisbon Story* (1994)
- ◢ *The Book of Disquiet* by Fernando Pessoa
- ◢ *The Last Kabbalist of Lisbon* (2000)
- ◢ *A Small Death in Lisbon* by Robert Wilson
- ◢ *Caitaes de Abril* (April Captains, 2000)
- ◢ *Requiem* by Antonio Tabucchi

IMPORT

- ◢ EU funds
- ◢ Citizens of its former colonies
- ◢ Investment money from John Malkovich
- ◢ Chillies
- ◢ Gold from South America

EXPORT

- ◢ Prince Henry the Navigator
- ◢ Vasco da Gama
- ◢ Catherine of Bragança
- ◢ Tea to the rest of Europe
- ◢ Five million people to Brazil from 1884 to 1963
- ◢ Painter Paula Rego
- ◢ Billions of natural cork bottle-stoppers each year
- ◢ Nobel prize–winning Author José Saramago
- ◢ The films of Manoel de Oliveira

SEE the central city from the low vantage point of 45m – the frilly, wrought-iron 19th-century oddity, the Elevador de Santa Justa.

EAT custard tarts from a secret recipe – they taste as though made by angels – at Pasteis de Belém.

DRINK *vinho verde* (green wine) – light, crisp dry wine (Portugal's signature wine).

DO take a stroll through Alfama, starting on tram No 28 to Miradoura da Senhora do Monte to avoid the uphill slog.

WATCH free Sunday-morning music and dance performances at Centro Cultural de Belém.

BUY *azulejos* and ceramics, sold all over, but check out styles first at the Museu Nacional do Azulejo.

AFTER DARK seek out the *fado* (Portuguese blues) experience in Bairro Alto or Alfama.

URBAN MYTH

The Portuguese don't actually drink much port – it's more of an English drop. The foreigners from the north were instrumental in the development of this wine, which is still commonly trod by human foot, and they've always been its chief market.

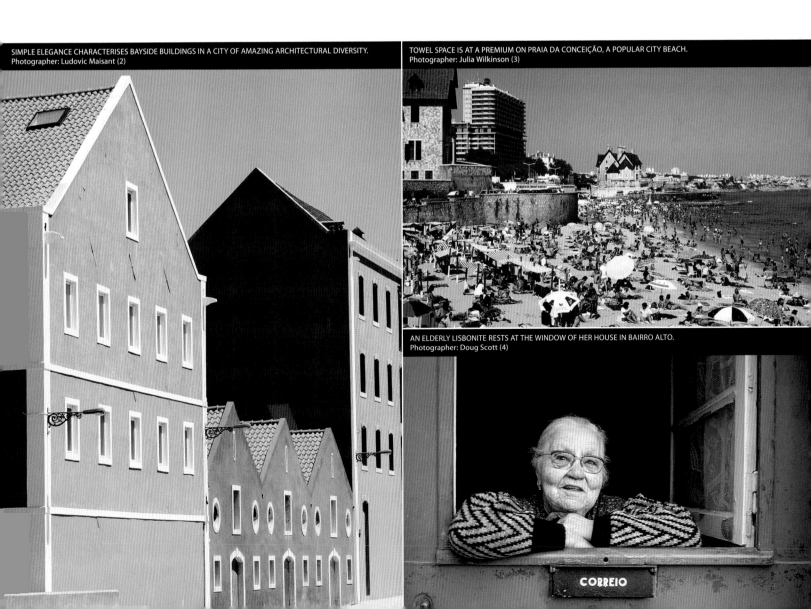

SIMPLE ELEGANCE CHARACTERISES BAYSIDE BUILDINGS IN A CITY OF AMAZING ARCHITECTURAL DIVERSITY.
Photographer: Ludovic Maisant (2)

TOWEL SPACE IS AT A PREMIUM ON PRAIA DA CONCEIÇÃO, A POPULAR CITY BEACH.
Photographer: Julia Wilkinson (3)

AN ELDERLY LISBONITE RESTS AT THE WINDOW OF HER HOUSE IN BAIRRO ALTO.
Photographer: Doug Scott (4)

CORREIO

Stockholm

051

VITAL STATISTICS

NAME: STOCKHOLM

NICKNAME: VENICE OF THE NORTH

DATE OF BIRTH: 1252; WHEN CHIEFTAIN BIRGER JARL ORDERED A FORT CONSTRUCTED ON A STRATEGICALLY PLACED ISLET

ADDRESS: SWEDEN (MAP 3, M2)

HEIGHT: 44M

SIZE: 188 SQ KM

POPULATION: 755,000

MODEL CITIZENS DISPLAY SEASONAL FASHIONS IN THE WINDOWS OF THE NK DEPARTMENT STORE.
Photographer: Jonathan Smith (1)

Without a doubt, Stockholm is one of the most beautiful national capitals in the world, and walking around the city's waterways and parks is a glorious way to spend a week-long stretch of European summer.

ANATOMY

Stockholm is built on islands, except for the modern centre (Norrmalm), which is focused around the ugly Sergels Torg. This business and shopping hub is linked by a network of subways to Centralstationen (central train station); the popular gardens of Kungsträdgården lie just to the east. The triangular island of Stadsholmen and its neighbours accommodate Gamla Stan, separated from Norrmalm by the narrow channels of Norrström near the royal palace, but connected by several bridges. On the south side of Stadsholmen, Centralbron (the main bridge) and the Slussen interchange connect with the southern city, Södermalm, and its spine, Götgatan. East of Gamla Stan is the small island of Skeppsholmen, and further down Strandvägen and past the berths you cross to Djurgården, topped by the Skansen museum.

PEOPLE

Most of Stockholm's population is of Nordic stock. There are also about 80,000 foreigners of more than 80 nationalities. The single largest group of foreigners are Finns, who number around 14,000 and form 18% of the total population. The next four largest groups are made up of Iraqis, Somalis, Turks and Iranians – including many Kurds who fled Kurdistan and settled in Sweden.

TYPICAL STOCKHOLMER

Naturally reserved and often shy, Stockholmers' lack of effusiveness in greeting strangers can seem rude but is seldom intentional. Extremely proud of their city, the populace is uniformly well educated and gender equality is advanced: families where the mother works while the father handles most childcare duties are common. Queuing by number is a favourite pastime, commonly done in shops, bakeries, banks, government offices, police stations and post offices. Rural connections are still strong: the summer cottage is almost *de rigueur*.

DEFINING EXPERIENCE

Breakfasting on *lussekatt* (saffron bun) and coffee at Thelins Konditori before visiting Moderna Museet, strolling along Strömkajen and through Kungsträdgården then lunching at Café Panorama, catching the changing of the guard at Kungliga Slottet, refuelling on *fika* (coffee and cake) prior to visiting the Hornspuckeln galleries, dining at Östgötakällaren, drinking at Kvarnen and checking out live music at Mondo.

STRENGTHS

- Compact but beautiful city
- 608-room Kungliga Slottet (Royal Palace)
- Quality of light
- Winding streets of Gamla Stan
- World leader in design and architecture
- Underground art – paintings, sculptures etc in over 90 *tunnelbana* (subway) stations
- *Fika*
- Salvaged 17th-century flagship *Vasa*
- Riddarhuset
- Ecological consciousness
- Stadshuset's mosaic-lined Gyllene Salen (Golden Hall)
- Shopper's paradise
- Haga Park
- Skogskyrkogården – World Heritage–listed cemetery
- Bohemian Södermalm
- Progressive political landscape
- Gay- and lesbian-friendly
- Eating out in Långholmen

WEAKNESSES

- A night on the town can be expensive
- Dumbed-down media/increased commercial influence
- Grim human filing-cabinet–style buildings, courtesy of the Million Program
- Kulturehuset – symbol of demolished history and soulless modern architecture

GOLD STAR

Skansen – step into another time at the world's first open-air museum, featuring around 150 traditional houses (inhabited by staff in period costume) showing how Swedes lived in previous times.

CITYSPEAK

- The euro: will they or won't they?
- Hammarby – no-one even seems to care *how* the club is doing – they just love being its fans
- Taxes: too high
- Which three parties will team up to lead Parliament this time?

STARRING ROLE IN...

- *Ondskan* (Evil, 2003)
- *Songs from the Second Floor* (2000)
- *The Seventh Seal* (1956)

IMPORT

- Jazz
- Machinery
- Chemicals
- Motor vehicles
- Iron and steel products
- Petrol and petroleum products
- Finns

EXPORT

- Ingmar Bergman
- Swedish design
- IKEA
- Bjorn Borg
- Ericsson
- ABBA
- The Hives
- Smörgåsbord
- The Cardigans
- August Strindberg
- Roxette
- Europe ('80s pop-rock group)
- Ace of Base
- Max Martin (producer/songwriter of Britney Spears, Backstreet Boys, *N Sync etc)
- Pippi Longstocking
- Olympic gold-winning skiers Ingemar Stenmark and Pernilla Wiberg

---

SEE Stockholm's waterways by boat.

EAT your fill of classic *husmanskost* (home cooking) at Den Gyldene Freden.

DRINK Staropramen at the steeped-in-history Pelikan.

DO lose yourself in the winding streets of Gamla Stan.

WATCH the changing of the guard at Kungliga Slottet.

BUY a variety of goods (and bads) from Skansen's market.

AFTER DARK rock the boat on warship-turned-restaurant/nightclub *Lady Patricia*.

URBAN MYTH

In 1912 tortured genius August Strindberg was awarded an 'Anti-Nobel prize' (funded by many Swedes) as compensation for not receiving the Nobel prize for literature.

RIDDARHOLMEN AND THE OLD TOWN FROM ABOVE DURING A GORGEOUS WINTER'S SUNSET.
Photographer: R Ryan (2)

STREETS IN THE OLD TOWN, NARROW YET WELCOMING AT THE SAME TIME.
Photographer: Preben Kristensen (3)

IT'S NOT THE RED-LIGHT DISTRICT, JUST A RED-LIT NIGHTSPOT IN MOSEBACKETORG.
Photographer: Jonathan Smith (4)

Kuala Lumpur

052

VITAL STATISTICS

NAME: KUALA LUMPUR

NICKNAME: KL

DATE OF BIRTH: 1857; WHEN A TROUPE OF TIN PROSPECTORS LANDED AT THE JUNCTION OF THE KLANG AND GOMBAK RIVERS AND DUBBED IT KUALA LUMPUR (MUDDY CONFLUENCE)

ADDRESS: MALAYSIA (MAP 5, L12)

HEIGHT: 39M

SIZE: 243 SQ KM

POPULATION: 1.5 MILLION

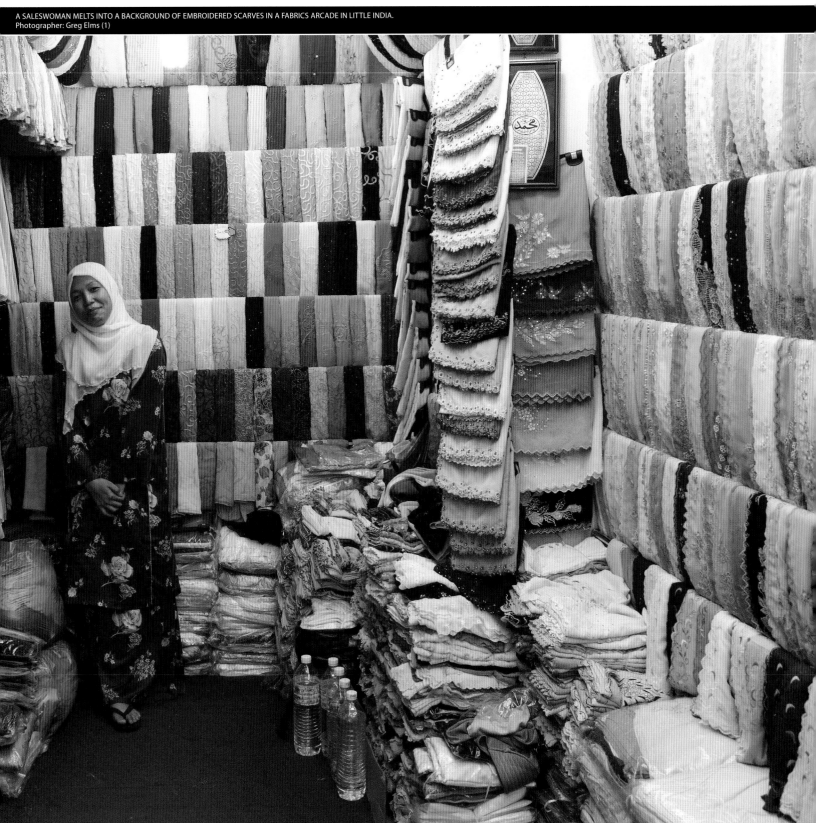

A SALESWOMAN MELTS INTO A BACKGROUND OF EMBROIDERED SCARVES IN A FABRICS ARCADE IN LITTLE INDIA.
Photographer: Greg Elms (1)

A BOY COPS AN OUTDOOR SHOWER AT SWIMMING POOLS BENEATH THE SOARING PETRONAS TOWERS. Photographer: Greg Elms (2)

THE QUIRKY COLONIAL ARCHITECTURE OF THE KUALA LUMPUR TRAIN STATION BUILT IN 1911. Photographer: Greg Elms (3)

AN IMPROMPTU BARBERSHOP QUARTET AT A HAIRDRESSING SALON IN LITTLE INDIA. Photographer: Greg Elms (4)

A triumphant and forward-looking city, KL vibrantly accommodates its traditional Malay, Chinese and Indian cultures with the buzz of thriving industry.

ANATOMY

KL's traditional heart beats at Merdeka Sq, marked by the world's tallest flagpole (100m), while the Golden Triangle represents modern KL; the Petronas Towers (now the world's *second* tallest, topped by Taipei 101) are dazzling beacons of industry. Southeast of Merdeka lies bustling Chinatown and southward is Masjid Negara (National Mosque) and the historic KL Train Station. Stretching west is KL's 'green belt', with the Lake Garden and Malaysian Parliament House. Beyond its mall culture, KL's maze of motorways can frustrate pedestrians – it's often easier to nab a cab or ride the slick LRT (Light Rail Transit) system.

PEOPLE

Kuala Lumpur truly is 'Little Asia', with 65% Malays, 20% Chinese, 10% Indians and 5% of other mostly Asian cultural groups. The official national language is Malay (Bahasa Melayu), and other languages spoken are Hokkien/Fukien, Cantonese, Hakka, Teochew, Tamil, Telugu, Malayalam, Hindi and English. Predominantly Muslim, Buddhists, Hindus, Sikhs and Christians all form part of KL's rich tapestry.

TYPICAL KUALA LUMPUR CITIZEN

Kuala Lumpur's citizens are proud, respectful and tolerant of different beliefs and cultural practices. They have triumphed at building a metropolis that retains local traditions and colour. Oppressed by dripping humidity, the citizens know how to relax, be it enjoying great food or bargain-hunting for fashion and electronic gadgets in KL's many air-conditioned malls.

DEFINING EXPERIENCE

Picnicking at the Lake Gardens among butterflies, birds and orchids, serenading your true love on a Tasik Perdana (Premier Lake) rowing boat, topped off by a balmy banquet and good-natured haggling at Chinatown's night market.

STRENGTHS

- ◢ Multiculturalism and diversity
- ◢ Tolerance
- ◢ Dazzling Petronas Towers
- ◢ Local colour and vibrancy
- ◢ Hawker markets and foodstalls
- ◢ Halal fast food
- ◢ Chinatown
- ◢ Little India
- ◢ Luscious gardens
- ◢ Bargain-hunting
- ◢ Exquisite pewter
- ◢ Nearby Batu Caves
- ◢ 'World's tallest' (flagpole *and* – almost – building)

WEAKNESSES

- ◢ Dripping humidity (though great for orchids)
- ◢ Traffic congestion and narrow streets
- ◢ Lack of sidewalks
- ◢ Unreliable bus service
- ◢ Smog
- ◢ Poor water quality
- ◢ The invasion of 'mall culture'
- ◢ (Some) less than honest cab drivers, preferring to go 'off meter'

GOLD STAR

Cheap, delicious and culturally diverse food – a hearty meal can be found in any one of KL's nooks, crannies and basements.

CITYSPEAK

- ◢ Reports of prowling tigers and mischievous monkeys on city outskirts
- ◢ KL's new monorail servicing 11 stations and posting a revenue loss of Rm46.24 million for its first year

STARRING ROLE IN...

- ◢ *Entrapment* (1999)
- ◢ *Connecting Faith* (2004)
- ◢ *The Big Durian* (2004)

IMPORT

- ◢ Chinese people
- ◢ Indian people
- ◢ British manicured gardens
- ◢ Moorish, Islamic and Buddhist architecture
- ◢ Japanese pop culture
- ◢ Rampant consumer culture
- ◢ LV and Gucci bags (the real deal)
- ◢ Shark fins (in brine and dried)

EXPORT

- ◢ Rubber
- ◢ Palm oil
- ◢ Tin/pewter
- ◢ Orchids
- ◢ PGA golfer Danny Chia
- ◢ Hollywood action star Michelle Yeoh
- ◢ LV and Gucci knock-offs
- ◢ Textiles
- ◢ Cheap (read 'pirated') DVDs

SEE the city lights from the Petronas Towers before getting a ride an hour northwest of KL to see the natural light show of *kelip-kelip* (fireflies) in the mangroves, best viewed on a river tour from Kuala Selangor.

EAT *bak kut teh* (a broth containing pork ribs and spices) from Jalan Petalin.

DRINK with friendly locals at *mamak* stalls (hang-out spot) dotting the city; run by Muslim Indians they are a great place for night owls to hang out late.

DO brave the indoor rollercoaster at Berjaya Times Sq if the heat gets too much.

WATCH Malay dance, Indian classical dance, Chinese dance and t'ai chi performances every weekend at the open-air Central Market.

BUY electronic gadgets, especially games, cheap DVDs, and mobile phones at Low Yat Plaza.

AFTER DARK doof-doof into the wee hours at Bangsar, KL's hub for clubs.

URBAN MYTH

It is rumoured that people have suffered strokes, aneurisms and heart attacks from mixing durian fruit (a popular if *very* malodorous treat) with alcohol. Purportedly, a deadly yeast can result when the two are added together. This is all unproven, and to the unseasoned but daring traveller, the best precaution taken before quaffing a durian-infused cocktail would be a peg on the nose.

By far Syria's largest metropolis, Damascus is a city of fascinating contrasts, with timeless oriental bazaars and Islamic monuments to enrapture romantics alongside the bustle of a busy capital.

ANATOMY

Damascus has two distinct parts: the Old City, tightly defined by its encircling walls, and modern Damascus, sprawled around it. The Old City is separated from the new by Sharia ath-Thawna, with the covered Souq al-Hamidiyy leading directly to the city's centrepiece, Umayyad Mosque. South of the mosque Shariah Medhat Pasha (Straight St) bisects the city on an east–west axis. Sights of interest are conveniently encapsulated within roughly 2 sq km. Handy microbuses cover set routes and the hundreds of taxis are cheap, though finding your way around this compact city on foot is simple.

PEOPLE

This ancient city has seen many previous tribes, from Mesopotamian Akkadians to the Egyptians and Hittites. Seventy-four percent of the population are Sunni Muslim, 16% are of Alawite, Druze and other Muslim sects, 10% are Christian (various sects), with a tiny Jewish community remaining. Damascenes have a literacy rate of 76.9%, while life expectancy is 69.71 years.

TYPICAL DAMASCENE

The typical Damascene speaks Arabic, is family-oriented, enjoys socialising over a meal and bathes communally in gender-segregated *hammams* (bathhouses). While males mingle over board games, water pipes and banter at coffee houses, women generally socialise in the home. The average day of the Muslim majority is punctuated five times by calls to prayer from minarets and mosques.

Damascus
053

VITAL STATISTICS

NAME: DAMASCUS

DATE OF BIRTH: 3000 BC; ONE OF THE OLDEST CONTINUOUSLY INHABITED CITIES IN THE WORLD, ITS PRIME POSITION IN THE VERDANT GHOUTA OASIS AND ITS PROXIMITY TO THE SILK ROAD LED TO IT BEING COVETED BY WAVES OF CONQUERING EMPIRES

ADDRESS: SYRIA (MAP 2, L1)

HEIGHT: 720M

POPULATION: 6 MILLION

SHHHH! THE SOUNDLESS STEPS OF MIMES IN REHEARSAL FOR A PERFORMANCE.
Photographer: Expuesto – Nicolas Randall (1)

DEFINING EXPERIENCE

Getting lost in the Old City and wandering among its souqs (markets), *medressas* (Islamic academies) and khans (inns), absorbing the serenity of Umayyad Mosque, exploring the treasures of the National Museum, witnessing the fine Azem Palace, viewing Damascene houses, steaming and sweating in a *hammam*, then whiling away some time in a coffee house before heading out to dine on superb food in enchanting surrounds.

STRENGTHS

- ◢ Intricate Arabesque design
- ◢ Mysterious and exotic souqs
- ◢ Dinnertime spread of *mezze* (a selection of hot and cold starters traditionally served at the beginning of meals) among friends
- ◢ Azem Palace
- ◢ Damascene houses
- ◢ The National Museum
- ◢ Deep-rooted culture of hospitality
- ◢ *Zalabiyya* (pastries dipped in rose water)
- ◢ Being invited in to eat or drink with locals
- ◢ *Hammams*
- ◢ Umayyad Mosque
- ◢ Coffee houses

WEAKNESSES

- ◢ Attempting to find a taxi between 2pm and 4pm on working days
- ◢ Saahat ash-Shodada, an ugly chicane for speeding cars in the city's heart
- ◢ Overfuelling on Bedouin coffee
- ◢ Smoke-clogged coffee houses for the nonsmoker

GOLD STAR

Immersing yourself in the scents of spices, coffee and perfume in Damascus' souqs, which seduce the eye with colour and glitter, and assault the hearing with trader's cries and porter's warning shouts.

CITYSPEAK

- ◢ Water, a precious commodity
- ◢ When will Washington drop Syria from its list of states supporting terrorism?

STARRING ROLE IN...

- ◢ *Train of Short Distances* (2003)
- ◢ *Damascus Bitter Sweet* by Ulfat Idilbi

IMPORT

- ◢ Lovingly restored '50s Buicks and Chevrolets
- ◢ Victorian adventurer Sir Richard Burton
- ◢ Indian 'B' movies
- ◢ St John the Baptist
- ◢ Egyptians
- ◢ Saul of Tarsus/St Paul the Apostle
- ◢ Hittites
- ◢ Romans
- ◢ Mongols
- ◢ Hong Kong martial-arts flicks
- ◢ Seljuk Turks
- ◢ Food and livestock
- ◢ Plastics

EXPORT

- ◢ Poet Nizar Qabbani
- ◢ Elaborate brassware
- ◢ Damascus steel (AD 900–1600)
- ◢ St John of Damascus
- ◢ Intricate, inlaid boxes
- ◢ Abbasid poet al-Mutanabi
- ◢ Singer Fairouz's first recording
- ◢ Crude oil
- ◢ Natural gas
- ◢ Damask fabric
- ◢ Figs and almonds
- ◢ The Damascus Declaration (1992)
- ◢ Damask rosewater, a prized medicine in the Arab world
- ◢ Writer/diplomat Constantine Zouraiq

SEE an *oud* (equivalent of classical guitar) craftsman at work at Sharia Bahsa in the Souq Saroujah.

EAT *tamarimoz* (pancakes with black honey and sugar, wrapped around a banana).

DRINK beer fountain-side at the Damascus Worker's Club.

DO experience the steaming and cleansing wonders of a *hammam*.

WATCH the street scene and ease into local time at Ash-Shams coffee house, formerly a *hammam*, armed with coffee and *narjileh* (water pipe).

BUY inlaid wooden boxes, Bedouin silver jewellery and elaborate copper work at the extensive Damascus Souq.

AFTER DARK team a restaurant meal with a floor show featuring whirling dervishes, musicians, singers-cum-sword fighters and human pyramid builders.

URBAN MYTH

Shariah Medhat Pasha, unique among the city's narrow winding streets, was one of the main streets of ancient Damascus and is believed to be the world's oldest known street. It's mentioned in the Bible (Acts 9:11) as a 'street called Straight', on which St Paul is supposed to have lived.

CLEANLINESS OF BODY AND PURITY OF SOUL IS THE OBJECT OF BATHING RITUALS AT THE HAMMAM EL MOKHADEM.
Photographer: Pascal Meunier (2)

SHEESHA SMOKERS BLOW THEIR TROUBLES AWAY IN A LOCAL COFFEE HOUSE.
Photographer: Nicolas Randall (3)

TOOTH-ROTTING TREATS DAZZLE THE EYES AND THE TASTEBUDS AT A CITY SOUQ.
Photographer: Russell Mountford (4)

Luang Prabang

054

VITAL STATISTICS

NAME: LUANG PRABANG

DATE OF BIRTH: 1512; WHEN THE CITY-STATE OF MUANG XIENG THONG (CITY OF GOLD) BECAME KNOWN AS LUANG (GREAT OR ROYAL) PHABANG (PRABANG)

ADDRESS: LAOS (MAP 5, L6)

HEIGHT: 287M

POPULATION: 26,000

Encircled by mountains and situated at the confluence of the Khan and Mekong Rivers, the city's stunning mix of gleaming temple roofs, crumbling French provincial architecture and multiethnic inhabitants is enthralling.

ANATOMY

Luang Prabang is dominated by Phu Si, a large hill near the middle of the peninsula formed by the confluence of the two rivers. Most of the longer roadways through Luang Prabang parallel the river. Shorter roads – once mere footpaths – bisect the larger roads and lead to the riverbanks, serving as dividing lines between different villages. Most of the historic temples are located between Phu Si and the Mekong, while the trading district lies to the south of the hill. The airport, speedboat landing and northern bus terminal are all northeast of the city, while the southern bus terminal and Sainyabuli terminal are to the southwest. Most of the town is accessible on foot and you can catch *jumbos* (motorised three-wheeled taxis).

PEOPLE

Lao is the official language, but Lao dialects (closely related to Thai) are also spoken, as are French and English. Sixty percent of the population is Buddhist, with 40% made up of animist and spirit cults.

TYPICAL LUANG PRABANG CITIZEN

Laid-back, relaxed, cruisey, slow paced, serene, unfussed and easy-going, the locals commonly express the notion that 'too much work is bad for your brain' and often say they feel sorry for people who 'think too much'. They avoid any undue psychological stress, choosing not to participate in any activity, whether work or play, unless it contains an element of *múan* (fun).

DEFINING EXPERIENCE

A morning spent playing *kátâw* (a game with a cane ball) with the locals, cruising through scenic villages on a motorcycle to the stunning Tat Kuang Si waterfalls and indulging in a soothing massage at the Lao Red Cross, before enjoying the tasteful chinoiserie décor and a sumptuous dinner of Lao, Thai and Pacific Rim cuisine at one of Luang Prabang's best restaurants, the Apsara.

STRENGTHS

- ◢ Gilded temple roofs
- ◢ Multiethnic marketplaces
- ◢ The ubiquitous Beer Lao
- ◢ Charming French colonial architecture
- ◢ The famous Pak Ou caves, crammed with images of the Buddha in all styles and sizes
- ◢ The wide, many-tiered waterfall of Tat Kuang Si, tumbling over limestone formations into a series of cool, turquoise pools
- ◢ Peaceful Buddhist traditions
- ◢ Lao women's more-or-less equal status in the workforce, inheritance, land ownership and so on
- ◢ Low cost of living/lazing
- ◢ Picturesque riverside setting
- ◢ The quaint Royal Palace Museum
- ◢ Trekking, rafting and cycling

WEAKNESSES

- ◢ Smoke from slash-and-burn agriculture in the surrounding mountains, causing red, watery eyes and breathing difficulties
- ◢ Crack-of-dawn roosters
- ◢ The high number of serious speedboat accidents, including fatalities, on the rivers

GOLD STAR

The traditional herbal sauna and/or hour-long Swedish-Lao massage at the Lao Red Cross

CITYSPEAK

- ◢ The calibre of competitors at boxing and Lao kick-boxing matches

STARRING ROLE IN...

- ◢ Short story 'The Boatman's Gift' by Pamela Michael
- ◢ *Het Bun Dai Bun: Laos Sacred Rituals of Luang Prabang* by Hans Georg Berger

IMPORT

- ◢ Theravada Buddhism
- ◢ French bread and pastries
- ◢ UXO (unexploded ordnance), which litters northeastern Laos and kills around 130 people each year
- ◢ *Nâm pạa* (a thin sauce of fermented anchovies from Thailand)
- ◢ Chinese and Vietnamese food

EXPORT

- ◢ Poached animals
- ◢ Teak and other hardwoods
- ◢ Garments
- ◢ Wood products
- ◢ Coffee
- ◢ Electricity
- ◢ Tin

SEE Wat Xieng Thong, Luang Prabang's most magnificent temple.

EAT *phák nâm* (a delicious watercress that's unique to Luang Prabang) and *khào nïaw* (the ubiquitous sticky rice).

DRINK *khào kam* – a local red, sweet, slightly fizzy wine made from sticky rice.

DO a walking tour around Luang Prabang's northeastern quarter to take in most of the historic attractions and sightseeing spots.

WATCH the boat races during Bun Awk Phansa (the End of the Rains Retreat) in October.

WATCH local performers put on a show that includes a *bqasïi* (spirit-blessing) ceremony, traditional dance and folk music at the Royal Theatre.

BUY beautiful handmade *săa* (mulberry bark) paper, naturally dyed house-woven Lao silk and cotton, handcrafted silverware, silk-lined cushions and embroidered rice mats.

AFTER DARK join a young Lao crowd dancing to bands playing Lao and Thai pop or DJs spinning rap and hip-hop in the cavernous club of Dao Fah.

URBAN MYTH

In the Royal Palace Museum (Ho Kham), a Buddha statue cast of a gold, silver and bronze alloy stands 83cm tall and is said to weigh 53.4kg. According to legend, the image was cast around the 1st century AD in Sri Lanka and later presented to Khmer King Phaya Sirichantha, who in turn gave it to King Fa Ngum in 1359 as a Buddhist legitimiser of Lao sovereignty. The Siamese twice carried off the image to Thailand (in 1779 and 1827) but it was finally restored to Lao hands by King Mongkut (Rama IV) in 1867. Persistent rumours claim that the image on display is a copy and that the original is stored in a vault either in Vientiane or Moscow. The 'real' one supposedly features a bit of gold leaf over the eyes and a hole drilled through one ankle.

GOTCHA! A CHEEKY CHILD PICKS A WATER FIGHT DURING CELEBRATIONS FOR THE LAO NEW YEAR.
Photographer: Chris Sattlberger (1)

A NOVICE MONK WITH A BIG GRIN TELLS YOU WHAT THE WORD IS.
Photographer: Jamie Marshall (2)

ANOTHER HEAVENLY DAY AT WAT XIENG THONG, LUANG PRABANG'S MOST FAMOUS TEMPLE.
Photographer: Bill Wassman (3)

ENTHUSIASTS WATCH A NIGHT MATCH OF PALENQUE, A POPULAR BOWLING GAME SIMILAR TO BOULES.
Photographer: Peter William Thornton (4)

Seattle 055

VITAL STATISTICS

NAME: SEATTLE

NICKNAME: THE PACIFIC NORTHWEST'S EMERALD CITY

DATE OF BIRTH: 1851; WHEN NEW YORKERS ARTHUR AND DAVID DENNY LED A GROUP OF SETTLERS HERE

ADDRESS: USA (MAP 1, G8)

HEIGHT: 38M

SIZE: 85 SQ KM

POPULATION: 571,900

SUITED UP, A KAYAKER PREPARES FOR A PADDLE ON PORTAGE BAY.
Photographer: Lawrence Worcester (1)

Mother of Microsoft, Nirvana and Starbucks, Seattle has stepped out of the limelight since the dot-com boom to enjoy a cornucopia of outdoor activities and a varied cultural scene.

ANATOMY

Seattle is stunningly sandwiched between the snowcapped Olympic Range to the west and the Cascade volcanoes, including towering Mt Rainier, to the south and east. The city is surrounded by water with Lake Washington to the east, Puget Sound to the west, and Lake Union and the Lake Washington Ship Canal slicing through the city. Downtown Seattle is fairly compact and contains Pike Place Market, Pioneer Sq and the Waterfront. The Space Needle is in Seattle Center, just north of downtown. Adjoining Seattle Center is the attractive, red-brick, residential Queen Anne area. The U district, home to the University of Washington, is on the northern side of Lake Union. Metro Transit buses blanket the metropolitan area.

PEOPLE

Almost three-quarters of Seattle's population are white. The rest are Asian-American, African-American, Hispanic and Native American (in decreasing numerical order). After San Francisco, Seattle has the smallest percentage of children of any large American city.

TYPICAL SEATTLEITE

Seattleites are laid-back and dress casually, even for the office. However, long hours and high pressure are the norm and people tapping on their WiFi-enabled laptops in coffee shops are a common sight. They like to party and bars are full pretty much all of the time. As well as drinking, book readings are popular. Seattleites are politically engaged and care about their environment. Outdoor activities are big news and it's not unusual for people to leave work early to head to the mountains for some skiing or hiking. Even if it's raining (and Seattleites swear it's more of a drizzle), you're bound to see them outside.

DEFINING EXPERIENCE

Zooming up to the top of the Space Needle for views of the Olympic and Cascade Mountains, the water and the city, then grabbing a tall, skinny, hazelnut latte in Pioneer Sq, before taking a walk in Discovery Park.

STRENGTHS

- Outdoor activities on tap
- Discovery Park
- Lakeside mega homes
- Opening Day of Yacht Season
- Pike Place Market
- Pioneer Sq
- The Waterfront
- Dim sum in the International District
- High salaries for tech types
- Profusion of vegan and vegetarian restaurants
- Easy recycling
- The Seattle Men's Chorus (180 gay members)
- Public art in Fremont
- Pacific Northwest Ballet
- The Space Needle
- Brewpubs
- Strong, tasty, ubiquitous coffee
- Skiing at nearby Whistler

WEAKNESSES

- Rain – and lots of it
- Traffic snarls
- Racial segregation
- Climbing house prices
- Struggling public transport

GOLD STAR

Coffee – Starbucks takes over the world but the coffee is good.

CITYSPEAK

- Politics and US foreign policy
- Microsoft's antitrust issues
- The Seattle Mariners baseball team

STARRING ROLE IN...

- *Sleepless in Seattle* (1993)
- *Singles* (1992)
- *Say Anything* (1989)
- *Snow Falling on Cedars* by David Guterson
- *Frasier* (1993–)

IMPORT

- Tech-savvy entrepreneurs (during the dot-com heyday)
- Software engineers
- Gary Larson, creator of *Far Side*
- Late 19th-century gold prospectors
- Novelist Tom Robbins

EXPORT

- Starbucks
- Nirvana
- Bill Gates, Paul Allen and Microsoft
- Amazon.com
- Boeing
- Adobe
- Savage Love sex-advice column
- Biotechnology
- Timber
- Jimi Hendrix
- Grunge (in the '80s and '90s)
- Pearl Jam
- Sherman Alexie
- Blown-glass sculptures

SEE market traders playing catch with live fish at Pike Place Market.

EAT scrumptious seafood at Belltown neighbourhood favourite Queen City Grill.

DRINK seasonal beers at the spacious Elysian Brewing Company on Capitol Hill.

DO take advantage of all that water and try windsurfing on Lake Washington.

WATCH hydroplane races, an airshow, a carnival and the arrival of a naval fleet at Seafair.

BUY weird and wonderful music from the knowledgeable owners at Wall of Sound.

AFTER DARK attend a reading at Seattle's favourite bookstore, Eliot Book Company.

URBAN MYTH

The city that gave birth to Starbucks is understandably obsessed with coffee. But ordering a cup of the black stuff in Seattle can be a minefield. If you just want a cup of regular coffee, ignore the surprised look of the barista and ask for a 'large drip'. When ordering your cappuccino consider whether you would like more foam than liquid ('dry') or the reverse ('wet'). Feel free to request the temperature of your coffee (though not in actual degrees). If the server queries 'room?' when you order, he's asking if you would like to add cream to your cup (we're still talking about coffee). Other terms should be familiar to the millions of regular Starbucks customers.

THE SUN SETS BEHIND THE MONUMENTAL MARKET SIGN AT PIKE PLACE.
Photographer: Lawrence Worcester (2)

CARNIVAL RIDES WHIRLING AND SWOOPING BENEATH THE SPACE NEEDLE, SEATTLE'S SIGNATURE ICON.
Photographer: Richard Cummins (3)

SHOPFRONT DETAIL OF ONE OF SEATTLE'S MANY GROOVY CAFÉS.
Photographer: Lawrence Worcester (4)

BEFORE HITTING TOWN, A WOMAN TAKES TIME OUT FOR ESSENTIAL HAIR CARE AT A BEAUTY SALON IN THE CITY CENTRE.
Photographer: Mark Henley (1)

Phnom Penh
056

VITAL STATISTICS

NAME: PHNOM PENH

NICKNAME: PENH

DATE OF BIRTH: 1430s; ANGKOR WAS ABANDONED AND PHNOM PENH WAS CHOSEN AS THE SITE OF THE NEW CAMBODIAN CAPITAL

ADDRESS: CAMBODIA (MAP 5, M9)

HEIGHT: 12M

SIZE: 290 SQ KM

POPULATION: 1.2 MILLION

At times beautiful and beguiling, at times chaotic and charmless, Phnom Penh is a crossroads of Asia's past and present, a city of extremes of poverty and excess, but one that never fails to captivate the visitor.

ANATOMY

Many of the city's most popular restaurants and bars are located along Sisowath Quay, which hugs Tonlé Sap river. The major boulevards of Phnom Penh run north–south, including Samdech Sothearos Blvd near the riverfront, which passes the Royal Palace, Silver Pagoda and National Assembly building. Most buses, taxis and pick-ups arrive in the centre of town around Psar Thmei. The train station is just a couple of blocks northwest of here.

PEOPLE

At first glance, Cambodia appears to be a nation full of shiny, happy people, but scratch the surface and you'll hear stories of endless personal tragedy, of dead brothers, mothers and babies, from which most Cambodians have never had the chance to recover. The nation's hellish years of the Khmer Rouge left a people profoundly shocked, suffering inside, stoical on the outside.

TYPICAL PHNOM PENHOIS

Older Phnom Penhois place family, faith and food at the centre of life, remembering a time when families were destroyed, food was scarce and faith got them through the nightmare that was the Khmer Rouge. The younger generation, however, are creating plenty of feisty friction in Phnom Penh. The rebellious teens, brought up in a postconflict, post-Communist period of relative freedom, dress as they like, date whom they choose and hit the town until all hours.

DEFINING EXPERIENCE

Strolling along the dawn-lit riverfront to see the mass t'ai chi and aerobics sessions, taking in the dazzling treasures of the Silver Pagoda at the Royal Palace and the wondrous Khmer sculpture at the National Museum, shopping for treasures at Psar Tuol Tom Pong, listening to soothing jazz, G&T in hand, at the Foreign Correspondents Club, cruising the Mekong at sunset then hitting the dance floor at the heaving Heart.

STRENGTHS

- The riverfront, lined with swaying palms and billowing flags
- The mighty Mekong
- 5000 silver floor tiles at the Silver Pagoda
- Art Deco Psar Thmei, Phnom Penh's central market
- Great nightlife and restaurants
- French colonial architecture
- Rubies wine bar
- Heart of Darkness nightclub
- Foreign Correspondents Club
- Wats (temples) galore
- Wandering monks in saffron robes carrying alms bowls
- Go-carting at Kambol F1 Go-carts
- Massages by blind masseurs at Seeing Hands Massage
- Phnom Penh Water Park on a stinking hot day
- Chaul Chnam (Khmer New Year), when the capital grinds to a halt for a massive celebration, with a lot of water and talc being thrown about
- Bon Om Tuk (Water Festival), when Tonlé Sap river comes alive with boat races and up to two million people flood the capital for fun and frolics

WEAKNESSES

- Overzealous bodyguards of the young elite in the city's clubs
- Risk of robbery
- Police fines for traffic violations
- Poverty
- Women currently make up just 10.9% of legislators in Parliament, even though they make up 56% of the voters
- The highest rate of HIV infection in the whole of Southeast Asia
- Air pollution

GOLD STAR

The Tuol Sleng Museum, a savage reminder of Cambodia's tragic past, and the Killing Fields of Choeung Ek, where prisoners from Security Prison 21 were taken for execution – a grim experience, but essential for understanding just how far Cambodia has come in the intervening years.

CITYSPEAK

- What time to meet at the karaoke bar

STARRING ROLE IN...

- *City of Ghosts* (2002)
- *One Night After the War* (1997)
- *Bophana, a Cambodian Tragedy* (1996)
- *S21 The Khmer Rouge Killing Machine* (2003)
- *The Killing Fields* (1985)

IMPORT

- Beer Lao
- Aid workers
- International films, shown at the Phnom Penh International Film Festival
- US-influenced Khmer pop music

EXPORT

- Rainforest timber
- Rubber

SEE an impressive traditional shadow-puppet performance at Sovanna Phum Arts Association.

EAT the closest thing to a Cambodian national dish, *amoc* (baked fish wrapped in banana leaf with coconut, lemongrass and chilli) – or if you're feeling brave, try eating crickets, duck foetus, durian, *prahoc* (fermented fish paste) or spiders from stalls around local night markets.

DRINK the very cheap and tasty Angkor beer, and make sure it's on the rocks!

DO jump on the back of a *moto* (small motorcycle) and zoom around the city.

WATCH the passing parade, including elephants, beggars, *moto* and *cyclo* (pedicab) drivers and occasionally the king, from the balcony of the sublimely relaxing Foreign Correspondents Club.

BUY handicrafts and textiles from shops raising money for projects to assist disadvantaged Cambodians.

AFTER DARK brave the happening Heart of Darkness, the place to be in Phnom Penh come midnight.

URBAN MYTH

Legend has it that the city of Phnom Penh was founded when an old woman named Penh found four images of the Buddha that had come to rest on the banks of the Mekong River. She housed them on a nearby hill, and the town that grew up here came to be known as Phnom Penh (Hill of Penh).

CHILDREN ESCAPE THE MIDDAY SUN IN THE COOL WATERS OF TONLÉ SAP RIVER.
Photographer: Nick Ray (2)

MOTORCYCLES BUZZ ALONG SAMDECH SOTHEAROS BLVD IN FRONT OF CHAN CHAYA PAVILION AT THE ENTRANCE TO THE ROYAL PALACE.
Photographer: Richard I'Anson (3)

ON THE EDGE OF THE CITY, WORKERS HARVEST RICE UNDER A RAINY SKY.
Photographer: David Alan Harvey (4)

St Petersburg

057

VITAL STATISTICS

NAME: ST PETERSBURG

NICKNAME: PETER; THE NORTHERN CAPITAL; VENICE OF THE NORTH

DATE OF BIRTH: 1703; WHEN PETER THE GREAT FOUNDED THE CITY AS RUSSIA'S 'WINDOW ON EUROPE'

ADDRESS: RUSSIA (MAP 3, S2)

HEIGHT: 4M

SIZE: 600 SQ KM

POPULATION: 4.7 MILLION

Hands down Russia's most stunning city, St Petersburg was built on a bog just three centuries ago, and has been relentlessly honed over 200 years to become one of Europe's most breathtaking cities.

ANATOMY

Laid out over 44 islands on the delta of the wide Neva River, St Petersburg is a city of water (and ice for about six months of the year). People zip under the rivers and canals on the super-efficient metro, and slightly less efficiently over them by bus, car, tram and trolleybus. The city centre is focused on Palace Sq and the Winter Palace, as well as the vast central boulevard, Nevsky Prospekt.

PEOPLE

The very homogeneous local population is almost entirely Russian, although there are significant Caucasian, Central Asian and Ukrainian minorities. There's also a large foreign community living and working in the city.

TYPICAL PETERSBURGER

Petersburgers are snobs, there's no other way of saying it. Polite, kind, welcoming snobs, but snobs nonetheless. Moscow, with its heady capitalism and fathomless size just strikes locals here as monstrous and best left to the 'big village' as they like to call their rival city. The Northern Capital is a city of culture and locals spend much of their time (or so they'd have you believe) visiting the stellar artistic entertainment on offer – from ballet at the Mariinsky Theatre to drama at the Maly Theatre.

DEFINING EXPERIENCE

Wandering along the Neva embankment, beer in hand, during the White Nights in late June, the sun dipping below the horizon but never far enough for it to get properly dark, and watching the vast bridges raised to allow boats to pass through the river delta into the Baltic Sea.

STRENGTHS

- The city never sleeps, especially in summer
- Every corner reveals breathtaking beauty
- The metro is super-fast and rather incredible looking
- Fantastic food and drink
- Every car is potentially a taxi (just hold your arm out and see them stop)

WEAKNESSES

- Insufficient public transport
- Collapsing/neglected buildings
- The foreigner pricing system (Russians usually pay up to 90% less for museums, the theatre and ballet)
- Drunks
- The general surfeit of men in uniform
- Nevsky Prospekt is ridiculously long and you are always at the wrong end!

GOLD STAR

The view downriver from the Troitsky Most, with the Winter Palace to one side, the magnificent Peter and Paul Fortress to the other and the Strelka of Vasilevsky Island straight ahead, is unforgettable.

CITYSPEAK

- Will the new Mariinsky Theatre be a success or a stupendous miscalculation?
- The latest controversial decisions of pro-Putin city governor Valentina Matvienko
- The times for the bridges going up – those who get caught out find they have a long wait to get home

STARRING ROLE IN...

- *October* (1928)
- *Golden Eye* (1995)
- *Brother* (1997)
- *Russian Ark* (2002)

IMPORT

- BMWs
- Foreign students learning 'pure' Russian
- Fruit and vegetables from the Caucasus
- Italian and French fashion

EXPORT

- Ballerinas
- Fur
- Caviar
- Vodka
- Baltika Beer
- Dostoevsky

SEE the mind-blowing art collections of the Hermitage and the Russian Museum.

EAT gourmet Russian food at the plutocrat's favourite, Onegin.

DRINK cheap Russian champagne with a cheap Russian crowd at Tsynik.

DO take a *banya* (wet steam bath) for the ultimate Russian experience.

WATCH world-class ballet and opera at the Mariinsky Theatre.

BUY the inevitable Russian nesting dolls for your friends.

AFTER DARK hang out at Dacha with the cool kids.

URBAN MYTH

One of St Petersburg's most famous bridges, the Anichkov Bridge, which crosses the Fontanka River on Nevsky Prospekt, is the subject of one of the city's most loved stories. The bridge is embellished on all four corners by elaborate and dramatic statues of rearing horses. A close look at the south-western horse's genitals will reveal that they're in the shape of a man's face. Here the story splits – one version has it that the face is that of the man who cuckolded the artist, while another claims that the features are those of one Napoleon Bonaparte.

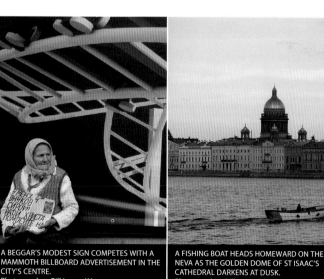

A BEGGAR'S MODEST SIGN COMPETES WITH A MAMMOTH BILLBOARD ADVERTISEMENT IN THE CITY'S CENTRE.
Photographer: Bill Lyons (1)

A FISHING BOAT HEADS HOMEWARD ON THE NEVA AS THE GOLDEN DOME OF ST ISAAC'S CATHEDRAL DARKENS AT DUSK.
Photographer: Bill Lyons (2)

THE WARM SMILES OF RUGGED-UP SOUVENIR VENDORS ON THE WINTRY STREETS OF THE CITY.
Photographer: Bill Lyons (3)

POET VLADIMIR MAYAKOVSKY MUSES ON THE STATE OF POST-SOVIET RUSSIA FROM THE WALL OF MAYAKOVSKY STATION.
Photographer: Bill Lyons (4)

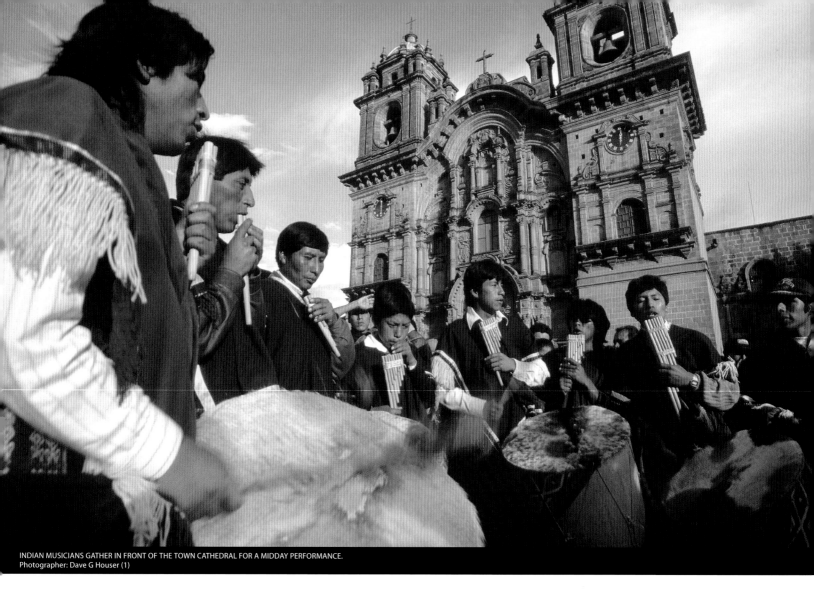

INDIAN MUSICIANS GATHER IN FRONT OF THE TOWN CATHEDRAL FOR A MIDDAY PERFORMANCE.
Photographer: Dave G Houser (1)

At the heart of the once-mighty Inca Empire, the magnetic city of Cuzco lies in exceptionally beautiful Andean surroundings.

ANATOMY

The heart of the city is Plaza de Armas, while nearby Avenida Sol is the main business thoroughfare. Just a few blocks north or east of the plaza are twisting, cobbled streets little changed for centuries. The pedestrian street between Plaza del Tricentenario and Huaynapata gives great views over Plaza de Armas. The central street leading from the northwestern side of the plaza is named Procuradores (tax-collectors' street). Local buses are slow, cheap and crowded.

PEOPLE

As with the rest of Peru, about 45% of Cuzco's population is Indian. A further 37% of the population is mestizo (mixed European and Indian descent), 15% is white (Spanish descent) and the remaining 3% is black, Asian or of other backgrounds. Spanish, Quechua and Aymara are spoken.

TYPICAL CUZQUEÑO

The *cuzqueños* are politically passionate, warm and hospitable, *fútbol*-crazy, unshakably patriotic but highly critical of their political leaders, energetic, never short of a smile, curious, very talkative, entrepreneurial and hard-working people. Cuzco is essentially a bicultural society, with one part containing the mainly white and mestizo middle and upper classes, and the other containing mainly the poor Indian *campesinos* (peasants or country people), many of whom live in poverty.

DEFINING EXPERIENCE

Starting the day at El Buen Pastor, which has a great selection of breads, cakes and wonderful hot chocolate, then exploring the Inca walls of the city, relaxing in the afternoon by cruising the area surrounding Plaza San Blas – Cuzco's artisan quarter, packed with the workshops and showrooms of local craftspeople.

Cuzco 058

VITAL STATISTICS

NAME: CUZCO

NICKNAME: NAVEL OF THE EARTH

DATE OF BIRTH: 12TH CENTURY; WHEN THE INCAS SETTLED IN THE CUZCO AREA

ADDRESS: PERU (MAP 1, M17)

HEIGHT: 3225M

POPULATION: 350,000

LOCALS IN TRADITIONAL DRESS MAKE THEIR WAY DOWN A CHARMING COBBLED STREET HEMMED BY COLONIAL BUILDINGS. Photographer: Krzysztof Dydynski (2)

WITH REVERENTIAL POISE AN INDIAN WOMAN HOLDS OUT AN OFFERING AT THE INTI RAYMI FESTIVAL, PLAZA DE ARMAS. Photographer: Nevada Wier (3)

IN A FRENZY OF MOVEMENT AND COLOUR, DANCERS SPIN UP A STORM AT THE VIRGIN OF CARMEN DAY PROCESSION. Photographer: Pablo Corral Vega (4)

STRENGTHS
- The continent's archaeological capital and oldest continuously inhabited city
- The craft workshops of San Blas
- Centuries of colonial treasures in Cuzco's cathedral
- Massive Inca-built walls
- Proximity to Machu Picchu
- Inti Raymi (Festival of the Sun)
- Fantastic Peruvian food
- Bird life
- Quechua-speaking descendants of the Incas
- 12-sided stone of Hatunrumiyoc

WEAKNESSES
- Treatment of animals
- Legacy of the disappeared
- Altitude sickness
- Strikes

GOLD STAR
Soaking up the amazing history and culture of this magnetic city, whether it be exploring the colonial and religious splendours built on the hefty stone foundations of the Incas or marvelling at the many fascinating and accessible archaeological sites.

CITYSPEAK
- The trial of Vladimiro Montesinos
- The push for disgraced former Peruvian president Alberto Fujimori's return from Tokyo to face murder and corruption charges

STARRING ROLE IN...
- *It Happened in Huayanay* (1981)
- *You Only Live Once* (1992)
- *The Dancer Upstairs* (2002)
- *The Green House* by Mario Vargas Llosa
- *Trilce* by César Vallejo

IMPORT
- *Fútbol* (football)
- *Mestizo* style of art
- Spanish conquistadors
- Colonial architecture
- *Corrida* (bullfighting)
- Roman Catholicism
- Kayaking
- Coups and military dictatorships
- Trance dancing to *techno-cumbia*

EXPORT
- Coffee
- Incan history
- Coca
- Mario Vargas Llosa
- *Pisco* sour
- Eating *cuy* (guinea pig)
- Alpaca woollens
- Silver jewellery with pre-Columbian designs

URBAN MYTH
Ever wondered what *cuzqueños* do to relax instead of whiling away the hours over a game of darts or pool in the local bar? Well next time you're in a local *picantería* (literally 'spicy place') or *quinta* (country houses serving typical Andean food) look out for a strange metal *sapo* (toad) mounted on a large box and surrounded by various other holes and slots. Men will often spend the whole afternoon drinking beer and *chicha* (fermented maize beer) while competing at this old test of skill in which players toss metal disks as close to the toad as possible. Top points are scored for landing it smack in the mouth.

SEE amazing views of Cuzco Valley from the Puca Pucara archaeological site.

EAT the Andean speciality tamales (boiled corn dumplings filled with cheese or meat and wrapped in a banana leaf) for lunch at a traditional *quinta*, such as Quinta Zárate, with its shady garden and good views.

DRINK a *pisco* sour at Los Perros, one of Cuzco's best drinking dens with a funky, laid-back couch bar and a top-notch music collection.

DO explore Plaza de Armas – surrounded by colonial arcades, it's fronted by a large flight of stairs and flanked by the cathedral and the churches of Jesús María and El Triunfo.

WATCH a live folklore music and dance show at Centro Qosqo de Arte Nativo.

BUY beautiful locally made items from a tremendous variety of woollens, textiles, pottery, jewellery and art at Centro Artesanal Cuzco.

AFTER DARK head to Ukuku's Bar for good, sweaty dance fun.

Dubrovnik

059

VITAL STATISTICS

NAME: DUBROVNIK

NICKNAME: THE CITY; THE PEARL OF THE ADRIATIC

DATE OF BIRTH: 7TH CENTURY; WHEN THE RESIDENTS OF THE ROMAN CITY OF EPIDAURUM (SITE OF PRESENT-DAY CAVTAT) FLED TO THE ROCKY ISLET (WHICH THEY DUBBED LAUS), LOCATED AROUND THE SOUTHERN WALLS OF PRESENT-DAY DUBROVNIK

ADDRESS: CROATIA (MAP 3, N13)

HEIGHT: 49M

SIZE: 143 SQ KM

POPULATION: 45,800

The lure of the magical walled city of Dubrovnik, adorned with fine Renaissance carvings and marble-paved streets, has given a boost to the entire region, creating a 'Dubrovnik Riviera' that is welcoming to residents and visitors alike.

ANATOMY

The city extends about 6km from the mouth of the Rijeka River in the west to the Cape of Sveti Jakov in the east and includes the promontory of Lapad, a leafy residential suburb popular with tourists thanks to its rocky beaches, hostel and hotels. The old walled town lies southeast of Lapad at the foot of Srd Hill, halfway between Gruž Harbour and the cape of Sveti Jakov. The entire old town is closed to cars and is divided nearly in half by the wide street of Placa, also referred to as Stradun. Pile Gate is the western entrance to the old town and the eastern gate is Ploče. The city boundaries also include the Elafiti Islands (Šipan, Lopud, Koločep, Olipe, Tajan and Jakljan). Walking or cycling is the best way to get around; public transport in Dubrovnik is pretty well limited to buses and taxis.

PEOPLE

Since the 1991–95 war Dubrovnik's population has been almost exclusively Croat and almost exclusively Catholic, with small minority groups of Serbs, Slovenians, Italians, Czechs and Muslims.

TYPICAL DUBROVNIK CITIZEN

Dubrovnik's residents are generally relaxed and cheerful; their Mediterranean character is evident in everything from their second language (likely to be Italian) to the casual office hours that allow people to enjoy the long hours of sunlight on a beach or in an outdoor café. They are proud of their city and its cultural heritage and generally have strong and passionate views on the 'Homeland' or 'Patriotic' war.

DEFINING EXPERIENCE

Strolling along the walls of the fortified city, taking in the patchwork of honey-coloured roofs, before making your way down the town's pedestrian promenade, Placa, where you'll be overwhelmed by the heady rush of cultural, religious and historic landmarks – not to mention some fantastic cafés.

STRENGTHS

- Dubrovnik's Summer Festival – the most prestigious in Croatia
- The visible results of a dedicated reconstruction effort since the bombs of 1991
- Fortified town walls and gleaming marble streets
- Proximity to the quiet Elafiti Islands and the beautiful beaches of Cavtat
- Vibrant street life

WEAKNESSES

- Located in a zone that is both geologically and politically seismic
- The scramble of private-accommodation owners at the bus station eager for the tourist dollar

GOLD STAR

The wide marble street, Placa, lined with businesses, cafés, churches and palaces, encourages the fusion of commerce, pleasure and faith into a vibrant community life.

CITYSPEAK

- The rise of apartment prices – how far will they climb?
- The new marina – was it worth the money?

STARRING ROLE IN...

- *Casanova* (2005)
- *The Ragusa Theme* by Ann Quinton
- *The Road to Dalmatia* by Christopher Dilke

IMPORT

- Cruise-ship tourists
- Investment in real estate

EXPORT

- Writer Marin Držić
- Poet Ivan Gundulić
- Scientist Ruđer Bošković
- Božidarević, Dobričević and Hamzić, Dubrovnik's finest 15th- and 16th-century artists

SEE the restored roofs of Dubrovnik from a walk around its walls.

EAT the local mussels at Kamenice, a convivial hang-out on one of Dubrovnik's more scenic squares.

DRINK a strongly brewed espresso at the inviting Café Festival, while watching the crowds ambling down Placa.

DO take the kids to the aquarium where they can 'ooh' and 'aah' at the electric rays, conger eels, scorpion fish and seahorses.

WATCH Shakespeare on the Lovrjenac fortress terrace during the Summer Festival.

BUY local products at the city's colourful market.

AFTER DARK head to the city's hippest bar, Troubadour, for Marko's jazz stylings.

URBAN MYTH

Carved in 1417, the Orlando Column in Luža Sq is a depiction of Roland, the legendary medieval knight whose forearm was the official linear measure of the republic – the ell of Dubrovnik, which measures 51.1cm.

LOOKING OVER ROOFTOPS FROM THE CITY WALLS REVEALS AN ORANGE THEME.
Photographer: Richard I'Anson (1)

THE CHURCH OF ST SAVIOUR'S STEEPLE TOWERS OVER THE PLAZA THAT ALSO, COINCIDENTALLY, BEARS HIS NAME.
Photographer: Richard I'Anson (2)

A SOLITARY PRIEST WENDS HIS WAY PAST THE ARCH OF THE FRANCISCAN MONASTERY.
Photographer: Richard I'Anson (3)

A BELLY-DANCER CREATES AN ARCH OF HER OWN AT THE TROUBADOUR CAFÉ AND BAR.
Photographer: Richard I'Anson (4)

Delhi 060

VITAL STATISTICS

NAME: DELHI

DATE OF BIRTH: 500 BC; HISTORICAL EVIDENCE INDICATES SETTLEMENT AT ABOUT THIS TIME; THE BRITISH MADE DELHI THE CAPITAL IN 1911

ADDRESS: INDIA (MAP 5, D2)

HEIGHT: 218M

SIZE: 1483 SQ KM

POPULATION: 12.8 MILLION

Don't let your first impressions of Delhi stick like a sacred cow in a traffic jam: get behind the madcap façade and discover the inner peace of a city rich with culture, architecture and human diversity, deep with history and totally addictive to epicureans.

ANATOMY

In Old Delhi there's the main Inter State Bus Terminal (ISBT), and to the south, the New Delhi train station. Near the station is Paharganj, packed with cheap accommodation and acting as a sort of buffer zone between the old and new cities. New Delhi can be broken into the business and residential areas around Connaught P1 (the city's core) and the government areas around Rajpath to the south. Running south from Connaught P1 is Janpath, which has the tourist office, hotels and a shopping strip. Dotted around are all the big tourist sights and enough crazy local flavour to keep you occupied while you're stuck in the congestion. Take your choice of buses, auto-rickshaws, motorised rickshaws or taxis to get around.

PEOPLE

Due to Delhi's extreme cultural diversity, very few city residents can lay claim to being 'real' Delhi-wallahs. Most of the population of New Delhi comprises Hindu-Punjabi families originally from Lahore, with a constant influx of new residents. The main languages spoken in Delhi are Hindi, English and Punjabi. After the violent Partition (1947), the largely Muslim city became mostly Hindu.

TYPICAL DELHI-WALLAH

Shrewd, wily, passionate and resourceful, the typical Delhi citizen is generally tolerant of religion and the lack of personal space. They are quite entrepreneurial. Arranged marriages are still the norm, though in Delhi more residents marry for love than ever before. Delhi-wallahs share a fondness for great food, good cricket and a big shindig, with some sort of festival to be found round every corner.

DEFINING EXPERIENCE

Rambling around Old Delhi's historic Red Fort and Jama Masjid before diving into the old city's rambunctious bazaars and recuperating later on in the serene surrounds of Humayun's Tomb.

STRENGTHS

- Chandni Chowk bazaar
- The Red Fort
- Cheap, delicious cuisine
- Fatepuri Mosque
- Humayun's Tomb
- Behemoth bazaars
- Jama Masjid
- Qutb Minar
- Coronation Durbar site
- Raj Ghat
- Mysticism
- Shalimar Bagh
- Spice Market (on Khari Baoli)

WEAKNESSES

- Scams
- Touts
- Pollution
- Extreme traffic congestion
- Crooked taxi-wallahs
- Stench
- Uproar
- Fumes
- Unscrupulous travel agents
- Poverty

GOLD STAR

Delhi's beguiling charm – lose yourself while unwinding the secrets of the city's Mughal past in the labyrinthine streets of Old Delhi before emerging into the wide open spaces of imperial New Delhi with its generous leafy avenues.

CITYSPEAK

- It's a monkey! It's a man! It's the Delhi 'Monkey-Man'! – whatever it is, Delhi's supposed Monkey-Man' is freaking out residents with his simian-like antics
- Sustaining Delhi's extraordinary population boom

STARRING ROLE IN...

- *Monsoon Wedding* (2001)
- *The Guru* (2002)
- *American Daylight* (2004)

IMPORT

- India's intelligentsia
- 'New' Delhi (courtesy of the British Raj)
- Punjabis
- Pakistanis
- A 50% increase in population in the past decade
- KFC
- McDonald's

EXPORT

- Exquisite Bengali and Punjabi cuisines
- Mukesh Chandra Mathur
- Garments
- MF Hussain
- Textiles
- Mohammad Adil
- Crockery and silverware
- Handicrafts
- IT-enabled services (and staff)
- Spices and incense

SEE India's largest mosque, the awe-inspiring Jama Masjid, the final architectural extravagance of Shah Jahan.

EAT fat, syrupy *jalebis* (fried, sweet 'squiggles') at Jalebiwala, near the Sisganj Gurdwara.

DRINK brutally good Bloody Marys at the Imperial Hotel, as you unwind from haggling hard at the nearby Janpath Market.

DO chill out from the traffic snarls, pesky touts and other vicissitudes of life in the pleasant grounds of Humayun's Tomb, a superb example of early Mughal architecture.

WATCH Bollywood blockbusters at the Imperial Cinema.

BUY eye-popping handicrafts, *agarbathi* (incense), spices and tea from Chandni Chowk, Old Delhi's famous stropping street of bazaars.

AFTER DARK catch the Dances of India at the Parsi Anjuman Hall, a one-hour performance of regional dances that includes *bharatanatyam*, Kathakali and Manipuri.

URBAN MYTH

Popular Hindu mythology claims that Delhi was the site of the fabled city of Indraprastha, which featured in the Mahabharata over 3000 years ago, but historical evidence suggests that the area has been settled for around 2500 years.

PRACTITIONERS OF YOGA RELAX AND CONTORT AT A MORNING CLASS IN LODI GARDENS.
Photographer: Palani Mohan (1)

HIGHWAY TO DEMOCRACY – RASHTRAPATI BHAVAN (PRESIDENT'S HOUSE) AT DUSK.
Photographer: Palani Mohan (2)

AFTER A HOT DAY, TWO MEN ENJOY A SHOWER AND A JOKE NEAR INDIA GATE.
Photographer: Palani Mohan (3)

A YOUNG BOY OPTS FOR A WINDOW SEAT ON A TRAIN LEAVING OLD DELHI STATION.
Photographer: Palani Mohan (4)

Russia's relentless economic motor and the biggest city in Europe by several million people, brutal, over-whelming, fascinating, Moscow is an absolute must for anyone wanting to see what's happened to Eastern Europe since the end of communism.

ANATOMY

The Moscow River weaves its way through the enormous city, with the Kremlin and Red Sq on the northern bank. The centre is defined by the enormous garden ring road around which you'll find many of the city's most important buildings. Controversial Mayor Luzhkov is a big fan of modern buildings and has little or no interest in heritage, leading to a shocking policy of destroying any building getting in the way of more high-rise apartment blocks or mega casinos for Moscow's new rich.

PEOPLE

With nearly three million unregistered inhabitants from elsewhere in Russia, it's hard to give an accurate breakdown of who lives here, but the city is fairly homogeneously Russian (and unlike other large European cities, it's almost entirely white). Despite this, there are significant and well-established groups of Caucasians, Central Asians and Ukrainians, not to mention a huge expat population of mainly businesspeople living and working in the city.

TYPICAL MUSCOVITE

Dour, mordant, sardonic – it's hard to overstate the initial hardness of your average Muscovite and this often skews the perception of locals for anyone here for just a few days. However, break the ice with a Muscovite (as with any Russian) and you'll be shown an entirely new set of characteristics: funny, warm, interested and welcoming.

MOSCOW
061

VITAL STATISTICS

NAME: MOSCOW

NICKNAME: THE THIRD ROME

DATE OF BIRTH: 1147; THE CITY WAS FIRST MENTIONED IN THE HISTORIC CHRONICLES WHEN PRINCE YURY DOLGORUKY INVITED HIS ALLIES TO A BANQUET THERE

ADDRESS: RUSSIA (MAP 3, U5)

HEIGHT: 156M

SIZE: 1035 SQ KM

POPULATION: 9 MILLION

A TRAIN PULLS INTO A REFINED METRO STATION OF CHANDELIERS AND DECORATIVE ARCHES.
Photographer: Kim Steele (1)

DEFINING EXPERIENCE

Red Sq in the snow, with flurries around the domes of St Basil's, soldiers goose-stepping around Lenin's pyramidal mausoleum, and escaping in the warmth of a side-street bar for some warming borscht.

STRENGTHS

- The super-efficient and aesthetically impressive Moscow metro
- The city's enormous architectural wealth (despite the mayor's best efforts)
- The smell of power lingering in the air
- History round every corner

WEAKNESSES

- The weather (snow on the ground for half the year)
- The city's sheer inhuman size
- The vast expense involved in staying here
- The huge gulf between the 'haves' and 'have nots'

GOLD STAR

The Moscow metro. Hands down the best in the world – over 150 stations, used by nine million people a day and breathtakingly efficient (you'll never wait more than two minutes for a train). Moreover, it's a joy to travel on, with elaborate chandelier and marble-clad platforms, socialist realist art and political sculpture to entertain the masses.

CITYSPEAK

- The astonishing scale and speed of building, often forcing residents out of their homes
- Who will replace Putin when he goes?
- The endless traffic jams and hassles from the corrupt traffic police
- Mayor Luzhkov's latest harebrained scheme

STARRING ROLE IN...

- *Irony of Fate* (1975)
- *Moscow Doesn't Believe in Tears* (1979)
- *The Saint* (1997)
- *The Barber of Siberia* (1998)
- *Night Watch* (2004)

IMPORT

- Limousines
- Fruit and vegetables
- Oligarchs arrested through Interpol

EXPORT

- Caviar
- Oil
- Fur
- Oligarchs on the run

SEE the magnificent cathedrals inside the Kremlin.

EAT wonderful Russian and Ukrainian peasant food at Shinok.

DRINK vodka – pretty much every bar or shop has a huge and unusual selection.

DO not miss your chance to see Lenin up close and personal at his mausoleum.

WATCH the offerings at the world-famous (and soon to be renovated) Bolshoi Ballet.

BUY everything and anything in Moscow's commercial heart, the Novy Arbat.

AFTER DARK head to friendly clubs Kitaysky Lyotchik or Propaganda for clubbing without the attitude.

URBAN MYTH

So fascinated with Lenin was Stalin that after Lenin's death he ordered Lenin's brain to be removed and experimented upon to see what made up the pure Communist mind. The experiments were rather fruitless (as you might expect), but Lenin's head was sewn up again and now sits on daily display in Red Sq. He's looking rather green around the gills, but can you blame him? Other cynics suggest that his entire head is made of wax these days anyway.

RED SQUARE, WHERE THE KREMLIN POWERS THE GOVERNMENT AND FACTORIES POWER THE REST OF THE COUNTRY. Photographer: Gerd Ludwig (2)

MUSCOVITES THAW THEMSELVES OUT IN THE STEAMING WATERS OF AN OPEN-AIR THERMAL SWIMMING POOL. Photographer: Liba Taylor (3)

A STUDENT GETS SOME EMERGENCY WARDROBE ASSISTANCE BEFORE FINAL EXAMINATIONS AT THE MOSCOW CIRCUS SCHOOL. Photographer: Bojan Brecelj (4)

Salvador da Bahia

062

VITAL STATISTICS

NAME: SALVADOR DA BAHIA

NICKNAME: BAHIA; SALVADOR; BLACK ROME

DATE OF BIRTH: 1549; WHEN TOMÉ DE SOUZA LANDED ON PRAIA PORTO DA BARRA UNDER PORTUGUESE ROYAL ORDERS TO FOUND BRAZIL'S FIRST CAPITAL

ADDRESS: BRAZIL (MAP 1, Q17)

HEIGHT: 19M

SIZE: 324 SQ KM

POPULATION: 2.4 MILLION

CAUGHT MOMENTARILY AGAINST THE SETTING SUN, A BOY LEAPS INTO THE BAY WHILE HIS FRIENDS QUEUE FOR THEIR TURN.
Photographer: David W Hamilton (1)

A MILITARY POLICEMAN MAKES A CALL FROM A PUBLIC PHONE SHAPED LIKE A *BERIMBAU*, A TRADITIONAL CAPOEIRA INSTRUMENT.
Photographer: Gianni Muratore (2)

TWO CHICKENS RE-ENACT A TIMELESS CLICHÉ IN THE HISTORIC QUARTER OF PELOURINHO.
Photographer: Sylvain Grandadam (3)

SPONTANEOUS DRUMMING AND DANCING EXPLODES IN THE FORMER SLAVE DISTRICT AS A PRELUDE TO *CARNAVAL*.
Photographer: Peter Turnley (4)

Salvador da Bahia is known as the African soul of Brazil: here, the descendants of African slaves have preserved their cultural roots more than anywhere else in the New World. This beautiful city thrives with culinary, religious, musical, dance and martial-art traditions.

ANATOMY

Salvador can be difficult to navigate as there are many one-way, no left-turn streets that wend their way through the hills and valleys. The centre is on the bay side of the peninsula and is divided by a steep bluff in two parts: Cidade Alta (Upper City) and Cidade Baixa (Lower City). The heart of historic Cidade Alta is the Pelourinho (or Pelô), which is also the heart of Salvador's tourism and nightlife. Cidade Baixa contains the Comércio (the city's commercial and financial centre), the ferry terminals and port. Linking Cidade Alta and Cidade Baixa are the historic Elevador Lacerda (four lifts that travel a set of 72m vertical cement shafts in about 20 seconds, shuttling 50,000 passengers daily) and the Plano Inclinado Gonçalves (funicular railway). You can catch buses around town.

PEOPLE

Bahia is Brazil's most Africanised state, and many inhabitants were forcibly brought here as part of the slave trade, while other ethnic groups were lured by the Portuguese to mine for gold. Seventy per cent of the population is Roman Catholic, with a significant proportion either belonging to various cults or practising Indian animism. Portuguese is the official language.

TYPICAL SALVADORENOS

Fun-loving, joyous, sensual and mystical all describe typical Salvadorenos, as does paradoxical. They are spiritual people who devoutly dedicate time to the activities of their church or *terreiro* (place of worship). On Sunday everyone dons something skimpy and heads outdoors to ogle the local eye-candy and, in turn, be ogled.

DEFINING EXPERIENCE

Drinking in a panoramic bay view from the Praça Municipal, then marvelling at the off-kilter icons in the baroque Igreja e Convento São Francisco before attending a Candomblé (an African-American religion, chiefly practised in Brazil) service at a *terreiro* in Casa Branca.

STRENGTHS

- Exciting, exhilarating *carnaval*
- Forbidden dances
- Capoeira
- Churches, churches, churches
- Idyllic white-sand beaches
- Colourful colonial façades
- Warm waters
- Enthusiastic, energetic locals
- Charming cobblestone streets

WEAKNESSES

- Sleazy, dangerous, volatile *carnaval*
- Rampant poverty
- Scams
- Muggings
- Pickpocketing
- Sexual harassment
- Begging
- Dengue fever

GOLD STAR

Mojo – Salvador da Bahia has a culture rich in hypnotic drum beats, fragrant spices, inherent sensuality and *axé* (divine energy that brings good luck).

CITYSPEAK

- Giving money to beggars – a helping hand or exacerbating the problem?
- The rapidly increasing population and the subsequent economic and social problems

STARRING ROLE IN...

- *That's My Face* (2002)
- *Dona Flor e Seus Dois Maridos* (Dona Flor and Her Two Husbands by Jorge Amado; film 1976)
- *Tenda dos Milagres* (1977)
- *Robinson Crusoe* by Daniel Defoe

IMPORT

- The Portuguese
- A rich African culture
- Tourism
- Party-goers
- Catholicism
- European luxury goods

EXPORT

- Petroleum
- Capoeira
- Chemicals
- Sugar
- Author Jorge Amado
- *Carnaval*
- Transport
- Tobacco
- Gold
- Diamonds
- Silver jewellery
- Leather goods
- Handicrafts

SEE city streets from the windows behind the lift (elevator) entrances at the beautifully restored Art Deco Elevador Lacerda.

EAT steaming plates of *bobó de camarão* (shrimp cooked in yucca cream) lowered down to you on a tray from the kitchen above in tiny Dona Chika-ka.

DRINK exquisite cocktails on the open-air patio at popular Cantina da Lua.

DO attend Salvador's raucous *carnaval*, the second largest in Brazil.

WATCH Bahia's beautiful people, skimpy togs and all, on beachside Praia Porto da Barra, bustling with vendors selling everything imaginable along the clear, calm waters.

BUY local handicrafts ranging from embroidery to musical instruments at Mercado Modelo on Praça Cayru.

AFTER DARK a long evening of Candomblé in Casa Branca, Salvador's oldest *terreiro*, is quite an experience.

URBAN MYTH

Forced to build their masters' church, the baroque Igreja e Convento São Francisco, and yet prohibited from practising their own religion, African slave artisans responded through their work: cherubs' faces are distorted, some angels are endowed with huge sex organs, while others appear pregnant.

Beijing 063

VITAL STATISTICS

NAME: BEIJING

NICKNAME: THE NORTHERN CAPITAL

DATE OF BIRTH: 500,000 YEARS AGO; WHEN THE SOUTHERN AREA OF BEIJING WAS INHABITED BY 'PEKING MAN'; THE CITY'S MODERN HISTORY DATES FROM 1045 BC

ADDRESS: CHINA (MAP 1, II10)

HEIGHT: 52M

SIZE: 750 SQ KM

POPULATION: 13.8 MILLION

The sheer size and scale of the capital of the world's most-populous nation is awe-inspiring, and if you look hard enough between the six-lane highways and skyscrapers you'll find fascinating Chinese imperial history dwarfed by everything around it.

ANATOMY

At the heart of the massive conurbation lies Tiananmen Sq and beyond it the vast imperial palace within the Forbidden City. The city's most controversial new building is the new National Theatre (dubbed 'the egg' by locals), just behind the Great Hall of the People and a stone's throw from the Forbidden City. The city is served by a small metro system (being extended for the Olympics) and an extensive bus network, but many visitors will find that the only way to truly get around is by cab.

PEOPLE

Like a magnet, Beijing attracts Chinese seeking their fortunes from all over the country, although the vast majority of the population is made up of Han Chinese speaking *beijinghua* – a dialect of the national standard dialect (Mandarin, or *putonghua*) unique to the capital. There's a big expat community centred on Sanlitun, which is a major nightlife draw and the one truly 24-hour area of town.

TYPICAL BEIJINGER

Beijingers know they live in the cultural, political and psychological centre of China. Unlike their mercurial Hong Kong and Shanghai cousins (whom they dismiss as calculating and stingy respectively), Beijingers are not showy and prefer understatement (as suggested by the city's skyline compared to those of China's two other pre-eminent economic centres). They are also extremely generous and will argue with ferocity over who gets to pay the bill in restaurants.

DEFINING EXPERIENCE

Thundering down one of the city's vast main avenues in a cab and suddenly turning into a side street where, between building sites and vast new structures, you'll be deposited at a medieval Lamasery (monastery), standing quite oblivious to the modernity around it.

STRENGTHS

- Superb food on every corner
- Pirate DVD menus available for you at restaurants while you wait for your food
- The *hutong* (side streets where traditional housing and ways of life continue as ever) give the city a human face
- Fantastic optimism and dynamism

WEAKNESSES

- Smog
- The city's sheer size and unmanageability
- Enormous building works everywhere
- The endless erosion of the *hutong* and the advance of concrete and asphalt

GOLD STAR

Coming across a genuine Beijing duck restaurant in a run-down *hutong*, and having a delicious meal without gawping tour groups present.

CITYSPEAK

- The latest multimillion dollar construction project creating havoc in the capital
- The dire state of CCTV
- The newest and best place to satisfy all your DVD needs
- Sandstorms crashing through the city, smog above it and that humidity…

STARRING ROLE IN…

- *The Last Emperor* (1987)
- *Farewell My Concubine* (1993)
- *The Gate of Heavenly Peace* (1995)
- *Beijing Bicycle* (2001)

IMPORT

- Starbucks
- McDonald's
- Tour groups

EXPORT

- Pirate DVDs
- Political dissidents
- Jade

SEE the astonishing imperial apartments and temples within the Forbidden City.

EAT Beijing duck with plum sauce, knocked back by a Yanjing beer.

DRINK green tea at a traditional teahouse.

DO make the effort to get out of town to a remote stretch of the Great Wall.

WATCH Beijing Opera for an unforgettably Chinese night out.

BUY your Mao Zedong watches at the not-very-Communist gift shop outside his mausoleum.

AFTER DARK head out for a midnight boat ride on magical Houhai Lake.

URBAN MYTH

By his later years, Mao Zedong – champion of the people – had moved himself and his entourage into the Forbidden City, having turned quickly from liberator into Communist emperor. Mao's final years were spent in virtual seclusion, receiving guests in a private chamber he never left and having only one young concubine who could translate his speech into Chinese, so debilitated was he by a rare disease of the nervous system. The preserved body of this deeply contradictory man is on public display in his Tiananmen Sq mausoleum.

CHARMING SILK LANTERNS SWAY IN THE LIGHT BREEZE AT THE PANJIAYUAN MARKET.
Photographer: Andrew J Loiterton (1)

HIGH TEA – A DRAMATIC DEMONSTRATION OF THE ART OF TEA POURING IN LAO SHE TEAHOUSE.
Photographer: Andrew J Loiterton (2)

PENNANT-WIELDING PATRIOTS FLY THE NATIONAL FLAG IN TIANANMEN SQ.
Photographer: Andrew J Loiterton (3)

RECLINING UNDER A RED CANOPY, A RICKSHAW DRIVER TAKES A WELL DESERVED NAP IN NANYAN *HUTONG* DISTRICT.
Photographer: Andrew J Loiterton (4)

MODESTLY DRAPED LADIES SAVOUR THE THERAPEUTIC HEAT OF A CITY SAUNA.
Photographer: Stephanie Maze (1)

Progressively high-tech Helsinki is a fascinating combination of Swedish and Russian influences, an intimate city that is fast becoming one of Europe's hottest destinations, with a strong cultural vein and a nightlife that's the envy of northern Europe.

ANATOMY

Helsinki is built on a peninsula, with links by bridge and ferry to nearby islands. The city centre is built around the main harbor, Eteläsatama. The *kauppatori* (market square) – also known as the fish market – is on the waterfront between the ferry terminals. Further inland, but still within walking distance, are the bus and train stations. The Meilahti area, northwest of the centre, gives you access to the museum island of Seurasaari.

PEOPLE

Most people from Helsinki speak Finnish as their mother tongue, though there's a sizable population of Swedish-speaking Swedish-Finns. Many Finns look very Scandinavian, with blonde hair and blue eyes. Recent immigrants include people from the Baltic States and the former USSR.

TYPICAL HELSINKI CITIZEN

The average Helsinki resident is well educated and reserved yet warm and friendly to visitors, surfs the Net, loves reading and drinks around nine cups of coffee per day. They relish outdoor pursuits, and flee the city for summer cottages around the lakes in July. They possess tremendous resilience and love their saunas.

DEFINING EXPERIENCE

Strolling around the imposing 19th-century Senate Sq and taking in the scene from the steps of the blue-domed Lutheran Chapel, poking around the harbour-side *kauppatori* in search of salmon chowder, ferrying to historic Suomenlinna Island, listening to gospel at the rock-hewn Temppeliaukio Church and partaking in the social ritual of relaxing in a Finnish-style sauna – hitting each other on the back with a bundle of birch twigs to get the circulation going, then rolling around in the snow or taking an invigorating dip in the cold lake before running back to the sauna – then drinking coffee and eating salty food to make up for the perspiration.

Helsinki
064

A MOTHER PUSHES A BABY CARRIAGE THROUGH A WINTRY LANDSCAPE IN FRONT OF THE LUTHERAN CHAPEL.
Photographer: Jodi Cobb (3)

HELLO SAILOR – THREE NAVY LADS WATCH THE PROGRESS OF THE GOOD SHIP *CINDERELLA*.
Photographer: Michael Jenner (2)

ART-LOVERS ENJOY A QUIET CUPPA IN THE AUSTERE ENVIRONS OF THE MUSEUM OF CONTEMPORARY ART.
Photographer: Jonathan Smith (4)

STRENGTHS
- The underground Itäkeskus swimming hall, carved from rock
- Multilingual 'Helsinki Helpers'
- Saunas – anywhere, anytime
- Fascinating museums such as Kiasma and the Ateneum
- Go-karting
- Diverse architecture
- Easy cycling on flat paths and free city bikes
- Helsinki's proximity to Tallinn
- Rambling around the ruins of the mighty fortress on Suomenlinna Island
- Coffee at the Kauppahalli (old market hall)

WEAKNESSES
- Waiting for a taxi in rush hour
- Parking, or attempting to

GOLD STAR
Ferrying out to explore the fortress at Suomenlinna Island and discovering Finland's heritage at the Seurasaari Open-Air Museum.

CITYSPEAK
- Pollution and other environmental issues
- The loss of biodiversity in Finland's native forests
- Is another recession on the cards?
- My best ever sauna…

STARRING ROLE IN...
- *The Man Without a Past* (2002)
- *Kites over Helsinki* (2001)
- *Spy Games* (1999)
- *Night on Earth* (1991)
- *Helsinki Napoli – All Night Long* (1987)
- *Born American* (1986)
- *Billion Dollar Brain* (1967)

IMPORT
- Coffee, and heaps of it
- Russian architecture
- Crude oil
- Natural gas
- Coal
- Nuclear energy

EXPORT
- Nokia mobile phones
- Finlandia vodka
- Leningrad Cowboys
- Formula One driver Mika Hakkinen
- Surf instrumentalists Laika & the Cosmonauts
- Tove Jansson's Moomin books
- The music of composer Jean Sibelius (particularly *Finlandia*)
- Classical musicians from the Sibelius Academy
- Designer Alvar Aalto
- The *Kalevala*, Finland's national epic mythology
- Paper and cardboard products
- Technology and engineering
- Metals

SEE the city from a different perspective by taking a ferry around its outlying islands.

EAT sautéed reindeer and Baltic herring.

DRINK vodka mixed with cranberry, or a beer and sauna combo at Saunabar.

DO a lap of Kaivopuisto Park on rollerblades or a bike, or a lap of a go-kart track.

WATCH and listen to gospel and classical concerts at the underground Temppeliaukio Church.

BUY traditional Sami handicrafts such as a *kuksa* (cup) and woven wall hangings, Moomintroll souvenirs, a 'Savoy' vase designed by Alvar Aalto, woven pine baskets and birdhouses.

AFTER DARK bar-hop around central Helsinki's many terraces, bars and clubs.

URBAN MYTH
On Wednesday nights restaurants are busy, music is playing at all the night-spots, the bars are full – Helsinki-ites are celebrating *pikku viikonloppu* (little weekend).

Kolkata

065

VITAL STATISTICS

NAME: KOLKATA

NICKNAME: CITY OF JOY

DATE OF BIRTH: 1690; WHEN IT WAS FOUNDED AS A TRADING POST FOR THE BRITISH EAST INDIA COMPANY; IT LATER SERVED AS THE CAPITAL OF BRITISH INDIA UNTIL 1912

ADDRESS: INDIA (MAP 5, G5)

HEIGHT: 6M

SIZE: 1036 SQ KM

POPULATION: 13.2 MILLION

A CONTEMPLATIVE RICKSHAW WALLAH WAITS FOR A FARE OUTSIDE VICTORIA MARKET.
Photographer: Tony Wheeler (1)

Kolkata is the centre of Bengali intellectual life and the cultural capital of India – the country's five Nobel Prize winners all come from Kolkata.

ANATOMY

Kolkata sprawls north–south along the eastern bank of the Hooghly River. South of the Howrah Bridge are BBD Bagh (the hub of the CBD, the central business district) and Chowringhee Sts. A new one-way system with streets flowing in different directions depending on the time of day, mean taxis, crowded trolleybuses or the subway (the oldest in Asia) are the way to get around.

PEOPLE

More than 80% of the population is Hindu. Muslims and Christians constitute the largest minorities, but there are also Sikhs, Jains, and Buddhists, and small Jewish and Christian communities.

TYPICAL KOLKATAN

Kolkatans are the poets and artists of India, with a penchant for art and culture and a level of intellectual vitality and political awareness unsurpassed in the rest of the country. No other Indian city can draw the kinds of thronging crowds to book fairs, art exhibitions and concerts. There is a lively trading of polemics on walls, which has led to Kolkata being dubbed the 'city of posters'. Elsewhere in India, the many millions of poor are largely shut out of this cultural life.

DEFINING EXPERIENCE

Soaking up an education at the Indian Museum and popping down to Park St (Mother Teresa Sarani) for a refreshing cappuccino or hot *kati* roll (marinated fillings in bread) and browsing in the Oxford Book Shop, then strolling along the east bank of the Hooghly River, passing several Hooghly Ghats, and finally, heading to the river for a ferry trip across the Hooghly for views of the Hooghly Bridge before dining at Peter Cat, a Kolkata institution.

STRENGTHS

- St Paul's Cathedral
- India Museum
- MP Birla Planetarium
- Asiatic Society
- Academy of Fine Arts
- Graveyard at St John's Church
- Eden Gardens
- Howrah Bridge
- Botanical Gardens

WEAKNESSES

- Traffic jams
- *Bandhs* (strikes), which happen with monotonous regularity
- Flooding

GOLD STAR

The Indian Museum covers an impressive range of subjects, from natural history to modern art. Highlights include a world-class gallery of religious sculptures and a life-size reproduction of the Barhut Gateway, built by Bihari Buddhists in the 2nd century BC. Also interesting – and possibly unique – is the gallery on plants and horticulture. The displays describe the varied uses of all the plants and crops grown in India.

CITYSPEAK

- Rickshaws – an inhuman practice or a necessary livelihood?
- Another strike?
- Road building – will the new flyovers ease congestion?
- Should the Communist Party (Maoist) of India be banned?

STARRING ROLE IN...

- *The Missionary Position: Mother Teresa in Theory and Practice* by Christopher Hitchens
- *Calcutta Chromosome* by Amitav Ghosh
- *City of Joy* by Dominique Lapierre
- *A Suitable Boy* by Vikram Seth

IMPORT

- Hindus from East Bengal at Partition
- Muslims from East Pakistan in the war of 1971
- Marxism
- Chronic labour unrest
- Mother Teresa and the Missionaries of Charity

EXPORT

- Nobel prize–winning author Rabindranath Tagore
- Satyajit Ray
- William Makepeace Thackeray
- Vikram Seth
- Author Amitav Ghosh
- Sri Aurobindo
- Photographer Julia Margaret Cameron
- Nobel prize–winning economist Amartya Sen

SEE a Bengali or foreign art-house film at the Nandan Cinema.

EAT sweets, Kolkata's culinary contribution to India, at a *mishtir dokan* (sweets shop).

DRINK at Cud Corner, where they whip up some of the best curd and lassis in town.

DO catch Kolkata's beautiful young things in their finest at Tantra or Shisha where you can dance and puff on a hookah.

WATCH the crowds stream over the Howrah Bridge and the flower sellers below.

BUY beautifully embroidered clothes and fabrics at the Women's Friendly Society.

AFTER DARK take in a dance-drama performance or Bengali poetry reading at Rabnidra Sadan.

URBAN MYTH

The Black Hole of Calcutta isn't a description of current living conditions. Having established a new trading post in Calcutta (now Kolkata) in 1690, the British expanded their trading activities rapidly, under the apprehensive gaze of the nawab (local ruler). Eventually, the nawab decided that British power had grown far enough. In June 1756 he attacked Calcutta and, having taken the city, locked some 70 British prisoners in a tiny cell. The space was so cramped and airless that by the time the prisoners were released the next morning, 43 had perished, and the cell became infamously known as the 'Black Hole of Calcutta'.

FAMILIES GATHER TO CELEBRATE THE NEW YEAR TOGETHER AT KALIGHAT TEMPLE.
Photographer: Richard I'Anson (2)

CURRY AND CONVERSATION AT THE BUSTLING FOOD MARKET IN FRONT OF THE TIPPU SULTAN MOSQUE.
Photographer: Richard I'Anson (3)

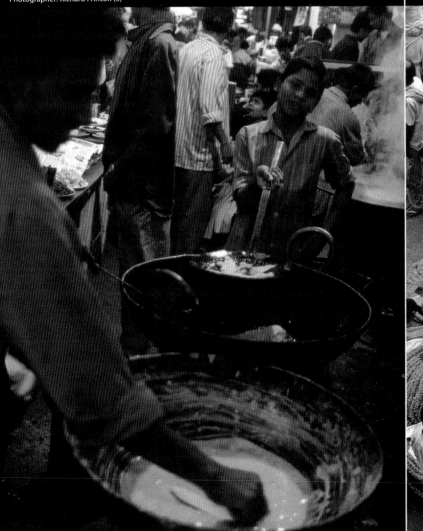

SEEN FROM ABOVE, THE FLOWER MARKET BENEATH HOWRAH BRIDGE BLAZES WITH COLOUR.
Photographer: Richard I'Anson (4)

Santiago de Chile 066

VITAL STATISTICS

NAME: SANTIAGO DE CHILE

NICKNAME: SANTIAGO

DATE OF BIRTH: 1541; FOUNDED BY CONQUISTADOR PEDRO DE VALDIVIA

ADDRESS: CHILE (MAP 1, M20)

HEIGHT: 520M

SIZE: 140 SQ KM

POPULATION: 5.5 MILLION

Santiago de Chile is a modern metropolis with a shiny face, but at the same time, struggling street vendors board city buses to hawk everything from pins to ice cream, and housemaids commute for hours to scrub floors and change nappies in exclusive suburbs.

ANATOMY

Greater Santiago is an immense bowl-shaped city jammed in between the Andes and the coastal cordillera. The most important axis is the east–west thoroughfare Av O'Higgins (popularly known as the Alameda), which in the east becomes Av Providencia and, further east, Av Apoquindo and Av Las Condes. The metro's Línea 1 also follows this main axis, leading 'up' to the residential areas at the foot of the mountains and 'down' in the direction of the coast.

PEOPLE

Santiago's people are mainly of Spanish ancestry, but the Irish and English also made a mark. Other immigrants came from Germany, France, Italy, Croatia and Palestine. Spanish is the official language.

TYPICAL SANTIAGUINO

Santiaguinos tend to be polite, well-dressed and somewhat restrained, despite their predilection for staying out late. They are hard-working, prosperous and business-minded. The lack of a law making divorce legal hasn't kept families together as much as it has increased the acceptance of couples living together and having children out of wedlock. While most Chileans are quite proud of their heritage, there's an obvious lack of patriotism and an increasing level of individualism.

DEFINING EXPERIENCE

Meandering in the city's historic centre, Plaza de Armas, a bustling square flanked by a clutch of colonial and neoclassical buildings and stopping off in one of the busy little arcades flanking the square for an *empanada de queso* (cheese-filled turnover), then heading to Bino, the city's finest museum, or Parque de las Esculturas, an open-air sculpture garden on the banks of the Río Mapocho.

STRENGTHS

- Bellavista's hip, energetic restaurant and club scene
- Quirky architecture in the atmospheric Barrios París Londres, Concha y Toro and Brasil
- Barrio Santa Lucía's laid-back bars and cafés
- Renowned wineries
- Skiing at Portillo
- *The* place to buy Chilean handicrafts
- Proximity to the Andes
- High literacy rate
- Producing Nobel Prize-winning poets
- Cerro San Cristóbal, whose 863m summit is crowned by a dazzling white statue of the Virgin Mary

WEAKNESSES

- Pollution
- History of human-rights violations
- Poor environmental record
- Past dictatorships
- The growing number of pickpockets, especially in the Centro

GOLD STAR

There's something kind of great about being smack in the middle of a metropolis and then looking up and seeing, to your surprise, the second-highest mountain range in the world just a few kilometres away.

CITYSPEAK

- Will Pinochet face the justice he deserves?
- Is Endesa (Chile's largest energy supplier) serious about green energy?

STARRING ROLE IN...

- *Johnny 100 Pesos* (1994)
- *El Chacotero Sentimental* (The Sentimental Teaser, 1999)
- *Taxi Para Tres* (A Cab for Three, 2001)
- *House of the Spirits* by Isabel Allende
- *Passions and Impressions* by Pablo Neruda

IMPORT

- Roman Catholicism
- Deforestation
- Obligatory military service (for all citizens aged 18 to 45)
- Guns
- Spaniards
- Neoclassical architecture
- Fast-food chains
- Ski resorts
- Tree-lined streets
- Bourgeois houses

EXPORT

- Pablo Neruda's poetry
- Copper
- Augusto Pinochet
- Novelist Isabel Allende
- Magic realism (literary genre)
- Wood chips

SEE the Barrio Brasil, a well-preserved traditional neighbourhood whose centrepiece is the relandscaped Plaza Brasil and its quake-damaged, neo-Gothic Basílica del Salvador.

EAT a hearty Chilean lunch at Galindo, a traditional, bohemian place that was one of Neruda's favourites.

DRINK a *pisco* sour while taking in some local theatre, poetry or live music at La Casa en el Aire.

DO catch the glass *ascensor* (lift) up the steep hillside to the beautiful gardens, footpaths and fountains of Cerro Santa Lucía.

WATCH a Chilean-style rodeo at Club de Huasos Gil Letelier.

BUY handicrafts from all over the country, including hand-woven alpaca shawls, Mapuche silver jewellery, lapis lazuli, black pottery and copperware at the artisans' village Centro Artesanal de Los Dominicos.

AFTER DARK head to the Tantra Lounge, where the cool folk go after drinks at Etniko.

URBAN MYTH

Café con piernas (café with legs) attract a male clientele by requiring its young female staff to dress in tight, revealing minidresses. While usually very tame, there does seem to be an ascending scale of risqué-ness; the serious stuff takes place in the cafés with mirror-glass windows (often in arcades), which are pretty much male-only venues. The only things customers can buy are nonalcoholic beer and hot, strong espresso (at least, that's the official story).

IN THE WAR AGAINST AIR POLLUTION, THE PEAK-HOUR SUBWAY SCRAMBLE PROVES TO BE A REAL BATTLE.
Photographer: Enrique Siqués (1)

A RELAXED PACE ON THE COBBLED STREETS OF DOWNTOWN PARÍS LONDRES.
Photographer: Enrique Siqués (2)

A MID-MORNING LULL AT A DESIGNER FURNITURE STORE/CAFÉ IN THE SANTA LUCÍA NEIGHBOURHOOD.
Photographer: Enrique Siqués (3)

THE SKYSCRAPERS OF THE VITACURA NEIGHBOURHOOD ARE DWARFED BY THE CITY'S NATURAL BOUNDARY, THE ANDES.
Photographer: Enrique Siqués (4)

CONCENTRATION ON THE FACE OF A YOUNG TANNER CARRYING A CURED HIDE IN THE MEDINA.
Photographer: Jose Manuel Navia (1)

Fès 067

VITAL STATISTICS
NAME: FÈS
NICKNAME: ATHENS OF AFRICA
DATE OF BIRTH: AD 789; FOUNDED BY IDRIS I
ADDRESS: MOROCCO (MAP 3, D17)
HEIGHT: 378M
SIZE: 16 SQ KM
POPULATION: 1 MILLION

As the first Islamic city in Morocco, Fès is the centre of Morocco's cultural and religious life and its calls to prayer five time a day serve as a strident reminder of this fact.

ANATOMY

Fès is a hotchpotch of twisting streets that are so narrow you can barely raise a decent yawn and stretch. Even smaller alleys venture off the main paths and people brush against people, overloaded donkeys, household goods and bags of wheat at every turn. The medina of Fès el-Bali (Old Fès), which is separated from modern Fès (the Ville Nouvelle) by the ancient walls, is where the city's mosques, shops, crafts, spices, and souq (market) are located along some 9000 streets. It is closed to motorised vehicles, so strap up your donkey.

PEOPLE

The majority of Fassis are Sunni Muslims of Arab, Berber or mixed Arab-Berber lineage. The Arab culture was established when Arabs invaded Morocco in the 7th and 11th centuries. While Arabic is the official language, Berber dialects are widely spoken and French is also seen as the language of business, government and diplomacy. In (much) earlier times, Fès was the scientific and religious centre of Morocco, where Muslims and Christians from Europe came to study.

TYPICAL FASSIS

The young Fassis have cast aside the trappings of their parents' lives, adopting fashions and lifestyles more readily identified with the West. However, many remain without work, and the smart, clean Ville Nouvelle disguises the sad lot of the poorer people living on the periphery. Fès' million or so inhabitants are straining the city to the utmost, and the old city, some experts have warned, is slowly falling apart. Fès continues to act as a barometer of popular sentiment – Morocco's independence movement was born here, and when there are strikes or protests, they are always at their most vociferous in Fès.

DEFINING EXPERIENCE

Walking through one of the medina's seven ancient gateways, then exploring its labyrinthine streets and crumbling grandeur before pulling up a goat-leather stool and tucking into a traditional *tagine*.

STRENGTHS

◢ Luxurious *hammams* (bathhouses)
◢ *Zellij* mosaics (hand-cut tiles arranged in geometric and/or abstract patterns)
◢ Ancient doorways and walls
◢ Islamic architecture

WEAKNESSES

◢ The overwhelming smell from the tanneries – sniffing mint might settle the nerves
◢ The plundering of ancient private homes for their doors and windows for exportation

GOLD STAR

The annual World Sacred Music Festival, which celebrates music from Sufi, Andean, Sephardic, Zulu, Pakistani *ghazal* chants, Renaissance, baroque Christian, spiritual music and American gospel songs.

CITYSPEAK

◢ The charter on the image of women in the media, which relates to the rights of women
◢ Health sector reforms to inject millions into new hospitals

STARRING ROLE IN...

◢ *The Mummy* (1999)
◢ *The Amazing Race 3* (2002)
◢ *Aziz and Itto: A Moroccan Wedding* (1991)
◢ *The Jewel of the Nile* (1985)
◢ *Kundun* (1997)
◢ *The Last Temptation of Christ* (1988)
◢ *This Blinding Absence of Light* by Tahar Ben Jelloun
◢ *Living in Morocco: Design from Casablanca to Marrakesh* by Landt and Lisl Dennis

IMPORT

◢ French
◢ American soft-metal tunes
◢ Henri Matisse
◢ Tunisian stone
◢ Eugene Delacroix

EXPORT

◢ Pottery
◢ Cous cous
◢ The fez (brimless felt hat)
◢ Writer Tahar Ben Jelloun
◢ Hash
◢ Farsi metalwork
◢ Architectural antiques
◢ *Babouches* (pointed slippers)
◢ Goat leather stools
◢ Fiery *harissa* sauce (made from chillies and tomatoes)

SEE the Blue Gate of the Old Fès.

EAT traditional tagines, *pigeon bastila* (a large pigeon pie) and mounds of hand-blended cous cous.

DRINK bladder-bursting amounts of *atay* (mint tea).

DO take a panoramic tour of the city in a taxi.

WATCH the day unfurl from a café in Old Fès.

BUY a traditional Moroccan carpet from Hamid's Carpet Shop.

AFTER DARK be serenaded in the courtyard of La Maison Bleue before eating a sumptuous feast of local fare under superb cedar ceilings.

URBAN MYTH

The hand is seen as a means of warding off the evil eye, which is a prominent theme. The 'hand of Fatima' is seen on everything. The *al-boua* (chameleon) is also thought to have special powers. It's said that if a wife suspects infidelity, she only has to blend chameleon meat or bones in his food and he will certainly never look the other way again. Fearing misfortune of an ethereal kind, throwing the poor creature into a wood-fired oven and walking around it three times might prove useful. If the chameleon explodes, the evil is gone, if it doesn't, best find a stronger solution.

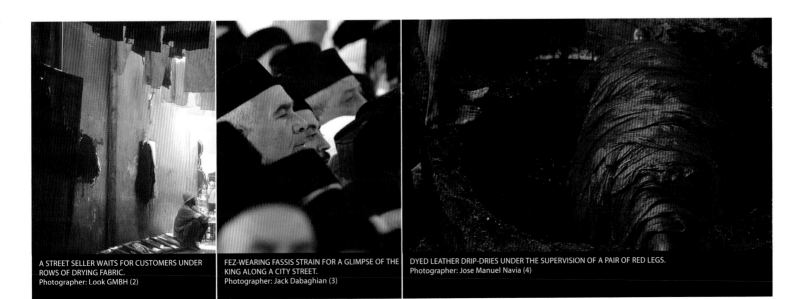

A STREET SELLER WAITS FOR CUSTOMERS UNDER ROWS OF DRYING FABRIC.
Photographer: Look GMBH (2)

FEZ-WEARING FASSIS STRAIN FOR A GLIMPSE OF THE KING ALONG A CITY STREET.
Photographer: Jack Dabaghian (3)

DYED LEATHER DRIP-DRIES UNDER THE SUPERVISION OF A PAIR OF RED LEGS.
Photographer: Jose Manuel Navia (4)

Auckland

068

VITAL STATISTICS

NAME: AUCKLAND

NICKNAME: CITY OF SAILS; *TAMAKI MAKAURAU* (IN MAORI)

DATE OF BIRTH: 1840; WHEN THE SETTLEMENT WAS MADE NEW ZEALAND'S CAPITAL (IT INDECISIVELY LOST THIS STATUS TO WELLINGTON IN 1865), BUT MAORI SETTLEMENT DATES BACK AT LEAST 800 YEARS

ADDRESS: NEW ZEALAND (MAP 1, OO21)

HEIGHT: 26M

SIZE: 502 SQ KM

POPULATION: 1.2 MILLION

With beaches in its backyard and an international gateway to Polynesia, Asia and, if you must, Australia – this is a truly relaxed world city.

ANATOMY

The commercial main street is Queen St stretching from QEII Sq near the waterfront to the hip wining and dining precinct around Karangahape Rd (known as K Rd to most Aucklanders). Get on the bus for posh Ponsonby Rd to the city's west, another hotspot for eating and shopping. A ferry ride across the harbour is Devonport, which is *the* Sunday afternoon spot with B&Bs, galleries and beaches. Public transport consists of buses, trains and ferries.

PEOPLE

With almost a third of the Kiwi population, Auckland has a huge cross-section of people from its traditional Maori communities to more recent Asian arrivals. Indeed, Auckland now has the world's largest concentration of Polynesians, which give the city a unique cultural make-up.

TYPICAL AUCKLANDER

Aucklanders certainly are a diverse lot migrating from Indonesia to Invercargill. 'Jafas', as Aucklanders are called by other Kiwis, have a reputation for being smugly cosmopolitan with the migration from New Zealand's regions to the big smoke triggered by work or cultural life. The longstanding rivalry with Wellington is shrugged off by many Aucklanders who are too busy enjoying their better weather and beaches to care for the windy city to the south.

DEFINING EXPERIENCE

Brunching on K Rd before a harbour sail, catcing a ferry over to Devonport to fossick among the art galleries, cycling up to Takapuna Beach for a well-deserved laze, having a relaxed dinner in one of Ponsonby's more exclusive eateries, and gearing up for a night of clubbing along Queen St.

STRENGTHS

- Harbourside views
- Volcanic hills pocked with *pa* (fortified villages)
- K Rd dining
- Beaches
- Maori culture
- Ponsonby
- Rugby
- Multicultural population of Polynesian and Asian peoples
- Latte bowls
- Stardome Observatory
- Hauraki Gulf Islands

WEAKNESSES

- Buses suffering from privatisation
- Weather
- Rush hour traffic
- Tough walking on hilly streets
- Howick Historical Village
- Sinking of the Rainbow Warrior

GOLD STAR

Yachting – they scored the America's Cup in 1995 and 2000, and the city's yachties are keen to show you why.

CITYSPEAK

- The 'brain drain' to the 'Western Island' (Australia)
- The coffee on K Rd – is it going downhill?
- Real estate prices – are there any harbour-front places left?

STARRING ROLE IN...

- *The Navigator: A Mediaeval Odyssey* (1988)
- *Whale Rider* (2002)
- *Once Were Warriors* (1994)
- *Shortland Street* (since 1992)
- *The Chronicles of Narnia: The Lion, the Witch and the Wardrobe* (2005)
- *An Angel at My Table* (1990)

IMPORT

- The America's Cup
- Over-sized latte bowls
- Polynesian people and culture
- Tim and Neil Finn
- Albert Wendt
- Bic Runga
- Scribe
- Carlos Spencer

EXPORT

- The America's Cup
- *Kina* (edible sea urchin)
- Marmite
- Mareko
- The Datsuns
- Sir Edmund Hillary
- Lucy Lawless (Xena)
- Russell Crowe
- Dave Dobbyn and DD Smash
- Deceptikonz
- Split Enz

SEE the view from Sky Tower.

EAT late-night kumara chips from the White Lady bus on Shortland St.

DRINK a glass of excellent white wine from the Marlborough region, such as Cloudy Bay.

DO the Two Volcanoes walk that takes in dormant Mt Victoria and a stunning panorama.

WATCH a cultural performance at Auckland Museum.

BUY Polynesian hip-hop bootlegs or other crafts from Otara Markets.

AFTER DARK be a doll in Papa Jack's Voodoo Lounge, a hard rock venue complete with skulls.

URBAN MYTH

Irish rock band U2 included a song called 'One Tree Hill' on their *The Joshua Tree* album that many assume was an acknowledgement either of the 'other' One Tree Hill in the UK or the band's appreciation of the spectacular views from the obelisk on Auckland's One Tree Hill. In fact it was a tribute to Greg Carroll, a Maori roadie who worked with the band until his tragic death in 1986. Members of the band accompanied his body back to Auckland and after the funeral dedicated their new album to him. Many U2 fans believe Carroll was buried atop One Tree Hill, but that honour went to Sir John Logan Campbell, known as the father of Auckland who named the hill in 1840.

GOING ON TILT IN WAITEMATA HARBOUR.
Photographer: Fergus Blakiston (1)

THE EXHILARATING LEAP FROM SKY TOWER.
Photographer: Peter Bennetts (2)

CHILLING OUT AT THE MINUS 5 DEGREES BAR, PRINCES WHARF.
Photographer: Peter Bennetts (3)

WARMING UP AT LION ROCK AND PIHA BEACH.
Photographer: Paul Kennedy (4)

The urban hub of the Philippines' 7000 islands, Manila is a megacity of skyscrapers, shantytowns and shopping malls with the ghosts of a Spanish colonial past lurking in the alleyways.

ANATOMY

Manila is huge. The so-called Metro Manila area is a vast district comprising 17 sprawling municipalities. At the centre of it all is the City of Manila, which gazes westward over the ocean. Intramuros is the oldest district in the city, perched on a thin peninsula that juts out into Manila Bay. This was the site of the original Muslim settlement, on top of which the Spanish built their walled fortress. From here you can venture east into the rest of the metropolis on foot or by *Jeepney* (local bus).

PEOPLE

Most Manilans are Catholic, and although the majority belong to the Tagalog ethnic group, Manila has become something of a microcosm of the Philippines ever since internal immigrants from all quarters of the archipelago settled in the city.

TYPICAL MANILAN

Manilans have a reputation for being warm and relaxed but they're never afraid to express their feelings or opinions. And it's hardly surprising. The city has been occupied successively by the Spanish, Americans and Japanese, and residents are well accustomed to struggling for their sense of self and political freedoms. The influence of the West remains strong, yet Manilans have adapted rather than surrendered to the outside world. Some locals speak 'Taglish', a dialect of Tagalog that subsumes elements of English vocabulary. The distinctly Filipino Jollibee restaurants are many times more popular than the imported fast-food chains they originally emulated.

Manila 069

VITAL STATISTICS

NAME: MANILA

NICKNAME: PEARL OF THE ORIENT

DATE OF BIRTH: 1571; WHEN IT WAS FOUNDED BY SPANIARD MIGUEL LOPEZ DE LEGAZPI, ALTHOUGH A MUSLIM SETTLEMENT HAD ALREADY EXISTED ON THE SITE FOR CENTURIES

ADDRESS: PHILIPPINES (MAP 5, R8)

HEIGHT: 14M

SIZE: 38.55 SQ KM

POPULATION: 10 MILLION

A COLOURFUL *JEEPNEY* GRIDLOCK ALONG THE MAIN ROAD AT DIVISORIA MARKET.
Photographer: Greg Elms (1)

DEFINING EXPERIENCE

Paying your respects at the bizarre Chinese Cemetery with its air-conditioned houses for the dead, strolling through the weird and wonderful markets and side streets of Quiapo, Santa Cruz and Binondo, then wandering along the walls of Intramuros in the evening and appreciating the legendary sunset over Manila Bay.

STRENGTHS

- *Jeepneys* – multicoloured local buses reconstructed from ex-US army jeeps
- Chinese Cemetery
- Dr José Rizal – national hero of the Philippines
- Intramuros – the walled Spanish city
- Fast-changing nightlife of the Malate and Ermita areas
- Fantastic clothing off the rack
- Extraordinary markets
- Trendy eateries
- Karaoke

WEAKNESSES

- Shantytowns
- Poverty
- Prostitution
- Traffic
- Stifling heat
- Pollution
- Overpopulation
- Ferdinand Marcos

GOLD STAR

Sunset – geographically Manila is perfectly poised to witness the brilliant sunsets over the bay, and the pollution in the air only enhances the light show!

CITYSPEAK

- The latest political scandal
- Traffic
- Are you up for karaoke tonight?

STARRING ROLE IN...

- *Seed of Contention* (2006)
- *Homecoming* (2003)
- *Too Hot to Handle* (1977)

IMPORT

- Mobile phones – Manilans love them
- Machinery
- Fuel
- Legal systems – from Spain and the US
- Hopeful workers from other parts of the Philippines

EXPORT

- San Miguel beer
- Kitsch religious souvenirs
- Herbal medicines
- *Parols* (traditional lanterns)
- *Barongs* (embroidered men's shirts)
- Electronic goods

SEE Intramuros, the old walled city that guarded Spain's Asian empire.

EAT typical dishes from all over the Philippines at a cheap and cheerful *turo turo* (a fast-food restaurant where patrons point to what they want to order).

DRINK San Miguel beer, the finest in Asia.

DO a tour of the Chinese Cemetery where mausoleums have running water and flush toilets for the deceased.

WATCH the sun set over Manila Bay.

BUY just about anything you can imagine – and much that you'd rather not – at a city market.

AFTER DARK hit the karaoke bars with the rest of Manila.

URBAN MYTH

It's more than likely that before the Japanese General Tomoyuki Yamashita was captured and executed, he organised the burial of masses of gold plundered during WWII. This may have been done when the Philippines seemed a safe, Japanese-held storage spot, or it may have been done in desperate haste as American troops closed in – or perhaps it was a bit of both. The vast majority of this loot was almost certainly dug up years later by one of the nastiest treasure hunters of all time – Ferdinand Marcos. In 1998 a lawsuit was filed against the Marcos estate in an attempt to retrieve some of the plundered and laundered gold. Meanwhile, avaricious enthusiasts still search for the loot that Marcos missed.

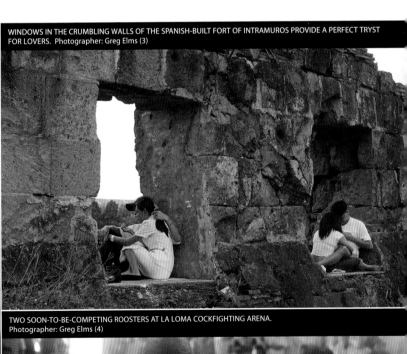

AS DUSK FALLS OVER MANILA BAY A TEENAGE GIRL SHOOTS OFF A QUICK TEXT MESSAGE.
Photographer: Greg Elms (2)

WINDOWS IN THE CRUMBLING WALLS OF THE SPANISH-BUILT FORT OF INTRAMUROS PROVIDE A PERFECT TRYST FOR LOVERS. Photographer: Greg Elms (3)

TWO SOON-TO-BE-COMPETING ROOSTERS AT LA LOMA COCKFIGHTING ARENA.
Photographer: Greg Elms (4)

Puerto Vallarta

070

VITAL STATISTICS

NAME: PUERTO VALLARTA

NICKNAME: PARTY VALLARTA; PV

DATE OF BIRTH: 1851; WHEN THE SÁNCHEZ FAMILY MOVED TO THE AREA FARMERS AND FISHERFOLK SOON FOLLOWED

ADDRESS: MEXICO (MAP 4, A3)

HEIGHT: 2M

SIZE: 5127 SQ KM

POPULATION: 166,000

Formerly a quaint fishing village, Mexico's most picturesque coastal city with its happy-go-lucky vibe and sweet-whispered promise of paradise has become a popular playground for tourists worldwide.

ANATOMY

Set among palm-covered mountains, the languid stretch of white-sand beaches on the Bahía de Banderas (Bay of Flags) coastline and the alluring azure sea, the old town centre is filled with cobblestone streets and traditional red-roofed whitewashed buildings. There are two main thoroughfares and the *malecón* – the main seaside promenade – lined with boutiques, bars, restaurants and nightclubs. The small elongated island of Cuale is downtown, surrounded by the two forks of Río Cuale that run into the nearby ocean. Amid the quaintness of the city are modern luxury hotels and resorts, with their attendant high-rises, sprawling out to the city fringes. While walking is the best way to take in the sights of the hilly city, buses or taxis service the walk-weary, and cars and motorbikes are available for hire; water taxis also operate in the area.

PEOPLE

While there are hundreds of thousands of international visitors to this township in the state of Jalisco every year, the live-in population is predominantly Mexican. They largely belong to the Roman Catholic faith, with around 5% Protestant and a smaller percentage belonging to other religions. Due to tourism, most of the population is bilingual: Spanish and English.

TYPICAL PUERTO VALLARTA CITIZEN

Most Mexicans in this town work in tourism – there really is no other main industry. They are religious. They are often poor. They are mainly young. They have been dubbed by international film crews and travel magazines as 'the friendliest people in the world'. They are keen to preserve their spectacular home from excessive development, but happy to share it with the world.

DEFINING EXPERIENCE

Exploring the coral reefs and underwater caves of pristine Isla Marietas, then re-fuelling at a beachside taco stand before heading out to Café Frankfurt & Biergarten for some icy-cold steins in a beer garden inhabited by fellow revellers and exotic tropical birds.

STRENGTHS

- Very gay friendly
- Tree-top canopy tour
- Great boutique shopping
- Excellent water sports
- The depths of the jungle close by
- Stunning views
- A handful of great fine art galleries
- Casa Kimberley (the house Richard Burton bought for Elizabeth Taylor)
- Swimming with dolphins
- Gorgeous nearby villages
- Beach of the Spirits – one of the most beautiful on the Bahía de Banderas
- Local festivals
- Free daily newspapers
- White-sand beaches
- Star-filled night sky
- Good variety of cosmopolitan restaurants
- Picturesque town
- Friendly locals
- Abundant marine life in the Bahía de Banderas
- Street stalls

WEAKNESSES

- Mega-luxury resorts destroying the view
- Lots of trashed tourists
- Hills
- Hurricane and cyclone risks

GOLD STAR

A living, breathing paradise – every activity you could possibly hope for in a tropical paradise is here by land or by sea: swimming with the dolphins, whale-watching, deep-sea fishing, sailing, windsurfing, bungee-jumping, hiking through tropical rainforest spotting exotic wildlife, horseback riding tours and touring archaeological sites and more.

CITYSPEAK

- Giant luxury mega-resorts taking over the city

STARRING ROLE IN...

- *Kill Bill Vol 2* (2004)
- *Puerto Vallarta Squeeze* (2003)
- *Harvest* (1992)
- *Predator* (1987)
- *Herbie Goes Bananas* (1980)
- *The Domino Principle* (1977)
- *Swashbuckler* (1976)
- *The Night of the Iguana* (1964)

IMPORT

- John Huston
- International film crews
- Fuel

EXPORT

- Textiles
- Beer
- Ceramics
- Gold and silver
- High quality crafts
- Resort wear

SEE the stunning city from the rails of the reproduction Spanish galleon *Marigalantes* – the cruise culminates in a mock pirate attack!

EAT jumbo shrimp while taking in the superb views of the bay at the hillside restaurant El Palomar de los González.

DRINK a strong morning coffee or yummy smoothie at the artsy Café San Angel.

DO try a freshly rolled cigar with a scotch at the Guantanamera Cigar Club.

WATCH a high-spirited performance of the contagious mariachi sounds at Tequlia.

BUY the strangely delicious mango slices seasoned with salt and chilli from the small-cart vendors on the beach.

AFTER DARK show the young things how it's done, with some table-top dancing at Kahlua.

URBAN MYTH

Bahía de Banderas was supposedly formed by an extinct volcano slowly sinking into the ocean. It now has a depth of some 1800m and is home to an impressive variety of marine life – almost every large marine animal is found here, except for sharks. Apparently dolphins mount an antishark patrol at the entrance to the bay, to protect the young dolphins that are born here all year-round.

A MAN WAITS FOR A BUS FROM BEHIND A CURTAIN OF TROPICAL RAIN IN ZONA CENTRO.
Photographer: Anthony Plummer (1)

THE MYSTERIOUS SILHOUETTES OF SERGIO BUSTAMANTE'S SCULPTURE 'IN SEARCH OF REASON' ON THE *MALECÓN* AT SUNRISE. Photographer: Anthony Plummer (2)

LOCALS ENJOY A HEALTHY LUNCH IN THE CHEERFUL SURROUNDINGS OF THE PLANETA VEGETARIANO RESTAURANT.
Photographer: Anthony Plummer (3)

A DOUGHNUT DELIVERY MAN DOES THE ROUNDS OF PLAYA DE LOS MUERTOS BEACH.
wPhotographer: Anthony Plummer (4)

Chiang Mai 071

VITAL STATISTICS

NAME: NOPBURI SI NAKHON PING CHIANG MAI
(SHORTENED TO CHIANG MAI)

NICKNAME: ROSE OF THE NORTH

DATE OF BIRTH: 1296; WHEN THAI KING MENGRAI TOOK
OVER A MON SETTLEMENT TO FOUND CHIANG MAI

ADDRESS: THAILAND (MAP 5, K6)

HEIGHT: 314M

SIZE: 4506 SQ KM

POPULATION: 170,300

SWEAT AND STEELY RESOLVE ON THE FACE OF A JUNIOR KICKBOXER AT A SPORTS CARNIVAL, JUGKHAM KHANATORN SCHOOL.
Photographer: Adam Pretty (1)

TO LAUGH IS DIVINE – YOUNG MONKS AT WAT PRASING TEMPLE.
Photographer: Adam Pretty (2)

SUSPENDED UNDERWEAR ON DISPLAY AT WOROROT MARKET FORM A CHEEKY HANGING MOBILE.
Photographer: Adam Pretty (3)

A RECLINING MOTHER AND CHILD ENJOY SOME TEMPLE TIME AT WAT SUAN DOK.
Photographer: Adam Pretty (4)

Chiang Mai is a small cosmopolitan metropolis with a striking mountain backdrop, over 300 temples, a quaint historical aura and its Thai culture firmly ingrained.

ANATOMY

More than 80% of Chiang Mai is covered by mountains and forests. The old city is surrounded by a moat and parts of the old city walls, which surround most of the city's important temples. Today the city is far larger than its ancient walls suggest and has especially expanded towards the Ping River in the east, the location of the Night Bazaar. Chiang Mai is easy to navigate once you've mastered the system of streets. Get around by flagging down one of the many red *songthaew* (a converted pick-up truck) or by túk-túk (motorised rickshaws).

PEOPLE

Only a small portion of Chiang Mai's population live within the city. Eighty percent are locals by birth, and speak a Thai dialect. People from China, Laos and Myanmar have long traded in Chiang Mai, thanks to its location along the northern region of Southeast Asia. Its Karen, Lahu, Hmong, Lisu, Lua, Akha, Mien and Palong cultures also enliven its heritage.

TYPICAL CHIANG MAIAN

Individual lifestyles in Chiang Mai vary tremendously according to family background and income. A Chiang Maian may work as a cleaner for a higher-income family, a civil servant, or they may be studying at university. High value is placed on education and there are private and international schools for the foreign and local elite. Thai men are expected to shave their heads and don monastic robes at least once in their lives.

DEFINING EXPERIENCE

Watching a puddle of sweat form at your feet as you perform a death-defying yoga pose in the early dawn from a first floor room overlooking the moat and the early traders.

STRENGTHS

- Easy to navigate
- Wats (temples)
- Starting point for Hill tribe treks
- *Mai pen rai* (take it easy) attitude
- Plenty of great food for vegetarians

WEAKNESSES

- Seedy bars lined with girls, girls, girls, some wearing numbers
- Staged hill tribe treks
- Too much to see, not enough time
- Traffic police blocking every corner, adding to the congestion

GOLD STAR

It is said that there are more than 300 temples within the walls of the old city. The wats are breezy and meditative and a reminder of the region's culture beyond the bazaars and go-go bars.

CITYSPEAK

- Traffic jams caused by a police crackdown on motorcyclists not wearing helmets
- Will there be a 15km cable car built along Doi Suthep?

STARRING ROLE IN...

- *Rambo 3* (1988)
- *Operation Dumbo Drop* (1995)
- *Smoking Poppy* by Graham Joyce
- *Fast Eddie's Lucky 7 A Gogo* by David Young
- *The Teachers of Mad Dog Swamp* by Khammaan Khonkhai

IMPORT

- Dunkin' Donuts
- Wikulpanich's Chinese steamed buns
- Exotic Burmese handicrafts
- Hip-hop
- Vespa scooters

EXPORT

- Thai silk
- Elephant art – literally, art made by elephants
- Saffron-clad monks
- Orchids
- Thai cooking classes
- Bamboo saxophones

SEE gold leaf artisans at work at the jungle wat, Ko Tao.

EAT freshly made *tom sam* (green papaya salad) from one of the many street stalls; *kaeo soy* (like laksa but different) in the Muslim quarter; or *kao lam* (sticky rice coconut milk and fried mung beans wrapped into a bamboo pole and roasted over coals) at the Tai Pei gate market.

DRINK long iced coffee from Aroon Rai made with a dark brew and sweetened condensed milk and a bucket of ice, or pull up a stool at a mobile cocktail van and slam back a tequila sunrise.

DO rent a scooter and take in the nearby villages of Bo Sang and get lost on roads with signs only in Thai.

WATCH a night of Muay Thai boxing at the Gawila Boxing Stadium – the highlight is the mounting frenzy of the bookmakers and gamblers alike as the main event draws near.

BUY art from contemporary young artists who converge at the weekly market at the Tai Pei gates.

AFTER DARK wander around the south side of the moat and sample some great street cuisine or fried grasshoppers, whatever floats your goat.

URBAN MYTH

According to legend, the site where Doi Suthep is located was chosen by an elephant after a monk placed half of a Buddha relic on an elephant's back and set it loose. A temple would be built wherever the elephant stopped its pilgrimage. Soon enough, the elephant began to climb a hill and Wat Prathat Doi Suthep was built on that very spot by King Kuna in 1388. Today, the temple is approached by climbing a steep *naga* (serpent) staircase of 304 steps.

A DEVOUT PILGRIM WADES INTO THE RIVER TO PRAY AT SUNRISE.
Photographer: Chris Beall (1)

India's holiest city attracts masses of Hindu pilgrims and visitors to the mighty Ganges to bathe, offer blessings, do yoga, wash clothes, get a massage, play cricket and witness cremations; and to drink in the spectacle of life's vibrancy on the riverbanks.

ANATOMY

The old city of Varanasi is situated along the western bank of the Ganges and extends back from the riverbank ghats in a labyrinth of alleys called *galis* that are too narrow for traffic. The *galis* can be disorienting but the hotels are usually well-signposted and however lost you become, you will eventually land up at a ghat where you can get your bearings. Catch crowed buses or a cycle-rickshaw or autorickshaw.

PEOPLE

As you'd expect, the majority of Varanasi's inhabitants are Hindu. Uttar Pradesh is an important political state and has produced half the country's prime ministers.

TYPICAL VARANASI CITIZEN

Despite Uttar Pradesh's prominent political position, poor governance has not made the citizens of Varanasi's life easy. Economic progress is slight, the erratic electricity supply causes problems and the state's overall literacy rate is low. Varanasi, however, has an excellent university and is a well-respected centre of learning attracting scholars from all over India. Family is important for Indian society and the birth rate is high – it is rare for people in their thirties to be unmarried or childless. Most Hindu marriages are arranged and although dowries are illegal, they are often still supplied, straining finances for the family concerned.

Varanasi

072

VITAL STATISTICS

NAME: VARANASI

NICKNAME: THE ETERNAL CITY; THE CITY OF SHIVA

DATE OF BIRTH: 1400 BC; VARANASI HAS BEEN A CENTRE OF LEARNING AND CIVILISATION SINCE THIS TIME

ADDRESS: INDIA (MAP 5, F4)

HEIGHT: 81M

SIZE: 74 SQ KM

POPULATION: 1.2 MILLION

BEFORE DESCENDING INTO THE WATERS OF THE GANGES A MAN HAS HIS HEAD SHAVED BY A RIVERSIDE BARBER.
Photographer: Chris Mellor (2)

LIKE NOTES ON A STAVE, WEARY GOATS RECLINE ON THE MULTI-COLOURED TULSI GHATS.
Photographer: Anders Blomqvist (3)

HINDU PILGRIMS IN GORGEOUSLY VIVID SARIS ON DARBHANGA GHAT.
Photographer: Richard I'Anson (4)

DEFINING EXPERIENCE

Watching pilgrims perform *puja* (prayer) at dawn on the ghats, before buying some *paan* (betel nut and leaves concoction) and heading to the International Yoga Clinic & Meditation Centre for a hatha lesson.

STRENGTHS

- ◢ The Ganges
- ◢ People-watching at Dasaswamedh Ghat
- ◢ Manikarnika Ghat – the most auspicious place for a Hindu to be cremated
- ◢ The Ganges *susu* (dolphin)
- ◢ The particularly holy water between the turrets of Trilochan Ghat
- ◢ Vishwanath Temple
- ◢ Benares Hindu University
- ◢ Ramnagar Fort & Museum
- ◢ Steam baths and massages
- ◢ Silk
- ◢ Noise and colour
- ◢ Hindi courses at Bhasha Bharati Language Institute
- ◢ International Music Centre Ashram
- ◢ International Yoga Clinic & Meditation Centre
- ◢ Hotel Ganges View
- ◢ Ram Lila (Sepember/October)

WEAKNESSES

- ◢ Pollution of the Ganges
- ◢ Blackouts caused by the power-hungry sewage treatment plants
- ◢ Rickshaw-wallahs and touts
- ◢ Street crime after dark
- ◢ Fishing the Ganges *susu*

GOLD STAR

Religious tradition

CITYSPEAK

- ◢ Plans for a better sewage system devised by the Sankat Mochan Foundation

STARRING ROLE IN...

- ◢ *Ganges Dreaming* (2004)
- ◢ *Ganges: River to Heaven* (2003)

IMPORT

- ◢ Foreign students at the university
- ◢ Hindu pilgrims
- ◢ Tulsi Das
- ◢ Mark Twain

EXPORT

- ◢ *Langda aam* (mangoes)
- ◢ *Sitafal* (custard apples)
- ◢ Silk brocades
- ◢ Benares saris
- ◢ Bhadohi carpets
- ◢ Ravi Shankar
- ◢ Rajul Mehta

SEE the incredible gold dome and tower of Vishwanath Temple – from the shop over the road if you're not Hindu, or from inside the temple if you are.

EAT local specialities at one of the city's best restaurants, Varuna Restaurant, and enjoy live sitar and tabla music.

DRINK a glass of history at Princep Bar, named after James Princep, illustrator of Varanasi's temples and ghats.

DO an uplifting boat trip down the Ganges from Dasaswamedh Ghat to Harishchandra Ghat at dawn.

WATCH cremations at Manikarnika Ghat.

BUY different types of beautiful silk at Ganga Silk.

AFTER DARK watch a sitar concert at the International Music Centre Ashram, and take lessons there if you feel inspired.

URBAN MYTH

Varanasi is the centre of the Hindu world, a crossing place between the physical and the spiritual, and the River Ganges is thought to offer salvation. Hindus believe that washing in the river will cleanse their bodies of sin. Varanasi is a popular place for Hindu cremations as the city is credited with a direct route to heaven. If a Hindu dies here they receive *moksha*, which is liberation from the cycle of life and death.

Cartagena

073

VITAL STATISTICS

NAME: CARTAGENA

NICKNAME: LA CIUDAD HEROICA (THE HEROIC CITY), ACCORDING TO SIMÓN BOLÍVAR

DATE OF BIRTH: 1533; WHEN IT WAS THE SECOND SPANISH CITY TO BE FOUNDED ON THE COLOMBIAN COAST

ADDRESS: COLOMBIA (MAP 4, K8)

HEIGHT: 5M

POPULATION: 1 MILLION

A SWEET VENDOR SELLS HANDMADE *COCADA*, A DESSERT MADE OF *PANELA* (CANE SUGAR) AND COCONUT OR PEANUTS.
Photographer: Patricia Rincon Mautner (1)

Cartagena de Indias is legendary both for its history and its beauty: it has been immortalised on countless canvases, glorified in hundreds of books and photographed a zillion times – and, as Colombia's most fascinating city and a World Heritage Site, it deserves every one of these tributes.

ANATOMY

The heart of Cartagena is the old town, facing the sea to the west and almost entirely separated by water from the mainland to the east. The old town's walled sections are separated by a channel, the Caño de San Anastasio. This was later filled up to make way for the construction of the wedge-shaped modern district, La Matuna. South of the old town is the L-shaped peninsula occupied by the trendy seaside resorts. Walk around town, or catch the large green-and-white buses.

PEOPLE

The majority of cartageneros are mestizos with Spanish background, with the rest of the population made up of afrocolombians. The more European your background, the higher your social status is, the greater your wealth and more stable your livelihood.

TYPICAL CARTAGENERO

They drink eternal coffees but their true love is rum. Their passions are their families, their *fútbol* (football) team and going out to rumba, in that order. They're isolated from the difficulties of most of the country, but never forget they are Colombians. They're relaxed and friendly to strangers, in good Caribbean fashion, but never forget that their family is first. They *always* know they live in the most beautiful city in Colombia.

DEFINING EXPERIENCE

Having a breakfast coffee with bread, a relaxing morning strolling around the streets, a big lunch then stopping for a *tintico* (short black coffee), dining on a good seafood meal at a *cantina* (bar) in el Centro, then heading off to Boca Grande for rum and rumba until dawn.

STRENGTHS

◢ *Chivos* (colourful local buses)
◢ Beautiful remnants of Spanish colonial history – La Ciudad Amurallada
◢ Perfect Caribbean climate all year-round
◢ Music – rumba, *vallenato, paseo…*
◢ Good seafood
◢ Dancing, partying and rum
◢ Festivals
◢ Glamour and Colombian fashion
◢ Isolation from the dark side of Colombia

WEAKNESSES

◢ Street moneychangers
◢ Fraudulent boat captains
◢ Bullfights
◢ Violent social history
◢ Machismo

GOLD STAR

Having the most stubborn military saviour – Blas de Lezo, who had lost a leg, an eye and an arm in various battles, but with only 2500 troops defended Cartagena against 25,000 British troops.

CITYSPEAK

◢ Who this year's winner of the national beauty pageant will be
◢ The Colombian situation (guerrillas, paramilitaries, drugs, money)
◢ The fortunes of the Real Cartagena *fútbol* team

STARRING ROLE IN...

◢ *Navy Seal* (1989)
◢ *Top Line* (1988)
◢ *The Mission* (1986)
◢ *Love in the Time of Cholera* by Gabriel García Márquez
◢ *Of Love and Other Demons* by Gabriel García Márquez
◢ *Chronicle of a Death Foretold* by Gabriel García Márquez

IMPORT

◢ Spanish colonists
◢ English pirates (Sir Francis Drake)
◢ The Inquisition
◢ Islamic-style building on Magna Island
◢ Rich Colombian tourists
◢ International films
◢ Colombian beauty queens
◢ Nuestra Señora de la Candelaria (the city's patron saint)
◢ African slaves

EXPORT

◢ Gabriel García Márquez
◢ Most of what comes out of Colombia (it's the country's major port)
◢ Composer Jaime R Echavarría
◢ Gold
◢ Emeralds
◢ Archaeological remains of indigenous Colombians

SEE films at the International Film Festival in March/April.

EAT sweets made from coconut, milk, tamarind and local fruits at el Portal de Los Dulces.

DRINK good Colombian coffee in any café.

DO take yourself on a tour of the old city, particularly the walled town.

WATCH the Reinado Nacional de Belleza (Colombia's national beauty pageant) on 11 November.

BUY emeralds at Las Bóvedas.

AFTER DARK take part in the street dancing, music and fancy dress parade at the Carnaval de Cartagena.

URBAN MYTH

In 1955, sailor Luis Alejandro Velasco was shipwrecked for 10 days on a raft without food or water. On his miraculous return, Cartagena feted him as a national hero. Gabriel García Márquez, at that time a cub journalist, conducted 20 six-hour interview sessions with Luis, and composed *Story of a Shipwrecked Sailor*. Unfortunately, Luis was not always to be so adored – it came out that his navy ship had been carrying contraband, which made it sink, the newspaper that published the interviews was closed, and the protests contributed to the downfall of the Rojas Pinilla government. On Luis's death, García Márquez erected a monument near his Cartagena residence, a book about the size of a double bed whose cover reads that Luis was 'kissed by beauty queens and made rich by the publicity, and later hated by the government and forgotten forever'.

STOCKED UP – SEASIDE VENDORS VIE FOR THE TOURIST DOLLAR ON THE CITY'S RESORT BEACHES.
Photographer: Patricia Rincon Mautner (2)

CARTAGENA'S COLONIAL CHARM IS NOWHERE MORE PERSUASIVE THAN ON THE NARROW STREETS OF THE WALLED CITY. Photographer: Patricia Rincon Mautner (3)

FORMERLY A PRISON, THE 23 VAULTS OF LAS BÓVEDAS NOW HOST A LINE-UP OF LOCAL ARTS AND CRAFTS.
Photographer: Patricia Rincon Mautner (4)

Zanzibar Town

074

VITAL STATISTICS

NAME: ZANZIBAR

DATE OF BIRTH: 8TH CENTURY; WHEN SHIRAZI TRADERS FROM PERSIA ESTABLISHED A SETTLEMENT

ADDRESS: TANZANIA (MAP 2, M16)

HEIGHT: 15M

SIZE: 1574 SQ KM

POPULATION: 990,000

Zanzibar's old quarter, Stone Town, could have been lifted directly out of a Persian fairy tale, bringing together a mesmerising and evocative mix of influences from the Indian Subcontinent, the Arabian Peninsula and mainland Africa, and all in a tropical setting.

ANATOMY

Stone Town juts into the Indian Ocean on the western side of Zanzibar Island. Mizingani Rd runs along the waterfront from the ferry terminal to Stone Town. Here is a magical jumble of cobbled alleyways where it's difficult to get your bearings. The best approach is to dive in and follow your nose – you'll either emerge on the waterfront or on Creek Rd on the eastern edge of Stone Town. There's no transport system in Stone Town (and no need for one). Crowded *dalla-dallas* (minivans) connect the town with the rest of Zanzibar Island.

PEOPLE

The residents of Zanzibar mirror the melting pot that is their Swahili culture: they trace a mix of Omani, Shirazi and African ancestors in their bloodlines. There are also sizable Asian (Indian) and Arabic communities. You may also encounter a few Maasai tribesmen, conspicuously clad in blue, unlike their red-robed Kenyan brethren.

TYPICAL ZANZIBARI

Zanzibar is the Swahili town par excellence, hence it retains a sedate Muslim atmosphere. Most Zanzibaris are relatively conservative, modest in dress and behaviour, yet friendly, welcoming and gregarious. The *baraza* on houses' outer walls exemplify the gregarious nature of Zanzibaris – these stone benches serve as focal points where people can sit, watch the world go by and catch up on gossip. Zanzibaris are given to long and elaborate greetings, love to discuss politics and take life at a languid, tropical pace.

DEFINING EXPERIENCE

Passing through the huge carved doors of the House of Wonders; pondering the horrors of the past at the Anglican Cathedral built on the old slave market; wandering the Darajani Market and inhaling the scents of spices and dried fish; strolling aimlessly and endlessly in Stone Town, getting deliciously lost in the maze of streets, discovering children chanting Koranic verses, or a beautiful mansion with overhanging balconies, or a coffee vendor with long-spouted pot clacking cups to drum up business; sampling the delights of the foodstalls in the Forodhani Gardens in the early evening.

STRENGTHS

- ◢ The scent of cloves
- ◢ The twisting, turning alleys of Stone Town
- ◢ Overhead lattice balconies, ornate doors and window frames
- ◢ Wandering barefoot on the cobbles
- ◢ Games of football on the beach
- ◢ Breakfasts of mango, pawpaw and chai
- ◢ Skipping ropes with local kids
- ◢ Lateen sails of dhows bobbing in the harbour
- ◢ Hearing the lap of the bay as you sleep
- ◢ Nearby beaches – azure waters and pristine white sand
- ◢ Diving the crystal seas
- ◢ Seafood, grilled or cooked with coconut milk

WEAKNESSES

- ◢ Humidity and monsoon rains
- ◢ Political tensions
- ◢ Security after dark (an issue in some parts of town)
- ◢ Street touts, known locally as *papasi* (ticks)

GOLD STAR

Tropical enchantment – it's hard to think of a more evocative place name than 'Zanzibar' and the reality doesn't disappoint.

CITYSPEAK

- ◢ Seceding from Tanzania – should we, shouldn't we?
- ◢ If only all the tourists could keep themselves nice
- ◢ What depravities will the resort developers come up with next?

STARRING ROLE IN...

- ◢ *Admiring Silence* and *By the Sea* by Abdulrazak Gurnah
- ◢ *Zanzibar* by Giles Foden
- ◢ *Revolution in Zanzibar: An American's Cold War Tale* by Don Petterson
- ◢ *Dhows & Colonial Economy In Zanzibar : 1860–1970* by Erik Gilbert
- ◢ *Zanzibar Stone Town: an Architectural Exploration* by Abdul Sheriff
- ◢ *Zanzibar Style* by Javed Jafferji and Gemma Pitcher

IMPORT

- ◢ Spices – originally from Asia
- ◢ Merchants from around the Indian Ocean
- ◢ Honeymooners from Europe
- ◢ Property developers lusting after idyllic beaches

EXPORT

- ◢ Slaves and ivory (in the bad old days)
- ◢ Cloves, cinnamon, cardamom
- ◢ Farokh Bulsara, better known as Freddie Mercury
- ◢ *Taarab* music – a fusion of African, Arabic and Indian rhythms
- ◢ Dr Livingstone, who set off to explore Africa's interior from his base in Zanzibar

SEE the Festival of the Dhow countries (every year in July), where participants come from around the Indian Ocean.

EAT savoury pilau at the Passing Show restaurant.

DRINK chai, milky and sweet.

DO a Spice Tour with Mr Mitu and learn all there is to know about the spice trade.

WATCH the moon rise over the dhow harbour and the House of Wonders.

BUY spices, silver jewellery or fabrics (*kangas* and *kikois*).

AFTER DARK head for any of the bars overlooking the bay.

URBAN MYTH

The 11th (and last) Sultan of Zanzibar was granted asylum in England after the revolution in 1964. He lived modestly in Portsmouth – in marked contrast to his earlier life on Zanzibar – on an annual stipend from the British government.

ON THE PROWL FOR FEATHERED BARGAINS AT THE CHICKEN MARKET IN STONE TOWN.
Photographer: Bethune Carmichael (1)

A SMILING WOMAN PEERS FROM A LAVISH WOODEN DOORWAY IN STONE TOWN.
Photographer: Ariadne Van Zandbergen (2)

AD FOR A BEAUTY STORE – EVERYTHING FROM MANICURES TO…ERR…MAKING BRIDES?
Photographer: Mitch Reardon (3)

A SCENE UNCHANGED THROUGH THE CENTURIES – ENCHANTING DHOWS MOORED AT SHANGANI POINT.
Photographer: David Else (4)

OLD MEETS NEW IN THE TOWN CENTRE WHERE STATELY 19TH-CENTURY HOUSES ARE REFLECTED IN THE WINDOWS OF A MODERN COMMERCIAL BUILDING.
Photographer: Glenn Beanland (1)

Innsbruck
075

VITAL STATISTICS

NAME: INNSBRUCK

NICKNAME: OLYMPIC TOWN

DATE OF BIRTH: 1180; WHEN THE SMALL MARKET SETTLEMENT ON THE NORTH BANK OF THE INN RIVER EXPANDED TO THE SOUTH BANK

ADDRESS: AUSTRIA (MAP 3, K10)

HEIGHT: 582M

POPULATION: 128,000

Innsbruck is an 800-year-old snow bunnies' paradise: laden with art treasures and stunning Gothic and baroque buildings, it's set against a postcard-perfect Alpine backdrop.

ANATOMY

In the valley of the Inn River, Innsbruck is scenically squeezed between the northern chain of the Alps (the Karwendel) and the Tuxer Vorberge (Tuxer Mountains) to the south. Extensive mountain transport facilities radiate from the city and provide ample walking and skiing opportunities, particularly to the south and west. The town centre is compact, with the *Hauptbahnhof* (main train station) just a 10-minute walk from the pedestrian-only *Altstadt* (old town). The main street in the *Altstadt*, Herzog Friedrich Strasse, connects with Maria Theresien Strasse, which is a major thoroughfare but closed to private transport. Getting around by foot is easy, but there also are buses and trams.

PEOPLE

Austrians are predominantly of Germanic origin (97%), and the remaining 3% are Slovene, Croat and Turkish. Austria's official language is German with Turkish, Slovenian, Croatian and English also spoken.

TYPICAL INNSBRUCK CITIZEN

Quietly confident, the typical Innsbruck citizen is friendly, intelligent and, like all Austrians, has a dollop of good-natured grumpiness thrown in. Hosting the Winter Olympics in 1964 and 1976, the people of Innsbruck are sporty, cosmopolitan and proud of their city, the largest in the European Alps. In summertime, locals swap their skis for hiking boots and mountain bikes to enjoy Innsbruck's spectacular surrounds. Almost one-sixth of the population of Innsbruck are university students.

DEFINING EXPERIENCE

Wandering the quaint cobblestone alleyways and baroque buildings of the *Altstadt*, then exploring the gardens and museum collections of Schloss Ambras, and topping it off by viewing the enchanting Goldenes Dachl (Golden Roof) against the Nordkette Mountains.

STRENGTHS

- Goldenes Dachl
- Medieval houses
- Snow!
- 25 nearby village resorts
- Picture-postcard views
- The new Bergisel Ski Jump
- Gothic and baroque architecture
- Rafting and canyoning
- Ambras Castle (Europe's oldest museum)
- Alpine air and flowers
- Quaint wooden chalets
- Sightseeing Trolley Tour
- Nordkettenbahn Cableway
- Pastries, cakes and strudel

WEAKNESSES

- Meat-and-dumpling-heavy meals
- Expanding waistlines
- Complicated Austrian etiquette
- (Some) old school attitudes and prejudices

GOLD STAR

The Olympic Ski World of Innsbruck – with 75 ski-lifts across seven ski fields, Innsbruck caters to everyone, from the daredevil seeking out the inkiest of black runs to the wannabe boarder who wouldn't know goofy from natural.

CITYSPEAK

- Pension reform (extending the compulsory retirement age)
- (Presently unfounded) fears of mass immigration from the East after the EU expansion

STARRING ROLE IN...

- *Die Freiheit des Adlers* (2002)
- *As In Heaven* (2003)
- *Crazy Canucks* (2004)
- *Overnight to Innsbruck* by Denyse Woods

IMPORT

- Students
- Tourists
- Busted-up skiers (the Innsbruck Medical University houses one of Europe's premier ski injury clinics)

EXPORT

- Embroidered textiles
- Film director Andreas Riedler
- Wrought-iron candlesticks
- SOS Children's Villages (one of the world's largest charities)
- Glassware
- Loden hats
- Woodcarvings
- Ingeborg Bachmann (graduate of University of Innsbruck)

SEE the magnificent Goldenes Dachl, constructed for Emperor Maximilian I as his box seat for tournaments in the square below.

EAT a tasty Wiener schnitzel at Goldener Adler, Innsbruck's 600-year old restaurant popular for both its history and Austrian and Tyrolean cuisine.

DRINK top-notch Alpine cocktails at the Hofgarten Café as you numb your ski-aches to the latest beats spun by local DJs.

DO brave the Nordkettenbahn Cableway all the way to the 2334m-high Hafelekar Top Terminal where you'll enjoy jaw-dropping views of the Zillertal, Stubai and Ötztal Alps.

WATCH home-grown opera, ballet, drama and comedy at Landestheater, Tyrol's seminal theatre.

BUY exquisite glittering trinkets at the Swarovski Crystal Gallery on Herzog Friedrich Strasse.

AFTER DARK get piste (*guffaw!*) with other snow hounds and adrenaline junkies at Jimmy's, a boisterous little bar in an inner courtyard near STA Travel.

URBAN MYTH

While much of the Western world has adopted the jolly fat guy in the red suit, Austrians offer a flip-side to Santa's generosity: the cranky Krampus. Around the 5th of December, you'll see a yuletide game of good cop versus bad cop: as St Nicholas walks from the St Nikolaus church to the Domplatz Sq giving presents to littlies, his demonic foe, the masked Krampus, threatens to punish them for any misdeeds and naughty behaviours throughout the year.

CAFÉ UMBRELLAS IN CAREFUL ROWS SEEN FROM HIGH UP ON THE CITY TOWER ON HERZOG FRIEDRICH STRASSE.
Photographer: Glenn Beanland (2)

AN EARLY MORNING CYCLIST HAS THE STREETS TO HIMSELF IN *ALTSTADT*.
Photographer: Glenn Beanland (3)

HOUSES ALONG MARIA THERESIEN STRASSE BASK IN THE STARK AFTERNOON LIGHT WHILE MOUNTAINS LOOM IN THE BACKGROUND.
Photographer: Glenn Beanland (4)

IN 1430 THIS MEDIEVAL HALL IN FOSSGATE BECAME THE HOME OF THE GUILD OF MERCHANT ADVENTURERS.
Photographer: Neil Setchfield (1)

York is a magical kind of place that makes you wish – if only for an instant – that the Industrial Revolution had never happened.

ANATOMY

Compact and eminently walkable, York has five major landmarks: the wall enclosing the small city centre, the minster at the northern corner, Clifford's Tower at the southern end, the River Ouse that cuts the centre in two, and the train station to the west. Just to avoid the inevitable confusion, remember that round these parts *gate* means street and *bar* means gate. York is easily walked on foot – you're never more than 20 minutes from any of the major sights.

PEOPLE

Traditional York has a very traditional demographic: 97.8% of the locals are white Brits. Although the University of York (established in 1963) heralded a 'return of the young people', York has an ageing population, with a higher proportion of elderly folks than anywhere else in England.

TYPICAL YORKIE

Possibly employed in the tourist industry (as over 9000 Yorkies are), the typical York citizen is a proud expert on their city's heritage, unfazed by the four million tourists that trod the narrow *snickets* (alleyways) each year. However, the newer breed of Yorkie might well be a person of science, as York's R&D laboratories steam full-speed ahead in the city's reinvention as a 'Science City'.

DEFINING EXPERIENCE

Marvelling at the tennis court–sized stained-glass Great East Window at York Minster before enduring the claustrophobic climb of 275 steps to the awesome central tower (the heart of the minster), then following the city walls clockwise to Monk Bar, York's best-preserved medieval gate.

York 076

VITAL STATISTICS

NAME: YORK

DATE OF BIRTH: AD 71; PRIOR TO THE ARRIVAL OF THE ROMANS WERE THE BRIGANTINES, A LOCAL TRIBE WHO MINDED THEIR OWN BUSINESS

ADDRESS: ENGLAND (MAP 3, E6)

HEIGHT: 17M

SIZE: 272 SQ KM

POPULATION: 137,505

SURVEYING THE SITES FROM A RESTFUL VIEWPOINT.
Photographer: Neil Setchfield (2)

BUILT BETWEEN 1220 AND 1472, THE MINSTER IS STILL YORK'S TALLEST BUILDING.
Photographer: Neil Setchfield (3)

CLIFFORD'S TOWER, THE KEEP OF THE OLD CASTLE BUILT IN 1245, IS NOW ALL THAT IS LEFT OF YORK CASTLE.
Photographer: Neil Setchfield (4)

STRENGTHS

- Oodles of history
- York Castle Museum
- York Minster
- Museum Gardens
- The Shambles
- Clifford's Tower
- Narrow *snickets*
- Jorvik Viking Centre
- Castle Howard
- Easily negotiable on foot
- National Railway Museum
- Medieval churches

WEAKNESSES

- Summertime traffic congestion
- Severe flooding from the River Ouse
- Demented tourism in the high summer season
- Cold, dark and grim winters

GOLD STAR

Resilience – garrisoned by the Romans, rampaged by Vikings, besieged by Parliamentarian forces in the Civil War of 1644 and blitzed by the Nazis in 1942, at almost 2000 years old York stands strong as a living museum – a true gem in England's crown.

CITYSPEAK

- The ongoing foot-and-mouth scare
- The 'new' York, 'Science City'

STARRING ROLE IN...

- *Elizabeth* (1998)
- *Harry Potter and the Philosopher's Stone* (2001)
- *All Creatures Great and Small* by James Herriot
- *Behind the Scenes at the Museum* by Kate Atkinson
- *Possession* by AS Byatt

IMPORT

- Romans
- Vikings
- William the Conqueror
- Four million tourists annually

EXPORT

- Kit Kats
- Smarties
- AS Byatt
- Terry's Chocolate Orange
- Dame Judi Dench
- The grand old Duke of York
- Yorkshire pudding
- Guy Fawkes

SEE Castle Howard, the palatially Palladian Vanbrugh/Hawksmoor creation surrounded by the rolling Howardian Hills, acres of terraced gardens, landscaped vistas and a scattering of monumental follies and obelisks.

EAT sandwiches and high tea, old-school style, at Betty's, a Yorkshire institution – a pianist tinkles Bett's ivories after 6pm (for added class).

DRINK an ale or few with the old blokes at Ackhorne on St Martin's Lane, a locals' inn that's as comfy as old slippers.

DO visit what is easily Yorkshire's most important historic building – the simply awesome York Minster.

WATCH well-regarded productions of theatre, opera and dance at the York Theatre Royal on St Leonard's Pl.

BUY unusual secondhand books from the Worm Holes Bookshop in Bootham, with a decent and far-reaching selection of old and new titles.

AFTER DARK join the 'ghost hunt' of York, an award-winning and highly entertaining 75-minute tour beginning at the Shambles.

URBAN MYTH

In AD 71, the Romans erected a walled garrison dubbed Eboracum (now York) at the strategically important confluence of the Rivers Ouse and Foss. The fort steadily increased in importance, becoming the Romans' British campaign headquarters and attracting visits by big-name emperors such as Hadrian, Septimius, Severus (who died there) and Constantine. It's thought that Constantine was proclaimed emperor on the future site of York Minster – spooky, because he went on to become the first Christian emperor.

Mumbai 077

VITAL STATISTICS

NAME: MUMBAI

NICKNAME: GATEWAY TO INDIA

DATE OF BIRTH: 1661; WHEN THE FEW FISHING VILLAGES
AND THE HARBOUR WERE ACQUIRED BY THE BRITISH

ADDRESS: INDIA (MAP 5, B6)

HEIGHT: 11M

SIZE: 440 SQ KM

POPULATION: 12 MILLION

EMPTY TABLES AND CHAIRS FORM PATTERNS
ON THE TORTURED LAWNS OF THE MUMBAI
CRICKET CLUB INTERNATIONAL.
Photographer: Will Chesser (1)

India's most liberal city is irrepressibly vibrant, with grand colonial and Art Deco architecture, double-decker buses, teeming bazaars, an unparalleled range of restaurants and Bollywood starlets and wannabes.

ANATOMY

The city sprawls across seven islands joined into an artificial isthmus. The principal part of the city is concentrated at the southern, claw-shaped end of the island known as South Mumbai and the southernmost peninsula is Colaba. Further north, across Mahim Creek, are the suburbs of Greater Mumbai, where many of the best restaurants and nightspots can be found. Taxis, double-decker buses on major routes, ferries and two suburban train lines are the way to get about.

PEOPLE

The majority of Mumbai's millions are Hindu (68%), but there is also a sizable Muslim minority (17%). There are also Christians, Buddhists, Jains and Parsis (followers of Zoroastrianism, who originally came from Persia). One-third of the population lives in squalid *chawls* (cramped, makeshift, miserable hovels) and many live on the streets.

TYPICAL MUMBAIKAR

Hustling, bustling, on the make, Mumbaikar lead India with outrageous wealth and astonishing poverty. They enjoy the most liberal and cosmopolitan city of India. Wealthier citizens work in Bollywood, the nuclear-research programme, industry, the media and advertising – and work is their focus; poorer citizens make of life what they can. Making no excuses for theirs being a city of such extremes, Mumbaikers are in equal turns relaxed and vivacious.

DEFINING EXPERIENCE

Taking a boat out to the Elephanta Caves from the Gateway of India, calling in at the Taj Hotel for tea, walking over to the Chhatrapati Sivaji Museum and Jehangir Art Gallery, wandering through the Chor (Thieves) Bazar, eating at the Revolving Restaurant and then driving down Marine Dr in the evening.

STRENGTHS

- Chhatrapati Sivaji Museum (formerly the Prince of Wales Museum)
- Rajabai Clocktower
- Gothic-style buildings
- Crawford Market
- Tiffin-box carriers – the *dabbawallahs*
- Chowpatty Beach
- Mahatma Gandhi Museum
- Towers of Silence
- Hanging Gardens
- Elephanta Island
- Knesseth Eliyahod Synagogue
- St Thomas' Cathedral
- Haji Ali's Mosque
- Cricket on the *maidan* (an open grassed area in a city)

WEAKNESSES

- Traffic
- Enormous wealth disparities
- Vicious gang warfare controlled by underworld dons
- The religious fault-line

GOLD STAR

Mumbai's transposed European building styles are fascinating. Many of the impressive Victorian buildings were constructed on the edge of Oval Maidan during the building boom of the 1860s and '70s. This and the Azad Maidan, immediately to the north, were on the seafront in those days, and a series of grandiose structures, including the Secretariat, Bombay University, the High Court and the Western Railway Building, faced directly onto the Arabian Sea. The reclaimed land along the western edge of the *maidans* out towards Marine Dr is now lined with an impressive collection of Art Deco apartment blocks.

CITYSPEAK

- Water – will it ever be easily available to all?
- Will we suffer sectarian violence again?
- Corruption in city and state government?
- Organised crime – how prevalent is it?

STARRING ROLE IN...

- *Midnight's Children by* Salman Rushdie
- *Family Matters by* Rohinton Mistry
- *Maximum City: Bombay Lost and Found* by Suketu Mehta
- *Shantaram* by Gregory David Robert
- *The Death of Vishnu* by Manil Suri
- *Love and Longing in Bombay* by Vikram Chandra
- *Salaam Bombay!* (1988)
- *Bride and Prejudice* (2004)

IMPORT

- Victorian architecture
- Film
- Advertising
- Parsis

EXPORT

- The Raj
- Bollywood
- Anish Kapoor
- Aamir Khan
- Salman Khan
- Rudyard Kipling
- Zubin Mehta
- Rohinton Mistry
- Ismail Merchant
- Merle Oberon
- Salman Rushdie
- Sachin Tendulkar

SEE the sun setting into the Arabian Sea from Marine Dr.

EAT *puri* (flat dough that puffs up when deep fried) with chickpeas at Santar.

DRINK chic cocktails at Flavours in the Ambassadors Hotel in Churchgate.

DO take a boat trip out to Elephanta Island for the caves and carved temples.

WATCH flamboyant wedding parties on Chowpatty Beach.

BUY silks and saris from all over India at Sheetal on B Desai Rd.

AFTER DARK head to the Beyond 1900s disco at the Taj Mahal Hotel, hang-out of well-heeled young Mumbaikar.

URBAN MYTH

Legend has it that long, long ago, when Mumbai was a tiny archipelago of seven islands, it was frequently plundered by a demon called Mumbaraka. The *kolis* (fisherfolk) appealed to Lord Brahma, creator of the universe, who produced an eight-armed goddess to vanquish the tyrant who was, of course, no match for her. Delighted, the *kolis* called the goddess Mumbadevi and named the island Mumbai, after their divine protectress.

LIGHTS, CAMERA, SONG! ACTORS IN GLITTERY COSTUMES PREPARE FOR ANOTHER TAKE ON THE SET OF A BOLLYWOOD FILM.
Photographer: George Georgiou (2)

MUSLIM WOMEN IN VIBRANT CLOTHING PRAY AT A CITY MOSQUE.
Photographer: Peter Adams (3)

SOME ARE BORN GREAT – THE GREAT PANI PURI SALESMAN UPHOLDS HIS REPUTATION ON CHOWPATTY BEACH.
Photographer: Greg Elms (4)

ALMONDS AND FERRIS WHEELS – THE PERFECT COMBINATION, HAMBURGER DOM.
Photographer: Martin Lladó (1)

Hamburg
078

VITAL STATISTICS

NAME: HAMBURG

NICKNAME: GATEWAY TO THE WORLD; CAPITAL OF LUST

DATE OF BIRTH: AD 9; A MOATED FORTRESS CALLED HAMMABURG WAS CONSTRUCTED IN WHAT IS TODAY THE CITY CENTRE

ADDRESS: GERMANY (MAP 3, J6)

HEIGHT: 22M

SIZE: 755 SQ KM

POPULATION: 2 MILLION

The entertainment capital of Germany, beautiful and historic Hamburg is both economically and culturally prosperous, with strong industry, an impressive music scene and a colourful and diverse local culture.

ANATOMY

Hamburg is a large city shaped by water, with a wonderful harbour at its centre, three rivers and canals running through it, a number of lakes and around 2500 bridges. Most of the attractions cluster around the bustling urban centre, with a good number of vast green spaces to break up the intensity of the busy port city. The Alsterfleet canal splits the urban centre into the Old City, which is full of historic churches and Renaissance-style arcades, and the New City, which contains the prominent city landmark, the baroque church of Michaeliskirche. The surrounding inner suburbs house a variety of popular entertainment districts, including the notoriously seedy Reeperbahn, as well as the residential suburbs of the young and trendy and those of the wealthy. A network of ferries, trains and other public transport is available.

PEOPLE

Hamburg's citizens are mostly German, with European immigrants making up around 15% of the population. About 30% of Hamburgers are Lutheran, 30% Hindu, 5% Muslim, 1% Jewish and around 30% are unaffiliated, atheist or of another faith. Pure German and local dialects are the main languages, though English is also widely spoken.

TYPICAL HAMBURGER

The city's population comprises more millionaires than any other German city, and the majority of Hamburgers live comfortably. They are proud of their city and relish Hamburg's green spaces. They love to shop and to eat out. Most are political with concerns ranging from social democracy to the environment, and few are shaken by the quirks of alternative subculture. While the pace in the city can be fast, they are welcoming to visitors.

DEFINING EXPERIENCE

Strolling bleary-eyed through the early-morning scene of the rowdy Fischmarkt while munching a *Bratwurst* (grilled sausage), balancing a beer and browsing for tulips and novelty T-shirts as store vendors noisily hawk their wares, then finding a bench to unload and finish breakfast while toe-tapping along to the locals joining in on the choruses of German pop tunes cranked out by bands at the market.

STRENGTHS

- Drinking holes around virtually every corner
- Excellent and free tourist maps
- Green areas of city
- Fischmarkt
- Cruises around the port
- Great music scene
- Historic buildings and churches
- Bridges
- The 'Art Mile' (string of art galleries and museums)
- Cool fashions
- Great café culture
- Flat city (good for cycling)
- German beer
- Nearby forests
- Good secondhand stores
- International cuisine
- Diverse character of the city
- Alternative scene
- Leafy streets
- Hamburger Dom festival

WEAKNESSES

- Junkies
- High cost of living
- Confusing train timetables

GOLD STAR

Entertainment central – whether you are up for clubbing, bar-hopping, a night of live music or a refined night at the theatre there are heaps of options… and it seems as though you are never more than a five-minute walk from a bar or pub in Hamburg.

CITYSPEAK

- Germany's chance in the 2006 FIFA World Cup (to be held in Hamburg)
- Whether the government measures to prevent terrorism in Germany are over the top

STARRING ROLE IN...

- *Mirador* (1978)
- *Tomorrow Never Dies* (1997)
- *Bella Marta* (Mostly Martha, 2002)

IMPORT

- The Beatles (for a time)
- The 2006 FIFA World Cup
- Coffee
- Chain restaurants
- EU citizens
- Arab citizens
- Fuel
- Fruit and vegetables
- Building materials
- Electronics

EXPORT

- The music of Felix Mendelssohn
- The music of Johannes Brahms
- The discovery of electromagnetic waves by Heinrich Hertz
- Biotechnology
- Schwarzkopf hair products
- Shipbuilding and aircrafts
- Steinway pianos
- Philips electronics
- Siemens
- Nivea beauty products
- Montblanc fountain pen
- Car manufacturing
- Commerce
- Holsten Pilsener Beer
- Print media and publishing
- Kraftwerk

SEE the saucy exhibits at the Erotic Art Museum, which showcases a collection of erotic art from the 16th century to the modern day.

EAT gourmet French at Chez Alfred, a charming restaurant housed in an old factory where railway tracks still run through the outdoor patio.

DRINK with punks and environmentalists in the politically charged and moody Fritz Bauch.

DO check out the animated collection of bars, sex clubs, restaurants and pubs in the 'sin centre' of St Pauli.

WATCH a cutting-edge adaptation of Goethe's *Faust* at Thalia Theater.

BUY a *Bratwurst* and a beer at the boisterous Fischmarkt.

AFTER DARK pay tribute at the famous basement of the Kaiserkeller – one of the local live venues gigged by the Beatles in the '60s.

URBAN MYTH

Before they became a household name, the Beatles built their musicianship and developed their stage performances in Hamburg – where their breakthrough finally came. First playing at the Indra Club in 1960, over the next three years the Beatles put in around 800 of hours of live performance at the Kaiserkeller, the Top Ten and the Star Club, and had a rollicking good time as they did it. As John Lennon famously said, 'I was born in Liverpool, but I grew up in Hamburg.'

THE HEAVILY INKED OWNER OF JUNGBLUTH PIERCING AND TATTOO SHOP POSES PROUDLY.
Photographer: Yadid Levy (2)

CHILE HAUS, FRITZ HOEGER'S EXPRESSIONIST TRIUMPH, MERCHANT DISTRICT.
Photographer: Andrea Schulte-Peevers (3)

CHECKING OUT THE ACTION AT THE STRAND PAULI BEACH CLUB.
Photographer: Yadid Levy (4)

At once relaxed and energetic, remote and cosmopolitan Oaxaca City is one of Mexico's most vibrant cultural capitals where ancient indigenous culture and modern artistic innovation intermingle in a charming colonial setting.

ANATOMY

Situated at a comfortable altitude at the juncture of three valleys, the city enjoys a sunny and stable climate, which suits its cheerfully laid-back vibe. Oaxaca City's Spanish colonial heritage is visible as much in the stunning stone buildings as in the town's gridlike planning. Streets open out into public gardens and airy plazas then disappear again into narrow cobbled lanes and winding back alleys. Oaxaca City's heart and soul is the broad *zócalo* (town square), a meeting place for its citizens and venue for its many cultural events. Most points of interest in the city are within walking distance of each other, but you can use city buses if your feet get tired.

PEOPLE

Almost all of Oaxaca City's citizens are descended from the indigenous Zapotec and Mixtec peoples who remain fiercely proud of their heritage; many continue to observe pre-Hispanic traditions, from cooking and music to healing practices.

TYPICAL OAXACAN

Oaxacans have the best of everything. They are well educated (thanks in part to the town's historic hero, Benito Juárez), artistically appreciative, discerning in matters culinary and lacking in the macho boisterousness that tends to confront visitors in other parts of Mexico. Locals are self-confident and friendly. They are as comfortable yelling at a football match as they are chatting at a café or wandering quietly through an art gallery. Nobody is in much of a hurry in Oaxaca. With thousands of years of colourful history behind it, what's the rush?

Oaxaca City

079

VITAL STATISTICS

NAME: OAXACA CITY

NICKNAME: IN THE NOSE OF THE SQUASH; THE LITERAL MEANING OF 'HUAXYÁCAC', OAXACA'S EARLIER AZTEC NAME

DATE OF BIRTH: 1529; WHEN THE SPANISH OFFICIALLY FOUNDED THE CITY, ALTHOUGH AN INDIGENOUS SETTLEMENT HAD ALREADY EXISTED AT THE SITE OF PRESENT-DAY OAXACA CITY FOR SEVERAL MILLENNIA

ADDRESS: MEXICO (MAP 4, D5)

HEIGHT: 1550M

POPULATION: 260,000

COWBOY-HATTED LOCALS FRAMED AGAINST THE CHARACTERISTIC PASTEL COLOURS OF A CITY DWELLING.
Photographer: Jeffrey Becom (1)

DEFINING EXPERIENCE

Getting up early and heading straight for the rowdy market to enjoy an invigorating bowl of hot *cacao* (chocolate) and sweet bread, stepping out again into the clear light that has inspired some of Mexico's most respected contemporary artists, crawling the galleries and the cafés for the rest of the day before losing yourself in the joyful mania of a festival.

STRENGTHS

- ◢ Chocolate
- ◢ Extraordinary arts and crafts
- ◢ Stunning galleries
- ◢ Indigenous culture
- ◢ Explosive festivals
- ◢ Unbeatable local cuisine
- ◢ Modern art
- ◢ Día de los Muertos (Day of the Dead) celebrations
- ◢ Colonial architecture
- ◢ Benito Juárez
- ◢ Handicrafts
- ◢ VW beetle taxis

WEAKNESSES

- ◢ Heavy-handed police
- ◢ Political unrest
- ◢ Former dictator Porfirio Díaz
- ◢ Traffic

GOLD STAR

Nowhere is the Mexican festival Día de Muertos taken more seriously than in Oaxaca City and the surrounding villages. In this Zapotec celebration, which has fused with Catholic traditions, Oaxacans honour their dead by setting off fireworks in the cemeteries, eating sugared skulls and dressing up in outrageous costumes.

CITYSPEAK

- ◢ Artist José Posada – overrated or underappreciated?
- ◢ Guelaguetza festival – have you got tickets?
- ◢ Salsa – who's dancing with whom?
- ◢ Día de Muertos – what are you wearing?

STARRING ROLE IN...

- ◢ Día de Muertos iconography

IMPORT

- ◢ Camera-happy tourists
- ◢ International fine-arts students
- ◢ Handicraft collectors
- ◢ American products
- ◢ Rural workers looking for a big-city break

EXPORT

- ◢ *Calaveras* (whimsical sculptures or images on a skeleton motif, abundant at markets prior to Día de Muertos)
- ◢ *Mole* (a sauce made with unsweetened cocoa and chilli)
- ◢ Benito Juárez' philosophy
- ◢ Pirated CDs
- ◢ Contemporary art
- ◢ Chocolate

SEE the Iglesia de Santo Domingo, the most splendid of Oaxaca's many churches.

EAT spiced grasshoppers from a street stall.

DRINK sickly sweet hot chocolate with cinnamon and crushed almonds.

DO a round of the contemporary art museums and wind up in an atmospheric café.

WATCH frenetic dancing at the Guelaguetza festival.

BUY Mexico's best folk art.

AFTER DARK hit Candela to catch some of the best live salsa you'll ever experience.

URBAN MYTH

Benito Juárez (1806–72) is literally synonymous with the city itself, as Oaxaca City was once named Oaxaca de Juárez in his honour. A Zapotec orphan, he began his impoverished childhood as a bookbinder and later rose to become justice minister. His liberal reforms, which reduced the power of the church and the military, provoked the War of Reform and briefly forced him into exile. One of Juárez' main political achievements was to make primary education free and compulsory. Today countless statues, streets, schools and plazas preserve his name and memory, and his sage maxim 'Respect for the rights of others is peace' is widely quoted.

IN A BLUR OF MOVEMENT A GRINNING DANCER STEPS TO A TRADITIONAL BEAT.
Photographer: Greg Elms (2)

SANTO DOMINGO CATHEDRAL RISES MAJESTICALLY ABOVE THE PALM LINED *ZÓCALO* IN THE TOWN CENTRE.
Photographer: Richard I'Anson (3)

PLASTIC BASKETS IN TRADITIONAL INDIGENOUS DESIGNS LINE THE COBBLESTONES OUTSIDE OAXACA MARKET.
Photographer: Greg Elms (4)

Galway

080

VITAL STATISTICS

NAME: GALWAY

NICKNAME: CITY OF TRIBES

DATE OF BIRTH: 1124; WHEN THE CASTLE OF BUN GAILLMHE WAS BUILT FOR THE KING OF CONNACHT

ADDRESS: IRELAND (MAP 3, B7)

HEIGHT: 21M

SIZE: 50 SQ KM

POPULATION: 209,077

Galway city is a rare confluence of elements: it's arty, romantic, youthful, eccentric and historic.

ANATOMY

Galway's tightly packed historic town centre lies on both sides of the fast-flowing River Corrib, and its curved, cobbled streets run down to the busy harbour. High St is closed to traffic most of the time, so often swarms with a festive crowd. The uninspiring Eyre Sq and the bus and train stations, as well as most of the main shopping areas, are on the river's eastern bank. To the southeast of Wolfe Tone Bridge is the historic, but now totally redeveloped, district of Claddagh; to the west is the faded beach resort of Salthill.

PEOPLE

Galway is one of Europe's most rapidly growing cities, with migrants from Eastern Europe, Asia and Sub-Saharan Africa mixing with a predominantly Irish Catholic community. Most notable, though, is the large percentage of students and a general skew towards those under 45. Although it's known as the gateway to the Gaeltacht (the Irish-speaking region), Galway has not had a solely Irish-speaking population since the 1930s.

TYPICAL GALWEGIAN

Galway has long been seen by the rest of Ireland, and beyond, as an essentially Celtic place. While Galwegians today are mostly young, and often progressive or even alternative in their outlook, it remains a city where historic cultural traditions are embraced and sustained. A local may be a musician, artist, thespian or intellectual, or combine an artistic pursuit with a boomtown professional life in IT or biotech. Galwegians have a high regard for a night out, and join the large number of students and, in the summer, tourists, in the pubs, restaurants and the streets.

DEFINING EXPERIENCE

Up early selling your hand-printed clothes at the Saturday markets, picking up some organic olives and brown bread after you've packed up your stall (it was a bit damp after all), grabbing a coffee at Bananaphoblacht, then taking your *bodhran* (traditional Celtic drum) to Taaffe's for a session and fitting in a few pints before a comedy act at the Kings Head.

STRENGTHS

- Galway Arts Festival and Galway Film Fleadh
- Lynch's Castle
- Traditional Irish music pubs
- Taibhdhearc na Gaillimhe (Irish-language theatre)
- Spanish Arch
- Salthill Golf Course
- Collegiate Church of St Nicholas of Myra
- Seafood
- The wild beauty of the surrounding landscape
- Street life in summer
- Cute painted houses

WEAKNESSES

- The rise of the super-pub
- Prodigious rainfall
- Petty crime
- Race Week crowds

GOLD STAR

Laid-back cool – Galway comfortably incorporates traditional and alternative lifestyles.

CITYSPEAK

- Eyre Sq – is it worth the trouble?
- The *Naked Galwegian* (satirical newspaper)

STARRING ROLE IN...

- *City of the Tribes* by Walter Macken
- *The Guards* by Ken Bruen
- *Belios* by Órfhlaith Foyle

IMPORT

- Crusties
- Spanish wine and oil in medieval times
- Folk musicians
- Students
- Jack B Yeats (poet Yeats' painter brother)

EXPORT

- Nora Barnacle
- John Lynch, signatory to the US Declaration of Independence
- Claddagh rings
- Fast-food chain Supermacs
- Connemara marble
- Aran sweaters
- Eamonn Ceannt, one of the leaders of the 1916 Easter Uprising
- Liam Mellowes
- Pottery and porcelain
- Novelist and dramatist Walter Macken
- Peter (Christopher) Yorke

SEE Galway Bay from the beach at Salthill, after eating your fill at the Oyster Festival.

EAT Cratloe Hills Gold, Irish ham and wild salmon, from Sheridans Cheesemongers.

DRINK locally made Johnny Jump-Up cider at Neáchtains.

DO a walk along the Corrib, past the Salmon Weir Bridge to the weir itself.

WATCH buskers on Shop or Quay Sts.

BUY *Anna Livia Plurabelle* by James Joyce at the Charlie Byrne Bookshop.

AFTER DARK catch a ceilidh session at Taylor's.

URBAN MYTH

A romantic icon in the hearts and songs of Irish-Americans for generations, Claddagh village was once Galway's main commercial fishing centre – up to 3000 people and 300 boats were based here. Claddagh once had its own costume and dialect, as well as its own king. Although the traditional Claddagh of thatched roofs, Irish speakers and fishing boats disappeared in the early 20th century, you'll still see many people wearing Claddagh rings. The rings depict a crowned heart nestling between two outstretched hands; it signifies friendship (the hands), loyalty (the crown) and love (the heart). If the heart points towards the hand, the wearer is taken or married; towards the fingertip means that he or she is looking for a partner. It has been the wedding ring used throughout much of Connaught since the mid-18th century.

KEEPING GOOD COMPANY – LOCALS SHARE A BENCH AND A CHAT WITH ONE OF IRELAND'S MOST FAMOUS WRITERS.
Photographer: Neil Setchfield (1)

COMPETING FOR CHANGE – ONE OF MANY TALENTED STREET MUSICIANS ENLIVEN THE CITY.
Photographer: Neil Setchfield (2)

FLESHING OUT A THOUGHT – AN INTROSPECTIVE LOCAL DAWDLES PAST A BUTCHER'S MOSAIC.
Photographer: Neil Setchfield (3)

LINING UP FOR WATERFRONT VIEWS – HOUSES ON THE HARBOUR AND RIVERSIDE ARE IN A HIGH DEMAND.
Photographer: Neil Setchfield (4)

Siena 081

VITAL STATISTICS

NAME: SIENA

DATE OF BIRTH: 1ST CENTURY BC; WHEN THE ROMANS ESTABLISHED A MILITARY SETTLEMENT HERE CALLED SENA JULIA

ADDRESS: ITALY (MAP 3, K13)

HEIGHT: 322M

POPULATION: 52,800

Stunning Gothic architecture, medieval city walls, the charmingly winding streets and that famous piazza (Il Campo) make peaceful Siena a Tuscan joy.

ANATOMY

At the heart of Siena is the large sloping Piazza del Campo, from which fan out the streets of the medieval town. Two of its main streets reveal Siena's history as a banking town – Banchi di Sopra and Banchi di Sotto. They form part of the Via Francigena pilgrims' route to Rome. Via di Città, another important thoroughfare, joins the other two behind Piazza del Campo. The town is enclosed by its original walls, which are punctured by eight city gates. There are no cars or motorbikes in Siena's city centre, which makes wandering through the streets a rare pleasure. Your only other option is to jump on a bus.

PEOPLE

Italy has one of the lowest birth rates in Europe and Siena's population is slowly dwindling. Eighty-four percent of its citizens are Roman Catholic, with 6% made up of Jewish, Muslim and Protestant communities.

TYPICAL SIENESE

Siena is one of Tuscany's main university towns, and the Sienese are a well-educated, hard-working bunch. Family is very important to them and small family-run businesses are common. Loyal to their neighbourhood, they are more likely to fly the flag of their *contrada* (town district) than the Italian colours. They are gastronomes and very proud of Tuscan wine and cuisine. Politically, they tend towards the left, and finally, like all Italians, they like to look good.

DEFINING EXPERIENCE

Tucking into a dish of *pici* (thick Sienese spaghetti) at Il Carroccio before getting lost in the snaking streets of the town and miraculously ending up at a recognisable landmark, the Palazzo Communale.

STRENGTHS

◢ Sienese-Gothic architecture eg Il Campo, Palazzo Communale, the cathedral
◢ Il Palio (Siena's famous horse race)
◢ The Sienese school of painting
◢ First European city to ban motorised traffic in its centre
◢ Rivalry with Florence
◢ The Council of Nine
◢ Monte dei Paschi di Siena bank, a big employer in Siena
◢ Slow Food movement
◢ Marble font by Jacopo della Quercia in the Battistero (baptistry)
◢ Museo dell'Opera Metropolitana
◢ Sienese art in the Pinacoteca Nazionale
◢ Frescoes depicting Santa Caterina's life in the Chiesa di San Domenico
◢ Settimana Musicale Senese (July)
◢ Stunning Tuscan countryside
◢ Nannini, the best place to buy cakes and ice cream
◢ *Cantucci* and *biscottini di Prato* (almond-based biscuits)

WEAKNESSES

◢ Accommodation is elusive in summer, particularly during Il Palio
◢ It's easy to get lost in the medieval town
◢ The plague in 1348 (it killed 100,000 people)

GOLD STAR

Gothic architecture

CITYSPEAK

◢ Who won the last Palio and how to win the next one
◢ Food, food, food
◢ Football and who AC Siena are playing next

STARRING ROLE IN...

◢ *The English Patient* (1996)
◢ *Stealing Beauty* (1996)
◢ *Prince of Foxes* (1949)

IMPORT

◢ Students attending the Università per Stranieri
◢ Visitors on a tour of Tuscany

EXPORT

◢ Santa Caterina (one of Italy's most famous saints)
◢ Sienese school of painting: Guido da Siena, Duccio di Buoninsegna, Ambrogio Lorenzetti, Simone Martini, Taddeo di Bartolo
◢ Embroidery
◢ Brunello di Montalcino (wine)
◢ *Panforte* (a rich fruit cake originally cooked for the crusaders)
◢ Textiles
◢ Leather goods
◢ Porcini mushrooms

SEE the marble- and mosaic-clad cathedral, one of Italy's great Gothic churches.

EAT what you fancy from the *menu degustazione* (a seven-course tasting menu) at Cane e Gatto.

DRINK a pricey glass of Brunello di Montalcino at a bar on Il Campo – you're paying for the view but it's worth it.

DO a jazz course at the prestigious Associazione Siena Jazz.

WATCH 10 horses fiercely hauling their riders around Il Campo and see who wins the *Palio* (silk banner).

BUY cheese, sausages and porcini mushrooms from Pizzicheria de Miccoli.

AFTER DARK watch a concert at the Settimana Musicale Senese.

URBAN MYTH

Twice a year jockeys and riders compete in the world's shortest horse race, Il Palio. It is so famous in Italy that it has become legendary. Each of the 10 riders represents one of the 17 *contrade* (not all 17 take part), and compete for the *Palio* (silk banner), and the glory, of course. Each *contrada* has its own costume, flag and *Palio* museum – yes, they mean business. The riders thunder around for approximately 80 seconds on a dirt track, which is laid around Il Campo. Horses can win without their riders (the jockeys ride bareback), but it is a noncontact sport – so no pulling at the reins of competing horses, please!

WINNING SMILE – GIRLS IN ROMAN GOWNS JOIN CELEBRATIONS IN HONOUR OF IL PALIO CHAMPION.
Photographer: Paolo Sacchi (1)

FRIENDS GATHER FOR A MORNING CHAT AT SUNRISE ON PIAZZA DEL CAMPO.
Photographer: Paolo Sacchi (2)

WARM LIGHTS LURE OUTSIDERS INTO THE POPULAR GRATTACIELO TAVERN.
Photographer: Paolo Sacchi (3)

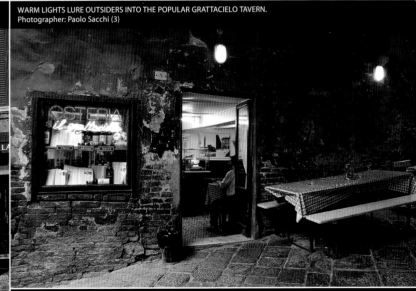

PIAZZA DEL CAMPO FRINGED BY THE CREEPING SHADOW OF THE PALAZZO PUBBLICO AND THE TORRE DEL MANGIA.
Photographer: Paolo Sacchi (4)

Esfahan 082

VITAL STATISTICS

NAME: ESFAHAN

NICKNAME: HALF THE WORLD (FROM THE PERSIAN RHYME, 'ESFAHAN NESF-E JAHAN': LITERALLY 'ESFAHAN IS HALF THE WORLD')

DATE OF BIRTH: 1587; WHEN SHAH ABBAS I CAME TO POWER AND HE SET OUT TO MAKE ESFAHAN A GREAT CITY

ADDRESS: IRAN (MAP 2, R2)

HEIGHT: 1773M

POPULATION: 1.6 MILLION

WOMEN IN FULL CHADOR LUG SHOPPING BAGS ACROSS IMAM SQ.
Photographer: Phil Weymouth (1)

KEEPING THE FAITH, AN ELDERLY MULLAH CLUTCHES A GOLD-EMBOSSED VOLUME OF THE HOLY KORAN. Photographer: Clint Lucas (2)

A MAN GAZES DOWN FROM ONE OF THE MANAR JOMBAN (SHAKING MINARETS), BUILT IN THE SAFAVIDS PERIOD. Photographer: John Borthwick (3)

THE BLUE-TONED MAJESTY OF IMAM SQ. Photographer: Phil Weymouth (4)

Iran's masterpiece, Esfahan is a stunning, colourful architectural gem, the centre of Persian arts and culture, brought to prominence by Shah Abbas the Great, set amid the desert of the central Iranian plateau.

ANATOMY

Chahar Bagh, 5km long, is the north–south artery through the centre of town. The Zayandeh River, crisscrossed by a series of historic arched bridges, runs roughly east–west. Northeast of the river are the expansive Imam Sq and the Bazar-e Bozorg (Grand Bazaar), while to the south lies the Armenian neighbourhood of Jolfa and the high-rises of the new town. Taxis and minibuses ply the main thoroughfares of the city, and if your haggling skills are good you could negotiate a private taxi.

PEOPLE

The population of Esfahan is as diverse as anywhere else in Iran. Besides Persians there are Azaris, occasionally visiting Bakhtiyari nomads, a sizable Armenian Christian community, Zoroastrians (the original monotheistic people of Persia), Afghan refugees, as well as small Jewish and Baha communities.

TYPICAL ESFAHANI

Esfahanis are fiercely proud of their home and its status as the capital of Persian arts and culture. Consequently, the typical Esfahani is likely to be articulate and urbane, educated and erudite, and as warm and welcoming as Iranians elsewhere. They will be conscious of their Muslim faith, and tend to be family oriented, living at home until – and perhaps after – they are married. An appreciation of all things artistic will be matched by a passion for football. Young people predominate in Esfahan – 70% of the Iranian population is younger than 30 years of age.

DEFINING EXPERIENCE

Wandering around the domed expanse of the Bazaar-e Bozorg, taking tea and smoking a *qalyan* (water pipe) at the outdoor tables of the Qeysarieh Tea Shop looking onto Imam Sq, poring over the exhibits at the Decorative Arts Museum of Iran, heading out to the Ateshkadeh-ye Esfahan to see the fire ceremonies of the Zoroastrians, strolling the banks of the Zayandeh River and fuelling up on tea in one of the teahouses under the bridges, musing on the elaborate frescoes of the Chehel Sotun Palace.

STRENGTHS

- The grandeur of Imam Sq
- The arts on show – calligraphy, tile making, metalwork, glassware, miniature paintings
- Carpets – where better to buy a Persian carpet?
- Haggling in the bazaar
- Teahouses and *qalyan*
- History at every turn
- Armenian cathedrals
- Architectural greatness – palaces, mosques, grand squares

WEAKNESSES

- Touts around Imam Sq
- The hard sell in the bazaar
- Scams involving impostor 'police'
- Pollution and hectic traffic
- Taxi drivers

GOLD STAR

Colour scheme – the symphony of royal blue, sunflower yellow and emerald tiles set atop the voluptuous domes and pointed arches of Imam Sq, all beneath a peerless, cloudless Persian blue sky.

CITYSPEAK

- With all this oil, do we really need nuclear power?
- The reformist agenda – it promised so much, but came to nothing
- How am I going to meet a spouse now that the conservatives are stifling all our freedoms again?
- Jobs, jobs, where are all the jobs?
- Should we really be afraid of the USA?

STARRING ROLE IN...

- *The Road to Oxiana* by Robert Byron
- *Travels in Persia* by Sir John Chardin
- *Honeymoon in Purdah* by Alison Wearing
- *The Siege of Isfahan* by Jean-Christopher Rufin
- *Portrait Photographs from Isfahan : Faces in Transition* by Parisa Damandan

IMPORT

- Armenian artisans

EXPORT

- Carpets
- Arts and crafts

SEE the view over Imam Sq from the elevated terrace of Ali Qapu Palace.

EAT *dolme bademjan* (stuffed eggplants) with rice, or *gaz* (nougat with pistachio and other chopped nuts).

DRINK *chay* (tea) while holding a sugar lump between your teeth.

DO spend time absorbing the frescoes of Chehel Sotun Palace, including the depiction of a man kissing the foot of a half-naked maiden.

WATCH craftsmen hammering copper pots, painting miniatures or enamelling copperware in the bazaar.

BUY a carpet or any traditional craftwork in the Grand Bazaar, but come prepared to haggle.

AFTER DARK loiter over a *qalyan* in one of the teahouses.

URBAN MYTH

The great travel writer Robert Byron remarked that the ornamental lake in the centre of Imam Sq was built to prevent Bakhtiyari tribesmen from playing polo or exercising their horses there.

WHILING AWAY A LAZY AFTERNOON AT CAFÉ L'AFFARE'S BAR.
Photographer: David Wall (1)

Hosting the *Lord of the Rings* world premieres put New Zealand's beautiful and blustering capital on the international movie map, but you don't have to be a film-star to enjoy 'Wellywood'– the bohemian vibe, great café scene and plentiful outdoor pursuits make it as attractive to civilians as it is to famous hobbits.

ANATOMY

Wellington's harbour sits between two peninsulas at the southern tip of New Zealand's North Island. Ferries regularly cross the Cook Strait from here to South Island. The main business street, Lambton Quay, used to sit on the waterfront but is now separated from the sea by reclaimed land. The city centre is bounded by the train station, at the northern end of Lambton Quay, and Cambridge and Kent Tce to the southeast. The historic and embassy area of Thornton lies just north of the centre. Wellington has an efficient local-bus system and suburban trains.

PEOPLE

New Zealand is a bicultural nation and Maori and English are the official languages. For most of Wellington's population at least one of these (probably English) is their mother tongue, but the number of Asian inhabitants in the city is on the increase.

TYPICAL WELLINGTONIAN

Wellingtonians enjoy a healthy rivalry with erstwhile capital Auckland. Like all Kiwis they are passionate about rugby and feel a great loyalty to New Zealand. Wellington is New Zealand's wealthiest region, and one in 25 earners pockets more than NZ$100,000 per year. Wellingtonians like outdoor activities and sports; they are also New Zealand's most culturally engaged people. The OE (overseas experience) is a rite of passage, although Australia is overtaking Britain as the most popular destination. Brain drain is allegedly receding, but proactive recruitment drives during the 2005 Lions tour suggest otherwise.

Wellington
083

VITAL STATISTICS

NAME: WELLINGTON

NICKNAME: WINDY WELLY

DATE OF BIRTH: 1840; EUROPEAN SETTLERS ARRIVED TO BUY LAND OFF THE MAORIS

ADDRESS: NEW ZEALAND (MAP 1, OO22)

HEIGHT: 127M

SIZE: 290 SQ KM

POPULATION: 205,500

A SURFER HANGS TEN – OR AT LEAST THREE – AT LYALL BAY.
Photographer: Paul Kennedy (3)

INDUSTRIAL-STYLE SCULPTURES ON THE EDGE OF WELLINGTON HARBOUR.
Photographer: Sally Dillon (2)

MAJESTIC VICTORIAN WEATHERBOARD HOUSES OVERLOOK ORIENTAL BAY.
Photographer: Peter Bennetts (4)

DEFINING EXPERIENCE

Taking a stroll around the Botanic Gardens before riding the cable car down to town for a steaming cup of coffee, grabbing your sailboard for some windsurfing in the harbour and going drinking later on Courtenay Pl.

STRENGTHS

- Radio New Zealand, based in Wellington
- Te Papa (Museum of New Zealand)
- City Gallery Wellington
- Old St Paul's Cathedral
- Government Buildings – among the world's largest all-wooden buildings
- Museum of Wellington City and Sea
- National Cricket Museum
- Beehive – the architectural emblem of New Zealand
- Katharine Mansfield's birthplace
- Botanic Gardens
- Red cable car
- Bill Manhire's creative writing course at Victoria University
- Live music from Fat Freddy's Drop
- View of the city from Mt Victoria
- Mountain biking at Makarara Peak
- Windsurfing
- Great café scene (more cafés per capita than New York City)

WEAKNESSES

- Houses are not insulated and have no central heating
- Wellington is on a fault line
- Windy weather
- Mad bus drivers

GOLD STAR

Cultural and physical activities on tap

CITYSPEAK

- What movie is being filmed in Wellington at the moment?
- When will we get the next big earthquake?

STARRING ROLE IN...

- *King Kong* (2005)
- *Lord of the Rings* trilogy (2001, 2002, 2003)

IMPORT

- Director Peter Jackson
- Architect Ian Athfield
- Rugby fans
- International movie stars on location

EXPORT

- Jane Campion
- Katharine Mansfield
- Director Lee Tamahori
- Author Catherine Chidgey
- Lamb
- Rugby players

SEE exhibits revealing New Zealand's history, and experience an earthquake at the fabulous Te Papa museum.

EAT a slap-up breakfast (often named after an All-Black) at Chocolate Fish café on Scorching Bay.

DRINK Pinot Noir and Sauvignon Blanc at Toast Martinborough, a food, wine and music bonanza.

DO take a ride in Wellington's red cable car up to the Botanic Gardens.

WATCH rock, Latin and soul in Wellington's oldest live-music venue, Bodega.

BUY retro fashion and funky furniture on Cuba St.

AFTER DARK take your pick of the bars and clubs on Courtenay Pl.

URBAN MYTH

Katharine Mansfield is New Zealand's most eminent author and is often compared to Chekhov and Maupassant. She spent five years of her childhood living at 25 Tinakori Rd in Wellington and this house, which pops up in her stories the *Aloe* (which became *Prelude*) and *A Birthday*, is open to the public. After leaving Wellington at the age of 19, she spent much of her time in Europe hanging out with famous scribes such as DH Lawrence, TS Eliot and Virginia Woolf and marrying the literary critic and author John Middleton Murry. A vicious bout of tuberculosis ended her life in 1923 in Fontainebleau in France when she was just 34. At Tinakori Rd you can see excerpts of her writing alongside photographs of her time there.

Ljubljana

084

VITAL STATISTICS

NAME: LJUBLJANA

NICKNAME: WHITE LJUBLJANA, AFTER THE NUMBER OF PALE-COLOURED CHURCHES AND MANSIONS BUILT BY THE HABSBURGS

DATE OF BIRTH: 1144; THE CITY WAS FIRST DOCUMENTED THEN BUT THE AREA HAD BEEN INHABITED FOR AT LEAST THREE MILLENNIA

ADDRESS: SLOVENIA (MAP 3, L11)

HEIGHT: 298M

POPULATION: 267,800

THE CHARMING DOLLS HOUSE-LIKE FAÇADE OF THE COOPERATIVE BANK BUILDING IN MIKLOŠIČEVA ST.
Photographer: Richard I'Anson (1)

Pocket-sized, picture-perfect Ljubljana punches above its weight with a thriving cultural scene, buzzing riverside bars and cafés and a photogenic Old Town – you just want to put it in your pocket and take it home with you.

ANATOMY

Ljubljana lies within the Ljubljana Basin (Ljubljanska Kotlina), which comprises the Ljubljana Marsh (Ljubljansko Barje) and the Ljubljana Plain (Ljubljansko Polje). It is positioned between the Polhov Gradec hills to the west and Golovec Hills (including Castle Hill) to the east and southeast. The combination of hills and marsh creates an early-morning fog in autumn and winter. The Ljubljanica River flows through the city and under several bridges, including Cobbler Bridge (Čevljarski Most), Triple Bridge (Tromostovje) and Dragon Bridge (Zmajski Most), which are the most interesting. On the western side of the river is Center, the commercial area, while the Old Town is on the eastern side. You can catch public buses around town.

PEOPLE

A typical native of Ljubljana is likely to speak not only Slovenian but also English, German and Italian. While around 83% of the population is Slovene, an increasing number of Croatians are popping over the border in search of work. Women make up 50% of the workforce but are unlikely to hold positions of authority. About 58% of the population is Catholic but as many as 33% are without specified religious beliefs.

TYPICAL LJUBLJANA CITIZEN

Despite the patina of imperial Austria, contemporary Ljubljana has a lively Slavic feel all its own, thanks to the temperament of its residents, which is influenced by both central Europe's penchant for orderliness and the Mediterranean's zest for life. Its inhabitants have always taken an active interest in the preservation of their city's character and rich cultural life. They are enthusiastic about the performing arts in general and are especially proud of their philharmonic academy, which is one of the oldest in Europe. Outdoor pursuits are also popular with the locals, who parade their pets in Tivoli Park and go swimming at Ilirija pool when not basking in the sauna at Zlati Klub. Over 27,000 students attend Ljubljana's university, which includes three art academies, so the city always feels young.

DEFINING EXPERIENCE

Buying an ice cream in Prešernov trg, licking it across the Triple Bridge and pottering around the Old Town between *burek* (small stuffed pastry) stands and umbrella-shaded outdoor cafés before heading up to Ljubljana Castle for a spot of lunch outside Bar Ljubljanski Grad and looking at those views.

STRENGTHS

- Proximity to the rest of Slovenia
- Riverside cafés
- Triple Bridge
- Skiing in Krvavec
- Swimming in the Adriatic
- Hot-air ballooning over the city
- Kayaking on the Ljubljanica
- Rafting on the Sava
- Cviček, a dry rosé from Posavje
- Varied and delicious cuisine
- Union beer
- Relatively low number of tourists
- Very pretty Old Town
- The multicoloured façade of the Cooperative Bank
- Ljubljana Castle
- National Gallery
- Slovenian National Opera and Ballet Companies
- Zlati Club sauna
- Union Olimpija basketball team
- Siddharta, a popular rock band
- The Ana Desetnica International Festival of Street Theatre
- Bird-watching
- Slovenian bread *(kruh)*
- Mushroom picking

WEAKNESSES

- Expensive laundrettes
- Increasing prices
- Peculiar, erotic souvenirs
- Confusing queuing system outside restaurants
- High sulphur dioxide levels
- Illegal waste dumping

GOLD STAR

Compact charm – simply wandering around the streets seems to be one of the local inhabitants' favourite pastimes, probably because the city still retains its human scale.

CITYSPEAK

- Refugees and economic immigrants from the former Yugoslav republics

STARRING ROLE IN...

- *Sign of the Cross: Travels in Catholic Europe* by Colm Tóibín

IMPORT

- Migrants from the former Yugoslav republics
- British tourists on no-frills flights
- James Joyce and Nora Barnacle (for one night, by mistake)
- Charles Nodier
- Ancient Greek mythological hero Jason, who is said to have founded the city when he stopped here with the Argonauts during their journey with the stolen Golden Fleece

EXPORT

- Poet Barbara Korun
- Impressionist painter Matija Jama
- Influential architect Jože Plečnik
- Ski-jumping world champion Primož Peterka
- Wine
- Realist painter Ivana Kobilca
- Industrial-techno group Laibach

SEE the city's biggest attraction, Ljubljana Castle, and peer over the Old Town from the ramparts.

EAT local cuisine at Pri Škofju, a delightful Krakovo restaurant.

DRINK award-winning Slovenian wines at the Movia Vinoteka wine bar.

DO go rafting on the Sava and experience the Slovenian outdoors.

WATCH open-air theatre at the highlight of the year, the Ljubljana Summer Festival.

BUY antiques and trinkets at the tempting Sunday-morning antiques flea market on Cankarjevo nabrežje.

AFTER DARK shake your funky stuff at Global Club on the 6th floor of Nama department store.

URBAN MYTH

The Dragon Bridge was funded by Vienna after a cunning mayor in the early 20th century persuaded his neighbour that the river required an additional crossing. Embellished with bronze dragons, locals claim that their tails wag when a virgin crosses the bridge.

COSMOPOLITAN CAFÉ CULTURE ON THE TRENDY RIVERSIDE STRIP.
Photographer: Richard I'Anson (2)

CONTRASTING STYLES OF STREET ART IN ONE OF THE CITY'S UNDERPASSES.
Photographer: Richard I'Anson (3)

EARLY MORNING DOG WALKING IN THE HILLS OVERLOOKING THE FOGGY CITY.
Photographer: Richard I'Anson (4)

A WOMAN IN A TRADITIONAL GOWN ACCESSORISES WITH FUR STOLE AND HANDBAG.
Photographer: Paul Chesley (1)

Seoul 085

VITAL STATISTICS

NAME: SEOUL

DATE OF BIRTH: 57 BC; DURING THE THREE KINGDOMS PERIOD, WHEN IT WAS RULED BY THE BAEKJE AND SILLA DYNASTIES

ADDRESS: SOUTH KOREA (MAP 1, JJ10)

HEIGHT: 87M

SIZE: 65 SQ KM

POPULATION: 10.7 MILLION

Seoul is the 600-year-old capital of a world-class economic powerhouse and a representation of a true rags-to-riches story – in every aspect of life and culture it is a fascinating melting pot of old and new, East and West.

ANATOMY

Bisected by the Hangang River, Seoul is surrounded by eight mountain peaks. The main historical, sightseeing and accommodation part of Seoul is the downtown area, with Namsan and Seoul Tower forming the southern perimeter. The touristy shopping and entertainment area of Itaewon is on the south side of Namsan. South of Itaewon, the Hangang River winds its way through the city. Within the river, to the west, is the small island of Yeouido, an important administrative centre. The Gangnam district, south of the river, is where upwardly mobile citizens aspire to live. To the east is Jamsil, home to the giant COEX Mall, Lotte World and Olympic Park. Seoul's subway system is modern, fast, frequent, clean, safe and cheap. There are also buses around the city.

PEOPLE

Birth rates are low, the population is getting older and there is a shortage of young females. Korea is ethnically and linguistically homogeneous and, although the number of foreigners visiting and working in Seoul is increasing, expats still comprise a very small percentage of the population.

TYPICAL SEOULITE

Seoulites work long hours, but also enjoy socialising and are generally more than kind to foreign visitors. Korean relationships are complicated by social hierarchy, and social status is very important. The concept of losing face is integral to Korean society. As a result Koreans are seemingly overly agreeable and pleasant, doing anything to smooth over potential disagreements or arguments that could lead to losing face. Seoulites are always very respectful and will greet each other with a short bow or nod. Seoul has over 40 top universities, and the Koreans' inexhaustible obsession with education and the social status it brings is nowhere more prevalent than here.

DEFINING EXPERIENCE

Exploring the royal palaces and War Memorial Museum and Seodaemun Prison for an introduction to Seoul's complex and tragic history, then sipping on ginseng tea in a tiny stall at Dongdaemun Market before adding the finishing touches to your wardrobe, and then climbing Inwangsan to the shamanist shrine at dusk to contemplate the lights of the city unfolding before you.

STRENGTHS

- ◢ Safe and friendly city
- ◢ Low crime rate
- ◢ High standard of living and clean streets
- ◢ Buzzing and modern Asian city
- ◢ Korean cuisine
- ◢ Ancient sculpture and architecture
- ◢ Leather goods
- ◢ Millions of trees (planted to try to improve the city's environment)
- ◢ Well-developed bicycle paths and sports facilities

WEAKNESSES

- ◢ Seoul is rated as the world's fifth most-expensive city
- ◢ Summer monsoon season
- ◢ Sometime conservative outlook on women in society
- ◢ Sometime conservative approach to Western and Korean relationships

GOLD STAR

Seoul is a fascinating melting pot of old and new, East and West.

CITYSPEAK

- ◢ Should the two-year national service be voluntary because it affects career development or is it a traditional rite of passage?
- ◢ Is the enforcement of the special law banning the sex trade doing more harm than good?
- ◢ The introduction of the 2005 Animal Protection Law affecting an age-old culture where dog is a popular menu item?

STARRING ROLE IN...

- ◢ *Chihwasun* (2002)
- ◢ *Taegukgi* (2003)
- ◢ *Eunuch* (1968)
- ◢ *Nowhere to Hide* (1999)
- ◢ *The President's Last Bang* (2005)
- ◢ *Sunday Seoul* (2005)

IMPORT

- ◢ All things European: food, wine, books, movies…
- ◢ Japanese popular culture (the importation ban was recently lifted)
- ◢ Australian indigenous art (Aboriginal art) – the latest hot commodity
- ◢ Christianity (about 25% of Koreans are Christians)
- ◢ Confucianism
- ◢ Buddhism (almost 25% of Koreans are Buddhists)

EXPORT

- ◢ North Korean missile technology
- ◢ Technology for cloning human embryos
- ◢ Hyundai and Daewoo automobiles
- ◢ Korean exchange students
- ◢ Leather jackets, belts, wallets, purses…anything leather
- ◢ Rice wines and Korean cuisine
- ◢ Cheap electronic goods
- ◢ Chemicals
- ◢ Textiles
- ◢ Machinery
- ◢ Lacquerware, made using a black paint that comes from the sap of the lacquer tree
- ◢ Reproduction Joseon Dynasty furniture

SEE the palaces of Gyeongbokgung and Deoksugung to soak up the atmosphere of the feudal royal court.

EAT temple food and take part in a tea ceremony with Buddhist monks at Jogyesa or Bongeunsa.

DRINK Geumsan Insamju, a rice wine made from a 600-year-old recipe.

DO a hike around the huge fortresses of Bukhansanseong and Namhansanseong that were built in the forest-covered mountains around Seoul.

WATCH the royal ancestral rites festival at Jongmyo, as well as other historical re-enactments that reveal an Asian society with its own very distinctive style.

BUY anything made of leather: jackets, belts, wallets, purses, bags and shoes are all Seoul specialities.

AFTER DARK head to one of the many tiny underground venues in Hongkik, Seoul's live indie-music hotspot.

URBAN MYTH

Every summer, Korean newspapers carry reports of people dying after sleeping in a room with the electric fan on and the doors and windows closed. It is widely believed that fans create an air current that seals the room, driving oxygen to the ceiling and carbon dioxide towards the floor, suffocating the person inside.

YOUNG BUDDHIST MONKS PUT THEIR HANDS TOGETHER TO COMMEMORATE BUDDHA'S BIRTHDAY AT THE CHOGYE TEMPLE.
Photographer: Chung Sung-Jun (2)

LIKE MINIATURE HOT-AIR BALLOONS, PAPER LANTERNS FLOAT IN THE BRANCHES OF A TREE AT THE CHOGYE TEMPLE.
Photographer: Craig Brown (3)

A CYCLIST SILHOUETTED AGAINST THE SUNRISE WITH THE SOARING DLI 63 BUILDING IN THE BACKGROUND.
Photographer: SETBOUN (4)

San Cristóbal de las Casas 086

VITAL STATISTICS

NAME: SAN CRISTÓBAL DE LAS CASAS

NICKNAME: SAN CRISTÓBAL

DATE OF BIRTH: 1528; WHEN DIEGO DE MAZARIEGOS FOUNDED THE CITY AS A SPANISH REGIONAL BASE

ADDRESS: MEXICO (MAP 4, E5)

HEIGHT: 2163M

POPULATION: 121,000

In the heart of Mexico's southernmost state, San Cristóbal de las Casas is a light and airy city; diverse indigenous communities flock here to trade goods and ideas in among crumbling colonial churches and pastel-coloured houses.

ANATOMY

Although San Cristóbal de las Casas is elevated several thousand metres above sea level, it still manages to rest in a broad, fertile valley. The town grid is framed on all sides by a chain of low hills dotted with indigenous villages. The serene heart of the city is Plaza 31 de Marzo where craft sellers, shoeshiners and lunch-breakers mill around in the sun. Commerce and industry have not left a strong architectural imprint: to this day the tallest structures are the lovely Spanish municipal buildings and centuries-old cathedrals. Combis go up Av Crescencio Rosas from the Pan-American Hwy to the town centre. You can also catch taxis within town.

PEOPLE

Due to their custom of wearing their hair in pony tails, the men of the early Spanish colonial town of San Cristóbal earned the nickname *coletos* (from the Spanish world *cola* or 'tail'). The word is still used to refer to a resident of the city although most citizens are mestizo (of mixed Spanish and indigenous ancestry). From its beginnings the town has been a regular meeting point for communities of Tzotzil and Tzeltal peoples, who continue to define the soul of the city.

TYPICAL COLETO

San Cristóbal is a city that wears its history on its sleeve, and residents have a strong sense of both their ancestral legacy and their place in the unfolding narrative. Largely untouched by the revolutionary land reforms of 1917, the inhabitants of the region continued to suffer under a punishing colonial structure until relatively recently. Indigenous pride is strong in the area and it's not unusual to see locals in their traditional dress going about their daily activities in the heart of the city. *Coletos* are confident but wary – cheerful faces veil simmering social tensions.

DEFINING EXPERIENCE

Getting up early to enjoy the freshest coffee from the city's own Museo Café (Coffee Museum), heading to the hills on a caffeine high to observe the unique lifestyles of San Cristóbal's neighbours, making it back to the market for an open-air lunch in the middle of the madness then winding down in the late afternoon sun at Plaza 31 de Marzo.

STRENGTHS

◢ Bartolomé de las Casas (early defender of indigenous rights; the city is partially named in his honour)
◢ Zapatista iconography
◢ Cobbled streets
◢ Clear highland light
◢ Plaza 31 de Marzo
◢ Mercado Municipal – the wonderfully chaotic city market
◢ Organic coffee
◢ Templo de Santo Domingo

WEAKNESSES

◢ Foreign missionaries
◢ Heavily armed soldiers
◢ Political tensions
◢ Intransigent councils
◢ Religious intolerance
◢ Culturally insensitive tourists

GOLD STAR

Weaving – Tzotzil weavers are some of the most skilled in Mexico and their distinctive needlework can be seen everywhere you wander.

CITYSPEAK

◢ Elections, elections, elections
◢ When will we hear from Marcos again?
◢ The Pueblo–Panama Plan – what will become of southeast Mexico?

STARRING ROLE IN...

◢ *A Place Called Chiapas* (1998)

IMPORT

◢ US-manufactured goods
◢ Crafts and textiles from neighbouring townships
◢ Tourists

EXPORT

◢ Amber
◢ Toy slingshots
◢ Marcos dolls
◢ *Huipiles* (traditional blouses)
◢ Zapatista ideology
◢ Coffee

SEE the charming Templo de Santo Domingo, a fine example of Spanish colonial architecture.

EAT rustic tortillas containing microscopic amounts of ground limestone.

DRINK organic coffee from locally harvested beans.

DO an excursion to the nearby indigenous villages.

WATCH a political demonstration in Plaza 31 de Marzo.

BUY expertly woven indigenous garments.

AFTER DARK check out the awesome live music at Creación, San Cristóbal's hippest nightspot.

URBAN MYTH

At midnight on 1 January 1994, a previously unknown leftist guerrilla army, the Zapatistas, emerged from the woods to occupy San Cristóbal de las Casas and other towns in Chiapas. Linking antiglobalisation rhetoric with Mexican revolutionary sloganism, their declared goal was to overturn a wealthy local oligarchy's centuries-old hold on land, resources and power and to fight to improve the wretched living standards of Mexico's indigenous people. The Zapatistas' charismatic pipe-puffing Subcomandante Marcos rapidly became a cult figure. His articulate dispatches – delivered in mocking, humorous and often self-deprecating tones – demanded justice and reform. Tensions continue to flare up between competing interest groups, and dialogue between the Zapatistas and the Mexican government is strained. A wry statement from the Zapatista leadership sums up the patient resilience of the people: 'For 500 years the authorities have failed to listen to us. We have time on our side.'

A WOMAN HAULS HER LOAD UP A STEEP HILLSIDE LANE.
Photographer: Macduff Everton (1)

A PUPPETEER IN A CROW COSTUME ACTS OUT A DRAMATIC SCENE FROM ONE OF THE ANCIENT MAYAN MYTHS.
Photographer: Macduff Everton (2)

SMILES ALL ROUND AT THE TIENDA DOÑA PANCHITA, A LOCALLY OWNED STORE ON CALLE DIEGO DUGELAY.
Photographer: Christian Heeb (3)

THE CROSS CASTS A LARGE SHADOW ON SAN CRISTÓBAL'S CATHEDRAL.
Photographer: Louis Grandadam (4)

MILES OF SMILES FROM A CHEERFUL SHOPKEEPER IN THE HEART OF TOWN.
Photographer: Brent Winebrenner (1)

The commercial and cultural heart of Taiwan, Taipei is regarded by many visitors as the friendliest big city in Asia – not to mention one of the world's great food capitals.

ANATOMY

Taipei city is divided into 12 districts that are then divided into neighbourhoods. It is also divided into compass points, much like most American cities. It's dissected at its north and south points by Chunghsiao and Pateh Rds, while its east and west grids are bisected by Chungshan Rd. Cab it, walk or take the MRT (Metropolitan Rapid Transit).

PEOPLE

Forty-two percent of Taiwan's entire population live in the Taipei area. The vast majority of Taiwanese are of Han Chinese origin, with 14% being immigrants who came from mainland China following the Communist Revolution. Around 2% of the population is indigenous, the nine main tribes being Ami, Atayal, Bunun, Paiwan, Puyuma, Rukai, Saisiyat, Tsao and Yami.

TYPICAL TAIPEI CITIZEN

Taiwanese are welcoming and friendly, particularly the younger set. Until the borders were relaxed in 1987, the typical Taipei citizen suffered from a severe case of workaholic behaviour. But they, too, are coming to learn the value of the 38-hour week.

DEFINING EXPERIENCE

Catching the 39-second lift (elevator) to the 89th floor of Taipei 101 (the world's tallest building), picking up some Hello Kitty merchandise, retreating from the noisy city to the beautiful lotus pond in the Botanical Gardens, then getting a late-night snack at the Shihlin Night Market.

STRENGTHS

- ◢ Subtropical weather
- ◢ Excellent (albeit expensive) seafood
- ◢ Excellent Chinese food available 24/7
- ◢ Traditional teahouses
- ◢ Lively night markets
- ◢ Wonderful shopping

WEAKNESSES

- ◢ Hazy skyline
- ◢ Summer typhoons

Taipei 087

VITAL STATISTICS

NAME: TAIPEI

NICKNAME: CITY OF AZALEAS

DATE OF BIRTH: 1709; WHEN SETTLERS FROM CHINA'S FUJIAN PROVINCE RECEIVED PERMISSION FROM THE QING GOVERNMENT TO EMIGRATE TO TAIWAN

ADDRESS: TAIWAN (MAP 5, R4)

HEIGHT: 9M

SIZE: 270 SQ KM

POPULATION: 2.64 MILLION

A TAXI TAKES OFF IN A BLUR.
Photographer: Hugh Sitton (3)

ELDERLY BUDDHIST NUNS KNEEL IN PRAYER AT LUNG SHAN TEMPLE, ONE OF THE OLDEST IN TAIPEI.
Photographer: Chris Stowers (2)

MYSTICAL SCENES AS LOCALS RELEASE LANTERNS TO BRING BLESSINGS AND GOOD FORTUNE AT THE CHINESE LANTERN
FESTIVAL. Photographer: Simon Kwong (4)

GOLD STAR

The National Palace Museum is home to the world's largest collection of Chinese artefacts – around 720,000 pieces. Around 15,000 pieces are on display at any given time and are rotated every three months. At that pace it would take something like 16 years to see everything. Bring a thermos and a packed lunch.

CITYSPEAK

- Police crackdown on online election gambling
- Drug use among teens on the rise
- Will aggressive Hollywood marketing continue to destroy the film industry in Taipei?

STARRING ROLE IN...

- *Eat Drink Man Woman* (1994)
- *The Red Lotus Society* (1988)
- *In Our Time* (1982)

IMPORT

- 7-11
- Pizza
- River tracing
- Baseball
- Glove puppets from China
- Jin Yong's martial-arts novels

EXPORT

- Computers and telecommunications
- Motorcycle parts
- Taiwanese opera
- Kuoshu martial arts

SEE the city at your feet from the 89th floor of Taipei 101, the world's tallest building.

EAT stinky tofu (tofu that has been fermented, deep-fried and served with pickled cabbage and hot sauce).

DRINK extra sugary milky tea from one of Taipei's teahouses (check out the Wisteria Tea House, where Ang Lee filmed *Eat Drink Man Woman*) or betel-nut juice from a street vendor.

DO visit snake handlers at the Huahsi Night market (aka Snake Alley) and try a couple of snake-penis pills or powdered gall bladder.

WATCH a performance by the Contemporary Legend Theatre established by Wu Hsing-guo, famous for his adaptations of Shakespeare's plays.

BUY shoes, bags, electronics and Hello Kitty paraphernalia from one of the myriad markets or shopping centres.

AFTER DARK buy, eat, drink, sniff and join the street peddlers at the Shihlin Night Market.

URBAN MYTH

Matsu, the Goddess of the Sea, is the predominant folk deity in Taiwan. It is said that she was a mortal originally, born during the Northern Sung dynasty (AD 960–1127). She only lived 28 years but she managed to remain pure and to take on the world's burdens, performing miracles, subduing evil spirits and averting sea disasters. Those who survived immigration by boat from mainland China believed that Matsu was looking over them. The Kuantu Temple in Taipei is the oldest Matsu temple, founded in 1661 on Mt Ling. According to legend, in 1895 three old banyan trees at the entrance of the temple suddenly died. Was this a message from Matsu of the impending Japanese occupation? Or just overwatering?

Tallinn 088

VITAL STATISTICS

NAME: TALLINN

NICKNAME: KOLUVAN; LINDANISA; REVALIA; REVEL; TALLSINKI

DATE OF BIRTH: 9TH CENTURY AD; WHEN AN ESTONIAN TRADING SETTLEMENT SPRANG UP

ADDRESS: ESTONIA (MAP 3, P2)

HEIGHT: 44M

SIZE: 158 SQ KM

POPULATION: 400,000

STRETCHING A LONG SHADOW BEHIND HIM, AN ELDERLY GENTLEMAN WALKS THROUGH THE STREETS OF TOOMPEA IN THE OLD TOWN. Photographer: Jonathan Smith (1)

Fairy-tale architecture and cobblestone streets, which seem made to give Hansel and Gretel a sugar rush, are sweetened by the quaint bay and gooey liqueurs.

ANATOMY

On the southern shore of the Gulf of Finland, Tallinn Bay protects this small city. The Old Town is the city's heart, divided into historic Upper Town on Toompea (the hill dominating Tallinn) and Lower Town, on the eastern side of Toompea. The centrepiece of the Old Town is the magnificent Raekoja plats (Town Hall Sq) hemmed by most of its 2.5km medieval wall. Around the Old Town is a belt of green parks following the line of the city's old defence moat. Radiating outwards from this old core is the New Town, dating from the 19th and early 20th centuries. Trams, trolleybuses and buses are the best way to get around.

PEOPLE

In the post-Soviet era the population has fallen, with immigration to Finland or Western Europe being popular. Predominantly still Estonian (49%), Tallinn has seen new arrivals from Russia (40%) and to a lesser extent the Ukraine and Byelorussia. Estonian is the official language, with the related language of Finnish usually understood. Russian is common, though it can be perceived as an uncomfortable reminder of the city's occupation.

TYPICAL TALLINER

Talliners have developed a strong sense of identity since independence when they peacefully ejected the Soviets in protests that became known as the 'Singing Revolution'. The spoils of the free market have been slow to arrive, with unemployment high and most Talliners still living in apartments. Working Talliners do get more in their pay packets than other Estonians, mainly due to large amounts of foreign investment and tourism. Some have dubbed the city Tallsinki for its multilingual leanings and large e-industry. Tourists and Russian immigrants are tolerated by Talliners who still recall the Soviet's control over the city.

DEFINING EXPERIENCE

Hopping off the ferry from Helsinki, breakfasting in Raekoja plats at a street-side café, strolling through the Old Town, hopping on a rattling tram across town, then lunching at the romantic Gloria restaurant, which once hosted Soviet canoodlers from St Petersburg, wandering along the docks then pausing for a mid-afternoon coffee and cake, taking dinner at the latest Thai or Nepali place, then finishing off the night with honey-brewed beer.

STRENGTHS

- Handy to Helsinki
- Raekoja plats
- Medieval buildings
- Historic trams
- Ecofriendly pedi-cabs (in the Old Town)
- Toompea
- Alexander Nevsky Cathedral
- Toomkirik (the Lutheran cathedral founded in 1233)
- Estonian Art Museum
- Kiek-in-de-Kök (a tall, stout tower built around 1475)
- Art Deco bars
- Backstreets of Pikk

WEAKNESSES

- Too handy to Helsinki
- Drunken Finns
- Street crime
- Cold, dark winters
- Reconstruction in Old Town

GOLD STAR

History – in 1997 Tallinn's Old Town was made a Unesco World Cultural Heritage site, so there are serious monuments in every alleyway.

CITYSPEAK

- Laws to limit the drunkenness of Finns
- The increasing drug culture of the city
- Old Town reconstruction – will it ever finish?
- Is the Uhispank building an eyesore or the 'way of the future'?

STARRING ROLE IN...

- *Darkness in Tallinn* (1993)
- *Fender Bender* (2003)
- *Lilja 4-ever* (2002)
- *Among the Russians* by Colin Thubron

IMPORT

- Finnish hedonists
- 'New' Russians
- McDonald's

EXPORT

- Alcohol to Finland
- Health products not covered by Finnish social services, such as glasses
- Vana Tallinn (the local liqueur)
- Knitwear
- Vaino Väljas
- Lennart Meri
- Internet-dating scams

SEE the sun setting over the Old Town from atop Toompea.

EAT a vampiric feast of blood sausage at the meaty Kuldse Notsu Kõrts, which has vegetarian (non-bloodsucking) options.

DRINK *Vana Tallinn* in the cosy ambience of Gloria Veinikelder.

DO sail the pretty Tallinn Bay or island-hop through the Finland Gulf.

WATCH an experimental play at Tallinn's epicentre of fringe, Von Krahli Theatre.

BUY a bargain snowflake sweater at the Kadaka Turg market.

AFTER DARK shake it with fellow starlets at Hollywood inside the Sõprus Cinema.

URBAN MYTH

One of the most photographed but least understood monuments of Pikk is the ornate doorway of the Brotherhood of Blackheads. Not a fraternity hell-bent on pimple-free hygiene, the brotherhood were a band of young, single merchants who had not been accepted into a larger guild. This building would have housed visiting merchants, keeping their wares and virtues safe behind the mighty door, under the protective gaze of St Mauritius, the patron saint of the brotherhood. His dark-skinned face (hence the Blackhead name) looks benignly down from above the doorway, keeping an eye on all of the footloose merchants' visitors.

SHAKE IT LIKE A POLAROID PICTURE – A GIRL GETS FUNKY AT A CITY NIGHTCLUB.
Photographer: Ingolf Pompe (2)

THE PUHAVAIMU KIRIK POKES A SHARP SPIRE ABOVE SURROUNDING BUILDINGS.
Photographer: Jonathan Smith (3)

FRIENDS STAY FIT FOR THE FOOTBALL SEASON NEAR THE OLD CITY WALLS.
Photographer: JA Schlosser (4)

A WOMAN SQUINTS AT A CELEBRATION OF LOSAR, THE TIBETAN NEW YEAR.
Photographer: Maria Stenzel (1)

Lhasa 089

VITAL STATISTICS

NAME: LHASA

NICKNAME: HOLY CITY; SUNLIGHT CITY

DATE OF BIRTH: 7TH CENTURY; WHEN LOCAL RULER SONGSTEN GAMPO MADE LHASA HIS CAPITAL

ADDRESS: TIBET (MAP 5, H2)

HEIGHT: 3595M

SIZE: 30,000 SQ KM

POPULATION: 240,000

The resilient heart of a nation and a city of unique heritage, Lhasa sits literally on the top of the world, seen by many as the homeland and jewel in the crown of Buddhism.

ANATOMY

The city divides clearly into a western (Chinese) section and an eastern (Tibetan) section. The Chinese side holds most of Lhasa's upmarket accommodation options, along with Chinese restaurants, bars and the Nepali consulate. The Tibetan eastern end of town is more colourful and has all the budget and mid-range accommodation popular with independent travellers. The main drag is the east to west–running Dekyi Nub Lam, which then becomes Dekyi Shar Lam in the east of town (in Tibetan, *nub* means west and *shar* means east). Jokhang Temple and Barkhor Sq are in between Dekyi Shar Lam and Chingdröl Shar Lam (Jiangsu Lu) and are connected to these two main roads by the Tibetan quarter – a web of winding alleyways lined with the whitewashed façades of traditional Tibetan homes. Bicycle is without a doubt the best way to get around (once you have acclimatised to the altitude). Otherwise, you'll find privately run minibuses are frequent on Dekyi Shar Lam and taxis are plentiful.

PEOPLE

The official figures for Lhasa's population are 87% Tibetan and just under 12% Han Chinese, though these are generally discounted by all except the Chinese government, which released them. More realistic estimates put the percentage closer to 50/50. The population of the city before the Chinese takeover was less than 30,000 and the recent influx of Han Chinese has been nicknamed 'China's second invasion'. There is also a 2000-strong Islamic community, based mostly in the Muslim Quarter.

TYPICAL LHASAN

Understanding the basics of Buddhism is essential in understanding any Tibetan and the citizens of Lhasa even more so. They are gentle in spirit, deeply religious and quietly unshakable in their resolve. Though they have lost so much to outside influence, they remain remarkably open and generous.

DEFINING EXPERIENCE

Following the flow of pilgrims around the Barkhor circuit with sustenance stops at nearby restaurants for *momos* (Tibetan dumplings) washed down with steaming yak-butter tea.

STRENGTHS

- ⊿ Potala, the deserted citadel of the Dalai Lama
- ⊿ Jokhang and its shrines
- ⊿ Walking tours
- ⊿ The nearby Drepung Monastery
- ⊿ Nam-tso Restaurant
- ⊿ Buddhist history
- ⊿ Tibet Museum
- ⊿ Barkhor Sq
- ⊿ A plethora of chapels
- ⊿ The Norbulingka

WEAKNESSES

- ⊿ Chinese cultural dominance
- ⊿ Altitude sickness
- ⊿ Modernisation
- ⊿ Chinese propaganda
- ⊿ Limited cuisine

GOLD STAR

To the Tibetans – for holding tight to what's left of Tibetan cultural and religious heritage after half a century of brutal and restrictive Chinese rule

CITYSPEAK

- ⊿ The controversial train line from Golmud, touted as a gift by the Chinese, but seen by many Tibetans as being potentially devastating for their culture, which has already been dwarfed by Chinese occupation

STARRING ROLE IN...

- ⊿ *Windhorse* (1998)

IMPORT

- ⊿ Buddhism
- ⊿ Chinese culture
- ⊿ Pilgrims

EXPORT

- ⊿ Lamas in exile
- ⊿ Buddhist teachers and teachings
- ⊿ Traditional handicrafts
- ⊿ Yak hair and leather

SEE the Potala, the deserted citadel of the Dalai Lamas.

EAT the local fare such as *momos*, *thugpa* (soup) and *shemdre* (potatoes and yak meat) at the Pentoc Tibetan Restaurant.

DRINK *bö cha* (Tibetan yak-butter tea).

DO cycle to the Drepung Monastery for an afternoon of exploring what remains of its 6th-century history.

WATCH traditional performances at the Tibetan Dance & Drama Theatre.

BUY a prayer wheel from one of the many stalls lining the Barkhor circuit.

AFTER DARK try the Music Kitchen or any of the other bars near the Lhasa Hotel for a good night out.

URBAN MYTH

It was Princess Wencheng, the Chinese wife of King Songtsen Gampo, who divined the presence of a vast, supine demoness whose body straddled all the high plateau. Through Chinese geomantic calculations she established that the heart of the demoness lay beneath a lake in the centre of Lhasa, while her torso and limbs lay far away in the outer dominions of the high plateau. It was decided that the demoness would have to be pinned down. The first task was to drain the lake in Lhasa of its water (read lifeblood of the demoness) and build a central temple that would replace her heart with a Buddhist heart. The temple built there was the Jokhang. A stake through the heart was not enough to put a demoness of this size out of action, however, and a series of lesser temples, in three concentric rings, were conceived to pin the extremities of the demoness forever.

PILGRIMS COMPLETE THEIR RITUAL CIRCUMAMBULATION OF JOKHANG MONASTERY.
Photographer: Angelo Cavalli (2)

NOVICE MONKS AT DREPUNG MONASTERY CROWD IN FOR A GROUP SHOT.
Photographer: Dennis Cox (3)

SUNBEAMS FILTER INTO THE RUSTIC SLEEPING QUARTERS OF A MONASTERY NEAR THE CITY.
Photographer: Hannah Levy (4)

With its emerald-green lake, islet with picture-postcard church, medieval castle clinging to a rocky cliff and some of the highest peaks of the Julian Alps and the Karavanke Mountains as a backdrop, Bled is simply magical.

ANATOMY

Surrounded by mountains, Bled's focus is its idyllic 2km-long lake, its beauty enhanced by a tiny island with a red-and-white-spired belfry rising above the trees. The built-up area to the northeast is the largest of the settlements located around the lake and contains most of the hotels. Bled's main road, Ljubljanska cesta, runs eastward from here. Bled is served by a bus station and two train stations.

PEOPLE

Slovenes are polyglots, and virtually everyone in the resort town of Bled speaks some English, German and/or Italian.

TYPICAL BLED CITIZEN

For centuries Bled was a mecca for pilgrims, and since the 19th century it has attracted hordes of tourists and health devotees – you're far more likely to encounter visitors than locals. There's nothing fuddy-duddy about Bled, but given that it is a spa town renowned for its curative waters, many of its visitors are, well, older. If you're lucky enough to find a real local, chances are they'll love a good polka and regular schnapps pick-me-ups. They will also be filled with pride at the achievements of the many world-class ski champions the mountains have produced. It is obvious, from the ship-shape state of the city, that its residents are eager to preserve its history.

DEFINING EXPERIENCE

Rising early to explore the lake at its most breathtaking before embarking on a romantic gondola trip to the island to wish for what you most desire on the wishing bell, then enjoying a lunch of good home-cooked food and local wine at a countryside inn.

Bled 090

VITAL STATISTICS

NAME: BLED

DATE OF BIRTH: EARLY IRON AGE; BLED WAS THE SITE OF A HALLSTATT SETTLEMENT

ADDRESS: SLOVENIA (MAP 3, L11)

HEIGHT: 501M

POPULATION: 5476

AFTER AN INVIGORATING DAY AT THE THERMAL SPA, SPIRITS ARE ENLIVENED AT THE DEVIL'S BAR.
Photographer: Richard I'Anson (1)

STRENGTHS

- The country's best golf course, and one of Europe's most beautiful
- Bled's precipitous medieval castle
- Hikes galore
- Ice skating on the lake in winter
- Trips on the Old Timer vintage steam train
- Crystal-clear warm water
- Hot-air ballooning over the town
- The Okarina Folk Festival of folk and world music
- Summertime concerts at the castle, Festival Hall and the parish church
- Excellent bread, especially the braided loaves at Christmas
- Clean air and mountain light
- Polka dancing
- A plethora of outdoor activities
- Panoramic flights in Cessna 172s
- Charming towns such as Radovljica – an easy day trip away

WEAKNESSES

- The congestion at the top of Slovenia's highest peak, Triglav
- Droves of tourists in midsummer
- Leaving

GOLD STAR

The spectacular Vintgar Gorge, just west and slightly north of Bled, is a peaceful bit of beauty hidden by steep canyons. A wooden walkway built in 1893 hugs the rock walls of the gorge for 1600m along the Radovna River, crisscrossing the raging torrent four times over rapids, waterfalls and pools before reaching the 13m-high Šum Waterfall.

CITYSPEAK

- Whether the national football team will continue to do as well as they did in the 2000 European championship
- The Union Olimpija basketball team
- Satellite TV shows

STARRING ROLE IN...

- The poetry of France Prešeren

IMPORT

- Olympic gold medal – Istok Čop and Luka Špik from the Bled Rowing Club won Slovenia's first Olympic Gold (in the double skull at the Sydney Olympic Games in 2000)
- International rowers – each year in mid-June they flock to Bled for the International Rowing Regatta
- Biathlon competitors – they arrive each winter to compete in the Biathlon World Championship of cross-country skiing and rifle shooting at the nearby Pokljuka Plateau
- Cuisine – Slovenian food is heavily influenced by Austria, Italy and Hungary

EXPORT

- Punk music in the late 1970s and early '80s
- France Prešeren, Slovenia's greatest poet, was born in Vrba, near Bled

SEE the stunning view from the summit of Velika Osojnica – over the lake, island and dramatic castle, with the peaks of the Karavanke in the background.

EAT Bled's culinary speciality, *kremna rezina* (cream cake), a layer of vanilla custard topped with whipped cream and sandwiched neatly between two layers of flaky pastry.

DRINK Zlatorog, Slovenia's best *pivo* (beer), at the friendly Pub Bled, the town's late-night venue of choice.

DO the polka – it only takes three minutes to learn.

WATCH the clouds roll by as you twirl around the lake or head to the castle in a horse-drawn carriage.

BUY a traditional beehive panel illustrated with folk motifs.

DO ring the wishing bell in the 15th-century belfry of Bled island's baroque church to ask a favour.

AFTER DARK try your luck at roulette, blackjack or baccarat at Casino Bled.

URBAN MYTH

Bled has been linked with the myths and legends of the early Slavs for centuries, particularly the ancient Slavic goddess Živa. The baroque Church of the Assumption is allegedly the site of Živa's temple, and archaeological excavations have found evidence of an ancient burial ground under the church.

A DREAMLIKE VISION AS DUSK SETTLES OVER BLED CASTLE.
Photographer: Richard l'Anson (2)

WITH GONDOLA RIDES INCLUDED, WEDDINGS ON PICTURESQUE BLED ISLAND ARE INCREASINGLY POPULAR.
Photographer: Richard l'Anson (3)

NESTLED IN THE PICTURESQUE MOUNTAINS IS THE CHARMING 100-YEAR-OLD TOWNSHIP.
Photographer: Richard l'Anson (4)

Hobart

091

VITAL STATISTICS

NAME: HOBART

DATE OF BIRTH: 1803; WHEN EUROPEAN COLONIALISTS ARRIVED, BUT THE AREA HAD PREVIOUSLY BEEN INHABITED BY THE SEMI-NOMADIC ABORIGINAL MOUHENEENNER TRIBE

ADDRESS: AUSTRALIA (MAP 1, LL22)

HEIGHT: 54M

SIZE: 1360 SQ KM

POPULATION: 128,600

Small but perfectly formed Hobart pulses with the energy of a young, contemporary city proud of its well-preserved historic buildings and beautiful natural setting.

ANATOMY

Hobart has an enviable location, perched over the mouth of the Derwent River in the shadow of the imposing 1270m-high Mt Wellington. The easily-navigated city centre is arranged on a grid pattern around the Elizabeth St mall, west of which awaits retail temptation. Most of the tourist attractions are on the picturesque waterfront and Battery Point. Following the river south you meet Sandy Bay, home to the university and Wrest Point casino. Towards the north of the centre lies the Domain area, which includes the Botanical Gardens. Cars, buses, boats and bicycles nip through and around the city.

PEOPLE

The majority of Hobart's inhabitants are of European (especially British) descent. Just 2.5% of Hobart's population is of Aboriginal descent – a legacy of the massacres that occurred in Tasmania.

TYPICAL HOBART CITIZEN

Hobart is Australia's second-oldest city, which makes its inhabitants some of the oldest Australians in terms of generations. Their home is also the country's southernmost capital and is in one of Australia's most picturesque settings – no wonder they like where they live and are keen to conserve their environment. The setting also encourages an active life, and cycling, walking and watersports are particularly popular. They are cultured and appreciate art-house and international films as well as the Tasmanian Symphony Orchestra, whose home is in Hobart. After all that activity a glass of Tasmanian wine and some fine seafood goes down a treat.

DEFINING EXPERIENCE

Wandering through the myriad stalls of the fantastic Salamanca Market, pottering and purchasing, people-watching and enjoying the street performers, before picking up some cheap but tasty fish and chips from a barge on the dock.

STRENGTHS

- Well-preserved colonial buildings
- Natural beauty
- Compact size
- The Georgian warehouses of Salamanca Pl
- Salamanca Arts Centre
- Salamanca Market
- Mt Wellington
- Excellent seafood
- Sailing activities including the Royal Hobart Regatta
- Fish and chip barges
- Tasmanian Museum and Art Gallery
- Tasmanian Symphony Orchestra
- Battery Point
- Royal Tasmanian Botanical Gardens, housing the largest collection of mature conifers in the southern hemisphere
- Gourmet food and wine
- Organic products
- Moorilla Estate Vineyard
- Cheap car rental (lower rates than on mainland Australia)
- Tasmanian Gothic literature
- Taste of Tasmania festival
- Henry Jones Art Hotel
- Surfing at Clifton Beach

WEAKNESSES

- Relatively expensive if good accommodation
- Aesthetically challenged Federation Concert Hall
- Tasmanian wine (more expensive than mainland wine)
- Aboriginal massacres by the colonialists

GOLD STAR

Australian colonial architecture: there are more than 90 buildings classified by the National Trust in Hobart.

CITYSPEAK

- Conservation issues, particularly logging, mining and hydroelectric power

STARRING ROLE IN...

- *The English Passengers* by Matthew Kneale
- *The Tilted Cross* by Hal Porter
- *The Fatal Shore* by Robert Hughes

IMPORT

- Convicts
- Discerning tourists who bother to cross the Bass Strait
- British immigrants

EXPORT

- Errol Flynn
- Designer Patrick Hall
- Painter William Piguenit
- Pinot Noir from Stefano Lubiana Wines
- Rock lobster
- Salmon
- Abalone
- Scallops
- Wasabi
- Cascade Premium Lager and Pale Ale
- Cheddar and other Tasmanian cheeses
- Jams and sauces made from Tasmanian fruit
- Tasmanian Symphony Orchestra
- Huon pine and sassafras wood
- Lavender
- Cadbury chocolate
- Leatherwood honey

SEE the flotilla of sails at the climax of the New Year Sydney to Hobart Yacht Race.

EAT a Vietnamese salad or an all-day breakfast while watching your washing spin at the Machine Laundry Café.

DRINK a free sample or two while on a tour of Australia's oldest brewery, Cascade.

DO one of the many walks up Mt Wellington and use the spectacular view as an excuse for a rest.

WATCH the city and southwest wilderness from the cosy comfort of a seaplane.

BUY a piece of Tasmanian art or something made of Tasmanian wood.

AFTER DARK preen and pose with the in crowd at fashionable waterfront bistro-wine bar, T-42°.

URBAN MYTH

If you want a first-hand experience of Hobart's mythical underworld, take a ghost tour of the Penitentiary Chapel, offered by the National Trust. Ghost Tours of Hobart also offers nightly ghoul-spotting. With Hobart's convict history don't be surprised if you come face to face with some nasty dead characters. Good luck!

KICK UP YOUR HEELS AT THE RENOWNED SALAMANCA MARKET.
Photographer: Ian Waldie (1)

THE FIRST SUNBEAMS OF THE DAY TOUCH HOUSES AT THE FOOT OF MT WELLINGTON.
Photographer: Ian Waldie (2)

THE ULTRAMODERN DIGS OF THE TASMANIAN SYMPHONY ORCHESTRA.
Photographer: Ian Waldie (3)

MAKING THE MOST OF HOBART'S NIGHTLIFE SCENE, SALAMANCA PL.
Photographer: Adam Pretty (4)

Jaipur 092

VITAL STATISTICS

NAME: JAIPUR

NICKNAME: THE PINK CITY

DATE OF BIRTH: 1727; WHEN JAI SINGH DECIDED TO MOVE HIS CAPITAL FROM AMBER

ADDRESS: INDIA (MAP 5, C3)

HEIGHT: 390M

POPULATION: 2.7 MILLION

Acid-bright colours punctuate the streets: crouched porters group by the station in red shirts and turbans, billowing saris catch the eye like butterflies and shopfronts glitter with fierce fabrics.

ANATOMY

The walled Old City is in the northeast of Jaipur, while the new parts spread to the south and west. The main tourist attractions are in the bazaar-lined old city and taxis and auto-rickshaws are the best way to get around.

PEOPLE

Jaipur's population is predominantly Hindu, with a sizable Muslim minority. There are small communities of Jains, Sikhs and Christians. Tribal (Adivasi) groups were the first inhabitants of this region, and today they form 12% of the population – the national average is 8%. The main languages are Hindi and Rajasthani.

TYPICAL JAIPURIAN

Heirs to a rich intellectual heritage, Jaipurians, Hindu and Muslim men alike have bright Rajput turbans and swashbuckling moustaches while the women wear colourful saris. Jaipurians go about their business among streets jam-packed with cars, cows, rickshaws, snuffling pigs, motorcycles and death-defying pedestrians. Street children beg outside huge jewellery shops and palatial hotels.

DEFINING EXPERIENCE

Taking a trip out to Amber Palace to see the elephants and architecture, lunching at Copper Chimney in the middle of the day and exploring the City Palace, then wandering through town to look at the Havelis, taking in a little shopping – textiles, carpets, handicrafts or jewellery – before eating on MI Rd and catching a Hindi film at Raj Mandir Cinema, with its shell-pink interior.

STRENGTHS

- Elephant Festival
- Gangaur (Harvest) Festival
- Teej festival
- Jantar Mantar, Jaipur's remarkable observatory
- Hawa Mahal (Palace of the Winds)
- Old City
- Maharaja Sawni Mansingh II Museum
- Central Museum
- Rajasthan Astrological Council & Research Institute
- Modern Art Gallery
- Nahargar (Tiger Fort)
- Amber Fort and Palace
- *Havelis* (traditional ornate residences)

WEAKNESSES

- The hassle
- The pressure to buy
- Gem scams
- Traffic jams
- Overzealous rickshaw wallahs
- Persistent hotel touts

GOLD STAR

The old city, which is partially encircled by a crenellated wall, is notable for its town planning: avenues divide the Pink City into neat rectangles, each of which specialises in certain crafts. At dusk the sunset-shaded buildings have a magical glow.

CITYSPEAK

- Desertification – how far will it go?
- Irrigation – how effective will it be?
- Pollution – how much more can we stand?
- Will the monsoon come in abundance this year?
- Will the train link to Pakistan ever reopen?

STARRING ROLE IN...

- *A Princess Remembers* by Gaytari Devi and Santha Rama Rau
- *Jaipur: The Last Destination* by Aman and Samar Singh Jodha

IMPORT

- The Raj
- Tourists
- Irrigation scientists

EXPORT

- Ex-royals
- Textiles
- Handicrafts

SEE a film at Raj Mandir Cinema, the world's only meringue-shaped film house.

EAT *lal maas* (mutton in a thick spicy gravy) at Copper Chimney, a classy place with the requisite waiter army and a big rollicking horse mural.

DRINK at the Polo Bar in the Rambagh Palace Hotel with its arched, scalloped windows overlooking perfect lawns.

DO make the trip out to the magnificent delicate-pink, fort-palace of Amber, a beautiful, ethereal example of Rajput architecture.

WATCH a polo match at the enormous polo ground next to the Rambagh Palace.

BUY precious and semiprecious stones – gold, silver and fine, highly glazed enamel work known as *meenakari*, a Jaipur speciality.

AFTER DARK head for the DJ bar Hightz in Mansingh Hotel; however you might find a Hammond organ as entertainment rather than the promised DJ.

URBAN MYTH

Jaipur's legendary pink colour was first instituted in 1876 when Maharaja Ram Singh had the entire old city painted pink – a colour associated with hospitality – to welcome the Prince of Wales (later King Edward VII).

CHARMED I'M SURE – A SNAKE CHARMER HYPNOTISES A COBRA AT THE GATES OF THE CITY PALACE.
Photographer: Paul Beinssen (1)

PREENING PALACE GUARDS FLAUNT COLOURFUL UNIFORMS IN FRONT OF THE LEGENDARY PEACOCK DOOR OF THE CITY PALACE.
Photographer: Liz Thompson (2)

THE STATELY WIND PALACE LOOKS DOWN OVER A BUSTLE OF ACTIVITY IN BADI CHAUPLE SQ.
Photographer: Noboru Komine (3)

A MOTHER ADDS FINISHING TOUCHES TO HER DAUGHTER'S FACE PAINT AHEAD OF THE GANGAUR FESTIVAL.
Photographer: Paul Harris (4)

Brussels 093

VITAL STATISTICS

NAME: BRUSSELS

DATE OF BIRTH: 695 AD; WITH A SETTLEMENT CALLED BRUOCSELLA, ALTHOUGH NEOLITHIC SETTLERS WERE THERE FROM AROUND 2250 BC

ADDRESS: BELGIUM (MAP 3, H8)

HEIGHT: 100M

SIZE: 161 SQ KM

POPULATION: 980,000

LIGHTS COME ON AS EVENING FALLS ON ST GORIK'S SQ AND WORKERS WIND DOWN WITH A REVITALISING APERITIF.
Photographer: Joost de Bock (1)

A SKYSCRAPER DWARFS AN ITINERANT WAFFLE VAN IN MIDI SQ.
Photographer: Joost De Bock (2)

THE MONOLITHIC EU BUILDING IN THE EUROPEAN QUARTER.
Photographer: Joost De Bock (3)

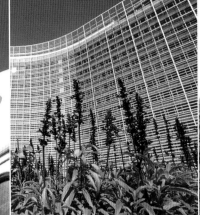

LOCALS RENDEZVOUS BENEATH THE CLASSICAL COLUMNS OF LA BOURSE.
Photographer: Joost De Bock (4)

Purveyor of gourmet treats such as mussels, beer and chocolate, capital of Europe, and showcase for cobbled streets and extravagant architecture, Brussels is much more than a Eurocrat conference room.

ANATOMY

The Ring, a large throbbing motorway, encircles the city while a polygon of busy boulevards called the Petit (Small) Ring hugs the old city centre. Central Brussels is made up of the Lower Town and the Upper Town. The former is Brussels' medieval heart, crisscrossed with pretty cobbled streets anchored in the Grand Place. The Upper Town is the old aristocratic quarter, complete with wide boulevards and large buildings. The EU area, towered over by the European Parliament and other high-rises, is east of the centre. Underground darts the metro, which contains a chapel, bars and nearly 60 works of art, as well as trains.

PEOPLE

Bilingual Brussels is in Flemish-speaking Flanders, yet the majority of the population speak French. The city is home to Europeans, Moroccans, Turks and Africans, most of whom come from the former Belgian colony of the Congo. Around 75% of Belgians are Catholic; Protestants, Jews and Muslims complete the picture.

TYPICAL BRUSSELS CITIZEN

Belgians dislike rules but can be surprisingly pedantic. They insist on efficiency yet seem unable to finish building and restoration projects on time. While nervous about change, they embrace technology. They are polite, helpful and extremely friendly. They are staunchly enamoured of the monarchy. Belgians come across as severe but have a cheeky sense of humour, evidenced by their treatment of the symbol of Brussels, Mannekin Pis, a statue of a naked boy that they regularly dress up in assorted outfits.

DEFINING EXPERIENCE

Spending your pennies on Avenue Louise, then exploring Ixelles' Art Nouveau streets before doing a circuit of the Musée Horta and relaxing with a beer in an old Brussels pub.

STRENGTHS

- Free museums on the first Wednesday of the month
- International restaurants
- Grand Place
- Centre Belge de la Bande-Dessinée
- Cathédrale des Sts Michel et Gudule
- Godiva and Neuhaus chocolates
- Belgian beer
- Belgian waffles
- *Moules et frites* (mussels and chips)
- Window boxes crammed with geraniums
- Gothic Hôtel de Ville
- EU importance – it's the capital of Europe
- Musée Bruxellois de la Gueuze (the old Cantillon Brewery)
- Long, tasty lunches
- Parc de Bruxelles
- Musées Royaux des Beaux-Arts de Belgique
- Art Nouveau Ixelles
- Traditional pubs

WEAKNESSES

- Expensive restaurants around Grand Place
- Ineffectiveness of pedestrian crossings
- Disappointing contemporary architecture
- Canine emissions

GOLD STAR

Beer – Belgium produces between 500 and 800 brews.

CITYSPEAK

- EU business: what size should our cucumbers be, and other more important questions
- Which beer should I drink now?

STARRING ROLE IN...

- *Meisje* (2002)
- *La vie sexuelle des Belges* (The Sexual Life of the Belgians, 1994)
- *Plenty* (1985)
- *Far West* (1973)
- *The good beer guide to Belgium & Holland* by Tim Webb

IMPORT

- Foreign businesspeople
- Students on EU work placements
- MEPs (Members of the European Parliament)

EXPORT

- Chocolate pralines
- Beer – Leffe, Hoegarden etc
- Tintin and Hergé
- Audrey Hepburn
- Liz Clairborne
- Jan Brueghel
- Jean-Claude van Damme
- Jacques Brel
- Claude Lévi-Strauss
- Diamonds
- René Magritte
- Adolphe Sax and the saxophone
- Handmade lace
- Tapestries

SEE the captivating façades of the Hotel de Ville (town hall) and the guildhalls on the Grand Place.

EAT *moules et frites* (mussels and fries) at local favourite, Aux Armes de Bruxelles.

DRINK a 3L magnum of Duvel at Beer Mania (but perhaps not by yourself).

DO admire fascinating zoological exhibits while pondering Belgium's actions in the Congo at the Musée Royal de l'Afrique Centrale.

WATCH the carpet of 800,000 begonias being laid in the Grand Place in August.

BUY slabs of delectable chocolate in Neuhaus and forget that diet.

AFTER DARK head to Music Village to hear Belgian blues singers and young European talent.

URBAN MYTH

Belgium's overzealous production of beer is credited to St Arnold, patron saint of brewers. In the Middle Ages he claimed that imbibing the brew would prevent the consumer from catching the plague. Apparently since the plague was spread through drinking unboiled water, drinking beer (which is boiled) was safer. His suggestion took off (why boil your drinking water when you have been advised to knock back a few?) and Belgium has been a brewery ever since.

ON THE SHOPPING STRIP OF ARTESANÍA ALLEY IS THE MERCADO DE HECHICERÍA, SPECIALISING IN LLAMA FOETUSES AND DRIED FROGS.
Photographer: Brent Winebrenner (1)

Standing at the edge of the canyon, the earth drops away, revealing, 400m below, the sprawling city of La Paz, which fills the bowl and climbs the walls of this gaping canyon.

ANATOMY

There's only one major thoroughfare in La Paz, called the Prado, and it follows the Río Choqueyapu canyon. Away from the Prado and its extensions, streets climb steeply uphill and many are cobbled or unpaved. Above the downtown skyscrapers, the adobe neighbourhoods and the informal commercial areas climb towards the city of El Alto, perched on the canyon's rim. La Paz is well served by public transport: basically you can choose between *micros* (buses) and *trufis* (either cars or minibuses).

PEOPLE

More than half of the city's population claims pure indigenous heritage; nearly 1% is of African heritage, mostly descendants of slaves conscripted to work in the Potosí silver mines. The remainder of Bolivia's citizens are largely of European extraction. Not all are descendants of the early Spanish conquerors; there are Mennonite colonies, Jewish refugees from Nazi Europe, Eastern European refugees and hordes of researchers, aid workers and missionaries. Spanish and Quechua are the official languages; Aymara is also spoken.

TYPICAL PACEÑO

The standard of living of most Bolivians is alarmingly low, marked by substandard housing, nutrition, education, sanitation and hygiene. Bolivia suffers from a Third World trifecta: a high infant mortality rate (57 deaths per 1000 births), a high birth rate (3.3 per woman) and a low female literacy rate (77%). Overall, 87% of primary-school-aged children are enrolled in classes, but attendance isn't a high priority. The people of La Paz are hard-working but generally underemployed, and many supplement their income by participating in the informal street-market and coca-production economy. Strikes among the public service and farmers are common.

La Paz 094

VITAL STATISTICS

NAME: LA PAZ

DATE OF BIRTH: 1548; LA CIUDAD DE NUESTRA SEÑORA DE LA PAZ (CITY OF OUR LADY OF PEACE) WAS FOUNDED AND NAMED BY SPANISH CAPTAIN ALONZO DE MENDOZA

ADDRESS: BOLIVIA (MAP 1, M18)

HEIGHT: 3658M

SIZE: 7 SQ KM

POPULATION: 1.5 MILLION

LOCAL BOYS PLAY A HIGH STAKES GAME OF FOOTBALL ABOVE THE CITY.
Photographer: Brent Winebrenner (3)

ALMOST AT EYE-LEVEL WITH THE ANDES, THIS WOMAN SURVEYS THE CAPITAL FROM ABOVE SOPOCACHI.
Photographer: Brent Winebrenner (2)

CHECKING THE INGREDIENTS FOR TODAY'S SPECIAL, A CHEF STANDS IN THE DOORWAY OF THE ANGEL CAFÉ.
Photographer: Brent Winebrenner (4)

DEFINING EXPERIENCE

Starting your day with a *salteña* (meat-filled pastry) around Plaza Isabel La Católica – the perfect spot for watching the world's highest city wake up, then strolling the historic cobblestone streets around Iglesia de San Francisco or wandering the nearby Artesanía Alley (or Calle Linares) and Mercado de Hechicería (Witches' Market) while shopping for fine alpaca wear.

STRENGTHS

- El Alto's sprawling markets
- Ancient ruins of Tiahuanaco
- *Peñas* (folk-music venues)
- Museo de la Coca
- Trendy Zona Sur
- Urmiri's hot springs
- The world's highest downhill skiing on the slopes of Chacaltaya
- Día de los Muertos (Day of the Dead, or All Souls' Day)
- Valle de las Ánimas
- The Cañón de Palca (aka Quebrada Chua Keri) gorge

WEAKNESSES

- Seventy percent of the population below the poverty line
- *Soroche* (altitude sickness)
- Machismo
- High infant mortality rate
- Unemployment
- *Lustrabotes* (shoeshine boys)

GOLD STAR

The Prado. On Sunday afternoon, when traffic is restricted and the city empties out, the Prado hosts promenading families, and the sidewalks fill with balloon and candy-floss sellers, and people renting kites, bicycles and toy cars.

CITYSPEAK

- Coca eradication
- Economic reform
- The privatisation of natural resources

STARRING ROLE IN...

- *Woman of Courage* (1993)
- *A Question of Faith* (1996)
- *Morder el Silencio* (The Biting Silence) by Arturo von Vacano
- *Los Fundadores del Alba* (The Breach) by Renato Prada Oropeza

IMPORT

- Bowler hats
- Missionaries
- Ice cream
- Foreign aid
- *Fútbol* (football)
- Roman Catholicism
- Non-governmental organisations (NGOs)
- Drug barons
- Aid workers
- Mennonites

EXPORT

- Marina Núñez del Prado, sculptor
- Gold
- Coffee
- Weaving
- Traditional Chola dress
- Plaits
- Alpaca sweaters
- Simón Bolívar
- Potosí silver

SEE La Paz on a clear, dark night and the cityscape will appear like a mirrored reflection of the glittering sky.

EAT a dinner of llama medallions with mushroom sauce at Tambo Colonial and enjoy the live acoustic folk-music performances.

DRINK a splendid local coffee at the cheery, little arty café Pepe's Coffee Bar.

DO explore the Mercado de Hechicería and pick yourself up a lucky llama foetus or dried toucan beak.

WATCH a folklore show at the Teatro Municipal Alberto Saavedra Pérez – a great old restored building with a round auditorium, elaborate balconies and a vast ceiling mural.

BUY fine woven wares at Artesanía Alley off Calle Sagárnaga.

AFTER DARK attend a *peña*, such as El Calicanto, for a taste of traditional Andean music, rendered on *zampoñas*, *quenas* and *charangos*.

URBAN MYTH

It's official: the road between La Paz and Coroico is 'the World's Most Dangerous Road' (WMDR), according to an Inter-American Development Bank (IDB) report. Given the number of fatal accidents that occur on it, the moniker is well deserved. An average of 26 vehicles per year disappear over the edge into the great abyss.

Québec City

VITAL STATISTICS

NAME: QUÉBEC CITY

DATE OF BIRTH: 1608; FOUNDED BY SAMUEL DE CHAMPLAIN ON THE SITE OF STADACONA, A FIRST NATIONS SETTLEMENT

ADDRESS: CANADA (MAP 1, M8)

HEIGHT: 90M

SIZE: 93 SQ KM

POPULATION: 167,000

IT'S ALL ABOUT OLD-FASHIONED SERVICE AT NORTH AMERICA'S OLDEST GROCERY STORE, JA MOISAN, FOUNDED IN 1871.
Photographer: Mario Tama (1)

Cradle and protector of French culture in North America and the heart that first beat the province's blood, captivating, historic Québec City is Canada's most European-flavoured destination.

ANATOMY

The city itself is surprisingly small, with nearly everything of interest packed into one compact, walkable district. Part of the city sits atop the cliffs of Cap Diamant (Cape Diamond), and part lies below. Québec City is thus divided into Haute Ville (Upper Town) and Basse Ville (Lower Town), each with old and new sections. The Citadelle, a fort and landmark, stands on the highest point of Cap Diamant. Together, the 10 sq km of these historic upper and lower areas, within the stone walls, form the appealing Vieux Québec (Old Town). Québec City is covered by a reasonably priced and efficient bus system.

PEOPLE

Québec City has a predominantly European population of French, British, Italian and Irish origin. A census report in 2001 detailed the ethnicity of the city as 98.7% white, 0.6% Aboriginal and 0.5% black, with a small percentage of Arab, Hispanic and Asian inhabitants. Many residents are bilingual, though the vast majority speak French and 94% claim French ancestry.

TYPICAL QUÉBÉCOIS

In general French Québécois tend to be down-to-earth and not big on ceremony or pretence. There is a sense of not wanting to seem better than others, and many project an earthy quality of straightforwardness often missing in their Anglophone counterparts. Francophones also have a reputation of being more fun-loving and raucous at get-togethers.

DEFINING EXPERIENCE

Breakfasting at Casse Crêpe Breton; exploring the old Haute Ville, including the fortifications, Parc de Champs de Bataille (Battlefields Park) and the Citadelle; then spending the afternoon wandering the old Basse Ville, before drinking beer at L'Oncle Antoine and later dining at a Basse Ville patio.

STRENGTHS

- Winter Carnival
- La Citadelle
- Parc de Champs de Bataille
- Musée du Québec
- Fortifications of Québec National Historic
- Parc d'Artillerie
- Festival de la Neige
- Musée d'Art Inuit
- Cathedrale de la Sainte Trinité (Cathedral of the Holy Trinity)
- Latin Quarter
- Basilica Notre Dame de Québec
- Musée de l'Amérique Française
- Le Château Frontenac
- Terrasse Dufferin
- Place Royale
- Musée de la Civilisation
- Antique shop district

WEAKNESSES

- 2001 Summit of the Americas conference, where 6000 police and 1200 soldiers used water cannons, tear gas, clubs and rubber bullets on protestors
- Exploitation of fauna reserves by the forest industry
- World's second-largest exporter of asbestos
- Xenophobic government hiring policies

GOLD STAR

With its striking architecture and well-organised permanent and temporary exhibits that cover both historical and contemporary concerns, the Musée de la Civilisation is not to be missed.

CITYSPEAK

- Forced municipal mergers
- Conflict-ridden French/English language debate

STARRING ROLE IN...

- *Le Confessional* (1995)
- *Black Robe* (Robe Noire, 1991)

IMPORT

- Tourists
- French culture
- 'New-economy' high-tech enterprises in photonics, geomatics, biotechnology and nutraceuticals
- Demonstrators against globalisation

EXPORT

- Maple syrup
- Celtic-tinged Québécois folk music
- Asbestos
- Dairy products
- Fruit
- Vegetables
- Cheeses, especially Oka and cheddar
- Paper
- Hydroelectricity

SEE newcomers or the occasional big name at Chez son Père, one of the best *boîtes à chanson* (informal singer-songwriter clubs).

EAT provincial fare including pea soup, duck or trout followed by maple-syrup pie at Aux Anciens Canadiens.

DRINK a selection of beers at L'Inox in the Old Port area, the city's only brewpub.

DO tweak snowman/mascot Bonhomme's nose at the Winter Carnival (January).

WATCH a classical concert at the Grand Théâtre de Québec.

BUY Inuit art from Galerie Brousseau et Brousseau.

AFTER DARK chill out (literally) at North America's first Ice Hotel, half an hour from central Québec City.

URBAN MYTH

When explorer Jacques Cartier left Stacadona (a village predating Québec City on the same site) he took with him basketfuls of iron pyrite (fool's gold) and quartz crystals, thinking they might be valuable. From this came the expression *'voilà un diamant de Canada'* (there's a diamond from Canada), meaning 'something's fake'.

THE SOARING STEEPLE OF THE 19TH-CENTURY CATHEDRALE DE LA SAINTE TRINITÉ DOMINATES THE SKYLINE OF VIEUX QUÉBEC.
Photographer: Chris Cheadle (2)

DUSK SETTLES ON VIEUX QUÉBEC.
Photographer: Chris Cheadle (3)

AN ALTERNATIVE TAKE ON AN ICONIC BOY–GIRL SCENARIO ON THE STREETS OF VIEUX QUÉBEC.
Photographer: Mario Tama (4)

A BIRD'S-EYE VIEW OF THE WINDING STAIRWAY OF THE MERCADO CENTRAL.
Photographer: Brent Winebrenner (1)

Valparaíso
096

VITAL STATISTICS

NAME: VALPARAÍSO

NICKNAME: VALPO, LA PERLA DEL PACÍFICO
(THE PEARL OF THE PACIFIC)

DATE OF BIRTH: 1536; WHEN IT WAS FOUNDED BY
THE SPANISH CONQUISTADOR JUAN DE SAAVEDRA,
THEN PERMANENTLY ESTABLISHED IN 1544 WHEN
PEDRO DE VALDIVIA MADE IT HIS OFFICIAL PORT

ADDRESS: CHILE (MAP 1, M20)

HEIGHT: 40M

POPULATION: 270,000

Valparaíso is a city of dramatic nature – narrow wave-cut terraces with steep, labyrinthine roads and crumbling mansions, precipitous cliffs and a rugged Pacific coastline.

ANATOMY

Chile's principal port and second-largest city, Valparaíso occupies a narrow strip of land between the waterfront and nearby hills. Its convoluted centre (known as El Plan) has distinctive, sinuous cobblestone streets and is overlooked by precipitous cliffs and hilltop suburbs, which are accessed by funicular railways and stairway footpaths. It is conducive to mazelike strolls and rides on the funicular, and its natural history, fine arts and maritime museums are justly famed. Muelle Prat, the redeveloped pier, is a lively market area.

PEOPLE

The lineage of Valpo residents is strongly European, particularly Spanish, English and German. The Catholic Church has a great deal of political power, and as a consequence many *porteños*, as locals are known, are quite conservative in their views.

TYPICAL PORTEÑO

Porteños are laid-back and cultured. They are known for their fine taste in seafood and wine, their prolific cultural output in films and literature, and their pride in their port city. They boast of their individuality but are as conservative as most other Chileans. Their parties are as raucous as their family feuds, and they love them both. They explore their own town and take the time to share it with visitors.

DEFINING EXPERIENCE

Having a *cafecito* (short black coffee) for breakfast, then a *paseo* (walk) through the winding streets and parks, shopping at the fresh fish market on the port and cooking up a *caldillo* (seafood soup), having a siesta in the afternoon and dancing until the wee hours on the waterfront.

STRENGTHS

- *Ascensores* (funicular lifts) and the quirky individuals who operate them
- Generally mild climate
- Views from the *cerros* (hills)
- Tangled, cobbled backstreets
- Spectacular Pacific coastline
- Excellent seafood
- Rich literary history
- Brightly coloured *barrios* (neighbourhoods) on the hillsides
- *Porteños* and their pride in their city's history
- The murals at the Museo a Cielo Abierto (Open-Sky Museum)
- *El Mercurio de Valparaíso* – the world's oldest Spanish-language newspaper

WEAKNESSES

- Social conservatism following the Pinochet years
- Earthquakes
- Shantytowns
- Machismo
- Petty theft
- Northern gales in winter

GOLD STAR

Often described as Chile's most distinctive city with its unique, faded gradneur and spontaneous, bohemian charm, the entire city has been named a Unesco World Heritage site.

CITYSPEAK

- Argentina's economic woes (and the feud with Argentina in general)
- The latest political scandal in Santiago
- The new divorce laws (which finally permit divorce, against the wishes of the Catholic Church)

STARRING ROLE IN...

- *El Wanderers de Valparaíso* (2003)
- *Valparaíso* (1994)
- *Valparaiso, Valparaiso* (1971)
- *Canto General* and *Confieso que he vivido* (I Confess That I Have Lived) by Pablo Neruda
- *Azul* by Rubén Darío

IMPORT

- Spanish colonists
- *Fútbol* (football)
- Rubén Darío
- British and German immigrants
- Chile's National Congress
- Nearly everything that comes to Chile via the sea

EXPORT

- Augusto Pinochet
- Salvador Allende
- Nobel prize–winning poetry by Pablo Neruda and Gabriela Mistral
- Experimental cinema
- Chilean folk musicians
- Wine
- Most of Chile's produce

SEE the final steps of 500,000 pilgrims walking the Virgen de lo Vasquez Pilgrimage in December each year.

EAT *curanto* – a hearty stew of fish, shellfish, chicken, pork, lamb, beef and potato.

DRINK good Chilean wines with the locals at Café Vinilo.

DO ride the *ascensores* to Cerro Concepción, both for the view and the neighbourhood.

WATCH the spectacular fireworks over the harbour on Año Nuevo (New Year).

BUY antiques in the market at Plaza O'Higgins.

AFTER DARK check out the live music at Valparaíso Eterno.

URBAN MYTH

The town of Valparaíso has certainly mythologised its most famous poet. Pablo Neruda maintained one of his three Chilean homes here in Valparaíso, known as La Sebastiana. Although it was his least-visited house, Neruda made it a point to watch Valparaíso's annual New Year's fireworks from his lookout on Cerro Bellavista. He heaped praise on Valpo in his works *Canto General* and *I Confess That I Have Lived*, and *porteños* have not forgotten his tribute. On the 100th anniversary of the birth of Pablo Neruda, *porteños* composed the world's largest poem in his honour. It was printed on a roll of paper 20m long and 1m wide, and included contributions from throughout Chile.

ESCAPING THE URBAN MADNESS AT THE PORT OF VALPARAÍSO.
Photographer: Brent Winebrenner (2)

COLOURFUL BUILDINGS CLUSTER ON THE HILLS ABUTTING TOWN.
Photographer: Brent Winebrenner (3)

PROTESTORS STILL INCENSED OVER THE NAVY'S REPRESSIVE ROLE DURING THE PINOCHET ERA.
Photographer: Brent Winebrenner (4)

Naples

097

VITAL STATISTICS
NAME: NAPLES
DATE OF BIRTH: 474 BC; WHEN GREEKS FROM NEARBY CUMAE FOUNDED NEOPOLIS
ADDRESS: ITALY (MAP 3, L14)
HEIGHT: 110M
SIZE: 117 SQ KM
POPULATION: 1 MILLION

Naples is a city for those who relish the intense urban experience: raucous, polluted, crowded and chaotic, but never dull.

ANATOMY

Naples has a heart-wrenchingly beautiful, if precarious, setting. Facing a crescent-shaped bay, Italy's largest port is watched over by a still-active volcano, Mt Vesuvius. The chaotic *centro storico* (inner city) follows the grid of its ancient counterpart that lies below: Via Toledo, Naples' main street, leads north from Piazza Trieste e Trento, next to the waterfront's central landmark, Castel Nuovo. Funiculars and the metro service residential neighbourhoods; in the rest of the city foot and scooter are more efficient than bus or, heaven forbid, cars.

PEOPLE

Naples' history is one of both occupation (as the local dialect flush with Arabic, Spanish, French and English words attests) and emigration (as the Neapolitan diaspora demonstrates). Neapolitans now stay, and although they imagine themselves as a homogeneous Italian-born group, they are increasingly joined by immigrants from Asia, North Africa and Eastern Europe.

TYPICAL NEAPOLITAN

Neapolitans embrace the Italian stereotype – noisy, theatrical, food-obsessed and passionate. They don't earn as much as most other Italians, but that doesn't stop them enjoying eating out and staying up late. They also manage to go to the theatre, rack up astronomical mobile-phone bills and drive like maniacs. The notion of family is still strong, and once young Neapolitans marry and move out of home, they will have more children than anywhere else in Italy.

DEFINING EXPERIENCE

Waking up after a siesta to a short, sweet, strong espresso, a chat with the local barista, hopping on your Piaggio and heading down to Mergellina for the evening *passeggiata* (promenade), grabbing a pizza and folding it in quarters, eating it as you stroll along staring out to Capri, then trying a new flavour of gelati.

STRENGTHS

- *Sfogliatella* – the staple *dolce* (sweet) of Naples, flaky and ricotta-filled
- The late-night *passeggiata*
- A Unesco-listed *centro storico* that's certainly historical, but also vividly alive
- Ferries to Capri, Genoa, Palermo or Tunisia
- *Mozzarella di bufala* (buffalo-milk mozzarella)
- Feeling like you have the Museo Archeologico Nazionale to yourself
- Leg- and lung-saving funiculars
- Ospedale delle Bambole – the delightfully kooky doll's hospital

WEAKNESSES

- The Camorra (Naples' home-grown Mafia)
- Cavalier attitude to the preservation and display of priceless artefacts
- Filthy and crumbling historic treasures
- Chaotic traffic
- Street hustlers and petty criminals
- Air pollution
- Soulless international hotels

GOLD STAR

Street life – Neapolitans take to the piazze and the *vicoli* (backstreets) for breakfast, lunch and dinner, and for a lot of the time in between.

CITYSPEAK

- Vesuvius – smoking or not smoking?
- My *nonna* (grandmother) swears she knows the winning lottery numbers, the Virgin came to her in a dream…
- Do you think they'll collect the rubbish this week?

STARRING ROLE IN...

- *Paisà* (Paisan, 1946)
- *L'Oro di Napoli* (The Gold of Naples, 1954)
- *Vito e gli altri* (Vito and the Others, 1991)
- *Il Postino* (The Postman, 1994)
- *The Talented Mr Ripley* (1999)
- *The Volcano Lover* by Susan Sontag
- *Midnight in Sicily* by Peter Robb

IMPORT

- In chronological order: Greeks, Romans, Normans, Saracens, Angevins, Napoleonic French and Bourbon Spanish
- Virgil
- Caravaggio
- South American soaps
- Bottled water
- Milanese and Roman media
- Poet Giacomo Leopardi
- Military bases: US Navy's 6th Fleet Naval Support Activity and the NATO Joint Force Command South
- Diego Armando Maradona

EXPORT

- Sophia Loren
- Domenico Scarlatti
- Totò
- Pizza
- Enrico Caruso
- Coral jewellery
- Bud Spencer
- The literary fairy tale – Giambattista Basile's *Lo cunto de li cunti*, published in Neapolitan dialect in 1634, was the first integral collection of fairy tales to appear in Western Europe
- Actor and director Massimo Troisi
- Shoes and leather goods
- Casertana, Salernitana and Pontina cheese, to Roman restaurants every morning

SEE the chaos below, and Vesuvius beyond, from the peaceful piazze of the Vomero.

EAT a *margherita* pizza at Da Michele, and wonder why it can't always be this good.

DRINK a locally made *limoncello* (lemon-based liqueur) on ice at Bar Lazzarella.

DO a run around Parco di Capodimonte.

WATCH the dancing to electro-pop on the beach at Arenile di Bagnoli on a hot July night.

BUY *presepi* (nativity scene) figures in Via San Gregorio Armeno – will you go trad with shepherds and sheep or cheeky with Berlusconi?

AFTER DARK stumble across the Argentinian tango dancers in the Galleria Umberto, and join them if your tango is up to it.

URBAN MYTH

Every year thousands of Neapolitans cram into the Duomo to witness the blood of their patron saint San Gennaro miraculously liquefy. Of course, few believe that it's a real miracle, and science has a ready explanation. To verify the theory of thixotropy, though, scientists would have to analyse the blood, something the church has effectively blocked by refusing permission to open the phial. Still, the fact remains that when the blood liquefies the city breathes a sigh of relief – another year safe from disaster. A coincidence maybe, but when the miracle failed in 1944, Vesuvius erupted and when it happened (or didn't happen) again in 1980 an earthquake struck.

NOT THE BEST PLACE TO GET A HANDLE ON THE BASICS – PIAZZA PLEBISCITO'S OBSTACLES INCLUDE PERFORMERS AND LARGE HERDS OF NERVOUS TOURISTS.
Photographer: Paolo Sacchi (1)

THE PRESTIGIOUS 16TH-CENTURY PROMENADE OF SANTA LUCIA NOW PLAYS HOST TO THE MOST EXCLUSIVE HOTELS IN THE CITY. Photographer: Paolo Sacchi (2)

A NEAPOLITAN SHOPKEEPER PROUDLY INFLATES ONE OF ITALY'S MOST FAMOUS FACES.
Photographer: Paolo Sacchi (3)

A GREENGROCER AMONG HIS PRODUCE IN THE ANCIENT ROMAN MARKETPLACE OF VIA TRIBUNALI.
Photographer: Paolo Sacchi (4)

CLASSIC CARS PRESERVE A SENSE OF HISTORICAL REALISM AT THE LORRAINE MOTEL WHERE MARTIN LUTHER KING JR WAS ASSASSINATED.
Photographer: Ray Laskowitz (1)

Where Elvis Presley lived and Martin Luther King died, Memphis reclines sleepily on the banks of the Mississippi, listening to its legendary blues and rock 'n' roll and watching the steamboats chugging past cotton mansions.

ANATOMY

Downtown Memphis hugs the eastern bank of the Mississippi, with Riverside Dr and a promenade running parallel to the river. Slightly inland is the main tourist area, roughly bordered by Beale St and Union Ave, 2nd and 4th Sts. Groovy neighbourhoods with shops, bars and restaurants lie to the east along Union Ave and Overton Sq. Graceland is 5km south of town on US51, also known as 'Elvis Presley Blvd'. Trolleys serve Main St downtown, and riverboat cruises ply the Mississippi.

PEOPLE

Memphis' population is almost evenly split between black and white. Minority groups include Native Americans, Asians and Hispanics.

TYPICAL MEMPHIAN

Memphis may be a big city, but Memphians enjoy a relaxed pace of life. Traffic jams and pollution are not as much of a problem as in other urban centres. The people are proud of their city and celebrate its musical heritage with a bevy of concerts and festivals. Outdoor activities are popular, with boating and water sports available on nearby lakes. Memphis has moved a long way from the racial tension of Martin Luther King's time and Memphians enjoy a generally peaceful, soulful existence.

Memphis
098

VITAL STATISTICS

NAME: MEMPHIS

NICKNAME: THE BLUFF CITY

DATE OF BIRTH: 1739; WHEN THE FRENCH FORT ASSUMPTION WAS ESTABLISHED, BUT THREE THOUSAND YEARS AGO THE LOESS BLUFFS ON THE EASTERN SHORE OF THE MISSISSIPPI RIVER WERE OCCUPIED BY NATIVE AMERICAN TRIBES

ADDRESS: USA (MAP 1, K10)

HEIGHT: 101M

SIZE: 723 SQ KM

POPULATION: 1 MILLION

A HIGHLY SKILLED WORKER IN THE GIBSON GUITAR FACTORY, WHICH HAS CRAFTED INSTRUMENTS FOR THE LIKES OF ERIC CLAPTON AND BB KING. Photographer: Ray Laskowitz (3)

THE MICROPHONE THAT ELVIS USED TO RECORD THE HIT 'THAT'S ALRIGHT MAMA' DISPLAYED LIKE A HOLY RELIC AT SUN STUDIO. Photographer: Ray Laskowitz (2)

A SAXOPHONE PLAYER AT BB KING'S BLUES CLUB RAISES THE ROOF UNDER THE GLOW OF RED STAGE LIGHTS. Photographer: Ray Laskowitz (4)

DEFINING EXPERIENCE

Wandering around Sun Studio where Elvis cut his first record, then grabbing a po'boy sandwich (French bread, usually filled with roast beef, oysters or prawns) at Sleep Out Louie's before boogying to the blues and soaking up some soul on Beale St.

STRENGTHS

- Graceland
- National Blues Foundation (based in Memphis)
- Blues on Beale St
- Memphis Rock 'n' Soul Museum
- National Civil Rights Museum
- Mississippi River Museum
- Sun Studio
- Steamboats
- Stax Museum of American Soul Music
- Victorian Village district on Adams Ave
- Pink Palace Museum and Planetarium
- Overton Park
- Memphis Zoo
- Pulled barbecue pork butt

WEAKNESSES

- Yellow-fever epidemic in 1878
- Street crime
- Mud Island

GOLD STAR

Elvis!

CITYSPEAK

- The latest results for Memphis Redbirds and Memphis Grizzlies
- The crowds of Elvis fans paying homage to Memphis' golden boy

STARRING ROLE IN...

- *Elvis by the Presleys* (2005)
- *21 Grams* (2003)
- *A Painted House* (2003)
- *Cast Away* (2000)

IMPORT

- Elvis Presley (he was born in Tupelo, Mississippi)
- BB King
- John Lee Hooker
- WC Handy
- Sam Phillips
- Martin Luther King
- Artists to record in Sun Studio eg Sheryl Crow and U2

EXPORT

- Elvis Presley
- FedEx
- Holiday Inn
- The supermarket (the world's first supermarket, Piggly Wiggly, opened here in 1916)
- The blues, rock 'n' roll and gospel
- Justin Timberlake
- Kathy Bates
- Aretha Franklin
- Morgan Freeman
- Cybill Shepherd

SEE the 5m couch, fake waterfall and more '70s décor at Graceland, and imagine living like the King.

EAT a Memphis staple – charcoal-broiled dry ribs – at the family-owned Rendezvous.

DRINK to steady your nerves before a guitar-pickin' contest at Kudzu's café.

DO visit the National Civil Rights Museum, where Martin Luther King was gunned down in 1968, and learn about his contribution to the civil-rights movement.

WATCH famous bands play at the Pyramid (the world's third-largest) – recognition that Memphis was named after the ancient capital of Egypt.

BUY Elvis memorabilia and a pair of those gold shades at Graceland.

AFTER DARK swing into the clubs of Beale St for the sounds of live soul, rock, country and jazz music.

URBAN MYTH

A visit to Memphis is not complete without a pilgrimage to Graceland, where Elvis Presley lived for 20 years. Among die-hard Elvis fans continual sightings of the King at liquor stores, friends' weddings and other unlikely spots (see www.elvissightingbulletin board.com) prove that he didn't really die in 1977. Other reports suggest his fatal cardiac arrest occurred while he was astride the toilet reading the *Scientific Search for the Face of Jesus*. Whatever – you can pay your respects at his flower-strewn grave by the swimming pool where he's buried with his closest relatives. As well as the diminutive but fabulous mansion, there's a memorabilia collection and car and aircraft museums. Watch out: uncontrollable pelvis twitching is a common side effect of visiting Graceland.

Heidelberg

099

VITAL STATISTICS

NAME: HEIDELBERG

DATE OF BIRTH: AD 765; WHEN SETTLERS CAME TO THE AREA

ADDRESS: GERMANY (MAP 3, J9)

HEIGHT: 110M

POPULATION: 141,000

Germany's oldest university city oozes dreamy charm with pretty 18th-century buildings, an alluring semi-ruined castle and a general air of intelligentsia – Goethe was enchanted, as you will be too.

ANATOMY

The main feature of Heidelberg is the Neckar River, spanned by the Alte-Brücke at the eastern end and the Theodor-Heuss-Brücke towards the west. South of the river lies the evocative *Altstadt* (old town), whose main street, the pedestrianised Hauptstrasse, known as the Royal Mile, runs from Bismarckplatz (the old town's epicentre) through the Markt to Karlstor. Dominating the city from a hill to the southeast is the fairy-tale Schloss (castle). Public transport consists of buses and trams.

PEOPLE

Heidelberg is a student town, with one in five residents reportedly there for learning. The city receives three million visitors every year, the majority of whom come from the USA and Japan, with the UK and other European countries also contributing. There are two US military communities southwest of the *Altstadt*. Approximately 20,000 of Heidelberg's inhabitants are not German nationals.

TYPICAL HEIDELBERG CITIZEN

Heidelberg is one of Germany's great centres of intellectual study, so the fact that its inhabitants are largely well educated and cultured will hardly come as a surprise. Concerts, which are held outdoors in summer, are well attended, and foreign films are popular. Well accustomed to receiving visitors, people are very friendly and most speak some English.

DEFINING EXPERIENCE

Taking the funicular up to the Schloss and admiring the city from up high, then descending to town, hiring a bicycle and exploring the surrounding countryside before retiring to the *Altstadt* for a refreshing litre of beer and a good book.

STRENGTHS

- Neckar River
- Schloss
- Ruprecht-Karl-Universität (Heidelberg university)
- Alte-Brücke
- Heiliggeistkirche
- 19th-century romantics eg Goethe
- Architectural unity (due to a total rebuild in the 18th century after invading French troops under Louis XIV devastated the city)
- Philosophising on Philosophonweg
- Students
- Cosy pubs
- Good beer
- Friendly locals
- Heidelberger Herbst, the massive autumn festival
- Christmas market
- Fireworks festivals
- Authentic charm
- Mild winters

WEAKNESSES

- Expensive and elusive accommodation
- Dull modern part of the city to the west (well, it can't all be gorgeous)
- Dearth of cheap eating options
- Students?

GOLD STAR

Intellectual charm: Heidelberg is the thinking person's crumpet.

CITYSPEAK

- Attractive foreign-exchange students
- Philosophy, literature and art

STARRING ROLE IN...

- *A Tramp Abroad* by Mark Twain
- *Heidelberg: Sunset* by William Turner

IMPORT

- Goethe
- Mark Twain
- William Turner
- Louis Armstrong
- Tourists
- Foreign students
- US military
- The Brothers Grimm
- Georg Wilhelm Friedrich Hegel

EXPORT

- Robert Bunsen and the Bunsen burner
- Educated people
- Printing

SEE the crumbling magic of the Schloss, one of Germany's best Gothic-Renaissance castles, and survey the town in a regal manner.

EAT 'student kisses' (chocolate-covered wafers) at Café Knösel.

DRINK dangerously addictive micro-brewed beer in the convivial bar, Vetter im Schöneck.

DO a summer German-language course at Heidelberg University and waft around the town enjoying your part in the city's academic tradition.

WATCH kaleidoscopic snap, crackle and pops at the triannual Fireworks Festivals.

BUY a ticket for a castle-spotting boat trip through the Neckar Valley.

AFTER DARK join the crooners in Germany's oldest jazz club, Cave54, where Louis Armstrong once played.

URBAN MYTH

Myths and legends are everywhere you turn in Heidelberg. The cracked iron ring by the gates of the Schloss was allegedly bitten by a witch following Ludwig V's pledge that he would give the castle to anyone who could chew through it. The footprint on the terrace apparently belongs to a knight escaping a lady's bedroom on the return of her husband, the prince. On a similar subject, the *Karl-Theodor* statue on the Alte-Brücke depicts a local legend that the prince sired 200 illegitimate offspring. If you would like the same results, touch the mice surrounding the brass monkey at the base of the bridge; touching the mirror promises wealth, and touching the fingers will ensure your return to Heidelberg.

A PARADE'S BRASH BRASS SECTION RINGS OUT AT THE MARKETPLACE BY THE TOWN HALL.
Photographer: Tina & Horst Herzig (1)

WELCOMING WINDOWS THROWN OPEN TO THE NEON PROMISE OF ICE CREAM.
Photographer: Martin Lladó (2)

A WOMAN TEARS PAST THE ALTE-BRÜCKE.
Photographer: Martin Lladó (3)

A STYLISED GIRAFFE PEERS INQUISITIVELY AT A MODERN BUILDING BY THE HAUPTBAHNHOF.
Photographer: Martin Lladó (4)

Dhaka100

VITAL STATISTICS

NAME: DHAKA

NICKNAME: CITY OF MOSQUES

DATE OF BIRTH: AD 4; AS A SMALL BUDDHIST TOWN

ADDRESS: BANGLADESH (MAP 5, H4)

HEIGHT: 8M

SIZE: 414 SQ KM

POPULATION: 12 MILLION

CHILDREN IMPROVISE A CRICKET PITCH IN AN ALLEYWAY OF OLD DHAKA.
Photographer: Chris Stowers (1)

AN ELDERLY RICKSHAW WALLAH CROUCHES BY HIS VEHICLE TO WAIT FOR HIS NEXT CUSTOMER.
Photographer: Dieter Telemans (2)

RICKSHAW GRIDLOCK ON A CITY STREET DURING A PUBLIC TRANSPORT STRIKE.
Photographer: Rafiqur Rahman (3)

MONSOON MONET – BOATMEN PICK A PATH THROUGH LUSH WATER HYACINTHS ON BURIGANGA RIVER DURING THE WET SEASON.
Photographer: Rafiqur Rahman (4)

Colourful and chaotic at a glance, Dhaka throbs with the raw (and infectious) energy of a spirited capital juggling civic deterioration, modern development and the realities of daily life as one the world's densest cities.

ANATOMY

Situated amid a maze of rivers and canals, Dhaka is both a city of relics and a melting pot of architectural styles. The frenzied – and yet curiously effective – network of bus services, trains and rickshaws will get you around town to see the main attractions. These sites are clustered in the three major sections of the city: Old Dhaka, a labyrinth of narrow streets lined with Moghul-era structures, including the premier attraction – the Lalbagh Fort on the expansive Buriganga River; Central Dhaka, which retains the whitewashed colonial buildings of its former role as the British part of the city but now forms the modern part of town and is home to the celebrated National Assembly building designed by American architect Louis Kahn; and suburban Dhaka, where the best restaurants in town are to be found.

PEOPLE

The nationality of Dhaka's citizens is almost 100% Bengali (Bengal being the regional entity that was split into West Bengal and East Pakistan at the time of Indian/Pakistani independence in 1947). The nation's official language is Bangla (also known as Bengali) and while around 16% of the population is Hindu, the vast majority – around 83% – is Muslim.

TYPICAL DHAKA CITIZEN

Most citizens are working-class Islamic men and women who, with indomitable patience, navigate their way through the gridlock of rickshaws to spend long hours in factories, on the river or in the fields. On the way home they may stop at one of the dilapidated floating restaurants on the river's edge for a quick bite. Despite their penchant for hard work, they are also prepared to strike, and demonstrations are common in the capital. While high unemployment (around 40%) is a continuing problem throughout Bangladesh, in the capital there is also a growing middle-class. This stratum is made up of young, educated Bangladeshis – often found lounging in hip cafés – or families from the well-to-do inner suburbs.

DEFINING EXPERIENCE

Riding into town for a leisurely hot breakfast at the Mango Café, followed by bird-watching in the Botanical Gardens, wandering along the riverbanks to see the Lalbagh Fort and the Pink Palace, and then heading to Gulshan Ave for an indulgent meal.

STRENGTHS

- The romantic Old Dhaka region
- Bazaars
- Tea
- Rickshaw art
- Handicrafts
- Cheap public transport
- Good variety of great local, Asian and European restaurants
- Cheap clothes
- *Shankaris* (Hindu artisans)
- Diversity of Eastern and Western-influenced architecture
- Botanical Gardens
- National Museum
- 'Asian Art Biennial' – a month-long cultural event attracting top artists
- Nothing seems to stand still

WEAKNESSES

- Air pollution
- Heat and humidity during the summer months
- Poverty
- Overpopulation, leading to crowded buses and frequent traffic jams
- Locals spitting on the street
- Pickpockets
- Workers' strikes (and often violent demonstrations)
- Frequent floods
- Can be hard to get a beer (aside from expat bars, alcohol is banned in this Islamic nation)
- No bacon or pig products
- Nothing seems to stand still

GOLD STAR

Its many faces – the Eastern and Western influences of the city's past are richly woven into the challenging realities of today, giving modern-day Dhaka a uniqueness that surmounts the apparent clutter of the city.

CITYSPEAK

- Double- and triple-parking in the city's streets
- Corruption in the government

STARRING ROLE IN...

- *The Clay Bird* (2002)
- *Tale of the Darkest Night* (2001)
- *Lajja* by Taslima Nasrin
- *The Shadow Lines* by Amitav Ghosh

IMPORT

- Coca-Cola
- Pepsi
- Fruit and vegetables
- Foreign aid
- Medical equipment
- Used cars
- International cricket

EXPORT

- Jute
- Pink pearls
- Tea
- 'Fashion for Development' fashion label
- Cheap ready-made garments
- Monica Ali (author of Man Booker prize short-listed novel *Brick Lane*)
- Fazlur Rahman Khan (structural engineer of international standing)
- Tarque Masud (film director)
- International cricketers
- Leather

SEE the vista of activity on the Buriganga River as people bathe, rest, fish and cook.

EAT Mexican at El Toro, the only Mexican restaurant in Bangladesh, and surely the best on the Indian subcontinent.

DRINK alcohol with a newly befriended expat in one of the few legal drinking establishments in Dhaka.

DO a walking tour around the historic Hindu artisan hub of Hindu St with an enthusiastic Shankari guide.

WATCH the moving gallery on Dhaka's streets as the rickshaws pass displaying the bright and varied artwork on their back panels.

BUY a personalised piece of rickshaw art from popular rickshaw artist Ahmed in Hossaini Dalan Rd.

AFTER DARK try to get into an international club.

URBAN MYTH

The famous Hindu temple Dhakeshwari, built in the 11th century, is situated at the point where Old Dhaka meets the modern Central Dhaka region. This is the oldest Hindu temple in Dhaka city and the meaning of 'Dhakeshwari' can be translated as 'Temple of the Goddess of Dhaka'. Legend has it that the city of Dhaka was named after this temple. The deity is said to have been found hidden at the site of the temple, thereby explaining the literal definition of the word 'Dhaka' which means 'concealed'.

More a modern Arab city than a great ancient metropolis, Amman comes to life in its earthy and chaotic Downtown district, with its markets and men smoking *nargileh* (water pipes) and playing backgammon, and in the leafy residential districts of Western Amman, with trendy cafés and bars and impressive contemporary art galleries.

ANATOMY

Amman was originally built on seven hills but has stretched out beyond these and now covers around 19. The area around the King Hussein Mosque is referred to as *il-balad* (downtown). Memorise the major landmarks or you'll find navigating the city a near impossibility, particularly in a short time. Restaurants, big hotels and shops are located around the main hill, Jebel Amman. The impressive Citadel is sits atop the city's highest point, Jebel al-Qala'a. You can catch buses around town.

PEOPLE

Most of Amman's residents are Arab, including Palestinian refugees as well as Iraqi and Kuwaiti refugees who arrived after the first Gulf War of 1990–91. Amman's population is also graced by a small number of Circassians, Chechens, Armenians and Bedouins. Around 50% of Ammanians are under the age of 18.

TYPICAL AMMANIAN

Ammanians, like all Jordanians, are a welcoming bunch, and Amman, like most countries, sees a great divide between the classes. The Bedouins, who have little, will give you the hair off their camel's back in the midst of all the gentrification.

DEFINING EXPERIENCE

Wandering around the large Roman Amphitheatre, an impressive remnant of ancient Philadelphia (as the city was known under the Romans), which was cut into a hill that once served as a necropolis, and later in the day crowding round a coffee-house TV in support of Amman's football teams.

Amman
101

VITAL STATISTICS

NAME: AMMAN

NICKNAME: AL-HAMAMA AL-BAYDA (WHITE PIGEON)

DATE OF BIRTH: 3500 BC; THE SITE OF AMMAN HAS BEEN CONTINUOUSLY OCCUPIED SINCE THIS TIME

ADDRESS: JORDAN (MAP 2, L2)

HEIGHT: 777M

POPULATION: 5.46 MILLION

DAILY LIFE TAKES CENTRE STAGE IN JORDAN'S THRIVING FILM INDUSTRY.
Photographer: Olivier Cirendini (1)

STRENGTHS

◢ Roman ruins
◢ Proximity to Israel
◢ A convenient base to travel around Jordan
◢ Jordanian hospitality

WEAKNESSES

◢ Drivers who insist that a white line down the centre of a road is just that, a white line
◢ Modernisation

GOLD STAR

While Amman might be a sprawling metropolis with fewer signs of the area's ancient past than its Arab neighbours, a performance in the 2000-year-old Roman amphitheatre will have you reaching for your toga and asking for directions to the Nymphaeum.

CITYSPEAK

◢ While the state wants to control the winds of change, liberalisation has taken a step forward in the form of satellite TV
◢ Amman is leading the way in Jordan's real-estate boom, which has sent prices per square metre soaring and the number of building contracts flying through the roof

STARRING ROLE IN...

◢ *Story of a City: A Childhood in Amman* by Abd Al-Rahman
◢ *The Desert and the Snow* by Gertrude Bell

IMPORT

◢ Mickey D's
◢ Western shopping centres
◢ Amman International Theatre Festival
◢ Fête de la Musique

EXPORT

◢ Coloured marble
◢ Amin Matalqa's short films about Jordanian life
◢ King Hussein
◢ Bedouin crafts
◢ Antiquities – actually it's prohibited

SEE the remains of a prehistoric Neolithic settlement near Ain Ghazal, which dates back to about 6500 BC.

EAT *mensaf* – a whole lamb, head included, on a bed of rice and pine nuts, eaten with *jameed* (sun-dried yoghurt).

DRINK coffee – Ammanians are said to have a serious caffeine addiction.

DO experience the contemporary art space, Darat al Funun.

WATCH or participate in the annual Dead Sea Ultra Marathon.

BUY hand-woven Bedouin rugs.

AFTER DARK see a free art-house film (undubbed) at Books@Cafe.

URBAN MYTH

Amman is considered the oldest capital in the world. Biblical references to city are numerous and indicate that by 1200 BC Rabbath Ammon (as it was then known) was the capital of the powerful Ammonites. King David, after being insulted by the Ammonite king Nahash, burnt many inhabitants alive in a brick kiln. Later the city fell under the sway of Rome, and Philadelphia became the seat of Christian bishops in the early Byzantine period. But the city declined and by the time a colony of Circassians resettled here in 1878, Amman was nothing more than a sad little village amid the ruins.

CHILDREN COMING OUT TO PLAY AT THE MAGNIFICENT ROMAN THEATRE, GUARANTEED TO DRAW A CROWD.
Photographer: Anthony Ham (2)

THE IMPRESSIVE ANCIENT CITADEL TOWERS ABOVE THE CITY FROM ATOP JEBEL AL-QALA'A.
Photographer: Clint Lucas (3)

ALL THAT GLITTERS IS NOT GOLD, BUT LOCAL MARKETS OVERFLOW WITH INTERESTING TREASURES.
Photographer: Olivier Cirendini (4)

Monaco102

VITAL STATISTICS

NAME: MONACO

DATE OF BIRTH: 1297; THE BEGINNING OF GRIMALDI RULE, BUT THE AREA WAS PROBABLY SETTLED IN PHOENICIAN TIMES

ADDRESS: MONACO (MAP 3, I12)

HEIGHT: 7M

SIZE: 1.95 SQ KM

POPULATION: 30,000

THE COOL WATERS OF PLAGE DU LARVOTTO ENTICE SUN SEEKERS THE WORLD OVER.
Photographer: Dallas Stribley (1)

Tiny but beautiful Monaco has the same relationship with glamour as its residents do with diamonds – easy, effortless and elegant – so be sure to dress appropriately.

ANATOMY

Monaco comprises six main areas: Monaco Ville (south of the port) with its pastel houses and Palais du Prince; Monte Carlo (north of the port), home to the casino and flash shops; La Condamine, southwest of the port; industrial Fontveille, south of Monaco Ville; Moneghetti, west of Condamine; and Larvotto beach, north of Monte Carlo. Elegant yachts stand proudly in the harbour, lifts (elevators) whisk people up to the higher levels and fast cars roar around before being carefully valet parked.

PEOPLE

Monaco is ruled by the Grimaldi royal family. Residents do not pay income tax so Monaco has become a tax haven for many foreign celebrities. Only 7000 residents are Monégasque – most of the others are French and Italian.

TYPICAL MONACAN

The citizens of Monaco live a lovely, tax-free, low-crime life. They have their own flag (red and white), national holiday (19 November), national anthem and country dialling code. The official language is French, but many street signs also appear in the local dialect, Monégasque. This dialect, which is a mixture of French and Italian, is taught in schools. Finally, of course, they are glamorous and expensively dressed, drive super-cars and own luxury yachts.

DEFINING EXPERIENCE

Coasting your private helicopter onto a friend's huge catamaran to drink cosmopolitans and fine dine, followed by a spot of blackjack in a private room at the casino.

STRENGTHS

- Monaco Grand Prix
- Casino de Monte Carlo (Europe's first casino)
- Palais du Prince
- Musée Océanographique de Monaco
- No income tax
- Low crime rate
- Grace Kelly
- Royal family
- Personal lives of Princesses Stéphanie and Caroline
- Chic shops
- Being a sovereign state
- Lifts up through the rock
- The Mediterranean
- Jardin Exotique
- Collection de Voitures Anciennes
- Local beaches – Plage du Larvotto and Plage de Monte Carlo
- Glitz and glamour

WEAKNESS

- If you don't have a gold or platinum card, this place will not be much fun

GOLD STAR

Glamour – Monaco never goes out of style.

CITYSPEAK

- The death of Rainier III
- Princess Stéphanie's love life
- Who will win the next Monaco Grand Prix?
- Is his yacht bigger and better than mine?

STARRING ROLE IN...

- *GoldenEye* (1995)
- *Herbie Goes to Monte Carlo* (1977)
- *L'Inconnue de Monte Carlo* (1938)

IMPORT

- Roger Moore
- David Coulthard
- Ringo Starr
- Björn Borg
- Helmut Newton
- Luciano Paravotti
- Julian Lennon
- Alain Ducasse

EXPORT

- The Grimaldi Royal Family
- Style and sophistication

SEE a slice of life under the sea at the world-famous aquarium Musée Océanographique de Monaco.

EAT fine cuisine at Alain Ducasse's three-Michelin-starred restaurant, Louis XV.

DRINK champagne and play count-the-limousine at the Café de Paris.

DO visit the lush Jardin Exotique and breathe in the incredible view.

WATCH one of the most thrilling car races in the world – Monaco's Grand Prix.

BUY designer togs and precious jewels in the lavish boutiques on ave des Beaux-Arts.

AFTER DARK be like James Bond and have a flutter in the beautifully ornate Casino de Monte Carlo.

URBAN MYTH

Grace Kelly is the legendary star of Monaco's history. After falling madly in love with Prince Rainier III, she married him in 1956 and became Princess Grace. On 14 September 1982 she was tragically killed in a car accident in Monaco Ville after reportedly suffering a stroke. She is buried in the Byzantine Cathédrale de Monaco and visitors keep her grave covered in flowers. Her beloved husband died on 6 April 2005 and was buried next to her.

FOR ELEGANT NIGHT DINING CAFÉ DE PARIS IN PLACE DU CASINO IS THE PLACE TO BE SEEN.
Photographer: Dallas Stribley (2)

TRENDY PORT HERCULE CAN BE VIEWED FROM THE BALCONY ROOMS OF THE STYLISH HERMITAGE HOTEL.
Photographer: Dallas Stribley (3)

SERVICE AT THE CASINO MONTE-CARLO ALWAYS COMES WITH A SMILE.
Photographer: Dallas Stribley (4)

Washington DC

VITAL STATISTICS

NAME: WASHINGTON DC

NICKNAME: DC, CAPITAL CITY

DATE OF BIRTH: 1791; WHEN CONGRESS CHOSE THE SITE FOR THE NEW FEDERAL CAPITAL

ADDRESS: USA (MAP 1, L10)

HEIGHT: 22M

SIZE: 177 SQ KM

POPULATION: 72,000

Washington DC is full of great monuments and museums but it's also one of North America's great culinary capitals.

ANATOMY

The city lies at the last navigable point on the Potomac River, where the coastal plain meets a higher, rockier plateau. The latter is the setting for DC's wealthy residents; monumental Washington sits on the coastal lowlands. It's a city of gridded streets and diagonal avenues radiating from ceremonial squares and elegant circles. The city proper is quite small, with much of the metropolitan population living in the Virginia and Maryland suburbs. The centre has wide sidewalks and few highways, ideal for walking to many destinations, and the subway is excellent, uncrowded and convenient.

PEOPLE

Washington is a predominantly black and fairly segregated city. The majority (60%) is of African-American descent; there are growing numbers of Asians (2.7%) and Hispanics (7.9%). A high proportion (13%) of the residents are foreign-born.

TYPICAL WASHINGTONIAN

This being a company town, and the industry being politics, there isn't one typical Washingtonian, although about a third of all residents work in government. Whites and blacks don't mix much socially or professionally. Driven and secular (although less so of late), the largely white political class is in stark contrast to the majority. Poverty affects 20% of the population, which is way above the national average – and this in a town with the second-highest per-capita income in the USA.

DEFINING EXPERIENCE

Breakfasting at Jimmy T's diner on Capitol Hill, wandering down the mall past the Capitol, picking a museum to explore before blowing your mind in the National Sculpture Garden, strolling along the Potomac to lunch at Dean & Deluca in Georgetown, and then taking in blues at Madam's Organ.

STRENGTHS

- Smithsonian Institution
- Vietnam Veterans Memorial
- Lincoln Memorial
- National Gallery of Art
- International Spy Museum
- Capitol Hill
- The White House
- Library of Congress
- The buzz of Dupont Circle
- Union Station
- The subway – it's a pleasure to ride
- DC Blues Festival
- Arlington Cemetery
- Funky jazz bars in Adams-Morgan
- Townhouses and cafés of Georgetown
- Watergate complex
- National Cherry Blossom Festival
- National Arboretum
- Eastern Market
- Black Fashion Museum

WEAKNESSES

- Politicians
- The contrived grandeur of Graeco-Roman monuments
- Segregation
- The murder rate
- The government (white, conservative)/populace (black, liberal) divide
- The long ride in from Dulles airport
- The hot air – humidity in summer and from the politicians

GOLD STAR

The National Mall has monuments and museums to occupy visitors for days. It's a history lesson in sod and stone, with a wide expanse of green that stretches from the Potomac in the west to Capitol Hill in the east. It is the scene of protests and celebrations, lined with gravel paths and bordered by tree-shaded avenues.

CITYSPEAK

- Hillary in 2008?
- When are they going to build a memorial to the veterans of the War of 1812?
- Will DC get a Major League baseball team again?
- What's the state of panda conception at the zoo?
- Can the kids fly kites next to the Washington Monument next year?

STARRING ROLE IN...

- *All the President's Men* (1978)
- *Mr Smith Goes to Washington* (1939)
- *Wag the Dog* (1997)
- *The Pelican Brief* (1993)
- *Enemy of the State* (2003)
- *In the Line of Fire* (1993)
- *Patriot Games* (1992)
- *Primary Colors* (1998)
- *Thirteen Days* (2000)
- *Advice & Consent* (1962)
- *Dave* (1993)
- *Being There* (1979)
- *Legally Blonde 2* (2004)
- *The Contender* (2000)
- *The West Wing* (2000–)
- *Lost in the City* by Edward Jones
- *Far East Suite* by Duke Ellington
- *In this Land* by Sweet Honey in the Rock

IMPORT

- Woodward and Bernstein
- Ambitious politicians
- Wily bureaucrats
- Oleaginous lobbyists
- Eager interns
- Presidents of varying quality
- Bullshit artists
- Journalists
- Mendacious diplomats
- Carpetbaggers of all types

EXPORT

- Portentous rhetoric
- CIA operatives
- The link between Saddam and Al Qaeda
- Operation Shock and Awe
- War in Iraq
- Novels of George Pelecanos
- Novels of Gore Vidal
- Polemic of Gore Vidal

SEE the suits arriving on Capitol Hill of a morning.

EAT adventurously – choose food from around the world at Dupont Circle or Adams-Morgan, or Southern cuisine at Georgia Brown's, a Clinton fave.

DRINK a fiery red Martini at trendy Degrees Bar & Lounge in Georgetown.

DO have your photograph taken under the Alexander Calder sculpture in the National Gallery of Art.

WATCH a game of football (it's a football town!) featuring the Washington Redskins.

BUY souvenirs, from rubber Nixon masks to shredded money, at the Bureau of Printing & Engraving.

AFTER DARK hit the sidewalks of Adams-Morgan and go clubbing: Heaven & Hell to tempt fate or vigorous Latino at Habana Village.

URBAN MYTH

Washington was torched by British troops in the War of 1812, and although the Capitol was eventually rebuilt, the city entered a slump from which it wouldn't recover for decades. A dispirited vote to abandon the capital lost by only nine votes.

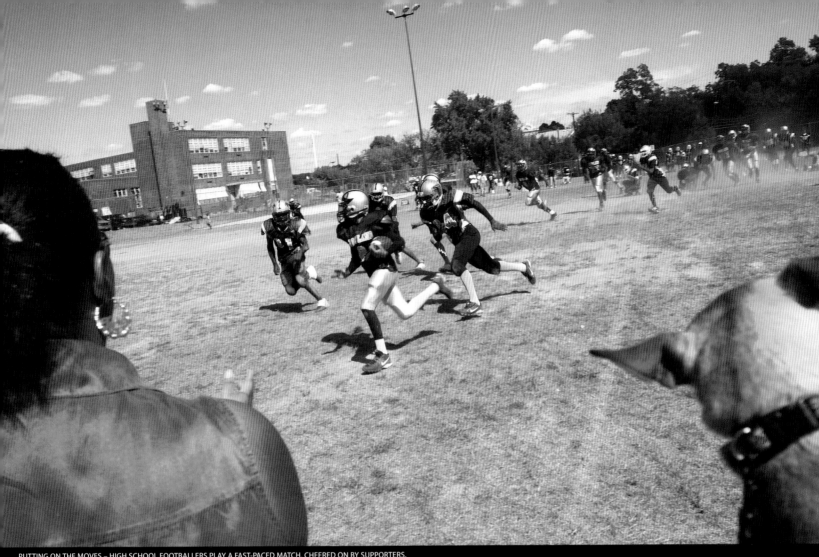

PUTTING ON THE MOVES – HIGH SCHOOL FOOTBALLERS PLAY A FAST-PACED MATCH, CHEERED ON BY SUPPORTERS.
Photographer: Jeff Hutchens (1)

THE BEST AND FRESHEST SEAFOOD FROM CHESAPEAKE BAY ON SALE AT WASHINGTON MARINA.
Photographer: Jeff Hutchens (2)

AN EXHAUSTED SIGHTSEER FINDS THE BENCH CAN OFFER A MUCH WELCOMED NEW PERSPECTIVE ON THE WASHINGTO MONUMENT. Photographer: Jeff Hutchens (3)

THE LIVELY STREETS OF GEORGETOWN MAKE CELEBRITIES AND POLITICIANS LOOK POSITIVELY TWO-DIMENSIONAL.
Photographer: Jeff Hutchens (4)

Quito 104

VITAL STATISTICS

NAME: QUITO

DATE OF BIRTH: PRE-COLUMBIAN; EARLY INHABITANTS OF THE AREA WERE THE PEACEFUL QUITU PEOPLE, WHO GAVE THEIR NAME TO THE CITY

ADDRESS: ECUADOR (MAP 1, L16)

HEIGHT: 2879M

SIZE: 17KM LONG AND 4KM WIDE

POPULATION: 1.4 MILLION

A HILLSIDE DESCENT REVEALS SPOTLIT QUARTERS OF THE OLD CITY.
Photographer: Pablo Corral (1)

A SWEET TOUCH – CANDIED APPLES RIPE FOR THE PICKING.
Photographer: Alison Wright (2)

THE CHRISTIAN IDEALS OF THE CONQUISTADORS ARE EMBEDDED IN LOCAL FAITH.
Photographer: Owen Franken (3)

THREE QUITEÑO TEENS GET ALL DOLLED UP FOR THE ARTS FESTIVAL, PLAZA DE SANTO DOMINGO.
Photographer: Pablo Corral Vega (4)

Tucked amid a high Andean valley and flanked by majestic mountains – when it comes to setting, Quito has it made.

ANATOMY

Quito lies along the central valley in a roughly north–south direction. It can be divided into three segments: the centre (El Centro) is the site of the old town, with its whitewashed, red-tiled houses and colonial churches; north is modern Quito, the new town, with its major businesses, airline offices, embassies, shopping centres and banks; and south of Quito consists mainly of working-class residential areas. The local bus network runs north–south. The speedy and efficient *El Trole* (the trolleybus) is Quito's most comfortable and useful transportation system. Trolleys run along Avenida 10 de Agosto, through the old town to the northern end of the southern suburbs.

PEOPLE

About 25% of the population is Indian, and another 65% is mestizo (of mixed Spanish and indigenous ancestry). It is difficult to accurately quantify how many pure-blooded Indians and how many mestizos there are – some sources give figures of 40% Indian and 40% mestizo. About 7% to 10% are white, and 3% to 10% are black, with a small number of people of Asian descent. Quechua and Spanish are spoken.

TYPICAL QUITEÑO

Quiteños are warm, welcoming and polite. Class division is an issue and blacks and indigenous people are sometimes discriminated against and treated as second-class citizens. While 95% of the population is Catholic, the Indians tend to blend Catholicism with their traditional beliefs.

DEFINING EXPERIENCE

Strolling along the old-town streets, where you'll pass an interesting sight on almost every block, then stopping at the hole-in-the-wall Heladería San Agustín, a 140-year-old ice-cream parlour, for a couple of scoops of nourishment before walking from the narrow colonial streets of the old town into the openness of Plaza San Francisco, revealing one of the finest sites in Ecuador – a sweeping cobblestone plaza backed by the long whitewashed walls and twin bell towers of Ecuador's oldest church, the Monasterio de San Francisco.

STRENGTHS

- Plaza San Francisco
- Vibrant indigenous cultures
- Spectacular setting
- World Cultural Heritage site status
- Virgin of Quito on El Panecillo
- Avenue of Volcanoes
- *Salsotecas* (salsa nightclubs)
- Monasterio de San Francisco
- Museo del Banco Central
- La Mitad del Mundo (The Middle of the World) monument
- Well-preserved colonial architecture

WEAKNESSES

- Altitude sickness
- Political unrest
- Class division
- Pickpockets, especially in the Ipiales market area
- Economic instability
- Deforestation

GOLD STAR

El Panecillo ('The Little Bread Loaf') – from the summit of this much-loved hill there are marvellous views of the whole city stretching out below, as well as views of the surrounding volcanoes.

CITYSPEAK

- The ousting of President Lucio Gutierrez, following weeks of intense street protests in Quito
- Interventionist policies of the USA

STARRING ROLE IN…

- *Between Marx and a Naked Woman* (1996)
- *Proof of Life* (2000)
- *The Villagers* by Jorge Icaza

IMPORT

- *Fútbol* (football)
- Armed rent-a-cops
- Colonial architecture
- Roman Catholicism
- Spaniards
- Colonial religious art
- Foreign debt
- Corrida (bullfighting)
- Volunteer organisations

EXPORT

- Oil
- Bananas
- Panama hats
- Coffee

SEE marvellous views of Quito by climbing the tower of La Basílica high on a hill in the northeastern part of the old town.

EAT *yaguarlocro* (potato and blood-sausage soup) for lunch at Tianguez, under the Monasterio de San Francisco.

DRINK the local firewater, *aguardiente* (sugar-cane alcohol), at the cozy *peña* La Taberna del Duende while listening to traditional *música folklórica* (folk music).

DO take a few salsa dance lessons at Ritmo Tropical before hitting the dance floor of one of Quito's *salsotecas*.

WATCH the spectacular Ballet Folklórico Nacional Jacchigua at Teatro Aeropuerto.

BUY superb Andean textiles on the weekend at Quito's biggest crafts market and sidewalk art show at the northern end of Parque El Ejido.

AFTER DARK head to Reina Victoria, around Santa María and Pinta, where there are several wildly popular bars with packed dance floors on weekends.

URBAN MYTH

New Year's Eve in Quito is celebrated by burning elaborate, life-size puppets (often representing politicians) in the streets at midnight.

THE VIEW FROM SUMNER CAPTURES THE NATURAL BEAUTY OF THE CITY AGAINST THE BACKDROP OF SOUTHERN ALPS.
Photographer: Peter Bennetts (1)

Closely bound to its English roots, with the willow tree–lined banks of the Avon and stone Gothic Revival buildings, the city has preserved its colonial heritage and its large central parks and gardens, but has also embraced the new in the form of inviting cafés, restaurants and bars and a swag of seasonal festivals.

ANATOMY

A flat grid of streets stretches in every direction from Cathedral Sq, the heart of the city. Much of the centre is pedestrianised, but little of it is busy, with the sprawl of malls tucked away in the suburbs. The city is bordered to the south by the Port Hills, to the east by the Pacific, and to the north and west by farmland. Compact and walkable, the city centre is also served by a re-created tram service; buses are the main form of public transport further afield.

PEOPLE

Mostly of solid Anglo-Celtic stock (83%), Christchurchians are increasingly from elsewhere too. The Dutch were the first to come in any numbers in the 1950s, followed by large Pacific Island (2%) and Southeast Asian (5%) communities. Maoris make up 7% of the population.

TYPICAL CHRISTCHURCHIAN

The typical Christchurchian is a rabid supporter of the provincial rugby team, wanting to get on in life and business without too much interference from the pollies in Wellington or those self-serving Aucklanders (inter-city rivalry is fierce). Locals are appreciative of just how important tourism is for their city, and are finally beginning to enjoy the food introduced from their Southeast Asian neighbours.

Christchurch

105

THE SCULPTURED WALLS OF THE ARTS CENTRE EVOKE THE GRACEFUL LINES OF THE AVON RIVER.
Photographer: Peter Bennetts (2)

PASTORAL BEAUTY REMINISCENT OF THE ENGLISH COUNTRYSIDE: THE AVON RIVER.
Photographer: Jon Davison (3)

ENTRANCED FANS ENJOY A SPECTACULAR SUNSET RUGBY MATCH AT JADE STADIUM.
Photographer: David Wall (4)

DEFINING EXPERIENCE

After a heart-starting coffee, wandering through Cathedral Sq before catching the tram to the Botanical Gardens for a stroll among mostly introduced flora and fauna, then lunching in the Arts Centre and browsing the work of local artists before lazily punting along the Avon River in the late afternoon, and, finally, dining at Alchemy.

STRENGTHS

◢ Colonial heritage
◢ Walking and mountain biking the trails on the Port Hills
◢ Arts Centre
◢ Academy Cinema
◢ Sumner Beach
◢ Botanical Gardens and Hagley Park
◢ The tram
◢ Avon River, twisting and turning through the city
◢ Afternoon tea at the Sign of the Takahe
◢ The drive through the tunnel to Lyttelton
◢ Spanish mission–style architecture of New Regent
◢ The Antarctica exhibits in the Canterbury Museum
◢ The Antarctic Centre

WEAKNESSES

◢ Smog in winter
◢ Movement of retail business out into the suburbs
◢ Suburban malls
◢ Excessive pedestrianisation of the inner city
◢ The Mayan monstrosity of the Park Royal Hotel in Victoria Sq
◢ 1980s architecture

GOLD STAR

Colonial architecture – the city's history has not been 'developed' out of existence and some graceful buildings remain, especially along the river in the city centre.

CITYSPEAK

◢ What school did you go to?
◢ House prices…Rising? Falling?
◢ The new art gallery – was it worth all the NZ$?
◢ How much nicer Christchurch is than Auckland.

STARRING ROLE IN…

◢ *Heavenly Creatures* (1993)
◢ *Closed, Stranger* by Kate de Goldi
◢ *The Colour* by Rose Tremain

IMPORT

◢ Class structure
◢ Sheep
◢ *Panini*
◢ Coffee machines
◢ Focaccia

EXPORT

◢ Lamb
◢ Wool
◢ New Zealanders
◢ Ngaio Marsh
◢ Ernest Rutherford

SEE the wizard, casting spells and pontificating during summer lunchtimes in Cathedral Sq.

EAT mod-Kiwi cuisine at Alchemy at the art gallery.

DRINK boutique brews at Dux de Lux.

DO punt along the Avon River into the lovely Botanical Gardens.

WATCH the sun set behind the Southern Alps, from atop the Port Hills.

BUY kiwi dub, hip-hop or even classical music from Radar Records in Cashel Mall.

AFTER DARK try the strip of bars and restaurants on Cambridge Tce, overlooking the river.

URBAN MYTH

'My Mum/Mum's bridesmaid/cousin/auntie/neighbour lived near/worked with/went to the same school as/sat next to on the bus the mother of one of those girls in *Heavenly Creatures*/the girls themselves/a neighbour of one of the girls.'

Glasgow

VITAL STATISTICS

NAME: GLASGOW

NICKNAME: GLESCA; RED CLYDESIDE

DATE OF BIRTH: 6TH CENTURY AD; WHEN GLASGOW GREW UP AROUND THE CATHEDRAL FOUNDED BY ST MUNGO

ADDRESS: SCOTLAND (MAP 3, D5)

HEIGHT: 8M

SIZE: 198 SQ KM

POPULATION: 689,000

Scotland's largest city is the original rough diamond, with a fair share of economic pressure to create dazzling live music, a 24-carat bar scene and the hardest dialect to decipher in English.

ANATOMY

Rambling Glasgow has sights scattered throughout it, though the city centre on the north side of the Clyde River has two train stations that link even the most distant quarters of the city via the UK's second-largest metropolitan train network. The main centre is George Sq, though Sauchiehall St (running along the ridge of the northern part of the city) is a popular pedestrian mall with shops and pubs. Parallel to the river, Argyle St is another important shopping strip, along with its tributary, Buchanan St. The aptly named Merchant City is the commercial district in the city's centre, while the university is near Kelvingrove Park to the northwest, in the area deceptively known as the West End. Pollok Country Park and the Burrell Collection are in the South Side, southwest of the centre.

PEOPLE

Glasgow's population is overwhelmingly Caucasian, with a small group of Asians (2.5%) and Afro-Caribbeans (1%). While English is theoretically the lingua franca, you could get confused by the slang and thick accents of Glaswegians.

TYPICAL GLASWEGIAN

Glaswegians are a tough, hard-working lot who love a pint and speak their own language, which they've cheerfully made impenetrable to visitors. There's a rough humour to it with a Glaswegian Kiss being a head butt and a lexicon that includes *wanner, stiffen* and *mollocate* for getting beaten up. Folk from Edinburgh refer to Glaswegians as *weegies* or *soap dodgers* – a dig at the city's working-class roots. Glaswegians are known for their fierce support of unions and the Labour Party, with huge protests against the poll tax in the 1990s, some of which ended in that other choice piece of Glaswegian patois, a *stoush*.

DEFINING EXPERIENCE

Brunching in the West End's finest cafés, strolling and spying out pirated software at the Barras, picnicking in Kelvingrove Park, sampling the best of the pubs along Sauchiehall St, and then rocking out to the next Franz Ferdinand at the Barrowlands.

STRENGTHS

- Glasgow Cathedral
- Live-music scene
- Merchant City
- Sauchiehall St
- Willow Tea Rooms
- St Mungo's Museum of Religious Life & Art
- Hunterian Art Gallery
- Burrell Collection
- Tenement House
- Mitchell Library
- Pubs and pints
- BBC Scotland studios

WEAKNESSES

- Orange marches
- Economic depression
- Unique dialect
- Neds (Non-Educated Delinquents)

GOLD STAR

Art – from Rennie Mackintosh to Franz Ferdinand there's no doubt Glasgow has made a huge impact on the arts.

CITYSPEAK

- Celtic/Rangers chances this year
- The state of the Clyde River – will it ever be clean again?
- There's really not much in Edinburgh is there?
- Will there ever be a band as great as Jesus and Mary Chain/Orange Juice?

STARRING ROLE IN...

- *Young Adam* (2003)
- *Wilbur Wants to Kill Himself* (2002)
- *Trainspotting* (1996)
- *My Name is Joe* (1998)
- *Shallow Grave* (1994)
- *The Borrowers* (1997)

IMPORT

- Daniel Defoe
- Ewan McGregor

EXPORT

- Franz Ferdinand
- Charles Rennie Mackintosh
- Teenage Fanclub
- Billy Conolly
- Travis, bis and Texas
- Robert Carlyle
- Irn Bru soft drink
- Angus Young
- Robbie Coltrane
- Gregor Fisher
- Darius Danesh
- Lulu
- Sir Thomas Lipton
- Kenny Daglish
- Adam Smith

SEE the architectural canniness of Mackintosh House and get the rest of the Hunterian Art Gallery into the bargain.

EAT seasonal Scottish organic produce in a swanky Victorian-era noshery, the Buttery.

DRINK one of a hundred whiskies at Uisge Beatha (the Gaelic nickname for whisky, literally 'water of life').

DO stroll the grounds and woodland trails of Pollok Country Park and imagine you're the monarch of the glen.

WATCH Glasgow's next big things at King Tut's Wah Wah Hut, where Oasis notoriously played their debut.

BUY a designer knock-off at the Barras on Gallowgate.

AFTER DARK hang under the Arches, the city's biggest club, which attracts visiting DJs and aspiring turntablists.

URBAN MYTH

The age-old rivalry between Glasgow and Edinburgh goes way back. In the late 19th century a group of Glaswegian painters took on the domineering artistic establishment of Edinburgh. Up to this point paintings were largely historic scenes and sentimental visions of the Highlands, but the Glasgow Boys (as they became known) saw the world differently. Painters such as Sir James Guthrie, EA Hornel, George Henry and Joseph Crawhall experimented with colour and themes of rural life, shocking Edinburgh's artistic society. Like Charles Rennie Mackintosh, the Glasgow Boys achieved success in Europe, where their work met with admiration and artistic recognition, but they were largely snubbed in the UK.

LOOKING DOWN THE FOOTBRIDGE ACROSS THE CLYDE RIVER.
Photographer: Neil Setchfield (1)

CLASSIC GLASGOW: TRADITION MEETS ATTITUDE.
Photographer: Neil Setchfield (2)

THE SUN MAKES A RARE APPEARANCE OVER THE BUSTLE OF BUCHANAN ST.
Photographer: Photolibrary (3)

THE FAMOUS SCOTTISH EXHIBITION AND CONVENTION CENTRE, AFFECTIONATELY NICKNAMED 'THE ARMADILLO' FOR REASONS OBVIOUS.
Photographer: Neil Setchfield (4)

THE ART OF MARRIAGE – A BRIDE CELEBRATES *LAYYAT AL-HENNA* ON THE EVE OF HER WEDDING.
Photographer: James L Stanfield (1)

Muscat 107

VITAL STATISTICS

NAME: MUSCAT

NICKNAME: THE THREE CITIES

DATE OF BIRTH: AD 1741; IMAM AHMED BIN SAID, HAVING EXPELLED IRANIAN RULE, MADE MUSCAT THE CAPITAL OF THE NEWLY INDEPENDENT OMAN

ADDRESS: OMAN (MAP 2, T5)

HEIGHT: 5M

POPULATION: 635,000

Elegance in a concealed harbour – Muscat is a dichotomy of tradition and progression, where camels cruise through the city on the back of Toyota pick-ups and the domed buildings of the walled city are inhabited by modern Omanians with mobile phones.

ANATOMY

Wedged between the sea and a jagged spine of mountains, Muscat comprises a string of suburbs, each with its own attractions. The gated city of Muscat sits on a natural harbour and is flanked on the coast by Mutrah, which stretches along an attractive corniche of latticed buildings and mosques. Inland lies Ruwi, Oman's 'little India', the commercial and transport hub of the capital. Plentiful public transport (buses) runs through the three cities. The giant sculptures on the roundabouts provide much-needed navigational aids for the city's unnamed streets, while the well-marked highway parallels the coast and passes through its main attractions.

PEOPLE

Although the city's population is predominantly Arab and Arabic speaking, an Indian merchant community has existed in Muscat for at least 200 years, and English is also enthusiastically spoken. Muscatians follow the Ibadi sect of Islam and are tolerant of other religious groups. Under the auspices of a progressive leader, Sultan Qaboos, the city has reawakened into a modern culture.

TYPICAL MUSCATIAN

Muscatians are as paradoxical as their beloved three cities. They will fashionably wear a headscarf and silk *abeyya* (black outer robe) over Western clothing; receive text messages on eating well while becoming increasingly obese on fast food; and contemplate genetically modified crop rotations, while looking at the cloudless sky and realising that they haven't been praying loud enough. They are hard-working and modern, the women motivated and politically active. They embrace rapid change with a healthy scepticism.

DEFINING EXPERIENCE

Visiting the Marina at dawn to inspect the daily catch, enjoying fresh juice and *shwarma* (meat stuffed in a pocket of pita-type bread with chopped tomatoes and garnish) at the souq (market), then stocking up on savoury pastries, *halwa* (halva) and dates to picnic like royalty by the water (or that old Muscatian favourite: the sewage farm) discussing the afternoon's wet-pitch football game.

STRENGTHS

- Sultan Qaboos
- Fishing-village feel
- (Almost) endless stretches of beach
- Domed buildings
- Mutrah's souq
- International-standard health care
- Walled city of Muscat
- Mountain walks
- Water sports
- The Muscat festival (mid-Janurary to mid-February)
- Excellent bird-watching
- Spotlessly clean streets
- Progressive attitudes

WEAKNESSES

- High cost of living
- Public beaches (which may make women feel uncomfortable)
- Long distances
- Limited shopping and entertainment
- Lack of Arabic coffee

GOLD STAR

Mutrah's souq – an outdoor warren of isle-like alleyways selling everything from frankincense to fruit juice, the souq is the essence of Muscat.

CITYSPEAK

- Football-fuelled stories of the Beckhams
- 'Made in Oman' pottery

STARRING ROLE IN...

- *The Icarus Agenda* by Robert Lidlum

IMPORT

- Islam
- Western medicine
- Portuguese rule
- Internet cafés
- Ships
- Camels
- Fast food
- Football
- Street names (in progress)

EXPORT

- Frankincense
- Slaves
- The arms trade
- Oman Today
- The Oman Bird List
- Fine-bone china
- Tableware
- Pottery skills
- Textiles
- Gold
- Kitsch knick-knacks
- Moving-forward attitude

SEE 125 years of graffitied records left by visiting sailors on the harbour walls.

EAT sizzling kebabs at the Khargeen Café.

DRINK snake coffee, which the head waiter performs by setting fire to an orange peel, at Mumtaz Mahal.

DO visit the perfect bathing spot at picturesque Jissah Beach.

WATCH the fireworks and dance displays at the fabulous Muscat Festival.

BUY and bargain for frankincense in Muscat's Mutrah souq.

AFTER DARK pop down to Al-Ghazal for some pub-grub, a quiz night and other expat festivities.

URBAN MYTH

The walled city of Muscat's gates remained resolutely locked and bolted against the inevitable encroachments of the outside world until 1970 when Sultan Qaboos opened the city again. To facilitate the growing number of cars needing access to the city, a hole was driven through the city walls. Goods and services flooded in and Muscat flooded out to occupy the surrounding coastline. Touchingly, the city gates continued to be locked at a specific time every evening, despite the adjacent hole in the wall, until the gates were replaced with an archway – a fitting metaphor for a city that has given access to modern conveniences while it holds on to the integrity of its character.

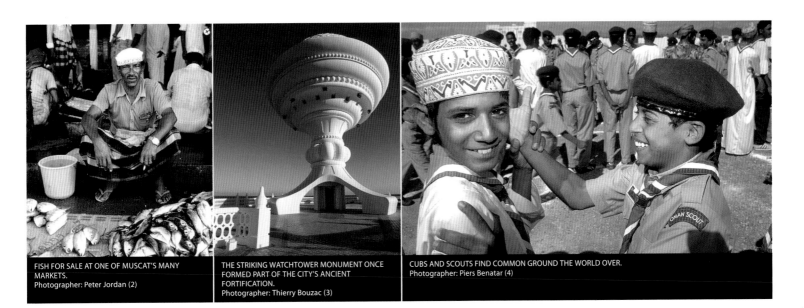

FISH FOR SALE AT ONE OF MUSCAT'S MANY MARKETS.
Photographer: Peter Jordan (2)

THE STRIKING WATCHTOWER MONUMENT ONCE FORMED PART OF THE CITY'S ANCIENT FORTIFICATION.
Photographer: Thierry Bouzac (3)

CUBS AND SCOUTS FIND COMMON GROUND THE WORLD OVER.
Photographer: Piers Benatar (4)

Panama City

VITAL STATISTICS

NAME: PANAMA CITY

NICKNAME: PANAMÁ, THE NAME OF THE FORMER CITY, RAZED TO THE GROUND BY THE PIRATE HENRY MORGAN IN 1671

DATE OF BIRTH: 1519; WHEN IT WAS FOUNDED ON THE SITE OF AN INDIAN FISHING VILLAGE BY THE SPANISH GOVERNOR PEDRO ARIAS DE ÁVILA

ADDRESS: PANAMA (MAP 4, J8)

HEIGHT: 13M

SIZE: 2561 SQ KM

POPULATION: 470,000

The bottleneck of the world's shipping routes, Panama City is a teeming capital in the heart of Latin America, touched by transient influences from all over the globe – sooner or later, everything comes to town.

ANATOMY

Panama City stretches about 20km along the Pacific coast, with the Bahía de Panamá to the south, the Panama Canal to the west, protected forest to the north and the stone ruins of Panamá Viejo (Old Panama, the city's original site) to the east. You can trace the history and personality of the city by walking from the crumbling old town neighbourhood of Casco Viejo through the hotel district of La Exposición to arrive eventually at the vertiginous skyscrapers of El Cangrejo, the thriving banking district. Panama City has a good network of local buses (nicknamed *diablos rojos* – or red devils). Taxis are also plentiful.

PEOPLE

Most of Panama City's population is mestizo (of mixed Spanish and indigenous ancestry). There is also a sizable Chinese community, and a considerable proportion of the population is descended from English-speaking West Indians.

TYPICAL PANAMANIAN

Just as the colonial decay of old-town Casco Viejo is thrown into sharp relief by the modern excess of new-town El Cangrejo, your typical citizen of Panama City is equally contradictory. The exceptionally tolerant Panamanian character weathers many disjunctions – the old and the new, the grave disparity between rich and poor, and the gorgeous natural environment and its rapid destruction. Much of this tolerance begins in the family, which is the cornerstone of Panamanian society and plays a role in nearly every aspect of a person's life.

DEFINING EXPERIENCE

Wandering aimlessly through the heavily atmospheric old-town district of Casco Viejo, peering in the doorways of old churches to admire the altar displays and escape the midday sun, rambling on towards the bustling market and finishing up with a sangria or coffee at an outdoor café.

STRENGTHS

- Bicycle-riding police
- Fabulously decorated public buses
- Mireya Moscoso, the country's first female president
- Artistic postage stamps
- Scrumptious international food
- The Panama Canal
- Diverse museums

WEAKNESSES

- High crime
- Psychotic drivers
- General Manuel Noriega
- Unemployment
- Government corruption

GOLD STAR

The Panama Canal, one of the seven wonders of the industrial world, is just a short distance from the city. Its construction was considered as early as 1524 and its early 20th-century system of giant lock gates remains a marvel of engineering.

CITYSPEAK

- The Miss Universe beauty pageant
- The destruction of rainforest in the Darién
- Unemployment and the economy
- The future of the Panama Canal and the nation in general

STARRING ROLE IN...

- *The Tailor of Panama* (2001)

IMPORT

- Shopping malls
- American fashions
- High-rolling entrepreneurs
- Manufactured goods
- Panama hats – actually made in Ecuador
- Illegal drugs
- Sailors
- Container ships laden with everything from the four corners of the Earth

EXPORT

- Bananas
- Fish
- Sugar
- Coffee
- Reggae – the earliest recordings were made by Jamaican labourers in Panama City
- Reggaeton – the hard-core new upstart in the Latin music scene, pioneered in Panama City
- Illegal drugs
- Sailors
- Container ships laden with everything from the four corners of the earth

SEE a ship passing through the giant locks of the Panama Canal.

EAT cuisine from all over the world.

DRINK sangría in Casco Viejo.

DO a dance course at the Latin Dance Company; this skill will get you places.

WATCH the thunderous, booty-shaking Carnaval parade.

BUY bargain jewellery.

AFTER DARK hit one of Panama City's pumping clubs and be prepared to dance till you drop.

URBAN MYTH

It is said that when the Welsh pirate Henry Morgan sacked Panamá in 1671, the only object of value that was salvaged was the Altar de Oro (Golden Altar) in the Iglesia de San José. According to local tales, when word came of the pirate's impending attack, a priest painted the altar black to disguise it. The priest told Morgan that the famous altar had been stolen by another pirate and even convinced Morgan to donate handsomely for its replacement. Morgan is said to have told the priest, 'I don't know why, but I think you are more of a pirate than I am'.

STRIKING A POSE, PANAMA-STYLE.
Photographer: Richard Quataert (1)

THE SPARKLING VIEW DOWN BALBOA AVE AT NIGHTTIME.
Photographer: José Fuste Raga (2)

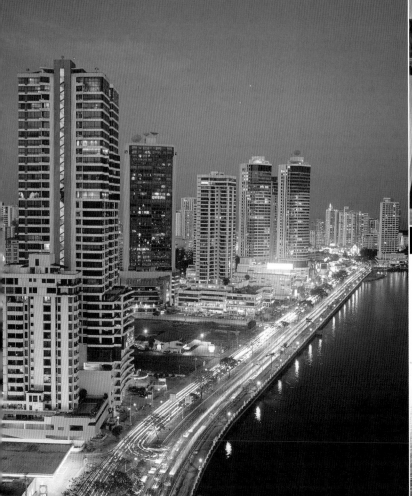

LOCALS RELAX IN THE CRUMBLING BEAUTY OF CASCO VIEJO.
Photographer: Alfredo Maiquez (3)

FISHING BOATS GET A REST AFTER DELIVERING THE DAY'S CATCH.
Photographer: Danny Lehman (4)

Dakar109

VITAL STATISTICS

NAME: DAKAR

DATE OF BIRTH: 1857; THE FRENCH ESTABLISHED DAKAR AT THE SITE OF A FISHING VILLAGE, AND IN 1895 IT BECAME FRENCH WEST AFRICA'S ADMINISTRATIVE CENTRE

ADDRESS: SENEGAL (MAP 1, S13)

HEIGHT: 40M

SIZE: 547 SQ KM

POPULATION: 2 MILLION

Relentless and complex, Dakar is a giant termite nest, tough on the outside and teeming with life on the inside.

ANATOMY

A massive square called Place de l'Indépendance (usually simply called the 'Place') is the city's heart. From here, major streets stem outwards, including ave Léopold Senghor (which passes the Palais Présidentiel) and ave Pompidou, the main street, which leads west to Marché Sandaga. From here, ave du Président Lamine Guéye goes north to the Gare Routière Pompiers and the autoroute, leading inland. The train station is 3km north of Place de l'Indépendance.

PEOPLE

Around 90% of Senegal's population is Muslim, including the Wolof and Mandinka. (The Fula, or Peul, and the Diola are animists by tradition, while many of the Sérèr are Catholics.) French is the official language and Wolof the principal African tongue. The Fula speak Pulaar (or Fula), while the Sérèr speak Sérèr. Arabic expressions are also widely used.

TYPICAL DAKAR CITIZEN

Like many African tribes, Senegal's main indigenous group, the Wolof, has a highly stratified society. At the top are traditional noble and warrior families, followed by the farmers, traders and persons of caste – blacksmiths, leather workers, woodworkers, weavers and *griots*. *Griots* are the lowest of the castes but are highly respected, as they are in charge of passing on the oral traditions. Many descendants of former slaves still work as tenant farmers for the masters of old. Few people would make a big decision without consulting their town's *marabout* (holy man), thought to link Senegalese Islam's disciples and Allah.

DEFINING EXPERIENCE

Quaffing tasty pastries at Pâtisserie Laetitia, bargaining at Marché Kermel before hightailing it to the floodlit landmark minaret of the Grande Mosquée.

STRENGTHS

- A glimpse of the African urban future
- Palais Présidentiel
- Marché Kermel
- Delicious *poisson yassa* (fish grilled with a sauce made from onions, lemon and mustard)
- Dakar's IFAN Museum
- Grande Mosquée
- Simple corner stalls selling bread with butter, chocolate spread, mayonnaise and sardines
- Senegalese beer (especially Gazelle and Flag)
- Urban storytellers
- Saying 'non merci!' three times (effective in staving off hustlers)
- Joggers running barefoot along urban thoroughfares

WEAKNESSES

- Muggings
- Scams
- Petty theft
- The sickeningly wealthy and sickeningly impoverished
- Aggressive street sellers
- Pickpockets (broad daylight is no deterrent to these light-fingered folk)

GOLD STAR

The IFAN Museum is one of the best museums in West Africa. The lively, imaginative displays show masks and traditional dress from the whole region (including Mali, Guinea-Bissau, Benin and Nigeria) and provide an excellent overview of styles, without bombarding you with so much that you can't take it all in. You can also see beautiful fabrics and carvings, drums and tools.

CITYSPEAK

- The government's bogged-down reform processes
- Senegal's rampant desertification from overgrazing and tree felling

STARRING ROLE IN...

- *Badou Boy* (1970)
- *Touki Bouki* (1973)
- *West Africa: An Introduction to Its History* by Michael Crowde
- *Topics of West African History* by Adu Boahen

IMPORT

- Western pop, rock and soul
- Progress, progress, progress
- An international jet-set crowd
- Chronic drug abuse

EXPORT

- Mbalax music
- Agricultural and fish processing
- Youssou N'Dour
- Phosphate mining
- Touré Kunda
- Petroleum refining
- Construction materials

SEE an impressive collection of masks, statues, musical instruments and agricultural implements from all over West Africa at the IFAN Museum.

EAT tasty, cheap and filling *fajayas* (similar to samosas) at Chawarma Donald.

DRINK budget-priced beer at Bar Gorée, opposite the Gorée ferry wharf, popular with sailors and anyone who wants a good time without busting the bank.

DO visit the fishing village of Soumbédioune, west of the city centre, especially at dusk to witness pirogues beach themselves.

WATCH traditional Senegalese wrestling matches (*les luttes* in French) at or near the Stade Iba Mar Diop.

BUY beautiful West African fabrics at Marché Sandaga.

AFTER DARK hit Club Thiossane, a hot, crowded place in La Médina owned by international music star Youssou N'Dour (who might just grace the stage).

URBAN MYTH

Once translators and diplomats to the royal courts, Dakar's modern-day *griots* are akin to singing historians and genealogists, invited to the most important social events such as weddings and naming ceremonies and lavishly paid to recite epics and family histories – the equivalent, perhaps, of a librarian, a gossipy grandmother and a sidewalk folk singer rolled into one.

A 15-MINUTE FERRY RIDE AWAY LIES GORÉE ISLAND WITH ITS CHARMING MEDITERRANEAN-STYLE ARCHITECTURE.
Photographer: David Else (1)

A LOCAL MUSICIAN ADDS SOME URBAN RHYTHM TO THE STREETS OF THE CAPITAL.
Photographer: Ariadne Van Zandbergen (2)

THE STRIKING MOSQUE AT PLAGE D'OUAKAM IS SET AGAINST THE STUNNING BACKDROP OF THE ATLANTIC OCEAN.
Photographer: David Else (3)

LOCAL SALT COLLECTORS PRACTISE THEIR TRADE AT LAC ROSE.
Photographer: David Else (4)

Bratislava
110

VITAL STATISTICS

NAME: BRATISLAVA

NICKNAME: BEAUTY ON THE DANUBE

DATE OF BIRTH: AD 1919 AND AGAIN IN 1993; BRATISLAVA WAS THEN NAMED THE CAPITAL OF THE NEWLY INDEPENDENT SLOVAK REPUBLIC (SEPARATED FROM CZECHOSLOVAKIA, NOW THE CZECH REPUBLIC)

ADDRESS: SLOVAKIA (MAP 3, M10)

HEIGHT: 153M

SIZE: 367 SQ KM

POPULATION: 452,288

A vibrant, pulsing city encapsulating the best of urban Slovakia, Bratislava's vibrant core lies beneath the capital's plain exterior – here you can immerse yourself in the country's finest museums, choose from an ever-increasing array of international cuisine and party till dawn in some of Eastern Europe's most progressive bars and clubs.

ANATOMY

The Staré mesto (old town), which sits on the north bank of the Danube, holds the city's historical heart and its life. A compact strip of cafés, restaurants and nightclubs fills this pedestrianised 500-sq-metre area. On a clear day from the castle hill, you can see Hungary and Austria, while the new town spreads northeastwards to the bland, high-rise suburbs beyond. South, across the Danube via the striking hypermodern Nový most (New Bridge), is the model socialist suburb of Petržalka, home to some 117,000 Bratislavans. Squeezed between the castle and the old town is what is left of the old Jewish quarter, pulled down to accommodate the Bridge. There is an extensive public transport system of trams, buses and trolleybuses.

PEOPLE

Having once been joined to the Czech Republic, Bratislava shares much of its history and people with that country. The persecution of Jewish Slovaks during WWII is silently expressed in every rebuilt stone – Nový most was built over the bulldozed remains of the city's old Jewish quarter. The slow rise of tourism and the influence of communism have kept this city fairly monoculturally Slovak, though international music, films and languages are now served up alongside old Slovak favourites.

TYPICAL BRATISLAVAN

Bratislavans are young, energetic Slovaks who work and play hard, enjoying the increasing buzz of their country's capital. They are business-minded and straightforward – a Bratislavan knows what he or she wants, that's why they are there. They are exceedingly polite, especially on public transport. They make a definite distinction between those that take their country seriously and those that don't. A troubled history only reinforces their sense of national identity and pride.

DEFINING EXPERIENCE

Taking an afternoon stroll through the old town to the Bratislava castle (stopping off at the excellent Museum of Jewish Culture on the way), enjoying a glass of wine and a meal at Hradná Vináreň before joining a film club for a night of well-trodden classics, and then dancing at Hlbočina till dawn.

STRENGTHS

- The old town
- Magnificent views
- Devin Castle's ruins
- Easy access to Hungary and Austria
- Great clubs
- The river cruise
- Pedestrian-friendly streets
- Slovak National Gallery
- The public transport system
- The Bratislava Lyre (festival)
- September jazz days

WEAKNESSES

- Communist-era architecture
- Comparatively pricey accommodation
- Strict driving rules
- Pickpockets
- Sky-high suburban sprawl

GOLD STAR

Superb museums – the Museum of Folk Music, the Museum of Clocks, the Decorative Arts Museum and the Museum of Jewish Culture, to name just a few

CITYSPEAK

- Whether the city's iconic sculpture, the *Peeper*, will lose his head
- If HC Slovan (Bratislava's ice hockey team) will win the next match

STARRING ROLE IN...

- *The Year of the Frog* by Martin M Simecka

IMPORT

- International dishes
- Vegetarianism
- Films
- Rural Slovaks
- Jewish pilgrims
- Communism
- Modernist architecture

EXPORT

- Weddings
- Folk handicrafts
- Football players
- Director Matej Minac

SEE the *Peeper*, the *Frenchman* and the *Photographer* – Bratislava's quirky and very photogenic bronze statues.

EAT Hradná Vináreň's *bryndzové halušky* (potato dumpling dish) at the candlelit tables overlooking the old town.

DRINK crisp Slovak beer while soaking up the jazzy atmosphere of the Buddha Bar.

DO escape the summer heat by hiring a rowing boat at Zlaté piesky (Golden Sands) lake resort.

WATCH the live summer performances at the Museum of Folk Music.

BUY Slovakian folk handicrafts and souvenirs at Uľuv.

AFTER DARK take in an opera that rivals anything in Europe at the lush Slovak National Theatre.

URBAN MYTH

Bratislava's Jewish cemetery has attracted Jewish pilgrims from all over Europe. Buried under rubble during Nazi occupation, the tomb of Chatam Sofer lies here. Born Moshe Schreiber in Frankfurt, Chatam Sofer (1762–1839) moved to Bratislava in 1806 to accept a position as rabbi. Here he founded a yeshiva (a school for rabbis) and in the course of his life trained over 150 rabbis. The school became one of the best known in Europe, and operated up until the first years of WWII, when it had to be moved to Israel. Recently reopened to the public, the cemetery is now Slovakia's most important Jewish site.

OLD TOWN STREETS PAVE THE WAY FOR MODERN LIFE.
Photographer: Glenn Beanland (1)

MICHAEL'S GATE IS ALL THAT REMAINS OF THE CITY'S ORIGINAL FORTIFICATION.
Photographer: Glenn Beanland (2)

CLOSING THE DOOR ON THE PAST.
Photographer: Glenn Beanland (3)

MOOD LIGHTING MAKES BLENDING IN EASY AT THE CAMOUFLAGE BAR.
Photographer: Glenn Beanland (4)

San Sebastián

111

VITAL STATISTICS

NAME: SAN SEBASTIÁN (BASQUE NAME: DONOSTIA)

DATE OF BIRTH: 1174; SAN SEBASTIÁN WAS GRANTED SELF-GOVERNING STATUS BY THE KINGDOM OF NAVARRA, FOR WHOM THE BAY WAS THE PRINCIPAL OUTLET TO THE SEA

ADDRESS: SPAIN (MAP 3, E13)

HEIGHT: 7M

POPULATION: 178,534

A SURFER WAITS TO SPREAD HIS WINGS ON PLAYA DE LA ZURRIOLA.
Photographer: Dallas Stribley (1)

BASQUE *PINTXOS*, WIDELY REGARDED AS THE BEST FOOD IN SPAIN.
Photographer: Dallas Stribley (2)

PAINT SPLATTERED ON THE WALL OF THE SPANISH COMANDANCIA NAVAL BY BASQUE SEPARATISTS.
Photographer: Dallas Stribley (3)

FAST-PACED *JAI-ALAI* ACTION IN PLAZA DE LA TRINIDAD.
Photographer: Dallas Stribley (4)

One of the oldest and most famous beach resorts in the world, San Sebastián's breathtaking natural beauty, warm inhabitants and extraordinary cuisine ensure that the gloss never wears off this quintessential haunt of the bronzed and beautiful.

ANATOMY

San Sebastián has three main centres of activity. The busy and modern centre surrounds the Catedral del Buen Pastor, while the heart of San Sebastián beats in the Parte Vieja (Old Town), squeezed below Monte Urgull Parque on the eastern spur of the superb Bahía de la Concha. The third area is Gros, east across the Río Urumea, which also has a good beach, and is home to the Renfe train station. The main bus station is about 1km south of the cathedral.

PEOPLE

The Basque people have become one of Europe's most prominent yet least-understood minorities. The Basques have retained a language, and with it a separate identity, whose origin still puzzles linguists.

TYPICAL SAN SEBASTIÁN CITIZEN

Chic, hard-working and fond of food and drink, the typical citizen of San Sebastián speaks both Castilian (Spanish) and Euskara (the Basque language) and keeps a pragmatic but proud grip on local traditions. Older men will often be members of a *txoko* (all-male eating societies) and capable of wearing berets with much style. Younger men will often be keen surfers of the nearby beaches.

DEFINING EXPERIENCE

Starting the day with a refreshing dip at the beach to get the blood pumping after the night before, which saw you tripping between *pintxos* (Basque tapas) bars until the wee hours, then spending the morning sussing out some of the edgy graphic arts on display around the city, followed by a very, very satisfying Michelin-starred lunch.

STRENGTHS

- Burying of the Sardine ritual at the end of *carnaval*
- Great local beaches
- Stylish places to stay
- San Sebastián Film Festival
- Innovative nouvelle cuisine
- International Jazz Festival
- Views from Monte Igueldo
- Eduardo Chillida's *Peine de Vientos* sculpture
- Mesmerising Euskara

WEAKNESSES

- Crowds in summer
- Trying to get a good night's sleep in the Parte Vieja
- Angry young drunks around closing time on some of the Parte Vieja streets
- Unmentionable politics
- Impenetrable Euskara

GOLD STAR

Food – Basque *pintxos* are the greatest snacks in the world and San Sebastián's are the best of the lot.

CITYSPEAK

- Great secret surfing spots
- Where to eat
- What are those clowns doing in Madrid?
- Who's coming out for the film festival?

STARRING ROLE IN...

- *The Sun Also Rises* (1926)
- *The Red Squirrel* (1993)
- *A Social Parade* (2004)

IMPORT

- Other Basques
- Surfboards
- Castellano (Castilian)
- Fireworks
- Jazz
- Cod (now)

EXPORT

- Loreak Mendian clothes
- *Pintxos*
- Beach chic
- Cod (then)
- Red berets
- *Jai-alai* (a Basque form of handball)
- Cider

SEE the world's prettiest city beach at Playa de la Concha.

EAT at Juan Mari Arzak's triple Michelin-starred Arzak.

DRINK red wine from nearby La Rioja.

DO a walk to the top of Monte Urgull by taking a path from Plaza de Zuloaga or from behind the aquarium.

WATCH hot cinema at the San Sebastián Film Festival.

BUY cutting-edge Basque fashion from the Loreak Mendian label.

AFTER DARK go bar-hopping in the Parte Vieja.

URBAN MYTH

On Christmas Eve, locals climb Mt Igueldo with an effigy of a sea bream – a pre-Christian ritual to ward off the character of Olentzaro, a charcoal burner who slithers down chimneys on that day and wreaks havoc. Locals keep their fireplaces well stocked with burning wood on the day to keep him at bay. A pastry shaped like a sea bream is also eaten on Christmas Eve, as the fish is strongly associated with Olentzaro.

A SMART WAY TO TRAVEL – 100 YEARS AFTER E=MC² THE WILD-HAIRED PHYSICIST BEAMS FROM THE SIDE OF AN ENERGY-SAVING TRAM.
Photographer: Glenn Beanland (1)

Bern is a charmingly quaint city despite its status as the capital of Switzerland, and boasts a medieval heart, a 15th-century town hall and a thriving alternative-arts scene.

ANATOMY

The compact town is contained within a sharp U-shaped bend, limiting some streets to pedestrian and public transport access. The main train station is at the mouth of the U and within easy reach of the main sights, and daily loan of city bikes is free.

PEOPLE

The majority of Bern's friendly residents speak Swiss German as a first language, while others speak French. Bernese German incorporates several words from *Matteänglisch*, a secret language that few people now speak, which was used in the former workers' quarter of Matte.

TYPICAL BERNESE

The typical Bern resident is modest, well-groomed, bilingual in French and German, predominantly Protestant and lives a quiet life in the pleasant Swiss capital. The Bernese enjoy the arts and regularly go to Bern's numerous cinemas to watch films in their original language.

Bern 112

VITAL STATISTICS

NAME: BERN

NICKNAME: BEAR (DUKE BERTHOLD V OF ZÄHRINGEN ALLEGEDLY NAMED THE CITY AFTER AN ANIMAL HE KILLED WHILE HUNTING; THE BEAR HAS BEEN BERN'S HERALDIC ANIMAL FOR SEVEN CENTURIES)

DATE OF BIRTH: 1191; WHEN IT WAS FOUNDED AS A MILITARY POST; BERN BECAME CAPITAL WHEN THE SWISS CONFEDERATION CAME TO LIFE IN 1848

ADDRESS: SWITZERLAND (MAP 3, I11)

HEIGHT: 509M

SIZE: 52 SQ KM

POPULATION: 127,000

A QUICK ONE-ON-ONE WITH SOME OF THE WORLD-CLASS ARTISTS IN THE COLLECTION OF THE KUNSTMUSEUM.
Photographer: Glenn Beanland (3)

A YOUNG COUPLE SHARE A PARTING KISS ON THE BUSY BERNASTRASSE.
Photographer: Glenn Beanland (2)

GRAFFITI AND GIG POSTERS SIGNPOST THE WAY TO BERN'S THRIVING UNDERGROUND SCENE AT THE REITSCHULE.
Photographer: Glenn Beanland (4)

DEFINING EXPERIENCE

Climbing the tower of Bern's Gothic Münster (cathedral) for fantastic views, joining a tour of the Bundeshäuser (Houses of Parliament), viewing the Paul Klee exhibition at the Kunstmuseum and watching the twirling figurines before the chiming of the Zeitglockenturm, an elaborate medieval clock tower with moving puppets.

STRENGTHS

- Bern's Unesco World Heritage–listed medieval city centre
- Summer rafting tours on the River Aare
- Ornate fountains every 150m or so
- Marking time at the Zeitglockenturm
- The impressively ornate Bundeshäuser
- The Bern Onion Market
- Kunstmuseum's collection, including Picasso, Hodler, Fra Angelico, Dalí and Paul Klee
- Swimming in the open-air, riverside Marzili pools
- Hotel Belle Epoque's opulent Art Deco rooms
- Reitschule's alternative scene
- Nougat-speckled Toblerone chocolate
- Covered shopping promenades

WEAKNESSES

- The thought of being eaten by the ogre in Ogre Fountain
- The Bear Pits displaying Bern's namesake (though some love it)
- Lofty prices

GOLD STAR

Stupendously vertiginous views of the medieval town, River Aare and Berner Alps from the lofty spire of Bern's Gothic 15th-century *Münster*.

CITYSPEAK

- Switzerland's adopted philosophy of 'harm reduction' rather than 'zero tolerance' in dealing with illicit drugs, and their use, in society
- Whether to limit the number of European asylum-seekers entering Switzerland

STARRING ROLE IN...

- *An Indian Idyll* (2000)
- *On Her Majesty's Secret Service* (1969)
- Ferdinand Hodler's artwork

IMPORT

- Tourists
- Vehicles
- University students
- South American musicians
- Albanian and Kosovite refugees
- Textiles

EXPORT

- Toblerone chocolate
- Einstein's theories from the Bern patent office where he worked
- Swiss army knives
- Pockmarked Emmental cheese
- Fondue sets
- Muesli
- Painters Ferdinand Hodler and Paul Klee
- Poet Albert Bitzius
- Scientist Albrecht von Haller
- Songwriter Mani Matter
- Pharmaceuticals
- Precision instruments, including watches and clocks
- Swiss Air

SEE why the medieval town centre attained its Unesco World Heritage listing by gaining a bird's-eye view from the Münster's spire.

EAT cheese in a fondue, coupled with *rösti* (fried potatoes) and followed by smooth Swiss chocolate.

DRINK Bärner Müntschi (Bern's kiss) beer, Rivella soft drink or Apenzeller Alpenbitter (Alpine bitters), a liquor made from the essences of 67 different flowers and roots, and make sure you look into someone's eyes when you chink glasses.

DO bathe at the open-air, riverside Marzili pools.

WATCH twirling figurines celebrating the passing of time on the Zeitglockenturm.

BUY a Swiss army knife.

AFTER DARK head past graffiti-adorned buildings to the Reitschule and its vibrant alternative-arts scene.

URBAN MYTH

Though it can never be tested fully, $E=MC^2$ is no myth. Legend has it that Albert Einstein came up with his theory of relativity while gazing into space instead of tending to his tedious job at the Swiss patent office in Bern in 1907. Today this theory lives on as one of the 20th century's most important scientific pronouncements and Einstein's reputation as a groundbreaking physicist endures.

San Juan

113

VITAL STATISTICS

NAME: SAN JUAN

DATE OF BIRTH: 1511; WHEN THE SPANISH COLONISED THE CITY

ADDRESS: PUERTO RICO (MAP 4, O4)

HEIGHT: 25M

SIZE: 300 SQ KM

POPULATION: 1.6 MILLION

THE PUERTO RICON FLAG EMBODIES THE NATION'S PRIDE.
Photographer: Tony Arruza (1)

Fulfilling all fantasies about tropical Caribbean coastal cities, San Juan offers all the fun and drama of a Latino holiday haven, played out against the backdrop of the spectacular fortressed walls of the old city.

ANATOMY

The city stretches from San Juan Bay across a coastal plain. The city's centre (Old San Juan) is crammed with Spanish colonial architecture. This walled city occupies the end of a small island on the eastern side of the entrance to the bay. East of Old San Juan are the red-hot resort districts of Condado and Isla Verde, with greater San Juan stretching south, east and west of the main centre. Walking is the best way to get around Old San Juan and the immediate vicinity, though there is a handy and free tourist trolley. There are also many *públicos* (shared taxis – mainly minibuses) available.

PEOPLE

In San Juan the majority of the population (around 80%) is of Spanish or mixed Spanish descent, while around 20% are of African descent. Most locals are Roman Catholic, with around 10% being Protestant and a small percentage following other faiths. The official language is Spanish, but English is widely spoken.

TYPICAL SAN JUAN CITIZEN

San Juan's citizens work predominantly in manufacturing industries or tourism. Despite the fact that Puerto Rico is a US territory, their hourly wage is significantly lower than in the USA and, thus, many work for US companies. They are increasingly prosperous. They have small families, are religious, love quick tempos and hot moves, and are friendly to visitors. After work they hang out at restaurants and bars that pulse with the lively rhythm of the night.

DEFINING EXPERIENCE

Sipping coffee and scrawling inspired notes for 'the novel' at the popular meeting place for writers and artists (Cuatro Estaciones café in Old San Juan), then heading to the beach for a splash and some well-deserved shut-eye in the sun before sprucing up for a sizzling night of salsa at La Rumba.

STRENGTHS

- Good offshore fishing
- World-class golf-courses close by
- Coral reefs offshore
- Thriving nightlife
- Rainforest nearby
- Gardens of the Casa Blanca
- World Heritage site of Old San Juan
- Beach weather year-round
- Coconut limber (home-made icy-pole in a cup)
- Radio Sol (good salsa station)
- Mercado de Río Piedras
- Cronopios (The Bookstore)

WEAKNESSES

- Confusing street signs (speed limit signs are in miles, even though distances are in kilometres)
- Traffic jams (and carjacking)
- Dangerous areas in and around the city
- Many restaurants closed on Sunday or Monday
- Drug dealers
- Heaps of tourists, virtually everywhere, most of the time

GOLD STAR

The walled city of Old San Juan – within its walls are the charms of over 400 years of Spanish colonial history, fine cultural institutions, a spirited community and a thriving nightlife. This fortress of fun offers travellers more entertainment per square kilometre than New York City, at a pace that is laid-back and distinctly Latin.

CITYSPEAK

- When and how will the government curb the bloody toll of Puerto Rico's ongoing drug wars?
- Petrol shortages on the island due to continuing truckie strikes

STARRING ROLE IN...

- *Havana Nights* (2003)
- *Bad Boys 2* (2002)
- *Under Suspicion* (1999)
- *Amistad* (1997)
- *Contact* (1997)
- *GoldenEye* (1995)
- *Assassins* (1995)

IMPORT

- Millions of tourist dollars each year
- Fast-food chains
- American chain stores
- Machinery and equipment
- Clothing
- Fish
- Fuel
- US businesses in search of cheap, plentiful labour and tax relief

EXPORT

- Chemicals
- Electronics
- Apparel
- Canned tuna
- Rum
- Beverage concentrates
- Medical equipment
- Low-wage workers to the US
- Rita Moreno
- Raul Julia

SEE the salsa heroes of tomorrow perform on the streets of the modern city of San Juan.

EAT your fill of fresh, cheap exotic fruits as you peruse the market stalls of the colourful Mercado de Río Piedras.

DRINK free rum on a boozed-up tour at the factory of world-famous Bacardi Rum.

DO devote as many days as possible to exploring Old San Juan – to fully soak up its bubbling tropical atmosphere and bold beauty.

WATCH surfers battle the swells east of the broad tropical beach of Isla Verde in the dusk of early evening.

BUY new-season items at the Ralph Lauren store in Old San Juan.

AFTER DARK join the vibrant crowds at the Tapas bar at Café Bohemio.

URBAN MYTH

Over the centuries, the Capilla del Cristo (Christ's Chapel) has been a popular place to pray for miracles. While one story goes that the chapel was primarily built to stop people falling over the city wall of the old city and into the sea, a less pragmatic explanation is that it was built to commemorate a miracle with a similar plot line. This account describes a rider participating in a horse race during festivities in the city. The horse galloped clean over the top of the wall into the sea, but the rider miraculously survived. While some historians dispute this, saying the rider died, believers continue to leave tokens of thanks at the chapel for the miracles in their own lives.

STEP BACK IN TIME – SPANISH COLONIAL ARCHITECTURE IS A FEATURE OF OLD SAN JUAN.
Photographer: John Neubauer (2)

CAFÉS AND TAPAS BARS SERVE UP CULINARY DELIGHTS ALONG WITH A VIBRANT SOCIAL SCENE.
Photographer: Jerry Alexander (3)

THEY MIGHT NOT BE CUBANS BUT SAN JUAN'S CIGARS ARE STILL WORLD CLASS.
Photographer: Ira Block (4)

Aleppo (Halab)

114

VITAL STATISTICS

NAME: ALEPPO (HALAB)

NICKNAME: HALAB (DERIVED FROM 'MILK' – LEGEND SAYS ABRAHAM MILKED HIS COW IN THE REGION)

DATE OF BIRTH: 1800 BC; THERE ARE RECORDS OF THE TOWN AT THIS TIME FROM THE HITTITE

ADDRESS: SYRIA (MAP 3, V16)

HEIGHT: 390M

POPULATION: 4 MILLION

Centre of commerce and trade since Roman times and possibly the oldest city in the world, Aleppo has a bountiful architectural heritage which has survived countless invasions and offers almost limitless opportunities for exploration.

ANATOMY

Aleppo has two distinct parts: the New City, where you stay and eat, and the Old City, where you go sightseeing. The New City is centred on sharias Al-Baron and Al-Quwatli, with the main travellers' area (containing inexpensive hotels and eating places) to the east and south. The Old City lies southeast, separated by two drab, wide avenues (sharias Al-Mutanabi and Bab Antakya). Its heart is the compress of streets making up the famed souq (market). Main thoroughfares run east–west, past the Great Mosque and terminating at the Citadel. North is the 16th- and 17th-century Christian-Armenian quarter of Al-Jdeida. Catch a microbus around town or walk.

PEOPLE

In line with the rest of the country, Aleppo's population is predominantly Arabic. There are also ethnic Syrians, who are of Semitic descent, and smaller groupings of Kurds, Armenians, Circassians and Turks. Aleppo is unique in that between 20% and 30% of its population is Christian – the greatest concentration of Christians in the Middle East.

TYPICAL ALEPPINE

Known for their hospitality, many Aleppines will welcome you into their homes for food or tea as a matter of course. Family-oriented, social life often revolves around food and bathing communally in (mostly) gender-segregated *hammams* (bathhouses). Sometimes described as serious or sober, Aleppines have a legendary mercantile bent best summed up in the proverb: 'An Aleppine can sell even a dried donkey skin.'

DEFINING EXPERIENCE

Visiting the New City's National Museum before setting off for the Old City and its souq to shop, exploring the Grand Mosque and Citadel before bathing at the Hammam Yalboughaan-Nasry, prior to dining on traditional Aleppine dishes in the Al-Jdeida quarter.

STRENGTHS

- Shopping the souq
- Great Mosque
- Al-Jdeida quarter
- The Citadel
- Hammam Yalboughaan-Nasry
- Khan al-Jumruk and Khan an-Nahaseen
- 40 Martyrs' Armenian Cathedral
- National Museum
- Beir al-Wakil (a Thousand and One Nights fantasy, with added air-con and minibar)
- Qala'at Samaan
- Dead Cities – shells of ancient towns and villages
- Comparatively undeveloped city, tourism-wise

WEAKNESSES

- Political straitjacketing of cultural scene
- Litter, especially plastic bags
- Newer roads pouring traffic into neighbourhoods never designed for it
- Incongruous high-rises looming over traditional courtyard houses
- The 'Aleppo button' (ulcers from sandfly bites)

GOLD STAR

While not as extensive as Cairo's Khan al-Khalili or as grand as Instanbul's Kapali Carsi, Aleppo's souq is the most vibrant and untouristy in the entire Middle East.

CITYSPEAK

- Turkey's plans to push ahead with dam projects on the Euphrates River
- What happens when President Assad finally goes?

STARRING ROLE IN...

- *That in Aleppo Once* by Vladimir Nabokov
- *Aleppo Tales* by Haim Sabato, Hayim Sabato and Philip Simpson

IMPORT

- Food and livestock
- Hong Kong kung-fu movies
- Trashy Indian B-movies
- Alexander the Great (took the city in 333 BC)
- Crusaders (unsuccessfully besieged Aleppo in 1118 and 1124)
- Saladin (captured the city in 1183)
- Mongols (held the city briefly under Hulagu Khan in 1260 and Timur in 1401)
- The Ottoman Empire (annexed the city in 1517)
- Agatha Christie (who wrote the first part of *Murder on the Orient Express* at the Baron Hotel)
- Machinery
- Chemicals

EXPORT

- Pistachios
- The Aleppo codex, an early manuscript of the Judaeo-Christian Bible
- Silks
- Cotton textiles
- Aleppo soap, a unique mix of olive and laurel oils
- Al-Kindo Ensemble
- Spices
- Carpets
- Muhammed Fares, Syria's first cosmonaut
- Olives
- Chess player and writer Phillip Stamma
- Poets al-Mutanabbi and Abu al-Firas
- Philosopher and scientist al-Farabi

SEE the beautifully maintained warren of Al-Jdeida's stone-flagged alleyways.

EAT cherry kebabs and mutton patties filled with fetta cheese at Beit al-Wakil.

DRINK at the Baron Hotel's bar while communing with the ghosts of guests past, including Charles Lindbergh, TE Lawrence, Theodore Roosevelt and Agatha Christie.

DO bathe at the Hammam Yalboughaan-Nasry.

WATCH whirling dervishes at the Bimaristan Arghan.

BUY gold, silver and carpets at the souq: geared to local trade, there's less pressure and better choice than in Damascus.

AFTER DARK Aleppo isn't a late-night city, but options include promenading around the Al-Azizah area or going on a bar-restaurant crawl in Al-Jdeida.

URBAN MYTH

The city is mentioned several times in Shakespeare's plays eg in *Macbeth* the witches say of a sailor's wife, 'Her husband's to Aleppo gone.'

A BEAUTIFUL DAY FOR A SONG AND A PICNIC, ST SIMEON.
Photographer: Mark Daffey (1)

HIGH CULTURE IN THE NEW CITY: THE STATELY OPERA CINEMA.
Photographer: Wayne Walton (2)

SUN ON THE HORIZON PAINTS THE OLD CITY A RICH SHADE OF ORANGE.
Photographer: Mark Daffey (4)

A VETERAN TAXI TAKES A WELL-DESERVED REST OUTSIDE THE BUS STATION.
Photographer: Mark Daffey (3)

SAVOURING THE SAND, FEMALE EMIRATI STUDENTS TAKE TIME OUT TO ENJOY THE BEACH.
Photographer: Allenby-Pratt (1)

Dubai 115

VITAL STATISTICS

NAME: DUBAI

NICKNAME: DO BUY

DATE OF BIRTH: 5000 BC; WHEN TRADE IN THE AREA BEGAN

ADDRESS: UNITED ARAB EMIRATES (MAP 2, S5)

HEIGHT: 5M

SIZE: 35 SQ KM

POPULATION: 1.1 MILLION

With a slightly surreal mix of dazzling consumerism and Arabian culture with an Islamic influence, Dubai has a cosmopolitan and easy-going charm that makes it the best introduction to the Middle East.

ANATOMY

Dubai is really two towns split by the Dubai Creek (Khor Dubai), an inlet of the Gulf. North of the creek lies Deira, an older city centred on creekside Baniyas Rd, while the north has the glittering new office buildings of Bur Dubai clustered along Sheikh Zayed Rd (also known as Trade Centre Rd). There's little public transport in the city, so to negotiate Dubai you'll pay out a small fortune for taxis.

PEOPLE

More than 80% of Dubai's residents are expats (many drawn from Asia and the Philippines), who were born in other countries and have chosen to make the city their home. UAE nationals (or Emiratis) are a minority. While the official language is Arabic, you can expect to hear English, Persian, Hindi and Tagalog spoken throughout the city.

TYPICAL DUBAI CITIZEN

Okay so Emiratis like to shop and Dubai is certainly the fashionista capital, with more Porsches than you're ever likely to see in a showroom, but the city is anything but superficial. The call to prayer is probably the only thing that will get people off their mobiles, but Muslims are very devout in the city. Every neighbourhood has its own mosque and Ramadan is a month that stops DJs spinning in town. Even partying expats respect the Muslim customs and restrict their drinking to a select group of hotels.

DEFINING EXPERIENCE

Snapping up a bargain at Deira City Centre, sailing in for a closer view of Burj al Arab, sniffing the richness of Deira Spice Souq, catching a dhow to Deira, and finally relaxing with *sheesha* (a tobacco water pipe often flavoured with honey or apple) in a courtyard café.

STRENGTHS

- Burj al Arab
- Fashion
- Duty-free shopping
- Dubai Museum
- Jumeirah Mosque
- The Palm Islands
- Deira Gold Souq
- Dhows
- Deira Spice Souq
- Grand Mosque
- Endless summer sunshine
- Bootleg brands (Readbok and Adiblas, anyone?)
- Sheikh Saeed al-Maktoum House
- Emirate Tower
- Nad al-Sheba Club
- Wild Wadi Waterpark
- Jumeirah Beach Park
- Dusit Dubai
- Jumeirah Archaeological Site

WEAKNESSES

- Limited alcohol
- Hard-to-find Emirati cuisine
- Beachfront resorts
- Searing summer heat

GOLD STAR

Wacky construction projects – whether it's the world's largest indoor ski slope, biggest mall or reclaiming islands in the shape of the globe, there's always design challenges being dreamed up in Dubai.

CITYSPEAK

- Dubailand – will it be the world's largest mall for long?
- Where to drink on the sly
- Smoking bans – what's wrong with smoking in the office?
- Whatever happened to the light-rail project?

STARRING ROLE IN...

- *Code 46* (2003)
- *Dubai Tales* by Mohammad al-Murr
- *Don't They Know It's Friday?* by Jeremy Williams
- *Father of Dubai: Shaikh Rashid bin Saeed al-Maktoum* by Graeme Wilson

IMPORT

- Tax-dodging corporations
- Accounting firms
- Tourists
- Latest fashions
- Marian Behnam
- Gold, perfume and spice
- David Beckham
- Bollywood movies

EXPORT

- Oil and gas
- Beverages, chemicals, paper, pharmaceuticals and rubber
- General Sheikh Mohammed bin Rashid Al Maktoum, the crown prince of Dubai
- Duty-free goods
- Masoud Amralla al-Ali
- Yaseer Habeeb

SEE the iconic glass sail of Burj al Arab.

EAT fish so fresh it's still flapping at the Fish Market, where you select the city's best seafood and pay by weight.

DRINK nothing but water as you sample apple or vanilla *sheesha* at Cosmo Café.

DO take a dhow cruise to see how spice, gold and perfume are still delivered to the souqs (markets).

WATCH the Bedouin dance *ayyalah* – a celebration of the tribe's courage, strength and unity – performed at the Heritage Village.

BUY spices at a souq, but only after haggling an hour to save five dirhams.

AFTER DARK hop into lush French bar Boudoir to rub shoulders with visiting supermodels.

URBAN MYTH

Even with the huge import of Ferraris and Mazeratis, dhows remain *the* vehicle of Dubai, just as they were centuries ago. The Dhow Wharfage is still piled high with assorted goods from Iran, India, Pakistan and East Africa. It's no surprise then that Dubai was once one of the most important dhow-building centres in the Gulf. The *al-galalif* (dhow builders) used basic materials and methods to construct a diverse range of vessels. The larger dhows used for long-distance journeys were called *al-boom*, *al-bateel* and *al-baglah*, and were up to 60m in length. Some of them have now been turned into cruise vessels and floating restaurants.

THE ART OF FALCONRY IS A PRESTIGIOUS SPORT IN THE UAE.
Photographer: Christine Osborne (2)

STRIKINGLY BEAUTIFUL JUMEIRAH MOSQUE IS AN EXQUISITE EXAMPLE OF ARABIAN ARCHITECTURE.
Photographer: Chris Mellor (3)

NOT YOUR AVERAGE FAMILY CAR – DUBAI'S WEALTH IS VERY VISIBLE.
Photographer: Phil Weymouth (4)

Rīga 116

VITAL STATISTICS

NAME: RĪGA

NICKNAME: THE PARIS OF THE BALTICS; PARIS OF THE EAST

DATE OF BIRTH: AD 1201; WHEN BISHOP ALBERT OF LIVONIA FOUNDED THE LIVONIAN KNIGHTS

ADDRESS: LATVIA (MAP 3, P4)

HEIGHT: 3M

SIZE: 307 SQ KM

POPULATION: 790,000

The Baltic States' biggest and most cosmopolitan city, Rīga exudes both medieval charm and contemporary cool, combining these qualities seamlessly in a welcoming environment that has not gone unnoticed by European tourists, who already flock here for weekend breaks.

ANATOMY

Rīga lies slightly inland from the massive Bay of Rīga, on the massive Daugava River. On the eastern bank is Vecrīga (Old Rīga), the city's historical heart, with a skyline dominated by three steeples: St Peter's, Dome Cathedral and St Jacob's. The river is crossed by three huge bridges, and joins Vecrīga to the city's more modern left bank and to the nearby seaside resort of Jūrmala. You can get around by bus, minibus, tram or trolleybus.

PEOPLE

Just as Latvia is the most Russian of the Baltic States, Rīga is the most Russian of the Baltic capitals, with some 42% of the city's residents being ethnic Russians. Many of the Latvians resident in the city also speak fluent Russian, too, so unlike Tallinn or Vilnius the city has an extremely Russian feel. Most Latvians are Lutheran, while the Russian population is generally Russian Orthodox Christian.

TYPICAL RĪGAN

Despite a very real Latvian feeling of colonisation and resentment towards Russians in general, anti-Russian feeling is hardly ever expressed by Rigans – a rare case of two very different peoples sharing a city in almost total harmony. While Latvians have a very Scandinavian approach to life – and this is evident in the incredible pace of change over the past two decades – the Eastern-looking Russian Rīgans have also been caught up in the developmental frenzy and profited from it equally. Your typical Rīgan will have both Russian and Latvian friends, be confident in both languages and be extremely proud of Rīga's pre-eminent position among the Baltic capitals.

DEFINING EXPERIENCE

Wandering the charming streets of Vecrīga, stumbling across ancient churches and colourful houses, always being surprised by something.

STRENGTHS

- ◢ Extremely clean streets
- ◢ Friendly people
- ◢ Easy to negotiate
- ◢ Superb Art Nouveau architecture

WEAKNESSES

- ◢ Some would say that Rīga has been cleaned up and restored into sterility
- ◢ Those freezing winters limit most visitors to just a few sunny months during the summer
- ◢ The stodgy and greasy national cuisine of Latvia leaves many people cold

GOLD STAR

The cleanliness of the city, its charming inhabitants and their extraordinarily good manners – this is a city where people clean up after themselves, always open doors for you and drivers bend over backwards to give way to each other at junctions. If nothing else, this will convince you just how Scandinavian Rīga is.

CITYSPEAK

- ◢ Which side of the river is the best to live on (there's a huge rivalry)
- ◢ The latest sleek DJ bar or fusion restaurant to be seen drinking at or eating in
- ◢ The most recent controversy to originate from the office of Latvia's popular love-her-or-hate-her president Vaira Vīķe-Freiberga

STARRING ROLE IN...

- ◢ *The Dogs of Riga* by Henning Mankell
- ◢ *The Merry Baker of Riga* by Boris Zemtzov

IMPORT

- ◢ Oil
- ◢ Natural Gas
- ◢ Machinery

EXPORT

- ◢ Timber
- ◢ Paper
- ◢ Agricultural products

SEE the stunning Art Nouveau architectural creations that line the streets of Vecrīga.

EAT everything infused with garlic (including desert) at Kiploka Krogs.

DRINK the local lethal tipple, Rīga Black Balsam, only if you dare…

DO visit the Dome Cathedral, the largest in the Baltics.

WATCH a production at the stunning National Opera House.

BUY exquisite amber jewellery from the Rīga Central Market.

AFTER DARK enjoy the sleek restaurants and cool bars of Vecrīga.

URBAN MYTH

It has often been claimed that Rīga is the home of the original Christmas tree, created by Martin Luther while he took a winter walk in the woods near the city. The truth is slightly different – the story has, in fact, two parts. The Latvians at the time were pagan and one of their rituals was worshipping the winter solstice (known as Yule), when they burned a log in honour of the sun. This later developed into a ceremony in which an evergreen tree was placed outside the town hall, decorated by men in black hats and later burned. Martin Luther, generally considered to have been the man who introduced the tradition to Europe, probably came across this annual ritual during the Christmas period while on his travels to Rīga in the early 16th century. To this day there's a magnificent Christmas tree in Vecrīga Sq every year.

TWO GUARDS TAKE THEIR JOBS AT THE FREEDOM MONUMENT VERY SERIOUSLY.
Photographer: Bruce Yuan-Yue Bi (1)

AN EQUALLY STERN ART NOUVEAU FAÇADE HANGS OVER AN OLD TOWN DOORWAY.
Photographer: Bruce Yuan-Yue Bi (2)

'LOOK, MA: I CAN FLY!' – A PERFORMANCE AT THE WATER PEACH INTERNATIONAL VIDEO FESTIVAL.
Photographer: Bruce Yuan-Yue Bi (3)

SOAKING UP THE NIGHTLIFE OUTSIDE THE RĀTSLAUKUMS (TOWN SQUARE), WITH THE HOUSE OF BLACKHEADS LIT UP IN THE BACKGROUND.
Photographer: Bruce Yuan-Yue Bi (4)

Asmara

VITAL STATISTICS

NAME: ASMARA

DATE OF BIRTH: 12TH CENTURY; ENCOURAGED BY THE PLENTIFUL SUPPLIES OF WATER, SHEPHERDS FROM THE AKELE GUZAY REGION FOUNDED FOUR VILLAGES ON THE HILL THAT IS NOW THE SITE OF AN ORTHODOX CHURCH

ADDRESS: ERITREA (MAP 2, M8)

HEIGHT: 2355M

POPULATION: 450,000

EDUCATION EQUALS OPPORTUNITY FOR THESE YOUNG GIRLS.
Photographer: Patrick Ben Luke Syder (1)

Like a film set from an early Italian movie, old espresso machines churn out macchiatos, Cinquecento taxis putt-putt about and all over town you can see outstanding examples of Art Deco architecture, Asmara is without doubt one of the safest, cleanest and most enchanting capital cities on the continent.

ANATOMY

Built according to a strict urban plan, Asmara was divided into four main areas: the administrative centre, the colonial residential quarter, the native quarter and the outbuildings. Liberation Ave, lined with majestic palms, striking architecture and busy cafés, is flanked by September 1 Sq at the eastern end and the Governor's Palace in the west. The old Italian residential quarter with its Art Deco villas is south of Liberation Ave. Central Asmara is small enough to walk everywhere, but even the locals have trouble keeping up with the changing street names.

PEOPLE

Asmarinos are a mix of nine colourful ethnic groups, each with its own language and customs. The Tigrinya make up the majority, and this is the language you'll hear widely spoken, although Arabic, English and Amharic are also prevalent. On a Sunday the clashing sound of cathedral bells and the Muslim call to prayer provide oral evidence of the communities' ability to coexist, notwithstanding all government efforts to the contrary.

TYPICAL ASMARINO

Cosmopolitan, dignified and welcoming are words often used to describe Asmarinos. Presentation is everything and it's not uncommon to see a well-groomed man walking out of his tin-roofed shack sporting a suit, leather jacket and gold galore. Locals love to dance, and the traditional style is unique, with lots of variations on shaking body parts, but if you give it a go, you'll win a lot of friends. Being a small city, and such social people, Asmarinos can't walk more than a block without running into somebody they know. Cycling is popular, but bikes seem to spend more time lined up outside the cafés than on the streets.

DEFINING EXPERIENCE

Watching the world go by and enjoying a cappuccino in one of the many 1930s Italian-style cafés, then taking a *gari* (horse-drawn cart) tour of Asmara's fascinating architecture before joining in the sunset *passeggiata* (promenade; when the whole town takes a turn around the streets) to catch up with friends, hear the latest gossip, window-shop and generally take things easy.

STRENGTHS

- Sublime architecture – from Art Deco to cubist, expressionist, functionalist, futurist, rationalist and neoclassical styles
- Impressive churches
- Mies (local honey wine)
- Blue skies eight months of the year
- Excellent coffee and pizza
- Medeber market
- Traffic-free streets
- Incredibly clean city
- Fresh juices
- Safe to walk the streets at night
- Endless dinner/lunch invitations to strangers' homes
- Gold shops
- Lively café culture
- *Injera* (spongy bread)

WEAKNESSES

- Asmara gin
- Lack of water
- No cheap flights
- No privately owned news media
- First-day altitude sickness
- Lack of tourist infrastructure
- Not a great diversity of food once you've had your fill of pizza, spaghetti bolognaise and *zigny* (a spicy meat stew)

GOLD STAR

The Cultural Assets Rehabilitation Programme (CARP) – set up in 1996 to record the city's architecture and to educate children, businesspeople and developers to look after their unparalleled urban heritage

CITYSPEAK

- Housing shortages
- Antismoking regulations
- What's showing at the Cinema Impero?

STARRING ROLE IN...

- *Towards Asmara* by Thomas Keneally
- *Who Said Merhawi Is Dead?* edited by Charles Cantalupo and Ghirmai Negash
- *Ciao Asmara* by Justin Hill

IMPORT

- Fiats
- Pizza
- Coffee – anyone for a macchiato or a cappuccino?
- Italian cheese and salami
- The nightly *passeggiata*
- Italian words in the vernacular
- Military materials
- Fuel

EXPORT

- Shellfish, snapper and groper
- Sesame seeds
- Salt
- Live sheep
- Gum Arabic
- Textiles
- Young football stars

SEE the entire population of Asmara strolling down the boulevards during the sunset *passeggiata*.

EAT *injera* and *tibs zil zil* (sizzling lamb) in the traditional back room of the Milano Restaurant.

DRINK an espresso from a vintage Italian coffee machine at one of the many outdoor cafés.

DO take the Eritrean State Railway steam train down the escarpment from Asmara to the Red Sea at Massawa.

WATCH a film in the 1800-seat, beautifully restored Art Deco Cinema Impero.

BUY a tailor-made leather jacket, or for something more traditional, a gorgeous basket made by ex-fighter Fattima Suleiman at Roble Gift Articles.

AFTER DARK dance up a storm with the locals at the Mocambo nightclub.

URBAN MYTH

It's hard not to stare at all the stunning women, particularly when their grins reveal tattooed gums. Fashionable teenagers prick their gums until they bleed, and then rub them with charcoal. The resulting blue colour sets off a dazzling set of teeth, and is considered a mark of great beauty.

THIS ART DECO APOTHECARY RETAINS ITS COLONIAL ITALIAN BEAUTY.
Photographer: Oliver Strewe (2)

RELIGIOUS FESTIVITIES GIVE THIS YOUNG PRIEST SOMETHING TO THINK ABOUT.
Photographer: Frances Linzee Gordon (3)

CHRISTIAN, MUSLIM AND ORTHODOX FAITHS LIVE SIDE BY SIDE IN ASMARA.
Photographer: Frances Linzee Gordon (4)(4)

Kabul 118

VITAL STATISTICS

NAME: KABUL

DATE OF BIRTH: AD 1772; WHEN IT WAS MADE THE CAPITAL OF AFGHANISTAN, THOUGH THERE HAS BEEN HUMAN HABITATION SINCE PREHISTORIC TIMES

ADDRESS: AFGHANISTAN (MAP 1, CC10)

HEIGHT: 1827M

SIZE: 250 SQ KM

POPULATION: 2.5 MILLION

A precious preserve of thriving Afghan culture, Kabul is one of the world's most ancient cities and continues to sparkle through tumultuous change.

ANATOMY

Kabul sits on a plain ringed by the mountains of the Hindu Kush. Little remains of the old city. The Koh-e Sher Darwaza mountains run south, topped by the old city walls, and then lead eastwards to the royal citadel of Bala Hissar. The Kabul River divides the capital. To the north is the prosperous Shahr-e Naw area, centred on its eponymous park and Pashtunistan Sq.

PEOPLE

Afghanistan's location at the crossroads of Asia has produced a jigsaw of nationalities. The largest ethnic groups are the Pashtun, Tajik and Hazara, but over a dozen smaller nationalities also live within Afghanistan's borders, from the Uzbek Baluchi and the blue-eyed Nuristanis, to the nomadic Kuchi and Kyrgyz. The majority of the population is Sunni Muslim, another 15% (mainly the Hazaras) follow Shiite Islam. Sufism has always been an important strand in traditional Afghan Islam.

TYPICAL KABULI

Through the many manmade disasters, tragedies and rebuilding, the people of Kabul have maintained a reputation of generosity and hospitality. However, travellers that have returned since the Taliban defeat have noted that these experiences have somewhat hardened the local people. Though encouraged by modern changes, many Kabulis remain fearful.

DEFINING EXPERIENCE

Brunching on a tasty chicken kebab from one of the many vendors on Cinema Zainab Rd while strolling through the park on your way to the Afghan Handicrafts Centre to peruse the local wares.

STRENGTHS

- Chicken St Markets
- Darulaman Palace
- Mausoleum of Abdur Rahman Khan
- Kabul Zoo
- Pul-e Khishti Mosque
- OMAR Land Mine Museum
- Ariana Graveyard
- The fortress of Bala Hissar
- The bird market
- Musical instrument makers

WEAKNESSES

- Sparse nightlife
- Few streetlights
- Strong presence of foreign armies
- Land mines
- Restricted drinking
- Fuzzy directions

GOLD STAR

Preservation of Afghan culture – Kabul has retained an ancient culture through a myriad of oppressions, rising above the terrible reputation given to the Afghani people by the Taliban and other extremist groups.

CITYSPEAK

- When will the promised rebuilding of the roads be finished?
- Will the Kabul police get paid this month?

STARRING ROLE IN...

- *Kandahar* (2001)
- *Osama* (2003)
- *Little Game* by Timor Shah

IMPORT

- Extremist rule
- Refugees from the provinces
- Land mines
- Foreign aid

EXPORT

- Heroin
- Musical instruments
- Refugees
- Terrorists
- Afghan carpets and rugs

SEE the bird markets and musical instrument makers in the old city for a taste of traditional Afghan life.

EAT *Qabli pulao* (pilaf of rice and fried vegetables topped with almonds, raisins and grated carrot) from any street vendor.

DRINK a discreet beer on the terrace bar of the Deutscher hof.

DO suck black tea through a sugar cube as you overlook the city from the beautifully restored terraces of Babur's Gardens, created in the 16th century as the last resting place of the first Mughal ruler.

WATCH the concerts of Afghan music and poetry recitals on Saturdays at the FCCS (Foundation for Culture & Civil Society).

BUY a genuine Afghan rug from the Carpet Bazaar.

AFTER DARK on Thursday is kebab night at the Mustafa Hotel, which includes a rooftop barbecue.

URBAN MYTH

Various regimes, most famously the Taliban, each took their turn to erode the rights of women. However, this hasn't always been the case; pictures from the 1920s show Queen Soraya unveiled and wearing a sleeveless dress. In the early 1970s, Afghan womens' rights were included in the national constitution. At the time, women were seen on the streets of Kabul in skirts, they attended university and studied to be doctors, while holding over 40% of government jobs. Afghanistan's former king Zahir Shah has said, 'Any country that covers the eyes of its women makes itself blind'. Then, in September 1996, the Taliban took Kabul. The numerous edicts they imposed were medieval and the punishments for breaking these were brutal. The burka was made mandatory from head to toe, a mere flash of ankle could result in a fatal beating. Womens' voices (even laughter) and footsteps were not to be heard by strangers. They could not buy from a male shopkeeper and were forbidden to leave their homes unless accompanied by a *mahram* (male relative).

DOING BUSINESS OUTSIDE THE KABUL MONEY EXCHANGE.
Photographer: Paula Bronstein (1)

A BOY SELLS FLOWERS AS SMOKE FROM GRILLED MEATS FILLS THE AIR.
Photographer: Paula Bronstein (2)

A 12-YEAR-OLD GIRL CARES FOR HER TWO-YEAR-OLD COUSIN IN AN ABANDONED, WAR-RAVAGED BUILDING.
Photographer: Paula Bronstein (3)

A TOILET-PAPER VENDOR DODGES SHOPPERS AS SHADOWS LENGTHEN AT THE MARKET.
Photographer: Paula Bronstein (4)

Bath 119

VITAL STATISTICS

NAME: BATH

DATE OF BIRTH: 800 BC; REPUTEDLY FOUNDED BY KING BLADUD, A TROJAN REFUGEE AND FATHER OF KING LEAR

ADDRESS: ENGLAND (MAP 3, E8)

HEIGHT: 181M

SIZE: 29 SQ KM

POPULATION: 85,500

FALLING IN LOVE WITH (AND AT) THE PARADE GARDENS, BY THE RIVER AVON.
Photographer: Scott Barbour (1)

BECKHAM IMPERSONATIONS ABOUND AT ROYAL VICTORIA PARK, OVERLOOKED BY THE ROYAL CRESCENT.
Photographer: Scott Barbour (2)

INDIANA JONES WOULD LOVE TO EXPLORE THE GREAT BATH, CENTREPIECE OF THE ROMAN BATHS.
Photographer: Scott Barbour (3)

A CONSTABLE ENSURES THAT BATH'S CREAM SUPPLY REMAINS SAFE FROM THREATS.
Photographer: Scott Barbour (4)

When sunlight brightens the honey-coloured stone, and buskers and strollers fill the streets and line the river, stylish and lively Bath, England's first spa resort, reveals all its charm.

ANATOMY

Bath is nestled at the bottom of the Avon Valley in the southern Cotswolds and is famed for its seven hills, with buildings climbing the steep streets. The River Avon, tamed by a series of weirs, runs through the town centre. The town's most obvious landmark is the abbey, across from the Roman Baths and Pump Room. Walk, cycle or catch a bus to get around.

PEOPLE

The typical Bath resident is healthy, comes from a white ethnic background (97.2%), has an average age of 39.9, and is predominantly of the Christian faith (71%), while 19.5% register no religion. The city has only small populations of other ethnic groups, including Asians (0.5%) and blacks (0.5%).

TYPICAL BATH CITIZEN

Citizens of Bath are much like their fellow countrymen – they drink tea, form orderly queues while awaiting service and enjoy a pint at the pub.

DEFINING EXPERIENCE

Strolling through the historic baths and enjoying luxurious spa treatments at Thermae Bath Spa, tasting the waters from the fountain before tea and scones in the elegant Pump Room, then visiting the Roman Baths Museum, wandering through the 500-year-old abbey, strolling through the riverside Parade Gardens and taking a boat tour at Poulteney Weir, before getting an architectural, gossip and trivia overview on a free walking tour of the city, viewing the crowning glory of Georgian Bath (Royal Crescent and The Circus), and travelling through four centuries of fashion at the Costume Museum.

STRENGTHS

- The thermal baths, which have attracted kings and queens over the centuries
- Exquisite mosaics
- Georgian splendour and original limestone buildings
- Wide parades
- The wonderful fan vaulting of Bath Abbey's nave
- The majestic sweep of Royal Crescent and the Circus
- Shopping
- Bath International Music Festival
- Abbey Ales brews
- Atmospheric restaurants and bars
- Hidden pockets of Georgiana found up steep streets
- The self-guided Jane Austen Bath Walk
- Free touch-screen information kiosks
- Carved mythical beasts in the choir stalls of the abbey
- The carnivalesque chaos of Walcot Nation Day
- Bath Fringe Festival

WEAKNESSES

- Florence-style tourist congestion
- Traffic
- Trying to read stone-carved street signs

GOLD STAR

Bath's star attraction, the Roman Baths, and their stunning mosaics.

CITYSPEAK

- The sensationalist 'news' stunts of the *Bath Chronical*
- Air pollution caused by open-topped tourist buses
- The lack of useful shops for the people living in Bath

STARRING ROLE IN...

- *Three Tenors Concert* (2003)
- *Vanity Fair* (2003)
- *Persuasion* by Jane Austen (film 1994)
- *House of Eliot* (1991–94)
- *The Music Lovers* (1969)
- *Ghost Train* (1931)
- *Northanger Abbey* by Jane Austen
- *Pickwick Papers* by Charles Dickens

IMPORT

- Richard 'Beau' Nash's 18th-century style codes
- Tourists
- Jane Austen devotees
- Organist and astronomer William Herschel

EXPORT

- Food writer and first TV celebrity chef Marguerite Patten
- Software
- New media and gaming magazines

SEE angels climbing up and down (head first!) a stone ladder on the exterior west façade of Bath Abbey.

EAT cream tea or a traditional English meal at Sally Lunn's, founded by the Huguenot refugee in 1680.

DRINK a Bellringer ale, home-brewed in Bath.

DO taste the waters in the elegant Pump Room.

WATCH the cinematic rendering of a Jane Austen classic for a view into the grand times of Georgian Bath.

BUY yourself some luxurious pampering at Thermae Bath Spa, bohemian treasures on Walcot St, or secondhand books from the covered Guildhall Market.

AFTER DARK take a 'ghost walk' of Bath, departing from the reputedly haunted Garricks Head pub.

URBAN MYTH

William Herschel arrived in Bath as an organist but was to become most noteworthy for his achievements in the field of astronomy. In 1781 he discovered the planet Uranus from the garden of his home in Bath.

Copenhagen

VITAL STATISTICS

NAME: COPENHAGEN

NICKNAME: WONDERFUL, WONDERFUL COPENHAGEN

DATE OF BIRTH: 1167; BISHOP ABSALON CONSTRUCTED A FORTRESS ON SLOTSHOLMEN

ADDRESS: DENMARK (MAP 3, K5)

HEIGHT: 9M

SIZE: 88.3 SQ KM

POPULATION: 500,000

Copenhagen is one of the few places left where the term 'fairy tale' can be used freely – from its most enduring literary legacy to its most recent royal romance. The old and the new combine to form an attractive, civilised, ergonomic and punctual confection.

ANATOMY

Copenhagen sits on the east coast of Denmark's largest island, Zealand (Sjælland). It is separated from Sweden by the Øresund and is largely low-rise, with few skyscrapers. Most of the city's obvious attractions are found near the main square of Rådhuspladsen and the islands of Slotsholmen and Christianshavn. Public transport can involve buses, boats or the shiny new metro system.

PEOPLE

The vast majority of Copenhageners seem to come from the same stock, ie the Teutonic ancestry so common to Scandinavia. However, there is also a substantial population of foreign nationals (11.9%) in Copenhagen, home to half of Denmark's immigrants.

TYPICAL COPENHAGENER

The clichéd local will have Jensen, Nielsen or Hansen for a surname, be tall, prepared to join a queue and fond of biting, irony-laden humour. They will have strongly held opinions on where to dine and what to dine on, and will give the impression that little else is of great importance. That and what you should sit on when you eat – beautiful chairs are a citywide obsession.

DEFINING EXPERIENCE

Thinking about your next feed, while taking advantage of even a hint of a sunny day by sitting outside at a café where the owners have thoughtfully provided blankets for their patrons, riding a bicycle across beautiful bridges such as Knippelsbro to funky Islands Brygge and taking a dip at the canalside public baths.

STRENGTHS

- Imaginative *smørrebrod* (buttered bread) toppings at Ida Davidsen
- Timely and tidy public transport
- Christianshavn
- Royal Palaces
- Staten Museum for Kunst
- Tivoli
- Local beers
- Islands Brygge Havnebadet (harbour bathing)
- Good-looking gene pool
- Modern architecture
- An easy-going monarchy
- Bakeries

WEAKNESSES

- 25% VAT
- Licensing laws
- Taciturn locals
- Daredevil cyclists
- Stubborn refusal to do things that aren't 'the Danish style'
- Long, cold, dark winters
- Smoke-filled bars and restaurants

GOLD STAR

Design – Copenhagen is always bang on the money when it comes to marrying form with function.

CITYSPEAK

- Crown Princess Mary
- How will the Little Mermaid be vandalised next?
- How much can you cram on to a piece of *smørrebrod*?

STARRING ROLE IN...

- *Miss Smilla's Feeling for Snow* by Peter Høeg
- *Smilla's Sense of Snow* (1977)
- *The Idiots* (1998)
- *Open Hearts* (2003)
- *Reconstruction* (2003)

IMPORT

- Drunken Swedes
- Mary and Alexandra
- German cars
- Tropical fruit
- Solariums
- Jazz
- Chemicals
- Pizza

EXPORT

- A relaxed attitude to porn
- Pork
- Carlsberg and Tuborg
- Claus Jensen
- Dogme films
- Aqua
- Arne Jacobsen chairs
- Christiania Cycles
- Georg Jensen
- Herring
- Dairy goods

SEE the citywide panorama from atop glorious Vor Frelsers Kirke in Christianshavn.

EAT at one of the city's 10 Michelin-starred restaurants.

DRINK Carlsberg beer in Carlsberg's microbrewery.

DO a long, lazy stroll down Strøget – the world's longest pedestrian mall.

WATCH a Dogme 95 film at the Danish Filmhuset.

BUY a stunning piece of silver from the Georg Jensen flagship store.

AFTER DARK watch the fireworks display at Tivoli.

URBAN MYTH

In 1834, Hans Christian Andersen applied for work at the Royal Library in Copenhagen in order 'to be freed from the heavy burden of having to write in order to live'. Apparently the library administrators weren't too impressed with his résumé, as he was turned down. Ironically, Andersen's unsuccessful application is now preserved as part of the library's valued archives, along with many of his original manuscripts.

A BUBBLE BOY EMERGES FROM A BURROW AT THE RABBIT LABYRINTH, COPENHAGEN ZOO.
Photographer: Martin Lladó (1)

A GRID OF SHADED WINDOWS ON THE FAÇADE OF THE SALMON PINK SPIES-HOUSE.
Photographer: Martin Lladó (2)

DREAMLIKE IMAGES OF LOVELY 19TH-CENTURY HOUSES REFLECTED IN THE SURFACE OF A CANAL.
Photographer: Brent Winebrenner (3)

A SERIOUS FIGURE TRUDGES BENEATH THE FRIVOLOUS SIGN FOR THE TIVOLI AMUSEMENT PARK ON HC ANDERSENS BLVD.
Photographer: Martin Moos (4)

MACAU'S ARCHITECTURE IS INSPIRED BY ITS FANTASTIC MIX OF CULTURES.
Photographer: Nigel Amies (1)

A rough diamond with a spit-and-polish, Macau fuses the Mediterranean and Asia with its Chinese temples, ancient stone fortresses, colonial villas and exotic street names etched on *azulejos* (Portuguese decorative glazed tiles).

ANATOMY

Most of Macau's attractions are clustered round the peninsula's centre – it's a hilly but rewarding walk from church to fort and back again. Land reclamation at the foot of the peninsula has created the two artificial Nam Van Lakes. Taipa Island is linked to the peninsula by two bridges, and a causeway links Taipa with Coloane. Aside from walking, the best way to get around the Macau Peninsula is by air-conditioned bus or minibus, taking in Lisboa Hotel, Avenida Almeida Ribeiro, the Barrier Gate, the Floating Casino, the A-Ma and Kun Iam temples, and Taipa and Coloane villages.

PEOPLE

The population is about 95% Chinese. Fewer than 2% of Macau residents are Portuguese and the rest are Macanese, with mixed Portuguese, Chinese, African and Filipino ancestry. Portuguese and Chinese (particularly Cantonese) are official languages of Macau. Taoism and Buddhism are the dominant religions, followed by Catholicism.

TYPICAL MACAU CITIZEN

Fond of a good meal and a punt, Macau citizens have a hearty, easy-going nature. Residents enjoy relaxed, laid-back pleasures, such as smoking a pipe or having their palm read in Mediterranean-style cafés filled with caged birds.

DEFINING EXPERIENCE

Escalating to the Monte Fort at the Macau Museum, followed by a leisurely stroll along Praia Grande before braving a game of baccarat at one of Macau's flashy new casinos (dress classy).

Macau 121

VITAL STATISTICS

NAME: MACAU

DATE OF BIRTH: 1557; WHEN IT WAS OFFICIALLY FOUNDED AS A COLONY OF PORTUGAL; IT WAS REBORN AS THE SPECIAL ADMINISTRATIVE REGION OF MACAU IN 1999

ADDRESS: CHINA (MAP 5, O5)

HEIGHT: 59M

SIZE: 24 SQ KM

POPULATION: 449,198

MOTORCYCLES ARE A GREAT WAY TO GET AROUND THE CENTRAL DISTRICT.
Photographer: Phil Carrick (2)

SIGNS OF PORTUGUESE COLONISATION STILL INFLUENCE THESE STREETS.
Photographer: Mark Henley (3)

THE SCENT OF RELIGION KEEPS THE JOSS STICK INDUSTRY IN BUSINESS.
Photographer: Hans Georg Roth (4)

STRENGTHS

◢ Unique Latin-Sino culture
◢ Cheap dim sum
◢ Fascinating cemeteries
◢ Guia Fort
◢ High-speed ferries to Hong Kong
◢ Kun Iam Temple
◢ Taipa House Museum
◢ Ruins of the Church of St Paul
◢ Macau Museum
◢ Chinese medicine shops
◢ Leal Senado
◢ Monte Fort

WEAKNESSES

◢ Rampant gambling culture
◢ The casino reigns supreme
◢ Progress, progress, progress
◢ Early dinners (many restaurants are empty by 9pm)
◢ False reputation as a sleepy, dirty, impoverished backwater

GOLD STAR

Extreme makeover – after years of Macau playing the dowdy Jan Brady to sassy big sister Marcia (Hong Kong), Macau's citizens have dolled her up in a pastel palette, wooing commerce and tourism like never before.

CITYSPEAK

◢ The lure of the tourism dollar, with proposed theme parks and more casinos
◢ The proposed 36km-long, US$3.7 billion bridge linking Macau and Zhuhai with Hong Kong, reducing the present four-hour journey to 20 minutes

STARRING ROLE IN...

◢ *The Corrupt Ones* (1967)
◢ *Fist of Fury* (1972)
◢ *Indiana Jones and the Temple of Doom* (1984)

IMPORT

◢ Casino culture
◢ Portuguese architecture and foods
◢ Hong Kong entrepreneurialism
◢ Western hotel chains

EXPORT

◢ Baskets
◢ Rattan goods
◢ Jade jewellery
◢ Old coins
◢ Specialist cigarettes

SEE into your future with one of the many fortune-tellers that throng the incense-infused Kun Iam Temple.

EAT spicy *piri-piri* (a type of chilli) prawns and clams at the Sailboat by A-Ma Temple.

DRINK a glass of *vinho verde* (a crisp 'green' wine from Portugal) at the Casablanca Café, an elegant watering-hole in the Vista Magnifica Court Building.

DO trek to the top of Guia Fort, as there are few better places in Macau to get your bearings (alternatively, ride the teeny cable car).

WATCH the transvestite show at the Jai Alai Show Palace as the showgirls strut around in a couple of beads and a feather or two.

BUY wonderful Macanese postage stamps, depicting everything from key colonial landmarks to roulette tables.

AFTER DARK hit the *Pai kao* (Chinese dominoes, similar to mah jong) tables at one of Macau's many casinos.

URBAN MYTH

The name 'Macau' is derived from the name of the goddess A-Ma. According to legend, A-Ma was a poor girl looking for passage to Guangzhou, but, after she was turned away by wealthy junk owners, a poor fisherman took her on board. Shortly afterwards a storm wrecked all the junks but left the fishing boat unscathed. When it returned to the Inner Harbour, A-Ma walked to the top of nearby Barra Hill and, in a glowing aura of light, ascended to heaven. The fisherman built a temple on the spot where they had landed (the A-Ma Temple was on the water's edge until land reclamation set it further inland).

Sofia 122

VITAL STATISTICS

NAME: SOFIA

DATE OF BIRTH: AD 29; WHEN THE ROMANS FOUNDED ULPIA SERDICA

ADDRESS: BULGARIA (MAP 3, P13)

HEIGHT: 160M

POPULATION: 1.1 MILLION

Glittering onion-domed churches, fascinating museums, leafy parks, gleaming hotels, Communist monuments, tacky casinos and seedy strip clubs – Europe's highest capital is an energising mix of old and new, East and West.

ANATOMY

Pl Sveta Nedelya, home to the church of the same name, is at the heart of the city. North of here bul Maria Luisa passes the Central Hali Shopping Centre and the Banya Bashi Mosque on the way to the main train and bus stations. To the south, Sofia's main shopping street, bul Vitosha, points the way to Yuzhen Park and the National Palace of Culture (NDK). East of the centre are pl Nezavisimost (aka the Largo) and bul Tsar Osvoboditel, overlooked by the former royal palace. Bul Tsar Osvoboditel continues past pl Narodno Sabranie and the Parliament building towards Borisova Gradina Park. Various forms of public transport (trams, buses, minibuses, trolleybuses, and the underground metro) will get you where you want to go.

PEOPLE

Around 14% of the national population (approx eight million) lives in Sofia. Bulgarians are of Slavic origin, and comprise roughly 85% of the country's people. The Turks (9%) and the Roma (formerly known as Gypsies; 4.5%) are the largest ethnic minorities.

TYPICAL SOFIA CITIZEN

The high unemployment and poor living standards of the 1990s are thankfully on their way out and Sofia is slowly smartening up. The rich-poor divide is, however, still evident and the sight of pensioners begging outside shops frequented by the young and wealthy is not uncommon. Despite the high literacy rate (90%) the average wage is very low. People hope EU membership will go some way to rectifying this. Bulgarians are warm, friendly people who like to party with friends and family. They are also cynical, and distrustful of bureaucrats and politicians (probably as a result of decades of totalitarian rule and corruption). Bulgarian stereotypes range from images of shot-putters to Cold War assassins and now that the country is becoming more outward looking, Bulgarians are frustrated by their lack of a tangible international image. To counteract this, a Bulgarian logo and brand are being created.

DEFINING EXPERIENCE

Sipping coffee alfresco in the City Garden before discovering Bulgarian folk art at the Ethnographical Museum, then taking in a show at the NDK.

STRENGTHS

- The beautiful Aleksander Nevski Memorial Church
- Archaeological Museum – a real treasure-trove
- Enormous Borisova Gradina Park
- Skiing at Dragalevtsi
- Delicious Bulgarian cooking
- National Museum of History
- Day-tripping to Koprivshtitsa
- Ethnographical Museum
- The changing of the guard at the President's Building
- Sofia Municipal Gallery of Art
- The murals inside the Church of St George
- Sveta Nedelya Cathedral
- The five gold domes of St Nikolai Russian church
- Monument to the Soviet Army
- Sofia monument

WEAKNESSES

- Crazy drivers who like to ignore pedestrian crossings and traffic lights
- Potholed pavements
- Beggars
- Toxic emissions from rather decrepit vehicles

GOLD STAR

Churches – stunning ecclesiastical domes are everywhere.

CITYSPEAK

- Football, football, football and which of Sofia's four teams are playing that night

STARRING ROLE IN...

- *The Other Possible Life of Ours* (2004)
- *Mila from Mars* (2003)
- *You're So Pretty, My Dear* (2004)

IMPORT

- International artists such as Buena Vista Social Club and Jerry Lee Lewis for concerts at the NDK
- Artist Genko Genkov
- Writer Ivan Vazov
- Artist Georgi Bozhilov
- Composer Dobri Hristov

EXPORT

- Icon paintings
- Artist Ivan Moudov
- Tennis star Magdalena Maleeva
- Artist Vladimir Dimitrov

SEE the elaborate interior of Aleksander Nevski Memorial Church (the symbol of Sofia and Bulgaria) and the huge array of religious icons in the crypt.

EAT the best Bulgarian food in Sofia at rustic tavern Pri Yafata and enjoy the evening entertainment.

DRINK in the so-hip-it-hurts Buddha Bar and dance around your designer handbags.

DO a spot of skiing on the slopes of Mt Vitosha.

WATCH the best of Bulgaria's warblers at the National Opera House.

BUY books on Bulgarian culture and Bulgarian novels at the Open-air Book Market on pl Slaveikov.

AFTER DARK go mad for the themed party nights and live music at Chervilo.

URBAN MYTH

Visitors to Bulgaria may be confused by people's head movements. Nodding the head means 'no' while 'yes' is indicated by a curved, almost bouncy, motion. Just when you have got your head around that, however, well-travelled Bulgarians may try and be helpful by doing the opposite. If in doubt, ask *da ili ne* (yes or no)?

FROM THE OUTSIDE LOOKING IN – A GLIMPSE INTO ONE OF THE CITY'S MOST EXCLUSIVE RESTAURANTS, THE BULGARI.
Photographer: Doug McKinlay (1)

TRADESMEN NARROWLY AVOID THE CRITICAL EYE OF THE FASHION POLICE ON TRENDY ALEXANDER STAMBOLISKI BLVD. Photographer: Doug McKinlay (2)

THE PARTY HOUSE – UNTIL 1990 THIS SOBER BUILDING WAS THE SEAT OF THE COMMUNIST PARTY, IT'S NOW AN EVENTS HALL. Photographer: Doug McKinlay (3)

COMPETITIVE SHOPKEEPERS MANAGE TO CONGEST THE ONLY PEDESTRIANISED STREET IN THE CITY, PIROTSKA ST.
Photographer: Doug McKinlay (4)

MODERN TECHNOLOGY CAN'T REPLACE A GOOD GAME OF CARDS FOR THESE OLD FRIENDS.
Photographer: Paul Souders (1)

Hoi An 123

VITAL STATISTICS

NAME: HOI AN

DATE OF BIRTH: 200 BC; THE LATE–IRON AGE SA HUYNH
CIVILIZATION ARE THOUGHT TO HAVE BEEN THE FIRST
INHABITANTS OF HOI AN

ADDRESS: VIETNAM (MAP 5, N7)

POPULATION: 75,800

Wander through Vietnam's past – with its traditional architecture and distinctive cuisine, Hoi An envelops you in a sense of history that oozes charm and culture from every corner.

ANATOMY

Hoi An is a living museum linked to the sea by the shallow Thu Bon River. Moss-covered pagodas and the pedestrian-friendly Old Town make many a visitor feel that they have been transported back centuries. Hoi An's brick-coloured *am* and *duong* (Yin and Yang) roof tiles, meticulously restored temples, and unique bridges can be explored on a day's walking tour, a bicycle ride or by boat.

PEOPLE

Hoi An's sea port has a rich history as a vibrant international trading centre and was the site of southern Vietnam's first Chinese settlement. Today, 1300 of Hoi An's population are ethnic Chinese. Relations between them and the ethnic Vietnamese have always been harmonious, with the Chinese here even speaking Vietnamese among themselves.

TYPICAL HOI ANIAN

Hoi Anians are entrepreneurial, with an almost aggressively competitive edge. They are traditional and family-oriented and many a restaurant or Internet café will be run by immediate and extended family. They are commonly devout in their everyday life. They are used to visitors and welcome them into their temples, pagodas and even their homes (occasionally for a fee). They are a solid community who gather together in times of trouble and joy.

DEFINING EXPERIENCE

Walking through Hoi An's pedestrian-friendly town centre to choose the silk for a new (and astonishingly cheap) tailored outfit, then crossing the sparse beauty of the Japanese Covered Bridge to take in a gallery or two before donning the finished clothes to walk along lantern-lit streets to the monthly Hoi An Legendary Night where hot 'white rose' (steamed prawns wrapped in rice paper) are eaten amid the sound and colour of traditional song, dance and games.

STRENGTHS

- Traditional Vietnam at its best
- Historical buildings
- Temples and pagodas
- Pedestrian-friendly streets
- Cheap tailors
- Local artisans
- Boat rides along the river
- Vietnamese cooking classes
- Waterside eateries
- Thirty kilometres of pristine, palm-lined beach

WEAKNESSES

- Unsafe swimming for six months of the year (November to March)
- Occasional late-night bag snatching
- Complicated ticketing systems to tourist attractions
- Fake antiques
- Quiet nightlife

GOLD STAR

Architectural history – Hoi An serves as a museum piece of Vietnamese history and more than 800 structures of historical significance have been officially identified here.

CITYSPEAK

- Building boom – turning this once bed-short city into a competitive mecca of places to stay
- Yearly flooding of waterfront residences and shops
- Whether the crackdown on street solicitation will last

STARRING ROLE IN...

- *The Quiet American* (2002)

IMPORT

- Japanese architecture
- English and French language
- Chinese culture
- Hinduism
- Christianity
- Vietnamese, Chinese, Western and vegetarian cuisine
- Commercialism
- Alexandre de Rhodes' *quoc ngu* script for the Vietnamese language

EXPORT

- Cotton and silk
- Woodcarving
- Ceramics
- Mass produced, hand-painted artworks
- *Cao lau* (a traditional noodle dish)

SEE the clear streams that run between the monuments of My Son.

EAT *cao lau* at the Ba La Well restaurant located conveniently by the well from which water is used to make genuine *cao lau*.

DRINK fine wine in the lovingly restored tea warehouse at Tam Tam Café and Bar.

DO a cooking course at the Red Bridge – buy from the market, take your groceries home on a river cruise, cook up local dishes and, of course, eat the results.

WATCH a traditional music concert in the historic Hoi An Old Town.

BUY local art and craft at the fair-trade gift shop, Reaching Out.

AFTER DARK eat fresh seafood from the bright line of kiosks leading to the moonlit beach.

URBAN MYTH

According to legend, there once lived an enormous monster called Cu, who had its head in India, its tail in Japan and its body in Vietnam. Whenever the monster moved, floods and earthquakes befell Vietnam. Hoi An's Japanese Covered Bridge is believed to have been built on the monster's weakest point and killed it; the temple within the bridge was built to pray for its soul. Constructed in the 1590s by the Japanese community of Hoi An, the bridge is very solid; apparently the builders were concerned about earthquakes (or the restless monster Cu!).

CHEEKY SMILES DELIGHT IN CHILD'S PLAY.
Photographer: Thomas Downs (2)

FLAVOURS OF DISTINCTION – THE UNFORGETTABLE EXPERIENCE OF DINING IN HOI AN.
Photographer: joSon (3)

SUPERHIGHWAY – THE THU BON RIVER PROVIDES EASY ACCESS TO TOWNS ALONG ITS BANKS.
Photographer: R Ian Lloyd (4)

Marseille is not pretty or quaint like some of its Provencal neighbours – it's a real, vibrant, cosmopolitan city with an endearing old port, great seafood and a ticking nightlife.

ANATOMY

Marseille's main artery is the wide boulevard of La Canebière, which carves through the city east from the Old Port. Bohemian cours Julien buzzes with trendy cafés, restaurants and theatres south of the boulevard. Further south stands the Basilique Notre Dame de la Garde, which proudly surveys the city from its spot on a hill. West from the Old Port and out to sea, boats sail to Corsica, Sardinia, Tunisia, Spain and Algeria. Also out to sea but closer to home stands Château d'If, the 16th-century fortress-turned-jail immortalised in Alexandre Dumas' *Le Comte de Monte Cristo*. Rumbling beneath the city are two metro lines, while buses cruise around above the surface. The overland train station is north of La Canebière.

PEOPLE

Due to its proximity to Tunisia and Algeria, Marseille is France's most North African city, with many immigrants from these countries. Immigrants also come from the Mediterranean basin and Indochina.

TYPICAL MARSEILLAIS

As citizens of France's second city and the capital of Provence, the Marseillais are predictably and justifiably proud. The city used to have a reputation for violence and racial tensions, but development projects and the TGV link to Paris are leaving this image behind. Smart Parisians are snapping up weekend homes and plugging into the cultural scene. In general, people are welcoming of visitors, but they do have a defensive streak, which can allow them to close ranks if they choose to. The people of Marseille were enthusiastic supporters of the revolution, and France's national anthem, 'La Marseillaise', was named after local revolutionaries who sang it on their march to Paris. Finally, the Marseillais are big fans of football and hip-hop.

Marseille
124

VITAL STATISTICS

NAME: MARSEILLE

DATE OF BIRTH: 600 BC; WHEN GREEK MARINERS FOUNDED A TRADING POST CALLED MASSILIA

ADDRESS: FRANCE (MAP 3, H13)

HEIGHT: 4M

POPULATION: 807, 071

THE TINY FISHING PORT OF VALLON DES AUFFES HAS A BIG REPUTATION FOR CHARMING SEASIDE RESTAURANTS.
Photographer: Eric Bouvet (1)

DEFINING EXPERIENCE

Delving into the city's Greek and Roman past at the Musée d'Histoire de Marseille, before tasting some *pastis* (a 90-proof, anise-flavoured cousin of absinthe) at La Maison de Pastis, grabbing some bouillabaisse down at the port and then making for place Jean Jaurès to pick up some vintage clothing.

STRENGTHS

- France's most important seaport
- Shopping heaven on rue Paradis
- Musée d'Histoire de Marseille
- Basilique Notre Dame de la Garde
- Château d'If
- Sunbathing at Calanques
- Îles du Frioul
- Musée des Beaux-Arts
- Musée de la Mode
- Centre de la Vieille Charité
- Harbourside restaurants
- Cosmopolitan vibe
- Old Port
- Bustling markets eg the fish market
- Tasty seafood
- TGV link to Paris
- Marseille Euroméditerrannée
- Hôtel le Corbusier
- Fiesta des Suds

WEAKNESSES

- Expensive car parks
- Some street crime
- Smelly backstreets

GOLD STAR

Bouillabaisse

CITYSPEAK

- Olympique de Marseille's latest results
- Hip-hop and rap music

STARRING ROLE IN...

- *La Vie est Tranquille* (2002)
- *Baise-Moi* (2000)
- *Taxi* (1998)
- *The French Connection* (1971)
- *Le Comte de Monte Cristo* by Alexandre Dumas

IMPORT

- Parisian weekenders
- Thriller writer Lee Child
- Marcel Pagnol

EXPORT

- Zinédine Zidane
- Eric Cantona
- Sébastien Grosjean
- Bouillabaisse
- Fish and seafood
- Olive-oil soaps
- IAM
- Hip-hop
- Tarot cards
- 'La Marseillaise'

SEE the absorbing view of Marseille from the highest point in the city, the Romano-Byzantine Notre Dame de la Garde.

EAT inventive cuisine at Une Table au Sud, and take a break from bouillabaisse.

DRINK home-made *pastis* or, if you're feeling brave, absinthe at L'Heure Verte.

DO stroll around the Old Port and spy the fishing craft, pleasure yachts and ferries.

WATCH or join in a game of *pétanque* (aka boules – similar to lawn bowls but played with heavy metal balls on a sandy pitch) in the late afternoon.

BUY African woodcarved animals at Marseille's best market, Marché aux Puces (flea market).

AFTER DARK salsa, samba and prop up the bar at steamy Le Cubaila Café.

URBAN MYTH

Heated discussions over the best way to prepare Marseille's speciality, bouillabaisse, are legendary in the city. Standard ingredients are fish, onions, white wine, tomatoes, fennel, saffron and croutons, and brief, vigorous boiling of the soup followed by simmering over a low heat are universally accepted practices. Most people agree that five or six types of Mediterranean fish plus crab or prawn (shrimp) should be included. However, to some people's horror, there are those who add mussels, lobster or *langoustines* to the mixture. Others dare to pop potatoes in. And the serving of the stew divides everyone – should the broth and the stew be served separately, or together?

WITH FIST-PUMPING ENTHUSIASM MARSEILLE SOCCER CLUB SUPPORTERS REACH FEVER PITCH IN THE STANDS.
Photographer: Eric Bouvet (2)

EVEN FROM THE HARBOUR THE GILDED 'GOOD MOTHER' OF NOTRE DAME DE LA GARDE CAN BEEN SEEN WATCHING OVER THE CITY. Photographer: Eric Bouvet (3)

ARGUING THE TOSS – A SUMMER AFTERNOON'S GAME OF *PÉTANQUE* HEATS UP WHEN THE TAPE MEASURE APPEARS.
Photographer: Eric Bouvet (4)

Zagreb 125

VITAL STATISTICS

NAME: ZAGREB

DATE OF BIRTH: 9TH CENTURY; WHEN SLAVIC SETTLEMENTS WERE FOUNDED

ADDRESS: CROATIA (MAP 3, M11)

HEIGHT: 163M

SIZE: 631 SQ KM

POPULATION: 770,000

A VIVID REMINDER OF THE CITY'S CHEQUERED HISTORY – THE TILED ROOF OF THE 13TH-CENTURY ST MARK'S CHURCH.
Photographer: Richard I'Anson (1)

Vibrant, cultured and laid-back in equal measure, Zagreb is the gateway to the Balkans, an often overlooked melange of Slavic, Central European and Austro-Hungarian (understated) grandeur.

ANATOMY

Upper Zagreb sprawls across the hills of Gradec and Kaptol, the sites of the city's original settlements. Dolac Market is the hub of the upper city, just near the imposing Cathedral of the Assumption of the Blessed Virgin Mary with its distinctive twin spires. The central square of Trg Josip Jelačića is the heart of Lower Town. Crisscrossed by tramlines, this is where old men meet for morning coffee and where teenagers congregate on Friday evenings. The tram system is an effective, if overcrowded, way to get around, although the city is so compact you can probably walk anywhere you need to go.

PEOPLE

Zagreb's citizens are uniformly Croatian; the era of Yugoslavian multiculturalism is now sadly passed.

TYPICAL ZAGREBIAN

The typical Zagreb local is resolutely Western in outlook – they see themselves as distinct from their Slavic Balkan counterparts – and staunchly Catholic. They are elegant, but casually so – although Croatia was the birthplace of the necktie, no self-respecting Zagreb habitué would be seen in anything other than an open-neck shirt. Remaining well dressed at all times is paramount for Zagrebians. They will forgo other extravagances to ensure that they can be suitably dressed for all occasions. Relishing the culture, history and artistic heritage of their city, Zagreb locals are given to conviviality and amiable chatter and enjoy the outdoor café lifestyle (especially during the summer months).

DEFINING EXPERIENCE

Wandering through Dolac market and choosing grapes as big as plums and plums as big as your fist, watching the changing of the guard at the Banski Dvori, contemplating the airy interior of the Cathedral of the Assumption of the Blessed Virgin Mary, taking your time to ponder Zagreb's long and eventful history and lively arts scene at the city's museums and galleries, and then bar-hopping with the crowds along Tkalčićeva after dark.

STRENGTHS

- Cobbled streets
- Elegant squares and gardens
- Cafés and streetlife on spring afternoons
- Streets not fouled with traffic
- A compact and conveniently walkable city
- People-watching
- Few tourists – Zagreb is generally overlooked by travellers
- Meaty cuisine

WEAKNESSES

- Bad coffee
- Shortage of reasonably priced accommodation
- Pockets of Soviet-era architecture
- Steep streets in Upper Town
- Meaty cuisine
- Shortage of green vegetables in restaurant meals (some may consider this a strength!)

GOLD STAR

Central European elegance (if somewhat faded) and architecture, without the hype and crowds of Prague

CITYSPEAK

- When can we join the EU?
- Everybody has rediscovered Dalmatia, when will they notice us?
- Actually, we like it better as it is – nice and tranquil

STARRING ROLE IN...

- *The Zahir* by Paulo Coelho
- *How We Survived Communism and Even Laughed* by Slavenka Drakulić
- *Black Lamb and Grey Falcon* by Rebecca West
- *Café Europa* by Slavenka Drakulić

IMPORT

- Fresh fish from the Dalmatian Coast
- European fashions
- A knack for making delicious pizzas (from near neighbours, the Italians)

EXPORT

- Neckties ('cravat' is a corruption of 'Croat')
- Ballpoint pens – invented by a Croat
- Basketball players (tall ones!)
- Electronics
- Machine tools
- Textiles

SEE the view from Lotrščak Tower, a 360-degree vista of the rooftops, spires and squares of Upper and Lower Towns.

EAT *čevapčiči* (meaty, garlicy Balkan sausages) with sliced onions or *ayvar* (capsicum paste) and flat bread.

DRINK *slivovica* (plum brandy) or locally brewed Ozujsko (beer).

DO visit Zagreb's museums and galleries for a view of a little-known, but surprisingly rich, culture.

WATCH any of the free, open-air performances of the Zagreb Summer Festival.

BUY embroidery in cheerful red-and-white geometric patterns.

AFTER DARK head for the bars on Tkalčićeva, or around Trg Petra Preradovića.

URBAN MYTH

When the all-conquering Ottoman Turks were approaching Zagreb in the 14th century, an inadvertently fired cannon shot smothered a rooster in full view of the Turkish camp. This was interpreted as an unusually bad omen by the hitherto fearless Turks, who immediately broke camp never to return, leaving Zagreb a bastion of Catholicism amid the Ottoman Empire.

TRG JOSIP JELAČIĆA, THE COLOURFUL HEART OF THE CITY, IS FILLED WITH FLOWER MARKETS, SHOPS, CAFÉS AND THEATRES.
Photographer: Richard I'Anson (2)

COFFEE, CIGARETTES AND A GOOD BOOK – A LEISURELY AFTERNOON IN ONE OF THE CITY'S MANY CAFÉS.
Photographer: Richard I'Anson (3)

THE NEO-GOTHIC BELL TOWERS OF THE CATHEDRAL OF THE ASSUMPTION OF THE BLESSED VIRGIN MARY WATCH OVER TKALČIĆEVA. Photographer: Richard I'Anson (4)

Manchester

VITAL STATISTICS

NAME: MANCHESTER

DATE OF BIRTH: AD 70; WHEN THE ROMANS ESTABLISHED A FORT CALLED MAMUCIAM

ADDRESS: ENGLAND (MAP 3, E6)

HEIGHT: 73M

SIZE: 1286 SQ KM

POPULATION: 394,270

THE CASTLEFIELD CANAL BOAT WAITS TO TAKE IT TO THE NEXT LEVEL.
Photographer: Neil Setchfield (1)

Manchester's pioneering spirit started the Industrial Revolution, a musical revolution and the *Guardian* newspaper, and its resilience shook off an IRA bomb to rise triumphant, with excellent museums, fine dining and top shopping.

ANATOMY

The city centre is easily navigable on foot or using the efficient Metrolink. The latter's hub is in Piccadilly Gardens, east of the cathedral. North of here is the hip Northern Quarter. To the southeast you'll find Canal St and the Gay Village, with Chinatown next door. Nineteenth-century canalside industrial buildings have been trendily developed at Castlefield and Deansgate Locks southwest of the centre. Further south are the Salford quays embellished by the fabulous Imperial War Museum North and the Lowry Centre. Old Trafford (the 'Theatre of Dreams') is nearby. Compact Manchester is fairly foot-friendly, but if you're not pounding the pavements you can either catch one of the many buses or trams that weave across the city or one of the trains that skirt the inner city area.

PEOPLE

Manchester's population is predominantly of British heritage, although the number of Pakistani and Bangladeshi inhabitants is increasing.

TYPICAL MANCUNIAN

Mancunians are justifiably proud of their city, from its industrial history as 'Cottonopolis' through to the musical mayhem of 'Madchester'. They believe Manchester is the best city in England, and are friendly and welcoming to visitors. The city of Hacienda fame knows how to party, and people are fun-loving and stylish. Despite housing Manchester United, the hugely successful football club and global brand, most people support Manchester City, its far less successful neighbour. In addition to a general rivalry with London, Manchester and Leeds sit on opposite sides of the historic Lancashire-versus-Yorkshire clash, which is reinterpreted every year with the Roses cricket match. The city bounced back after the 1996 IRA bomb and many now say the city looks much better for it.

DEFINING EXPERIENCE

Breathing in the view of the city from little-visited Godlee Observatory before heading down for some shopping heaven in the Northern Quarter, followed by a reviving beer in Bar Centro and a spot of live music at the Manchester Roadhouse.

STRENGTHS

- Civic pride
- Harvey Nichols
- Successful urban regeneration
- Canals
- Manchester Pride
- Football
- Imperial War Museum North
- Lowry Centre
- Manchester Art Gallery
- Manchester Smithsonian
- University of Manchester
- Old Trafford
- Canal St after dark
- Lancashire County Cricket Club
- Large choice of restaurants
- Manchester airport
- Granada TV studios

WEAKNESSES

- Working conditions in the 19th century
- Weather
- Lack of low-cost airlines
- Manchester City Football Club

GOLD STAR

Pioneering and resilient spirit

CITYSPEAK

- Manchester City's latest results
- The new bar/club/shop that has recently opened

STARRING ROLE IN...

- *24-Hour Party People* (2002)
- *Cold Feet* (1998–2003)
- *Coronation Street* (1960–)
- *The Queen is Dead* by the Smiths

IMPORT

- Footballers' wives
- Students
- Friedrich Engels (to work in a family cotton factory)
- Scientist Ernest Rutherford

EXPORT

- Manchester United
- Oasis
- The Stone Roses
- Happy Mondays
- The Smiths
- Artist LS Lowry
- Cotton (but not since World War II)
- *Guardian* newspaper
- Caroline Aherne
- Steve Coogan
- Mick Hucknall
- Anna Friel
- Joanne Whalley-Kilmer

SEE the Daniel Libeskind–designed Imperial War Museum North and the audiovisual displays inside.

EAT at the best Indian restaurant on Curry Mile, Shere Khan.

DRINK a whisky in Temple of Convenience, a converted public toilet.

DO a tour of Old Trafford and imagine wearing one of those red shirts.

WATCH the heavens above and the city below from the Godlee Observatory.

BUY stylish clothes and must-have accessories in Millennium Quarter.

AFTER DARK don your dancing shoes for a club night at Music Box.

URBAN MYTH

The origins of 'Madchester' can be traced to Tony Wilson, founder of factory records – the label that in 1983 released New Order's *Blue Monday*, Britain's bestselling 12-inch single. With his pockets getting fatter, he opened the Hacienda nightclub but it was slow to take off. The turning point came with house music from Chicago and Detroit, DJs Mike Pickering, Graeme Park and Jon da Silva, and ecstasy – everyone in town became 'mad for it'. Local bands the Stone Roses, Happy Mondays and the Charlatans joined in. But the party couldn't last forever. In 1992 the Haçienda closed and the bands went quiet, making room for Manchester's most successful band, Oasis. Today new groups expound their individuality, reluctant to belong to a particular movement. Madchester is no more, but it has gone down in legend as a wild time.

PLENTY OF SPACE TO CONTEMPLATE: THE JANE BROWN EXHIBITION AT SALFORD QUAY'S LOWRY CENTRE.
Photographer: Neil Setchfield (2)

THE JAUNTY PEAK OF THE URBIS, MANCHESTER'S URBAN MUSEUM.
Photographer: Neil Setchfield (3)

MURAL DEPICTING VARIOUS FAMOUS MANCUNIANS.
Photographer: Neil Setchfield (4)

Antigua

127

VITAL STATISTICS

NAME: ANTIGUA

DATE OF BIRTH: 1543; WHEN IT WAS FOUNDED AND SERVED AS THE COLONIAL CAPITAL FOR THE NEXT 233 YEARS

ADDRESS: GUATEMALA (MAP 4, F6)

HEIGHT: 1480M

POPULATION: 40,000

One of the oldest and most beautiful cities in the Americas, Antigua thrives as an eclectic arts hub and magnet for students of its many language schools.

ANATOMY

Nestled in the Ponchoy Valley, Antigua is dramatically set between three volcanoes: Volcán Agua to the southeast, Volcán Fuego to the southwest and Volcán Acatenango to the west. Antigua served as the capital until it was moved to Guatemala City following the 1773 earthquakes, and a few buildings remain from this era. The central point of the city is Parque Central and *calles* are labelled east and west of this point. Buses arrive at the Terminales de Buses, four blocks west of Parque Central.

PEOPLE

The majority of Antigüeños are of a mestizo (of mixed Spanish and indigenous heritage; 56%) and are practising Roman Catholics. The region's indigenous Mayan people speak Cakchiquel and continue to practise their nature-based religion along with Roman Catholicism.

TYPICAL ANTIGÜEÑO

Antigüeños typically start the day early the same way they finish it – with a meal of eggs, beans, fried plantains and plenty of tortillas. A two-hour siesta follows lunch, the main meal. They are social, polite and refined in the arts, and enjoy the marimba and mariachi music played at frequent festivals and celebrations.

DEFINING EXPERIENCE

Visiting the museums and ruins strewn about town, studying Spanish while living with a Guatemalan family, summiting Volcán Pacaya, hiking or horse-riding to the Cerro de la Cruz vista point, buying vividly coloured, traditional handmade *traje* (clothing) in the market, and watching the passing parade during elaborate religious celebrations.

STRENGTHS

- Cathedral of San Francisco
- Elaborate religious celebrations during Holy Week
- Intensive Spanish-language courses
- Climbing the stunning Volcán Agua
- Charming Spanish baroque architecture
- Parque Central
- Intricately beaded crafts
- Embroidered *huipiles* (embroided blouses)
- Unique and weathered doorknobs and knockers
- Colourful, cobblestone streets
- Shopping for Mayan crafts
- Volcanoes
- Mayan water-lily blossoms and vegetable motifs adorning the church of La Merced

WEAKNESSES

- Twisting ankles on cobblestone streets after a drink
- Leaving
- Pleading for accommodation in the busy season
- The sheer number of tourists in the busy season

GOLD STAR

Parque Central – the gathering place for locals and visitors alike. On most days the plaza is lined with villagers selling handicrafts to tourists; on Sunday it's mobbed and the streets on the east and west sides are closed to traffic. Things are cheapest late on Sunday afternoon, when the peddling is winding down. At night, mariachi or marimba bands play in the park.

CITYSPEAK

- Will it be an earthquake or volcanic eruption next?

STARRING ROLE IN...

- *Riotous Rhymes 'n' Remedies* by Sylvanus Barnes
- *Garden of Life* by LHC Westcott

IMPORT

- Spanish-language students
- Cafés
- Colonial architecture
- The Spanish

EXPORT

- Coffee – some of the world's best
- Ceramics
- Beaded handicrafts
- Singer Ricardo Arjona
- Handmade *traje*
- Carved ceremonial masks
- *Huipiles*

SEE Samuel Franco Arce's photographs and recordings of Mayan ceremonies and music at Casa K'Ojom.

EAT the Sunday buffet in the Café Condessa.

DRINK Zacapa Centenario (a fine Guatemalan rum).

DO enrol in an intensive Spanish-language and culture course.

WATCH the afternoon handicrafts trade around the 1738 fountain in Parque Central, to the sounds of mariachi or marimba bands.

BUY colourful beaded and embroidered handicrafts, ceramics and carved wooden masks.

AFTER DARK explore Antigua's atmospheric bars and see if you can practise some of that new-found Spanish.

URBAN MYTH

Antigua really comes alive in Semana Santa (Holy Week), when hundreds of people dress in deep-purple robes to accompany the most revered sculptural images from the city's churches in daily street processions remembering Christ's Crucifixion. Dense clouds of incense envelop the parades and the streets are covered in breathtakingly elaborate *alfombras* (carpets) of coloured sawdust and flower petals.

DAY MAKES FOR LONG SHADOWS IN ANTIGUA.
Souders (1)

EW OF VOLCÁN AGUA OVERLOOKING THE OLD CITY.
Maiquez (2)

TWO INFECTIOUSLY HAPPY DENIZENS OF THE ANTIGUA HIGHLANDS.
Photographer: Greg Johnston (3)

SPOILT FOR CHOICE: ANTIGUA'S FRUIT AND VEGETABLE MARKET.
Photographer: Jon Arnold Images (4)

BATHERS AT THE LAUGADALUR COMPLEX DEMONSTRATE WHY ICELAND IS SO POORLY NAMED.
Photographer: Anders Blomqvist (1)

Tiny and often very cold, Reykjavík surprises with its exuberance, cultural savvy and otherworldly setting.

ANATOMY

The world's northernmost capital lies on a small peninsula, framed by the snowcapped Mt Esja and the windswept waters of the Atlantic. Recent generations of young architects have filled the capital with intriguing modern buildings, which sit neatly juxtaposed against the coloured-roofed, tin-clad wooden houses. The old town centre lies between a picturesque harbour and a large pond, the Tjörn, to the southwest. Reykjavíkers bike, bus or traverse their compact city on foot, but favour 4WDs for the sprawling suburbs.

PEOPLE

Reykjavíkers usually know each other and are often distantly related. Around 94% are of mixed Scandinavian and Celtic stock – a legacy of early settlement. The remaining 6% are either transplanted spouses or temporary workers, mainly from Poland (as immigration is strictly controlled). Most Reykjavíkers will be as fluent in English as they are in Icelandic.

TYPICAL REYKJAVÍKER

National traits of self-reliance and reserve may well apply, but young Reykjavíkers also tend to be somewhat bohemian. They are more likely to be interested in poetry, painting or their band's upcoming performance than traditional outdoor pursuits. They work hard but love nothing more than to go out for long drinking sessions come the weekend. Increasingly, they don't mind living in debt (with the price of a night out, how would they ever afford that new 4WD otherwise?), or 'in sin' – over a third of babies are born out of wedlock.

Reykjavík
128

VITAL STATISTICS

NAME: REYKJAVÍK

DATE OF BIRTH: AD 874; ACCORDING TO ARI THE LEARNED, NORWEGIAN VIKING INGÓLFUR ARNARSON SET UP HOUSE NEXT TO A SET OF GEOTHERMAL VENTS, NAMING THE SETTLEMENT REYKJAVÍK (SMOKY BAY)

ADDRESS: ICELAND (MAP 1, S5)

HEIGHT: 18M

SIZE: 275 SQ KM

POPULATION: 181,746

GAZING OVER AT REYKJAVÍK AND TJÖRN FROM CITY HALL.
Photographer: Anders Blomqvist (3)

Q: HOW DO YOU KEEP A GLASS-CEILINGED RESTAURANT WARM? A: BUILD IT ON TOP OF REYKJAVÍK'S HOT-WATER TANK
Photographer: Anders Blomqvist (4)

HOW CIGARETTES AND SHADES CAN OFFSET THE STYLE EFFECTS OF THOSE HATS.
Photographer: Anders Blomqvist (2)

DEFINING EXPERIENCE

Belly-flopping the warm waters of the Luagadalur thermal pool, hoping to forget how late you stayed out the night before, then browsing the Kolaportið flea markets, grabbing the obligatory hot dog with *remúladi* (a mayonnaise sauce) and crispy-fried onion from Bæjarins Bestu before heading off to an opening of contemporary sculpture at Hafnarhúsið with friends just back from New York.

URBAN MYTH

Stories of hidden races of wee people have been handed down through generations, and although some Icelanders today will roll their eyes at the mention of elves, many have no doubt about their existence and gardens often feature small wooden *alfhol* (elf-houses) 'just in case'. Hafnarfjörður, a suburb of Reykjavík, is believed to lie at the confluence of several strong ley lines (thought to be the lines of prehistoric tracks) and therefore particularly rife with these twilight creatures. Construction of roads and homes is strictly prohibited if a site is deemed to be populated by little folk.

STRENGTHS

- ⊿ Long summer days
- ⊿ The Raðhús
- ⊿ Surprisingly short flying times to New York, London or Oslo
- ⊿ Perlan parkland
- ⊿ Rex Bar
- ⊿ Alternative attitude
- ⊿ Excellent fresh produce and innovative chefs
- ⊿ Hallgrímskirkja
- ⊿ Eco-consciousness
- ⊿ Geothermal swimming pools and beaches
- ⊿ Ingibjörg Pálmadóttir's Icelandic-minimal interiors
- ⊿ Unique moonscapes close to town

WEAKNESSES

- ⊿ Summer temperatures that never leave the teens
- ⊿ Legless drunks and vomit
- ⊿ Hideously high cost of living
- ⊿ Chewing gum
- ⊿ Everyone hears what you got up to last weekend
- ⊿ Ubiquitous corrugated iron

GOLD STAR

Friday nights: for a small, chilly city, it's amazingly energetic and uninhibited.

CITYSPEAK

- ⊿ You're building a summerhouse in Árnessýsla too?
- ⊿ Whale – should it be on the menu?
- ⊿ I'm so over Damon Albarn…
- ⊿ Power plants, dams, smelters
- ⊿ Just how independent is Iceland from Denmark anyway?

STARRING ROLE IN…

- ⊿ *Reykjavík Guesthouse: Rent a Bike* (2002)
- ⊿ *101 Reykjavík* (2000)
- ⊿ *Icelandic Dream* (2000)
- ⊿ *Children of Nature* (1992)
- ⊿ *Rokk í Reykjavík* (Rock in Reykjavík, 1982)

IMPORT

- ⊿ US genomics research companies
- ⊿ Vikings
- ⊿ Polish labourers
- ⊿ Alcoa
- ⊿ Punk
- ⊿ Vladimir Ashkenazy
- ⊿ French-trained chefs
- ⊿ Pan-Scandinavian political policies
- ⊿ Irish slaves
- ⊿ Driftwood from Siberia and South America; used to build most of Reykjavík's traditional timber houses

EXPORT

- ⊿ Björk
- ⊿ Fish
- ⊿ Singer Emiliana Torrini
- ⊿ Parliamentary democracy
- ⊿ Hydrogen-powered transport expertise

SEE, as you sit by the harbour at midnight, the summer sun dip slightly below the horizon before it makes its way up again.

EAT Siggi Hall's take on *skyr* – a yoghurt-like concoction most often paired with lush local berries – at his eponymous restaurant (especially if you can't face puffin pie).

DRINK vodka-spiked beer with the Friday night *runtur* (literally, 'round tour') crowd around Laugavegur in the town centre – the ultimate pub-crawl.

DO chess at Grand Rokk bar with the Hrokurinn Chess Club when it's too cold to horse-ride, hike or whale-watch.

WATCH an international rock act, preferably from the comfort of a geothermal pool, during the Airwaves Festival in October.

BUY Icelandic CDs at Japis or Skifan – both stock the entire Björk back catalogue.

AFTER DARK discuss the sagas or the songs of Sigur Rós, at the volcanic-monochrome bar of the 101 Hótel.

VITAL STATISTICS

NAME: YOGYAKARTA

NICKNAME: YOGYA

DATE OF BIRTH: 1755; WHEN PRINCE (LATER SULTAN) MANGKUMBI BUILT THE KRATON OF YOGYAKARTA

ADDRESS: INDONESIA (MAP 1, HH17)

HEIGHT: 106M

SIZE: 33 SQ KM

POPULATION: 450,000

COLOURFUL KITES FLY OVER TAMAN SARI.
Photographer: Dimas Ardian (1)

PICKING UP A NIGHTTIME SNACK OF *GUDEG*.
Photographer: Dimas Ardian (2)

SHAKING TO THE BEAT OF THE NIGHTLIFE AT
PURAWISATA AMUSEMENT PARK.
Photographer: Dimas Ardian (3)

A DANCER PREPARES TO PERFORM THE RAMAYANA, A TRADITIONAL HINDU EPIC.
Photographer: Dimas Ardian (4)

If Jakarta is Java's financial and industrial powerhouse, Yogyakarta is its soul: central to the island's artistic and intellectual heritage, Yogyakarta is where the Javanese language is at its purest, Javanese arts are at their brightest and Javanese traditions at their most visible.

ANATOMY

Jalan (Jl) Malioboro, named after the Duke of Marlborough, is Yogya's main road, running from the train station to the *kraton* (walled palace) at the far end. The road becomes Jl A Yani further south, but is generally referred to as Jalan Malioboro. The tourist office and many souvenir shops and stalls are along this street and most of the budget places to stay are west of it, in the Jl Sosrowijayan area near the railway line. The old, walled *kraton* is the centre of old Yogya, where you will also find the Taman Sari (Water Castle), Pasar Ngasem (Bird Market) and numerous batik galleries. While easy to navigate, it is impossible to go to any tourist areas without being greeted by *becak* (auto-rickshaw) drivers. Regular taxis are metered and efficient.

PEOPLE

With a mix of Javanese, Sundanese and Madurese peoples, the main languages spoken in Yogya are Javanese, Sundanese, Madurese and Bahasa Indonesian. While the predominant religion is Muslim, there are Hindu, Buddhist and Christian minorities.

TYPICAL YOGYAKARTA CITIZEN

Living in a cultural and intellectual centre crammed with prestigious universities and academies, the typical Yogya citizen is used to living in a city enduring a Westernised puberty. While the town swings moodily between fast-food joints, shopping malls and satellite TV, locals have a traditional focus, centred around the family, the 'village' and religious piety.

DEFINING EXPERIENCE

Scoffing down a street-stall *gudeg* (Yogya's signature dish: it's sweet and made with jack fruit, coconut, eggs among other ingredients), meandering the grounds of the *kraton*, then being enchanted by one of the many *wayang kulit* (shadow-puppet) plays at night.

STRENGTHS

- The *kraton*
- The Gerebeg festivals
- Pasar Ngasem
- Pasar Beringharjo (Yogya's main market)
- The Dutch-era fort Benteng Vredeburg
- First-class Javanese art
- Shadow-puppet plays
- Museum Kareta Kraton
- Sumptuous spices
- The Affandi Museum
- Purawisata amusement park
- Kota Gede
- Museum Sansana Wiratama

WEAKNESSES

- 'Last chance' batik scammers
- Copycat batik painting galleries
- Bag snatchers
- Bike bandits
- Pickpockets

GOLD STAR

Location – aside from being Java's premier tourist city, Yogya is an ideal base for exploring nearby attractions, including Indonesia's most important archaeological sites, Borobudur and Prambanan Temples.

CITYSPEAK

- 'Special rates!' – be warned: these wily *becak* drivers are trying to get you into a batik gallery
- 2004's reconstruction efforts to renew the neighbourhood around the *kraton*

STARRING ROLE IN...

- *Agung Gives Ivor a Haircut* (1991)
- *Becak driver – Superimposed* (1998)

IMPORT

- Tourism
- Rapid Westernisation
- Burger joints
- Bar girls
- Big hotels

EXPORT

- Affandi (Indonesia's best-known artist)
- Batik
- Silverwork
- Leather puppets and wooden masks
- Traditional and contemporary Javanese art

SEE hundreds of budgerigars, orioles, roosters, singing turtledoves and pigeons, all in ornamental cages at Pasar Ngasem on the edge of Taman Sari.

EAT anything from nasi goreng to greasy-spoon fry-ups at the FM Café on Jl Sosrowijayan, with stacks of atmosphere and an eclectic, well-priced menu.

DRINK draught Heineken with homesick Hollanders at the Dutch Café on Jl Tirtodipuran, a venerable traveller and expat haunt.

DO marvel at the restored 1760s bathing pools in the Taman Sari, and imagine the sultan and harem members relaxing in this one-time pleasure park.

WATCH the spectacular Ramayana ballet held in the open air at Prambanan in the dry season.

BUY exquisite leatherwork, batik bags, *topeng* (masks) and *wayang golek* (wooden puppets) from all over the archipelago in Jl Malioboro.

AFTER DARK *wayang kulit* performances can be seen at several places around Yogya every night.

URBAN MYTH

In the *kraton's* southern square are two similar banyan trees, which are said to bring great fortune if you walk through them without mishap while blindfolded. The *kraton* is closed on national holidays and for special *kraton* ceremonies, yet batik touts after a bonanza of their own will advise it's closed to lure you to Taman Sari and a batik gallery.

Carcassonne

130

VITAL STATISTICS

NAME: CARCASSONNE

DATE OF BIRTH: 3500 BC; WHEN THE FIRST NEOLITHIC SETTLEMENTS APPEARED

ADDRESS: FRANCE (MAP 3, G13)

HEIGHT: 130M

POPULATION: 46,250

One of the largest and best preserved walled towns in the world, Carcassonne enfolds centuries of history within the defensive ramparts of La Cité.

ANATOMY

The River Aude separates the Ville Basse (Lower Town) from La Cité, located on a hill 500m southeast and surrounded by two concentric walls. Pedestrianised rue Georges Clemenceau leads from the train station and Canal du Midi southwards through the heart of the lower town. You can catch buses around town.

PEOPLE

The inhabitants of Carcassonne live mostly in the Ville Basse and surrounding suburbs, with only a small percentage living in La Cité itself. Ninety percent are Roman Catholic and some speak Catalan rather than French. In recent years the population has been greatly boosted by British migrants.

TYPICAL CARCASSONNAIS

Carcassonne's residents go about their daily lives seemingly oblivious to the hordes of tourists and the cacophony of buskers, tour guides and souvenir vendors. While celebrating their proud Cathar history at every chance, they certainly don't adopt the austere lifestyle of their predecessors, preferring to cultivate a convivial café culture, a predilection for local wine and *cassoulet* (a piping hot dish blending white beans, juicy pork cubes, sausage and – in the most popular local variant – duck).

DEFINING EXPERIENCE

Admiring the charming carousel just outside the entrance to La Cité, then literally walking around the city (along 3km of defensive ramparts), visiting Porte Narbonnaise, Basilique St-Nazaire and Château Comtal, dining on *cassoulet* at L'Écu d'Or, followed by a twilight walk outside the now-illuminated castle walls, for a different perspective.

STRENGTHS

- Your first glimpse of La Cité's witches-hat turrets as you approach
- World Heritage listing
- Basilique St-Nazaire
- 12th-century Château Comtal
- Musée Lapidaire
- Massive bastion of Porte Narbonnaise
- L'Embrasement de la Cité (Setting La Cité Ablaze) – Bastille Day celebrations
- Magnificent reconditioned 19th-century carousel
- Elaborate tombs and graves in the cemetery
- *Cassoulet*

WEAKNESSES

- Hellishly overcrowded with tourists (over two million) in high summer
- An oversupply of kitsch souvenir shops
- Cheesy/tacky private museums
- Can be expensive
- Variable quality of Château Comtal guided tour

GOLD STAR

La Cité itself, dramatically illuminated at night and enclosed within its two rampart walls punctuated by 52 towers, is simply breathtaking.

CITYSPEAK

- The ever-increasing number of tourists
- Who's winning the rugby?

STARRING ROLE IN...

- *Robin Hood: Prince of Thieves* (1991)

IMPORT

- Tourists
- McDonald's
- Rugby

EXPORT

- Wine
- Shoes
- Rubber
- Textiles
- Tacky souvenirs

SEE graceful Gothic transept arms and superb 13th- and 14th-century windows at Basilique St-Nazaire.

EAT *cassoulet* at Au Bon Pasteur, where simple décor belies the sophistication of the cooking.

DRINK your favourite coffee from the huge selection available at La Cité des Arômes.

DO take in the view of La Cité from the Pont Neuf or Pont Vieux, straddling the River Aude.

WATCH birds of prey dive and swoop in falconry demonstrations at Les Aigles de La Cité (The Eagles of La Cité), 800m south of the city walls.

BUY kitsch souvenirs, or better yet, save your money for some of the region's wines.

AFTER DARK most tourists have left, so enjoy a quiet post-dinner stroll and experience the city anew under floodlights.

URBAN MYTH

When Carcassonne was besieged in AD 760, the inhabitants soon began to starve. But Dame Carcas, widow of one of the castle's nobles, devised a clever bluff. Feeding all their remaining grain to one pig, the fattened creature was catapulted over the walls to the army outside. When they saw that the Carcassonnais could apparently still expend large amounts of grain just to feed livestock, the besiegers became demoralised and withdrew. Bells were then rung in Dame Carcas' honour, and many historians believe this legend is the source of the city's name, 'Carcas sonne', meaning 'Carcas rings'.

THE FAIRY-TALE WALLS OF THE MEDIEVAL OLD CITY GLOW MAGICALLY AT NIGHT.
Photographer: Dallas Stribley (1)

A HORSE MERRILY MAKES IT WAY AROUND A CAROUSEL IN THE JARDIN DU PRADO, WHILE THE TOWERS OF THE PORTE NARBONNAISE LURK OMINOUSLY OVERHEAD.
Photographer: Dallas Stribley (2)

THE BLUE FAÇADE OF A BUILDING IN VILLE BASSE IS OFFSET BY SASSY PINK WASHING HUNG OUT TO DRY.
Photographer: Dallas Stribley (3)

A VERY WELL CARED FOR POODLE BASKS WITH HER PERSON IN PLACE CAMOT.
Photographer: Dallas Stribley (4)

Lübeck 131

VITAL STATISTICS

NAME: LÜBECK

DATE OF BIRTH: AD 1000; WHEN THE WENDS ESTABLISHED A ROYAL SEAT CALLED LIUBICE

ADDRESS: GERMANY (MAP 3, J6)

HEIGHT: 17M

POPULATION: 213,000

Lübeck's medieval architecture is as mouth-watering as its marzipan, and for a relatively small city it packs a powerful punch – it's a Unesco World Heritage site and in days gone by its famous Holstentor (gate) used to grace the DM50 note.

ANATOMY

The twin, pointy-roofed circular towers of the Holstentor form the main entry to Lübeck's *Altstadt* (old town) on the western side. The northern and eastern parts of the *Altstadt* belonged to craftspeople in the Middle Ages. Now this area is characterised by small low-rise homes in *Höfe* (courtyards) that are accessed by little *Gänge* (walkways) from the street. Not far from the Holstentor is the *Markt* (marketplace), where you'll find the *Rathaus* (town hall) and the Marienkirche, Germany's third-largest church. The pedestrianised shopping area leads off from here. The whole of the *Altstadt* is surrounded by the Trave River and its canals. Travemunde ferry port is 16km from the *Altstadt*. Buses and trains service the city.

PEOPLE

Lübeck still calls itself a Hanseatic city, referring to the commanding medieval Hanseatic League that united more than 150 merchant cities in an 'association'. It may now be a provincial city, but the people of Lübeck have powerful roots.

TYPICAL LÜBECK CITIZEN

Lübeck is the main attraction for visitors to Schleswig-Holstein, Germany's answer to the Côte d'Azur (weather aside), and inhabitants of Lübeck escape the crowds by sailing to islands offshore and relaxing on the attractive beaches along the coast. The city may be old and picturesque, but it also hums with life, particularly in the warm and inviting bars that are popular with the locals. The people also enjoy culture and the city has connections to two Nobel prize-winning authors – Thomas Mann, who was born in Lübeck in 1875, and Günter Grass, who is a current resident.

DEFINING EXPERIENCE

Musing on creative genius in the Günter Grass-Haus, then seeking inspiration for your novel among the fairy-tale architecture of the *Altstadt*, before taking the kids to the *Marionettentheater* (puppet theatre).

STRENGTHS

- Marzipan
- Holstentor
- Medieval merchant's homes
- 1000 historical buildings
- Hanseatic League
- Marienkirche and its shattered church bells, now a peace memorial
- *Rathaus*
- Museum für Puppentheater
- Literary tradition
- Café Niederegger
- Füchtingshof and Glandorps Gang
- Nearby beaches
- Boat trips through the canals
- Gothmund, a charming fishers' village

WEAKNESSES

- Lots of temptation for those on a diet
- Cold winds and dark clouds (even in summer)

GOLD STAR

Marzipan – don't you just love those chocolate-covered marzipan delights…

CITYSPEAK

- The weather – is it good enough to go to the beach?
- Will the airport get the runway expansion proposed?

STARRING ROLE IN…

- *The Buddenbrooks* by Thomas Mann
- *Holstentor* by Andy Warhol

IMPORT

- Günter Grass
- Discerning tourists

EXPORT

- Willy Brandt
- Thomas Mann
- Horst Frank
- Marzipan

SEE the magical city gate, Holstentor, and imagine letting down your Rapunzel hair from the circular towers.

EAT modern German cuisine in Markgraf, a perfectly elegant historic restaurant.

DRINK home-brewed beer in Brauberger, which has made and served its own since 1225.

DO a boat tour of the canals that surround the *Altstadt* – well, with all that water you have to really, don't you?

WATCH a spellbinding organ concert in the Marienkirche, home to the world's largest mechanical organ.

BUY some of that lovely sweet stuff at Café Niederegger – and, yes, we're talking about marzipan.

AFTER DARK watch a play in the Art Nouveau Theater Lübeck.

URBAN MYTH

The Hanseatic League is a legendary part of Lübeck's history. Its initial aim was to protect shipping and trade in the North Sea and Baltic regions, but as more and more members signed up its sheer size made it a powerful political force in Europe. During meetings in Lübeck, the league effectively dictated policy by fixing prices of commodities such as grain, fur and ore or threatening to withhold trading privileges. It was known to bribe foreign officials and in 1368 it even went to war with Denmark after being challenged by Danish King Vlademar IV for control of the south-western Baltic. In general it was a positive force, though, and provided stability and prosperity to members. In the 16th century the league started to erode and the 17th-century Thirty Years' War was the final nail in the coffin. Bremen, Hamburg and Lübeck still call themselves Hanseatic cities despite no meeting of the league taking place since 1669.

THE VIEW FROM ABOVE REVEALS HOW LÜBECK'S CATHEDRAL ANCHORS THE OLD TOWN.
Photographer: Manfred Gottschalk (1)

A DARK FIGURE CONTEMPLATES THE LIGHT SIDE AS SUN SETS ON HEILIGEN-GEIST-HOSPITAL.
Photographer: Martin Lladó (2)

A MANNEQUIN COOLLY AWAITS FINAL SALE.
Photographer: Martin Lladó (3)

MODERN AND FUNKY, TEL AVIV IS A CITY KNOWN FOR ITS OPENNESS AND TOLERANCE.
Photographer: Stephane Victor (1)

Tel Aviv 132

VITAL STATISTICS

NAME: TEL AVIV

NICKNAME: THE WHITE CITY; THE BIG ORANGE

DATE OF BIRTH: 1909; WHEN IT WAS FOUNDED BY 60 FAMILIES AS A JEWISH NEIGHBOURHOOD NEAR JAFFA

ADDRESS: ISRAEL (MAP 2, L2)

HEIGHT: 34M

SIZE: 52 SQ KM

POPULATION: 371,000

While Jerusalem is considered the spiritual centre of Israel, Tel Aviv, conversely, is the pop-cultural centre, with its cafés, Mediterranean beaches and Israeli trance music, which is loud and unavoidable.

ANATOMY

Hayarkon St, Herbert Samuel Rd and Ibn Gvirol St are the main streets of Tel Aviv, running north–south and parallel to the seafront. Dizengoff Sq, Rabin Sq and Hamedina Sq are critical reference points. The New Central Bus Station is officially the world's biggest bus station and buses will take you practically everywhere in Israel.

PEOPLE

Around a third of Israel's population lives in Tel Aviv. It is a predominantly Jewish city.

TYPICAL TEL AVIVIAN

Tel Avivians are youthful and brash and totally unlike their neighbours in Jerusalem, which is only around 45 minutes away but may as well be on another continent. As a Tel Aviv shopkeeper once said, 'In Jerusalem they like their religion, in Tel Aviv we like our drugs'. It may not ring true for the entire city, but it certainly provides an insight.

DEFINING EXPERIENCE

After you've taken in the spiritual teachings of the kabbalah and eaten an icy pole (ice lolly) on the beach, head over to Nachalat Binyamin (street of artists) for a look at the work of the city's artisans and street performers.

STRENGTHS
- Weather
- Beaches
- Proximity to the country's amazing sights and relics
- Museum of the Diaspora
- Cafés spilling out onto the streets and beaches

WEAKNESSES
- Young soldiers carrying machine guns
- Drivers on mobile phones
- The occasional market-place bombing

GOLD STAR

Behind some drab façades is an incredible collection of Bauhaus buildings along Rothschild Blvd, Ahad Ha'am St, Engel St, Nachmani St, Melchett St and Balfour St, making it the Bauhaus capital of the world.

CITYSPEAK
- Orange as the colour of protest – despite world opinion, fashion designers in Tel Aviv are packing the orange palate away in opposition to disengagement
- Will Madonna ever perform in Tel Aviv?
- Crowds at Queer Pride Day getting smaller – could it be the 1000-strong assembly of police and security guards?

STARRING ROLE IN...
- 'Tel Aviv' by Duran Duran
- *Tel Aviv-Berlin* (1987)
- *Walk on Water* (2004)
- *The Flower of Anarchy* by Meir Wieseltier

IMPORT
- New York bagels
- T'ai chi in Yarkon Park
- Italian *gelati*
- The usual fast-food suspects (but with inflated prices)
- Cable TV
- US culture
- Mobile phones
- Bauhaus architecture
- Poet Meir Wieseltier
- Tim Tam biscuits (around 700,000 packets a year)

EXPORT
- Kabbalah
- Diamonds
- Jaffa oranges
- Israeli trance music
- Tomato-growing technology
- Jazz musician Avi Leibovitz
- Fertilisers

SEE fresh-faced soldiers, lads and lasses in shopping malls and nightclubs bandying about their machine guns.

EAT halva ice cream down along Ibn Givrol and Frishman Sts.

DRINK home-brewed ale at the Tel Aviv Brewhouse.

DO walk along powder-fine sand beaches – you'll find sand in every nook and cranny for days to come.

WATCH avant-garde and new wave films at the Cinematheque.

BUY secondhand goods at Shuk Hapishpeshim, Jaffa's flea market.

AFTER DARK take your *darbuka* (drum) and pound the night away on drum beach.

URBAN MYTH

According to the Bible, Jonah departed from Jaffa on that fateful day in an attempt to escape from God. But then he was swallowed by a whale, where he spent three days and nights. Let that be a lesson. And if you have any doubts about the legend, a statue of the whale in Jaffa serves as a portentous reminder.

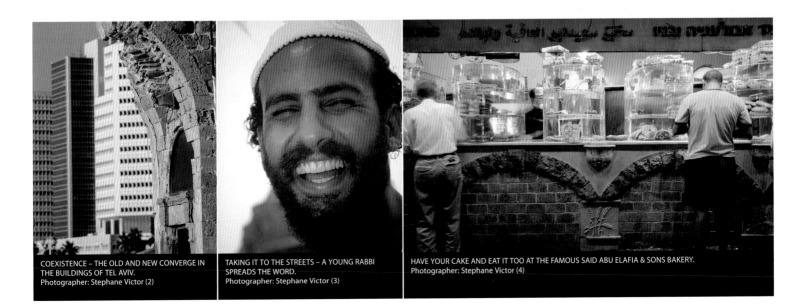

COEXISTENCE – THE OLD AND NEW CONVERGE IN THE BUILDINGS OF TEL AVIV.
Photographer: Stephane Victor (2)

TAKING IT TO THE STREETS – A YOUNG RABBI SPREADS THE WORD.
Photographer: Stephane Victor (3)

HAVE YOUR CAKE AND EAT IT TOO AT THE FAMOUS SAID ABU ELAFIA & SONS BAKERY.
Photographer: Stephane Victor (4)

A one-of-a-kind example of the true Japanese experience and so much more than a tasteful reminder of one of the modern world's darkest hours, Hiroshima's cherry blossom–lined streets, local artisans and vivacious entertainment venues embrace a city sparkling with hope and tradition.

ANATOMY

Hiroshima (meaning 'broad island') is built on a series of sandy islands on the delta of Ota-gawa river. JR Hiroshima Station is east of the city centre and, although there are a number of hotels around the station, the central area, with its very lively entertainment district, is much more interesting. Hiroshima's main east–west avenue is Heiwa-Ōdōri (Peace Blvd). Parallel to it runs the busiest road (with the main tram lines from the station), Aioi-dōri. Just south of this is the busy Hon-dōri shopping arcade. There is an extensive tram system.

PEOPLE

The only way to be Japanese is to be born of Japanese parents. This leaves the nearly two million migrant workers throughout Japan out in the cold when it comes to obtaining rights to health care and education. Chinese, Korean and Filipinos constitute about 75% of the migrant community, while another 20% hail from Peru and Brazil. A small city for a Japanese metropolis, Hiroshima affords its constituents an element of Japanese traditional rural charm.

TYPICAL HIROSHIMAN

Like most Japanese people, Hiroshimans are hard-working and obstinately polite. Their dedication to etiquette can be daunting to the uninitiated, but they are also warmly hospitable. Though their city's name is tied to the horrors of 6 August 1945, when it was the victim of the world's first atomic attack, it is by no means their whole story. The people of Hiroshima hold steadfastly to their traditions all the more for this experience and look optimistically forward.

Hiroshima
133

VITAL STATISTICS

NAME: HIROSHIMA

DATE OF BIRTH: AD 1589; WHEN FEUDAL LORD MORI TERUMOTO NAMED THE TOWN AND ESTABLISHED A CASTLE

ADDRESS: JAPAN (MAP 1, KK11)

HEIGHT: 4M

SIZE: 742 SQ KM

POPULATION: 1.1 MILLION

A QUIET MOMENT OF CONTEMPLATION AS PAPER LANTERNS REFLECTING SOULS OF THE FALLEN ARE SET OUT TO SEA.
Photographer: Karen Kasmauski (1)

DEFINING EXPERIENCE
Relishing a lunch of *kaki-ryōri* (oyster cuisine) at Aini Kinchaya Organic Dining before touring the town in a streetcar to take in the heroic collection of tributes and memorials, most notably Peace Memorial Park.

STRENGTHS
◢ Hijiyama Park, noted for its cherry blossoms
◢ City Manga Library
◢ Nearby Miyajima
◢ A-Bomb Dome
◢ Asa Zoo
◢ Mazda Museum
◢ DJ scene
◢ Hiroshima-jō (also known as Carp Castle)
◢ Hiroshima Museum of Art
◢ Japanese baseball

WEAKNESSES
◢ Omnipresent history
◢ Expensive accommodation
◢ Very cold winters
◢ Westernisation

GOLD STAR
Hope – Hiroshima is a hopeful and optimistic beacon to the rest of the world and a living argument against war and the use of nuclear weapons.

CITYSPEAK
◢ Japan joining the nuclear-arms race
◢ Naturalisation of migrants

STARRING ROLE IN...
◢ *Shockwave : Countdown to Hiroshima* by Stephen Walker
◢ *Hiroshima* by John Hershey
◢ *Hiroshima Mon Amour* (1959)

IMPORT
◢ Buddhism
◢ Karaoke
◢ Western fashion
◢ Migrants from China, Korea and the Philippines
◢ Pop music

EXPORT
◢ Mazdas
◢ Hopes of peace

SEE the Flame of Peace, which will only be extinguished once the last nuclear weapon on earth has been destroyed.

EAT *Hiroshima-yaki*, a local version of *okonomiyaki* (egg-based savoury pancakes), from one of the 30 mini-restaurants at Okonomi-mura.

DRINK sake or a cocktail at Bar Alcoholiday in the Casablanca building.

DO visit the popular Mazda Museum and see the world's longest assembly line – 7km.

WATCH a memorial service held in Peace Memorial Park on 6 August, where thousands of paper lanterns for the souls of the dead are floated down the Ota-gawa.

BUY unique *ukiyo-e* (wood-block prints) from local artisans.

AFTER DARK check out the latest local DJ playing everything from hard techno to reggae at the cool and cosy Commune.

URBAN MYTH
A 10-year-old local girl named Sadako, who like many others after the atomic bomb attack developed leukaemia, decided to fold 1000 paper cranes – an ancient Japanese custom through which it is believed that a person's wishes will come true. The crane is the symbol of longevity and happiness in Japan, and Sadako was convinced that if she could achieve that target she would recover. Though she died before reaching her goal, her class-mates folded the rest. The story in-spired a nationwide bout of paper-crane folding, which continues to this day. This was also the impetus behind the Children's Peace Memorial, where strings of paper cranes from all over Japan are kept on display.

TRADITIONALLY DRESSED WOMEN MULL OVER HOW BLUE THE DAY IS.
Photographer: Paul Quayle (2)

FAST TIMES AT MORNING PRAYERS, MIYAJIMA.
Photographer: Michael Freeman (3)

HUNDREDS OF PAPER CRANES ON DISPLAY.
Photographer: Chase Swift (4)

Mendoza

134

VITAL STATISTICS

NAME: MENDOZA

DATE OF BIRTH: 1561; WHEN IT WAS FOUNDED BY PEDRO DE CASTILLA

ADDRESS: ARGENTINA (MAP 1, M20)

HEIGHT: 801M

SIZE: 110 SQ KM

POPULATION: 130,000

A town that offers wine tasting, a sunny clime, tree-lined streets and parks just made for roaming, mountain jaunts…Mendoza offers all this and more amid the company of relaxed and friendly mendocinos.

ANATOMY

First you'll notice the trees: giant sycamores forming a canopy over the wide avenues of downtown, shading Mendoza's lively inhabitants from the blistering summer sun. With all those leaves, you'd never know it's a desert. But the *acequias* (open irrigation channels) burbling along every street give it away. They carry snow-melt from the Andes, visible evidence of the city's indigenous and colonial past, even where modern quake-proof construction has replaced fallen historic buildings. Mendoza's architecture, hidden behind the trees, is almost an afterthought. Without the trees, Mendoza would be hell. With them, it's one of Argentina's finest cities, with outdoor cafés crowded with coffee drinkers, five beautiful central plazas, a bustling shopping district and an exciting nightlife. And above the city are the Andes. Mendoza is more spread out than most Argentine cities, so you'll need to tighten your shoelaces or catch a bus to get around.

PEOPLE

Mendocinos are mostly European descendants (especially Spaniards and Italians) and mestizos, with some indigenous people. They speak Spanish, as well as Quechua, Araucanian and Guaraní. They are predominantly Roman Catholic (93%) with smaller percentages of Protestant, Jewish, Ukrainian Catholic and Armenian Orthodox communities.

TYPICAL MENDOCINO

Mendocinos have city charm but country tranquillity. They're laid-back but full of passion, their relaxed natures concealing the party animal within. They'll dance until 7am and still make time for a family *asado* (barbecue) for lunch. They'll boast of the surrounding natural wonders but probably won't bother to leave the city to look at them. They believe they're more European than Argentine, except when it comes to World Cup Football.

DEFINING EXPERIENCE

Waking up late after a night dancing in a *boliche* (nightclub), starting the day with a maté, going for a walk in the shaded streets and plazas, gorging yourself on an *asado* until late afternoon, drinking bottle after bottle of Quilmes and dancing the night away to *cumbia* (Colombian dance tunes), then returning home after the sun comes up to sleep through half the weekend.

STRENGTHS

- Damn fine Malbec wines
- Laid-back atmosphere
- Wide, shady avenues
- Sun
- Snow
- The Italianate character
- Inner-city greenness
- Proximity to the Andes and all its adventure sports
- Outdoor cafés
- Open-air and handicraft markets

WEAKNESSES

- Wide irrigation channels on both sides of every street
- Climatic extremes
- Clichéd Argentine egotism and machismo
- Earthquakes

GOLD STAR

For being the city that converted Argentina's wine industry from a local shame to an international success

CITYSPEAK

- *Fútbol* (football)
- Chileans and Argentines – who's right, who's wrong?
- The effects of the economic crisis

STARRING ROLE IN...

- *The Motorcycle Diaries* (2004)

IMPORT

- International mountaineers
- Adventure sports
- The Virgin of Cuyo, patron of San Martín's Ejército de los Andes (Army of the Andes)
- British railways (linking Chile and Argentina)
- Italian culture

EXPORT

- General San Martín's troops – they were trained here before the liberation of Chile in the Wars of Independence
- Wine
- Olive oil
- Tourism to Cerro Aconcagua
- Oil and gas

SEE the Museo Popular Callejera on Av Las Heras – an innovative sidewalk museum.

EAT *lomitos* (beef sandwiches) at Toblao.

DRINK a good Malbec at Mendoza's Vendimia (grape-harvest) festival on the first Saturday of March each year.

DO a relaxing walk around the parks and lakes of the Parque General San Martín.

WATCH the underwater freak show at the Acuario Municipal Mendoza (Municipal Aquarium).

BUY indigenous weavings at the Mercado Artesanal (Handicraft Market).

AFTER DARK dine, drink and dance on Avenida Aristides Villanueva.

URBAN MYTH

Puente del Inca (Bridge of the Inca), the site of spectacular hot springs a little outside of Mendoza, got its name from this Inca legend. Long before the arrival of the Spanish, a great Inca chief had a paralysed daughter, and all cures had failed her. The king heard that curative waters were located to the south, and without hesitation he collected his best warriors to accompany him and his daughter on the quest. When they arrived at the famous waters, the troop saw that the way was blocked by a torrential river. Out of loyalty to their king, the warriors stretched themselves across the river in a human bridge. The king, carrying his daughter, walked across their backs to the source of the water, and when he turned back to thank his warriors he saw that they had been turned to stone – hence the name.

LIVING HISTORY – TRIBAL INDIANS HAVE EXISTED ON THIS LAND FOR THOUSANDS OF YEARS.
Photographer: Michael Coyne (1)

COLONIAL ARCHITECTURE MAINTAINS ITS STYLE ON THE TREE LINED AVENUES OF MENDOZA.
Photographer: Michael Coyne (2)

BEADS, STRING AND FEATHERED THINGS CATCH THE EYE AT AN OPEN AIR MARKET IN PLAZA INDEPENDECIA.
Photographer: Michael Coyne (3)

MATÉ, A POWERFUL, REJUVENATING TEA, HAS BEEN ENJOYED BY LOCALS FOR CENTURIES.
Photographer: Michael Coyne (4)

Nairobi 135

VITAL STATISTICS

NAME: NAIROBI

NICKNAME: SAFARI CAPITAL OF THE WORLD

DATE OF BIRTH: 1901; AFTER EMERGING AS THE ADMINISTRATIVE CENTRE FOR THE UGANDA RAILWAY, NAIROBI BECAME THE CAPITAL OF THE BRITISH PROTECTORATE

ADDRESS: KENYA (MAP 2, M15)

HEIGHT: 1820M

SIZE: 680 SQ KM

POPULATION: 2.5 MILLION

From a rugged iron-roofed frontier town with rhinos and lions roaming in the streets, Nairobi has, in the last 100 years, emerged as a bustling cosmopolitan city set among the vast wilderness of Africa.

ANATOMY

As the gateway to East Africa, the busy Kenyan capital is surrounded by the breathtaking snowcapped Mt Kenya and the open plains of the Masai Mara National Reserve. This young city, with its ultra-modern skyline and few remaining colonial-era buildings, spreads out from the city centre – where the main touristy sights are located – into the energetic working-class suburbs, the wealthy garden suburbs of expats and the notorious sprawl of shantytowns. Getting around Nairobi is easy, but sometimes treacherous: there are crowded but cheap and plentiful speed-demon *matatus* (shared minibus taxis), trains and frequent buses.

PEOPLE

The population comprises many indigenous tribes, a significant number of expats and an increasing number of refugees from surrounding nations. Besides English (the official language) and the widely spoken Swahili, there are also many ethnic languages. The religious demographics of the population are approximately 35% Protestant, 30% Roman Catholic, 30% Muslim and 5% Animist.

TYPICAL NAIROBIAN

Narobians are largely working-class, even though there are extremely rich and poor elements of the population. They like going out for a drink after work and socialising in cafés, restaurants and clubs. Sport is very popular – especially athletics, golf, rugby and cricket – as are Indian and mainstream movies, and shopping in the malls and markets.

DEFINING EXPERIENCE

Sharing a table with locals while enjoying coffee, cake and a newspaper at the overpopulated Nairobi Java House, then heading *Out of Africa* to wander around the colonial house and gardens of the Karen Blixen Museum before heading down the road to the fashionable pub and stylish restaurant in the Karen Blixen Coffee Garden.

STRENGTHS

- Excellent nightspots and good music scene
- Hot, but not extreme, temperatures (due to the high altitude)
- Air-conditioning
- Westlands Triangle Curios Market
- White-water rafting on the Tana River
- Western luxuries in malls
- Many craft emporiums
- Good selection of restaurants and bars
- Text Book Centre (one of the best bookshops in East Africa)
- Excellent outdoor activities

WEAKNESSES

- Poverty
- Rampant crime (the city is often referred to as Nairobbery by the locals)
- Few laundrettes
- Political instability (and attendant violent demonstrations)
- Ever-present prostitutes
- AIDs epidemic

GOLD STAR

Proximity to Africa's natural wonders – just a few kilometres from the air-conditioned luxury of the city is the species-rich Nairobi National Park, full of famous African beasts, hundreds of species of birds and exotic plant life, while only an hour out of town the thrills and spills of white-water rafting await the adventurous. Trekking and mountain-climbing fun on Mt Kenya (5199m) is also close by – only a couple of hours out of town.

CITYSPEAK

- To use or not use condoms to curb the AIDS epidemic
- What will the rewriting of the constitution amount to?

STARRING ROLE IN...

- *Nowhere in Africa* (2003)
- *Nairobi Affair* (1988)
- *Out of Africa* (1985)
- *Present Moment* by Marjorie Oludhe Magoye

IMPORT

- Indian and Western blockbusters
- Fast-food chains
- International cuisine
- Air-conditioning
- Heaps of expats

EXPORT

- World-champion athletes
- Coffee
- Exotic flora and fauna
- Batteries
- Textiles
- Flour
- Chemicals
- Beer
- Tea

SEE Western blockbusters cheaply in open-air Africa at the Belle-Vue drive-in.

EAT excellent Swahili stews and curries at the Smart Place.

DRINK an ice-cold Tusker on the rooftop of the Wheels Restaurant & Bar.

DO some lion- and rhino-spotting at Nairobi National Park.

WATCH a range of lively African bands at popular bar-restaurant Simmers.

BUY wonderful – albeit pricey – African souvenirs at Kumbu Kumbu.

AFTER DARK join the steamy drinkin' and dancin' mayhem at the bizarre spacecraft-like New Florida, locally known as the 'Mad House'.

URBAN MYTH

While robbing from churches is unfortunately not an uncommon event in Nairobi, one singular tale goes that a middle-aged man received divine retribution when he was killed after accidentally running in front of a bus. At the time he was escaping from the Nairobi All Saints Cathedral after stealing the contents of collection plates.

SHARE A DRINK AT THE LORD DELAMER BAR IN THE NORFOLK HOTEL.
Photographer: Mark Daffey (1)

NAIROBIAN CHILDREN CLAP TO THEIR OWN TUNE.
Photographer: Eric L Wheater (2)

THE CURIOSITY OF YOUTH SPARKS AN UNUSUAL FRIENDSHIP IN THE NAIROBI NATIONAL PARK.
Photographer: David Wall (3)

MAASAI FOR THE MASSES – THIS COLOURFUL JEWELLERY IS POPULAR WITH TOURISTS.
Photographer: Tom Cockrem (4)

PUTTING ON THE FINISHING TOUCHES AT THE CRYSTAL NIGHTCLUB.
Photographer: Stephanie Sinclair (1)

Beirut 136

VITAL STATISTICS

NAME: BEIRUT

NICKNAME: THE PEARL; PARIS OF THE MIDDLE EAST

DATE OF BIRTH: STONE AGE; THE EARLIEST TRACES OF
HUMANS DATE FROM THIS TIME, WHEN BEIRUT WAS TWO
ISLANDS IN THE DELTA OF THE BEIRUT RIVER

ADDRESS: LEBANON (MAP 2, L1)

HEIGHT: 34M

POPULATION: 1.5 MILLION

Beirut is a city of contrasts: beautiful architecture exists alongside concrete eyesores, traditional houses set in jasmine-scented gardens are dwarfed by modern buildings, and swanky new cars vie for right of way with vendor carts.

ANATOMY

Bound north to south by the Mediterranean Sea, the west of Beirut is very hilly, flattening out to the east. The Hamra district in West Beirut is one of the city's hubs, where you'll find the ministry of tourism, major banks, hotels and restaurants. North of Hamra is Ras Beirut, filled with coffee bars and cheap restaurants. The Corniche is the area where Beirutis come to promenade. On the hill to the southeast is the prosperous Achrafiye; here many older buildings are still intact and it is a great place to wander. Most people use service taxis to get around, a huge number of which run like buses on set routes, carrying around five passengers.

PEOPLE

Beirut's population is 60% Muslim and 40% Christian. Ethnic groups comprise Arabs, Palestinians, Kurds and Armenians, and Arabic, French, English and Armenian are spoken.

TYPICAL BEIRUTI

After 15 years of living in a battle zone, the typical Beiruti does their best to forget their troubled past by eating well, dancing and enjoying life, imbuing Beirut with a buzz that is absent from every other city in the region. Warm of heart, it's rare to see any interaction between people that doesn't begin with profuse greetings, inquiries into the other's health and myriad niceties. As an *ajnabi* (foreigner), if you make the effort to come up with the right expression at the appropriate moment, you'll be warmly regarded for it.

DEFINING EXPERIENCE

Exploring the shattered remains of the civil war along the city's former Green Line, experiencing 6000 years of history at the National Museum then watching dusk descend over the Mediterranean at one of the city's many seafront cafés.

STRENGTHS

- The Corniche
- The National Museum
- A city reborn at the Beirut Central District
- Ottoman houses
- American University of Beirut Museum
- Genuine hospitality
- Pigeon Rocks
- Martyrs Statue
- Souq el Barghout
- Seafront cafés
- Vibrant arts scene
- St George Cathedral
- Religious and social diversity

WEAKNESSES

- The political situation is often tumultuous and tense – stay informed
- Land mines outside of Beirut – avoid off-road and unmarked areas
- Oppressive summers
- Wild traffic
- Potholes
- Unlicensed taxis (it is recommended women avoid these at night)
- Lack of street numbers and conflicting street names

GOLD STAR

Optimism – a city well on the mend, visitors to Beirut can see a phoenix-like transformation in progress.

CITYSPEAK

- Ongoing tensions with Israel
- Syria's continued presence in Lebanon

STARRING ROLE IN...

- *The Hills of Adonis* by Colin Thubron
- *A House of Many Mansions* by Kamal Salibi
- *Pity the Nation* by Robert Fisk

IMPORT

- Assorted Muslim and Christian denominations
- A glut of designer stores
- Tourists

EXPORT

- Agriculture
- Banking and finance
- Construction
- (American-Lebanese) Paul Anka and Yasmine Bleethe

SEE modern Lebanese plays in Arabic, French and occasionally English at the Al-Medina Theatre.

EAT a delicious fusion of Eastern and Western cuisines in Casablanca (Rue Ain al-Mraisse), set in one of the few intact Ottoman houses left on the Corniche.

DRINK (if you dare) three whole cups of potent Arabic coffee for the price of one at Modca.

DO peruse the traditional Palestinian embroidery at Al-Badia; the shop has garments handmade by refugee women who benefit from the proceeds.

WATCH horse racing of a Sunday at the Hippodrome, one of the only places in the Middle East where you can legally place a bet.

BUY melt-in-your-mouth baklava and other pastries from Amal al-Bohsali, Beirut's most famous pastry shop for decades.

AFTER DARK be part of Beirut's social mosaic on an evening stroll along the Corniche.

URBAN MYTH

Following the 11 September 2001 attacks, a pro-Palestine Beirut news network, Al-Manar Channel, falsely reported to Lebanon that 4000 Israelis who worked in the World Trade Center did not show up for work that day. The implication was that Israel was somehow responsible for the attack and had provided its nationals with a tip-off. The falsehood is indicative of the continuing tensions in the region.

HEAVENLY RAYS SHOW OFF THE SPLENDOUR OF THE GRAND MOSQUE.
Photographer: Bethune Carmichael (2)

LIVING THE HIGH LIFE AT THE RIVIERA BEACH CLUB.
Photographer: Naftali Hilger (3)

DAY'S END AT THE CORNICHE, BEIRUT'S SEAFRONT.
Photographer: George Georgiou (4)

LOCAL BOYS PRACTICE THEIR MOVES AGAINST THE BACKDROP OF VILNIUS CATHEDRAL.
Photographer: Bruce Yuan-Yue Bi (1)

Vilnius is kooky, mysterious and spooky, a spectacular city with astonishing contrasts: eerie shadowy courtyards, a thriving bohemian community of artists, and beautiful baroque buildings (the Old Town is a World Heritage site).

ANATOMY

The centre of Vilnius is on the south side of the Neris River. Its heart is Katedros aikšatė (Cathedral Sq), with the cathedral on the north side and Gedimino kalnas (Gediminas Hill) rising behind. South of Katedros aikštė are the cobbled Old Town streets *(senamiestis)*; to the west, Gedimino prospektas cuts straight across the newer part of the centre to Parliament. The train and bus stations are beyond the Old Town's southern edge, 1.5km from Katedros aikštė. The city has tourist signs in English and Lithuanian pointing to sites around the Old Town, making it impossible to get lost!

PEOPLE

Lithuania has the most ethnically homogeneous population of the three Baltic countries, with Lithuanians accounting for 81% of inhabitants. About 8% are Russian, 7% Polish and 0.1% Jewish. Lithuanian is the official language, though locals are willing to speak English, German and even Russian (in stark contrast to Latvia and Estonia).

TYPICAL VILNIUS CITIZEN

Living in a self-proclaimed (albeit unofficial) independent republic, the typical Vilnius citizen is spirited, artistic, bohemian, fiercely proud of their bizarre, beautiful and bewitching city, and, as well as being a purveyor of rockin' baroque, is also a committed custodian of the world's only bronze Frank Zappa statue.

DEFINING EXPERIENCE

Cruising the blue lagoon around Trakai Castle in a yacht before getting lost in the cobbled streets of the Old Town and hiking up Gedimino kalnas to the tower for a sublime sunset over the city spires.

Vilnius 137

VITAL STATISTICS

NAME: VILNIUS

DATE OF BIRTH: 1323; WHEN IT WAS FOUNDED BY THE LITHUANIAN DUKE GEDIMINAS

ADDRESS: LITHUANIA (MAP 3, P6)

HEIGHT: 189M

SIZE: 401 SQ KM

POPULATION: 600,000

UNESCO WORLD HERITAGE–LISTED VILNIUS OLD TOWN IS ADMIRED FOR ITS STUNNING GOTHIC ARCHITECTURE.
Photographer: Bruce Yuan-Yue Bi (2)

HUMOUR SIGNALS THE WAY FOR ARTISTS, DRUNKS AND DREAMERS AT THE BORDER OF UZUPIO REPUBLIC.
Photographer: Bruce Yuan-Yue Bi (3)

THE PEOPLE OF VILNIUS ARE PROUD OF THEIR LITHUANIAN HERITAGE.
Photographer: Bruce Yuan-Yue Bi (4)

STRENGTHS
- Baroque Old Town
- World Heritage site status
- Spires of Orthodox and Catholic churches
- Bohemian locals
- Strange bars in dim courtyards
- Narrow cobbled streets
- Gates of Dawn
- Pilies gatvė (Castle St)
- Applied Art Museum
- World's only Frank Zappa statue
- New rail links
- English signage (easy to navigate)
- The artists' Republic of Užupis, the Montmartre of Vilnius
- Ausros Vartu gatvė
- Great sense of humour
- Settling disputes with former neighbours

WEAKNESSES
- Some undercurrents of anti-Semitism
- Accusations of 'cashing in' on dark past eg the Soviet Sculpture theme park at Grūtas
- Uncomfortable KGB jokes
- The older generation's antiquated views of gays and ethnic/minority groups
- Western excesses – burgeoning strip clubs and casinos

GOLD STAR
Chocolate-box baroque – decadent and fragile, bohemian and tough, devilishly attractive Vilnius seduces visitors with its Old Town charm and a warm, wizened soul.

CITYSPEAK
- The controversial restoration of the Jewish Quarter and ghettos
- The relentless brainwaves of whacky mayor Artūras Zuokas

STARRING ROLE IN...
- *Koridorius* (The Corridor, 1995)
- *The Necklace of Wolf's Teeth* (1998)
- *The Book of Sorrow* by Josif Levinson
- *Forest of the Gods* by Balys Sruoga
- *Bohin Manor* by Tadeusz Konwicki
- *The Theology of Rain* by Alfonsas Nyka-Niliūnas

IMPORT
- The ill-fated concept of 'community' bicycles
- Remnants of Soviet-era architecture
- Casinos
- Strip bars
- Entrepreneurial outlook
- Frank Zappa (well, his statue), as a prodigal son
- Tourists
- Other bohemians

EXPORT
- Folk art (particularly carved wooden crosses)
- Jazz
- Pianist Gintautas Abarius
- Saxophonist Petras Vysniauskas
- The Ganelin Trio
- Amber
- Crosses

SEE the treasure-trove of religious jewels on display at the Applied Art Museum.

EAT smoked pigs' ears at Rotis Smuklė while the spit roast turns, no Coca-Cola in sight.

DRINK a 'Neprisikashkopustelaujancho punch' at funky studenty hang-out Mano Kavinė, then try pronouncing it!

DO catch a free performance of the Vilnius String Quartet in the courtyard of Grybas House every Wednesday.

WATCH the sun set over Vilnius' Gothic-steepled skyline from the tower on Gediminas Hill.

BUY pottery bells, woven wicker baskets, wooden toys and painted eggs from the artisan stalls that line the length of Vilnius' Pilies gatvė.

AFTER DARK head to Bix, formed by the eponymous Lithuanian hard-rock band – with an avant-garde industrial décor, it remains a favourite among the city's youngsters and funsters.

URBAN MYTH
According to legend, Vilnius was founded in the 1320s, when Lithuanian grand duke Gediminas, while camping on a hunting trip, dreamt of an iron wolf that howled with the voices of 100 wolves. His interpretation was to build an impregnable city as mighty as their cry. In fact, the site had been occupied at least 1000 years before and may also have been a political and trade centre.

Montevideo

VITAL STATISTICS

NAME: MONTEVIDEO

DATE OF BIRTH: 1726; WHEN THE SPANISH FLEET ESTABLISHED A CITADEL IN THE SHELTERED PORT OF MONTEVIDEO REACTING TO THE BURGEONING PORTUGUESE IN THE RIO DE LA PLATA AREA

ADDRESS: URUGUAY (MAP 1, O21)

HEIGHT: 22M

POPULATION: 1.3 MILLION

A picturesque blend of colonial Spanish, Italian and Art Deco styles paired with superb sandy beaches on the city's outskirts, Montevideo is South America's well-kept secret.

ANATOMY

Lying almost directly east of Buenos Aires on the west bank of the Río de la Plata (River Plate), Montevideo's Ciudad Vieja (Old Town) attracts most visitor attention. The Rambla (riverfront road) rambles eastward past numerous public parks (including Parque Rodó) at the southern end of bulevar Artigas. Well within the city limits are the sandy beaches, a little further east. Montevideo's bus fleet is reliable, but most stop running by 11pm. If you're out late, taxis are safe and on the meter but a little pricey.

PEOPLE

Predominantly white (88%) with 8% mestizo (with mixed Spanish and indigenous blood) and 4% black, Montevideo's population includes many European immigrants, mostly from Spain and Italy. Economic stagnation and political decline in the mid-20th century also saw many rural folk flood into Montevideo's city slums.

TYPICAL MONTEVIDEANOS

A city of lovers (of the arts and big drinking) not fighters (bar-room brawls are rare), Montevideanos pride themselves on being the opposite of the hot-headed Latin-American stereotype. Sunday is family day, a time to throw half a cow on the *asado* (spit roast), sip some maté and stroll along the river.

DEFINING EXPERIENCE

Perusing the opulent furnishings of Montevideo's 19th-century elite at the Museo Romántico, riding the No 64 bus along the riverfront Rambla, then tucking into a seriously sumptuous steak in the Mercado del Puerto.

STRENGTHS

- Historical Ciudad Vieja
- Laid-back atmosphere
- Museo Histórico Nacional
- White sandy beaches
- Mercado del Puerto
- Rich artistic and cultural heritage
- Teatro Solís (superb acoustics and a quality roster of local and international performers)
- Spanish, Art Deco and Italian styles
- The neoclassical Palacio Legislativo (Parliament)

WEAKNESSES

- A throbbing decades-old hangover from economic stagnation
- Dependency on Argentine tourism
- Increasing social divide
- Shabby (not chic) city appearance
- Rising street crime

GOLD STAR

Montevideo's port market, Mercado del Puerto – it was the continent's finest when it opened back in 1868. The impressive wrought-iron superstructure bustles with craftspeople, street musicians, outstanding seafood restaurants and traditional *parrillas* (steakhouses).

CITYSPEAK

- The long rebuild after the 2001 US bans on Uruguayan beef exports (due to the spread of foot and mouth disease)
- The still turbulent economy after the Argentine crisis

STARRING ROLE IN...

- *State of Siege* (1973)
- *Burnt Money* (2000)
- *Between the Moon and Montevideo* (2001)

IMPORT

- The Spanish
- The Italians
- *Candombe* (an African-derived rhythm brought to Uruguay by slaves)
- Argentine holidaymakers

EXPORT

- The football World Cup in 1930 (well, Uruguay were the first-ever hosts and winners)
- Beef
- Writer Juan Carlos Onetti
- Painter Juan Manuel Blanes
- Playwright Mauricio Rosencof
- Tango legend Carlos Gardel
- Software and IT services

SEE the crumbling vestiges of grand 19th-century neoclassical buildings, legacies of the beef boom, in Ciudad Vieja.

EAT obscenely big steaks at *parrillas* inside the Mercado del Puerto.

DRINK *medio y medio* (a knockout blend of local sparkling and white wines) in Bartholomew Mitre, Montevideo's most happening bar precinct.

DO ride bus No 64 along the riverfront Rambla – Montevideo's beaches get better the further you go.

WATCH local football rivals Nacional and Peñarol at Montevideo's Estadio Centenario stadium.

BUY everything from antique knick-knacks to fried fish at Montevideo's sprawling outdoor market, the Feria de Tristán Narvaja.

AFTER DARK whip that rose between your chompers and take on the tango at Fun Fun in the Mercado Central.

URBAN MYTH

Montevideo's full name is San Felipe y Santiago de Montevideo. According to one definition, it's derived from the Portuguese *'Monte vide eu'* (I see a mountain). Another definition is that Spanish cartographers noted the location as *'Monte VI de Este a Oeste'* (The sixth mountain from east to west). Regardless, Montevideo's moniker has something to do with mountains and absolutely nothing to do with that thing that killed the radio star.

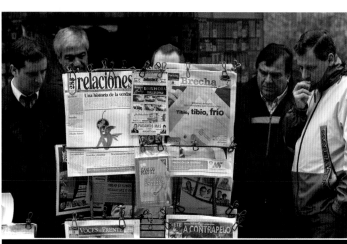

MEN CLUSTER ROUND TO FIND OUT WHAT'S NEWS IN THE CIUDAD VIEJA.
Photographer: Michael Coyne (1)

IT TAKES TWO TO ATTEND CLASSES AT THE JOVEN TANGO (YOUNG TANGO) DANCE SCHOOL.
Photographer: Michael Coyne (2)

A SOLITARY PALM LENDS SOME SHADE TO THOSE WORKING WITHIN THE INDEPENDENCE BUILDING AT PLAZA INDEPENDENCIA.
Photographer: Michael Coyne (3)

WILD AND WET AT THE NEW YEAR WATER FESTIVAL.
Photographer: Alison Wright (1)

Yangon
139

VITAL STATISTICS

NAME: YANGON (FORMERLY RANGOON)

NICKNAME: THE GARDEN CITY OF THE EAST

DATE OF BIRTH: 1755; WHEN KING ALAUNGPAYA CONQUERED CENTRAL MYANMAR AND BUILT A NEW CITY ON THE SITE OF YANGON, WHICH AT THAT TIME WAS KNOWN AS DAGON

ADDRESS: MYANMAR (BURMA)

HEIGHT: 6M

SIZE: 400 SQ KM

POPULATION: 4.5 MILLION

Situated in the fertile delta country of southern Myanmar on the Yangon River, Yangon is a city of golden pagodas, colonial edifices and wide boulevards that come alive at night with hordes of stalls selling delicious food and piles of huge cigars.

ANATOMY

Located in the Irrawaddy Delta, Yangon is a lush paradise in comparison to most of its Southeast Asian counterparts. Central Yangon is easy to navigate. The main streets are set in grids and the best way to plot a course is to flag down a trishaw, walk or catch one of the myriad, albeit unreliable, means of transport. Yangon's battered buses are crowded but colourful.

PEOPLE

By far the majority of Yangon's citizens are Bamar. A small portion of the population is of Shan and even fewer are Karen, Rakhine, Indian, Mon and Chinese. While Buddhists comprise 85% of the population, Muslims, animists and Christians make up the rest of its religions, along with a handful of other indigenous beliefs.

TYPICAL YANGONESE

Deprived of more than a few civil liberties, Yangon's citizens hope for a brighter future when their heroine, Aung San Suu Kyi, is released from a lengthy house arrest and will hopefully bring democracy. The Yangonese are optimistic and it shows in their questions and relaxed conversations.

DEFINING EXPERIENCE

Handling some of the finest lacquerware in the world at the Bogyoke Aung San Market followed by a moment's reflection inside a prayer hall of the Shwedagon Paya, then taking a class in Burmese kick boxing at Yangon University and winding down with a cup of syrupy tea and *mohinga* (a fish-based noodle-soup) in the balmy afternoon at one of Yangon's famous tea shops.

STRENGTHS

⊿ Unspoilt by mass tourism
⊿ Shrines to *nat* (animist spirits)
⊿ British colonial architecture on leafy streets
⊿ Shwedagon Paya
⊿ Tea shops and sickly sweets

WEAKNESSES

⊿ The government
⊿ A virtually nonexistent nightlife
⊿ No ATMs, credit-card or travellers-cheque facilities
⊿ Censorship of the democratic voice
⊿ Ban on foreign films
⊿ Betel nut–spit on the ground
⊿ Soaring HIV rates
⊿ Teak logging

GOLD STAR

Shwedagon Paya, the most sacred of Buddhist sites in Myanmar, is the highlight of a trip to Yangon. Kipling once called it 'a golden mystery…a beautiful winking wonder'. The glittering gold-leaf covered stupa is said to house eight of Buddha's hairs.

CITYSPEAK

⊿ Will Yangon remain deaf to global criticism over slow reforms and the detention of democracy icon Aung San Suu Kyi?
⊿ A greener Yangon: the government challenges developing countries to address urban-environment issues

STARRING ROLE IN...

⊿ *Beyond Rangoon* (1995)
⊿ *Burmese Days* by George Orwell
⊿ *Secret Histories: Finding George Orwell in a Burmese Tea Shop* by Emma Larkin
⊿ *Letters from the East* by Rudyard Kipling
⊿ *True Love* (2005)

IMPORT

⊿ George Orwell
⊿ Hip-hop
⊿ Rudyard Kipling
⊿ Chinese-style buildings
⊿ Martin Sheen
⊿ Cars

EXPORT

⊿ Shan shoulder bags (seen on a Southeast Asian traveller near you)
⊿ Poetry
⊿ The father of modern Burmese art, Aung Myint
⊿ The New Light of Myanmar, the government's English-language mouthpiece
⊿ Gilded marionettes
⊿ Rubies
⊿ Opium

SEE t'ai chi practised at the crack of dawn at Mahabandoola Garden.

EAT *lethouq* – a spicy salad of raw vegetables dressed with lime juice, onions, peanuts, chillies and a variety of spices.

DRINK *lahpeq ye* (tea water) poured from the cup and drunk from the saucer at the Sei Taing Kya Teashop or any one of Yangon's renowned tea shops.

DO have a go at rolling a *cheroot* (like a cigar) and, if you're up for it, try the 2cm-thick variety.

WATCH an impromptu game of *chinlon* (cane ball) on any street at any time of day and watch the players perform gravity-defying pirouettes.

BUY a *longyi* (the Bamar version of the sarong) from the sprawling Bogyoke (Scott) Market.

AFTER DARK wander barefoot along the cool stone floor of the Shwedagon Paya and watch the many-coloured jewels sparkle at its tip.

URBAN MYTH

During the New Year water festival, Thingyan, it's not uncommon to walk around Yangon soaked to the bone after a drenching by a local. The belief is that the water will purify the believer both spiritually and physically for the coming year. Taking it that one step further, the Yangonese may purchase live fish and cows and release them into rivers or sanctuaries on Thingyan Ah-Tet Day (the final day of the festival). For extra karmic points, kids like to wash an old person's hair – you get bonus points if you wash their body as well.

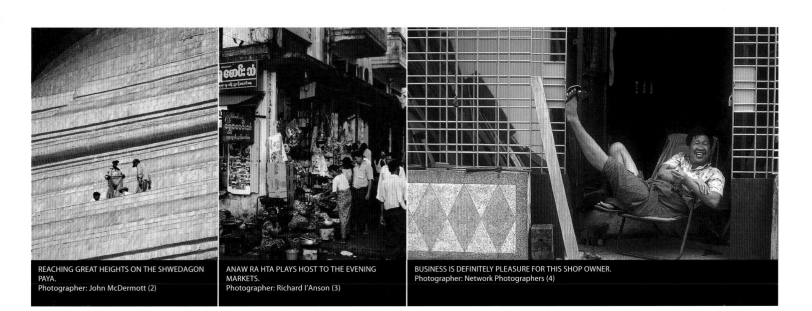

REACHING GREAT HEIGHTS ON THE SHWEDAGON PAYA.
Photographer: John McDermott (2)

ANAW RA HTA PLAYS HOST TO THE EVENING MARKETS.
Photographer: Richard I'Anson (3)

BUSINESS IS DEFINITELY PLEASURE FOR THIS SHOP OWNER.
Photographer: Network Photographers (4)

Arequipa is a one-of-a-kind example of South American life – the lanes, museums, churches and rich culture of the town and its resilient people are resplendent after nearly 500 years of volcanic earthquakes and tumultuous politics.

ANATOMY

At over 2km above sea level, Arequipa nestles in a fertile valley under the perfect cone-shaped volcano of El Misti (5822m). The Río Chili flows around the northern boundary of the town. The city centre is easily navigable as it is based on a colonial checkerboard pattern around Plaza de Armas. Addresses, however, can be confusing, as streets change names every few blocks. Walk, cycle or catch minibuses, buses and taxis to get around the city.

PEOPLE

About half of Arequipa's population is Indian (*indígenas* is an appropriate term; *indios* is insulting). A further 37% of the population is mestizo, 15% is white and the remaining 3% black, Asian or of other backgrounds. As is clear from the many religious buildings and churches, Christianity is the dominant religion and a significant part of daily life. Though the Peruvian constitution allows complete religious freedom, its citizens remain almost exclusively Christian, with 90% identifying themselves as Roman Catholic.

TYPICAL AREQUIPAN

The Arequipans are rugged and proud people, fond of intellectual debate, especially about their fervent political beliefs, which find voice through regular demonstrations in the main plaza. In fact, their stubborn intellectual independence from Lima is so strong that at one time they even designed their own passport and flag.

Arequipa
140

VITAL STATISTICS

NAME: AREQUIPA

NICKNAME: THE WHITE CITY

DATE OF BIRTH: AD 1540; REFOUNDED BY THE SPANISH AT THE SITE OF A PRE-INCAN SETTLEMENT

ADDRESS: PERU (MAP 1, M18)

HEIGHT: 2325M

POPULATION: 750,000

TAXIS PATIENTLY AWAITING THEIR TURN IN THE PLAZA DE ARMAS.
Photographer: Brent Winebrenner (1)

DEFINING EXPERIENCE

Spending the morning exploring the Museo Santuarios Andinos, the home of Juanita, 'the ice princess' and numerous other ice mummies, artefacts and curiosities, then savouring a leisurely lunch of the invigoratingly spicy *rocoto relleno* (hot peppers stuffed with meat, rice and vegetables) at one of the balcony restaurants overlooking Plaza de Armas.

STRENGTHS

- Alpaca knitwear
- *Criollo* cuisine (spicy local fare)
- Ice mummies
- Gateway to El Misti
- Dazzling *sillar* (a light-coloured volcanic rock) stonework
- The nearby Cañón del Colca and its condor residents
- River running the Ríos Chile
- Vibrant locals
- La Catedral
- Stately colonial sillar mansions

WEAKNESSES

- Petty theft
- Volcanoes
- Sparse midweek nightlife
- Animal cruelty (bullfights and cockfights)
- Illegitimate tour rip-offs

GOLD STAR

Tradition – Arequipa is a preserve of the uniquely eclectic Peruvian culture; so much more than a transit stop to the mountains, it has carved its own niche in the South American psyche.

CITYSPEAK

- Workers' rights – especially wages
- The next earthquake

STARRING ROLE IN...

- *Parelisa* (1999)
- *Path to Arequipa* by Mark Jacobi

IMPORT

- Spanish and African culture
- VW kombis
- Indians from Lake Titicaca and the Peruvian highlands
- Mountaineers

EXPORT

- Alpaca textiles
- Leather goods

SEE the astonishing views of Arequipa and Mt Misti flanked by its two siblings, Chachani (6075m) and Pichu Pichu (5571m) from the mirador (observation tower) in the suburb of Yanahuara.

EAT *chupede camarones* (prawn soup) or *chancho al horno* (suckling pig) at the lively Sol de Mayo.

DRINK *chicha* (fermented maize beer) at the tourist mecca Déjà Vu.

DO go on a guided tour of La Catedral, which dominates Plaza de Armas.

WATCH the bullfights, which are not as bloodthirsty or cruel as their Spanish counterparts (the Peruvian way is to pit two bulls against each other for the favour of a female, usually culminating in one making a sensible exit).

BUY a high-quality alpaca sweater from Patio El Ekeko.

AFTER DARK catch the very latest blockbuster movie at Cinessur el Portal.

URBAN MYTH

The Monasterio de Santa Catalina was founded in 1580 by a rich widow, María de Guzmán, who very selectively chose her nuns from the best Spanish families, who paid a hefty dowry for the privilege. Traditionally, the second daughter of upper-class families would enter a nunnery to live in chaste poverty, but in this privileged convent each nun had between one and four servants or slaves, and the nuns would invite musicians, have parties and generally live it up in the style to which they had always been accustomed. After about three centuries of these hedonistic goings-on, the pope sent Sister Josefa Cadena, a strict Dominican nun, to straighten things out. She arrived like a hurricane in 1871 and set about sending all the rich dowries back to Europe and freeing the myriad of servants and slaves, many of whom stayed on as nuns.

THE BLESSEDLY TRANQUIL EXTERIOR OF THE MONASTERIO DE SANTA CATALINA.
Photographer: Brent Winebrenner (2)

STARING PAST STEEPLES AT THE MOUNTAINS FLANKING AREQUIPA.
Photographer: Brent Winebrenner (3)

ALL OUT OF ICE CREAM, TWO VENDORS LUG THEIR PORTABLE MARKETS BACK TO HOME BASE.
Photographer: Brent Winebrenner (4)

Bucharest

VITAL STATISTICS

NAME: BUCHAREST

DATE OF BIRTH: 70 BC; GETO-DACIAN TRIBES INHABITED THE REGION THAT IS NOW MODERN-DAY BUCHAREST

ADDRESS: ROMANIA (MAP 3, Q12)

HEIGHT: 92M

SIZE: 228 SQ KM

POPULATION: 2.3 MILLION

Emerging from a tumultuous and sometimes tragic past, Bucharest is blossoming into one of Eastern Europe's most cosmopolitan cities, where a flourishing music scene and lively nightlife complement the rich historical feel of the city.

ANATOMY

Despite two devastating earthquakes and allied bombings in WWII, much of Bucharest's rich and chequered history is preserved in the blend of neoclassical architecture, Romanian Orthodox churches, Parisian-style parks and the stony-faced buildings of the Communist era, including the monstrous Palace of Parliament. The main attractions cluster in the heart of the city and are easily accessible via Bucharest's transit system – one of the largest in Central and Eastern Europe – which includes buses, trolleybuses, trams and the underground urban railway, the Metro.

PEOPLE

The capital's population mirrors that of the nation and comprises some 90% Romanian citizens, while the remaining 10% is made up of Hungarians, Roma (formerly known as Gypsies), Germans and Ukrainians. The official language is Romanian and the vast majority of the citizens follow the Eastern (Romanian) Orthodox religion.

TYPICAL BUCHAREST CITIZEN

With a low unemployment rate (around 2%) most locals work and, as Bucharest is the least expensive city in Europe, the citizens of the post-Communist capital are also voracious consumers. They love to show-pony the latest-model cars in the streets of the capital, and take great pride in their personal appearance – shopping is an increasingly popular pastime. Etiquette is important, and affectionate public embraces are common. They are both a traditional and dynamic population, with a resilience and optimism born of hard-won freedom.

DEFINING EXPERIENCE

Breathing in the morning air atop the Triumphal Arch, then catching a train to the monastery by Snagov Lake to see the supposed tomb of Dracula before heading back into town to dine with expats on the terrace of the decadent Athénée Palace Hilton, and ending the evening with some sexy dance moves at Cuban club Salsa 2.

STRENGTHS

◢ Live music
◢ Ice-skating on lakes in winter
◢ Greenery of the urban parklands
◢ Low cost of living
◢ Mainstream and art-house cinemas
◢ History round every corner
◢ Variety of pubs, clubs and cafés
◢ Friendly locals
◢ Sailing across Herăstrău Lake in summer
◢ Selection of tasty, hearty local and international cuisine
◢ Local beer and wine
◢ Museum of the Romanian Peasant
◢ Stavropoleos Church
◢ Patriarchal Cathedral
◢ Triumphal Arch

WEAKNESSES

◢ Stray dogs
◢ Daredevil drivers and the worst potholes in Romania
◢ State buses for long-distance travelling
◢ Poorly signposted train stations
◢ Flirty taxi drivers (ladies: take the back seat)
◢ Crowded transit system during peak hour

GOLD STAR

After-dark music scene – whether it's checking out live rock, getting into the traditional sounds, dancing to your favourite '70s tunes, toe-tapping at a jazz bar or a more refined experience with the George Enescu Philharmonic Orchestra, there is something for all tastes in Bucharest. Plugging into the local scene is easy – advertisements posted around the city promote clubs and hot DJs.

CITYSPEAK

◢ Will Romania be accepted into the EU in 2007?
◢ The ongoing political and civic impact of the 2005 flooding across Romania

STARRING ROLE IN...

◢ *Philanthropy* (2002)
◢ *The Wild Dogs* (2002)
◢ *Children Underground* (2000)

IMPORT

◢ Designer clothes
◢ Music from around the world
◢ Cars
◢ Oil
◢ Gas
◢ Greek olives
◢ American poultry and pork
◢ Pot plants
◢ McDonald's
◢ Tobacco
◢ Fruit and vegetables
◢ Machinery

EXPORT

◢ George Enescu's music
◢ Fashion
◢ Wine
◢ Textiles

SEE the crystal chandelier in the decadent Palace of Parliament that weighs 2.5 tonnes.

EAT exquisite French/Thai fusion at Balthazar, the best and hippest restaurant in the city.

DRINK Guinness at the Dubliner as you swap stories with other travellers.

DO head into the residential areas of Bucharest to see the old-style Bucharest housing – before the apartment blocks of Ceauşescu's era.

WATCH some fine jazz acts at the intimate Green Hours 22 Jazz Club Amzei.

BUY a bottle of the famous anti-ageing magic potion – Gerovital face cream – (allegedly used by Elizabeth Taylor and JFK) available at pharmacies.

AFTER DARK soak up the flavour of Romania's cultural scene with a ballet performance at the Opera House.

URBAN MYTH

The myth is that Michael Jackson stood on the balcony of Bucharest's monumental Palace of Parliament and said 'Hello Budapest, I'm so glad to be here' – he actually made the legendary error at Bucharest's National Stadium!

ENJOY A SPOT OF SHOPPING AT THE TRADITIONAL CITY MARKETS.
Photographer: Richard I'Anson (1)

MAGNIFICENT LAKE CISMIGIU PARK IS THE CAPITAL'S OLDEST PUBLIC GARDEN.
Photographer: Richard I'Anson (2)

MUSIC TAKES ON A LIFE OF ITS OWN IN BUCHAREST'S LIVE MUSIC VENUES.
Photographer: Richard I'Anson (3)

PATRIACHAL CATHEDRAL IS THE CENTREPIECE OF THE ROMANIAN ORTHODOX FAITH.
Photographer: Richard I'Anson (4)

Apia 142

VITAL STATISTICS

NAME: APIA

DATE OF BIRTH: 1820S; WHEN THE RESIDENT EUROPEANS ESTABLISHED A SOCIETY IN APIA

ADDRESS: SAMOA (MAP 1, QQ18)

HEIGHT: 2M

SIZE: 1.2 SQ KM

POPULATION: 40,000

TOP BRASS – THE SAMOAN POLICE BAND BELT OUT A MARCHING TUNE.
Photographer: Peter Hendrie (1)

SUBMERGED SIGNPOST AT PALOLO DEEP NATIONAL MARINE RESERVE, A POPULAR SNORKELLING LOCATION.
Photographer: Mark Daffey (2)

THE WELCOMING SMILE OF AN OLDER APIAN.
Photographer: Will Salter (3)

THE COLONIAL GRANDEUR OF ROBERT LOUIS STEVENSON'S METICULOUSLY RESTORED FORMER RESIDENCE.
Photographer: John Borthwick (4)

With its run-down colonial buildings, big old pulu trees and easy-going pace, Apia retains a certain shabby and romantic charm.

ANATOMY

From the centre of town, Apia's neat villages spread west along the level coastal area and climb up the gentle slopes towards the hills and into the valleys. Travelling by public bus is the most common method of getting around. Taxis are also cheap and plentiful.

PEOPLE

The indigenous people of the Samoan islands are large and robust folk of Polynesian origin. Samoans account for 93% of the population and Euronesians 7%. There is a substantial Chinese Samoan community centred in Apia. Most of the Europeans and Asians residing in the country are involved in UN development projects, business investment, or volunteer aid organisations, such as the Peace Corps.

TYPICAL APIAN

Samoans are tradition-oriented and follow closely the social hierarchies, customs and courtesies established long before the arrival of Europeans. They are outwardly friendly and responsive people. The social system can produce as much pressure as it does wellbeing. Beneath the light-heartedness, a strict and demanding code of behaviour is upheld with expectations that can stifle individuality and creativity.

DEFINING EXPERIENCE

Spending a lazy morning exploring the Flea Market and Maketi Fou (main market) and snacking on *palusami* (coconut cream wrapped in taro leaves), visiting the churches along the city's waterfront, then snorkelling the afternoon away at Palolo Deep National Marine Reserve.

STRENGTHS

◢ Laid-back atmosphere
◢ Palolo Deep National Marine Reserve
◢ The Madonna-topped Catholic cathedral
◢ Madd Gallery
◢ Friendly people
◢ Samoan buses, with names such as 'Don't Tell Mum'
◢ The traditional Polynesian feast cooked in an *umu* (above-ground oven)
◢ Samoan *fiafia* (dance performances)
◢ Aggie Grey's Hotel
◢ Tomb of the Tu'imaleali'ifano dynasty

WEAKNESSES

◢ Year-round humidity averaging 80%
◢ Cyclones
◢ Deforestation
◢ Traffic congestion due to lack of town planning
◢ Stray dogs

GOLD STAR

The pace of life – it's so laid-back it's only a heartbeat away from being a nice little snooze.

CITYSPEAK

◢ The encroachment of the reef-wrecking crown-of-thorns starfish
◢ The development of an increasing number of ecofriendly industries

STARRING ROLE IN...

◢ *A Chief in Two Worlds* (1992)
◢ *Island of Lost Souls* (1993)
◢ *Where We Once Belonged* by Sia Figiel
◢ *Leaves of the Banyan Tree* by Albert Wendt

IMPORT

◢ Christian missionaries
◢ Pirates
◢ Robert Louis Stevenson
◢ Foreign aid
◢ Margaret Mead
◢ Tax breaks for foreign manufacturers
◢ Junk food
◢ The Chinese
◢ Rugby
◢ Mormons
◢ Peace Corps members

EXPORT

◢ Coconut products
◢ *Siapo* (bark cloth made from the inner bark of the paper mulberry tree)
◢ Kava
◢ Taro
◢ Writer Sia Figiel
◢ *Fale* (traditional thatched house)
◢ Va'aiga Tuigamala (the 'million dollar man') – the highest-paid rugby union player in the world in the late '90s
◢ Laid-back vibe

SEE Apia from the Mt Vaea Scenic Reserve, where you'll find the beautifully restored home of Robert Louis Stevenson, the botanical gardens and rainforest trails.

EAT a breakfast of Samoan pancakes (more like small doughnuts) washed down with a cup of addictive *koko Samoa* (locally grown cocoa served hot and black with lots of sugar) at the Maketi Fou or the foodstalls behind the Flea Market.

DRINK Independent Samoa's excellent locally brewed lager, Vailima, at the happening Coast Bar & Grill.

DO go snorkelling in Palolo Deep to experience the sudden drop from the shallow reef into a deep blue hole flanked by walls of coral and densely populated by colourful species of fish.

WATCH a spectacular *fiafia* at Aggie Grey's Hotel.

BUY locally made *siapo*, kava bowls and coconut jewellery at the Flea Market.

AFTER DARK see Cindy, the indomitable drag queen of Samoa, who performs at the Hotel Kitano Tusitala every Saturday.

URBAN MYTH

In December 1889 the already famous Scottish author and poet Robert Louis Balfour Stevenson and his wife, Fanny Osborne, arrived in Apia aboard the schooner *Equator*. Stevenson had left Europe in search of relief from worsening tuberculosis and the general sickliness that had plagued him all his life. He was enchanted by Samoa, and in 1890 he paid £200 for 126 hectares of land in the hills above Apia. Stevenson spent four years in Samoa before he died of a stroke. When the Samoan chief Tu'imaleali'ifano spoke of Stevenson's death, he echoed the sentiments of many Samoans: *Talofa e i lo matou Tusitala. Ua tagi le fatu ma le 'ele'ele,'* he said. ('Our beloved Tusitala. The stones and the earth weep'.)

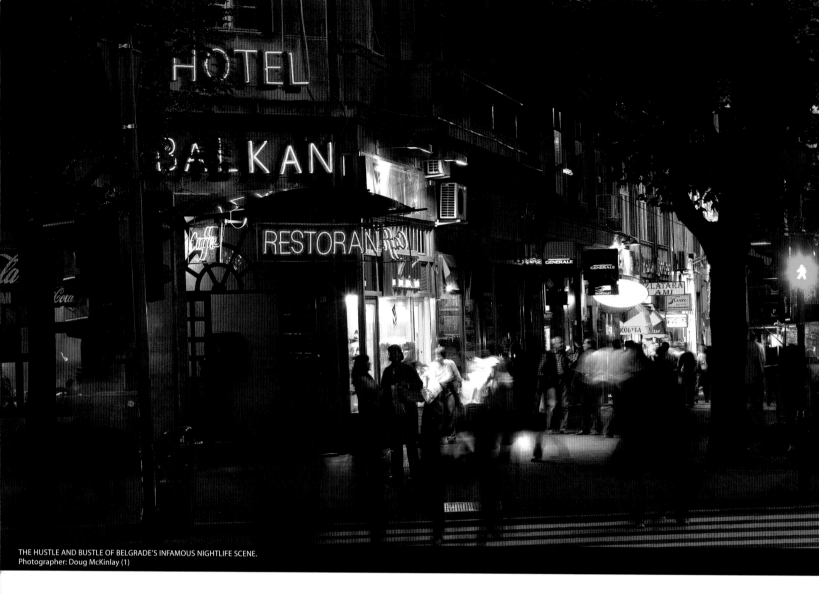

THE HUSTLE AND BUSTLE OF BELGRADE'S INFAMOUS NIGHTLIFE SCENE.
Photographer: Doug McKinlay (1)

With its underground nightlife scene and enchanting above-ground Stari Grad (old town), unpretentious Belgrade is like a dishevelled teenager compared with its slick European cousins, but it's fast reinventing itself.

ANATOMY

Terazije is the heart of modern Belgrade. Knez Mihailova, Belgrade's lively pedestrian boulevard, runs northwest through Stari Grad from Terazije to the Kalemegdan Citadel, which lords over the Sava and Danube Rivers estuary. Buses and a new underground metro train network will get you around town.

PEOPLE

The country is a rich tapestry of ethnicities made up of Serb (63%), Albanian (14%), Montenegrin (6%), Hungarian (3%), Croatian, Romano and Magyar communities, and Belgrade is equally diverse. The official tongue is Serbian.

TYPICAL BELGRADER

Belgraders are a proud, forthright and strong-willed bunch with a melancholic core. Tourists are only now returning to Belgrade and foreign visitors are warmly greeted. In fact, it is not uncommon for Belgraders to offer to show you round their city, and treat a newcomer to family-oriented hospitality, which revolves around eating, football and partying. Hopelessly romantic, Belgraders love to fall in love and then overdramatise it all.

DEFINING EXPERIENCE

Checking out the Kalemegdan Citadel before wandering along vibrant Knez Mihailova, a café-lined pedestrianised boulevard, and chatting with a bunch of curious university types who are likely to warmly welcome you to their student digs for a poetry reading coupled with plenty of *pivo* (beer).

Belgrade
143

VITAL STATISTICS

NAME: BELGRADE

NICKNAME: WHITE CITY

DATE OF BIRTH: 2300 YEARS AGO; SINCE THEN BELGRADE HAS BEEN DESTROYED AND REBUILT 40 TIMES

ADDRESS: SERBIA AND MONTENEGRO (MAP 3, O12)

HEIGHT: 132M

SIZE: 360 SQ KM

POPULATION: 1.58 MILLION

A LADY IN RED PROVIDES ANOTHER SPLASH OF COLOUR TO A GRAFFITIED STAIRWELL.
Photographer: Doug McKinlay (2)

SLOW DESCENT AT THE KALEMEGDAN CITADEL.
Photographer: Doug McKinlay (3)

A MOMENT OF PRAYER AT THE SVETI MARKO CATHEDRAL.
Photographer: Doug McKinlay (4)

STRENGTHS

◢ World-class nightlife
◢ A living history
◢ Go-anywhere bus and train network
◢ Grandiose old buildings
◢ Deli central: melt-in-your-mouth *kajmak* (a salted cream turned to cheese) and delectable grilled meats (*pljeskavica* and *ražnjići*)
◢ Multilingual population
◢ Affordability
◢ Outstanding museums
◢ Polite and gregarious young people
◢ A smorgasbord of fun-filled festivals, from summer jazz to film festivals
◢ Cheap taxi fares
◢ Religious celebrations held in honour of the city saint and protector, Spasovdan

WEAKNESSES

◢ A lingering postwar sadness
◢ US-wannabe gangsters
◢ Daytime traffic congestion
◢ Next to no vegetarian options (they will ask what sickness you're suffering from)
◢ Corbusier-era concrete blocks of New Belgrade

GOLD STAR

The city boasts the kind of effortlessly cool nightlife that promoters the world over can only dream of recreating. Belgraders are happy to dance all night and go straight to work the next day.

CITYSPEAK

◢ Serbian football team line-up
◢ The future of Kosovo
◢ The exodus abroad of Belgrade's talented young professionals
◢ Health and education skills shortage

STARRING ROLE IN...

◢ *The Wounds* (1998)
◢ *Cabaret Balkan* (1998)
◢ *Loving Glances* (2003)
◢ *Underground* (1995)
◢ *Black Lamb & Grey Falcon* by Rebecca West
◢ *Balkan Blues: Writing out of Yugoslavia* edited by Joanna Labon

IMPORT

◢ All things Italian fashion: Gucci, Benneton, Sisley…
◢ All things Italian automotive: Vespa, Alfa Romeo

EXPORT

◢ Monica Seles
◢ Basketball players
◢ Serbian lovers
◢ Baby-soft leather
◢ A medley of berry fruits
◢ Top-notch cheeses
◢ Anything and everything *šlivovitz* (plum), including plum-infused *rakija* (brandy)
◢ Drop-dead gorgeous models
◢ Labour: brainy professionals to do-anything workers

SEE Belgrade's ancient Kalemegdan Citadel.

EAT the famed *burek*, a greasy pie made with *sir* (cheese), *meso* (meat), *krompiruša* (potato) or occasionally *pečurke* (mushrooms), at one of the alfresco cafés along Trg Republike.

DRINK the current apéritif of choice, bittersweet Pelinkovac, at Ben Akiba, a chic and liberal watering hole.

DO saunter along Knez Mihailova, a treasure-trove of historical buildings with great people-watching.

WATCH summer musical, theatrical and cabaret performances at Skadarska – Belgrade's answer to Paris' Montmarte.

BUY something lacy to perk up your table life or hand-knitted woollens from the vendors in Kalemegdan Park.

AFTER DARK dance hands-in-the-air style to Belgrade's very own 'turbo folk' at one of the cities many night-owl haunts, such as Andergraund or Plastic.

URBAN MYTH

Belgrade is the meeting place of two rivers, the Danube and the Sava. Belgraders' love of all things romantic is typified in their belief that the rivers are like lovers whose passion exploded into Belgrade.

Dar es Salaam

144

VITAL STATISTICS

NAME: DAR ES SALAAM

NICKNAME: DAR

DATE OF BIRTH: AD 1866; WHEN THE ARAB SULTAN OF ZANZIBAR SAW THE POTENTIAL OF DAR AS A DEEP WATER PORT

ADDRESS: TANZANIA (MAP 2, M17)

HEIGHT: 14M

SIZE: 165 SQ KM

POPULATION: 2.5 MILLION

A total escape from the big-city hustle, a week in Dar is chilling out on the coast Robinson Crusoe–style with the crystal-green waters, palm-fringed white beaches and coral reefs that frame Tanzania's unofficial capital.

ANATOMY

Dar's city centre, with most of the cheaper hotels and restaurants, is spread out around the harbour. The green and pleasant area around Shaaban Robert St holds foodstalls and hole-in-the-wall cafés, and hotels line Libya St. Suburbs spread out west and north, and a ferry connects the centre with the tranquil southern beaches outside the village of Kigamboni. To the north are resorts and white-sand tropical beaches. Dar's city centre is fairly compact, and if you can stand the relentless heat, you should have no problems getting around on foot. Otherwise, catch city buses, *dalla-dallas* (pick-up or minibus) or taxis, which are everywhere.

PEOPLE

Niney-nine percent of the local population is native African (over 100 tribes), while 1% is made up of Asians, Europeans and Arabs. Kiswahili (Swahili) is the language of Dar es Salaam, though some English is spoken due to the huge influx of expatriates attracted to Dar's beaches. A vibrant Asian population spices up the city and its food, while a Middle Eastern influence is still present here. Around 40% are Christian, with another 40% Muslim, and 20% following indigenous beliefs.

TYPICAL DARIEN

Dariens are open, warm and unfailingly generous. They are predominantly married and very family-oriented. They are as hospitable as they are conservative and might just as easily take you on a hand-held guided tour through the dusty streets as look askance at your piercings and tattoos. Regardless, the word 'welcome' is on every Darien's lips.

DEFINING EXPERIENCE

Sipping spiced tea over a lavish breakfast at Awale Haad restaurant, then heading south to the stunning Kim Beach to alternate swimming and strolling along the white sand before checking out the thriving local hip-hop scene at the latest off-the-beaten-track venue.

STRENGTHS

- Beaches second to none
- Safaris
- Cheap hotels
- The National Museum of Tanzania
- Shaaban Robert St
- International flights
- Plentiful taxis
- Global cuisine
- Chilled-out atmosphere

WEAKNESSES

- Relentless heat
- Horrendously late trains
- The *bhangi* (marijuana) scam
- Muggers

GOLD STAR

Beaches – Dar is blessed with glorious lost-in-a-tropical-paradise beaches just a few kilometres from the city centre.

CITYSPEAK

- The latest cool suburban bar frequented by expats
- Muggings at night

STARRING ROLE IN...

- *Zanzibar* by Giles Foden
- *Uharu Street* by MG Vassanji
- *Dar es Salaam by Night* by Ben Mtobwa

IMPORT

- Western expatriates
- Internet
- French-language films
- Food from around the world
- German, Asian and British architecture
- Beach lovers

EXPORT

- Coffee
- Cotton
- Hides
- Crafts
- Sculpture
- Recycled paper
- Secondhand books
- Safaris

SEE the art exhibitions, witchcraft and ritual items from all over the country at the attractive National Museum of Tanzania.

EAT the famous *mishkaki* (grilled meat) with the locals at Chef's Pride.

DRINK a liquid lunch in the fun beach-front bar at Coco Beach.

DO Gendayeka Beach for a gloriously chilled-out day by the water.

WATCH the local dance and theatre performances on Friday night at Nyerere Cultural Centre & Nyumbaa Ya Sanaa.

BUY sculptures carved from ebony grown in sustainable plantations from the Nyerere Cultural Centre & Nyumbaa Ya Sanaa.

AFTER DARK jump in a taxi heading to the trendy 4Twenty bar at Oyster Bay.

URBAN MYTH

Beware the *bhangi* scam! Several travellers have fallen prey to hustlers in Dar who approach them offering *bhangi*. Whether they say yes or no, within a few minutes they're stopped by two 'undercover policemen' who claim to have caught them in the act of purchasing drugs. They are then asked for a hefty on-the-spot fine to avoid going to the police station and/or jail. This is a hard scam to avoid and a harder one to get out of, as the 'policemen' can sometimes be the real thing doing a bit of hustling on the side. Insist on going to the police station, which will eliminate any fake police, and if you do end up negotiating a 'fine' with some corrupt real police, start low – locals caught like this will get away for around US$20.

THE FLAVOURS OF INDIA HAVE INFUSED THE LOCAL CUISINE.
Photographer: Ariadne Van Zandbergen (1)

A WINDOW FULL OF SWEET SEDUCTIONS ENTICES PASSERS BY.
Photographer: Ariadne Van Zandbergen (2)

INDIAN BUSINESS FINDS ITS NICHE IN DOWNTOWN DAR ES SALAAM.
Photographer: Ariadne Van Zandbergen (3)

THE LIFE OF A FISHERMAN IS NOT ALL HARD WORK AND NO PLAY.
Photographer: Ariadne Van Zandbergen (4)

A TOUCH OF MADNESS HELPS THESE WINTER BATHERS BRAVE THE COLD.
Photographer: Stringer (1)

Kyiv 145

VITAL STATISTICS

NAME: KYIV

NICKNAME: NORTHERN ROME

DATE OF BIRTH: AD 5–6; THE STORY ABOUT THE ORIGINS OF THE CITY ARE DISPUTED, BUT ACCORDING TO OFFICIAL SOVIET HISTORY THE CITY WAS FOUNDED AT THIS TIME

ADDRESS: UKRAINE (MAP 3, S8)

HEIGHT: 179M

SIZE: 780 SQ KM

POPULATION: 2.5 MILLION

This ancient city has undergone a face lift in the wake of the nation's independence around 20 years ago, and modern Kyiv is a fast-paced capital – glamorous, consumerist, cosmopolitan and rich in the treasures of history and culture.

ANATOMY

Situated on the Dnipro River, Kyiv's city centre and old city are on the western bank, while grey residential blocks sit on the eastern bank. The old town lies along the high bank, with the main commercial centre of town sitting behind it. The city's wide boulevards are lined with a curious mix of architecture that reflects the rich historical influences in the capital: plain Stalinist buildings and stunning medieval, baroque, Gothic, Russian and Byzantine monuments and churches. As the main attractions are mostly found beyond the centre of town, the Kyiv Metro is a good way to get around, with river cruises, buses and car hire also available.

PEOPLE

The capital's population is composed of a Ukrainian majority (about 78%), as well as approximately 17% of Russians, and a small percentage of Eastern European immigrants. The majority of the population belongs to one of several national Orthodox churches or to the Russian Orthodox Church, with minority faiths including Roman Catholicism, Judaism and Islam. Ukrainian is the official language, but English is also quite widely spoken in Kyiv.

TYPICAL KYIVAN

The city attracts more than its fair share of wealthy and talented Ukrainians as well as the political elite and stunning fashionistas. These moneyed groups are flashy. They are pushy and don't like to queue. They are fast and frantic and voracious consumers. They love to be seen at the hot clubs, bars and restaurants of Kyiv. They do, however, like the more 'ordinary' people of the city, have strong social connections and are proud of their culture and city.

DEFINING EXPERIENCE

Indulging with a lavish breakfast and jaw-dropping views of Kyiv's golden church domes on the 18th floor of the Premier Palace Hotel, then meeting friends at Independence Sq for some quick shopping before going to see a high-stakes match featuring the resident football team, Dynamo Kyiv.

STRENGTHS

⊿ Culinary capital of Ukraine
⊿ Very cheap food
⊿ Beer considered a soft drink and can be drunk on the streets
⊿ St Andrew's Church
⊿ Caves Monastery
⊿ Street performers during Kyiv Days celebrations
⊿ Mosaics and frescoes at the 11th-century St Sophia Cathedral
⊿ Museum of the Great Patriotic War
⊿ Mariyinsky Palace
⊿ Independence Sq
⊿ Pyrohovo Museum of Folk Architecture
⊿ Street-food kiosks
⊿ River cruises
⊿ Kitsch-themed restaurants
⊿ Wild nightlife
⊿ Shevchenko Opera & Ballet Theatre
⊿ Clean Metro

WEAKNESSES

⊿ Wild traffic
⊿ Swinging glass doors on the metro
⊿ Pushy locals in queues
⊿ Confusing street numbers
⊿ High cost of living
⊿ Covert sex industry

GOLD STAR

Caves Monastery – to Orthodox pilgrims this site is holy land, the holiest in the country, and to all other visitors this place is at the very least something truly spectacular. With the earliest buildings dating from as far back as AD 1051, the monumental monastery is set on grassy hills above the river and clustered with gold-domed churches, fascinating museums and monks' quarters. Underground is an intriguing labyrinth of caves lined with the naturally preserved bodies of monks.

CITYSPEAK

⊿ Ukraine's EU membership quest
⊿ The controversial sales pitch of selling the city of Kyiv via 'sex tours'

STARRING ROLE IN…

⊿ *Mamai* (2003)
⊿ *A Prayer for Hetman Mazepa* (2002)
⊿ *Est-ouest* (East-West, 2000)
⊿ *Defending the Honour of Kyiv* by Andy Dougan
⊿ *The White Guard* by Mikhail Bulgakov

IMPORT

⊿ SUVs and luxury cars
⊿ Catwalk fashion
⊿ Eurovision Song Contest
⊿ Fast-food chains

EXPORT

⊿ Chemicals
⊿ Fur products
⊿ Vodka
⊿ Fashion models
⊿ Machinery and transport equipment
⊿ Vehicle manufacture
⊿ Fuel
⊿ Mail-order brides
⊿ Football stars
⊿ Chicken Kiev (Kyiv)

SEE the mummified monks by candlelight in the underground passages of the Caves Monastery.

EAT traditional Ukrainian food served up in Cossack-themed Kozak Mamay, one of Kyiv's best restaurants.

DRINK 'real coffee' at Kaffa, one of the few cafés that don't just serve instant coffee.

DO meet at the ever-lively and noisy, fountain-filled Independence Sq, the meeting place it seems for every citizen in Kyiv, day or night.

WATCH the 'walruses' (swimmers) wake up to themselves with a winter swim in the freezing Dnipro River.

BUY tasty *Kievsky Tort* (a nutty, layered sponge) at the train-station stalls.

AFTER DARK get into the latest hip-hop and R&B at the glam Tchaikovsky club.

URBAN MYTH

In summer the beaches on the mid-river islands of the Dnipro are packed with thousands of locals and tourists. The river is contaminated to some unknown extent with radioactive silt from Chornobyl, and an enduring urban myth is that the waters are inhabited by a family of huge, mutated crocodiles. While this story is unlikely, it is probably better just to sunbathe than to swim.

STATELY ST MICHAEL'S MONASTERY IS SURE TO LEAVE A LASTING IMPRESSION.
Photographer: Peter William Thornton (2)

MAKING A SPLASH IN THE PARKS OF CENTRAL KYIV.
Photographer: Gleb Garanich (3)

EXTINCT IS FOREVER – SIGNS OF REMEMBRANCE FOR THE MANY TOWNS LOST TO CHORNOBYL.
Photographer: Carol Ann Wiley (4)

Central Asia's holiest city and a place uniquely preserved from pre-Russian Turkistan, Bukhara is a sprawl of truly fascinating Islamic architecture.

ANATOMY

The *shakhristan* (old town) lies at the centre of sprawling modern Bukhara and its streets and squares probably haven't changed much in two centuries. The very centre of the city is the Lyabi-Hauz, a square with a pool in the middle of it (Lyabi-Hauz means 'around the pool' in Tajik) where people congregate for tea and conversation. Buses and taxis service the city.

PEOPLE

Bukhara is primarily Uzbek, but also has significant numbers of Tajiks and other Central Asian ethnic communities.

TYPICAL BUKHARAN

The pride the locals take in their city is hard to overstate. Its recovery in the past decade and a half of Uzbek independence has been quite amazing. Neglected by the Soviet government, for whom the city represented Islam in all its counter-revolutionary glory, the restoration programme initiated since the early 1990s has made the city a highlight of Central Asia. Bukharans are conservative but generally very hospitable and kindly people who are always happy to see visitors in their ancient city.

Bukhara
146

VITAL STATISTICS

NAME: BUKHARA

DATE OF BIRTH: AD 900; WHEN IT WAS THE CAPITAL OF THE SAMANID STATE AND CENTRAL ASIA'S RELIGIOUS AND CULTURAL HEART

ADDRESS: UZBEKISTAN (MAP 1, CC10)

HEIGHT: 230M

POPULATION: 255,000

SHAPING UP – UZBEKISTAN IS A COUNTRY RICH IN SPORTING ACHIEVEMENT.
Photographer: Peter Turnley (1)

DEFINING EXPERIENCE

Drinking tea by the Lyabi-Hauz and having a quiet chat in the shade as you watch the city bustle go on about you.

STRENGTHS

- Fascinating architecture
- The sheer scale and awe-inspiring devotion of the mosques and *medressas* (Islamic academies)
- Extremely open and welcoming attitude to tourists

WEAKNESSES

- Pushy children selling souvenirs and begging
- The extreme heat and dust in summer
- The good restaurants in the old town are block-booked by tour groups for months throughout the summer

GOLD STAR

The Char Minar, the gatehouse of a long-gone Bukhara *medressa* – this is one of the most perfect buildings anywhere in the world, surely?

CITYSPEAK

- The eviction of US forces by Parliament
- Troops firing on demonstrators

STARRING ROLE IN...

- Bukhara has yet to grace the silver screen in any major way, although when a city is as superbly preserved as this, it really only can be a matter of time…

IMPORT

- Tour groups
- Ever-growing numbers of backpackers

EXPORT

- Carpets
- Fruit and veg

SEE the Ark, the royal town-within-a-town, for an insight into how the all-powerful emirs of Bukhara lived.

EAT delicious and cheap *laghman* (noodles) and *samsas* (samosas) at the alfresco teahouses around the old town.

DRINK tea in the blissful quiet of a summer afternoon by the Lyabi-Hauz.

DO climb the astonishing Kalon Minaret for an amazing view – Genghis Khan was so impressed that he didn't destroy it.

WATCH puppetry at the amateur theatre by the Lyabi-Hauz.

BUY jewellery, silk, carpets and trinkets from one of the fabulous bazaars.

AFTER DARK you'll be limited to a belly-dancing show or some beers in one of the few bars of the *shakhristan*.

URBAN MYTH

During the days of the 'Great Game', when the British and Russian empires ground up against each other in Central Asia, a British emissary named Charles Stoddart arrived in Bukhara to placate the emir about Britain's invasion of next-door Afghanistan. However, things didn't quite go to plan: Stoddart quickly offended the emir's vanity (he rode up to the Ark – the emir's palace – rather than dismounting, as protocol dictated) and ended up in the bug pit (the name just about says it all) for three long years. When the British finally got a second emissary to Bukhara to secure Stoddart's release, the emir (apparently offended this time at having had no reply from Queen Victoria, to whom he had written a letter earlier) executed both unfortunates in front of a huge crowd outside the Ark.

IMPRESSIVE ARCHITECTURE INSPIRES SCHOLARS AT MIR I ARAB MEDRESSA.
Photographer: Gavin Hellier (2)

EDUCATING BUKHARA'S YOUNG MINDS.
Photographer: Janet Wishnetsky (3)

THIS ROMANTIC OLD SILK ROAD CITY IS AN IMPORTANT CENTRE FOR ISLAMIC STUDIES.
Photographer: Network Photographers (4)

Male' 147

VITAL STATISTICS

NAME: MALE'

DATE OF BIRTH: 2000 BC; EVIDENCE OF THE EARLIEST SETTLEMENT ON MALE'

ADDRESS: THE MALDIVES (MAP 5, C12)

HEIGHT: 2.1M

SIZE: 2KM

POPULATION: 75,000

ISLAM IS THE DOMINANT RELIGION OF MALE'.
Photographer: Hilarie Kavanagh (1)

The only city in this Indian Ocean archipelago nation, Male' is the transit point for divers and honeymooners: a laid-back stop atop a coral reef.

ANATOMY

Two kilometres long and only one wide, the island is flat but half of it has been reclaimed in the last century as the reef has been filled in with dredged coral to create more land. The atoll is now all filled in, packed to the edges with buildings, roads and a few well-used open spaces, and there's nowhere to go but up – high-rises are growing. Taxis are the way to get around, if not on foot. The increasing number of cars is causing the not unexpected but wholly unwelcome inconvenience of traffic jams. Male' experienced only minor flooding from the tsunami in the Indian Ocean in December 2004. International and domestic flights and boat services around the islands resumed almost immediately after the disaster.

PEOPLE

Male''s citizens are liberal Muslims who until recently had the highest rate of divorce in the world. They start their families at a young age and population growth is quite high, compounded by urbanisation and by Maldivians flocking to the capital for education and work opportunities. A century ago only 5000 people lived on the much smaller land area of Male'.

TYPICAL MALE' CITIZEN

Maldivians make up at least 75% of the city's population. They are laid-back, friendly, sober and accustomed to living in fairly cramped quarters. Other ethnic groups include South Indians, Sinhalese and Arabs.

DEFINING EXPERIENCE

Strolling around the island on Boduthakurufanu Magu, one of the loveliest street names, late in the afternoon, watching a game of football, basketball or maybe cricket, on the manmade sports grounds at the eastern end, then stopping for refreshments at a teahouse.

STRENGTHS

- The *dhoni* (a traditional all-purpose vessel now usually powered by a diesel engine) ride from the Male' airport island, Hulhule
- The gold-domed Grand Friday Miskiiy (mosque)
- The coral-stone–walled Hukuru Miskiiy, which dates from 1656
- Curious street names rather than numbers – watch for Crabtree, Sweet Rose, Sun Dance, the grand River Nile, the strange Ozone or even Aston Villa
- The Artificial Beach built on reclaimed land at the eastern end of the island

WEAKNESSES

- Traffic
- No alcohol

GOLD STAR

The Hukuru Miskiiy (Old Friday Mosque), which dates from 1656. Its walls, built with coral stones, are intricately carved with Arabic writings, ornamental patterns and expert lacquer works, especially in the domes.

CITYSPEAK

- Should we move to a newly created residential island, as close as a 15-minute *dhoni* ride away, or not?
- When will the tourists come back?
- Is democratic reform on the cards?

STARRING ROLE IN...

- *The Strode Venturer* by Hammond Innes

IMPORT

- Land reclamation
- Tourists
- Motor vehicles
- Almost all food other than fish
- Aid workers

EXPORT

- Happy honeymooners
- Bronzed holidaymakers

SEE the rounded corners of walls and buildings so vehicles can negotiate tight corners more easily.

EAT *hedhikaa* (short eats) – a selection of sweet and savoury counter items including rice pudding, tiny bananas, curried fish cakes and frittered dough balls, which are usually fishy and mostly spicy.

DRINK *raa*, the local brew, a sweet and delicious toddy tapped from the crown of the palm-tree trunk.

DO dive to the wreck of the *Maldive Victory*, with its wheelhouse underwater at around 15m and propeller at 35m.

WATCH football or cricket at the National Stadium.

BUY fine-woven *kunaa* (mats) with elegant, abstract geometric patterns and subdued natural colouring.

AFTER DARK catch a movie or hang out in a tea shop.

URBAN MYTH

The accent in the city's name isn't an 'e' acute, although pronunciation would suggest it. Pronounced *Mah*-leh, the most common local spelling has an apostrophe following the 'e' – a contraction of the name of an early dynasty, Malei. It is often assumed the apostrophe was used because there was no acute accent on the old English typewriter; however, even with modern software, local publishers still prefer the apostrophe ending.

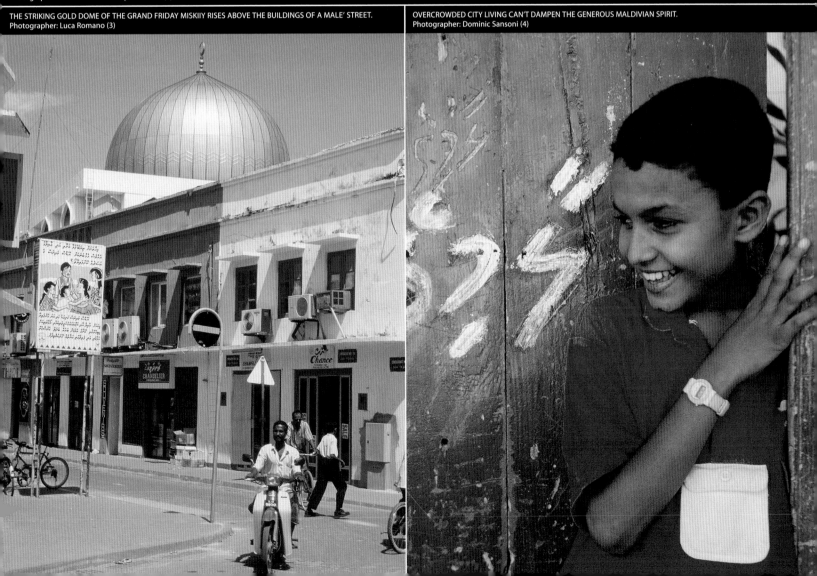

LOCALS WATCH THE SUN BID A FLASHY FAREWELL TO THE DAY.
Photographer: Anuruddha Lokuhapuarachchi (2)

THE STRIKING GOLD DOME OF THE GRAND FRIDAY MISKIIY RISES ABOVE THE BUILDINGS OF A MALE' STREET.
Photographer: Luca Romano (3)

OVERCROWDED CITY LIVING CAN'T DAMPEN THE GENEROUS MALDIVIAN SPIRIT.
Photographer: Dominic Sansoni (4)

Caracas

148

VITAL STATISTICS

NAME: CARACAS

DATE OF BIRTH: 1560; WHEN EXPLORER FRANCISCO FAJARDO FOUNDED A SETTLEMENT, WHICH HE CALLED SAN FRANCISCO

ADDRESS: VENEZUELA (MAP 4, N8)

HEIGHT: 1042M

SIZE: 78 SQ KM

POPULATION: 4.6 MILLION

The capital of Venezuela is a huge, vibrant, energetic South American city, bringing together the tremendously wealthy and the desperately poor.

ANATOMY

Caracas sprawls for 20km along a long and narrow coastal valley, bordered to the north by the verdant and refreshingly unpopulated Parque Nacional El Ávila. To the south it's quite a different story, with modern suburbs and precariously poised shantytowns invading the steep hillsides. The city's pride and joy, the metro, is fast, easy, well organised, clean and cheap. Caracas' bus system isn't bad either, covering all suburbs within the metropolitan area as well as major neighbouring localities.

PEOPLE

About 70% of the population is a blend of European, Indian and African ancestry, or any two of the three. The rest are whites (about 20%), blacks (8%) and Indians (2%). Spanish is the official language.

TYPICAL CARAQUEÑO

An estimated 75% of *caraqueño* families live below the poverty line. It's common for haphazardly built barrios (shantytowns) to sit directly alongside opulent hillside mansions. Despite this, everyday life is remarkably open and public and often takes place outside the home. People may dance to the tune of the car stereo in the street or drink a leisurely beer together on the sidewalk curb. Personal affairs are discussed loudly and without embarrassment. Of central importance to *caraqueños* is the family, and especially the mother figure. Young *caraqueños* almost always live with their families until they are married.

DEFINING EXPERIENCE

Strolling around the green haven of Parque del Este, before heading to the gastronomic hub of Las Mercedes, then chilling out at the 200-year-old coffee hacienda at La Estancia and finishing the day at the ultra-cool nightclub Loft, with the cream of suave, young *caraqueños*.

STRENGTHS

- The *teleférico* (cable car) to the summit of El Ávila
- Bars and clubs of Las Mercedes and La Castellana
- Winding streets of El Hatillo
- Museo de Arte Contemporáneo and Museo de Arte Colonial
- Cuisine scene of Las Mercedes, Altamira and La Candelaria
- Tomb of national treasure Simón Bolívar in the Panteón Nacional
- The steep, wooded slopes of Parque Nacional El Ávila, where miles of walking trails wind through scented forests
- Vibrant arts scene
- Mosaics and murals gracing the streets
- Salsa aficionados

WEAKNESSES

- Barrios
- Poverty
- Petty crime
- Pollution
- Bulldozing the past
- Traffic jams
- Political instability

GOLD STAR

The bright lights of Caracas' stylish nightlife – there are myriad opportunities for clubbers, bar-hoppers and live salsa aficionados to mingle with the city's famously die-hard party crowd

CITYSPEAK

- Will plans go ahead to develop nuclear technology for the medical, industrial and oil sectors with the possible cooperation of Iran?
- Where is this week's strike?

STARRING ROLE IN...

- *Shoot to Kill* (1991)
- *Sicario* (1995)
- *Little Thieves, Big Thieves* (1998)
- *Huelepega* (1999)
- *Pais Portatil* (Portable Country) by Adriano González León

IMPORT

- *Telenovelas* (soap operas)
- US cars
- The latest gadgets
- *Béisbol* (baseball)
- Salsa
- Multiculturalism
- Corrida (bullfighting)
- Shopping malls
- Plastic surgery

EXPORT

- Machismo
- Oil
- Miss World winners
- Simón Bolívar
- Papillon

SEE the Capitolio Nacional (National Capitol) with its golden domes, neoclassical pediments and, most famously, its Salón Elíptico, an oval hall with a mural-covered dome and walls lined with portraits of the country's great and good.

EAT delicious seafood dishes at the decorative *tasca* (Spanish-style bar-restaurant) La Castañuela.

DRINK excellent, strong espresso coffee at Gran Café – an open-air café right in the thick of a bustling street market, alive with sharp-eyed urchins and energetic haggling.

DO take a trip up El Ávila mountain on the newly reconstructed *teleférico*.

WATCH a *béisbol* game at the Estadio de Béisbol on the grounds of the Universidad Central de Venezuela.

BUY hammocks, papier-mâché devil masks or stuffed piranhas at the biggest craft shop of them all at Hannsi in El Hatillo.

AFTER DARK head to the hedonistic clubs of Caracas and bear testament to the *caraqueños'* religious devotion to having a good time.

URBAN MYTH

Remember the story that Caracas has the highest female–male ratio in the world? Well the ratio is only 10:9, and that difference is in the over 50s. Sorry boys!

THE URBAN JUMBLE OF CARACAS FLOWS ALONG THE CONTOURS OF THIS NARROW, FORESTED VALLEY.
Photographer: Zigy Kaluzny (1)

SLAM DUNK! THE COMPETITION HEATS UP ON THIS FRIENDLY GAME OF BASKETBALL.
Photographer: Henry Horenstein (2)

SHOPPING FOR YOUR DOLLAR ON THE BOULEVARD DE SABANA GRANDE.
Photographer: Krzysztof Dydynski (3)

ESCAPING THE SUN FOR A LONG GAME OF CHESS IS A FAVOURITE PASTIME.
Photographer: Pablo Corral Vega (4)

Tirana

149

VITAL STATISTICS

NAME: TIRANA

DATE OF BIRTH: 1614; WHEN THE CITY WAS FOUNDED BY A TURKISH PASHA

ADDRESS: ALBANIA (MAP 3, N14)

HEIGHT: 89M

SIZE: 41 SQ KM

POPULATION: 550,00

ENJOYING SUNSHINE AND GOSSIP IN THE BLLOKU AREA, FORMERLY THE DOMAIN OF THE COMMUNIST ELITE BUT NOW A PLAYGROUND FOR THE URBAN HIP.
Photographer: Doug McKinlay (1)

BRIGHT, NEWLY CONSTRUCTED BUILDINGS ARE BEGINNING TO PUSH STALINIST GREY OUT OF THE CAPITAL.
Photographer: Doug McKinlay (2)

THE INSPIRING ET'HEM BEY MOSQUE, SHESHI SKËNDERBEG.
Photographer: Doug McKinlay (3)

LACK OF URBAN INFRASTRUCTURE MEANS THAT SOME PEOPLE STILL RELY ON COMMUNAL WATER SUPPLIES.
Photographer: Doug McKinlay (4)

The proud and plucky capital of Albania is charming and surprising, with colonial Italian villas interspersed with monolithic Communist-era structures and traditional Turkish mosques.

ANATOMY

The tiny Lana River is little more than a stream that runs unobtrusively through the city, barely noticed by most people. The central square is the busy Sheshi Skënderbeg (Skënderbeg Sq) from where streets radiate like spokes on a wheel. The city's main street, Bulveardi Dëshmorët e Kombit (Blvd of Heroes and Martyrs) runs from here to Tirana University, hiding ministries and hotels behind its plentiful trees. Near here is the Blloku – once the closed-off residential area of Tirana's Communist elite and now the trendy bar and nightclub quarter. Crowded city buses operate in Tirana.

PEOPLE

Traditionally Tirana has been almost entirely Albanian, particularly as foreigners were almost barred from even visiting until the end of communism in 1990. Since then, though Tirana has been swamped by a succession of outsiders. First came ethnic Albanian refugees from the conflict in Kosovo and second the waves of aid workers and military peacekeepers who used Tirana as a base in the aftermath of the crisis created. Both have had a large influence on what was in many ways a total backwater and – for better or worse – have contributed to the rapid modernisation and Westernisation of Tirana.

TYPICAL TIRANA CITIZEN

Tirana continues to breed surprisingly conservative people – although this is doubtlessly changing. The influence of both Muslim and Christian mores and the later wave of extremist Stalinism since the end of WWII has had an effect, and while being exceptionally kind and friendly, Tirana's residents are far more easily shocked than their cousins in other European capitals.

DEFINING EXPERIENCE

Wandering the pleasant tree-lined avenues on a summer evening when everyone's out for their evening stroll, and soaking up the charming atmosphere of this friendliest of European capitals.

STRENGTHS

- Compact city
- Undiscovered by the tourist hoards
- A great base for exploring this totally overlooked European country

WEAKNESSES

- Still a large amount of poverty despite the progress
- Litter is a huge problem – civic pride is still something that very few people attach importance to
- Plenty of petty crime
- Gaping potholes in the streets to twist ankles

GOLD STAR

Mt Dajti, the mountain overlooking the city, has some beautiful walking and great spots for weekenders leaving the heat of the capital for more alpine climes.

CITYSPEAK

- The latest drive to improve the city's appearance from popular and controversial mayor Edi Rama
- The economic nose dive and ever-remote possibility of joining the EU
- Rumours of the slightest ethnic unrest in Kosovo

STARRING ROLE IN...

- *Slogans* (2001)

IMPORT

- Foreign aid workers
- Refugees from Kosovo

EXPORT

- Fruit and vegetables
- Natural gas
- Oil

SEE the impressive Et'hem Bey Mosque – one of the few religious buildings in the city to survive the Hoxha dictatorship.

EAT pretty much anything you want in Tirana's ever-evolving restaurant scene.

DRINK Albanian *rakia* (similar to cognac) if you want a truly rough hangover.

DO make an effort to visit Kruja, the pleasant mountain town a short trip out of Tirana, for an insight into the Albanian struggle for independence.

WATCH the nightly processions of Skënderbeg Sq as the entire city takes an evening stroll during the summer months.

BUY anything and everything emblazoned with the impressive Albanian flag – this is one proud country.

AFTER DARK head to the Blloku area for bar-hopping, outdoor cocktails or a boogie at the latest nightspot.

URBAN MYTH

So paranoid was former dictator Enver Hoxha that he found a man who looked just like him and sent him regularly to stand in for him at public events, convinced that he was going to be assassinated at any moment. When Hoxha finally died and communism was overthrown a few years later, the doppelgänger was greeted by such terror from everyone he met who thought the dictator had come back to life, that he went mad and cut off his own face. Nice.

Suva 150

VITAL STATISTICS

NAME: SUVA

DATE OF BIRTH: 1882; WHEN THE FORMER CAPITAL, LEVUKA, WAS DEEMED TOO SMALL BY THE BRITISH COLONIALISTS

ADDRESS: FIJI (MAP 1, PP18)

HEIGHT: 6M

SIZE: 15 SQ KM

POPULATION: 358,495

An island city with a young cosmopolitan edge, Suva is charmingly laid-back yet tainted by some of the trappings of Western society; however, the mix of Fijian and Indo-Fijian cultures, a beautiful landscape and a generous people outweigh these pitfalls.

ANATOMY

A lush and bustling port on the island of Viti Levu, Suva is Fiji's political and administrative centre. Suva houses the University of the South Pacific; the fascinating Fiji museum; Fiji's tallest building, the Reserve Bank of Fiji; and interesting colonial-era buildings. Much of Suva's city centre was built on former mangrove swamps. Express buses run from Suva to major cities and towns, and local buses stop at every village they pass. For island-hopping, ferries are cheap, frequent and reliable.

PEOPLE

Suva is an interesting blend of Melanesian, Polynesian, Micronesian, Indian, Chinese and European cultures. Of these groups, 50% are indigenous Fijian and 45% are Indo-Fijian. The population is predominantly Christian (53%); other religious groups include Hindus (38%), Muslims (8%) and Sikhs (1%). The official language is English, with Fijian and Hindi widely spoken.

TYPICAL SUVA CITIZEN

Savvy, good-humoured and proud, Suva's citizens have held onto their traditional rights and practices, including *meke* (traditional dance), *bure* (house construction), *kava* ceremonies, tapa-cloth making and pottery. Most citizens are young: about half of the Fijian population is under 20, with about two-thirds aged under 30.

DEFINING EXPERIENCE

Listening to uplifting Sunday gospel Fijian-style at a local church, hitting the markets for tropical fruit, vegetables, kava, saris and handicrafts, and later, marvelling at the collection of curious cannibal curios at the Fiji Museum.

STRENGTHS

- 'Bula!' (Cheers!) with a smile
- Easy to navigate on foot (daytime only)
- Cheap local buses
- The Government Craft Centre
- Suva Municipal Market
- Victoria Pde on a Friday or Saturday night
- Colo-i-Suva Forest Park
- Hole-in-the-wall curry joints
- Hibiscus Festival (August)
- Dawali, the Hindu festival of lights (October/November)
- Surf-break near Suva lighthouse
- Trips to Bega Lagoon

WEAKNESSES

- Racial strife
- Political and economic uncertainty
- Turtle meat and turtle shells freely available at Suva market
- Polluted waters around Suva
- Skyrocketing youth unemployment
- Pickpockets
- Changeable and inclement weather

GOLD STAR

Suva Municipal Market – *the* place to buy kava and local delicacies, as vendors jostle to sell exotic fruit and vegetables, *nama* (seaweed), multicoloured fish, bound crabs, pungent spices and neon Indian sweets.

CITYSPEAK

- Indigenous Fijian landowners turfing Indo-Fijian farmers off property where their families have toiled for generations, rendering them homeless
- Youth unemployment (only one in eight school-leavers finds a job)

STARRING ROLE IN...

- *Blue Lagoon* (1979)
- *Contact* (1997)
- *Cast Away* (2000)
- *Anacondas: The Hunt for the Blood Orchid* (2004)

IMPORT

- Tourist-fuelled water sports
- Tourists
- Indian cultures
- Western TV and youth culture
- Foreign aid/debt
- Cane toads

EXPORT

- Golfer Vijay Singh
- Sugar
- Molasses
- Gold
- Trochus-shell buttons
- Timber
- Fish
- Ginger
- Coconuts and coconut oil
- A skilled and educated workforce
- Forest woodchips
- Sawn timber
- Clothing
- The *bure*-look hut (adopted by chichi Western island resorts)

SEE glorious views of Suva and its surrounds from Mt Korobaba.

EAT scrumptious seafood at one of Suva's most atmospheric nosheries, Tiko's Floating restaurant, anchored at the sea wall across from Ratu Sukuna Park.

DRINK delicious fruit concoctions from the glass tanks at the Suva Municipal Market.

DO experience a touch of the Indiana Jones with rope swings and stone steps across streams and three natural swimming holes in the Colo-i-Suva Forest Park.

WATCH a game of rugby (and the fervent spectators!) at Suva's National Stadium.

BUY exquisite souvenirs from the Government Craft Centre and support rural artisans.

AFTER DARK shake your groove thang at one of the many establishments on Victoria Pde.

URBAN MYTH

In 1842, 'exotic' Fiji was thrust into the world's spotlight courtesy of an elaborate hoax, the 'Fejee Mermaid'. The mermaid 'skeleton' displayed in New York's American Museum was purportedly discovered by Japanese fishermen in the Fiji islands. However, this sea-faring beauty was in fact cobbled together by American showman PT Barnum using fish parts, the torso of a baby orang-utan and a monkey's head. After two decades of touring America, the Fejee Mermaid was destroyed by fire in 1865.

FRESH LOCAL PRODUCE IS AVAILABLE AT SUVA MUNICIPAL MARKET.
Photographer: Peter Solness (1)

LISTENING TO A SUNDAY GOSPEL CHOIR IS AN UPLIFTING EVENT.
Photographer: Peter Solness (2)

LIVELY TEAROOMS ARE POPULAR WITH THE LOCALS.
Photographer: Peter Solness (3)

SHOOTING THE BREEZE ON A LOCAL BUS.
Photographer: Peter Solness (4)

STUNNINGLY BEAUTIFUL, TBILISI IS A CITY OF MYSTERY AND ENCHANTMENT.
Photographer: Stephane Victor (1)

Hands down the most beautiful city in the Caucasus, the mysterious and historic Georgian capital enchants with its beautiful old town, dramatic cliff-side setting and wealth of historic churches.

ANATOMY

A long, slim city built into the gorge of the Mtkvari River, Tbilisi is eminently manageable on foot. The right bank of the river is home to the charming old town, the sulphur baths and the dramatic *Mother Georgia* monument, while the more modern left bank is perched on a clifftop giving stunning views of the old town. An efficient Soviet-built metro system connects the city to the suburbs.

PEOPLE

The cultural centre of Georgia, Tbilisi is excessively cosmopolitan, with large Russian, Armenian, Azeri and Jewish minorities all living peacefully side by side. Most people speak both Russian and Georgian, and often more languages on top of that.

TYPICAL TBILISIAN

Just as likely to speak Russian as Georgian, your typical resident of this city is a hardened cynic, having lived through a turbulent two decades and seen pretty much everything in that time, from food shortages and starvation to civil war and mass protest. Used to days without electricity, running water and gas, they never lose their sense of humour about the post-Communist chaos into which Georgia was plunged under former president Eduard Shevardnadze. Things might be looking better today under pro-US President Mikhail Saakashvili, but locals still need to be convinced.

Tbilisi 151

VITAL STATISTICS

NAME: TBILISI

DATE OF BIRTH: NEOLITHIC PERIOD; ALTHOUGH LOCALS LIKE TO BELIEVE IT WAS FOUNDED IN THE 5TH CENTURY, ACCORDING TO A MUCH-LOVED LOCAL LEGEND

ADDRESS: GEORGIA (MAP 3, Y14)

HEIGHT: 490M

SIZE: 140 SQ KM

POPULATION: 1.7 MILLION

BUILDING A BETTER FUTURE – TBLISIANS HAVE LIVED THROUGH A TURBULENT PAST.
Photographer: Stephane Victor (2)

FOOD FOR THOUGHT – WELL, THE BREAD'S GOT TO GET THERE SOMEHOW!
Photographer: Stephane Victor (3)

KEEPING THE FAITH AT ST MARY'S DAY PRAYERS.
Photographer: Stephane Victor (4)

DEFINING EXPERIENCE

Having an invigorating bath and massage at the famous Tbilisi sulphur baths (where Pushkin and Dumas both took the waters), then a bracing walk up to *Mother Georgia*, the vast metallic lady who overlooks the city, and the fascinating Narikala Fortress, before finding the way back down through the old town, checking out some of the beautiful churches and then settling on a traditional Georgian restaurant for the full Georgian culinary experience.

STRENGTHS

- Food, oh! the food…
- Decent wines
- Kind people
- Sioni Cathedral Church, dating from the 5th century
- Ancient Narikhala fortress
- Famous and long-established theatres
- Paliashvili Opera House
- Gorgeous architecture
- Fascinating history

WEAKNESSES

- Petty crime
- Unique alphabet that makes getting around rather tough
- Steep hills that make walking hard work
- Street muggings
- Potential instability

GOLD STAR

Dominating the city skyline (until the TV tower came along, anyway), the Narikala Fortress is an ancient symbol of Tbilisi's defensive brilliance. Its walls date from various periods, the earliest being the 4th-century Persian citadel. The tower foundations and much of the present walls were built on the orders of the Arab emirs in the 8th century.

CITYSPEAK

- How is Saakashvili doing? Is he definitely better than Shevardnadze?
- The building spree in the city and shady financiers behind it
- The Russians still haven't left Georgia, and now there are already American troops here…

STARRING ROLE IN…

- *Since Otar Left* (2003)

IMPORT

- Electricity
- Gas
- Mercedes Jeeps
- American-trained lawyers (who become president)

EXPORT

- Wine
- Stalin
- Polyphonic singing
- Aubergines
- Kate Melua

SEE the astonishing collection at the Treasury of the Janashia State Museum of Georgia.

EAT as much as you can – try a full Georgian feast at Dzveli Sakhli.

DRINK some of the country's wine – Saperavi tends to get the best reaction from visitors with a Western palate.

DO take a day trip to nearby religious centre Mtskheta.

WATCH a show at the beautifully ornate Paliashvili Opera House, founded in 1851.

BUY *cha cha* (Georgian firewater) from the market if you want a memorable introduction to Tbilisi.

AFTER DARK head down to Akhvlediani kucha for the late-night bars.

URBAN MYTH

Despite a history of settlement in the area stretching back to Neolithic times, Georgians prefer the legend of King Gorgasali, who remains honoured as a saintlike figure today, and is said to have founded Tbilisi in the 5th century. The legend runs that the king was hunting (either for deer or pheasant, depending on whom you believe) and that either the pheasant fell into a hot sulphur spring and was conveniently cooked for dinner, or that the wounded deer fell into the hot sulphur spring and was miraculously healed. Either way, the name 'Tbilisi' derives from the Georgian word *tbili* (warm), and there seems to be little doubt that it was the magnificent hot springs, which still lure visitors today, that attracted the king.

Agadez

VITAL STATISTICS

NAME: AGADEZ

DATE OF BIRTH: AD 1100; STEMMING FROM ITS PRIME LOCATION ON THE TRANS-SAHARAN CARAVAN ROUTES

ADDRESS: NIGER (MAP 2, C8)

HEIGHT: 529M

POPULATION: 122,000

Niger's premier ancient city, Agadez offers the romance of the Sahara and the allure of exotic mud minarets, swarming markets and nomadic culture.

ANATOMY

In Niger's central west sits Agadez. The centre of the city is taken up by the extraordinary Grande Mosquée, which affords spectacular views over the town and the surrounding desert. From here you can see the Old Town (Vieux Quartier) and to the south lies the main focus of town life – the Grand Marché (the main market). Head west for a good price on a camel or just to absorb the sights and sounds of the Tuareg Camel Market. Rising out of the Sahara to the north are the majestic Aïr Mountains, dotted with hospitable Tuareg villages, lush valleys and enough rough terrain to delight any budding mountaineer. A motley selection of minibuses, *taxis-brousses* (bush taxis) and Toyota 4WDs service the city's public-transport needs.

PEOPLE

The small but active nomadic Tuareg population has strong roots in and around Agadez, emerging from outlying areas to do business with the Hausa traders from the south at the city's Grand Marché. Pastoral populations such as the well-known Wodaabe also live in areas west of Agadez. Although French is the official language, some tribal languages are also spoken. Muslim dress is taken very seriously by Agadezers, and foreign women in particular should wear modest clothing.

TYPICAL AGADEZER

Agadezers are friendly and lively and are eager for tourism to take off in their city. They are traders, farmers and marketers – nomadic and agricultural. They are festive and as such, festivals thrive in Agadez. While they hold religion dear to their hearts and are Muslim in dress and belief, they readily indulge their liking for drinking, gambling and sport. The national obsessions of *la lutte traditionelle* (traditional wrestling) and table football are alive, well and flourishing thanks to Agadezers.

DEFINING EXPERIENCE

Wandering the labyrinth of narrow alleyways between the traditional single-storey *banco* (mud-brick) buildings of the Old Town to the small night market opposite Place de la Fraternité to eat and watch the bustle of the medicine men, foodstalls and people while contemplating a game of table football or another brochette.

STRENGTHS

- Camel markets
- Desert trips
- The nearby Aïr Mountains
- Ténéré Desert
- Camping
- Plentiful festivals and festivities
- Sealed roads going out and in
- Mud-brick architecture
- Grande Mosquée
- The Old Town
- Table football

WEAKNESSES

- Agadez airport
- Fierce competition (for the tourist dollar)
- The distinct lack of beer
- Occasional scams, thievery and armed hold-ups
- Requests for a *cadeau* ('gift' or bribe)

GOLD STAR

The Grande Mosquée – standing in the centre of Agadez, this stunning mosque is for many people the single most definitive image of Niger.

CITYSPEAK

- The reopening of Agadez airport
- *La lutte traditionelle* (traditional wrestling) – always a hot topic
- Tourism – on the increase or decrease?

STARRING ROLE IN...

- *The Sheltering Sky* (1990)
- *Agadez* by Jonathan Bennet
- *Seven Words for Sand* by Allen Serafino

IMPORT

- Camels
- Tour groups
- Internet
- French and Middle Eastern cuisine
- Imported beer

EXPORT

- Camels
- Tour guides
- *Croix d'Agadez* (traditional Tuareg currency)
- Local medicine and wisdom
- Brochettes
- 4WD expeditions

SEE the stomping bustle of the Tuareg camel market at sunset.

EAT home-made ice-cream surrounded by the traditional semi-open design at Restaurant Le Pilier.

DRINK nomadic Tuareg 'desert tea', strong and sugared in small glasses, in one of the scattered Tuareg villages.

DO take a camel ride through the lush valleys and rough, stony Aïr Mountains.

WATCH the artisans in action at the Centre Artisanal.

BUY *croix d'Agadez* at the Grand Marché.

AFTER DARK sit in the small night market opposite Place de la Fraternité eating brochettes and watching the world go by.

URBAN MYTH

The colourful Cure Salée event is held after the rains in August or September, when farmers take their herds to pastures rich in mineral salts. In the ceremony called the Gerewol, young men of the nomadic Peul-Fulani group adorn and beautify themselves so that only the most obstinate female can resist them. With luck, each will find a wife – a woman brave enough to move forward and demand his services, at least for a night. But furthermore, Cure Salée also involves the Soro, a virility test requiring initiates to be beaten with big sticks while maintaining an inane grin. Though difficult for outsiders to witness the events themselves, if you're in the region around this time you will undoubtedly run into plenty of spectacularly garbed nomads preparing for their big day.

ELEGANTLY DECKED-OUT MEMBERS OF THE WODAABE TRIBE.
Photographer: Imagestate (1)

A GROCERY-LADEN CYCLIST MAKES HIS WAY HOME.
Photographer: Frans Lemmens (2)

INVESTIGATING THE NARROW STREETS BETWEEN MUD HOUSES IS A REAL TREAT.
Photographer: Anthony Ham (3)

PATIENT MOTHERS WAIT AT THE HOSPITAL.
Photographer: Alvaro Leiva (4)

Ushuaia 153

VITAL STATISTICS

NAME: USHUAIA

NICKNAME: THE CAPITAL CITY OF ANTARCTICA;
THE END OF THE WORLD

DATE OF BIRTH: 1884; WHEN A MISSION WAS FOUNDED

ADDRESS: ARGENTINA (MAP 1, M24)

HEIGHT: 14M

POPULATION: 58,000

THE SUPERLATIVE COASTLINE OF THE BEAGLE CHANNEL CAPTIVATES.
Photographer: Michael Coyne (1)

TAKING A DIFFERENT VIEW, THE CHAIRLIFT IS A POPULAR WAY FOR VISITORS TO SEE THE CITY.
Photographer: Michael Coyne (2)

BE AWED BY THIS SKY SHOW ON YOUR JOURNEY TO THE END OF THE EARTH.
Photographer: Michael Coyne (3)

WATCHING TIME PASS IN THE VOLVER RESTAURANT.
Photographer: Michael Coyne (4)

This southernmost city in the world has brightly coloured houses sitting toylike against the dramatic backdrop of the Cerro Martial and the Fuegan Andes, and is surrounded by awesome scenery.

ANATOMY

The harbour city, whose name means 'bay overlooking the west' in the local Yamaná language, is situated on the Beagle Channel and sprawls untidily along the coast. It's easy to walk around the town, as all its sights are close together, but you can also catch local buses or taxis.

PEOPLE

The citizens of Ushuaia are mostly descendants of pioneers who came here to settle, explore or serve prison terms. Only artefacts, shell mounds, Thomas Bridges' famous dictionary of the Yamaná language and memories remain of the Yamaná people who once flourished here. The populace is augmented by Antarctic researchers. Ninety-three percent of the population is Roman Catholic.

TYPICAL USHUAIAN

Ushuaians tend to be easy-going, laid-back and sociable. While they are friendly and passionate, they can also have a subtle broodiness to their nature. Argentina has a large middle class, though it has struggled greatly since the recession that began in 1999. Many locals work as fishers or in the tourism industry. A devotion to family is something all Argentines have in common.

DEFINING EXPERIENCE

Walking around town and checking out the many mansions, then exploring the national park and spotting geese, Magellanic woodpeckers and austral parakeets, before taking a boat out to the penguin colony on Isla Martillo and then eating at any one of the excellent fish restaurants.

STRENGTHS

- Mansions throughout the city
- Casa Beban Exhibition Centre – built in 1911, prefabricated from a Swedish catalogue
- Museo del Fin del Mundo (The End of the World Museum) – a very Win Wenders name
- Museo Penitenciario
- The End of the World Train – the world's southernmost steam train
- Estancia Haberton – the oldest sheep station in Tierra del Fuego

WEAKNESSES

- The long, cold winters
- The short, cool summers
- The difficulties getting here
- The rough trip on the Beagle Channel

GOLD STAR

Museo Marítimo & Museo del Presidio – housed in the national prison, which was built by convicts who were moved from Staten Island to Ushuaia in 1906. The spokelike halls of single cells were designed to house 380 prisoners, but during the prison's most active period it held up to 800 inmates. It closed as a jail in 1947 and now houses the museums. It makes a fine port of call on a blustery day. Some of the more illustrious prisoners included author Ricardo Rojasand and Russian anarchist Simón Radowitzky. Halls showing penal life are intriguing, and on the upper floor of one hall is a display on Antarctic exploration.

CITYSPEAK

- The exchange rate – has it gone to hell in a handbasket?

STARRING ROLE IN...

- *Happy Together* (1997)
- *Uttermost Part of the Earth* by Lucas Bridges

IMPORT

- Food
- Missionaries
- City types
- Cruise ships
- Expectant penguin-spotters
- Eager Antarctic visitors
- Adventurous skiers and hikers

EXPORT

- Cruise ships
- Happy penguin-spotters
- Contented Antarctic visitors
- Tired skiers and hikers

SEE the museum in the old prison.

EAT Tierra del Fuego *centolla fueguina* (spider crab) at Kaupé.

DRINK the traditional beverage of yerba maté.

DO take a trip to the Beagle Channel – the majestic, mountain-fringed sea passage to the south of the city – for sea lions' lairs and cormorant colonies.

WATCH the surroundings from the Cerro Martial chairlift.

BUY duty-free goods at Atlantico Sur.

AFTER DARK drink at U! Bar, with trendy orange plastic décor and chilled ambience.

URBAN MYTH

As Charles Darwin saw it, the Yamaná (or Yahgan) of the Beagle Channel – naked except for a loincloth and seal-skin cape, and paddling about in canoes with all their most important possessions, including bows, dogs and even fire – were 'subhuman beings…without spiritual life.' Perhaps, had old Chuck spent more time on land rather than concocting his theories aboard ship, he might have noticed that the Yamaná had a rich system of spiritual beliefs. They believed in a Supreme Being, Watauinewa, and had shamans who talked to spirits that the Yamaná believed controlled the weather and the hunt. Darwin might have seen that during the Kina ceremony, in which boys are initiated to adulthood, the men dressed themselves as gods, painting their bodies with black carbon and the region's white and red clays, holding tall masks and dancing to represent the different spirits: Kina-Miami, the guardian; Tulema-Yaka, the tutor; and Hani-Yaka, the energy giver.

THE CHAOTIC BUSTLE OF LIFE IS PLAYED OUT DAILY ON THE RED STREETS OF KAMPALA.
Photographer: Robert Caputo (1)

In 1907 a pioneering tourist named Winston Churchill dubbed Uganda the 'Pearl of Africa' and 100 years on, though much has transpired, it's still Africa's best-kept secret and Kampala is by far the jewel in its crown.

ANATOMY

Like Rome, Kampala is said to be built on seven hills. Nakasero Hill, encompassing the city centre, is where much of the action is. Between Nakasero and the lower part of the city is Kampala's main thoroughfare, Kampala Rd (which turns into Jinja Rd to the east and Bombo Rd to the west). Here you'll find banks, the main post office, plenty of shops and a few hotels and restaurants. Below this are a hotchpotch of shops, markets, budget hotels and eateries. Minibuses and taxis are the best way to get around.

PEOPLE

Uganda has a kaleidoscopic range of tribes and Kampala displays this wonderfully. The most prominent is the Buganda, with substantial representation from the Lango, Acholi and Teso people. There are also the Karamojong from the northeast of Uganda and Pygmies from the forests in the west. The church is a guiding light and often interwoven with traditional beliefs. There is also a small minority of Muslims, which once included Idi Amin, who converted to Islam to win financial support from Arab states in the 1970s.

TYPICAL KAMPALAN

Kampalans are educated, informed and globally aware. Their home remains one of the continent's great centres of learning. They love to engage visitors in conversations about their impressions of Africa and the world beyond. Both ethnically and culturally diverse, they take pride in their cosmopolitan lifestyle.

Kampala
154

VITAL STATISTICS

NAME: KAMPALA

DATE OF BIRTH: AD 1894; DECLARED BRITISH PROTECTORATE, THOUGH LOCAL TRIBES HAVE INHABITED THE AREA SINCE PREHISTORIC TIMES

ADDRESS: UGANDA (MAP 2, K14)

HEIGHT: 1312M

POPULATION: 1.2 MILLION

BEAUTIFUL AFRICAN PRODUCE, ON SALE DOOR TO DOOR.
Photographer: Eric L Wheater (2)

THE FEET OF MANY PILGRIMS HAVE TRAVELLED ALONG THE ROAD TO THE LUBAGA CATHEDRAL.
Photographer: Dennis Johnson (3)

THE BUSY STREETS OF KAMPALA, ALIVE WITH COLOUR.
Photographer: Doug MacLellan (4)

DEFINING EXPERIENCE

Whiling away the afternoon at the City Bar & Grill's grand Art Deco setting, then planning a gorilla spotting and white-water rafting adventure in the surrounding area.

STRENGTHS

- Uganda Museum
- National parks
- Speed-boating and white-water rafting
- Entebbe Botanic Gardens
- Lake Victoria
- Local gorillas
- Owino Market
- Ethiopian restaurants
- Uganda Wildlife Education Centre
- Kibuli Mosque

WEAKNESSES

- Security searches in government buildings
- Limited shopping
- A bloody history
- Some expensive tours
- Thrill-seeking tourists

GOLD STAR

Survival – after Uganda's many troubled years of war and political turmoil, Kampala has carefully forged its own unique culture and remains strongly linked to world politics.

CITYSPEAK

- The prospect of multiparty politics
- The civil wars in neighbouring countries

STARRING ROLE IN...

- *The Last King of Scotland* (2005)
- *ABC Africa* (2001)

IMPORT

- English
- Refugees
- Curries

EXPORT

- Traditional handicrafts
- Former leaders

SEE the Ndere Troupe performing traditional Ugandan dances every Sunday evening at the Nile Hotel.

EAT the house vegetarian masala or a *tilapia* (fish) curry at Haandi.

DRINK a beer in the relaxed, local atmosphere of the Wagadougou Bar.

DO visit the Kasubi Tombs, the huge traditional reed and bark-cloth buildings trumpeted as the largest thatched mausoleum in Africa.

WATCH the chimps frolic at Ngamba Island Chimpanzee Sanctuary, located on Ngamba Island in Lake Victoria and nicknamed 'Chimp Island'.

BUY bargain secondhand clothes at the vibrant Owino Market.

AFTER DARK the Speke Hotel has a popular terrace bar out the front and within the hotel is On the Rocks, a major player on the nightlife scene and always packed with people.

URBAN MYTH

Idi Amin staged a coup to prevent his arrest in January 1971, and so began Uganda's first reign of terror. All political activities were quickly suspended and the army was empowered to shoot on sight anyone suspected of opposition to the regime. Over the next eight years an estimated 300,000 Ugandans lost their lives, often in horrifying ways. Amin's main targets were the educated classes, the Acholi and Lango tribespeople of Obote and the country's 70,000-strong Asian community. In 1972 Asians were given 90 days to leave the country; they departed with little more than the clothes they wore. Meanwhile, the economy collapsed, infrastructure crumbled, prolific wildlife was machine-gunned by soldiers for meat, ivory and skins, and tourism evaporated. The stream of refugees across the border became a flood, inflation hit 1000% and the treasury ran out of money to pay the soldiers. Faced with a restless army, Amin had to seek a diversion. He chose a war with Tanzania, ostensibly to teach that country a lesson for supporting anti-Amin dissidents. The Tanzanians defeated the Ugandan army and pushed on into the heart of Uganda in early 1979. Amin fled to Libya and later to Saudi Arabia, where he lived in exile until his death in 2003.

THE MUSEO DEL ORO, HOME TO THE WORLD'S FINEST COLLECTION OF PRE-HISPANIC GOLD.
Photographer: Patricia Rincon Mautner (1)

Bogotá 155

VITAL STATISTICS

NAME: BOGOTÁ

DATE OF BIRTH: PRE-COLUMBIAN; INHABITED BY ONE OF THE MOST ADVANCED PRE-COLUMBIAN INDIAN GROUPS, THE MUISCA

ADDRESS: COLOMBIA (MAP 4, L10)

HEIGHT: 2645M

SIZE: 25 SQ KM

POPULATION: 7 MILLION

Bogotá is a city of futuristic architecture, a vibrant and diverse cultural and intellectual life, splendid colonial churches and brilliant museums.

ANATOMY

Bogotá is bordered to the east by a mountain range topped by the two peaks of Monserrate and Guadalupe. Bogotá's northern sector consists mainly of upmarket residential districts, while the city's southern part is a vast spread of undistinguished lower-income suburbs, culminating in the vast shanty towns on the southernmost outskirts. The urban bus service TransMilenio is efficient and fast.

PEOPLE

About 75% of the population is of mixed blood, composed of around 55% mestizos (of mixed Spanish and indigenous heritage) and 20% mulattos (with one black and one white parent). There are also about 3% *zambos* (of African-Indian blood). Indians represent just a bit more than 1% of the population. Spanish is the official language.

TYPICAL BOGOTANO

Bogotanos are courteous, polite and hospitable. Everyday life is remarkably open and public, and much family life takes place outside the home: in front of the house, in the street, in a bar or at the market. As a result Colombians may seem indiscreet about their behaviour in public places. Someone in a bar may discuss personal problems at a volume that allows all the patrons to follow the conversation. A driver may urinate on the tyre of his bus after he has stopped for a break on the road. Couples hug and kiss passionately in parks and in the street.

DEFINING EXPERIENECE

Strolling around La Candelaria, Bogotá's charming historic quarter, and stopping off for a *santafereño* (hot chocolate served with cheese and local bread) at Pastelería Florida, then exploring the Museo del Oro (Gold Museum), before conducting a night crawl around the pubs and discos of Zona Rosa.

STRENGTHS

- Friendliness of the locals
- Museo del Oro
- Donación Botero
- Festival Iberoamericano de Teatro de Bogotá – one of the best theatre festivals in Latin America
- Colonial churches such as the Iglesia Museo de Santa Clara
- Cerro de Monserrate
- The nightlife
- Amazing variety of fruits, some of which are endemic to the country
- Futuristic architecture
- *El Señor Caído* (the Fallen Christ) statue
- Intellectual life

WEAKNESSES

- Guerrillas
- Cocaine thugs
- Vast shantytowns
- Street urchins
- Traffic
- Graffiti

GOLD STAR

The view of the city from the top of Cerro de Monserrate – on a clear day you can even spot Los Nevados, the volcanic range in the Cordillera Central, 135km away, noted for the symmetrical cone of the Nevado del Tolima.

CITYSPEAK

- The arrest of Ferney Torres, a Marxist rebel who engineered the smuggling of 300 tonnes of cocaine
- Air pollution from vehicle emissions

STARRING ROLE IN...

- *The People at Universal* (1991)
- *Maria Full of Grace* (2004)
- *El Rey* (The King, 2004)
- *One Hundred Years of Solitude* by Gabriel García Márquez

IMPORT

- *Telenovelas* (soap operas)
- African rhythms of the Caribbean
- Roman Catholicism
- Columbus
- Car bombings
- Drug trafficking
- Spaniards
- Cuban salsa
- Corrida (bullfighting)
- Slavery

EXPORT

- Gabriel García Márquez
- Marijuana
- Shakira
- Emeralds
- Revolutionary Armed Forces of Colombia (FARC)
- Magic realism (literary genre)
- Álvaro Mutis
- Cocaine
- Illegally exported wildlife

SEE more than 34,000 gold pieces from all the major pre-Hispanic cultures in Colombia at the most important gold museum in the world, Museo del Oro.

EAT the Bogotano speciality *ajiaco* (soup made with chicken and potato) at Restaurante La Pola.

DRINK the excellent *tinto* (a small cup of black coffee) – the number one drink in Bogotá – first thing in the morning.

DO go to Galería Café Libro, a popular *salsoteca* (salsa nightclub) always packed with salsa fans.

WATCH a local theatre production at the inspiring Teatro de la Candelaria.

BUY emeralds at one of the many *joyerías* (jewellery shops) in the city centre.

AFTER DARK head to Gótica, a large nightclub offering different musical ambiences on different levels, including salsa, techno and trance.

URBAN MYTH

The Palacio de Justicia (Palace of Justice) has had a tragic history. The first court building, erected in 1921, was burnt down by a mob during El Bogotazo in 1948. A modern building was then constructed on Plaza de Bolívar, but in 1985 it was taken by M-19 guerrillas and gutted by fire in a fierce 28-hour offensive by the army in an attempt to reclaim it. The ruin stood untouched for four years until authorities decided to construct a new building.

CERRO DE MONSERRATE PROVIDES A HEAVENLY PLACE TO VIEW THE CITY.
Photographer: Patricia Rincon Mautner (2)

TAKING FLIGHT IN SIMON BOLÍVAR PARK.
Photographer: Patricia Rincon Mautner (3)

POMP AND CEREMONY ACCOMPANY THE CHANGING OF THE GUARD AT PLAZA DE BOLÍVAR.
Photographer: Patricia Rincon Mautner (4)

Bridgetown
156

VITAL STATISTICS

NAME: BRIDGETOWN

NICKNAME: LITTLE ENGLAND

DATE OF BIRTH: 1628; FOUNDED BY THE BRITISH – PURPORTEDLY THE ONLY EVIDENCE OF PREVIOUS INDIGENOUS OCCUPATION WAS A SIMPLE BRIDGE (THAT PUT THE 'BRIDGE' IN BRIDGETOWN) SPANNING THE CONSTITUTION RIVER

ADDRESS: BARBADOS (MAP 4, Q6)

HEIGHT: 55M

POPULATION: 80,000

Amid the white-sand and turquoise-water tropical idyll, Barbados's only city is a modern and colonial architectural mishmash with, a hubbub of side streets sprinkled with rum shops and chattel houses.

ANATOMY

Bridgetown is a busy commercial city set on Carlisle Bay, developed around an inlet known as the Careenage. True to the island's British heritage, there are obelisks, Gothic Parliament buildings, and a large Anglican cathedral. Broad and Swan Sts are thick with vendors catering to every souveniring whim. Bridgetown is easily covered on foot, while taxis can be flagged on the street.

PEOPLE

Bajan culture displays some trappings of British life, such as cricket, polo, and horse racing yet, on closer examination, Barbados is deeply rooted in Afro-Caribbean tradition. The typical Bridgetown citizen's roots are African (90%), with the rest made up of a mix of English, Scottish and East Indian cultures. Religions observed are Protestantism (67%), Roman Catholicism (4%) and other (12%). Seventeen percent are atheists.

TYPICAL BRIDGETOWN CITIZEN

Like other Caribbean cultures, Bridgetown's citizens are relatively conservative and the men are macho, but the ongoing bond with London has made Barbados more socially progressive than its neighbours. Special events are carried out with a great deal of pomp and ceremony, and older ladies are fond of donning prim little hats. However, for all its surface 'Britishness', family life, art, food, music and dress have more in common with the nearby Windward Islands than with West London.

DEFINING EXPERIENCE

Snorkelling the coral-encrusted tug *Berwyn* in Carlisle Bay and lazing on Pebble Beach followed by an afternoon trip of spiritual healing, Calypso-cocktail style, at the Malibu beachfront distillery.

STRENGTHS

- Congaline Carnival (late April)
- Blissful beaches
- Rum!
- The Bridgetown Synagogue
- Payne's Bay Beach
- Barbados Museum
- Crop-Over Festival (mid-July)
- Flying-fish sandwiches
- Calypso rhythms
- Harry Bayley Observatory
- National Heroes Sq
- Workin' up (dancing)
- St Michael's Cathedral

WEAKNESSES

- Sparse accommodation
- A somewhat macho culture
- Densely populated beaches
- Berthing 'super cruise ships'
- The well-oiled pre-fab tourist machine
- Soil erosion
- Ship pollution

GOLD STAR

'British' Bridgetown is West Indian to the core – with calypso rhythms and its own quirky characteristics, it has enough local flavour to feel 'exotic' yet has enough of the familiar to feel comfortable.

CITYSPEAK

- Cruise-ship pollution and the continuing soil erosion threatening Bridgetown's pristine water supply
- The major social problem of crack cocaine that has insidiously clawed its way to Barbados' youth

STARRING ROLE IN…

- *The Castle of My Skin* by George Lamming
- *Treasures of Barbados* by Henry Fraser
- *Island in the Sun* (1957)

IMPORT

- Anglo culture
- Cricket
- Polo
- New York hip-hop fashion
- Saturday at the races
- Queen Elizabeth portraits in every scout hall and municipal building
- Around 500,000 cruise-liner passengers every year

EXPORT

- Tourism
- Sir Frank Worrell
- Sugar
- Rum
- Molasses
- Garfield Sobers
- Light manufacturing
- Calypso artist the Mighty Gabby
- Component assembly
- Agriculture
- Fishing

SEE engaging displays on all aspects of Bajan history, with exhibits on early indigenous inhabitants, slavery, emancipation, military history and plantation-house furniture at the excellent Barbados Museum.

EAT local specialties flying fish and coconut prawn (shrimp) at the Rusty Pelican – the 2nd-floor balcony affords a pleasant view over the Careenage.

DRINK with the locals at Bridgetown's many rollicking rum shops along Baxter Rd, just north of the centre.

DO tussle with the crowds on the pristine white sands of Pebbles Beach on Carlisle Bay.

WATCH world-class cricket at Kensington Oval, Fontabelle, just outside Bridgetown.

BUY pottery, leather, wood and fabric handicrafts at Pelican Craft Village, between downtown and the cruise-ship terminal.

AFTER DARK view the gorgeous Caribbean night sky from the Harry Bayley Observatory, the headquarters of the Barbados Astronomical Society.

URBAN MYTH

In 1751, at age 19 – some 38 years before he would become the first US president – George Washington visited Barbados as a companion to his half-brother Lawrence, who suffered from tuberculosis. It was hoped that the tropical climate would prove therapeutic. The two rented a house in the Garrison area south of Bridgetown (where the Bush Hill House now stands) and stayed on the island for six weeks. Unfortunately, George contracted smallpox while on Barbados, which left his face permanently scarred, and Lawrence died the following year. The Barbados trip was the only overseas journey that George Washington ever made.

MAKING SHADE ON THE WAY HOME, MARHOLE RD.
Photographer: John Neubauer (1)

INNOCENTS' PURSUITS IN POLLARD'S BAR.
Photographer: John Neubauer (2)

A SEDATE CHATTEL HOUSE IN EVANS VILLAGE…
Photographer: John Neubauer (3)

…AND A RIOTOUS NEIGHBOURHOOD SHOPFRONT.
Photographer: John Neubauer (4)

Ulaanbaatar

VITAL STATISTICS

NAME: ULAANBAATAR

NICKNAME: UB

DATE OF BIRTH: 1693; ALTHOUGH THE CITY WAS LARGELY NOMADIC, SO IT ACTUALLY CHANGED LOCATIONS REGULARLY UNTIL THE 20TH CENTURY

ADDRESS: MONGOLIA (MAP 1, HH8)

HEIGHT: 1325M

SIZE: 1368 SQ KM

POPULATION: 900,000

Definitely one of the world's most unusual capitals, UB is the furthest capital city in the world from the sea; it's the decidedly rough-and-ready capital of a seminomadic country, at a vast remove from the rest of the world.

ANATOMY

The city is a sprawl without much natural definition. It's centred around the vast Sükhbaatar Sq, named after Mongolia's Stalinist leader during early Communist times. The Trans-Mongolian railway runs right through the city too, and provides a useful landmark, running parallel to the Dund River. Local public transport is reliable and departures are frequent, but buses can get crowded. Green minivans run along a similar route to the buses, and for short trips it's just as cheap to take a taxi.

PEOPLE

UB is bursting at the seams these days, with more and more people from the countryside coming in to find work in the overstretched capital. Almost half of the country's population lives here, which, given the country is twice the size of France, is quite indicative of just how empty the Mongol plains really are. The capital's population is 99% Mongolian.

TYPICAL ULAANBAATAR CITIZEN

This sprawling city's residents are different from most other city dwellers in every way. On the city's outskirts are *ger* (tent) suburbs, where mangy mongrels patrol the unpaved lanes and most residents still live in traditional circular felt tents. Some districts still serve their traditional role as the protective ring around a monastery. Of great contrast are the narrow lanes off Sükhbaatar Sq that are undergoing a renaissance of ultra-progressive fashion shops and trendy cafés. The city is still spirited, with a heady cross section of society – crimson-robed monks rub shoulders with sombre-suited politicians and businesspeople, while mobile-phone–toting teenagers skip past bewildered nomads fresh off the steppes.

DEFINING EXPERIENCE

Visiting the market to see the colours and the excited bartering, wandering the unusual streets of this extraordinary city as the houses give way to *ger*, where you'll as likely as not be invited in by one of the families living there, then checking out some Mongolian throat singing or the circus in the evening after some hearty fare in a traditional Mongolian restaurant.

STRENGTHS

- Extremely friendly local population
- Very well set up for tourism
- You really do feel like you've reached the end of the earth
- Superb trips to the surrounding stunning countryside

WEAKNESSES

- Unbelievable litter – Mongolians aren't used to nonbiodegradable materials and still simply throw everything onto the floor once they've done with it
- UB has become such a huge tourist draw that sometimes you feel you're in India or Thailand come the summer months

GOLD STAR

The monasteries here are spectacular. Visiting the Gandantegchinlen Khiid is a humbling and memorable experience, as is seeing the interior of the Winter Palace of the Bogd Khaan.

CITYSPEAK

- Rapid globalisation and the fashion boutiques, elegant restaurants and Korean taxis taking over the streets
- Mongolia's 800th anniversary of statehood in 2006 and the International Tourism Fair held in UB to welcome the influx of visitors

STARRING ROLE IN...

- There have been several very successful films shot in Mongolia including *Urga* (1991) and *The Weeping Camel* (2003), but they tend to focus on rural life and as such have not been shot in Ulaanbaatar.

IMPORT

- Korean cars
- Processed and consumer goods
- Oil

EXPORT

- Copper
- Cashmere
- Leather
- Gold

SEE wrestling and other traditional sports during the Nadaam Festival in July.

EAT *buuz* (steamed mutton dumplings) and *khuushuur* (fried mutton pancakes) for a taste of Mongolia.

DRINK the ubiquitous local brew, Chinggis Beer.

DO not miss the staggering exhibits of dinosaurs at the National History Museum.

WATCH extraordinary performances of unique Mongolian throat singing.

BUY traditional Buddhist good-luck trinkets at the shops around any monastery or religious building.

AFTER DARK be aware that much of the city isn't lit at night!

URBAN MYTH

Unfortunately this is not so much a myth as a terrible reality, which has attained its own morbid fame. Thousands of Mongolian children – orphans or those abandoned by families unable to feed them – live beneath the city in underground slums, congregating around heating pipes to keep themselves alive during the extremely harsh Mongolian winter, when it regularly goes below minus 20°C. Despite the best efforts of local aid workers, the problem doesn't seem to be going away and child beggars are still extremely common on the streets.

WRESTLING FOR INDEPENDENCE – IT'S ALL ABOUT THE SHOWMANSHIP.
Photographer: Bradley Mayhew (1)

RIDING, WRESTLING, ARCHERY – THE THREE MANLY SPORTS OF THE ANNUAL NADAAM FESTIVAL.
Photographer: Felicity Volk (2)

TRADITIONAL YURTS FORM THIS SUBURB WITH A DIFFERENCE.
Photographer: Olivier Cirendini (3)

A SLOW GAME OF DRAUGHTS OR CHESS PASSES TIME.
Photographer: Scott Darsney (4)

One of the newest cities on the planet, Abuja was imagined in the 1970s on the back of oil revenues, and building began in the 1980s at the geographical centre of Nigeria.

ANATOMY

The very character of this purpose-built city has been shaped by the two renowned rock formations around it – Zuma Rock, the 'Gateway to Abuja', and Aso Rock, located at the head of Abuja, with the city extending southwards from the rock. The rolling landscape is dotted with hills and plains, canopied with scenic greenery and virgin forests. As a new city it is serviced by a very good road system, but it's too new to have a bus system; numerous cheap taxis and vans are the main method of getting around and the adventurous take *okada* (bike taxis).

PEOPLE

Several indigenous groups live in Abuja, the largest among them are the Gbabyi (also known as the Gwari) and the Koro. Several smaller indigenous groups are the Gade, Egbura, Gwandara, Bassa and the Gana gana.

TYPICAL ABUJAN

A civil servant, a politician, a diplomat, or a member of the domestic staff of the aforementioned.

DEFINING EXPERIENCE

Meeting early at the International Conference Centre, going hiking in the hills around the city, playing a round of golf in the afternoon, then finding one of the local botanic garden–styled drinking spots in town and sampling some local fare before a spot of dinner at an international hotel.

Abuja 158

VITAL STATISTICS

NAME: ABUJA

DATE OF BIRTH: 1976; WHEN THE NIGERIAN GOVERNMENT KICKED OUT THE LOCAL GWARI INHABITANTS AND DECIDED TO UP-AND-MOVE THE CAPITAL FROM LAGOS TO ABUJA

ADDRESS: NIGERIA (MAP 2, B11)

HEIGHT: 360M

SIZE: 250 SQ KM

POPULATION: 500,000

TRADITIONAL TRANSPORT CLASHES WITH THE ULTRAMODERN ARCHITECTURE OF ABUJA.
Photographer: Pascal Maitre (1)

STRENGTHS

- Wide-open streets
- Few cars
- A good golf course
- The imposing Zuma Rock
- Aso Rock, the largest rock formation, nearly 400m above sea level
- The Dutse hill range, a sanctuary for baboons and other forms of wildlife

WEAKNESSES

- Its comparative emptiness
- Few people
- Domestic flights are unscheduled, as they are mainly charter flights, even to Lagos

GOLD STAR

Aso Rock, the city's spine, a granite monolith that towers over the gleaming green dome of Nigeria's new National Assembly building

CITYSPEAK

- Debt relief for this oil-producing country
- Sotto voce: will the country once again top the list of the most corrupt countries?
- Will the city ever be finished?

STARRING ROLE IN...

- The plans of international architecture practices!

IMPORT

- Architects
- Town planners
- Builders
- Tradesmen
- Road builders
- Civil servants
- Bureaucrats
- Politicians
- Diplomats
- Oil companies
- Lobby groups
- Non-governmental organisations (NGOs)

EXPORT

- Conference agreements – Abuja is the site of several international conferences, for example for Unicef and the Commonwealth, on HIV/AIDS in Africa and debt relief

SEE the flowering bougainvillea and other exotic greenery that conceal the high walls and razor wire protecting the office towers, apartment buildings and villas dotting the landscape.

EAT *edikang ikong*, a rich, leafy delicacy from the southeast; probably Nigeria's most famous and most cosmopolitan meal, it's served in many restaurants and the biggest hotels.

DRINK the popular traditional brew *brukutu* – a chocolate-coloured, faintly sour fermented drink made from sorghum.

DO attend Asofest in November, an annual festival of traditional arts and culture.

WATCH baboons in the nearby Dutse hill range.

BUY music by Fela Kuti or King Sunny Ade – leaders of the West African music scene.

AFTER DARK have a drink at Elephant Bar or Dazzles in the Sheraton.

URBAN MYTH

Nigerian Internet scams aren't really from Nigeria. Although commonly referred to as 'Nigerian', the various international financial scams that first appeared in 1989 don't necessarily originate here. Many scams originate in other countries including Angola, Sierra Leone, the Congo, South Africa, Mauritius, the Philippines, Zimbabwe and Azerbaijan.

FILING OUT OF THE NATIONAL MOSQUE FOLLOWING FRIDAY PRAYERS.
Photographer: Jacob Silberberg (2)

CHECKING OUT THE GOODS: A CATTLE MARKET ON THE CITY'S OUTSKIRTS.
Photographer: Jacob Silberberg (3)

TAKING A QUICK BREAK IN THE FIELDS.
Photographer: Chris Illemassene (4)

Christiansted

159

VITAL STATISTICS

NAME: CHRISTIANSTED

DATE OF BIRTH: 1733; CHRISTIANSTED SERVED BRIEFLY AS THE CAPITAL OF THE DANISH WEST INDIES

ADDRESS: US VIRGIN ISLANDS (MAP 4, O4)

HEIGHT: 5M

SIZE: 1572 SQ KM

POPULATION: 2800

Christiansted is beautiful, historical, easy to travel around and, best of all, totally Caribbean in look and feel.

ANATOMY

Pressed between hills and a shallow, reef-protected harbour, Christiansted, on the island of St Croix, is a traveller's delight. For decades, its greatest appeal lay in its six-block historic district, but in recent years, Christiansted has evolved into a vibrant entertainment district. With its historical significance, cleanliness, walkability and array of dining and nightlife opportunities, Christiansted embodies almost everything many travellers hope for in a West Indies town – you can kick back at a waterfront brewpub or in a courtyard restaurant and make friends with the West Indians at the next table. You can walk around town and catch buses to get around the island, or hire a car to be your own tour guide.

PEOPLE

The majority of Christiansted residents (75%) are of African descent, with 13% made up of expats from the US mainland – often young whites who run hotels, inns and sports operations. Don't forget to add a smattering of immigrants from Puerto Rico, the Leeward Islands and the Dominican Republic, and even the odd Danish plantation family or French land holder. English is the official language.

TYPICAL CHRISTIANSTED CITIZEN

Cruzans, as the residents of Christiansted and the rest of St Croix call themselves, consider their home-island the 'stepchild' of the US Virgin Islands. The origins of the image are rooted in St Croix's isolated location, and Christiansted residents show an independence and self-motivation that comes from this separation. They're proud of their wealth and comfortable status, and always ready for a party as soon as you crank up the music. People from Christiansted know how to eat well, party well and live well – get in there with them!

DEFINING EXPERIENCE

Drinking a quick coffee on a Saturday, then heading to Market Sq for fresh fruit and vegetables, taking a leisurely walk along the Kings Wharf boardwalk, an exploration of duty-free shopping in Gallows Bay, dining on seafood delicacies overlooking the harbour and then dancing the night away at a full-moon party.

STRENGTHS

- Historic yellow buildings and their stories
- Vibrant music scene
- The Saint Patrick's Day Parade
- Duty-free shopping
- Cruise ships and the yacht-charter industry
- The red-light district in Kings Cross St (a change from the clean-cut mainstream scene)
- One of the highest standards of living in the Caribbean
- Steel-drum bands
- Danish street signs
- Maps that still show the names and boundaries of old plantations

WEAKNESSES

- Hurricanes
- Perpetually exorbitant 'tourist' prices for everything
- Swanky resorts
- An armada of cruise ships

GOLD STAR

For tourism achievement – the successful blending of centuries of colonial history with natural beauty to make a genuinely relaxed and attractive tourist destination.

CITYSPEAK

- US-sourced welfare payments – are they good enough?
- Property prices on the bay – going up? Going down?
- Which hurricane will be the next to (hopefully) pass them by?

STARRING ROLE IN...

- *Treasure Island* by Robert Lewis Stevenson
- *Sunfon Calypso* by Julian Putley
- *Don't Stop the Carnival* by Herman Wouk

IMPORT

- Wining, dining and sailing à la megarich
- French quadrille dances
- Colonial management
- Roulette and other casino fun

EXPORT

- Rum
- 'Mix' music – a rollicking blend of calypso, reggae and hip-hop
- Yacht-charter services
- Refined oil
- Sugar

SEE 'Jump Up' – a carnival-like evening (held four times a year) filled with steel bands, dancing, local arts and crafts, island food, and fun in the streets and on the waterfront.

EAT yellowfin tuna with mango salsa and rum-fried plantains at the elegant Indies Restaurant.

DRINK local Cruzan Estate Diamond Rum.

DO a late-night turtle-watch during the nesting and hatching seasons, sponsored by the St Croix Environmental Association.

WATCH the waves lapping the deserted beaches of nearby Buck Island.

BUY a gold or silver bracelet with a 'Cruzan hook' from the Caribbean Bracelet Company.

AFTER DARK see some mean jazz guitar at the Usual Suspects on Kings Wharf.

URBAN MYTH

Once upon a time, when the French, British and Danish were fighting to colonise the island of St Croix, Christiansted was merely a tiny French village called Bassin. After the French sold the island to the Danish in 1733, the town had its 15 minutes of diplomatic fame as capital of the Danish West Indies from 1755 to 1871. The town was designed to have the layout of Christiana (now Oslo), Norway, and the size of Copenhagen. Thanks to the Danes and their sugar industry, the town's population swelled to 5284. Since the handover of St Croix to the USA, only 2800 Cruzans overlook the picturesque harbour.

MEDICAL MEMOIR – THIS APOTHECARY MUSEUM WAS ONCE A WORKING PHARMACY.
Photographer: John Neubauer (1)

A PROUD HISTORY IS IMMACULATELY MAINTAINED ON COMPANY ST.
Photographer: John Neubauer (2)

CRUISIN' WITH THE CRUZANS – THE LAID-BACK STYLE OF ISLAND LIFE.
Photographer: John Neubauer (3)

FORT CHRISTIANSVAERN, BUILT TO KEEP OUT MARAUDERS FROM THE SEA.
Photographer: John Neubauer (4)

URBAN
THREADZ

San'a

160

VITAL STATISTICS

NAME: SAN'A

NICKNAME: SAM CITY

DATE OF BIRTH: BIBLICAL TIMES; LEGEND SAYS
IT WAS FOUNDED BY NOAH'S SON SHEM

ADDRESS: YEMEN (MAP 2, O9)

HEIGHT: 2250M

POPULATION: 1.1 MILLION

SAN'ANIS WEAR THEIR CULTURE WITH PRIDE.
Photographer: Chris Stowers (1)

THE GRACIOUS SMILE OF AN OLDER SAN'ANI LOCAL.
Photographer: Bethune Carmichael (2)

DISTINCT ARCHITECTURE MAKES THIS ONE OF THE WORLD'S MOST BEAUTIFUL CITIES.
Photographer: Noboru Komine (3)

ANCIENT STREETS PAVE THE WAY FOR MODERN SAN'A.
Photographer: Chris Stowers (4)

San'a is the capital of one of the last untouched corners of Arabia; the Old City is a perfectly preserved realm of traditional architecture with the stone foundations of some houses thought to date back 1000 years.

ANATOMY

San'a expands vigorously in all directions from its original heart, the walled Old City. The clamorous Midan at-Tahrir sits at the western edge of the Old City, while Az-Zubayri St defines its southern limits. Bab al-Yaman leads into the vibrant Souq al-Milh. Traffic is frantic and anarchic – to enter the fray your best options are taxis and motorbike taxis.

PEOPLE

The population of San'a is almost exclusively Arab – residents are said to have descended from different stock from the tribes that live in the rest of Yemen. The city's once-notable Jewish community has departed for Israel. There is a small and eclectic population of expats who call San'a home.

TYPICAL SAN'ANI

As a rule, San'anis are welcoming, spontaneous and gregarious to a fault. They are noted throughout the Middle East for their quick sense of humour. Tribe still plays an important role in the consciousness of Yemenis, although less so in San'a, but all Yemenis are proud of their distinctive culture.

DEFINING EXPERIENCE

Starting the day with a strong coffee at a Turkish coffee house near the Bab al-Yaman; pondering the exhibits, including examples of San'ani building styles, at the Museum of Traditional Arts and Crafts; diving in and getting lost in the labyrinth of the Souq al-Milh; chewing *qat* (a mild stimulant) with the locals in the afternoon; getting soapy and washing away the grit of the desert in a *hammam* (bathhouse).

STRENGTHS

◢ History around every corner
◢ Very safe for visitors and locals alike
◢ Free of touts and other tourism-related hassles
◢ Easy-going traders in the souqs (markets) – no hard sell

WEAKNESSES

◢ Dust
◢ Traffic and exhaust fumes
◢ Monsoon rains
◢ Kidnappings (only occasional!)
◢ Stray dogs
◢ Everything closing down every afternoon for the daily *qat*-chewing session

GOLD STAR

Architecture – San'a is home to prototypical skyscrapers built of mud and stone; the entire Old City has been declared a Unesco World Heritage Site.

CITYSPEAK

◢ Why are the Americans so interested in us?
◢ Was the unification of Yemen such a great idea?
◢ The price of *qat*

STARRING ROLE IN...

◢ *Arabian Nights* (1974)
◢ *A New Day in San'a* (2003)
◢ *Travels in Dictionary Land* by Tim Mackintosh Smith
◢ *Eating the Flowers of Paradise* by Kevin Rushby
◢ *The Southern Gates of Arabia* by Freya Stark
◢ *Motoring with Mohammed* by Eric Hansen

IMPORT

◢ 'Authentic' Bedouin silver jewellery
◢ Rhino horn – for ceremonial *jambiyah* (daggers)
◢ *Qat* from the provinces

EXPORT

◢ Frankincense
◢ Labourers to work in the Saudi oil business
◢ Yemenite Jews
◢ Oil
◢ Coffee

SEE the Museum of Traditional Arts and Crafts.

EAT *shwarma*, or *salta*, a fiery stew of lamb, peppers and coriander.

DRINK coffee flavoured with cardamom, but don't come here for an alcoholic tipple.

DO a course in the Arabic language or Islamic culture at the Sana'a Institute for Arabic language.

WATCH the sun set over the domes and towers of the Old City.

BUY spices, fabrics, incense or coffee in the Souq al-Milh.

AFTER DARK wander the Old City – the stained-glass windows of the traditional buildings illuminate the city like a mass of coloured lanterns.

URBAN MYTH

In 2003 parliamentary sessions were disrupted by the intercession of a raging bull. The beast, intended for slaughter in a public display of protest outside the Parliament, broke free and crashed through the Parliament. It gored an official and knocked down a child, all the while being chased by disgruntled tribesmen, whose protest perhaps took on a more slapstick aspect than originally intended.

UNIFORMED STUDENTS STRIKE A POSE OUTSIDE THE TOWN'S EPONYMOUS SCHOOL.
Photographer: Dave Bartruff (1)

Africa's adventure capital, the humble, dusty city of Livingstone is only a stone's throw from the magnificent Victoria Falls, where bungee-jumping, white-water rafting and abseiling end in sunset booze cruises on the mighty Zambezi.

ANATOMY

Livingstone lies only 11km north of one of the world's greatest natural wonders: the Victoria Falls. Mosi-oa-Tunya Rd is the city's tourist mecca, with shops, banks, *bureaux de change*, a post office, the Zamtel public-phone office and, most importantly, travel and tour agents. South of the town centre is Livingstone's main produce market (Maramba Township). Past the train station the town fizzles out but the trail of minibuses and taxis heading south lead to the Zambezi River, Victoria Falls and the Zambia–Zimbabwe border.

PEOPLE

More than 50% of Zambia's population lives in urban areas such as Livingstone, which lies on the border of the traditional territories of the Lozi, Tonga and Leya peoples. Although the main language group and people are Lozi, English is the official language and widely spoken due to Livingstone having become a major hub for travellers in southern Africa. The dominant religion is Christianity, though the majority also adhere to the traditional Zambian beliefs.

TYPICAL LIVINGSTONIAN

If Zambians have a reputation for being laid-back, Livingstonians are decidedly tranquil. They are notoriously friendly and easy-going and live happily in the present. They are blasé and indifferent to the buzz and hype of the falls and more interested in what tourism has done for Livingstone than what Livingstone has done for the tourist. They party hard and won't begrudge you a space on the dance floor. They are both colonial and very African.

Livingstone

161

VITAL STATISTICS

NAME: LIVINGSTONE

NICKNAME: MARAMBA

DATE OF BIRTH: AD 1905; FOLLOWING THE COMPLETION OF THE RAILWAY BRIDGE ACROSS THE ZAMBEZI RIVER

ADDRESS: ZAMBIA (MAP 2, I21)

HEIGHT: 985M

POPULATION: 97,000

THE VICTORIA FALLS BRIDGE'S BUNGY-JUMP STATION COMMANDS A SPECTACULAR VIEW OF THE WATERFALL.
Photographer: Andrew Woodley (2)

A STATUE OF DR LIVINGSTONE (WE PRESUME), KEEPING WATCH OVER VICTORIA FALLS.
Photographer: Adrian Arbib (3)

GRUBBY HANDS GET CLEANED UP BEFORE MEAL TIME.
Photographer: Jenny Matthews (4)

DEFINING EXPERIENCE

Waking up in a lush oasis, having a light breakfast with strangers discussing spine-tingling adventures, then sharing a minibus to the adrenaline junkie's paradise, bungee-jumping into the Batoka George, and white-water rafting through the seething turmoil that is the Zambezi.

STRENGTHS

- Victoria Falls
- Gateway to Zambia's wildlife parks
- Vast array of activities
- Laid-back atmosphere
- Tourist-friendly layout
- A raw-edged Africa
- Stone's throw from Zimbabwe
- Livingstone Museum
- Mukuni Village
- Wooden sculpture
- Great backpacker accommodation

WEAKNESSES

- Regular muggings between Livingstone and Victoria Falls
- Touts
- Rougher than usual wilderness
- It-can-wait attitude
- Losing capital-city status (to Lusaka)

GOLD STAR

Victoria Falls on the Zambezi River – the mesmerising waterfall spans nearly 2km, drops a dramatic 100m over a cliff and accommodates an amazing range of activities, from the tranquil to the terrifying.

CITYSPEAK

- The rise of tourism (again)
- The latest adrenaline-pumping activity over the falls

STARRING ROLE IN...

- *Stanley and Livingstone* (1939)

IMPORT

- Adventure seekers
- David Livingstone
- Christianity
- Tourism
- English
- US dollar
- Victorian era names
- Pizza

EXPORT

- Safaris
- Tours
- Batik fabrics
- Wooden sculptures
- Locally made furniture
- Falls activity T-shirts
- Visas

SEE the natural wonders of the Victoria Falls section of Mosi-oa-Tunya National Park.

EAT the Friday barbecue at Hippo's open-air restaurant.

DRINK as much as you can handle on a sunset booze cruise on the Zambezi.

DO a heart-stopping gorge swing over Batoka Gorge.

WATCH traditional dance performances from Zambia and neighbouring countries at Falls Craft Village.

BUY carved-wood pieces by the Leya people at Mukuni Village craft market.

AFTER DARK rock to the roof with Western hits and Congo rumba at the loud and gregarious Ravestone.

URBAN MYTH

Before being asked that famous question ('Dr Livingstone, I presume?'), British explorer David Livingstone travelled up the Zambezi River. It was the 1850s and Livingstone hoped to introduce Christianity and commerce to combat the horrors of the slave trade. In 1855 local people showed him a magnificent waterfall of torrents of water thundering into the Zambezi, which Livingstone later described as 'the ceaseless roar of the cataract, with the perpetual flow, as if pouring forth from the hand of the Almighty'. This natural wonder was called 'Mosi-oa-Tunya' (smoke that thunders). To Dr Livingstone, however, Victoria Falls seemed a more appropriate name, and Victoria Falls it remains.

Alexandria

162

VITAL STATISTICS

NAME: ALEXANDRIA

NICKNAME: THE PEARL OF THE MEDITERRANEAN

DATE OF BIRTH: 332 BC; WHEN ALEXANDER THE GREAT COMMISSIONED HIS ARCHITECT DEINOCRATES TO CONSTRUCT A NEW CAPITAL CITY ON THE COAST

ADDRESS: EGYPT (MAP 2, J2)

HEIGHT: 32M

SIZE: 300 SQ KM

POPULATION: 3.3 MILLION

A PENSIVE MOMENT ON THE TRAM.
Photographer: Bill Lyons (1)

As much Mediterranean as Middle Eastern, Alexandria has stood the test of time; although its early 20th-century European-influenced cosmopolitanism and decadence have faded, with Cleopatra's Palace and the ruins of the Pharos lighthouse emerging from the seabed and its dazzling new library, this confident Mediterranean city of cafés and promenades is making waves again.

ANATOMY

A thin, ribbonlike city, Alexandria runs along the Mediterranean coast for 20km without ever venturing more than 5km inland – a true waterfront city. The Great Corniche sweeps along the eastern harbour, with a string of city beaches. Trams travel at a snail's pace across the city, supplemented by buses and minibuses. The busy central area is small enough to walk around.

PEOPLE

Alexandria's citizens no longer include the extraordinary prerevolutionary mix of Egyptians, Greeks, English, French and Italians that gave the city its 19th- and 20th-century vitality. There were 300,000 people here in the 1940s, of whom about 40% were foreigners; today's millions are almost exclusively Egyptian.

TYPICAL ALEXANDRIAN

Alexandria is currently undergoing something of a regeneration, courtesy of an enlightened and free-spending municipality and the high-profile activities of a bunch of foreign archaeologists whose discoveries keep the city in the news. Its citizens are more laid-back than Cairenes, and have an immense pride in simply being Egyptian. Large extended families and close-knit neighbourhoods act as social support groups, strangers fall easily into conversation with each other, and whatever goes wrong, somebody always knows someone somewhere who can fix it.

DEFINING EXPERIENCE

Breakfasting at Trianon, downstairs from Cavafy's old offices, before exploring the Roman amphitheatre and Pompey's Pillar, the Catacombs of Kom ash-Shuqqafa – creepy tombs out of a horror film set – then wandering along the Corniche to the Royal Jewellery Museum for a taste of recent excess before going for a swim at Mamoura, resting in the late afternoon, and dining at the 1950s-style Elite.

STRENGTHS

▲ Beautiful beaches
▲ Antoniadis Gardens
▲ Old-world cafés
▲ Creepy catacombs
▲ The Biblioteca Alexandrina
▲ The Corniche
▲ The Mediterranean

WEAKNESSES

▲ Summer crowds
▲ Beautiful beaches as overcrowded asset
▲ Its rejection of cosmopolitanism

GOLD STAR

The library, with a reading room stepped over 14 terraces, re-creates the repository for literature and history founded 2500 years ago by the Macedonian conqueror of the world. It resembles a giant discus embedded in the ground at an angle, representing a second sun rising from the Mediterranean.

CITYSPEAK

▲ Have you paid your overdue fines at the library?
▲ Cairenes: thanks for the money – but so many of you?

STARRING ROLE IN...

▲ *Alexandria: A History & Guide* by EM Forster
▲ *Death on the Nile* by Agatha Christie (film 1978)
▲ *Alexandria Quartet* by Lawrence Durrell
▲ *Lawrence of Arabia* (1962)
▲ *Farewell to Alexandria: Eleven Short Stories* by Harry E Tzalas

IMPORT

▲ Greek mathematician Euclid
▲ Greek poet Apollonius
▲ Greek scholar Aristarchus
▲ Greek mathematician and astronomer Eratosthenes
▲ Greek physician Herophilus
▲ Julius Caesar
▲ Marc Anthony
▲ Augustus Caesar
▲ Gustave Flaubert
▲ Hordes of Cairenes in the summer
▲ Millions of foreign tourists attracted to the city's jaded historical and literary mystique
▲ Archaeologists busy uncovering splendours on the harbour floor

EXPORT

▲ The great love story of Cleopatra and Marc Anthony
▲ Cleopatra's Needles (two red-granite obelisks), now in London and New York
▲ Rudolf Hess
▲ The exiled King Farouk
▲ The mass flight in the 1950s of non-Egyptians
▲ The poetry of Constantine Cavafy
▲ Omar Sharif
▲ Demis Roussos

SEE the ancient royal remains submerged in the surrounding sea (scuba equipment needed).

EAT the freshest seafood at Gezeirit El-Maleka and sample the whole menu – feel free to use your fingertips.

DRINK coffee at the classic and very elegant Trianon Le Salon.

DO visit the new Alexandria Library, two millennia after the world's first library was founded here.

WATCH the Alexandrians promenading along the Corniche overlooking the sea, enjoying the cool of the evening.

BUY leather goods, including shoes, in the shopping area south and west of Mian Sa'ad Zaghool.

AFTER DARK catch the belly dancing at the Palace Suite in the Plaza Hotel.

URBAN MYTH

The theory that the original library initiated by Ptolemy I in 288 BC was destroyed by later Christian mobs – or any other group – is disputed. It is thought more likely to have gradually declined due to a lack of support.

TWILIGHT TRAFFIC FRINGES THE MEDITERRANEAN.
Photographer: Bill Lyons (2)

A TRADITIONALLY DRESSED MANNEQUIN IS OUTRAGED BY HER NUDE COUNTERPART.
Photographer: Bill Lyons (3)

TEA DRINKERS IN REPOSE UNDER A WATCHFULLY DECORATED RUG.
Photographer: Bill Lyons (4)

Belfast has earned its stripes; after years of violence and stagnation, there's a palpable positive energy, plus interesting industrial architecture and a slew of glorious drinking holes.

ANATOMY

Belfast's compact city centre curls around the undulating west bank of the River Lagan, with the steep slopes of Black Mountain and Cave Hill beyond. It's a child of the Industrial Revolution; imposing Victorian architecture and leafy gardens are set against the cranes of the Harland and Wolff shipyards, restored warehouses and row upon row of workers' terraced houses. Buses and trains do the job, and chartered black cabs – the people's taxis – ply the main roads of sectarian West Belfast.

PEOPLE

Historically, Belfast's only ethnic divisions were those between Catholics and Protestants. Today there is greater equality between the two groups, and sectarian tensions are often linked to issues of class. As in other large Irish cities, there are now significant migrant communities, mainly from China, the Philippines, Africa, the Middle East and Pakistan. This influx of new cultures, as well as a large student population (from the rest of Ireland and abroad), has contributed to the decreasing importance of religion. But the transition isn't an easy one, with ongoing violence towards ethnic minorities, especially those living in poorer Protestant neighbourhoods.

TYPICAL BELFASTIAN

Belfastians surprise visitors with their infectious confidence and gregariousness. Like their Dublin neighbours they take their social lives seriously but, more than anywhere in Ireland, really do dress up for a night out. They remain vitally interested in politics, but are more likely to talk about their favourite DJ or the next sun holiday to Portugal than casually discuss the peace process. They are masters at taking the piss but don't take it personally; they're also known for asking any new-found acquaintances to a party on pub closing.

Belfast 163

VITAL STATISTICS

NAME: BELFAST

DATE OF BIRTH: 1611; WHEN CHICHESTER'S COLONY OF ENGLISH AND SCOTTISH SETTLED HERE, THOUGH THERE WAS A NORMAN CASTLE BUILT IN 1177; CELTIC OCCUPATION DATES BACK TO THE IRON AGE

ADDRESS: NORTHERN IRELAND (MAP 3, C6)

HEIGHT: 67M

SIZE: 115 SQ KM

POPULATION: 279,240

A PICTURE OF IRISHNESS: YOUNG BELFAST BOYS LOOK THE PART.
Photographer: Vehbi Koca (1)

DEFINING EXPERIENCE

Hitting Topshop for some gear, fixing up the fake tan then off to Spring & Airborne for that new alt-country band and wee pint before going to BT1, hanging out in the unisex toilets because it's where the action is, then heading home for a few hours' sleep and a fry-up, grabbing the steamer and heading away to the coast – the East Strand at Portrush is pumping.

STRENGTHS

- Amazing Victorian architecture: City Hall and the Grand Opera House
- Beautiful Botanical Gardens
- Views of the encircling mountains
- Queen's University
- Ulster Museum
- Compact but still resolutely urban centre
- Friendly to visitors
- Lagan Towpath
- Burgeoning restaurant scene
- City Hall
- Belfast Art College
- Resilience

WEAKNESSES

- July
- Undeserved grim reputation
- Brian Kennedy
- The marriage of old-school sectarianism and millennial xenophobia
- *Spides* (the Belfastian term for local male hoodlums)

GOLD STAR

Black, black sense of humour: Belfastians love to laugh, and the humour tends towards the surreal and sarcastic.

CITYSPEAK

- Why can't we have an Ikea too?
- Revitalisation of the city centre
- Have you seen her new Louis Vuitton handbag?

STARRING ROLE IN...

- *Divorcing Jack* (1998)
- *The Most Fertile Man In Ireland* (1999)
- *The Mighty Celt* (2005)
- *This Human Season* by Louise Dean

IMPORT

- Day-tripping Dubliners
- Students
- Black cabs
- Mural art
- British high-street chains
- English and Scottish footballers
- Italian craftsmen (in the 1880s)

EXPORT

- Mary McAleese (President of Ireland)
- Van Morrison
- Wayward sporting stars: George Best, Alex Higgins
- Paul Hill
- Ships
- Linen
- Bushmills
- Ash
- Therapy
- Actor Stephan Rea
- James Nesbitt
- Kenneth Branagh

SEE Samson and Goliath, the giant yellow cranes of the Harland & Wolff shipyards, from a boat on the River Lagan.

EAT posh – perhaps local game cooked up by Michael Dean in his eponymous Michelin-starred restaurant.

DRINK a hot whiskey with cloves and lemon while ensconced in a snug in the high-Victorian camp of the Crown Liquor Saloon.

DO the Falls and Skankills Rds by people's taxi and take in the murals.

Watch a big-name act play the Ulster Hall or an up-and-coming one at the Limelight.

BUY an edgy new Brit label from the Clothes Agency.

AFTER DARK hear harder and heavier beats at Shine, a venerable club night at the Queen's Student Union.

URBAN MYTH

The Crown Saloon, a heavily touristed but still authentic city pub, has a sectarian love story all of its own. When the establishment was being renovated in 1885, the Catholic owner, Patrick Flanagan, argued with his Protestant wife over a new and fitting name. She eventually got her way and they opted for 'The Crown', despite the fact that it was symbolic of the British regime. Flanagan's acquiescence came with a cheeky subversion though: he ordered a crown mosaic for the doorstep so that each and every punter would trample it upon entering.

THE ORNATE MAJESTY OF BUILDINGS AT QUEEN'S UNIVERSITY.
Photographer: Richard Cummins (2)

GLASSY WATERS REFLECT THE MODERN MASTERPIECE OF THE RIVER LAGAN WEIR.
Photographer: Richard Cummins (3)

A REPUBLICAN MEMORIAL MURAL HONOURS THE DEAD, FALLS RD.
Photographer: Richard Cummins (4)

THE COLOUR OF LIFE IN THE VIVID HEART OF THE SOUTH.
Photographer: Ray Laskowitz (1)

Savannah
164

Savannah is a city rich in history, charm and Southern hospitality with one of the largest historic districts in the USA. It features thousands of beautiful buildings, including classic examples of Federal, Italianate and Victorian architecture.

ANATOMY

The city lies on the Savannah River, 29km from the Atlantic Coast amid moors and mammoth oak trees dripping with Spanish moss. Careful urban design, both widely studied and admired, makes for a liveable, beautiful and expandable city, with a gridlike pattern of streets, and houses and public buildings built around tree-filled squares. The city is pedestrian-friendly and there are also plenty of buses.

PEOPLE

This is the South, so about 30% of the population is African-American. Demographic changes across the continent are felt here too, with Latino and Asian-Americans (4%) becoming a growing force in Savannah. Disease, war and forcible removal have meant that Native Americans form only 1% of modern-day Savannah's populace.

TYPICAL SAVANNAH CITIZEN

The majority of voters are right-leaning conservatives, although in the early 1960s the city drew on its liberal traditions and became perhaps the first fully integrated city in the South. These contradictions are evidenced in a city culture where tradition battles with debauchery – pleasure and its indulgence are as much a part of tradition as the glorious façades of yesteryear. And while the city is now almost as cosmopolitan as Martha's Vineyard, Miami Beach or San Francisco, the legendary hospitality remains, as does a certain formality and politeness – opening doors for women is expected and the locals do like to dress up for special events.

DEFINING EXPERIENCE

Starting the day with a leisurely breakfast in the Historic District at Clary's Café then visiting the Savannah History Museum and taking a walking tour before the day heats up too much, catching lunch at an outdoor café then beating the heat by heading out onto the river aboard a paddle wheeler.

STRENGTHS

- Historic District
- Riverfront
- Paddle-wheeler trips on the river
- Cobblestone streets
- Carriage rides around town
- City Market
- History Museum
- Mercer House
- Wonderful African Baptist churches and the oldest Reform Judaism temple in the USA (dating from 1733)
- The sea islands
- Great tours at all times of day and night
- Telfair Art Museum

WEAKNESSES

- The sticky height of summer
- Petty crime

GOLD STAR

Savannah's vast historic districts show off extraordinary collections of 18th- and 19th-century buildings and a collection of immense Victorian townhouses.

CITYSPEAK

- Continuing disparity between poor blacks and affluent whites.
- How many tourists can we cope with?

STARRING ROLE IN...

- *The Gift* (2000)
- *The Legend of Bagger Vance* (1999)
- *Forces of Nature* (1998)
- *The General's Daughter* (1998)
- *Midnight in the Garden of Good and Evil* by John Berendt (film 1997)
- *Forrest Gump* (1993)
- *Glory* (1989)
- *The Return of Swamp Thing* (1988)
- *Roots* (1976)

IMPORT

- Damn Yankees
- Five million tourists a year

EXPORT

- Johnny Mercer
- 'Moon River'
- Poet Conrad Aiken
- Flannery O'Connor

SEE the city, river and nearby Tybee Island from one of the replica riverboats plying the waters from River St.

EAT Southern cuisine (black-eyed peas, turnips, fried chicken, sweet potatoes, green beans and rice) at Mrs Wilkes' Dining Room.

DRINK with pleasing ease – drinking alcohol outdoors is OK on city streets, unlike other cities in the South.

DO take a tour of the houses and gardens to see legendary mansions and secret gardens.

WATCH great drama at the Savannah Shakespeare Festival or listen to musicians at the Savannah Jazz Festival.

BUY antiques from more than 100 registered dealers, or Civil War artefacts from True Grits.

AFTER DARK enjoy the sumptuous nightlife, go clubbing at City Market and the Riverfront or catch a drag show at Club One Jefferson.

URBAN MYTH

Books and films have glamorised Savannah as a surreal remnant of the old South, where tradition beds down with sweet decadence. Now most of the world knows Savannah through its roles in *Forrest Gump*, John Berendt's hugely successful 1994 murder-mystery travelōgue *Midnight in the Garden of Good and Evil*, and the subsequent film directed by Clint Eastwood. Books such as *Wise Blood* by Savannah-born Flannery O'Connor, songs like 'Moon River' by native-son composer Johnny Mercer and the 2002 hit movie the *Legend of Bagger Vance* have added to the city's mythology. These days, hardly a year goes by without another feature film being made in Savannah with a gaggle of stars moving about incognito in the city's bars, clubs and restaurants and dipping into the local real-estate market to buy a little piece of this garden of good and evil.

THE HAUNTING BEAUTY OF BONAVENTURE CEMETERY – A JEWEL IN SAVANNAH'S GLITTERING CROWN.
Photographer: Ray Laskowitz (2)

SAVANNAH'S GRACIOUS SPIRIT FLOWS INTO HER BUILDINGS AND WELL PLANNED STREETS.
Photographer: Ray Laskowitz (3)

ENJOYING SOME OF THAT SOUTHERN HOSPITALITY.
Photographer: Ray Laskowitz (4)

Nuuk 165

VITAL STATISTICS

NAME: NUUK

NICKNAME: GODTHÅB (LITERALLY 'GOOD HOPE' IN DANISH)

DATE OF BIRTH: 1728; THE TOWN WAS FOUNDED BY THE NORWEGIAN MISSIONARY HANS EGEDE AS THE FIRST ALL-YEAR EUROPEAN COLONY AND TRADING POST IN GREENLAND

ADDRESS: GREENLAND (MAP 1, O5)

HEIGHT: 20M

SIZE: 87,000 SQ KM

POPULATION: 16,200

Nuuk is the perfect base for discovering Greenland and its culture – explore the Inuit culture and people, then head off into the mountains or onto the fjords for spectacular adventure tourism.

ANATOMY

Situated on the mouth of the Godthåbsfjord, Nuuk commands an impressive if spread-out fjord system and is backed by a splendid panorama of mountains, particularly Mt Sermitsiaq. The architecture is a mix of older homes of real Greenlandic charm and rows of spirit-crushing housing. Explore the world's northernmost capital city by boat and snowmobile.

PEOPLE

This city's population is bicultural, with 87% Greenlander (Inuit) and 13% Danish. The two thought systems are often almost diametrically opposed, but Greenlanders of Danish, Inuit and mixed origin share a bond of objective, philosophical realism, and they mock incoming Danes and foreigners alike for their unrealistic belief in clocks, appointments and deadlines. Danish is the official language.

TYPICAL NUUK CITIZEN

Nuuk's inhabitants have adapted to the development from a traditional Greenlandic society to a modern industrial town in a unique way. The economy functions for and because of administrators, but tools lie where they're dropped once the cash arrives on payday. Time will be spent with friends, but in comfortable silence – the key is in the body language. Smiles are common, but don't always mean pleasure. Adults in villages will ignore you, but children won't stop examining you. Your race and origins will be observed, but you'll be judged on your actions. Nuuk is the only place to be for family, friends and the hunt.

DEFINING EXPERIENCE

Morning fishing on the fjords, then *kaffemik* (coffee and, usually, seven types of cakes or biscuits) with the entire community, sitting in blissful silence with friends and leaving when you've had you're second cup of coffee, eating your day's catch, then heading out for a night of live music and dancing at the pub.

STRENGTHS

⊿ Vibrant Inuit culture
⊿ Aurora borealis
⊿ Braedet Market (fresh fish and game sold on open-air tables)
⊿ World's hardest golf course
⊿ Photogenic Qornup Suvdula fjord
⊿ Traditional costumes worn on the first day of school
⊿ Snow, ice and water sports galore
⊿ Oldest rocks (3.8 billion years old) ever discovered on earth
⊿ Ghosts of Herrnhut missionaries in the University of Greenland
⊿ Humpback whales in the harbour
⊿ Greenlandic modern art

WEAKNESSES

⊿ Long-slab apartment blocks, such as Block P
⊿ Pervasive sense of economic apartheid
⊿ Children on the streets all night from parental neglect
⊿ Alcoholism
⊿ *Perlerorneq* ('the burden' in Greenlandic) – depression during the long, dark winters

GOLD STAR

The Arctic Marathon – Nuuk hosts the world's most challenging snow-bound marathon for locals and internationals.

CITYSPEAK

⊿ The controversial new airport extension
⊿ The perpetual, unsubstantiated rumours that Denmark is somehow siphoning off secret profits from 'something' in Greenland…but what?
⊿ Greenland's dreams of national independence

STARRING ROLE IN...

⊿ *Nuuk* (2004)
⊿ *Miss Smilla's Feeling For Snow* by Peter Høeg
⊿ *Smilla's Sense of Snow* (1977)
⊿ *Last Places* by Lawrence Millman
⊿ *Tales and Traditions of the Eskimo* by Henry Rink
⊿ *Eskimo Folk-tales* collected by Knud Rasmussen
⊿ *An African in Greenland* by Tété-Michel Kpomassie

IMPORT

⊿ Anything (product or food) that can't be made from Arctic critters or territory
⊿ Beer
⊿ Ridiculously expensive hashish
⊿ Vikings
⊿ Missionaries
⊿ Danish welfare payments
⊿ Evangelical Lutheran beliefs and hymns
⊿ Music styles

EXPORT

⊿ Fish, prawns and other fish products
⊿ Inuit culture
⊿ Fur craft and clothing
⊿ Mummified six-year-old girls on the cover of *National Geographic*
⊿ The Nuuk Declaration on Arctic nations and its role in protecting the Arctic environment
⊿ Nuuk Posse, Greenland's most popular hip-hop band
⊿ Big-budget Arctic tourism
⊿ Santa Claus
⊿ Packaged whale steaks

SEE Kolonihavn – an 18th-century fishing village in the heart of Nuuk.

EAT gourmet Arctic gastronomy (like musk steak) at Restaurant Nipisa.

DRINK genuine Greenlandic coffee at Café Tuap.

DO explore ancient and modern Inuit art at the Katuaq Cultural Centre.

WATCH snow sculptors at work at the annual Nuuk International Snow Festival.

BUY a piece of black *Nuummiit*, the 'Greenland opal', found only in the Nuuk region.

AFTER DARK drink up in Kristinemut, Greenland's first pub, then party on in the electro-throbbing rock bar Afterdark.

URBAN MYTH

An indefinable distance from Nuuk is Kongsgaarden, a world-famous workshop full of consumer goods that are given away on a seasonal basis, especially in late December. This behaviour brings unprecedented popularity to the manager, a certain Mr S Claus, who receives more mail than anyone else in the whole of Greenland. Alas, reindeer-sleigh services are notoriously unreliable, so Santa Claus can only be accessed via the web (www.santa.gl) or through mail posted in the world's biggest postbox, located outside the post office in Nuuk.

BASKING IN THE AFTERNOON SUN – UNIFORM APARTMENT BLOCKS ARE A COMMON SIGHT IN NUUK.
Photographer: Anders Blomqvist (1)

SEAL MEAT IS A STAPLE OF THE LOCAL DIET, ON SALE HERE IN THE BRAEDET MARKET.
Photographer: Anders Blomqvist (2)

THE INUIT PEOPLE TRY TO PRESERVE THEIR CULTURE DESPITE THE CRUSH OF MODERNISATION.
Photographer: Anders Blomqvist (3)

GOLFERS DO IT TOUGH AGAINST THE BACKDROP OF SERMITSIAQ PEAK.
Photographer: Anders Blomqvist (4)

Jeddah

166

VITAL STATISTICS

NAME: JEDDAH

NICKNAME: JIDDAH

DATE OF BIRTH: AD 646; THE CALIPH UTHMAN OFFICIALLY ESTABLISHED JEDDAH AS THE GATEWAY TO MECCA

ADDRESS: SAUDI ARABIA (MAP 2, M6)

HEIGHT: 6M

SIZE: 560 SQ KM

POPULATION: 2.82 MILLION

A microcosm of the Islamic world and the pulse of modern Saudi Arabia, Jeddah has all the vibrancy of a liberal, fast-moving, modern commercial capital, with the added charm of century-old alleyway souqs (markets), the waterfront corniche and the gateway to the holy Islamic cities of Mecca and Medina.

ANATOMY

Jeddah's heart is its Al-Balad district, with enchanting buildings made of coral overlooking the narrow lanes of the souqs. The city has bloated to 1000 times its original size. King Abdul Aziz St is its main north–south thoroughfare and has a host of restaurants, banks and shops. The bulk of the urban sprawl is north of Al-Balad, and Medina Rd is the principal street running north from the centre, flanked to the west by Al-Andalus St – all reached by a network of buses and taxis. Not far away, the waterfront corniche (Al-Kournaish Rd) runs the length of Jeddah's coastline from Jeddah Islamic Port (in the southern part of town) to the city's northern outskirts.

PEOPLE

Although no official census exists in the kingdom, it would be safe to say that Jeddah's citizens are both typically and atypically Saudi. The bustling city reflects the largely urbanised Saudi Arabia – Jeddah boasts residents from all over the world, including a large expatriate business population. Although Islam prevails, expatriate compounders very quietly retain Christian and other beliefs. Jeddah is on the path to Mecca for thousands of haj pilgrims, and, as such, Jeddahns retain the essence of one of the most essential and historic aspects of Islam.

TYPICAL JEDDAHN

Cosmopolitan, modern and as swift as the traffic, Jeddahns are a sleeker, more progressive version of their Saudi counterparts. They work hard and speak a multitude of languages. Typical Saudi wariness is relaxed here – Jeddahns have been opening their city to pilgrims for centuries. Jeddahns hold dear the Islamic traditions of dress, strict gender roles and prayer, but young Saudis, who gently push the boundaries of the kingdom's traditions, push a little harder here.

DEFINING EXPERIENCE

Soaking up Arabia at its best at the enchanting Souq al-Alawi during the haj season, as wonderful old houses tower above and pilgrims from across the sea and desert follow the calls to prayer, which fill the lanes at sunset, as they have done for more than a millennia.

STRENGTHS

- Internet
- Banks
- Souqs (markets)
- Comparatively relaxed *mutawwa* (religious police)
- Diving and windsurfing
- Casual private resorts
- Haj pilgrims
- Heritage architecture
- Hotels for every budget
- Cosmopolitan attitudes

WEAKNESSES

- Reckless driving
- Lack of trees
- Dilapidated buildings
- Ordinary beaches
- Limited freedoms for women

GOLD STAR

The haj pilgrimage – Jeddah has been the historical gateway for pilgrims travelling to the holy Islamic cities of Mecca and Medina for almost 15 centuries.

CITYSPEAK

- The August 2005 death of King Fahd, Saudi Arabia's ruler since 1982, succeeded by the former crown prince Abdullah
- Saudi women's rights

STARRING ROLE IN...

- *Seven Pillars of Wisdom* by TE Lawrence
- *Eight Months on Ghazzah Street* by Hilary Mantel
- *Exit Only* by Liam Bracken

IMPORT

- Pilgrims
- Fast food
- American cars
- Sheep
- Camels
- Syrian jewellery
- Thai food
- TE Lawrence

EXPORT

- Oil
- Iron
- Steel
- Bricks
- Furniture
- Tiles
- Afghan rugs
- Big business

SEE the delightfully restored Naseef House, standing in the centre of the Al-Alawi souq.

EAT from the delicious seafood buffet at Al-Bouhaira Restaurant.

DRINK coffee at a traditional coffee house.

DO dive in the Red Sea, at the popular and relaxed Al-Nakheel Beach Resort.

WATCH a classic flick in the makeshift cinema at the Italian Cultural Centre.

BUY Syrian silver jewellery from the friendly and informative owners of Old Jeddah Arts & Crafts.

AFTER DARK stroll along Jeddah's corniche and catch a Red Sea breeze amid the eclectic collection of sculptures, which includes a Henry Moore.

URBAN MYTH

Jeddah's history is the stuff of legend, and one of those legends goes back to the theological beginnings of the human race. The name 'Jeddah' means 'grandmother', supposedly named after Eve, who went to live in and eventually died in Jeddah, following her exile from paradise. Her grave, in the shadow of the city gates, survived the perils of history until 1947, when the gates were destroyed to accommodate the rapid population growth. Although reverence of the site is not encouraged, many still pause to ponder the place where the tomb is rumoured to have been.

ENOUGH DATES TO FILL A CALENDAR.
Photographer: Chris Mellor (1)

THE TRADITIONAL ARABIAN FAÇADE OF SHORBATLY HOUSE.
Photographer: Tony Wheeler (2)

TIME FOR SOME MALE BONDING (NO LADIES ALLOWED) AT A LOCAL TEAHOUSE.
Photographer: Nikolai Ignatiev (3)

A WOMAN AND CHILD ENJOY QUALITY TIME AT THE BEACH IN THE SHADOW OF A MINARET.
Photographer: Lynsey Addario (4)

Johannesburg

167

VITAL STATISTICS

NAME: JOHANNESBURG

NICKNAME: JO'BURG; JOZI

DATE OF BIRTH: 1886; FOUNDED WHEN GOLD WAS DISCOVERED IN THE TRANSVAAL

ADDRESS: SOUTH AFRICA (MAP 2, J24)

HEIGHT: 1665M

SIZE: 2500 SQ KM

POPULATION: 4.9 MILLION

CELEBRATING MARRIAGE THE TRADITIONAL WAY IN SOWETO'S FAMOUS REGIONAL MUNDI CHURCH.
Photographer: Brent Stirton (1)

KEEPING THE PEACE AT THE POPULAR COLOR BAR.
Photographer: Brent Stirton (2)

SOWETO – THIS LEGACY OF THE APARTIED REGIME WAS ONCE THE HOME OF NELSON MANDELA.
Photographer: Brent Stirton (3)

THE RHYTHM OF THE NIGHT IS FELT IN JOHANNESBURG'S LIVELY CLUB SCENE.
Photographer: Brent Stirton (4)

The huge beating heart of the Rainbow Nation, Johannesburg is a cosmopolitan African city, at once untamed and sophisticated, hazardous and welcoming, now shedding its shameful past and embracing the richness and lessons of its history.

ANATOMY

Johannesburg is built on a high-altitude inland plateau, with winding river systems and natural reserves breaking up the cityscape. Unfolding from the office-block jungle of the city centre, the main sights in this expansive city spread across the cultural and social hub of Newtown, past the ring of black neighbourhoods and out into the wealthy white suburbs of the north and the black township of Soweto in the southwest. While the African flavour of Jo'burg is virtually absent in the shopping mall–centred northern suburbs, it crowds the streets of the city centre by day with street stalls and vendors. Johannesburg is big and best navigated by car, though there are buses, minibus taxis and an efficient, yet sometimes dangerous, train system.

PEOPLE

The population of Johannesburg is 73% black African and 17% white, with the remaining 10% made up of other nationalities, including a significant Indian portion. While South Africa has no fewer than 11 official languages, the most common in Johannesburg are Afrikaans, English, Zulu and Sesotho. The religious demographics of Johannesburg are similarly diverse, with around 53% belonging to mainstream Christian churches, 24% atheist, 14% belonging to African Independent churches, 3% Muslim, 1% Jewish and 1% Hindu.

TYPICAL JOHANNESBURGER

In a city still economically segregated, the typical Johannesburger can range from the unspeakably poor to the grossly affluent. They travel mainly by cars, love music and the entertainment scene and tend to live it up in ethnically distinct areas. They love to drink, watch sport and relax in the great outdoors. Though acutely aware of their infamous history, they disarm visitors with their open and friendly manner.

DEFINING EXPERIENCE

Sifting through crafts at Rosebank Rooftop Market, then soaking up the exuberant hospitality of Soweto with a fabulous buffet meal and some African brews at the infamous Wandie's Place before manning the *braai* (barbecue) pitch-side while watching an international test at the Wanderers Cricket Ground or heading to Codfather for some of Johannesburg's best-value seafood dishes.

STRENGTHS

- Thriving music scene
- Weather
- City street stalls selling corn and beef
- Many free art galleries
- Arts Alive Festival (showcasing hot, new talent)
- Over six million trees
- Ethnic diversity
- Mary Fitzgerald Sq
- Gay-friendly
- *Mail & Guardian* entertainment guide in Friday's paper
- Soweto
- World-class theatre
- International sporting events
- Apartheid Museum
- Great shopping in the malls
- Botanical Gardens

WEAKNESSES

- Carjacking
- Dangerous neighbourhoods
- High unemployment
- Wearing a camera round your neck signals 'Mug me'
- AIDS epidemic

GOLD STAR

The high-life – cigar lounges, stylish restaurants, world-class theatre productions and excellent shopping are all part of the fun of high living in one of the cheapest major cities in the world.

CITYSPEAK

- The ongoing theft and falsification of thousands of South African identity documents and, in particular, the 2005 incident of US actor Wesley Snipes trying to leave South Africa using a fake South African passport
- Jo'burg's preparations for hosting the 2010 FIFA World Cup

STARRING ROLE IN...

- *Stander* (2004)
- *Cry, the Beloved Country* (1995)
- *Cry Freedom* (1987)
- *Long Walk to Freedom* by Nelson Mandela

IMPORT

- Luxury goods
- International brand names
- Mahatma Gandhi (for a time)
- European and Asian cuisine
- Cars

EXPORT

- Gold
- The wisdom of Nelson Mandela
- Humankind (depending on the theory)
- Finance
- Insurance
- Processed food
- Diamonds
- Charlize Theron

SEE the Cradle of Humankind site – 50km out of city centre – where human ancestor fossils up to 3.5 million years old have been excavated.

EAT African-Asian fusion at Gramadoela's – join Hillary Clinton and Denzel Washington on the list of diners at this classic restaurant.

DRINK a couple of pints on the terrace of Jo'burg's oldest pub, Guildhall Bar & Restaurant.

DO – if you can afford it – spend a night at the luxurious Saxon Hotel, where Nelson Mandela put the final touches to his autobiography.

WATCH rugby at the hallowed Ellis Park and get religious with the fanatical fans.

BUY traditional medicine at the Faraday Market.

AFTER DARK join Jo'burg's recent reggae revival with some thumping rhythms at Cool Runnings.

URBAN MYTH

It has been said that Johannesburg's premier residential and business district, Sandton – often described as the richest square kilometre in Africa – has so many swimming pools and landscape gardens that on some satellite pictures it looks like a tropical forest…even though it is built on the dry African grassland.

BACKS TO THE WALL – THE MEDINA WALL AND GREAT MOSQUE DATE BACK TO AD 761.
Photographer: Mark Henley (1)

Tunisia's spiritual heart, ancient Kairouan is serene, magnetic, lively and proud: this ancient beauty of exquisite arches, columns and stonework enthrals the mind and eyeballs.

ANATOMY
Easy to navigate by foot, the old walled holy city of Kairouan encloses crumbling, whitewashed, blue- and green-edged houses, some hung with birdcages and many marked by the hand of Fatima. Away from the main souvenir drag, it's lovely to wander through the narrow cobblestone streets and big doorways of the medina (old quarter).

PEOPLE
Ninety-eight percent of Kairouans are Arab-Berber, with the remaining 2% made up of European and Jewish nationals. Islam is the dominant religion, with Kairouan historically known as 'the City of 100 Mosques'.

TYPICAL KAIROUAN
In an ancient city revered as one of Islam's holiest of holiest, it shouldn't be surprising that Kairouans are a traditional people, home to a civilisation that was closed to outsiders for many years. Men get about in red-felt hats and many local women are wrapped in the traditional Berber cream shawls, their faces marked with traditional tattoos.

Kairouan
168

VITAL STATISTICS
NAME: KAIROUAN

NICKNAME: LITTLE CAIRO

DATE OF BIRTH: AD 670; WHEN ARAB CONQUEROR UQBA IBN NAFI ESTABLISHED MILITARY POSTS ACROSS NORTH AFRICA AND SET UP A TEMPORARY ENCAMPMENT AT WHAT LATER BECAME KAIROUAN

ADDRESS: TUNISIA (MAP 3, J17)

HEIGHT: 60M

POPULATION: 110,000

THE GREAT MOSQUE AREA – A STARK, WHITE SHRINE TO MUSLIM IDEALS.
Photographer: Kevin O'Hara (3)

BRINGING HOME THE DAILY BREAD.
Photographer: Veronica Garbutt (4)

WHITE-WASHED BUILDING SPRAWL LIKE MODERN ART UPON THE CANVAS OF KAIROUAN, ISLAM'S FOURTH
HOLIEST CITY. Photographer: Roger Wood (2)

DEFINING EXPERIENCE

Coveting carpets woven by artisans in the medina, then picnicking with a feast of *makhroud* (honey-soaked pastry stuffed with dates) market-stall sweetmeats by the Aghlabite Basins' 9th-century reservoirs, and admiring the breathtaking pillars and columns of the Roman and Byzantine buildings and Grande Mosquée by twilight.

STRENGTHS

◢ Grande Mosquée and its ancient minaret (said to be the oldest in the world)
◢ Mosque of the Three Doors
◢ Carpet museum
◢ Zaouia Sidi Abid el-Ghariani
◢ Kasbah
◢ Barber mosque – Zaouia Sidi Sahab
◢ *Makhroud*

WEAKNESS

◢ Poor treatment of animals

GOLD STAR

Koran kudos – many Muslims, particularly Sunni Muslims, consider Kairouan to be Islam's fourth-holiest city (after Mecca, Medina and Jerusalem).

CITYSPEAK

◢ All manner of trade – the word on the street often involves grain, livestock, cereals, olives and animal products

STARRING ROLE IN...

◢ *Raiders of the Lost Ark* (1984)
◢ *The Great Mosque of Kairouan* by Paul Sebag
◢ *Sleepless Nights* by Ali Duaji
◢ *Pillar of Salt* by Albert Memmi
◢ *Will to Live* by Abu el-Kacem el-Chabbi

IMPORT

◢ The pilgrim faithful
◢ Byzantine and Roman buildings
◢ Tourists

EXPORT

◢ Carpets
◢ Brasswork
◢ Leatherwork
◢ Handicrafts
◢ Grain
◢ Livestock
◢ Olives
◢ Thirteen centuries of Islamic culture
◢ Berber cream shawls

SEE the Mosque of the Three Doors, famous for the rare intertwined floral and Arabic inscriptions carved in its façade.

EAT local delicacies at the Restaurant Sabra, a friendly popular local eatery with a piercingly loud bird in a cage.

DRINK espresso shots in school chairs in the delightful tree-shaded café of Hôtel Sabra.

DO brave Kairouan's side streets and get among the animated locals going about their daily lives.

WATCH the fascinating flux of faithful pouring out of afternoon prayer at the Grande Mosque on Friday afternoon.

BUY exquisite hand-knotted pile Alloucha carpets, Kairouan's local specialty, from one of the hundreds of shops in the medina's souq (market).

AFTER DARK hightail it out of the city walls to get a view from the outside as the sun sets over this mind-bogglingly ancient holy city.

URBAN MYTH

Kairouan was established as a pilgrimage destination largely due to a legend that tells of a warrior's horse discovering a golden goblet in the sands of Kairouan. It was recognised as a goblet that had disappeared from Mecca years before and, when it was extracted, a spring emerged from the ground. These gushing waters were claimed to have come from the same aqueduct feeding the sacred Zamzam well in Mecca.

Austin

169

VITAL STATISTICS

NAME: AUSTIN

NICKNAME: LIVE MUSIC CAPITAL OF THE WORLD

DATE OF BIRTH: 1842; WHEN IT BEGAN LIFE AS THE VILLAGE OF WATERLOO

ADDRESS: USA (MAP 1, J11)

HEIGHT: 178M

SIZE: 651 SQ KM

POPULATION: 567,000

Skip the bighorn of Houston and the Ala-ho-hum – Texas is all about its weird and wonderful capital, which hosts innovative IT, live music that's more than just alt-country, a burgeoning film industry and the best Tex-Mex you can gobble down in the state.

ANATOMY

Downtown Austin is laid out in an easily navigable grid, with Congress Ave running from the city's south, across the Colorado River and continuing to the Texas State Capitol. Parallel to Congress, Guadalupe St becomes the Drag, a student mecca for cheap eats and music stores. East 6th St – also running alongside Congress – is known as the Strip and boasts an array of clubs, bars and nightspots. The Warehouse District to the southwest of Congress is another entertainment district, catering for an older hootenanny, often with gay and lesbian nights. The city's public bus network is a solid system of inexpensive neighbourhood, express and downtown routes.

PEOPLE

Austin is relatively cosmopolitan by Texan standards with almost two-thirds of the population identifying as Caucasian. Hispanic and Latin Americans make up 30%, with Spanish spoken amid the predominant English. African-Americans are 10% of the population, with Asian and Native Americans also making up the diverse background of the capital.

TYPICAL AUSTINITE

After being bucked from the dot-bronco, Austinite digital cowboys have had to take a breather, but the city is still the shining star of teched-up Texas. GPS is the new cowboy hat (though the city has never been into uniforms – there's an unspoken 'no-suits' policy). Almost 50,000 residents attend UT (as University of Texas is better known), making for a massive student population to keep the music live and the art cutting edge. Yep, Austinites prize their strangeness, even going so far as to stage protests to 'Keep Austin weird', and see themselves as very different from their oil-rich, cowpoke Texan neighbours. 'I don't live in Texas', local troubadour Jerry Jeff Walker once said, 'I live in Austin'.

DEFINING EXPERIENCE

Grabbing a barbecue breakfast – a spicy start to any day – then working it off with Frisbee golf through Zilker Park, attending a seminar on film at UT, then hoeing-down at a hootenanny, sinking a few margaritas in a honky tonk on 6th St, and being spooked by the 1.5 million-strong bat colony under Congress Ave Bridge.

STRENGTHS

- South by Southwest (SXSW)
- Zilker Park and Barton Springs Pool
- McKinney Falls State Park
- UT
- Colorado River
- Bikes Not Bombs (free bikes for visitors)
- Pennybacker Bridge
- Frisbee golf courses
- Texas State Capitol
- Free Silver 'Dillo (short for armadillo) buses
- Moonlight Towers

WEAKNESSES

- Good ol' boys
- Boiling heat
- Dull chain hotels lining I-35

GOLD STAR

Live music – every other bar has tunes to get your foot tapping and your boot scooting.

CITYSPEAK

- They don't make tacos with a real kick any more do they?
- Is it un-American that Willie Nelson's bus runs on bio-diesel?
- Who's playing at SXSW this year?

STARRING ROLE IN...

- *Armadillos and Old Lace* by Kinky Friedman
- *Slacker* (1991)
- *Dazed and Confused* (1993)
- *Spy Kids* (2001)
- *Secondhand Lions* (2003)
- *Miss Congeniality* (2000)
- *Office Space* (1999)
- *Sin City* (2005)

IMPORT

- Lance Armstrong
- Michael Dell
- Sandra Bullock
- Matthew McConaughey
- Tacos, burritos and *cervezas* (beer)

EXPORT

- Hootenannies
- Richard Linklater films
- Oil
- Slacking
- Lyndon B Johnson
- Laid-back music

SEE the eerie view from the 9m-tall UT Tower.

EAT a dripping taco *al pastor* (pork and pineapple) washed down with a margarita or 12 at Guero's Taco Bar.

DRINK a few Buds at Shady Grove Café on Thursday evening with Austin's local bands rocking the stage.

DO a warm-up lap with Lance Armstrong on the Town Lake Trail, a 10-mile loop that takes in the Stevie Ray Vaughan statue.

WATCH (and maybe get dragged onto the floor yourself) for Texas dancehall at Broken Spoke.

BUY a 'Keep Austin Weird' bumper sticker from any cigar store.

AFTER DARK check out the best retro country (and the cheap brews) at Ginny's Little Longhorn, a genuine honky tonk.

URBAN MYTH

Being state capital has been a tough gig for relaxed Austin, with the title almost disappearing in 1842. Attributing the move to the danger of local Comanche attacks, President Sam Houston tried to shift the government to Houston in 1842 and later to the catchy-named Washington-on-the-Brazos. The only thing sly Sam left behind were the archives of Texas, which he sneakily sent his Texas Rangers to reclaim in the dead of night. The history (a seat of government) was saved by local innkeepr Mrs Angelina Eberly, who raised the alarm by lighting a cannon with her cigar. Without the archives, the government had to return to Austin in 1845 and Sam Houston never looked at a cigar the same way again.

TIME TO SAY YOUR PRAYERS AT SIMPSON UNITED METHODIST CHURCH.
Photographer: Joe Raedle (1)

PROVE YOU AIN'T NO CHICKEN BY ENTERING THE 'WHERE WILL THE POOP LAND' COMPETITION AT GINNY'S.
Photographer: Joe Raedle (2)

SIX FINE LOOKIN' LEGS AT THE REGULAR JO FASHION SHOW, JO'S HOT COFFEE.
Photographer: Joe Raedle (3)

TUCKING INTO SOME DAMN FINE CHICKEN, GREEN MESQUITE BBQ & MORE.
Photographer: Joe Raedle (4)

GETTING SOME CHEEKY INK AT CUSTOM TATTOOS FROM THE SOUL.
Photographer: Joe Raedle (5)

WHISPERED PRAYERS RISE UP TO GREET THE BEAUTIFUL INTERIOR OF IGLESIA LA CIBA DE GUADALUPE.
Photographer: Anthony Plummer (1)

San Salvador

170

You can come to be one of the few tourists to see San Salvador's spectacular natural sights, or to watch Salvadoran society reconstruct itself after the ravages of civil war, but really, just come for the people – San Salvadorans are friendly, helpful, curious and generous, the best reason to visit the city.

ANATOMY

Built on a volcanic slope that parallels the Pacific coast and located beneath the San Salvador volcano, the city of San Salvador is El Salvador's largest, and its principal crossroads. It functions as the transportation and economic hub of the nation, and is home to one-third of the population and half of the nation's wealth. Crossed by the Pan American Hwy, the city's modern downtown area has many high-rise buildings, but sadly earthquakes have destroyed the majority of historic landmarks. San Salvador's extensive bus network, from large smoke-spewing monsters to zippy microbuses, can get you just about anywhere you need.

PEOPLE

San Salvadorans are among the more European-looking Central Americans – the vast majority is undoubtedly mestizo (of mixed Spanish and indigenous ancestry), but fair skin and green and blue eyes are not uncommon. Nine percent of San Salvadorans are considered of full European ancestry, while only 1% is indigenous. Spanish is the official language.

TYPICAL SAN SALVADORAN

San Salvadorans are straight-talking, strong-minded and hard-working. They're extremely helpful and almost universally friendly, with a powerful sense of justice; few are shy about expressing their opinion. The civil war still looms large for many, but they're genuinely dismayed to learn that foreigners know little about their country *other* than war, and will talk with pride about El Salvador's natural virtues.

DEFINING EXPERIENCE

Beginning the day with bread and *cafecito* (short black coffee), stocking up on food in the Mercado Central, cooking a beans-and-rice lunch then snoozing away the siesta, drinking Pilsener and getting down to some *cumbia* (Colombian dance tunes) and salsa.

STRENGTHS

- San Salvadorans
- Few foreign tourists
- The Mayan community
- Creative street vendors
- The Festival of El Salvador del Mundo (the Saviour of the World)
- Lake of Ilopango
- Museo de Arte de El Salvador (MARTE)
- San Salvadorans' unity post–civil war
- Adventure of travelling a relatively unvisited city
- Great literary history
- Year-round summer climate
- Positive attitudes to the future

WEAKNESSES

- Petty theft
- High population growth
- Poverty
- Guns everywhere
- Shanty towns
- Pollution
- Earthquakes
- Bitter political history
- Crossing the street
- Environmental destruction
- Traffic

GOLD STAR

Most improved – San Salvadorans have a strong work ethic and have quickly raised their country from the wreckage of civil war to close to the top of Central America's economic ladder.

CITYSPEAK

- The political situation following the last elections
- Money and survival
- The growth of Protestant evangelism (a full 20% of the population has converted from Catholicism)
- Family members who've migrated to the USA

STARRING ROLE IN...

- *Salvador* (1986)
- *Romero* (1988)
- *One Day of Life* by Manlio Argueta
- *Salvador* by Joan Didion
- *San Salvador* by Roque Dalton

IMPORT

- Conquistadors
- Guerrilla warfare
- Baseball
- Football
- Foreign aid

EXPORT

- Liberation theology
- Pilsener and Suprema beers
- Tobacco products
- Textiles
- Soaps
- Political activists worldwide
- Coffee

SEE the view of the city from the rim of Boquerón volcano.

EAT *pupusas* (meat or cheese pastries) from a street stall.

DRINK Pilsener beer at a bar with the locals.

DO check out the MARTE.

WATCH the maelstrom of crowds scurrying through sprawling markets, music blaring from every direction and buses zipping around at breakneck pace.

BUY handicrafts, hand-woven textiles and ceramics at the Mercado Ex-Cuartel.

AFTER DARK see live jazz and salsa at La Luna Casa y Arte.

URBAN MYTH

The much-loved Archbishop Oscar Romero was an outspoken supporter of the poor and in public opposition to the government. As he gave mass in the chapel of the Hospital La Divina Providencia one day in March 1980, Romero was assassinated by government agents. The chapel is still used, and exhibitions in his former living quarters in the hospital display his blood-soaked robes and the typewriter he used to type his famously stirring homilies. The Centro Monseñor Romeros at the Universidad Centroamericana José Simeón Cañas also pays homage to his memory.

A LIFE OF POVERTY HAS NOT TARNISHED THE BEAUTY OF THIS SAN SALVADORAN WOMAN'S FACE.
Photographer: Anthony Plummer (2)

THE SPIRIT OF THE REVOLUTION LIVES ON IN THE HEARTS OF SAN SALVADORANS.
Photographer: Anthony Plummer (3)

IN FULL VOICE – WASHED DOWN WITH RUM, LIME AND COKE AT ONE OF THE CITY BARS.
Photographer: Anthony Plummer (4)

Stunning scenery, historic, battle-scarred castles, a menu of outdoor activities, and gleaming bars and shops make the modern yet traditional capital of Wales a compelling place to visit.

ANATOMY

Central Cardiff's main landmarks are Cardiff Castle and the Millennium Stadium, by the River Taff. High St, St Mary St, Queen St, Bridge St and Charles St are a shopper's paradise, while the Civic Centre north of the castle houses government buildings. The harbour area to the south, once the world's top coal port, is now a redeveloped commercial centre called Cardiff Bay. The bus and train stations are near the stadium.

PEOPLE

Only one-fifth of Wales' population now speak Welsh and just over one-fifth of people come from England. Young people are migrating from the country to the city. Butetown is Cardiff's most multicultural area. Wales does not receive many asylum seekers.

TYPICAL CARDIFF CITIZEN

Welsh people are very proud of their national identity. They are supportive of the National Assembly, despite its limited powers, and are keen to maintain their flagging language (Welsh is taught in schools). Cardiff residents work long hours and are relatively affluent. They enjoy sport and are passionate about rugby. They are friendly and good fun, and confident and positive about Wales's future.

DEFINING EXPERIENCE

Sipping a shot of caffeine with the papers at Café Bar Europa, before wandering over to Bute Park to sunbathe near the ruins of Blackfriars Priory, then heading to Cardiff Central Market to refuel and Queen St for some retail therapy.

Cardiff 171

VITAL STATISTICS

NAME: CARDIFF

DATE OF BIRTH: AD 75; WHEN THE CITY BEGAN AS A ROMAN FORT – IT WAS ONLY MADE A CITY IN 1905 AND A CAPITAL IN 1955

ADDRESS: WALES (MAP 3, D8)

HEIGHT: 62M

SIZE: 120 SQ KM

POPULATION: 327,700

CHOICES, CHOICES: DIFFICULT DECISIONS AT CARDIFF MARKET'S SECONDHAND RECORD STORE.
Photographer: Neil Setchfield (1)

STRENGTHS

- National pride
- Cardiff Festival (July/August)
- Winning the Six Nations Rugby Championship in 2005
- Millennium Stadium
- National Museum & Gallery of Wales
- Cardiff Bay
- Cardiff Castle
- Caerphilly Castle
- Castell Coch
- Roman fortress at Carleon
- Brecon Beacons National Park
- Artes Mundi Award (Arts of the World)
- Museum of Welsh Life
- National Assembly
- Rugby – Cardiff Blues and the Welsh team
- Cycling the Lôn Las Cymru trail
- St Davids Hotel & Spa
- Surfing off the Gower Peninsula
- Welsh rarebit
- Welsh cheese eg Caerphilly and Celtic Blue
- Cardiff University
- Llandaff Cathedral
- Bute Park
- Techniquest
- EU financial aid
- Lower prices than in the rest of the UK
- Royal National Eisteddfod

WEAKNESSES

- Inclement weather
- Political apathy
- Rural economic problems
- Dwindling number of Welsh speakers

GOLD STAR

Castles – Wales is famous for them and Cardiff doesn't let the side down.

CITYSPEAK

- Rugby – we've won the Six Nations; can Wales win the World Cup?
- The new National Assembly building designed by Richard Rogers – will it ever be finished?

STARRING ROLE IN...

- *Human Traffic* (1999)
- *Twin Town* (1997)
- *Doctor Who* (2005–)
- *Dat's Love* by Leonora Brito

IMPORT

- Sir Anthony Hopkins
- Rugby (from England originally)

EXPORT

- Dame Shirley Bassey
- Charlotte Church
- Ryan Giggs
- Ioan Gruffyd
- Griff Rhys-Jones
- Cerys Matthews
- Shakin' Stevens
- Ivor Novella
- Brains Beer
- Penderyn Single Malt Whisky
- Roald Dahl
- Coal (until World War II)
- Mail-order businesses (the first one began in Newtown)
- Kissing under the mistletoe, a druidic tradition
- S4C
- Welsh National Opera
- Captain Robert Scott (launched his expedition to the South Pole from Cardiff in 1910)

SEE Cardiff Castle complete with Great Hall and minstrel's gallery, as well as a Norman keep.

EAT innovative Welsh cuisine at the Armless Dragon Restaurant.

DRINK vodka till you drop at the Russian bar Moloko.

DO visit the National Museum & Gallery of Wales for impressionist art, volcanic eruptions and the world's largest turtle.

WATCH international football and rugby matches at the Millennium Stadium or do a tour and check out the players' tunnel.

BUY love spoons, dragons and souvenir T-shirts at Castle Welshcrafts or explore the trendy shops of High St Arcade.

AFTER DARK check out the latest local bands at Clwb Ifor Bach.

URBAN MYTH

Cardiff and Wales are awash with myths. King Arthur is said to have held his first court at Caerleon; the capstone of the Cefyn Bryn burial chamber on the Gower Peninsula is known as Arthur's stone; and legend has it that the Holy Grail hides at Llangollen's Castell Dinas Brân. Arthur's sidekick, Merlin, was apparently born in Carmarthen. In Cardiff, they say if you dance around Tinkinswood on a Sunday you will be turned to stone – and that the stones surrounding the burial chamber are, in fact, women who did just that.

WORDS AND REFLECTIONS ON THE CARDIFF BAY OPERA HOUSE.
Photographer: Neil Setchfield (2)

STRUMMING CHORDS IN BUTE PARK – YES, THEY PROBABLY ARE SINGING TOM JONES SONGS.
Photographer: Neil Setchfield (3)

A PEACEFUL TRIBUTE: CATHAYS PARK WAR MEMORIAL.
Photographer: Neil Setchfield (4)

Minsk 172

VITAL STATISTICS

NAME: MINSK

NICKNAME: THE OUTPOST OF TYRANNY

DATE OF BIRTH: 11TH CENTURY AD; FOLKLORE SAYS A GIANT NAMED MENESK (OR MINCZ) HAD A MILL ON A NEARBY RIVERBANK, WHEREBY HE MADE BREAD TO FEED HIS WARRIORS

ADDRESS: BELARUS (MAP 3, R6)

HEIGHT: 234M

SIZE: 15 SQ KM

POPULATION: 1.8 MILLION

With more Soviet iconography and statues than you can shake a sickle at, Minsk offers a refreshing respite from the consumerist glut of Western Europe.

ANATOMY

Most of Minsk's buildings have only been around since 1944 (following the USSR's violent recapture) and it's probably the best standing example of grand-scale Soviet planning. The main drag, praspekt Nezalezhnastsi (formerly praspekt Francyska Skaryny), is a huge and hectic promenade: at the southwestern end sits the 500m-long ploshcha Nezalezhnastsi (Independence Sq), surrounded by government buildings and the attractive Polish Catholic Church of St Simon. Public transport consists of trams, trolleybuses and buses.

PEOPLE

Ethnic Belarusians make up 81.2% of the population, with 11.4% Russian, 4% Polish and 2.4% Ukrainian nationals comprising the rest. Eighty percent of the populace is Eastern Orthodox and the remaining 20% are Roman Catholics. Everyone speaks Russian in public, saving their native Belarusian tongue for home.

TYPICAL MINSK CITIZEN

Urbane and savvy even as their government does its best to block all Western influence, Minsk citizens serve up communism with a cappuccino. Belarusians have a reputation of being exceptionally neat, tidy and law-abiding – even tipsy teens assiduously use rubbish bins for their beer bottles. Many locals have fair hair and piercing round blue eyes.

DEFINING EXPERIENCE

Taking snaps of tiny Traetskae Prodmestse (Trinity Suburb) on the eastern bank of the Svislach River, then ogling the best architectural examples of Soviet monumentalism on praspekt Nezalezhnastsi, and, after dark, people-watching on the block between vulitsa Lenina and vulitsa Enhelsa.

STRENGTHS

- Astounding Soviet architecture
- The sheer girth of praspekt Nezalezhnastsi
- The Red Church
- Museum of the Great Patriotic War
- Tsentralny Skver (Central Sq)
- The tank outside Dom Ofitserov (Officer's Building)
- Booming slogan: The Feats of the People Will Live Forever!
- Trinity Suburb
- The monument on the Ostrov Slyoz (Island of Tears), a tribute to those who died in war
- The Belarusian State Art Museum

WEAKNESSES

- Astoundingly ugly Soviet architecture
- A long history of human-rights abuses
- Lukashenka (self-proclaimed autocrat and authoritarian)
- The Outpost of Tyranny
- Open forum and gay websites blocked for 'technical reasons'
- Rude, blunt service
- Paranoia and suspicion
- '70s time-warp fashions

GOLD STAR

History – for better or for worse, Minsk is bursting with a rich cultural heritage, bloodstained or not.

CITYSPEAK

- The opening of three new and architecturally unique metro stations.
- The controversial plan to move inmates from Volodarka Prison out of the city centre and to turn the old building into a prison-themed hotel.
- The opening of three new and

STARRING ROLE IN...

- *Babi Yar* (2003)
- *Mysterium Occupation* (2004)
- *The Locals* by Janka Kupala
- *Two Souls* by Maxim Haradsky

IMPORT

- As a cloistered state-controlled economy, there aren't a great many imports. However, Belarus is almost entirely dependent on Russia for its oil and gas supplies and on Lithuania for its electricity.

EXPORT

- Weapons (for the past decade, Belarus has made the world's top five of arms exporters)
- Potassium fertilisers
- Chemicals
- Wooden fibreboards
- Refrigerators
- Tractors
- Trucks

SEE Dinamo Minsk, Belarus' top football club, play in its home stadium in central Minsk, and witness wary locals loosen up a little as they get into the game.

EAT some of the best cheesy mushroom dishes in town amid the lacklustre interior of Staroe Rusloe on vulitsa Uljanauskaja.

DRINK the city's finest coffee and tea at Stary Mensk on praspekt Nezalezhnastsi as you spy on the KGB building across the street.

DO forgo the romance of them thar cracked hotel walls and goonish doormen by renting your own flat.

WATCH the Belarusian Ballet, which during Soviet times was considered second only to Moscow's Bolshoi Ballet.

BUY Belarusian folk art, particularly the wooden boxes intricately decorated with geometric straw patterns, from any of Minsk's department stores.

AFTER DARK take in a kick-ass live rock show in the inimitable Graffiti on per Kalinina, where the vibe is garage meets army surplus.

URBAN MYTH

In Lukashenka's nationalist sledge-hammering, non-Belarusian faces are outlawed from public advertising. Consequently, the handful of foreign companies doing business in Minsk can no longer use posters featuring foreign models.

KEEPING UP THE TRADITION – NEWLY RENOVATED HOUSES NEAR SVABODY SQ MAINTAIN THEIR STYLE.
Photographer: Bruce Yuan-Yue Bi (1)

PRAYING AT THE FEET OF ST PETER & PAUL CHURCH, ONE OF FEW TO SURVIVE THE RAVAGES OF WAR.
Photographer: Bruce Yuan-Yue Bi (2)

THE INNOCUOUS-LOOKING MUSEUM OF THE GREAT PATRIOTIC WAR HOUSES THE HARROWING STORY OF BELARUS' SUFFERING IN WWII.
Photographer: Bruce Yuan-Yue Bi (3)

BRIGHT YOUNG THINGS STROLL IN FRONT OF THE HOLY SPIRIT CATHEDRAL.
Photographer: Bruce Yuan-Yue Bi (4)

Thimphu 173

VITAL STATISTICS

NAME: THIMPHU

NICKNAME: SHANGRI-LA

DATE OF BIRTH: 13TH CENTURY; WHEN A HUGE FORTRESS WAS BUILT, BUT THE SMALL TOWN ONLY BECAME THE NATIONAL CAPITAL IN 1961

ADDRESS: BHUTAN (MAP 5, H3)

HEIGHT: 2300M

POPULATION: 50,000

WEIGHING UP THE COSTS – WEEKEND MARKETS ARE GREAT PLACE FOR LOCAL PRODUCE.
Photographer: Richard I'Anson (1)

With one foot in the past and one in the future, the last Buddhist Himalayan kingdom strolls confidently towards modernisation on its own terms.

ANATOMY

Thimphu lies in a beautiful, wooded valley, sprawling up a hillside on the bank of the Thimphu Chhu River. Several north–south streets run through the town, and numerous smaller streets weave their way uphill to government offices and the posh suburb of Motithang at the top of the town. In the central district, numerous lanes and alleys lead off the north–south streets to provide access to the new shopping centres as well as shops, bars and small restaurants. For those on a normal tourist visa, you will have a car, driver and guide available throughout your stay in Bhutan; and it's easy to pop out for a drink or a round of shopping on foot.

PEOPLE

Thimphu's people, like that of the country, are fairly homogeneous, comprising Drukpas (Ngalops and Sharchops; 65%) and indigenous or migrant tribes (15%). The main language is Dzongkha, but Tibetan and Nepali are also spoken. The religious divide is nominally Buddhist (75%) and Hindu (25%).

TYPICAL THIMPHUITE

Bhutanese people are very friendly, open and polite. Despite the fact that Bhutan is not a rich country, the Bhutanese people seem to be content – full of inner and outer beauty, dignity and power. Thimphu, as the capital and only real city, also has the lion's share of bureaucrats, diplomats, politicians and non-governmental organisations (NGOs).

DEFINING EXPERIENCE

Wandering Norzin Lam, lined with shops, restaurants and retail arcades, taking in the view of the river and climbing the Telecom tower to see the valley below before letting your guide choose a restaurant and bar followed by a good night's sleep.

STRENGTHS

◢ Weekend market
◢ Tourism as a low-volume, high-cost affair
◢ Trashi Chhoe Dzong (Fortress of the Glorious Religion)
◢ Pristine mountain air
◢ No advertising
◢ Mobile phones have arrived, but are blissfully rare – the mountainous terrain renders them generally useless
◢ Rugged mountains
◢ Enchanting valleys
◢ Meandering rivers
◢ Crystal lakes
◢ Dense forests

WEAKNESSES

◢ The cost of getting there
◢ The cost of being there

GOLD STAR

The weekend market – village people jostle with well-heeled Thimphu residents, Bhutanese housewives and monks from nearby monasteries. In one section of the market is an odoriferous collection of dried fish, beef and balls of *datse* (home-made soft cheese that is used to make sauces). During the winter you can even pick up a leg of yak (with the hoof still attached). At the northern end of the market is a collection of indigenous goods and handicrafts. Here you will find locally produced goods, including religious objects, cloth, baskets and strange hats from various minority groups.

CITYSPEAK

◢ Is Chang Jiji – the first housing project in Thimphu – a success or not?
◢ What's happening on the latest soap?
◢ Queen Ashi Sangay Choden Wangchuck's nation-wide HIV-awareness campaign

STARRING ROLE IN...

◢ *Travellers and Magicians* (2003)
◢ *The Other Final* (2002)
◢ *Dreams of the Peaceful Dragon* by Katie Hickman and Tom Owen Edmonds

IMPORT

◢ TV – finally, in the 21st century
◢ NGOs
◢ Very wealthy tourists
◢ Mobile phones, but few

EXPORT

◢ Philately
◢ Feature films directed by high-ranking Buddhist lama Khyentse Norbu

SEE the spectacular view of Thimphu Valley from the Telecom tower.

EAT green chilli for breakfast – or maybe not.

DRINK Tsheringma, a safflower-based herbal tea.

DO take a day walk up to either Tango Goemba or Cheri Goemba monastery.

WATCH a *tsechu* (festival) at a *dzong* (monastery) in honour of Guru Rinpoche, who brought Buddhism to Bhutan.

BUY contemporary paintings and handmade paper at the Jungshi Handmade Paper Factory or Mangala Paper House.

AFTER DARK stay up late and sample Bhutanese nightlife in Thimphu's friendly discos and bars.

URBAN MYTH

It is often said that Thimphu is the only world capital without traffic lights. One was installed several years ago, but the residents complained that it was impersonal and ugly and it was removed within days. Traffic continues to be directed by policemen stationed at two traffic circles, one at the north end and another near the south end of Norzin Lam, Thimphu's wide, tree-lined main street. They keep Thimphu's traffic flowing throughout the day using elegant, exaggerated gestures. They disappear at night and leave drivers to sort things out for themselves.

HOPES AND DREAMS SPIN IN A RIOT OF COLOUR ON GIANT PRAYER WHEELS.
Photographer: Izzet Keribar (2)

TIME IS SLOW TO CATCH UP WITH THE PAST IN THIS BEAUTIFUL CITY.
Photographer: Richard I'Anson (3)

THE PHALLUS, PAINTED ON THE WALL OF THIS HOUSE, BRINGS FERTILITY AND PROTECTION TO THE OCCUPANTS.
Photographer: Alison Wright (4)

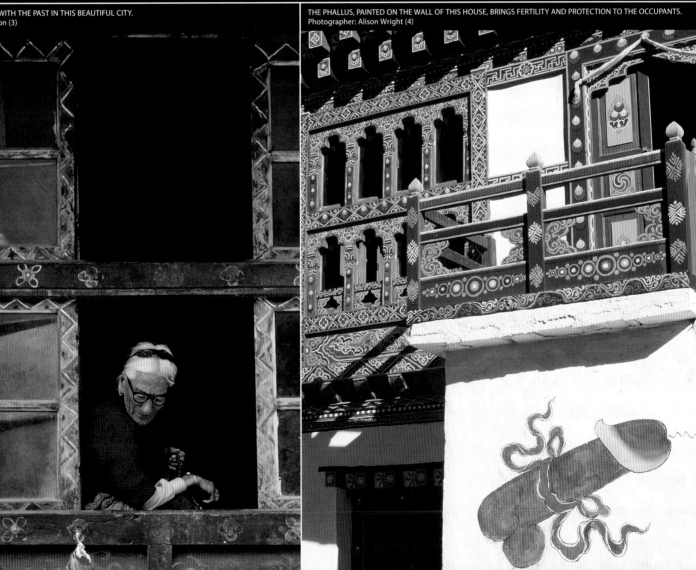

Khartoum174

VITAL STATISTICS

NAME: KHARTOUM

DATE OF BIRTH: AD 1821; ESTABLISHED AS
AN EGYPTIAN ARMY CAMP

ADDRESS: SUDAN (MAP 2, K8)

HEIGHT: 390M

POPULATION: 3 MILLION

LOCAL BOYS SPOT THE CAMERA WHILE FILLING UP THEIR WATER TANKS.
Photographer: Eric L Wheater (1)

A BUSINESSMAN STRIKES A JAUNTY POSE OUTSIDE HIS JEWELLERY SHOP.
Photographer: Eric L Wheater (2)

THE EVERYDAY BUSTLE OUTSIDE AL-KABIR MOSQUE, SHARIA AL-JAMI.
Photographer: Anthony Ham (3)

A REFUGEE FROM DARFUR WITH SOMETHING TO SMILE ABOUT.
Photographer: Finbarr O'Reilly (4)

Where the azure and pale waters of the Blue and White Niles meet lies Sudan's modern capital – Khartoum is a haven of hospitable people, tree-lined boulevards and bustling souqs (markets) lining the banks of the legendary river.

ANATOMY

The two Niles converge in the centre of Khartoum, splitting the capital into three main wedges: Khartoum, Bahri (Khartoum North) and Omdurman. Omdurman is Khartoum's most traditional suburb and home to the largest souq in the country. Buses, minibuses and shared taxis cover most points in the city and it is a short ride from the airport to central Khartoum and UN Sq, south of which are countless informal joints serving up Sudanese classics.

PEOPLE

As 75% of Sudan's population, including around two million nomads, live in rural areas, the residents of Khartoum form an urban minority. More than 100 languages are spoken around the country, but Arabic is the official language and the mother tongue of Khartoum, and Islam is the predominant religion, in keeping with much of northern Sudan. English, widely used here, is by no means universal.

TYPICAL KHARTOUMAN

For Khartouman read hospitality. Khartoumans will pay for everything, share their meals and even invite you to stay in their homes. They are among the friendliest people in Africa, with a natural generosity that entirely belies their poverty. They are strictly Islamic nondrinkers but will discreetly enjoy a *chicha* (a water pipe infused with apple or tobacco) after a meal. Frequent street clashes and revolts reflect a city whose people, justifiably or not, remain passionate about past and present conflicts and continue to fight for their beliefs.

DEFINING EXPERIENCE

Eating *ta'amiya* (falafel) while picking through the wares at the souq in Omdurman, watching the colours of the Blue and White Niles swirl into one from the White Nile Bridge, and then going to Hamed el-Nil Mosque to see the traditional Nubian wrestlers going through their paces for the last two hours before sunset.

STRENGTHS

◢ Convergence of the Niles
◢ Nubian history
◢ The National Museum
◢ Omdurman
◢ The souq
◢ The camel market
◢ Mahdi's Tomb
◢ The Ethnographical Museum
◢ Cheap (if basic) hotels
◢ Fast, low-priced Internet
◢ Pyramids

WEAKNESSES

◢ War zone
◢ Death penalty (maximum) for homosexuality
◢ Extreme poverty
◢ Nonexistent nightlife
◢ 40°C summer heat

GOLD STAR

The souq – this market is a dusty, vibrant relic of Sudanese life. At home in Khartoum's traditional suburb of Omdurman, it is the largest souq in the country.

CITYSPEAK

◢ Conflict in the south – ceased or renewed?
◢ Sudanese–American tensions

STARRING ROLE IN...

◢ *Khartoum* (1966)
◢ *Triumph of the Sun* by Wilbur Smith
◢ *The Translator* by Leila Aboulela

IMPORT

◢ Camels
◢ Internet
◢ Islam
◢ Christianity
◢ English texts
◢ US missiles (unwanted)
◢ Colonialism
◢ The water of the Blue and White Niles

EXPORT

◢ Camels
◢ Chicha
◢ Nubian wrestlers

SEE the sun setting on the narrow pyramids that fill the ancient royal cemetery of Meroe.

EAT *fuul* (beans) and *ta'amiya* on the riverside at El-Shallal.

DRINK the famously fresh fruit juices at Lem Prost restaurant.

DO ride the fast-moving Ferris wheel in the Al-Mogran Family Park for an original perspective of the converging Niles.

WATCH the Halgt Zikr stir up the dust in celebration of Allah at the Hamed el-Nil Mosque every Friday afternoon.

BUY almost anything from the amazing variety of wares at the Khartoum souq.

AFTER DARK enjoy a post-dinner smoke at the tiny *chicha* terrace on Sharia as-Sayed Abdul Rahman.

URBAN MYTH

Mahdi's Tomb, housed in a striking postwar onion-domed building, is not the original. According to Muslim prophesy, the Mahdi would rid the world of evil and when, in 1881, Mohammed Ahmed proclaimed himself to be the Mahdi he carried out the legacy by ridding Khartoum of General Gordon, the British-appointed governor. The Mahdists then ruled Sudan until 1898. They were defeated by Lord Kitchener and his Anglo-Egyptian army who ordered Mahdi's tomb to be destroyed. General Gordon's nephew 'Monkey' then carried out the deed by, somewhat unsportingly, throwing the Mahdi's ashes into the Nile!

TAKING THE TIME TO CATCH UP ON CURRENT EVENTS AT PEGGY'S CAFÉ.
Photographer: Brent Winebrenner (1)

Anchorage is an outpost of wilful humanity crafting more than survival from this unforgiving yet beautiful land. In this unparalleled urban wildness polar bears take no notice of city limits and outdoor adventure is as easy to have as theatre, great food and a rocking nightlife.

ANATOMY

Sprawling across a broad triangle of a peninsula, the city is embraced by Cook Inlet and the 1500m-plus peaks of Chugach State Park, a backyard getaway to wilderness adventure. Anchorage's excellent public-bus system shuttles you from the grid of flower-filled Downtown streets where you'll find more than enough museums to keep you happy, and through the interesting Midtown neighbourhoods with their diverse eateries and lively nightlife. But get off the bus and explore the 196km of paved bicycle paths, the stunning tracts of green (or white, depending on the season) parkland and the lakes that dot the city.

PEOPLE

Fifteen years ago barely a quarter of Anchorage residents were born in Alaska but these days the city's population is a lot less transient. That said, the lure of the final frontier never diminishes, and the typical resident is young (average age is 32), mobile and often from the US West Coast. Ethnic communities are growing fast in this previously male and very Caucasian town, but Alaskan natives are the largest minority group, making up 8% of the population.

TYPICAL ANCHORAGITE

Anchoragites have the frontier spirit of most Alaskans, but with the urban edge of big-city dwellers. They are independent, practical people who answer extreme weather with extreme living, whether it's indulging in arctic diving, bear hunting and back-country snowboarding, or just drinking until the sun goes down. Looked down upon by rural Alaskans, Anchoragites can't wait to hit the mountains on the weekend, but they always get back in time for a trip to the theatre or to catch a local band.

Anchorage
175

VITAL STATISTICS

NAME: ANCHORAGE

NICKNAME: LOS ANCHORAGE; THE RAGE

DATE OF BIRTH: 1914; ANCHORAGE WAS FOUNDED WHEN IT SERVED AS A HEADQUARTERS AND WORK CAMP FOR THE ALASKA RAILROAD

ADDRESS: USA (MAP 1, D6)

HEIGHT: 40M

SIZE: 4396 SQ KM

POPULATION: 261,446

TOTEMS KEEP A STERN WATCH OVER THE ENTRANCE TO THE ANCHORAGE COURTHOUSE.
Photographer: Brent Winebrenner (2)

BRIGHT MODERN ARCHITECTURE BRINGS A RAY OF SUNSHINE TO 4TH AVE.
Photographer: Brent Winebrenner (3)

TROPHIES THAT WOULD HORRIFY RUDOLPH AT THE GENERAL STORE.
Photographer: Brent Winebrenner (4)

DEFINING EXPERIENCE

Wandering through the Saturday market to the Snow City Café for a breakfast of Ship Creek Benedict and a Kaladi coffee while tossing up whether to bike the Tony Knowles Coastal Trail or hike the tundra in the Chugach State Park, then heading down to the Beer Tooth Theatre Pub for an evening meal/movie/beer.

STRENGTHS

- ◢ Big, green parks
- ◢ Proximity to mountains, glaciers, lakes – this is a nature lover's paradise!
- ◢ Alaska Zoo
- ◢ Beluga whales in Cook Inlet
- ◢ Being able to catch an 18kg salmon from under a highway bridge
- ◢ A multitude of microbreweries
- ◢ Title Wave Books
- ◢ The aurora borealis – when you can see it!
- ◢ Good music scene

WEAKNESSES

- ◢ Winter
- ◢ No major league sports teams
- ◢ 'Our Alaska' with Governor Frank Murkowski
- ◢ Ravenous summer mosquitoes
- ◢ One of the most expensive cities in the USA

GOLD STAR

You're only 20 minutes from Alaska! It's the best base location for outdoor adventures.

CITYSPEAK

- ◢ Speculation on the construction of the bridge across the Cook Inlet
- ◢ The weather – is summer over or not?
- ◢ Ariel wolf hunting

STARRING ROLE IN...

- ◢ *About Grace* by Anthony Doerr
- ◢ *Mystery, Alaska* (1999)
- ◢ *Sidney Laurence, Painter of the North* by Kesler E Woodward
- ◢ 'Anchorage' by Michelle Shocked

IMPORT

- ◢ Pilot bread
- ◢ 'Chicago's Best' food wagon
- ◢ Retirees from the lower 48 on cruise holidays
- ◢ Mountain men
- ◢ Nature film crews

EXPORT

- ◢ Salmon and halibut
- ◢ Oil
- ◢ Jewel
- ◢ Softball-size radishes and giant cabbage
- ◢ Water
- ◢ Morel mushrooms
- ◢ Malamutes
- ◢ Moose 'nugget' jewellery
- ◢ Reindeer antlers

SEE the start of the Iditarod, the last great trail sled-dog race, charge up 4th Ave at the beginning of March each year.

EAT Coconut-beer–battered Spam (or not).

DRINK an ice-cold pint of Alaskan Amber on the deck of the Snow Goose and soak up the midnight sun.

DO hear ancient Alaskan songs, once thought lost forever, performed at the Alaska Native Heritage Centre.

WATCH the *Whale-Fat Follies* at Mr Whitekey's Fly by Night; a fun and raunchy musical about duct tape, spawning salmon and Alaska's official state fossil, the woolly mammoth.

BUY a Qiviut scarf or cap from the Oomingmak Musk Ox Producers' Co-operative.

AFTER DARK head to the 10 bars at Chilkoot Charlie's (Koot's) – the place for unbridled Anchorage debauchery for the last 35 years.

URBAN MYTH

US airman Ted Winnen shoots a larger than normal grizzly while out deer hunting in Prince William Sound and suddenly his escapades and photos end up in about half a million email inboxes around the world and, according to the Alaska Forest Service, the enquiries about the monster bear of impossible proportions (think 3.8m and 725kg) just keep on coming, even four years after the incident.

Mecca

176

VITAL STATISTICS

NAME: MECCA

NICKNAME: FORBIDDEN CITY

DATE OF BIRTH: APPROXIMATELY 2000 BC; POSSIBLY FOUNDED BY THE PROPHET IBRAHIM (ABRAHAM)

ADDRESS: SAUDI ARABIA (MAP 2, N6)

HEIGHT: 277M

POPULATION: 1.8 MILLION

Mecca is an icon of inestimable religious and historic importance; to spend time in Islam's first city is a truly unforgettable experience.

ANATOMY

The ancient city nestles on the slopes of the narrow valley of Abraham, surrounded by dusty hills and mountains on three sides. The Sacred Mosque dominates the centre of the city and contains the Kaaba (the first temple of God constructed by Adam, later rebuilt by Ibrahim). Mecca has a fairly efficient infrastructure to cater for pilgrims, whose numbers are concentrated during the main pilgrimage, known as the haj, when two million Muslims descend on the city.

PEOPLE

By law non-Muslims cannot enter Mecca. The city's permanent residents are mainly Arabs (around 80%) but there is a significant minority of nationals from other Islamic countries, mainly Africa and Asia, who come here to study the Koran. Mecca is Saudi Arabia's third most populous city after the capital, Riyadh, and Jeddah. Arabic is the main language, with English spoken by staff in some hotels.

TYPICAL MECCAN

During the haj you might only get to meet other pilgrims, whose extraordinary numbers give real meaning to the term 'sea of humanity'. The city's students give the place a welcoming cosmopolitan vibe and everyone who lives here considers themselves seriously blessed. The Arab Meccans, in particular, have a remarkable ability with languages and may be scornful of those who don't at least try to begin conversations in Arabic.

DEFINING EXPERIENCE

Dropping your jaw upon realising the sheer size of the Grand Mosque, using sign language to communicate with pilgrims of every nationality, quenching a burning thirst with chilled water from the public fountains, and returning to the Grand Mosque at twilight when everything is bathed in an eerie blue light.

STRENGTHS

- Radiating holiness
- The Kaaba
- The Black Stone of Kaaba
- The Sacred Mosque (al-Masjid al-Haram)
- Almost zero crime
- Like-minded people
- Unparalleled sense of history and religious importance
- Must for Muslims
- Incredible ornamentation
- Breathtaking architecture
- Lifts (elevators) in mosques
- Street vendors
- Huge shopping arcades
- Gates to the Sacred Mosque (there are almost 100)
- Multilevel ablution complex (over 2000 toilets and ablution units)

WEAKNESSES

- Ban on non-Muslims
- Overcrowded
- Stampeding pilgrims
- Public executions
- Judicial amputations
- Zero nightlife
- Expensive

GOLD STAR

The Kaaba – Muslims pray in the direction of the Kaaba all their lives and seeing it for the first time is an unforgettable spiritual experience that will permeate life forever.

CITYSPEAK

- Kentucky Fried Chicken – a bad influence on young Meccans?
- Heritage or idolatry? Developers want to build apartment blocks on sites of historic and religious interest, which they say can encourage idolatry
- Floods – will the new drainage system cope when put to the test?

STARRING ROLE IN...

- The Koran
- The Bible (the city has been controversially identified as the ancient city Bakkah, the Biblical 'valley of Baca' in Psalm 84)
- *Personal Narrative of a Pilgrimage to Al Madinah and Meccah* by Richard Burton
- *One Thousand Roads to Mecca* edited by Michael Wolfe

IMPORT

- Pilgrims
- Food: with scarce arable land and water, not much is grown in Mecca itself

EXPORT

- Islam
- Mohammed
- Textiles
- The cloth covering the Kaaba
- Dates

SEE the narrow streets of the old quarter, the original heart of Mecca.

EAT like a local and grab a cheap chicken or camel *shwarma* (meat sliced off a spit and stuffed in a pocket of pita-type bread with chopped tomatoes and garnish) from the street vendors.

DRINK holy water from the Zamzam well, referred to in the Koran.

DO wander out into the suburbs where you can see enormous excavations as more buildings are cut into the rock.

WATCH the *tawaf* (pilgrims circling the Kaaba) from a viewing platform at the Sacred Mosque.

BUY Ajwa Kajoor dates, said to contain healing powers.

AFTER DARK visit the Sacred Mosque when it is less crowded and brilliantly lit up by stadium lights.

URBAN MYTH

The origin of the famous Black Stone which, mounted in silver, forms the cornerstone of the Kaaba, is shrouded in mystery. Legend has it that the stone fell to earth during the time of Adam, or that he brought it with him after he was kicked out of God's Kingdom. This fits in with the scholarly assumption that the stone is a meteorite, although tests to confirm this will never be permitted. The stone was stolen by Ismaili warriors in AD 930 and was returned in pieces 22 years later, hence the necessity of mounting it in silver. Although not venerated by Muslims (idolatry is forbidden), pilgrims kiss the stone in memory of the same act carried out by Mohammed.

GOING WITH THE FLOW – A SEA OF PILGRIMS CIRCLE THE KAABA IN THE SACRED MOSQUE.
Photographer: Reza (1)

CAPTURING THE MOMENT.
Photographer: Reza (2)

MUSLIM WORSHIPPERS MUST PRAY FIVE TIMES A DAY IN THE DIRECTION OF KAABA.
Photographer: Zainal ABD Halim (3)

SPREADING THE FAITH – RUGS ARE LAID OUT IN PREPARATION FOR MORNING PRAYERS.
Photographer: Reza (4)

Aswan

177

VITAL STATISTICS

NAME: ASWAN

DATE OF BIRTH: 300 BC; ELEPHANTINE ISLAND (ADJACENT TO ASWAN) WAS THE ORIGINAL SETTLEMENT AND A NATURAL FORTRESS

ADDRESS: EGYPT (MAP 2, K5)

HEIGHT: 112M

SIZE: 679 SQ KM

POPULATION: 2 MILLION

Once the gateway to Africa and a crossroads for the ancient caravan routes, Aswan is a mellow winter resort boasting sun-filled days, jostling markets and sweeping views of the desert on the most picturesque part of the Nile.

ANATOMY

The Nile flows down from the dams and around the giant granite boulders and palm-studded islands that protrude from the waters at the edge of Aswan. There are only three main avenues, and most of the city runs parallel to the Nile, making it easy to navigate. The train station, at the northern end of town, is only three blocks east of the river and the Corniche el-Nil, and is fronted by Aswan's market street, where the souqs (markets) overflow with colourful, tempting and aromatic wares. Running parallel to this is Sharia Abtal at-Tahrir, where you'll find the youth hostel and a few hotels. Across the river on Elephantine Island, modern Nubian culture thrives. Hire a bike or a taxi to get around.

PEOPLE

Beside the Egyptians, there are a handful of separate indigenous groups with ancient roots in Aswan. The city is finely threaded with Nubian culture. The traditional lands of Nubia, home to the tall, dark-skinned Nubian people, were drowned with the building of the High Dam in the 1970s to provide a water supply for the region. Despite this, Egyptians and Nubians live relatively harmonious, if independent, lives.

TYPICAL ASWANIAN

Aswanians distinguish themselves from the rest of Egypt by being particularly laid-back and pleasant. They love their souqs and their slice of the Nile and enjoy nothing more than watching the water move by after a long day of working numerous jobs to support their large families. Their laughter lubricates the wheels of social exchange and transactions are done with a smile. While religion cushions life's blows, in Aswan jokes and wisecracks are its parlance.

DEFINING EXPERIENCE

Spending the morning in the narrow alleyway souqs, tasting life as it has been for many centuries, before sailing gently across the Nile on a felucca to the cliffs of Elephantine Island and Nubian House for henna tattoos, Nubian music and a sunset 'tea' buffet overlooking the river and the desert beyond.

STRENGTHS

- Sunset on the desert
- The Nile
- Nubian culture
- Elephantine Island
- The tombs of the Nobles
- The Nubian Museum
- Feluccas
- Souqs
- Relaxed, friendly atmosphere
- Top-quality henna
- History-packed streets

WEAKNESSES

- Expensive tours
- Lecherous souq tattooists
- Unbearable 38ºC to 45ºC summer heat (June to August)
- Cheap camel meat
- Safflower sold as saffron

GOLD STAR

Feluccas – you haven't seen Aswan, or Egypt for that matter, until you've seen it from a felucca on the Nile.

CITYSPEAK

- Tight policing of tourists
- The Aswan Oberoi hotel's hideous extensions – and resulting lawsuit

STARRING ROLE IN...

- *Death on the Nile* by Agatha Christie
- *Elephantine: The Ancient Town* by the German Archaeological Mission

IMPORT

- Camels
- Nubians and their culture
- Western food
- Foreign guests (considered lucky) for Nubian weddings
- British design for the High Dam
- International sculptors
- Christianity
- Caravans
- Indian and African botany

EXPORT

- Camels
- Henna and henna tattoos
- Spices
- Ivory
- Granite
- Roasted peanuts
- *Karkadai* (dried hibiscus drink)
- Nubian *tahtib* (stick dancing)
- Colourful skull caps

SEE the sun set over the desert from the peaceful Ferial Gardens.

EAT *daoud basha* (meatballs in tomato sauce) as the Nile slides slowly past the Aswan Moon Restaurant.

DRINK delicious fruit cocktails and take in the views at Emy Restaurant.

DO visit the breathtaking history, art and culture of the Nubian Museum.

WATCH the *tahtib* on a winter's eve by the Aswan folkloric dance troupe.

BUY the best henna in Egypt in Aswan's colourful souqs.

AFTER DARK take a boat ride to Philae (Agilkia Island) to experience the sound and light show and wander through the temple at night.

URBAN MYTH

Mohammed Shah Aga Khan, the 48th imam of the Ismaili sect of Islam, had Aswan as his favourite wintering place. When he died in 1957, his widow, the Begum, oversaw the construction of his domed granite-and-sandstone mausoleum, opposite Elephantine Island. For over 40 years she placed a single red rose on her husband's sarcophagus each day. The Begum continued her floral tribute every day until her death in 2000. Now she lies inside, reunited with her husband for eternity.

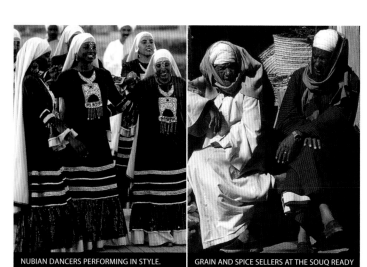

NUBIAN DANCERS PERFORMING IN STYLE.
Photographer: Anders Blomqvist (1)

GRAIN AND SPICE SELLERS AT THE SOUQ READY TO WRAP UP THE DAY.
Photographer: John Elk III (2)

A CAMEL AND FRIEND TRAVERSE THE DUNES, WITH A VIEW OF THE CITY ACROSS THE NILE.
Photographer: John Elk III (3)

DREAMS OF PAST SPLENDOUR – A SLEEPY GUIDE NODS OFF BENEATH THE SUPERB RELIEFS OF THE TEMPLE OF ISIS.
Photographer: Becca Posterino (4)

ARMENIANS ENJOY A HEIGHTENED SENSE OF CULTURE.
Photographer: Stephane Victor (1)

Yerevan
178

VITAL STATISTICS

NAME: YEREVAN

DATE OF BIRTH: 782 BC; WHEN KING ARGISHTI BUILT
THE TOWN FORTRESS OF EREBUNI ON THE ARARAT PLAIN

ADDRESS: ARMENIA (MAP 3, Y14)

HEIGHT: 990M

SIZE: 210 SQ KM

POPULATION: 1.1 MILLION

Yerevan is the cultural heart of the Armenian people, one of the surviving ancient peoples of the Near East; it is a proud, cultured and enterprising city stunningly situated in the mountainous realm of the Caucasus.

ANATOMY

The centre of Yerevan sits on the east bank of the Hrazdan River. Streets are arranged in a strict grid system, and the heavily trafficked Opera Sq where Mashtots, Marshall Baghramian and Sayat-Nova Aves meet is often patrolled by female traffic cops in high heels. The city itself is surrounded on three sides by mountains. To the southwest stands Mt Ararat, holy mountain of the Armenian people, in full view, yet poignantly sited just across the Turkish border. Yerevan has tonnes of public transport, including buses, minibuses, trolleybuses and a metro.

PEOPLE

Yerevan is populated almost entirely by Armenians; there are some Russians, Kurds (including the little-known Yezidis, a Gnostic sect sometimes mistakenly called devil-worshippers) and nationals from other Caucasian republics.

TYPICAL YEREVANI

The typical Yerevanis is hospitable and eager to help visitors. They are likely to be adherents of the Armenian Apostolic Church (Armenia was the first nation to convert to Christianity – in AD 301). They are resourceful, industrious and resilient, if a little melancholy, in the face of hardship (to which Yerevan, and Armenia as a whole, is no stranger). Members of a nation of stonemasons, philosophers and poets, they are fiercely proud of their culture and artistic traditions. Yerevanis tend to linger over meals and have a relaxed attitude to work, happy to stay out late at night, turn up at work around 10.30am and then take a long lunch. In fact, attitudes to time are pretty relaxed. Punctuality isn't *de rigueur* in Yerevan.

DEFINING EXPERIENCE

Visiting Matenadaran, a repository of the country's culture and literature and home to tens of thousands of documents and manuscripts in the elaborate Armenian script; heading to Echmiadzin, the spiritual heart of the Armenian church, just a few kilometres out of Yerevan; pondering Armenia's traumatic past at the Genocide Memorial; climbing the Cascade to enjoy the view over the entire city; getting melancholy as you watch the sun set over Mt Ararat, tantalisingly close yet unreachable across the Turkish border; then following your nose and choosing a delicious and sizzling *khoravats* (barbecue) somewhere along Proshyan Poghots.

STRENGTHS

- Cafés at every turn
- Thriving heart of Armenian art and culture
- Hospitality and generosity of the locals
- Intriguing atmosphere – a city poised between East and West, Europe and Asia
- Proximity to all of Armenia's attractions – it's a small country!
- Long lunches and dinners

WEAKNESSES

- Vodka toasts – fine, until you realise it is poor form to reveal any sign of drunkenness
- Power shortages
- Bitterly cold winters
- Earthquakes
- Soviet-style customer service (or lack thereof)
- Stalinist architecture
- Corruption and local mafia

GOLD STAR

Art and culture – a city of museums and galleries in a nation of writers, poets and artists

CITYSPEAK

- How much lower can Lake Sevan's water level go?
- Will we find a reliable power supply before next winter?
- We all have university degrees, so why do we have to drive taxis to survive?

STARRING ROLE IN...

- *The Claws of the Crab* by Stephen Brook
- *The Crossing Place* by Philip Marsden
- *Among the Russians* by Colin Thubron
- *Imperium* by Ryszard Kapuscinski
- *Calendar* (1993)

IMPORT

- Armenians – children of the diaspora returning to discover and reinvigorate their homeland

EXPORT

- Armenians – the nation's traumatic past saw massive emigration (and flight) to Russia, Eastern Europe, America and elsewhere
- Notable people of Armenian extraction: Andre Agassi, Charles Aznavour, Cher and chess master Gary Kasparov

SEE the intermingled influences of East and West at the National Folk Art Museum of Armenia.

EAT *khoravats* (barbecued lamb or pork).

DRINK Armenian cognac – smooth and potent.

DO visit Sarian Park on the weekend to see the gatherings of contemporary artists who critique each other's work.

WATCH a performance of the Yerevan Ballet Company.

BUY local handicrafts and lacework at the market at Vernissage, or an Armenian carpet.

AFTER DARK check out the casinos at Argavand, slightly seedy and very garishly lit, or visit Astral, Yerevan's ground zero for dance music.

URBAN MYTH

The National Chamber Orchestra of Armenia was formed in 1997. At their first meeting (held in a public square) there weren't enough chairs for all members to sit down. By 1998 they had released their first CD; by 2003 they had toured three continents.

A PAUSE FOR REFLECTION – SURP GRIGOR LUSAVORICH CATHEDRAL RESTS IN THE SHADOW OF MT ARARAT.
Photographer: Stephane Victor (2)

YEREVANIS TAKE PLEASURE IN THEIR CULTURAL TRADITIONS.
Photographer: Stephane Victor (3)

THE STATELY PEAKS OF MT ARARAT OFFER A STRIKING BACKDROP TO THE CITY.
Photographer: Stephane Victor (4)

Luxembourg City 179

VITAL STATISTICS

NAME: LUXEMBOURG CITY

DATE OF BIRTH: AD 963; WHEN COUNT SIGEFROID OF ARDENNES ERECTED A CASTLE HERE

ADDRESS: LUXEMBOURG (MAP 3, H9)

HEIGHT: 330M

POPULATION: 90,000

The entire ancient core of this 1000-year-old city has been preserved and provides spectacular vistas over lush parklands and atmospheric old quarters, spanned by a series of imposing bridges.

ANATOMY

The Alzette River passes through Luxembourg City and gives the capital its geographic charm. A medieval street plan mixes with 18th- and 19th-century buildings in the Old Town. The city's central area is divided by gorges; the lower town is at the base of the Old Town's Bock fortifications. Walking is the best way to get around.

PEOPLE

Lëtzebuergesch, closely related to German, was proclaimed the national language in 1984. French and German are also official languages. A whopping 97% of the population is Roman Catholic. The population is about 30% foreigners, predominantly Italian and Portuguese, the highest ratio of any EU country.

TYPICAL LUXEMBOURGER

Luxembourgers are wealthy; the country's per-capita GDP was the world's highest in 1997 and the standard of living consistently rates among the best. Luxembourgers are likely to work in the new service-based economy, as the country has morphed from an industrial producer by wooing big spenders from abroad with favourable banking and taxation laws. Luxembourgers are a confident lot. Their motto? *'Mir wëlle bleiwe wat mir sin'* (We want to remain what we are.)

DEFINING EXPERIENCE

Wandering the pedestrianised heart of the Old Town, investigating history and art in the new Musée National d'Histoire et d'Art, delving into the dark Bock Casemates and taking the lift (elevator) carved into the rock at Plateau du St Esprit to Grund for an apéritif before returning to the Chemin de la Corniche and dining outside for a fabulous view.

STRENGTHS

- Place d'Armes
- Musée National d'Histoire et d'Art
- Chemin de la Corniche
- Breedewee
- The equality of three official languages: French, German and Lëtzebuergesch

WEAKNESSES

- Conservative attitudes
- Very Eurocentric
- Eurocratic

GOLD STAR

With its impressive state-of-the-art museums, its Moorish Palais Grand-Ducal, its cathedral and free lift dug into the rock, the pedestrianised centre is a pleasant way to while away the time. Unesco obviously thought so when it added the fortifications and older quarters of the city to its list of World Heritage sites.

CITYSPEAK

- Rising immigration
- The state of the economy
- Levels of air and water pollution
- The new-look royal family

STARRING ROLE IN...

- *The Moon of the Big Winds* by Claudine Muno
- *Aleng* by Cathy Clement

IMPORT

- Employees from neighbouring countries
- The Commission of the European Community
- The Court of Justice of the European Communities
- The General Secretariat of the European Parliament
- The European Investment Bank
- The Nuclear Safety Administration
- 1300 investment funds
- 220 banks

EXPORT

- Edward Steichen
- Richard Schuman
- Happy personal investors
- Busy Eurocrats

SEE the startling white building of the Musée d'Histoire et d'Art, with collections of prehistoric relics and contemporary local and international artists.

EAT the national dish, *judd mat gaardebounen* (slabs of smoked pork served in a thick, cream-based sauce with broad beans and huge chunks of potato).

DRINK local specialist brews, Gamorinus, a blond beer and Diekirche's Grand Cru.

DO promenade on the Chemin de la Corniche and the pedestrianised heart of the Old Town.

WATCH the city from the terrace of Breedewee, perched high on the Corniche, the French-cuisine restaurant with an unbeatable view.

BUY porcelain from the House of Villeroy & Boch, the world-famous manufacturer of china and crystal.

AFTER DARK try out the techno and house at funky nightclub Didjeridoo in Hollerich.

URBAN MYTH

When the founder of Luxembourg City, Count Sigefroid, married the beautiful Melusina, he was so smitten with his new bride that he agreed to her request to spend one day and one night alone every month. As the years went on, though, the Count's curiosity grew and grew. One day the Count could take it no more – he peeked into Melusina's room. What the Count saw was his wife lying in the bath with a mermaid's tail draped over the edge. Melusina repaid the intrusion by leaping out of the window into the Alzette River. Occasional sightings of mysterious beautiful women with fish tails in the Alzette persist.

A NEON SIGN ON CASINO LUXEMBOURG REMINDS US THAT EVERYTHING WAS NEW ONCE.
Photographer: Martin Lladó (1)

SUNRISE REFLECTS OFF THE SPIRE OF NEUMÜNSTER ABBEY.
Photographer: Martin Lladó (2)

CAFÉ-GOERS THRONG PLACE D'ARMES.
Photographer: Richard Elliott (3)

MODERN GLASS ARCHITECTURE BEDECKS PLACE GUILLAUME II.
Photographer: Richard Klune (4)

Georgetown 180

VITAL STATISTICS

NAME: GEORGETOWN

DATE OF BIRTH: 1786 ; WHEN IT WAS
FOUNDED BY BRITISH EAST INDIA COMPANY
TRADER CAPTAIN FRANCIS LIGHT

ADDRESS: MALAYSIA (MAP 5, K11)

HEIGHT: 3.9M

POPULATION: 220,000

BREAKFAST OF CHAMPIONS AT THE MORNING MARKET ON JALAN KUALA.
Photographer: Jeff Yates (1)

LOCKED BICYCLES REST AGAINST THE COLUMNS OF AN ARCADE IN THE CENTRE OF TOWN.
Photographer: David Ryan (2)

A YOUNG BASKETBALLER PEERS FROM THE BALCONY ON WASHING DAY.
Photographer: James Braund (3)

MONKEY BUSINESS – A BOY HANGS OUT IN PENANG.
Photographer: Eric L Wheater (4)

Georgetown, capital of Pulau Penang, is an easy-going, colourful, good-time port city full of crumbling old shop houses, trishaws and ancient trades, such as carpentry, seal-making and prostitution.

ANATOMY

The old colonial district centres on Fort Cornwallis. Lebuh Pantai is the main street of the 'city', a financial district crammed with banks and stately buildings that once housed the colonial administration. You'll find many of Georgetown's popular cheap hotels along Lebuh Chulia in Chinatown, packed in among travel agencies, budget-priced restaurants and Internet cafés. At the northern end of Lebuh Chulia, Jl Penang is a main thoroughfare and a popular shopping street. A compact city, most places in Georgetown can easily be reached on foot or by trishaw.

PEOPLE

People of Chinese origin account for almost two-thirds of Georgetown's population, while Malays, Thais, Indians and Europeans comprise the rest. Languages spoken are English, Chinese, Malay and Tamil. Georgetown is home to a lively mix of Buddhists, Taoists, Muslims, Christians and Hindus.

TYPICAL GEORGETOWN CITIZEN

Georgetown has a long tradition of attracting adventurers, artists, intellectuals, scoundrels and dissidents, making for a spirited town ethos. From a fisher to a street hawker, the typical Georgetown resident is good-humoured and open-minded, embracing the long colourful legacy of the 'melting pot of Asia' (perhaps better realised as a hot and spicy curry laksa) their city enjoys.

DEFINING EXPERIENCE

Sitting down to a fine tiffin lunch at Sarkies Corner in the grand Eastern & Oriental Hotel, before riding a trishaw around the colonial heart of Georgetown and stepping back in time at the dazzling Cheong Fatt Tze Mansion.

STRENGTHS

- ◢ Trishaws
- ◢ Colonial district
- ◢ Penang Museum
- ◢ Eastern & Oriental Hotel
- ◢ Cheong Fatt Tze Mansion
- ◢ Fort Cornwallis
- ◢ Batu Ferringhi resort strip
- ◢ Kek Lok Si Temple
- ◢ Snake Temple
- ◢ Little India
- ◢ Chinatown
- ◢ Hawker stalls
- ◢ Khoo Kongsi clan house
- ◢ Affordable international-standard golf courses
- ◢ Temple of the Reclining Buddha

WEAKNESSES

- ◢ Pickpocketing
- ◢ Petty crime
- ◢ Polluted beaches
- ◢ Scams
- ◢ Attacks and muggings in dimly lit (and not a whole lotta) Love Lane

GOLD STAR

Old-school Chinese flavour – in its older neighbourhoods you could be forgiven for thinking that the clock stopped in Georgetown at least 50 years ago.

CITYSPEAK

- ◢ More autonomy – many citizens consider the decision-makers in Kuala Lumper as being too far from Georgtown's local situation to form appropriate policies
- ◢ Traffic congestion – it can take over an hour to drive 12km downtown during peak hour

STARRING ROLE IN...

- ◢ *Indochine* (1992)
- ◢ *Paradise Road* (1997)
- ◢ *Anna and the King* (1999)
- ◢ *The Touch* (2002)

IMPORT

- ◢ British East India Company
- ◢ Tourists
- ◢ Japanese golfers
- ◢ Chinese
- ◢ Indians
- ◢ Thais

EXPORT

- ◢ Tin
- ◢ Rubber
- ◢ Palm oil
- ◢ Timber
- ◢ Tropical fish
- ◢ Oil
- ◢ Textiles

SEE awesome views from the pagoda at the Kek Lok Si Temple.

EAT cheap Chinese noodles, satay and *popiah* (rice-paper rolls) courtesy of the many vendors in Chinatown's popular outdoor Hawker Centre, Hsiang Yang Fast Food.

DRINK an Eastern & Oriental Sling at Farquhar's Bar, an upmarket British pub inside the E&O Hotel.

DO take in the sights, sounds and exotic scents of Georgetown's lively Little India.

WATCH local girls throw oranges into the sea from the esplanade on Chap Goh Meh, the 15th day of the New Year celebrations.

BUY Penang pewter (a more affordable version of the better-known Selangor pewter, though of equal quality) from a number of stores along J1 Penang.

AFTER DARK go gigging Georgetown-style at Rock World as local Chinese bands hit the stage each weekend – you can't miss the gargantuan neon spider web hanging out the front.

URBAN MYTH

'Curry Kapitan' is a popular Penang chicken curry dish that is supposed to have been named when a Dutch sea captain asked his Indonesian mess boy what there was to eat that night. The young boy winsomely chimed 'Curry, Kapitan!' and it's been on the menu ever since.

One of Africa's most alluring cities for rest and relaxation, Maputo has distinctly Mediterranean atmosphere, white sandy beaches and friendly locals that give the busy capital a resort feel.

ANATOMY

Set on a small cliff overlooking the large harbour in Maputo Bay, the city is circled by stunning beaches, the scenic Inhaca and Portuguese Islands, the 'reed cities' – the overpopulated slums – various sized farm plots as well as species-rich coastal wetlands. The city's ample avenues, lined with red acacia and lilac jacaranda trees, are populated by worse-for-wear colonial buildings – the result of almost two decades of civil war – many modern constructions and a flourishing café culture. The best way to see Maputo is by foot, but minibus tours and car hire are options. It's only been a couple of years since traffic lights arrived in Maputo and many drivers have a relaxed observance of road laws, so take care.

PEOPLE

Indigenous tribal groups comprise about 99% of the population, with Europeans and Indians making up the final 1%. Fifty percent of the population adheres to indigenous beliefs, 30% is Christian and 20% Muslim. Although Portuguese is the official language, there are many local dialects spoken, and English is quite common in the city.

TYPICAL MAPUTO CITIZEN

Unlike their rural counterparts, these urban Mozambicans have disposable income, which they like to spend. Going out for coffee is a popular pastime, as is hanging out at the beach. They have strong religious beliefs, are resilient and optimistic, enthusiastic about music and love to dance and play sport. They are always smiling and friendly towards visitors.

Maputo 181

VITAL STATISTICS

NAME: MAPUTO

DATE OF BIRTH: 1787; THE TOWN DEVELOPED AROUND A PORTUGUESE FORTRESS, WHICH WAS COMPLETED AT THIS TIME

ADDRESS: MOZAMBIQUE (MAP 2, K24)

HEIGHT: 59M

POPULATION: 1.5 MILLION

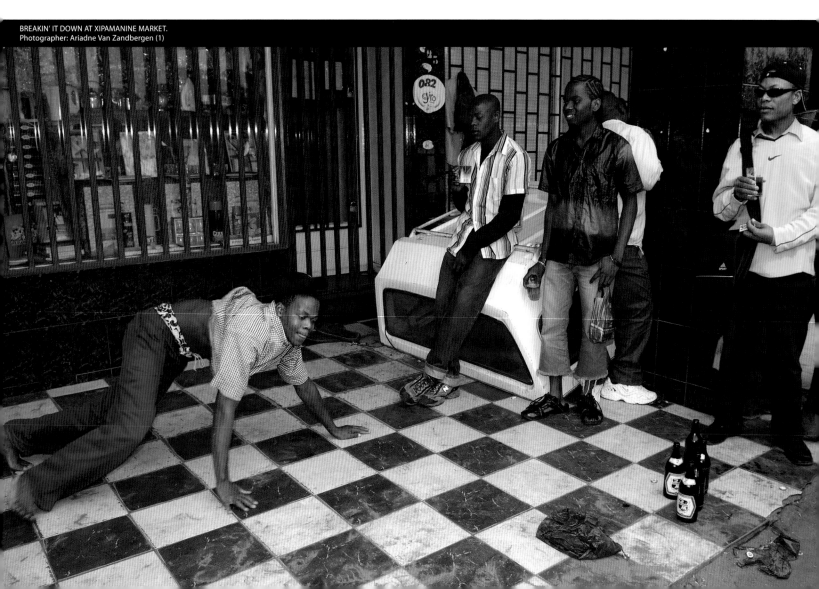

BREAKIN' IT DOWN AT XIPAMANINE MARKET.
Photographer: Ariadne Van Zandbergen (1)

DEFINING EXPERIENCE

Sunbathing with a book on the white sands of Praia de Maceneta beach, then taking in the bustling street life over a protracted beer and spicy tiger-prawn feast, picking up the Latino rhythm with some hot moves at the Mini-Golfe disco and cutting it up almost till dawn…before hot-footing it to the bay to take in a glorious sunrise.

STRENGTHS

- Locals
- Relaxed atmosphere
- Beach weather year-round
- Cheap-as-chips seafood
- Huge, colourful street murals
- Excellent water sports
- Palm tree–lined beaches
- Lively nightlife
- The Portuguese fort Nossa Senhora da Conceiao (Our Lady of Conception)
- Maputo Bay sunrises
- Café culture
- Maputo Elephant Reserve
- Colourful markets
- National Art Museum
- Local football matches
- Species-rich wetlands close by
- National Company of Song & Dance

WEAKNESSES

- Street crime
- Dodgy police officers
- Lawless drivers
- Poverty
- Central Railway Station
- Expensive supermarkets
- Poor-quality souvenir items

GOLD STAR

Pristine beaches – they're full of marine life and coral reefs, are within close reach of the city centre and have heaps of water sports available, including snorkelling, surfing, diving, fishing and windsurfing.

CITYSPEAK

- Maputo's mean streets – increasing violent attacks and carjacking – and how to clean them up
- Resumption (in July 2005) of train services in the Greater Maputo area and what their impact will be on the general population

STARRING ROLE IN...

- *Ali* (2000)
- *The Gaze of the Stars* (1997)
- *Under the Frangipani* by Mia Couto
- *Half a Life* by VS Naipaul

IMPORT

- Lots of South African tourists
- Fast-food chains
- Food
- Foreign aid
- Western-style billboards
- Clothing
- Mobile phones
- Farm equipment
- Petrol
- Air-conditioning

EXPORT

- Aluminium
- Cashews
- Prawns (shrimp)
- Cashews
- Cotton
- Sugar
- Citrus fruits
- Timber
- Electricity

SEE the impressive 95m-long mural opposite the Praça dos Heróis Moçambicanos, commemorating the Revolution.

EAT spicy *piri-piri* (a sauce made from a particular type of chilli) chicken at the famous 1960s-feel Restaurante Piri-Piri.

DRINK the local beers – Laurentina, Manica and 2M – street-side, under the shade of an acacia tree.

DO a camping trip to Inhaca Island and explore its offshore coral reefs.

WATCH an energetic performance of the first-rate National Company of Song & Dance.

BUY up-to-the-minute import items delivered straight from the docks of Maputo Bay to the city's air-conditioned shopping centres.

AFTER DARK check out the local jazz scene at Cinema Gil Vicente.

URBAN MYTH

The imposing Central Railway Station is an enormous palace-like structure. The story goes that the building was designed by Alexandre Gustav Eiffel (of Eiffel Tower fame), but as Eiffel himself never stepped foot in the city, some suggest it was in fact designed by one of his associates.

A POOL SHARK CONSIDERS HIS NEXT MOVE.
Photographer: Ariadne Van Zandbergen (2)

BROWSING THROUGH AN ASSORTMENT OF TRADITIONAL MEDICINES AT THE MARKET.
Photographer: Ariadne Van Zandbergen (3)

STREET MURAL DEPICTING THE CHAOS OF THE CIVIL WAR.
Photographer: Ariadne Van Zandbergen (4)

Baku 182

VITAL STATISTICS

NAME: BAKU

DATE OF BIRTH: BRONZE AGE; THERE IS EVIDENCE OF HABITATION SINCE THIS TIME, ALTHOUGH THE FIRST HISTORICAL REFERENCE TO BAKU WAS ONLY MADE IN THE 9TH CENTURY

ADDRESS: AZERBAIJAN (MAP 3, AA14)

HEIGHT: 1M

SIZE: 86,600 SQ KM

POPULATION: 1.7 MILLION

The ancient walled city at Baku's heart is a magnificently preserved collection of mosques and imposing Moorish architecture, while just outside the city fascinating relics of Zoroastrianism will astound anyone with an interest in religion.

ANATOMY

Baku curls majestically around the Bay of Baku, an inlet from the oil-rich Caspian Sea, from which the scent of black gold wafts through the city. The very heart of the town is the Içəri Şəhər, the old Muslim walled city, which contains several beautiful mosques and the famous Maiden's Tower. The modern city is congregated around the Içəri Şəhər and provides a stark contrast in its mercurial modernity. There is a range of public transport, including a metro, buses and trolleybuses.

PEOPLE

While Azerbaijan is a multicultural nation, 88% of Baku's population are ethnic Azeris. Seven percent are Russians and the rest are made up of minorities including Tatars, Lezgins, Kurds and Armenians. Azerbaijan is a Shiite Muslim nation, though Sunni Muslims and Russian Orthodox Christians comprise a significant proportion of the population. Fiercely proud of the young republic of Azerbaijan, many of the most educated people in the city nevertheless speak Russian rather than Azeri at home – a not uncommon contradiction in the post-Soviet world.

TYPICAL BAKUNIAN

Cosmopolitan and bilingual, Bakunians are well known for their sly business instincts, and the city's economic boom can be attributed as much to the character of the city's natives as it can to the oil wealth beneath the Caspian. That said, most Bakunians you meet are exceptionally laid-back, hospitable and talkative people who love nothing more than to engage in drawn-out debates and discussions. Whatever you do here, you'll come away feeling like you've got some new friends to visit on your return.

DEFINING EXPERIENCE

Leaving bustling downtown Baku with its busy oil men, glass-and-steel tower blocks and fast food, and slipping into another world entirely by wandering into the Içəri Şəhər, seeing the carpet sellers and fruit stalls, watching families going about their daily lives in the narrow backstreets and hearing the call to prayer at the grand mosques contained within the city's ancient walls.

STRENGTHS

- Cool breeze from the sea, which keeps the city pleasant even during the stifling summer months
- The friendly çayxana (traditional teahouse) society will convert even ardent espresso-fans to the delights of tea
- You'll see very few tourists but plenty of Western businesspeople
- The food is delicious and markets overflow with fresh fruit and vegetables

WEAKNESSES

- The smell of oil from the Caspian
- Corrupt officials always on the lookout for some extra earnings
- The dismal political situation

GOLD STAR

The fascinating world of the Içəri Şəhər

CITYSPEAK

- The most recent prodemocracy demonstrations and speculation about the president's game plan
- The latest cool-clime locations outside the city to spend the weekend during the hot summer
- New developments on the oil front – who's moving in, who's shipping out, new oil rigs and failed joint ventures

STARRING ROLE IN...

- *The World Is Not Enough* (1999)

IMPORT

- Oil-company employees from all over the world

EXPORT

- Oil
- Rostropovich

SEE the majestic view from the top of the mysterious Maiden's Tower.

EAT fresh and delicious *lula* (kebab) at any restaurant in town.

DRINK tea over a game of *nard* (backgammon) in a Bakunian *çayxana*.

DO explore the fascinating Palace of the Shirvan Shahs in the Içəri Şəhər.

WATCH out when discussing politics – the war with Armenia remains a taboo subject.

BUY carpets galore at the open-air market in the Içəri Şəhər.

AFTER DARK enjoy a display of live music and belly dancing in any smart restaurant.

URBAN MYTH

The mysterious Maiden's Tower remains an object of fascination. What was it actually used for? Some claim it was a lookout tower, some a prison, and others claim the flat circular room was a place to leave the city's dead in order that vultures might clean their bones.

MODERN LIVING IS EASY IN THIS ANCIENT METROPOLIS.
Photographer: Stephane Victor (1)

A MAZE OF NARROW ALLEYS MAKES EXPLORING THIS CITY A TREAT.
Photographer: Stephane Victor (2)

SHOP TILL YOU DROP IN THE BEAUTIFUL DISTRICT AROUND FOUNTAIN SQ.
Photographer: Stephane Victor (3)

FRIENDLY BREW – TRADITIONAL TEAHOUSES ARE A GREAT PLACE TO OBSERVE EVERYDAY LIFE.
Photographer: Stephane Victor (4)

Belize City

183

VITAL STATISTICS

NAME: BELIZE CITY

DATE OF BIRTH: 1779; WHEN 'BELIZE TOWN'
BECAME THE BRITISH HEADQUARTERS IN BELIZE

ADDRESS: BELIZE (MAP 4, G4)

HEIGHT: 5M

SIZE: 2 SQ KM

POPULATION: 60,000

ETHNIC DIVERSITY IS A PROUD HERITAGE OF
BELIZE'S INTRIGUING HISTORY.
Photographer: Anthony Plummer (1)

Belize City's ramshackle, untidy streets are alive with colourful characters representing every facet of the city's amazing ethnic variety, especially the Creoles whose culture has always been rooted here.

ANATOMY

Haulover Creek, running across the middle of the city, separates the downtown commercial area (focused on Albert St) from the slightly more genteel Fort George district to the northeast. The Swing Bridge – hub of the city – crosses Haulover Creek to link Albert St with Queen St. North up the coast from the Fort George district are the Newtown Barracks and Kings Park neighbourhoods. West of Albert St is the Southside, the poorest part of the city. There is a bus network, but walking is often your best option.

PEOPLE

Belize City enjoys a fabulous, improbable ethnic diversity. Creoles – descendants of British loggers and colonists and African slaves – now form about 25%. Racially mixed and proud of it, Creoles speak a fascinating, unique version of English, the country's official language. Over the last couple of decades, mestizos (of mixed Spanish and indigenous descent) have become Belize's largest ethnic group, now at 53%. The rest is a mix of the Maya, the Garifuna, 'East Indians' (people of Indian subcontinent origins), Chinese, Arabs (generally known as Lebanese), North Americans and Europeans.

TYPICAL BELIZEAN

Because of the mix of ethnicities and cultures in Belize, its people are very open, tolerant and accepting of the differences of others. Poverty is still widespread and crime is almost a way of life for some people in Belize City. You can admire lovely, large, breezy, two-storey, old-Caribbean-style wooden houses in parts of Belize City, but most Belizeans live in smaller dwellings, and new houses are often small, cinder-block boxes, while old ones may be composed of warped and rotting wood. Labour – whether washing dirty hotel sheets, cutting sugar cane or packing bananas – is poorly paid, and prices are high in comparison. It is estimated that one third of the population live below the poverty line.

DEFINING EXPERIENCE

Visiting the centre of activity in Belize City, the Swing Bridge, enjoying the traditional Belizean dish of rice and beans, then taking in the colonial architecture and cooling sea breezes of the Fort George district.

STRENGTHS

- Swing Bridge – the only remaining working bridge of its type in the world
- Multiculturalism
- Free education
- Image Factory art gallery
- Street vibe
- Crooked Tree Wildlife Sanctuary
- Lovingly cooked Creole-style fish
- Tolerance
- Calypso music
- Relaxed atmosphere
- Environmentally friendly focus

WEAKNESSES

- The 29-seat House of Representatives contained only two women at last count
- Low wages
- Poor housing
- All too frequent shootings and murders around the Southside district
- Heat
- Influx of cruise-ship tourists
- Divide between rich and poor

GOLD STAR

The atmosphere and street life, more than anything, are what make Belize City worth exploring.

CITYSPEAK

- How is it that a government that espouses low taxation can raise taxes and still get Belize's finances into a mess?
- Strong voices argue for stricter controls over cruise tourism and for its economic benefits to be spread more widely

STARRING ROLE IN...

- *The Dogs of War* (1980)
- *Mosquito Coast* (1986)
- *Heart of Darkness* (1993)

IMPORT

- Mennonites
- Football
- Cruise-ship visitors
- Bird-watching enthusiasts
- Racial diversity
- Scuba divers

EXPORT

- Punta rock
- The Garifuna
- Bananas
- Oranges
- Ecotourism
- Howler monkeys, jaguars and toucans

SEE the heart and soul of Belize City life, the Swing Bridge, which is crossed by just about everyone here just about every day.

EAT spicy jerk chicken; pork with rice, beans and vegetables; tasty shrimp Creole or a lobster-and-fish combo at Jambel's Jerk Pit.

DRINK a 'seaweed shake' sold by a street vendor – a blend of condensed milk, spices and extract of the seaweed *Eucheuma isoforme*, which grows underwater as a tangle of yellow branches.

DO encounter howler monkeys at close quarters at the Community Baboon Sanctuary.

WATCH Belize's amazing wildlife at the Belize Zoo.

BUY exquisite carvings made from the strikingly streaked wood zericote at the National Handicraft Center.

AFTER DARK catch a concert of traditional Belizean music at the 600-seat Bliss Centre for the Performing Arts.

URBAN MYTH

Some believe the name 'Belize' comes from the Mayan word *belix*, meaning 'muddy water', referring to the Belize River.

FRIDAY NIGHT LIGHTS – CLUBBING IN BELIZE IS A HIGH POINT.
Photographer: Anthony Plummer (2)

WATCHING THE GRASS GROW – MANY OLDER BUILDINGS SUFFER FROM NEGLECT.
Photographer: Anthony Plummer (3)

SIGHT-SEEING ON THE SWING BRIDGE IS NOT THE EXCLUSIVE DOMAIN OF TOURISTS.
Photographer: Anthony Plummer (4)

AFTERNOON SUN CASTS A SPELL OF LIGHT ON THE FORTIFIED WALLS OF THE ANCIENT PORT.
Photographer: Jose Manuel Navia (1)

Essaouira

184

VITAL STATISTICS

NAME: ESSAOUIRA

NICKNAME: WINDY CITY

DATE OF BIRTH: LATE 1500s; WHEN IT WAS FOUNDED BY THE PORTUGUESE

ADDRESS: MOROCCO (MAP 3, B18)

HEIGHT: 7M

POPULATION: 40,000

Deemed a Unesco World Heritage site, this picture-perfect town is an elegant marriage of Arabic and Mediterranean architecture. Bustling spice markets and winding whitewashed streets filled with artisan workshops combine a European sensibility with careful attention to Moroccan heritage.

ANATOMY

Essaouira has a marvellous setting between the Atlantic Ocean, a dune forest and river-mouth wetlands, and all attractions are within walking distance. The medina (old city), enclosed by walls with five main gates, is the main attraction. The walled town is pretty compact, split into the mellah (the old Jewish quarter), medina and kasbah, all laid out on a surprisingly simple grid system. The main thoroughfare, Ave de l'Istiqlal, merging into Ave Mohammed Zerktouni, runs from Bab Doukkala in the northeast to the main square, Place Moulay Hassan, in the southwest. Beyond the square is the historic port, fish market and bastion of Skala du Port, where there are panoramic views of the harbour, sweeping beaches to the east, and the offshore islands, Illes Purpuraires. The bus stations and taxis are 1km northeast of town.

PEOPLE

The official language is Arabic, but both French and Berber are spoken. About 70% of Morocco's population (30.7 million) is under 30. As in the rest of Morocco, 98% of Essaouira's population is Muslim, 1% is Christian and 1% Jewish.

TYPICAL ESSAOUIRA CITIZEN

The Moroccan people's love of the theatrical is most prominent in Essaouira, where you'll find a musician on every corner (some of them only just knee height…). Bodily contact plays an important role in communication: handshakes are a crucial icebreaker and affectionate public greetings are an art form. They are also big on community. Family loyalty and responsibility extends to everyone in the neighbourhood: beggars are always offered money and a displaced woman always has a place to sleep.

DEFINING EXPERIENCE

Getting lost in the labyrinth of narrow whitewashed lanes and discovering tranquil squares, spice markets and artisans in tiny workshops, then watching the sun set behind the picturesque stone ramparts of the historic port and sating your appetite at the sizzling seafood stalls lining the harbour.

STRENGTHS

◢ Recently classified as a World Heritage site by Unesco
◢ Pedestrian-only (apart from donkeys and bicycles) medina
◢ Mediterranean-style architecture and atmosphere
◢ World-class surfing destination
◢ Endless sandy beaches
◢ All attractions are within walking distance
◢ Labyrinthine backstreets filled with artisan workshops and markets
◢ Thriving local and international music and arts scene
◢ Fresh seafood

WEAKNESSES

◢ Essaouira has become a gloriously distorted fantasy-land for countless Western baby boomers
◢ Hordes of day-trippers because of its proximity to Marrakech
◢ Relentless, strong coastal wind
◢ Lack of environmental awareness

GOLD STAR

Seemingly more Mykonos than Morocco, Mediterranean Essaouira has something for everyone – it is both a windsurfing mecca and a cultural hub for music and international and local art.

CITYSPEAK

◢ The influx of expatriates to Morocco who buy up all the medina mansions
◢ Is the lure of European opportunities causing a brain drain in Morocco?
◢ Who is playing at the next Gnawa Music Festival?
◢ What the recent classing of Essaouira as a historic centre means to locals trying to start businesses or buy property

STARRING ROLE IN…

◢ *Kingdom of Heaven* (2004)
◢ *Alexander* (2005)

IMPORT

◢ Hippies in the '60s, the likes of Jimmy Hendrix and Cat Stevens
◢ European expats buying up picturesque medina mansions
◢ Internationally renowned artists
◢ International acts for the Gnawa Music Festival

EXPORT

◢ Exquisite marquetry work made from local fragrant thuja wood (now an endangered species)
◢ Argan-oil products
◢ Spices
◢ Raffia work made from the fibres of the doum palm
◢ Gnawa music (a mystical form of music that draws its roots from the Gnawas, descendants of black slaves)
◢ Paintings by local artists
◢ Skin lamps

SEE the Gnawa Music Festival, Essaouira's four-day musical extravaganza.

EAT freshly caught seafood sizzling on outdoor grills down in the port.

DRINK mint tea in Moulay Hassan Sq.

DO a camel-riding excursion through the sand dunes or break your first sweat in a classic *hammam* (bathhouse).

WATCH the sun set over the Atlantic from the historic 18th-century clifftop ramparts and turrets of Skala de la Ville.

BUY a painting by a local up-and-coming artists, or a beautifully designed raffia work.

AFTER DARK chill out at the laid-back bar on the lamp-lit roof terrace of Taros Café.

URBAN MYTH

In 1766 the Sultan Sidi Mohamed ben Abdallah commissioned a French engineer named Théodore Cornut to design a town that could compete with the rebel port of Agadir. Cornut is believed to have been a prisoner who earned his freedom through his design of the city.

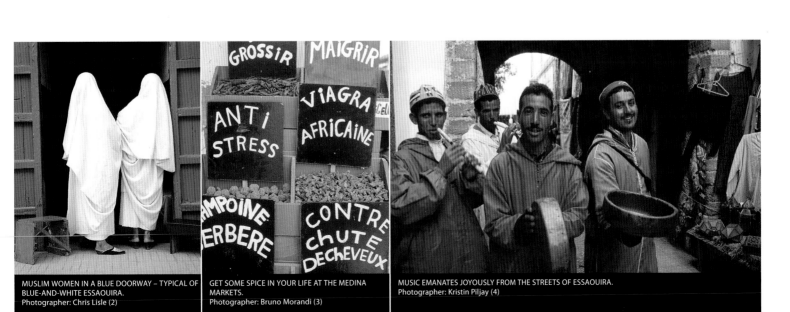

MUSLIM WOMEN IN A BLUE DOORWAY – TYPICAL OF BLUE-AND-WHITE ESSAOUIRA.
Photographer: Chris Lisle (2)

GET SOME SPICE IN YOUR LIFE AT THE MEDINA MARKETS.
Photographer: Bruno Morandi (3)

MUSIC EMANATES JOYOUSLY FROM THE STREETS OF ESSAOUIRA.
Photographer: Kristin Piljay (4)

Santo Domingo

185

VITAL STATISTICS

NAME: SANTO DOMINGO

DATE OF BIRTH: 1498; WHEN IT WAS FOUNDED BY BARTOLOMÉ COLOMBUS, BROTHER OF CHRISTOPHER

ADDRESS: DOMINICAN REPUBLIC (MAP 4, M4)

HEIGHT: 17M

POPULATION: 2.2 MILLION

The oldest Spanish city in the Americas has luscious natural surroundings, is profoundly festive and full of joyous, welcoming souls.

ANATOMY

Santo Domingo began as the birthplace of European colonies in the New World, and is now the political, economic and social centre of the Dominican Republic, which occupies the eastern side of the island of Hispaniola (Haiti occupies the western side). It's packed with gorgeous green blue waters crashing against its cliff-lined coast, couples overlooking the surf, whispering sweet everythings to each other, and buses belching long trails of spent diesel. It's an urban city with a vast cave system beneath it, a huge old fort and a park that fills daily with hundreds of joggers and cyclists.

PEOPLE

Santo Domingans may have adopted the Spanish language and the Catholic religion of their founders, but racially they're predominantly mulattos (with one white and one black parent; 73%), with the rest of the population comprised of those of African and European descent.

TYPICAL SANTO DOMINGAN

Maintaining close family ties and cultivating friendships are top priorities to Santo Domingans, and the quintessential merengue (folkloric dance of the Dominican Republic) is more like a tool for fostering relationships than music. Santo Domingans are flexible enough to live with profound contrasts, such as the immensely wealthy coexisting with those caught in grinding poverty. They maintain many traditions and revere their rich history, yet most watch American TV with awe and readily adopt the latest US trends. It's a city of Catholics with no shortage of brothels, five-star hotels that function despite frequent power outages and heat that can be downright oppressive, but Santo Domingans remain optimistic and patient.

DEFINING EXPERIENCE

Strolling and dining on savoury Dominican food on the *malecón* (waterfront promenade), watching Licey play at Quisqueya Stadium, then dancing merengue at Guacara Taina until dawn.

STRENGTHS

- Not one, but two crazy carnivals a year – in February and August
- Latin Music Festival
- Two merengue festivals
- Historic buildings
- Baseball games
- Obelisco del Malecón
- Generous, smiling locals
- Calle de las Damas (Ladies' Street)
- All-night, or any-time, dancing
- Fantastic views over the cliffs
- Roba La Gallina (enormous chicken character in the carnivals)

WEAKNESSES

- Petty crime
- Hurricanes
- Cockfighting
- Exterminated Arawak Indians
- Violent political history
- Aggressive police
- One third of the country below the poverty line
- Racism against Haitians

GOLD STAR

Most mobile 'founding city' – Santo Domingo was originally located in La Villa de Navidad in Haiti, moved 100km east to La Isabela, then onto the east bank of the Río Ozama, and finally settled itself on the Ozama's west bank.

CITYSPEAK

- The state of the peso and how expensive everything has become
- Dominican Republic versus Haiti – how's the dispute going now?
- Heroes – political (Leonel Fernández) and baseball (Vladimir Guerrero)

STARRING ROLE IN...

- *Santo Domingo Blues* (2004)
- *In the Time of the Butterflies* by Julia Álvarez
- *Sucre amer* (Bitter Sugar) by Maurice Lemoine
- *Santo Domingo, Past and Present* by Samuel Hazard

IMPORT

- Spanish and French culture
- US-trained dictators
- Slaves
- Baseball
- Poorly paid Haitian labourers
- Toussaint L'Ouverture (when he took the city in 1801)

EXPORT

- Rum
- Gold
- Hernando Cortés (before setting off to Mexico)
- Francisco Pizarro (before leaving for Peru)
- Julia Álvarez
- Cigars
- Merengue
- Baseball players to the US leagues

SEE *tabacos* (cigars) being rolled at the Boutique del Fumador or the Museo del Tabaco.

EAT *empanadas* (Chilean-style turnover stuffed with meat or cheese and raisins) and *pastelitos* (meat- and cheese-filled pastries) from street stalls.

DRINK rum at sunset at Plaza de Hispanidad.

DO bargain at the Pulga de Antigüedades (Antique Market) on Sunday.

WATCH a baseball game played by either Licey or Escojido at Quisqueya Stadium.

BUY amber or *larimar* (an opaque blue stone found only in the Dominican Republic) jewellery in the Zona Colonial.

AFTER DARK dance to music ranging from African drumming to French rock and Dominican dance music at Nowhere.

URBAN MYTH

To celebrate the 500th anniversary of Colombus' arrival in the Americas, President Belaguer planned to construct a lighthouse (the Faro a Colón). The plan was pilloried as ridiculously expensive and a show of megalomania; protests intensified, demonstrators were killed and foreign powers quietly withdrew their support. Two days before the inauguration, the president's 73-year-old sister, Doña Emma, had one last inspection, only to die mysteriously a few hours later. Belaguer refused to attend the inauguration, and Santo Domingans whispered of a *fukú* (curse) and reminded themselves that Columbus' name was always known to bring bad luck.

FRIENDSHIP IS ONE OF LIFE'S TRUE RICHES: A MOTORCYCLIST CHATS WITH NEIGHBOURS ON THEIR PORCH.
Photographer: Jeremy Horner (1)

LIFE ON DUARTE AVE SHOWS SIGNS OF CHAOS.
Photographer: Alfredo Maiquez (2)

BE ENCHANTED BY SANTO DOMINGO'S OLD-WORLD CHARM AND LATIN CHARISMA.
Photographer: Kevin O'Hara (3)

BLENDING IN AS ONLY A LOCAL CAN.
Photographer: Jeremy Horner (4)

Addis Ababa

186

VITAL STATISTICS

NAME: ADDIS ABABA

NICKNAME: ADDIS ABABA MEANS 'NEW FLOWER' IN AMHARIC

DATE OF BIRTH: 1886; FOUNDED BY EMPEROR MENELIK ON LAND CHOSEN BY HIS EMPRESS, TAYTU, FOR ITS PLEASANT CLIMATE IN THE FOOTHILLS OF THE ENTOTO MOUNTAINS

ADDRESS: ETHIOPIA (MAP 2, M11)

HEIGHT: 2450M

SIZE: 250 SQ KM

POPULATION: 5 MILLION

Ethiopia has been called the 'cradle of civilisation': one of the few countries on the continent never to be colonised, its unique culture is vibrantly expressed in its teeming capital, the third-largest city in Africa.

ANATOMY

Addis lies over a series of folds in the hills, but these have little effect on its sprawling mass, clustered round the Piazza to the north and Meskel Sq to the south. High-rise blocks stand next to fields of thatched, wattle-and-daub huts, air-conditioned taxis ferry businesspeople and bureaucrats while the rest of the population crowds into the fleet of tiny minibuses.

PEOPLE

Addis' population speaks 80 languages: Galla from the south comprise 40% of the total population, Amhara are the second-largest group at 30%, and others include Tigrayans (15% of the total), the Somali, Gurage, Borana, Awi, Afar, Wolayta, Sadama and the Beja.

TYPICAL ADDIS ABABAN

Like the city itself, Addis' citizens are a strange mix of the ancient and modern: priests in medieval robes bearing ceremonial umbrellas mingle with diplomats from across Africa visiting the African Union; street kids in filthy football shirts play among Oromo warriors attending tribal conferences, their elaborate hairpieces representing their prowess as hunters.

DEFINING EXPERIENCE

Joining in the week-long celebrations of the Feast of the True Cross in September, when huge bonfires are lit in Meskel Sq, topped by crosses made of flowers, and the singing and dancing goes on long into the night.

STRENGTHS

- Warm, temperate climate
- One of the safest cities in Africa
- Friendly locals

WEAKNESSES

- Extreme poverty
- Corruption
- The lack of education, employment, decent housing…

GOLD STAR

Ethiopians really are among the most welcoming people around: sit down for a natter and a strong, sweet coffee in one of the numerous cafés around the Piazza and just try and get away in a hurry.

CITYSPEAK

- New mayor Arkebe Oqubay, who has instituted a range of radical reforms since 2003
- The reduction of the omnipresent Ethiopian bureaucracy

STARRING ROLE IN...

- *Shaft in Africa* (1973)
- *500 Years Later* (2005)

IMPORT

- Jazz – while the '50s to the '70s were the foremost years of the Ethio-jazz movement, a love of brass and swing still persists in Addis' nightclubs.

EXPORT

- Coffee – Ethiopia claims to have discovered it, and buyers come to Addis from all over the world to procure the best.
- Hides and skins
- Handicrafts
- Gold
- Oil seeds
- Pulses and spices

SEE the rest of Ethiopia while you're there: from the Great Rift Valley to the Central Highlands, and the 1700-year-old obelisks of Axum to the rock churches of Lalibela, Ethiopia is one of the most fascinating and least visited countries on earth.

EAT Ethiopia's delicious national staple of *wot* (a spicy stew) and *injera* (a soft, spongy bread) at the Addis Ababa Restaurant, housed in a former *Ras* (duke's) residence.

DRINK a flask of *tej*, the powerful local mead brewed from honey, in one of the numerous *tej beats* (Ethiopian pub).

DO visit one of our oldest ancestors in the National Museum: 'Lucy', an almost complete hominid, was discovered in northeast Ethiopia in 1974, and she's at least 3.2 million years old.

WATCH a football match at Addis San Giorgis stadium in the centre of town, complete with barefoot players, live animal mascots, fire-breathing spectators and lashings of St George beer.

BUY anything you like at the sprawling, open-air Merkato, the largest market in East Africa, from Kalashnikovs to camels and spices.

AFTER DARK head to the bars on the Bole Rd for music and dancing in all styles – everything from *azmaris* (traditional Addis tunes) to international stars such as the adored Gigi Shibabaw.

URBAN MYTH

It may be cruel, but Ethiopian Airlines, one of Africa's most successful national carriers, still fields queries from potential passengers worried that they won't get anything to eat on the flight. In fact, both the airline and the city feature some of the finest cooking in Africa.

MAKING ENDS MEET ON THE STREETS OF ADDIS ABABA.
Photographer: Dave Bartruff (1)

FOOD FOR THE MASSES – THE UNIQUE FLAVOURS OF ETHIOPIA.
Photographer: Frances Linzee Gordon (2)

A TRADITIONAL OCTAGON, THE ORTHODOX CHURCH OF ST GEORGE IS ALSO A MUSEUM FOR RELIGIOUS ART.
Photographer: Caroline Penn (3)

RICH AND VIBRANT, ADDIS ABABA IS A CITY BUILT ON CULTURAL DIVERSITY.
Photographer: Nitu Mistry (4)

Pyongyang

VITAL STATISTICS

NAME: PYONGYANG

DATE OF BIRTH: AD 427; WHEN THE GOGURYEO
DYNASTY BUILT ITS CAPITAL HERE

ADDRESS: NORTH KOREA (MAP 1, JJ10)

HEIGHT: 27M

SIZE: 200 SQ KM

POPULATION: 2.7 MILLION

ON GUARD IN THE DEMILITARISED ZONE – NORTH KOREAN SOLDIERS ON PATROL AT TRUCE VILLAGE.
Photographer: Lee Jae-Won (1)

KIM JONG IL IS A CULT FIGURE IN HIS COUNTRY.
Photographer: Lee Jae-Won (2)

A LONE WORKER WALKS BY JUCHE TOWER, THE DEFINING SYMBOL OF NORTH KOREAN COMMUNISM.
Photographer: Anthony Pletts (3)

THE STRANGE BALLET OF THE MASS GAMES IS A WELL CHOREOGRAPHED SPECTACLE.
Photographer: Tony Wheeler (4)

Monumental and monolithic, the North Korean capital is one of the most impressive and unique cities on earth.

ANATOMY

Clustered around the massive Taedong River, Pyongyang's streets are eerily empty of traffic – most people walk or take buses, but only the privileged few have access to private motor cars. The centrepiece is Kim Il Sung Sq, the vast public space where military parades of fanatic precision take place under the shaded gaze of Communist emperor Kim Jong Il.

PEOPLE

Pyongyang must be one of the most homogeneous cities on earth. Its scant foreign population is billeted in the restricted diplomatic quarter, while the Chinese workers who run some of the city's hotels are unable to leave the establishments they work as it is feared they may adversely influence the locals. Pyongyang inhabitants are therefore fascinated by any foreigner, and will wave and smile, but rarely dare speak to you. Only those of an ideologically pure background are given permits to live in the capital, so the people you see here are among the most privileged in the country.

TYPICAL PYONGYANGER

Despite their relatively high status in North Korean society, the vast majority of Pyongyang's inhabitants live austere lives. Every household will have a portrait of Kim Il Sung and his son Kim Jong Il. While food is no longer scarce, most people will live on a frugal diet of rice and noodles. Electricity is in short supply and the capital is often pitch black at night. Whenever the lights go off, locals shout 'blame America!' in response.

DEFINING EXPERIENCE

Finding Pyongyang's heart and soul is challenge indeed. So much of what you see is façade designed to interpret the government's vision of the country, but often bearing nothing in common with reality. In itself this is the defining experience of the city – trying to see through the cracks and chinks in the city's ideological armour.

STRENGTHS

- The North Koreans, when you are lucky enough to spend time with them, are delightful
- Lack of traffic pollution
- No crime problems

WEAKNESSES

- Appalling human-rights record
- No contact with the locals at all (you'll only really speak to your North Korean guides)
- The fact that you can't leave the hotel without your guide
- Little nightlife beyond pool and karaoke in your hotel
- Bugged hotel rooms

GOLD STAR

Monumental buildings: few cities can compete with Pyongyang's exceptional ability to produce vast socialist-realist-meets-Asia architecture.

CITYSPEAK

Quite what Pyongyang residents speak to each other about is pretty much anyone's guess, as contact with locals is so restricted that such subtleties of ordinary life are simply off-limits to foreigners. However, you can be sure that conversations you have in your hotel will be recorded through bugs in rooms, so the North Korean security services will have a much better idea of what you are discussing.

STARRING ROLE IN...

- *The Game of Their Lives* (2002)
- *State of Mind* (2004)

IMPORT

- Aid workers
- Chinese weekenders looking to relive the Cultural Revolution in all its glory
- UN food relief

EXPORT

- Plutonium
- Refugees escaping over the border to China
- Diplomatic endgame

SEE the view of this incredible city from the top of the Tower of the Juche Idea.

EAT at the Pyongyang Boat Restaurant, which cruises the Taedong River while you eat.

DRINK Taedong beer, and reflect that it was made in a factory bought and shipped wholesale from Trowbridge, England.

DO make an effort to learn the Korean for 'hello' and 'thank you', as it will mean the world to any North Korean with whom you do have fleeting contact.

WATCH the annual 'Mass Games' – a weird North Korean team sport in which thousands of participants perform ideological worship as ballet.

BUY plenty of propaganda, including exquisite hand-painted agitprop posters.

AFTER DARK enjoy the facilities in your hotel, as you're unlikely to be going anywhere else.

URBAN MYTH

Most visitors are taken to see the Pyongyang metro as part of their city tour. However, the fact that groups are only ever taken to two stations and ride between them has fuelled rumours that the entire system normally lies dormant due to electricity shortages, only rumbling into life (complete with conscripted passengers hurrying about purposefully) when tour groups pay the system a visit.

LAHORE RAILWAY STATION CONNECTS PEOPLE FROM THE FARTHEST CORNERS OF THE COUNTRY.
Photographer: Mike Goldwater (1)

Although not Pakistan's administrative capital, Lahore wins hands down as the cultural, intellectual and artistic jewel of Pakistan, sparkling with effervescent local culture and studded with historic monuments.

ANATOMY

The second-largest city in Pakistan, Lahore sits high on an alluvial plain near the Ravi River and the Indo-Pakistani border. A peculiarly attractive vista, the city bears the stamp of its former status as the capital of the Mughal Empire, with fearsome Mughal constructions as well as the British Raj legacy of Gothic Victorian styles, and modern buildings. A railway and air transport nerve-centre of Pakistan, Lahore's local transport comprises frequent buses and minibuses as well as *tongas* (two-wheeled horse or pony carriages), taxis and auto-rickshaws.

PEOPLE

As capital of the Punjab province, Lahore's demographics are dominated by the Punjabi ethnic group but also include other ethnic groups, most notably Afghan refugees. The city comprises a Muslim majority (around 97%), with Hindu and Christian minorities. Punjabi is the language of the city, with English also widely spoken.

TYPICAL LAHORI

Lahoris are fiercely patriotic and proud of their city and culture. They are highly skilled professionals, sportspeople and craftspeople. They love their traditions but are open to and embrace many aspects of Western culture, including cricket, and are high-spirited spectators. Lahori women also fight for civil rights. They are generous, warm and open to travellers but expect visitors to be respectfully dressed. They don't drink but are indulgent eaters.

Lahore 188

VITAL STATISTICS

NAME: LAHORE

NICKNAME: HEART OF PAKISTAN

DATE OF BIRTH: AD 630; WHILE THE DATE IS OFTEN DISPUTED, THE FIRST RELIABLE REFERENCE TO THE CITY WAS IN THE WRITINGS OF HSUAN TSNAG, A CHINESE TRAVELLER

ADDRESS: PAKISTAN (MAP 5, C1)

HEIGHT: 214M

SIZE: 185 SQ KM

POPULATION: 5.1 MILLION

EXOTIC AND ROMANTIC, BADSHAHI MOSQUE IS ONE OF THE WORLD'S ARCHITECTURAL TREASURES.
Photographer: Martin Puddy (3)

BE AMAZED BY THE OPULENT SPLENDOUR OF THE NATION'S RELIGIOUS ARCHITECTURE.
Photographer: Ed Kashi (2)

ACTION AND ADVENTURE ARE ALIVE IN LOLLYWOOD, PAKISTAN'S THRIVING FILM INDUSTRY.
Photographer: Izzet Keribar (4)

DEFINING EXPERIENCE

Lazily reading in the restful garden of the gorgeous Jinnah Library, chowing down on calamari and alcohol-free piña colada at Café Aylanto, then firing up for a showcase of electrifying *qawwali* (Islamic devotional singing) at the shrine of Data Ganj Bakhsh Hajveri.

STRENGTHS

- Open and friendly locals
- Skilled artisanship
- Qawwali
- Private gardens
- Local music
- Basant – the kite-flying festival
- 'Time & Fare' – Pakistan's train timetable
- Mughal architecture of the Old City
- Mela Chiraghan (Festival of Lights)
- Jehangir's Tomb
- Royal Fort
- Shalimar Gardens
- Badshahi Mosque

WEAKNESSES

- Indifferent attitude to the treatment of animals
- Steady rain and oppressive humidity during the monsoon season (July to September)
- Pollution
- Dry zone
- Persistent mosquitoes (during the monsoon)
- Crowded buses

GOLD STAR

Lahore Museum – touted as the best in Pakistan, if not the subcontinent. It is definitely worth a couple of hours' snooping. Its exhibits span the recorded history of the subcontinent, dating from the Stone Age to the present day and include a haunting statue, the *Fasting Buddha*.

CITYSPEAK

- In a city full of journalists, writers and intellectuals, Lahore is abuzz with talk about London bombings and its possible repercussions on Pakistan and world
- How Lahore will accommodate its rapidly increasing population

STARRING ROLE IN...

- *Veer Zaara* (2004)
- *Eating Grass* (2003)
- *Earth* (1998)
- *Bhowani Junction* (1956)

IMPORT

- Petrol
- Edible oil
- Tea
- International cuisine
- Cricket
- Hockey
- Squash
- Fast-food outlets

EXPORT

- News media
- Electrical goods
- Leather garments
- Turkoman, Persian and Caucasian carpets
- Lollywood (Pakistan's film industry based in Lahore) films
- Lahori diaspora of medical professionals
- Investment
- The cricketing skills of Imran Khan and Wasim Akram

SEE the wildly ecstatic spectators as you take in an international cricket match at Qaddafi Stadium.

EAT *boti kebab* (meat grilled on a spit) under a clear night sky twinkling with stars at Coco's Den and Café.

DRINK up at the upmarket Pearl Continental to celebrate your newly acquired drinking permit.

DO attend 'Sufi Night' and get caught up in the frenzied rhythms of mystical bliss and traditional drumming.

WATCH the outlandish theatrics of the daily border-closing from the grandstands – filled with pumped-up patriots.

BUY a traditional Punjabi *dhal* (drum) at Langay Mandi.

AFTER DARK check out the impromptu rooftop jams at the Regale Internet Inn, which attracts some of the finest musicians in Lahore.

URBAN MYTH

The origins of the city's name are shrouded in legend. One story goes that the city was founded by and named after Loh, the son of Rama, hero of the Hindu epic *Ramayana*, while another suggests that the name comes from the ancient word *loha* (iron), suggesting that the city was at some stage strongly armed.

Cayenne

VITAL STATISTICS

NAME: CAYENNE

DATE OF BIRTH: 1643; WHEN IT WAS FOUNDED BY THE FRENCH, WHO SET UP A FORT ON THE HIGHEST HILL

ADDRESS: FRENCH GUIANA (MAP 4, T10)

HEIGHT: 6M

POPULATION: 50,750

AN OPEN WINDOW LETS THE BREEZE IN AND THE BLUES OUT.
Photographer: Philippe Colombi (1)

Pretty French colonial buildings, flowered balconies, vibrant markets, fantastic Creole and Guianese cuisine and a multicultural population make Cayenne one of South America's most charming capitals.

ANATOMY

Place des Palmistes in the northwest of Cayenne is the beating heart of the city, filled with cafés, outdoor foodstalls and beckoning palm trees. Place Léopold Héder (aka Place Grenoble), to the west of Place des Palmistes, is one of the oldest parts of Cayenne. The city itself sits at the western end of a small hilly peninsula between the Mahury and Cayenne Rivers. There are limited buses and taxis may be more reliable.

PEOPLE

Cayenne is a melting pot of French people, Brazilians, Haitians, American Indians, Vietnamese and Chinese people. The Boni are the only endemic tribe of Surinamese Maroons (descendants of escaped African slaves), although members of the Aucaner (Djuka) and Paramaccaner tribes live in French Guiana. There are also two Hmong groups who originally hailed from Laos. Most of French Guiana is Catholic.

TYPICAL CAYENNE CITIZEN

French Guiana is the smallest of the Guianas. It is an overseas department of France and therefore part of the EU. Significant wads of euros from its mother country mean the people of Cayenne enjoy a good lifestyle and an infrastructure comparable to rural France; the interior of the country is less developed. Some people advocate greater freedom from France, but most appreciate the cash injections too much to support this. Guianese people are warm, friendly and proud of their ethnic mix. Not surprisingly, considering their French parentage, they also love their food.

DEFINING EXPERIENCE

Pottering around the varied stalls at the market, before tanning on Plage Montjoly then returning to town for some irresistible crepes from the night-time footstalls on Place des Palmistes.

STRENGTHS

- Plage Montjoly – Cayenne's best beach and home to spawning leatherback turtles in summer
- Musée Départemental
- Musée des Cultures Guyanaises
- *Carnaval* (February and March)
- The lively market
- French colonial architecture
- Ecotourism
- Office Culturel de la Région Guyane
- Virgin rainforest in French Guiana's interior
- Wildlife, such as tapirs, jaguars, poison-arrow frogs and caymans
- Good roads
- Îles du Salut penal settlement ruins
- Centre Spatial Guyanais (Guianese Space Centre) – launch site for the European Space Agency's Ariane rockets

WEAKNESSES

- Hunters of leatherback turtles
- Brutal penal system until 1953
- Shady characters after dark in the Village Chinois (Chinatown) area

GOLD STAR

French-Latin-Caribbean vibe

CITYSPEAK

- How can we shake off our reputation as a penal colony and attract ecotourists and wildlife enthusiasts?

STARRING ROLE IN...

- *1ère Compagnie* (First Company, 2005–)
- *Papillon* by Henri Charrière (film 1973)

IMPORT

- 70,000 French prisoners from 1852 eg Captain Alfred Dreyfus, Henri Charrière
- Scientists and technicians working at the Centre Spatial Guyanais
- Food
- Consumer goods
- Energy

EXPORT

- Cayenne pepper
- Rainforest timber
- Fish and seafood eg prawns (shrimp)
- Gold
- Henri Salvador

SEE what's left of 17th-century Fort Cépérou and check out the views of the town and river.

EAT delectable pastries and sandwiches Parisian-style, at Le Café Crème.

DRINK at Harry's Bar, a congenial bar offering 50 brands of whisky and multiple beers.

DO visit Montsinéry (45km west of Cayenne) and spot caymans, jaguars, tapirs and toucans at the Réserve Animalière Macourienne.

WATCH the city go mad for live music and parades at *carnaval* (carnival).

BUY tropical fruits and sizzling Vietnamese soup at Cayenne's main market.

AFTER DARK listen to the tinkling of the ivories or try your luck with a pool cue at the piano bar at La Case Café Show.

URBAN MYTH

According to Dr Mark Plotkin the name 'Guianas' does not mean 'Land of Many Waters' as is commonly believed. Instead it came from a series of errors. First of all, the Spanish misspelt the name of the Surinamese Indian tribe Wayana, writing it as 'Juayana' or 'Guayana'. The English then misread their misspelling (still with us?) and turned it into Guyana.

BEST FRIENDS FOREVER: TWO GIRLS ENJOYING LIFE BY THE FISH MARKET.
Photographer: Roger Ressmeyer (2)

A SNACK-SHOP OWNER AWAITS CLIENTELE.
Photographer: Philippe Giraud (3)

ALL DOLLED UP FOR MARDI GRAS.
Photographer: Jeremy Hunter (4)

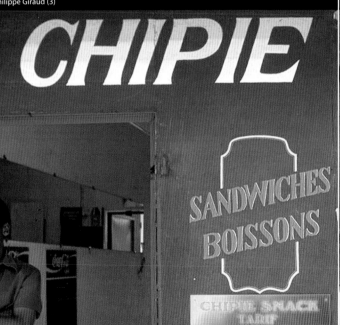

CHIPIE

SANDWICHES
BOISSONS

CHIPIE SNACK
TARIF

TWO BUSINESSMEN PROUD OF THE WARES THEY HAWK AT THE VEGETABLE MARKET.
Photographer: Anthony Plummer (1)

Almaty 190

VITAL STATISTICS

NAME: ALMATY

DATE OF BIRTH: AD 1854; A RUSSIAN FRONTIER FORT ON THE SITE OF THE SILK-ROAD OASIS, ALMATU

ADDRESS: KAZAKHSTAN (MAP 1, DD9)

HEIGHT: 775M

POPULATION: 1.5 MILLION

The honey pot of Kazakhstan, cosmopolitan Almaty is a city so European you would think you were in a leafy part of London, where you can sift through eclectic markets, pomp it up in fine old hotels, or make like a Soviet speed skater on the massive ice rink and best ski slopes in Central Asia.

ANATOMY

The Zailiysky Alatau Range rises like a wall along the southern fringes to form a superb backdrop to this clean, forested city. Almaty's long, straight streets are easy to navigate, running north–south and east–west, with mountains to the south and the city sloping upward from the north. There is a crowded network of *marshrutnoe* (minibus), bus and tram routes encompassing Zhibek Zholy, Almaty's pedestrianised shopping centre.

PEOPLE

Almaty's people are a typical mix of dozens of nationalities but, atypically for southern Kazakhstan, Russians and Ukrainians form the majority. To the ear, the sound of Russian, spoken even by most Kazakhs here, reveals the continuing hold of the colonising culture over the city. Several thousand Western and Asian expatriates, all after a foothold in the developing Kazakhstan economy, have also added to the mix in recent years – making Almaty Central Asia's most cosmopolitan city.

TYPICAL ALMATYAN

Almatyans are a people on the upswing. They are modern and European, having long moved away from rural Kazakhs in their dress, work habits and home life. Their former nomadic lifestyle, however, has bequeathed a certain attitude – laid-back and open – which separates them from their Russian brethren. Their middle-class incomes fuel the expansion of movie complexes, fashion shops, malls, sporting-goods stores and amusement parks. While the rich build themselves mansions up in the valleys around Almaty, some typically Kazakh traits remain and many an Almaty home will still be decorated with colourful carpets and tapestries, a tradition inherited from the brightly decorated yurts they once lived in.

DEFINING EXPERIENCE

Eating apples and *shashlyk* (kebab) in Central 'Gorky' Park before lazing on heated stone platforms at the Vostochnaya banya (Turkish baths) and then catching the infamous Otrar Sazy Kazakh Folk Orchestra and loudly discussing it afterwards.

STRENGTHS

- Zenkov Cathedral
- Altyn Adam (Golden Man)
- Eclectic museums
- Ski resorts
- State-of-the-art theatre scene
- Finest cafés and restaurants in Kazakhstan
- Arasan Baths
- Horse racing
- Pedestrian-friendly
- Cosmopolitan

WEAKNESSES

- Prostitution
- Police shakedowns
- Taxi scams
- Avalanches
- Waning national identity

GOLD STAR

Skiing – a hop, skip and jump from Almaty lies the powdered glory of the best skiing in Central Asia and the vertical 900m drop of Shymbulak ski resort.

CITYSPEAK

- Almaty's international airport (following the lines of a Kazakh traditional royal hat!)
- Ultimate Frisbee, the latest fad

STARRING ROLE IN...

- *Moksham* (2004)
- *The Place on the Grey Triangle Hat* (1993)
- *The Hiker's Guide to Almaty* by Arkady Pozdeyev

IMPORT

- The Golden Man
- International flights
- Nuclear warheads
- Weapon-grade uranium
- Ecotourism
- Big business
- Russian culture
- Cosmopolitan lifestyle
- Rich Kazakhs

EXPORT

- Oil
- Apples
- Vegetables
- Tobacco
- Rice
- Hemp
- Cotton

SEE the lolly-coloured, tsarist-era Zenkov Cathedral, built entirely of wood (and apparently without nails) in Panfilov Park.

EAT from the eclectic menu at PBC (RVS), the funky restaurant for the retro Soviet.

DRINK pints of beer on a crisp Sunday afternoon at the festivities in Central 'Gorky' Park.

DO catch a cable car to the viewing platform at Köktyube, the foothills of Zailiysky Alatau.

WATCH *dombra* (a two-stringed instrument) recitals at Almaty's Philharmonic Central Concert Hall.

BUY traditional Kazakh felt slippers and hats from the artisans in Sheber Aul artisans' village.

AFTER DARK line up with the young A-listers for pints of beer at the teeming Soho urban bar.

URBAN MYTH

The Golden Man is a warrior's costume. It is made of over 4000 separate gold pieces finely worked with animal motifs and a 70cm-high head-dress bearing skyward-pointing arrows, a pair of snarling snow leopards and a two-headed winged mythical beast. Found in a Saka tomb near Almaty, and now Kazakhstan's greatest archaeological treasure, the Golden Man resides in the vaults of Kazakhstan's National Bank. There's some confusion about its age – the Central State Museum cites the 12th century AD but most other sources put its origins at about the 5th century BC. The real confusion however, is who, or what, this Golden Man really was. Recent studies show that Kazakhstan's adopted symbol of war and strength was mostly likely a woman.

WORSHIPPING IN THE STATELY ZENKOV CATHEDRAL, ONE OF ALMATY'S FEW REMAINING TSARIST BUILDINGS.
Photographer: Ashley Gilbertson (2)

FINDING THE HIDDEN RAINBOW IN THE MIDDLE OF SUMMER'S HEAT.
Photographer: Shamil Zhumatov (3)

THIS COUPLE MAKES SURE TO LOOK TIDY IN THE WINTER CHILL.
Photographer: Donata Pizzi (4)

A thriving port city, Mombasa is a steamy, tropical entrepôt where life unfurls languidly.

ANATOMY

Mombasa is an island, connected to the mainland by causeways to the north and west and a ferry to the south. Digo Rd, and its southern extension, Nyerere Ave, is the main north–south thoroughfare. East of Digo Rd is the main market, which then leads on to the warren of narrow streets of the Old Town. On the fringe of the Old Town, overlooking the old harbour, are the fish markets and the almighty bulk of Fort Jesus. *Matatus* (minibuses, always jam packed) buzz around town, and connect Mombasa to the beach resorts to the north and south.

PEOPLE

As befits a port city, Mombasa has seen peoples – Persian, Omani and Portuguese, all of whom mixed with local African populations – come and go for millennia. The city is now one of the biggest Swahili cities, with a distinctive coastal culture that is a melange of African, Asian and Arabic influences. Along with the mosques of the Swahili populace there are Hindu and Sikh temples. There is a sizable English community as well as refugee communities from the Horn of Africa – Somalis, Eritreans and Ethiopians.

TYPICAL MOMBASAN

A tropical, coastal people, the Mombasans approach life at a languid pace. The humidity and a laid-back mind-set mean that there is no need to rush. That said, Mombasa is the biggest port in East Africa and it bustles (albeit at its own pace). Locals are convivial and gregarious – life occurs on the street, particularly in the evening as the cool descends. Etiquette is paramount, and greetings are long and elaborate. Mombasa is one of the oldest settlements in Kenya, so locals have a strong sense of identity.

Mombasa
191

VITAL STATISTICS

NAME: MOMBASA

DATE OF BIRTH: AD 150; WHEN PTOLEMY PLACED THE CITY ON HIS MAP OF THE KNOWN WORLD

ADDRESS: KENYA (MAP 2, N15)

HEIGHT: 16M

SIZE: 30 SQ KM

POPULATION: 653,000

GOING FOR A STROLL UNDER DRYING RAIMENTS.
Photographer: Carl & Ann Purcell (1)

DEFINING EXPERIENCE

Strolling the streets of the Old Town, admiring the ornately carved doorways, window frames and fretwork balconies of the coastal colonial houses, stopping for chai, then exploring the battlements of Fort Jesus, including Omani House, which dates back to the late 18th century, heading north to watch the comings and goings at the dhow harbour, or turning south on Mama Ngina Dr, passing the mighty baobab trees and gazing out across the Indian Ocean.

STRENGTHS

- Chai flavoured with cardamom
- Lazily spinning fans as you sleep under a mosquito net
- The scent of frangipani flowers in tropical rain
- The elaborate (slightly fading) glory of Swahili architecture
- Starched tablecloths on the Mombasa–Nairobi train
- Football on the gravel beneath Fort Jesus
- Lateen sails of dhows putting out to sea
- Tropical fruits – mangoes, pawpaws, pineapples

WEAKNESSES

- Street hassle from touts
- Mosquitoes when you're trying to sleep
- Humidity during the monsoon
- Disappearance of dhows from the dhow harbour
- Security after dark – some areas are best avoided
- Sex tourism

GOLD STAR

Coastal indolence – Mombasa is the place to take life languidly and watch the world pass by.

CITYSPEAK

- Are our politicians as corrupt as they say?

STARRING ROLE IN...

- *The Portuguese Period in East Africa* by Justus Strands
- *A Tourist in Africa* by Evelyn Waugh
- *Lunatic Express* by Charles Miller
- *The Weather in Africa* by Martha Gellhorn

IMPORT

- Arabic and Persian architectural styles
- Indian know-how and industriousness
- Expats looking for an idyllic coastal life

EXPORT

- Any and all produce from East Africa
- Oil
- Coffee
- Tea

SEE the sun rise over the Indian Ocean.

EAT traditional Swahili fare: grilled fish, beans in coconut milk, spiced pilau.

DRINK delicious lime soda in Fort Jesus.

DO a luxury dhow cruise around the harbour.

WATCH the colourful floats and parades at the annual carnival.

BUY a *kanga* or a *kikoi* (colourful traditional woven cloths).

AFTER DARK check out the bars on Moi Ave or Mama Ngina Dr.

URBAN MYTH

An Arab visitor in 1400 noted that Mombasa was being held to ransom by gangs of roaming monkeys. It was alleged the apes 'attack men in their own homes' and 'when they enter a house and find a woman they hold congress with her'.

SQUEEZING INTO THE SHOT DURING A BREAK FROM SCHOOL.
Photographer: Eric L Wheater (2)

A GAME OF FOOTBALL AT SUNSET AT FORT JESUS.
Photographer: Robert Caputo (3)

AN ELOQUENT TOUR GUIDE ELABORATES ON MOMBASA'S ATTRACTIONS.
Photographer: Paul Souders (4)

Valletta

VITAL STATISTICS

NAME: VALLETTA

DATE OF BIRTH: 1566; VALETTA WAS BUILT BY THE KNIGHTS OF THE ORDER OF ST JOHN

ADDRESS: MALTA (MAP 3, L16)

HEIGHT: 70M

SIZE: 0.6 SQ KM

POPULATION: 7030

The capital of Malta is a World Heritage site whose neat streets are crammed with signs of its history, including enlightening museums; forts, fortifications and monuments testifying to a valiant past; and remnants of British rule, such as red telephone- and postboxes.

ANATOMY

Perched on the tip of the Sceberras Peninsula, Valetta's grid-like pattern of streets makes it easy to navigate. Entering through City Gate, where you'll find the bus terminus, the main street, Triq ir-Repubblika (Republic St) runs northeast to Fort St Elmo. Parallel with Repubblika run Triq ir-Merkanti (Merchant St) to the southeast and Triq ir-Ifran (Old Bakery St) to the northwest. Triq ir-Repubblika and Triq ir-Merkanti are on the highest point of Valetta and the side streets run downhill. The main landmarks, St John's Co-Cathedral and the Grand Master's Palace, are on Triq ir-Repubblika. Valletta is easily explored on foot, although there is a bus service if you're feeling lazy.

PEOPLE

Over 95% of Malta's population was born on the island. The majority of the foreign community is British but there is a growing North African Muslim community.

TYPICAL VALETTA CITIZEN

The Maltese are proud of their country's rich history. Since their independence from Britain in 1964, they have shown themselves to be politically engaged (around 90% of people vote). The Roman Catholic Church still has a large influence, although this is decreasing, and family values are very strong. Unemployment is low at around 5% and there is free education for under-16s. Most people are friendly towards tourists and speak English; the native language is Malti. Football, horse racing and water polo are popular spectator sports.

DEFINING EXPERIENCE

Remembering Malta's WWII experiences in the National War Museum and spying that George Cross medal, before walking around the fortifications past the Siege Bell Memorial then into town for a coffee at Caffè Cordina and a trip around the Grand Master's Palace.

STRENGTHS

- ◢ Grand Harbour
- ◢ St John's Co-Cathedral
- ◢ The Malta experience
- ◢ 300 days of sunshine per year
- ◢ Mediterranean film studios – Europe's biggest film-production water tanks
- ◢ The city's fortifications
- ◢ The Grand Master's Palace
- ◢ National War Museum
- ◢ Ghana nights (Maltese folk music) at the St James Cavalier Centre for Creativity
- ◢ Church of St Paul's Shipwreck
- ◢ Excellent scuba-diving eg HMS *Maori*
- ◢ Rich marine life, such as sea horses and bottlenose dolphins
- ◢ Warm sea (over 20°C in summer)
- ◢ Kinnie orange-and-herb soft drink
- ◢ Cisk lager
- ◢ Hopleaf beer
- ◢ Agius Pastizzerija for pastries
- ◢ Carnival (February/March)
- ◢ National Museum of Archaeology

WEAKNESSES

- ◢ The Maltese Falcon – not spotted since the 1980s
- ◢ Rubbish in landfill sites

GOLD STAR

History

CITYSPEAK

- ◢ Malta's recent membership to the EU – what effects will this have?
- ◢ Bird hunting and Malta gaining special dispensation from the EU to continue this tradition
- ◢ What blockbuster is being filmed here at the moment?

STARRING ROLE IN...

- ◢ *Troy* (2004)
- ◢ *Gladiator* (2000)
- ◢ *The Spy Who Loved Me* (1977)

IMPORT

- ◢ Mattia Preti
- ◢ Caravaggio
- ◢ Jean Parisot de la Vallette (hero of the 1565 Great Siege and founder of Valletta)
- ◢ The Knights of the Order of St John

EXPORT

- ◢ Oliver Friġġieri
- ◢ Edward Bono, inventor of 'lateral thinking'
- ◢ Handmade lace
- ◢ Silver filigree
- ◢ Glassware

SEE where the knights used to worship, St John's Co-Cathedral, and admire Caravaggio's paintings in the Cathedral Museum.

EAT seasonal Maltese cuisine at local favourite Rubino.

DRINK and taste local wines in the Castille Wine Vaults underneath the stock exchange.

DO walk around the city's fortifications for views of the Grand Harbour and the Three Cities.

WATCH historical pageants and re-enactments at Fort St Elmo.

BUY locally produced glassware, lace and ceramics at the Malta Crafts Centre.

AFTER DARK see concerts, plays and art-house films in the St James Cavalier Centre for Creativity.

URBAN MYTH

Malta has been under siege more than once. Indeed it was a siege that prompted Valetta to be built in the first place (the Great Siege of 1565). But possibly the worst battle experienced by the island was in 1942, when they were bombed for 154 consecutive days and nights (when London's Blitz was at its worst, there were 57 days of continuous bombardment). Operation Pedestal was launched to rescue the island. Under heavy attack only five supply ships made it through, but this was enough for Malta to be saved. On 15 April 1942 King George VI awarded the George Cross to the population of Malta, for their bravery.

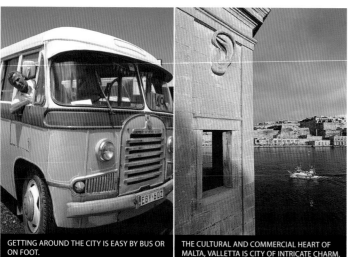

GETTING AROUND THE CITY IS EASY BY BUS OR ON FOOT.
Photographer: Bethune Carmichael (1)

THE CULTURAL AND COMMERCIAL HEART OF MALTA, VALLETTA IS CITY OF INTRICATE CHARM.
Photographer: Doug Scott (2)

THE MAJORITY OF CITIZENS WERE BORN ON MALTA AND REMAIN FIERCELY PROUD OF THEIR HERITAGE.
Photographer: Network Photographers (3)

VALLETTA IS A FASCINATING MASTERPIECE OF BAROQUE ARCHITECTURE.
Photographer: Doug Scott (4)

Antananarivo

VITAL STATISTICS

NAME: ANTANANARIVO

NICKNAME: TANA; LITERALLY 'CITY OF A THOUSAND' (WARRIORS)

DATE OF BIRTH: 1610; AFTER THE MERINA RULER, KING ANDRIANJAKA, CONQUERED SEVERAL VILLAGES IN THE AREA

ADDRESS: MADAGASCAR (MAP 2, P21)

HEIGHT: 1372M

POPULATION: 1.7

Often eclipsed by the natural beauty of the rest of the country, Tana offers a glimpse into the edgy, urban side of Malagasy culture, plus the chance to indulge in fine French colonial cuisine.

ANATOMY

Renault 4 taxis whine up and down the cobblestone hills, belching blue exhaust fumes over the crowds of pedestrians. In spring, purple jacaranda trees blaze into life, raining nectar onto the heads of skipping children and strolling couples. Terracotta mansions are stacked on the hillsides, turning gold under the setting sun. Beyond the city sprawl, paddy fields glint in the pale sunshine.

PEOPLE

The majority group in Tana is the indigenous Merina community. They and the other indigenous groups of Tana are joined by a very few French descendants, with the languages of choice being Malagasy and French.

TYPICAL TANA CITIZEN

The typical Tana resident is rooted in traditions and community but flexible enough to make room for tourists and their beliefs. The people of Tana are proud of their illustrious history but a little reserved about sharing it. Your best understanding of the Malagasy will come from the locals you encounter in your travels – ladies selling embroidered tablecloths on the pavement, men hawking rubber stamps from improvised stalls, or taxi drivers sharing peanut cake bought from a roadside kiosk.

DEFINING EXPERIENCE

Breakfasting *à la française* with coffee and bread, spending the day shopping or selling wares at the markets, eating dinner at a *hotely* (local foodstall), sampling local rums at Restaurant Sakamanga with friends, and, finally, dancing away to contemporary Malagasy music.

STRENGTHS

◢ The zoo at Tsimbazaza
◢ Zebu-drawn carts
◢ Merina history, living and dead
◢ Rice paddies in the middle of town
◢ On-foot exploration
◢ Antaimoro paper (tree-pulp parchment inlaid with flowers and leaves and left to dry under the moon's shade, as tradition dictates)
◢ The Marché Artisanal (Handicrafts Market) at La Digue
◢ Blended African and French heritage
◢ Access to the rest of Madagascar
◢ Views from the city down to the plains

WEAKNESSES

◢ Steep streets and steps
◢ Crowds, noise, pollution
◢ Only two published maps, neither of which is up-to-date
◢ Train tracks that cross the runway of the airport
◢ Continual advances of beggars and street vendors
◢ 55% living below the poverty line

GOLD STAR

Having the most amazing names for people and places – the queen's palace at the Rova is called Manjakamiadana (A Fine Place to Rule). It was designed for Queen Ranavalona I, and is located next to a replica of the palace of King Andrianampoinimerina, founder of the Merina kingdom.

CITYSPEAK

◢ When will we see the tourism sparked by the movie Madagascar?
◢ How are the play-offs going for the Madagascar Cup?
◢ The administrative war over the rights of 'residents' and 'nonresidents'

STARRING ROLE IN...

◢ *Madagascar* (2005)
◢ *Le Tricheur* (The Cheat) by Claude Simon
◢ *I Vola* by Andry Andraina
◢ *Fofombadiko* (My Fiancée) by Emilson Daniel Andriamalala

IMPORT

◢ Ancestor worship and rice worship from the city's Indonesian ancestors
◢ The African obsession with zebu
◢ Arabic words for books, money and music
◢ French pastries
◢ Anything that comes from European culture
◢ Naturalists from all over the world

EXPORT

◢ Tobacco
◢ Merina burial rituals
◢ A new appreciation for royalty with short names
◢ Textiles
◢ Lemurs and chameleons
◢ The concept of Madagascar as 'the eighth continent'

SEE the view from the Rova at sunset.

EAT at Chez Mariette – gourmet Malagasy cuisine based on the banquets served to Madagascan royalty.

DRINK tea, coffee or hot chocolate at a *salon de thé* (tearoom).

DO stroll down the steep, narrow streets to the Ave of Independence.

WATCH a traditional Malagasy performance of acrobatics, music and speeches.

BUY handicrafts from the revamped Zoma markets.

AFTER DARK dance to a mixture of American hip-hop, Malagasy chart hits, and French soft-rock anthems at Le Pandora Station.

URBAN MYTH

Everyday life in Tana is regulated by numerous *fady* (taboos), which differ from those of other regions in Madagascar. They can forbid foods (pork, lemur, turtle), wearing clothes of a particular colour, bathing in a river or a lake, etc. *Fady* are attributed to ancestors, to whom the Malagasy owe a respectful worship whatever their religion. It is preferable to respect these beliefs so as not to offend.

NIGHTTIME TRAFFIC LIGHTS UP THE AVE OF INDEPENDENCE.
Photographer: David Curl (1)

MARKET TRADERS RELAX UNDER A HOMAGE TO COFFEE.
Photographer: Jeremy Horner (2)

PLAYTIME IN MOTION, PLAYTIME AT REST.
Photographer: Reagan Pannell (3)

AN AERIAL VIEW REVEALS TANA'S HAPPILY COLOURED ROOFTOPS.
Photographer: Yann Arthus-Bertrand (4)

Miami

VITAL STATISTICS

NAME: MIAMI

DATE OF BIRTH: 1870; WHEN WILLIAM B BRICKELL ESTABLISHED AN INDIAN TRADING POST

HEIGHT: 8M

SIZE: 93 SQ KM

ADDRESS: USA (MAP 1, L12)

POPULATION: 376,815

INSIDE OUT – THE QUIRKY EXTERIOR DECORATION OF A FURNITURE STORE IN THE DESIGN DISTRICT.
Photographer: Richard Cummins (1)

A HAND-PAINTED TRUCK ON MIAMI BEACH PUTS THE LEMON BACK INTO LEMONADE.
Photographer: Jeffrey Becom (2)

THE SHADOW OF A PALM TREE EMBELLISHES THE FAÇADE OF A BUILDING IN THE ART DECO HISTORIC DISTRICT.
Photographer: Lawrence Worcester (3)

FIGURES IN A MURAL SWELL THE CROWD OF ONLOOKERS AT A DOMINO MATCH IN MÁXIMO GÓMEZ PARK, LITTLE HAVANA.
Photographer: Jeff Greenberg (4)

Miami is a fabulous melting pot of Latin immigrants, A-list celebrities and buffed, surgically enhanced beauties, all soaking up the city's sexy image (a magnet for tourists and style magazines), booming development and great museums and art galleries – not to mention the sun, sand and sea.

ANATOMY

Miami and Miami Beach are separated by the Intracoastal Waterway – Miami is on the mainland, while Miami Beach sits on a strip of white sand 6km to the east. Miami Beach is home to the world-renowned Art Deco Historic District and South Beach (SoBe), drawcards for the rich, famous and fabulous. Multicultural Miami has Little Havana, initially populated by Cubans but now home to a pan-Latin community, and Little Haiti, a medley of Haitian markets and eateries. The Miami River runs through downtown Miami. Miami's port, which regularly welcomes cruise ships, is the busiest in the world. Get around by bus or double-decker train.

PEOPLE

Sixty percent of the population was born outside the USA and the largest community in Miami is Latino (particularly Cuban). The average age of inhabitants is 39. Miami is bilingual (English and Spanish).

TYPICAL MIAMIAN

Miamians are hard-working, style-conscious people who tend to dress casually unless going out in the evening, when they pull out all the stops. It's not unusual to see A-list celebrities in Miami, but Miamians would never let on that they've noticed. Almost 40% of inhabitants own a property and real estate is more expensive in Miami Beach. Luxury condo high-rises are going up all the time. SUVs are the vehicle of choice. Miamians are a tolerant lot; in 2004 a law was passed to allow gay and straight couples living together to register their partnership. Gay adoption is still illegal though.

DEFINING EXPERIENCE

Inhaling the odours of cigar shops on Little Havana's Calle Ocho, watching old men playing dominoes in Máximo Gómez Park, then heading to South Beach for a bite in the News Café, some time on the beach and cocktails at the Delano Hotel.

STRENGTHS

- Art Basel Miami Beach
- Carnaval Miami
- Art Deco Historic District
- Argentine-Italian food in Normandy Isle
- Floribbean cuisine (a mix of Caribbean, Latin and local traditions)
- Mojitos (Miami's favourite cocktail: rum, lime, sugar, mint and soda water)
- Fashion Week of the Americas
- Clothes shopping at Lincoln Rd Mall
- Miami Heat (basketball)
- Miami Dolphins (football)
- *Miami Herald*
- Tropical weather
- Environmentally Endangered Lands (EEL) program
- Everglades National Park
- Art galleries of the Design District, particularly Moore Space
- Museum of Contemporary Art
- Public art eg Holocaust Memorial, The Living Room
- Latin music
- Delano Hotel
- Rollerblading on the Promenade
- Photo shoots on Glitter Beach
- MiMo architecture eg Fontainebleau Hilton
- Wolfie Cohen's Rascal House
- Miami Seaquarium
- Venetian Pool

WEAKNESSES

- Around a fifth of Miamians live below the poverty line
- It's easy to spend money here
- Lack of affordable housing
- Higher unemployment than the national average
- Political scandals
- Mosquitoes in summer
- Hurricanes

GOLD STAR

Fabulousness – beautiful Art Deco architecture and beautiful people

CITYSPEAK

- North Miami – the place to buy property?
- Should we get hurricane insurance?
- Have you seen Jennifer Lopez-Anthony at Skybar recently?

STARRING ROLE IN...

- *Nip/Tuck* (2003–)
- *Miami Vice* (1984–1989)
- *The Birdcage* (1996)
- *Scarface* (1983)
- *Cold Case Squad* by Edna Buchanan

IMPORT

- Paris Hilton
- Cameron Diaz
- Gloria Estefan
- Gianni Versace
- Ricky Martin
- Edna Buchanan
- Anti-Castro immigrants (after the 1959 Cuban revolution)

EXPORT

- LanChile Airline
- Embraer – Brazilian aircraft company
- Televisa – Mexican TV conglomerate
- MTV Latin America
- Telemundo
- Latin Music Conference and Awards
- Dr Arthur Agatston and the South Beach Diet
- Perry Ellis International
- Esteban Cortezar

SEE contemporary art exhibitions and live music at the Design District's monthly Art and Design Night.

EAT succulent steaks at Prime 112, in the oldest inn on Miami Beach, the 1915 Browns Hotel.

DRINK mojitos with famous faces in the upstairs garden at Skybar.

DO a walking tour of the South Beach Art Deco Historic District.

WATCH topless men gyrating on dance floors at the gay extravaganza, Winter Party Week.

BUY, buy, buy at Coconut Grove's popular outdoor malls: Coconut Walk and Streets of Mayfair.

AFTER DARK indulge in all-night drinking and dancing at enormous Space.

URBAN MYTH

The Biltmore Hotel in Miami's Coral Gables is the stuff of legend. So many murders, plots and dodgy dealings have taken place here there's a ghost-story-telling session every week in the hotel lobby. Al Capone had a speakeasy here during Prohibition and if you visit the Capone Suite you may be joined by the ghost of Fats Walsh who met his bloody end in this set of rooms. The hotel is hard to miss – its tower, modelled on the Cathedral of Seville's Giralda belltower, and designed by George Merrick, is 95m high. In 2002 Kyle McLachlan's wedding reception was held in the hotel. The Dade Heritage Trust runs guided tours of the property – check out the hotel pool, it's the largest in the USA.

SHARING GOOD TIMES IN THE SHADE.
Photographer: Crispin Hughes (1)

Bamako is a riot of sound and colour: women in flamboyant clothing with towers of tomatoes on their heads; men selling plastic combs, toys and bottles; table football games; the scorching sun overhead; and a rousing soundtrack of Bambara music.

ANATOMY

Sitting on the north bank of the River Niger, Bamako city centre is a triangle formed by Ave Modibo Keita, Blvd du Peuple and the train tracks. At the heart of the city off Rue Baba Diarra is the train station. The main road out of town is Route de Ségou. You reach this by heading south from Ave Modibo Keita to Square Lumumba then taking Pont des Martyrs. Catch one of Bamako's yellow taxis or a green *dourounis* (vans).

PEOPLE

Approximately 80% of Malians are Muslim, but animist beliefs are widespread. The main tribal groups in Bamako are Bambara, Malinke and Soninke.

TYPICAL BAMAKO CITIZEN

Mali is one of the world's poorest nations. Two-thirds of Mali's population struggle below the poverty line, and infant mortality is very high at 10%. The civil war in the Côte d'Ivoire, Mali's biggest trading partner, has caused the country massive problems. Despite all of this, Bamako is a harmonious place. The government is stable and popular and committed to stamping out corruption, and the media is relatively free. Women are revered, although genital mutilation and polygamy are still practised. Bamako's citizens are proud of Mali's history. They are warm, friendly and as loud as their clothing. And in such a musical city it's no surprise that they like to party.

Bamako
195

VITAL STATISTICS

NAME: BAMAKO

DATE OF BIRTH: 1700S; WHEN THE NIARÉ CLAN ARRIVED IN THE REGION AND NAMED THE TOWN 'CROCODILE RIVER' (BAMA-KO IN BAMBARA) AFTER THE NUMEROUS CROCODILES THEY SAW IN THE NIGER

ADDRESS: MALI (MAP 1, T14)

HEIGHT: 340M

POPULATION: 935,400

BAMAKO SITS PROUDLY ON THE NORTH BANK OF THE RIVER NIGER.
Photographer: John Elk III (2)

MARKET EXTRAVAGANZAS ARE AN EXPERIENCE WORTH ENJOYING.
Photographer: Peter Ptschelinzew (3)

THE PEOPLE OF BAMAKO REMAIN PROUD AND NOBLE DESPITE THE PRESSURES OF POVERTY.
Photographer: Finbarr O'Reilly (4)

DEFINING EXPERIENCE

Wandering through the markets, spying the dead-animal potions at the Fetish Market before buying henna decorations at the Marché de Médina and heading to Djembe for a drink and a dance to the sound of *griots* (poets, musicians and historical storytellers).

STRENGTHS

- Bambara woodcarvings eg the *chiwara* (antelope) mask
- *Griots*
- The library and concerts at the Centre Culturel Français
- Kora (traditional 12-string instrument)
- Grand Marché
- Woodcarvings at the Maison des Artisans
- Artisans' work at the Institut National des Arts
- Fetish Market
- Bogolan (hand-painted mud cloth)
- Marché de Médina
- Musée National
- The streets at prayer time, full of genuflecting people
- Bold, colourful clothing
- The Niger
- Table football

WEAKNESS

- Muggings around the train station, riverbanks and near the Maison des Jeunes de Bamako

GOLD STAR

Live music – Bamako has rhythm.

CITYSPEAK

- Where shall we get down to some live music this evening?
- What has the marabout (holy man) suggested for your aches and pains?

STARRING ROLE IN...

- *Bamako Sigi-Kan* (2002)
- *Je chanterai pour toi* (2002)
- *Yeleen* (1987)

IMPORT

- Damon Albarn of Blur
- Jackson Browne
- Bonnie Raitt
- Salif Keïta

EXPORT

- Film maker Souleymane Cissé
- Musician Toumani Diabaté
- Fashion designer Xuly Bët (Kouyaté Lamine Badian)
- Photographer Seydou Keïta
- Woodcarvings

SEE the stunning views from Point de Vue Touristique above Bamako.

EAT fantastic cakes with real coffee at the Pâtisserie le Royaume des Gourmands.

DRINK at old favourite Byblos and watch male expats chatting up high-heeled hookers.

DO take drumming or dancing lessons at the Carrefour des Jeunes.

WATCH the vibrant dealings of the Grand Marché, whose stalls are crammed with dried fish, extravagant fabrics and potions.

BUY fabulous woodcarvings and jewellery from the Maison des Artisans.

AFTER DARK dance under the stars and watch Toumani Diabaté take to the stage at Le Hogon.

URBAN MYTH

Cousinage (loosely translated as 'joking cousins') is something of an institution in Mali. Certain family names or ethnic groups have other groups as counterpoints. When people are introduced they immediately know from their names whether or not they are 'joking cousins', and if they are, an exchange of mock insults ensues. But this is not just random trading of abuse; *cousinage* breaks the ice and literally ridicules the idea of animosity between different families.

Saint-Denis

196

VITAL STATISTICS

NAME: SAINT-DENIS

DATE OF BIRTH: 1668; FOUNDED BY THE GOVERNOR REGNAULT, WHO NAMED THE SETTLEMENT AFTER A SHIP THAT RAN AGROUND HERE

ADDRESS: RÉUNION (MAP 3, K13)

HEIGHT: 12M

SIZE: 423 SQ KM

POPULATION: 140,000

Dominating life on the tropical island, Saint-Denis is Réunion's historic cosmopolitan capital with a chilled vibe and wicked café culture that is unparalleled anywhere in the Indian Ocean.

ANATOMY

The city centre, conveniently arranged in a grid pattern, is built on a coastal plain that drops gently north towards the sea. Life revolves around the vibrant seafront area, Le Barachois, with its cafés and bars, and Ave de la Victoire, the main thoroughfare heading inland that leads to the grand Creole mansions along Rue de Paris. St-Denis is relatively small and getting around the centre on foot is a breeze, but there is nevertheless a good and comprehensive city-bus service.

PEOPLE

The population of Saint-Denis is predominantly descended from 17th-century French settlers and successive waves of migrants from Madagascar, East Africa, India and Indochina who were either brought to the island as slaves, arrived as mutineers, or came to trade. The official language is French but Creole is widely spoken. Creoles (people of Afro-French ancestry) are the largest ethnic group, comprising around 40% of the population.

TYPICAL SAINT-DENISIAN

The city is a veritable melting pot and over the years has supported an abundance of interracial marriages that led to the emergence of its unique Creole culture. Whatever their ethnicity, locals tend to share a strong sense of community and family values, which bind them together. Most would refer to themselves as Creole, not in the narrow sense of having Afro-French ancestry, but simply meaning one of 'the people'. Saint-Denisians have a casual approach to life and often come across as being reserved, although they are disarmingly polite when approached. In this town it's very much a case of 'you have to show respect, to get respect'.

DEFINING EXPERIENCE

Marvelling at the *Cathédrale* sculpture as you drive in from the airport, sniffing your way through the perfumed plants at the Botanical Gardens, filling up on pastries from Le Castel, then heading to Le Barachois to knock back a few evening tumblers of rum while swapping fantasies about what you'd like to do to the mosquitoes.

STRENGTHS

- Creole mansions
- *Pétanque* (a bit like lawn bowls but played with heavy metal balls on a sandy pitch)
- Culturally diverse
- Bird-watching
- The Hindu temple
- Hearing Creole spoken
- Jurassic Park backdrop
- The Préfecture
- *Bonbons piments* (deep-fried balls of lentils and chilli)
- Botanical Gardens
- Amazing ice cream

WEAKNESSES

- Mosquitoes
- Everything's expensive
- Cyclones
- Everything's in French
- Finding a seat in a restaurant at lunchtime

GOLD STAR

Food – thanks to the French passion for *la gastronomie* (gastronomy), there's a restaurant or café around virtually every corner.

CITYSPEAK

- Religion – does the St Expédit voodoo cult really exist?
- Sustainability – how long will the island's resources last?
- Unemployment – nearly a third of the population rely on state welfare

STARRING ROLE IN...

- *Paul and Virginie* by Bernardin de Saint-Pierre

IMPORT

- Whisky
- Made-up saints
- Welfare state
- Animal species
- Slavery
- Modern art (paintings by Picasso, Renoir, Gauguin etc)

EXPORT

- Rum
- Vanilla tea
- Coffee
- Sugar

SEE the impressive Creole mansions on Rue de Paris, many of which feature elaborate verandas and intricate *lambrequins* (ornamental window and door borders).

EAT a storming traditional Creole curry at the funky-cool Cyclone café.

DRINK blinding mojitos (a cocktail made of rum, lime, sugar, mint and soda water) while posing at the ultra-modern Moda Bar.

DO play *pétanque* before sunset at the seafront park at Le Barachois.

WATCH a Hollywood blockbuster that's been hilariously dubbed into French at Gaumont cinema.

BUY the luscious local *rhums arrangés* (flavoured rums) from Le Petit Marché.

AFTER DARK get into the groove by taking an Afro-Caribbean dance class at Si Señor.

URBAN MYTH

St Expédit is one of Réunion's most popular saints, though some scholars argue that he never even existed. Instead, they attribute the origins of this 'saint who ain't' to a box of religious relics that was shipped from Rome in a parcel bearing the Italian word *espedito* (expedited). When the box arrived in Paris, the nuns mistakenly assumed that this was the saint's name and christened their new chapel La Chapelle de St Expédit. Whatever the truth, the idea was brought to Réunion in 1931 when a local woman erected a statue of the 'saint' in the Notre Dame de la Délivrance church in Saint-Denis, in thanks for answering her prayer to return to Réunion. There are now more than 350 shrines in Réunion dedicated to St Expédit.

CONSUMERS BUSTLE TO AND FRO IN SEARCH OF RETAIL THERAPY IN THE OPEN-AIR MARKET.
Photographer: Enrico Bartolucci (1)

IF YOU'RE AFTER A SEAFRONT PROPERTY, SAINT-DENIS MIGHT JUST BE YOUR TOWN.
Photographer: Reagan Pannell (2)

KIDS TAKING ADVANTAGE OF PARENTAL ABSENCE.
Photographer: Enrico Bartolucci (3)

A BREAK-TIME SNACK DURING INTERMISSION AT THE THEATRE.
Photographer: Enrico Bartolucci (4)

PASSION FLOWS IN EVERY MOVE OF THESE FLAMENCO DANCERS.
Photographer: Paco Ayala (1)

Granada
197

VITAL STATISTICS

NAME: GRANADA

DATE OF BIRTH: 1238; WHEN IT WAS FOUNDED BY
IBN AHMAR, A PRINCE OF THE ARAB NASRID TRIBE

ADDRESS: SPAIN (MAP 4, H7)

HEIGHT: 680M

POPULATION: 238,000

If there were a beauty contest lining up all the towns and cities of Spain, Granada would surely be declared the fairest of them all – it's a heart-stealer!

ANATOMY

Encapsulating Spanish allure, Granada is closer to Morocco's Tangier than Spain's capital of Madrid. Granada is a myriad of atmospheric streets and masterful architectural feats. The two major central streets, Gran Vía de Colón and calle Reyes Católicos, meet at plaza Isabel La Católica. From here, calle Reyes Católicos runs southwest to Puerta Real, an important intersection, and northeast to plaza Nueva. The street Cuesta de Gomérez leads northeast up from plaza Nueva towards the Alhambra on its hilltop. The Albayzín rambles over another hill rising north of plaza Nueva, separated from the Alhambra hill by the valley of the Río Darro. Below the southern side of the Alhambra is the old Jewish district, Realejo. The bus station (north–west) and train station (west) are out of the centre but linked to it by plenty of buses.

PEOPLE

Granada boasts a buzzing Spanish and international student population. Spanish is the language of choice but many tourism operators dabble in English.

TYPICAL GRANADINO

Granadinos are a gregarious, close-knit bunch, deeply rooted in their families and communities, and age-old traditions such as religious festivals, fairs and flamenco music. Like their fellow Andalucians, the people of Granada have a great capacity for enjoying themselves and give little emphasis to timetables and schedules.

DEFINING EXPERIENCE

Witnessing the Moorish splendour of the 11th-century Alhambra, the famed fortress and palace complex, and exploring the city's mystical old quarter where Gypsy music floats through the labyrinthine streets and households gather for late-afternoon feastings.

STRENGTHS

- Old-world atmosphere
- Compact and made for walking
- Interesting past: history buffs rejoice!
- University-town vibe
- Complimentary tapas with drinks in bars
- Colourful nightlife
- The Alhambra's Palacio Nazaries (Nasrid Palace), dubbed the best Islamic building in Europe
- Gay-friendly
- Festivals and events from holy celebrations to classical music extravaganzas
- Hiking and skiing aplenty in Sierra Nevada National Park

WEAKNESSES

- Stifling summer heat
- Tourist hordes
- Accommodation headaches
- Queues for the Alhambra
- Downtown noise
- Bag snatchers who loiter at some tourist sights

GOLD STAR

Experiencing a taste of North Africa at calle Calderería's many Arab-style cafés and Albayzín teahouses.

CITYSPEAK

- When are the kids getting married and moving out?
- Unemployment figures
- Wages below the national average
- Tourism booms
- Rising living costs

STARRING ROLE IN...

- *Doctor Zhivago* (1965)
- *Time Bandits* (1981)
- *Tales of the Alhambra* by Washington Irving
- *Driving over Lemons: An Optimist in Andalucia* by Chris Stewart
- *Moorish Spain* by Richard Fletcher
- *Andalucia* by Michael Jacobs
- *The Assassination of Federico García Lorca* by Ian Gibson

IMPORT

- Beige-clad, loafer-wearing tourists
- Celebrities on holiday, namely Posh and Becks and former couple Brad and Jen
- Islamic style
- Falafels in pitta

EXPORT

- Funky jewellery
- Tobacco
- *Jamón serrano* (cured ham)
- Olive oil
- Granadino village crafts: embossed leather, pottery, copper ware…
- Hand-crafted guitars
- Flamenco dancing and recordings
- Postcard-perfect tourist photos
- *Mantoncillos* (flamenco scarves)
- Hand-painted *azulejos* (decorative glazed tiles)

SEE Capilla Real, Granada's outstanding ode to late-Gothic splendour, mid-morning to soak up the atmosphere minus the tourist masses.

EAT in the narrow streets of Albayzín at El Agua where first-rate views of the Alhambra are guaranteed.

DRINK *cava* (sparkling wine) at hip 'n' happening El Círculo tapas bar on Calle de Elvira.

DO get lost while exploring the Darro Valley and the bohemian Albayzín.

WATCH flamenco at Peña de la Platería, a genuine aficionados' club in an Albayzín warren.

BUY some *taracea* (marquetry; tiny pieces of bone and hardwoods arranged in geometric patterns), used on boxes, tables, chess sets and frames – the best pieces have shell, silver or mother-of-pearl inlays.

AFTER DARK dance the night away with the oh-so-groovy student set at Granada 10, which opens at midnight.

URBAN MYTH

The Alhambra's Palacio de los Leones (Palace of the Lions), built under Mohammed V, is tipped to have doubled as the royal harem.

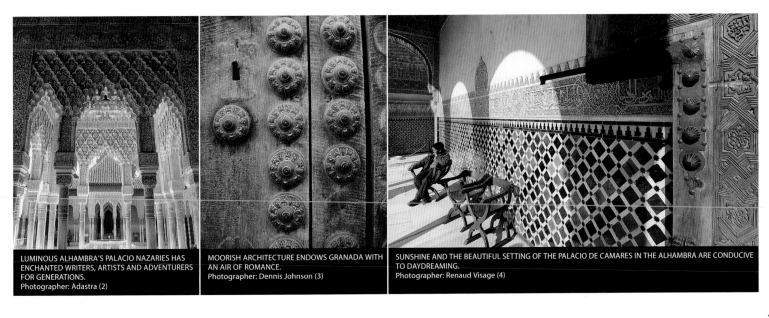

LUMINOUS ALHAMBRA'S PALACIO NAZARIES HAS ENCHANTED WRITERS, ARTISTS AND ADVENTURERS FOR GENERATIONS.
Photographer: Adastra (2)

MOORISH ARCHITECTURE ENDOWS GRANADA WITH AN AIR OF ROMANCE.
Photographer: Dennis Johnson (3)

SUNSHINE AND THE BEAUTIFUL SETTING OF THE PALACIO DE CAMARES IN THE ALHAMBRA ARE CONDUCIVE TO DAYDREAMING.
Photographer: Renaud Visage (4)

The ultimate coastal chill-out zone, Beira's laid-back blend of sandy beaches, outdoor nightlife, live music and dilapidated colonial heritage bestows a subtle and authentic flavour on the city.

ANATOMY

One of Southern Africa's oldest cities, Beira is a major port and rail terminus at the mouth of the River Pungwe. The city spreads along the coast from the port to the famous lighthouse overlooking paradisal Macuti Beach. Navigation can be difficult through its unnamed maze of streets, mostly built in a Mediterranean style with colonial buildings, patios, city squares and market areas. The architecture is prettiest near the pulsating Praça (main square) where you will find the banks, shops and other handy facilities. Catch buses or *chapas* (minibuses) to get around.

PEOPLE

Ships passing through the port ensure there is always a steady flow of different nationalities in addition to Mozambique's usual array of African, Arabic, Portuguese and Chinese ethnic communities. Portuguese is the official language and Bantu and Swahili are also spoken.

TYPICAL BEIRAN

Beira emerged from nearly two decades of civil war only to be hit by catastrophic floods in 2000 and again in 2001, but remarkably the people remain sanguine and are inspiringly strong. The city is now starting to experience rapid and much-needed economic development. As a result the people are confident, positive, friendly and laid-back, even for Africa, and will often welcome the chance to practise their English and share intriguing stories over a cold beer.

Beira 198

VITAL STATISTICS

NAME: BEIRA

NICKNAME: THE HEART

DATE OF BIRTH: 1891; FOUNDED AS THE HEADQUARTERS OF THE PORTUGUESE COMPANHIA DE MOZAMBIQUE ON THE SITE OF AN OLD MUSLIM SETTLEMENT

ADDRESS: MOZAMBIQUE (MAP 2, L21)

HEIGHT: 10M

POPULATION: 350,000

A SHOE SELLER STARTS THE DAY OFF ON THE RIGHT FOOT.
Photographer: Ariadne Van Zandbergen (1)

DEFINING EXPERIENCE

Losing yourself among the labyrinthine streets, stumbling unexpectedly into Largo do Município, playing beach volleyball under the searing sun before cooling off with a swim in the shadow of the *Macut* shipwreck on Macuti Beach, gorging on a different prawn curry every night of the week, getting blown away by the live percussion acts, and trying not to get emotional as you listen to locals telling you what life was like during the civil war.

STRENGTHS

- Awesome beaches
- Endless smiles
- Best facilities for many kilometres
- Casa Infante de Sagres
- Unofficial 'parks' everywhere
- Tropical climate
- Culturally diverse
- Gaudy 1930s-inspired Art Deco
- The shipwrecks
- Farol do Macuti, the lighthouse
- Inspiring locals

WEAKNESSES

- AIDS
- Malaria
- No street signs
- Water pollution
- Floods and cyclones
- Poverty

GOLD STAR

Beaches – dazzling hot sand, broad-leaved palm trees and spectacular shipwrecks make Beria's beaches sing like sirens.

CITYSPEAK

- Child poverty and petty crime
- Cyclones – can the city withstand another battering?
- Access to clean water – Beiran homes are below the national average when it comes to access to safe drinking water

STARRING ROLE IN...

- *Lumumba* (2000)
- *Carlos Cardosa – Telling the Truth in Mozambique* by Paul Fauvet and Marcello Mosse
- *The Veranda under the Frangipani* by Mia Couto

IMPORT

- Marxism
- Portuguese marble
- Shipwrecks
- Foreign aid

EXPORT

- Cashew nuts
- Prawns (shrimps)
- Sugar
- Lessons from tragedy

SEE the desolate shipwrecks off beautiful Macuti Beach at dusk.

EAT rice and chicken on your favourite stretch of beach.

DRINK a cup of 'real' coffee at Biques restaurant.

DO check out, but don't purchase, the contraband on sale in the market at Tchunga Moyo (literally, 'brave heart').

WATCH the masters at work in a woodcarving workshop at Makonde.

BUY a locally made drum from the market and learn to play while you're still feeling the rhythm.

AFTER DARK shake your booty to kitsch disco beats at Bar Africa.

URBAN MYTH

Rusty shipwrecks abound around Beira's port area and several more are dotted along the coast. But perhaps most surprising are the two hulking vessels washed up in the shadow of the famous red-and-white striped lighthouse on Macuti Beach. This would seem to suggest that old Farol do Macut, as they say in Portuguese, was something of a failure. However, the criticism is unfounded as the ships were intended to be breakwaters and were intentionally manoeuvred into their current beachside resting places. The 28m lighthouse is the only one in Mozambique that is close to a major town, and until recently the horizontal stripes were always painted black. It was erected in 1904 and if it hadn't been you could be pretty sure there would be more than two ships adorning Macuti Beach.

A HEADSTRONG MAN MAKES HIS WAY THROUGH THE BEACH MARKET.
Photographer: Ariadne Van Zandbergen (2)

NO ONE EVER KICKS UP A STINK ABOUT THE DRYING FISH CARCASSES LINING THE BEACH.
Photographer: Ariadne Van Zandbergen (3)

ART DECO HIGH-RISES PROVIDE PANORAMIC VIEWS.
Photographer: Ariadne Van Zandbergen (4)

Madang

VITAL STATISTICS

NAME: MADANG

DATE OF BIRTH: 1884; WHEN THE GERMAN NEW GUINEA COMPANY BRIEFLY ESTABLISHED A BASE HERE BEFORE MALARIA DROVE THEM OUT

ADDRESS: PAPUA NEW GUINEA (MAP 1, LL16)

HEIGHT: 4M

POPULATION: 30,000

Often dubbed the 'Prettiest town in the Pacific', Madang has a mega-chilled resort-style feel coupled with excellent facilities, and provides easy access to nearby volcanoes, islands and legendary dive sites.

ANATOMY

This small town of parks and ponds nestles snugly on a lush peninsula surrounded by harbours, bays and nearby islands. Luxuriant vegetation and lily-capped waterways flourish alongside the main thoroughfares. The aquatically inclined will find spectacular scenery beneath the surrounding coastal waters – the perfect accompaniment to this surreally beautiful township. Buses gather around the market at 8am and the door guys yell out their destinations 'LaeLaeLaeLae' and 'HagenHagenHagen' with a great sense of theatre. Once full, they head off.

PEOPLE

As capital of Madang province, the city attracts coastal people, islanders, highlanders, and river-dwellers in search of prosperity. More recently, Europeans and Chinese settlers have entered the mix. There are 30 main tribal languages spoken in Madang, but the official languages are English, Tok Pisin (the Pidgin language) and Motu, with Tok Pisin being the most widely used.

TYPICAL MADANGESE

Each of Madang's 30-plus tribal groups has its own traditional ideas and practices, and belief in supernatural forces and ancestral spirits is strong despite two centuries of missionary activity in the region. In the main, locals are extremely friendly. Petty crime is not uncommon – there is no safety net for those drifting into Madang from nearby villages in search of work, and even unemployed graduates often fall into gangs of *raskols* just to survive.

DEFINING EXPERIENCE

Snorkelling in the warmest water ever off Lion's Reserve Beach, drip-drying as you follow the picturesque trail south of the Coastwatcher's memorial, heading back to the beach for more deep soul chilling, before hitting a slow round of golf at sunset and being treated to one of nature's spectacles as swarms of giant bats take flight from their home among the towering casuarina trees.

STRENGTHS

- Luxuriant vegetation
- Jaw-dropping beauty
- World-class snorkelling and diving
- Smiles everywhere
- Mabarosa Festival
- Giant butterflies
- Giant bats
- Bamboo bands
- Volcanic activity
- Warm coastal waters
- Unique cultures

WEAKNESSES

- Malaria zone
- Spitting locals
- Sea urchins
- Volcanic activity
- Litter
- Missionaries

GOLD STAR

Diving – excellent visibility, stunning tropical coral and fish life, plus countless WWII wrecks make the diving and snorkelling around Madang world-famous.

CITYSPEAK

- Political double standards – Madangese have a deep-rooted distrust of politicians and their motives
- Ecoforestry – how the people of Madang are doing it for themselves
- Volcanic refugees – whenever there's an eruption nearby islanders are relocated to Madang

STARRING ROLE IN...

- *Robinson Crusoe* (1996)
- *Bekim* by Rosalie Ann Christensen
- *The Cannibal Cookbook: Low Cal Meals to Die for* by Liva Kabok

IMPORT

- Christianity
- Western clothes
- Motors for boats
- English
- Anthropologists

EXPORT

- Copra
- Coffee
- Gold
- Cannibalism
- Oral history

SEE the truly amazing four-day Mabarosa Festival (held annually in August or September), which features *singsing* (performance/dance) groups from all over the country.

EAT fresh seafood daily at the water's edge at Madang Lodge.

DRINK a cocktail as you stroll around the Orchid Gardens at the Madang Resort Hotel.

DO take a photograph of the horizon at sunset so you can reminisce about your time spent in paradise.

WATCH the canoe race from Krangket Island to Madang during the Marabosa Festival.

BUY curious artefacts from the carver's hut at the Madang Resort Hotel.

AFTER DARK head out to the reefs for an exhilarating night dive.

URBAN MYTH

Before white settlers arrived, some of the tribes in Madang province practised cannibalism. Successive waves of missionaries put an end to the practice but locals occasionally like to play up to their fearsome past. Micronesian celebrity chef Liva Kabok was clearly having a laugh when he wrote *The Cannibal Cookbook: Low Cal Meals to Die for*, which contains, among others, a recipe for Irish stew cooked with Irish missionaries. However, a bizarre double murder that took place in Madang in 2000 put an end to jokes about cannibalism, for a while at least. After a heated exchange a man killed another man and then ate his eyes, testicles and heart in a shocking act of cannibalism before shocked villagers. After regaining their composure the villagers chased the killer into the bush, caught and tied him up. On learning of the murder the victim's family then proceeded to hack the murderer to pieces, killing him. When police were called in to investigate, the villagers all fled into the bush, taking both bodies with them.

TRADE ROUTE – PASSENGER BOATS ARE ALWAYS BUSY AS PEOPLE MAKE THEIR WAY TO AND FROM THE MARKETS.
Photographer: Peter Solness (1)

YOU DON'T GET MUCH FRESHER THAN FISH SOLD RIGHT ON THE SHORELINE.
Photographer: Peter Solness (2)

PICK UP INTERESTING PRODUCE AT LOCAL MARKETS.
Photographer: Peter Solness (3)

MADANG LIFE REVOLVES AROUND THE MARKETS.
Photographer: Peter Solness (4)

Ashgabat 200

VITAL STATISTICS

NAME: ASHGABAT

NICKNAME: THE CITY OF LOVE (THE MEANING OF ASHGABAT IN ARABIC)

DATE OF BIRTH: 1881; AS A RUSSIAN FORT

ADDRESS: TURKMENISTAN (MAP 1, BB10)

HEIGHT: 226M

POPULATION: 550,000

Definitely one of the world's oddest cities, Ashgabat is a desert oasis devoted entirely to the cult of Turkmenistan's megalomaniac dictator, Saparmyrat Niyazov – known to one and all as Turkmenbashi, the leader of the Turkmen.

ANATOMY

The old Russian town was wiped off the face of the earth in a 1948 earthquake and the rebuilt city is entirely a product of dictatorship. The city's main thoroughfares are dotted with recently added white-stone residential buildings that seem permanently empty. These are broken up with fantastically elaborate palaces and monuments, including those of the stunningly weird world of Berzengi, Turkmenbashi's new suburb south of the city centre.

PEOPLE

The population is a mix of Russians left behind after the end of the Soviet Union and native Turkmen. Ashgabat is by far the most Russian city in Turkmenistan.

TYPICAL ASHGABAT CITIZEN

Your typical Ashgabat dweller shrugs passively at the latest ridiculous act of President Niyazov, and is used to finding that many of the main roads in the capital have been closed off for a presidential motorcade. They try to maintain a sense of humour despite being constantly under threat of being evacuated from their homes and watching them be destroyed so that Turkmenbashi's massive 'regeneration' can continue apace.

DEFINING EXPERIENCE

Standing beneath the Arch of Neutrality with a golden revolving Turkmenbashi overhead and the fantastically Orwellian ensemble of marble buildings around Independence Sq.

STRENGTHS

- Very green
- Friendly locals
- Extremely safe at all times
- The best restaurants and hotels in the country
- Almost no tourists

WEAKNESSES

- Constant road closures for the presidential entourage
- Bugged hotel rooms

GOLD STAR

Tolkuchka Bazaar, a few kilometres outside the city in the nearby desert, is one of the most colourful and fascinating markets on earth, where you can buy anything from carpets to camels.

CITYSPEAK

- My house has been knocked down, has yours?
- Have you heard the president's latest extraordinary command?
- Will you keep your dual Russian citizenship? Or will you go back to Russia?

STARRING ROLE IN...

- There's no modern movie industry here, but Ashgabat is crying out to be used in a Bond movie of the future. Dr Evil himself appears to be on display on every street corner.

IMPORT

- Water
- Italian marble
- French architects
- BMWs
- Gold leaf

EXPORT

- Oil
- Gas
- Carpets
- Political dissenters
- *Rukhnama* (President Niyazov's 'Book of the Soul')

SEE the 'Path of Health' – stairways built into the side of the mountains to encourage people to go for long, invigorating walks.

EAT at expat favourite the Iranian Truck Stop for a real culinary treat.

DRINK national beers Zip and Berk, both of which go down very well in the heat of the late desert afternoon.

DO some riding in the lush countryside around the city on traditional Akhal-Teke horses.

WATCH a traditional Turkmen opera at the spanking new National Theatre.

BUY stunning Turkmen carpets at Tolkuchka Bazaar for a fraction of their price at home.

AFTER DARK your best bet is to head to the Florida nightclub for Turkmenistan's one and only drum and bass night.

URBAN MYTH

Perhaps the most enduring of the many myths surrounding the president is that of his heart bypass in 1997. Having gone in grey haired, Turkmenbashi emerged, bypass complete and his hair mysteriously jet black again. The local media, at a loss to explain such an event, immediately hailed the bypass as rejuvenating to the extent that the leader's hair had followed suit. This led to lots of local muttering about Turkmenbashi being a patient of Dr Schwarzkopf – particularly among the workers who had to spend the next few years repainting all the official portraits of Niyazov.

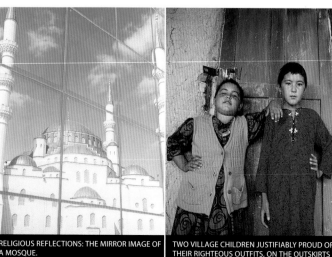

RELIGIOUS REFLECTIONS: THE MIRROR IMAGE OF A MOSQUE.
Photographer: Nevada Wier (1)

TWO VILLAGE CHILDREN JUSTIFIABLY PROUD OF THEIR RIGHTEOUS OUTFITS, ON THE OUTSKIRTS OF ASHGABAT.
Photographer: Nevada Wier (2)

DAZZLING JEWELLERY ON DISPLAY AT THE SUNDAY BAZAAR.
Photographer: David Samuel Robbins (3)

AN ASHGABAT WOMAN DEFIES NIYAZOV'S EDICT TO AVOID THE TRADITIONAL PENCHANT FOR GOLD-CAPPED TEETH – IN FULL VIEW OF HIS OWN GOLD-PLATED STATUE.
Photographer: Shamil Zhumatov (4)

Tony's Top Ten
Additional Cities

Detroit

VITAL STATISTICS

NAME: DETROIT

NICKNAME: MOTOR CITY

DATE OF BIRTH: 24 JULY 1701; WHEN FRENCH EXPLORER ANTOINE DE LA MOTHE CADILLAC SET UP A FUR-TRADING POST ON THE DETROIT RIVER

HEIGHT: 177M

SIZE: 219 SQ KM

ADDRESS: USA (MAP 1, L9)

POPULATION: 951,270

Detroit is the Motor City, Tamla Motown and home to Henry Ford's Greenfield Village, but it's also the doughnut city, a symbol of urban decay whose centre was abandoned as people moved out to a fringe of rich, thriving suburbs, trying to turn their collective backs on a core that might as well have been nuked. As a child I spent four great years there, back when what must have been half the world's chromium production was rolling down GM, Ford and Chrysler assembly lines, car fins were flying high, and the Detroit Tigers were the hottest baseball team around. It's never going to recover those glory days, but Detroit is still worth a look and Greenfield Village remains a truly fantastic museum, incorporating not only the laboratory where Thomas Edison conducted his pioneering work on electric lighting but also the bicycle shop where the Wright brothers built their first aircraft, quite apart from all the Model T stuff.

Jakarta

VITAL STATISTICS

NAME: JAKARTA

NICKNAME: BIG VILLAGE

DATE OF BIRTH: 22 JUNE 1527; WHEN IT WAS NAMED JAYAKARTA (CITY OF GREAT VICTORY) BY FATAHILLAH, A LEADER FROM A NEIGHBOURING SULTANATE

HEIGHT: 1M

SIZE: 661 SQ KM

ADDRESS: INDONESIA (MAP 1, HH16)

POPULATION: 9.3 MILLION

Indonesia's sprawling capital is yet another city considerably overshadowed, in the popularity stakes, by a smaller and more glamorous sister city, in this case tourist favourite and cultural capital Yogyakarta. Nevertheless, Jakarta is, in its own fashion, a mega-city that works from its teeming freeways to its old Dutch colonial capital, the one-time Batavia now known simply as Kota ('city' in Indonesian). No visit to Jakarta is complete without a stroll past the incredible line-up of brightly painted Makassar schooners (*pinisi*) in the old port district of Sunda Kelapa, living proof that the age of sail is definitely not finished. The city is also home to an impressive collection of imposing Stalinist-style socialist-era monuments, including the towering column in the centre of Merdeka (Freedom) Sq, popularly known as 'Soekarno's last erection'.

Karachi

VITAL STATISTICS

NAME: KARACHI

NICKNAME: CITY OF LIGHTS

DATE OF BIRTH: 1795; WHEN THE MIRS OF TALPUR CONSTRUCTED A MUD FORT AT MANORA

HEIGHT: 4M

SIZE: 1994 SQ KM

ADDRESS: PAKISTAN (MAP 1, CC12)

POPULATION: 9.3 MILLION

From my first birthday to my fifth this was home and, like any childhood memories, my pictures of Pakistan's troubled port city are rose-tinted: a melange of camels, sailboats, sandy beaches and exotic colours. Way back then Karachi was going through wrenching changes as India and Pakistan tore themselves apart and floods of refugees propelled the city's rocketing growth. To my pleasant surprise, when I returned to Karachi after an absence of 40 years, the city still had some of the charm I remembered. I could still hire a sailing boat and crew, drift out on the harbour and dangle a line over the side to pull up crabs to be cooked on the deck, just as I had done with my father all those years ago.

Mandalay

VITAL STATISTICS

NAME: MANDALAY

NICKNAME: CITY OF GEMS

DATE OF BIRTH: 1857; WHEN IT WAS ESTABLISHED AS A NEW CENTRE FOR THE TEACHING OF BUDDHISM

HEIGHT: 74M

ADDRESS: MYANMAR (MAP 5, J5)

POPULATION: 801,000

Kipling never actually took the 'Road to Mandalay'; the road to Mandalay is really a river, the mighty Ayeyarwady, but this is still the heart and soul of Myanmar. Quite apart from the huge Mandalay Fort (gutted during the closing phases of WWII), there are a host of temples and assorted Buddhist sites around the city. Plus it's the home of street theatre (*pwe*), and no visit to Mandalay is complete until you've caught a performance by the subversive Moustache Brothers. Nevertheless, it's outside Mandalay where the real surprises lie: the abandoned royal capitals of Inwa (Ava), Amarapura and Sagaing, and the massive Mingun Paya (pagoda), all a short boat ride north up the Ayeyarwady. Further afield there's the British colonial-era hill station of Pyin U Lwin (formerly Maymyo), or you can jump abord a river ferry and head downriver all the way to the amazing ancient city of Bagan.

Oslo

VITAL STATISTICS

NAME: OSLO

NICKNAME: TIGER CITY

DATE OF BIRTH: AD 1048 (ACCORDING TO THE NORSE SAGAS); HOWEVER, ARCHAEOLOGICAL RESEARCH HAS UNCOVERED CHRISTIAN BURIALS DATING FROM BEFORE AD 1000

HEIGHT: 629M

SIZE: 454 SQ KM

ADDRESS: NORWAY (MAP 3, J2)

POPULATION: 529,407

Cold, conservative and mouth-droppingly expensive, it's hardly surprising that Norway's capital and largest city doesn't feature on the city hit parade. Choose a sunny summer day, however, and Oslo can still charm you with leafy parks, busy cafés and restaurants, plenty of outdoor sculpture (Gustav Vigeland is the big name) and a simply dazzling collection of museums and art galleries. The Viking Ship Museum with its collection of longboats is my favourite, but ship lovers can also visit the Kon-Tiki Museum with Thor Heyerdahl's balsa raft and the *Polarship Fram*, which carried Roald Amundsen down to Antarctica for his epic journey to the South Pole in 1911. Of course, walking out of an Oslo art gallery with a Munch masterpiece under your arm seems to have become a Norwegian tradition.

MOTOR CITY TEST DUMMIES LINE UP FOR THEIR LAST DAY ON THE JOB.
Photographer: Louie Psihoyos (1)

BOATS DOCKED AT SUNDA KELAPA, JAKARTA'S PORT.
Photographer: Glenn Beanland (2)

SELLING CAKES TO KARACHI'S HUNGRY PORT WORKERS.
Photographer: Martin Puddy (3)

DELICIOUS STEAMED BUNS AWAIT IMMEDIATE CONSUMPTION.
Photographer: Jerry Alexander (4)

HOLMENKOLLEN, SITE OF THE WORLD'S OLDEST SKI JUMP.
Photographer: Galen Rowell (5)

It's easy to love cities like Paris and San Francisco – I've lived for a year in each of them, written guidebooks to them and am a total enthusiast – but there are lots of things to like about cities that don't pop up on anybody's favourites list. Here are 10 cities, in alphabetical order, that didn't make the cut but where I've still managed to leave a piece of my heart.

– Tony Wheeler, Cofounder, Lonely Planet

Papeete

VITAL STATISTICS

NAME: PAPEETE

DATE OF BIRTH: 1824; WHEN THE LONDON MISSIONARY SOCIETY (LMS) SETTLED HERE

HEIGHT: 2M

ADDRESS: TAHITI (MAP 1, D18)

POPULATION: 26,181

The capital of Tahiti and French Polynesia has a reputation as an overpriced, shonky Pacific disaster zone, a mere jumping-off point to the much more beautiful (though equally overpriced) attractions of neighbouring islands such as Bora Bora. Yeah, sure, but this is still a great place to buy a baguette, sip a glass of wine, sit by the harbour and watch the pirogues (six-man outrigger canoes) charge across the harbour. Meanwhile those dramatic green-draped mountains rise up right behind you, cruising yachts drift in from all over the world, catamaran ferries surge out to nearby Moorea, cargo ships steam out to towards the exotic Marquesas (Gauguin's final retreat), the *roulottes* (vans) set up to turn out bargain-priced food beside the docks in the evening, the towering *mahu* (Polynesian cross-dressers) totter off in their high heels and it's all done with a certain French style. What's not to like?

Stanley

VITAL STATISTICS

NAME: STANLEY

NICKNAME: CAPITAL OF 'THE CAMP' (FALKLAND ISLANDS)

DATE OF BIRTH: 1843; WHEN THE BRITISH ABANDONED PUERTO DE LA SOLEDAD AND ESTABLISHED STANLEY AS THE CAPITAL

HEIGHT: 135M

ADDRESS: FALKLAND ISLANDS (MAP 1, O23)

POPULATION: 2100

Some of my neglected favourites are those mega-cities few people can warm to, but Stanley is the polar opposite (and not that far from the South Pole). The capital 'city' of the Falkland Islands may be home to 75% of the 'kelpers' (as outsiders sometimes call the islanders), but that still means it can barely scrape together 2000 people. Despite this small population base, colourful Stanley (the islanders love decorating their houses with a technicolour paintbox) has plenty to see. There's a church fronted by a whalebone arch, a line-up of wrecked or dumped ship hulks along the shoreline, several noisy pubs, an iconic hotel (the Upland Goose),and a world-class garden-gnome collection in one front garden.

Tehran

VITAL STATISTICS

NAME: TEHRAN

NICKNAME: CITY OF 72 NATIONS

DATE OF BIRTH: 1553; WHEN RAMPARTS WERE CONSTRUCTED AROUND THE VILLAGE OF TEHRAN

HEIGHT: 1200M

SIZE: 1500 SQ KM

ADDRESS: IRAN (MAP 3, BB17)

POPULATION: 12 MILLION

The Islamic Republic of Iran has a long list of cities that score more highly than its chaotic capital. Sophisticated Shiraz has culture, and gave its name to one of the world's great wine varieties. Nearby lie the ruins of mighty Persepolis (whisper it). Mashhad and Qom far outscore Tehran when it comes to religious piety, Yazd and Kashan are way ahead when it comes to beautiful old traditional buildings and, of course, Esfahan is everybody's favourite and truly one of the world's most stunning cities. But there's no denying Tehran's energy and enthusiasm, from trendy shopping centres where teenagers raise a tentative finger to the fundamentalist mullahs, to madhouse traffic where women at the wheel give no quarter as they fight it out with their male counterparts, and all the time the magnificent Alborz Mountains (if you can see them through the pollution) rise up like a lodestone to the north – a clear reminder that the ski slopes on Mt Damavand are only a couple of hours away.

Tunis

VITAL STATISTICS

NAME: TUNIS

DATE OF BIRTH: 814 BC; FOUNDED BY PHOENICIAN SETTLERS

HEIGHT: 4M

SIZE: 346 SQ KM

ADDRESS: TUNISIA (MAP 3, J16)

POPULATION: 985,300

The sprawling Mediterranean capital of Tunisia is not going to win any beauty contests – although there's a fine World Heritage–listed medina (the ancient walled city) and some great restaurants. But Tunis also has one attraction that alone makes the trip across the Mediterranean from Europe worth the fare: the Bardo Museum. Even if you've never had an enthusiasm for Roman mosaics you will be a convert after you've wandered this treasure house. The Romans left mosaic treasures everywhere they built, from the frigid north of England to the warm Turkish coast, but it was in Tunisia where the art reached its apogee. The glowing artwork, which studs the Bardo's walls, underlines the fact that the colony's rich Roman settlers clearly knew how to build with style.

Warsaw

VITAL STATISTICS

NAME: WARSAW

NICKNAME: BIG POTATO

DATE OF BIRTH: 13TH CENTURY; IN 1413 IT BECAME CAPITAL OF THE DUCHY OF MAZOVIA AND, IN 1596, CAPITAL OF POLAND

HEIGHT: 106M

SIZE: 512 SQ KM

ADDRESS: POLAND (MAP 3, O7)

POPULATION: 1.69 MILLION

Poland's capital city, the 'Big Potato', ranks nowhere in the country's glamour stakes – as a tourist attraction Kraków gets all the votes. In fact, this is a city that has clearly gone through hell, and come out the other side throwing high-fives. The Old Town Sq was totally destroyed by Hitler's storm troopers during the closing days of WWII and so flawlessly rebuilt you'd have trouble telling where medieval Europe segues into the reconstruction of the 1970s and '80s. Weep at the poignant reminders of the Warsaw Ghetto; rage at the incredible story of the Warsaw Uprising, meticulously detailed in the Museum of the Warsaw Uprising; laugh at the 'Elephant in Lacy Underwear', the USSR's unwanted gift and for years the tallest building in Europe outside Moscow. And then hit the city's clubs and bars, where the Poles party as though they've got 50 depressing years to make up for.

LOCAL MUSICIANS TAKE SOME OF THE HEAT OFF A LONG BUS RIDE.
Photographer: Barry Lewis (6)

CUNNING GARDEN GNOMES PLOT A TAKEOVER OF THE FALKLAND ISLANDS.
Photographer: Tony Wheeler (7)

BEND IT LIKE BRANKO: HALFTIME AT A WOMEN'S FOOTBALL MATCH.
Photographer: Caroline Penn (8)

ROMAN MOSAICS ADORN THE PALAIS D'ORIENT'S TERRACE.
Photographer: Charles Bowman (9)

CANDLES BURN FOR THE FALLEN SOLDIERS OF THE WARSAW UPRISING.
Photographer: Krzysztof Dydynski (10)

Index

THE CITIES BOOK
A Journey Through the Best Cities in the World
March 2006

Published by:
Lonely Planet Publications Pty Ltd
ABN 36 005 607 983
90 Maribyrnong St, Footscray,
Victoria 3011, Australia

www.lonelyplanet.com

Printed through Colorcraft Ltd, Hong Kong. Printed in China.

Photographs:
Many of the images in this book are available for licensing from Lonely Planet Images.
www.lonelyplanetimages.com

ISBN 1 74104 731 5

Lonely Planet Offices

Australia Locked Bag 1, Footscray, Victoria, 3011
tel: 03 8379 8000 fax: 03 8379 8111
email: talk2us@lonelyplanet.com.au

USA 150 Linden St, Oakland, CA 94607
tel: 510 893 8555 TOLL FREE: 800 275 8555
fax: 510 893 8572 email: info@lonelyplanet.com

UK 72-82 Rosebery Ave London EC1R 4RW
tel: 020 7841 9000 fax: 020 7841 9001
email: go@lonelyplanet.co.uk

Publisher: Roz Hopkins
Senior Commissioning Editor: Laetitia Clapton
Commissioning Editors: Bridget Blair and Ben Handicott
Project Manager: Jenny Bilos
Production Manager: Jo Vraca
Print Production: Graham Imeson
Pre-press Production: Ryan Evans
Designer: Daniel New
Design Team: Brendan Dempsey and Daniel New
Layout Designers: Kaitlin Beckett and Vicki Beale
Image Commissioners: Rebecca Dandens, Glenn Beanland and Jane Pennells
Image Researcher: Pepi Bluck
Editors: Martine Lleonart and Adrienne Costanzo assisted by Elizabeth Swan
Cartographer: Wayne Murphy

Text:
The text in this book is partially based on Lonely Planet's guidebooks, trade and reference books and website content, which is researched and written by a global team of staff and authors. Content for this book was researched and compiled by:

Holly Alexander, Samone Bos, James Bridle, Laetitia Clapton, Karina Coates, George Dunford, Susannah Farfor, Will Gourlay, Robert Harding, John Hinman, Niki Horin, Piers Kelly, Martine Lleonart, Ian Malcolm, Jodie Martire, Tom Masters, Laura McKay, Sally O'Brien, Miriam Raphael, Craig Scutt, Jo Vraca, Katrina Webb, Donna Wheeler, Sarah Wintle

Image captions: Tenar Dwyer, Niki Horin, Piers Kelly, Vivek Wagle
Cities Past, Present & Future: Craig Scutt